MW01618068

Christian Images and Their Jewish Desecrators

JEWISH CULTURE AND CONTEXTS

Published in association with the Herbert D. Katz Center for Advanced Judaic Studies of the University of Pennsylvania

Series Editors

Beth Berkowitz,

Shaul Magid,

Francesca Trivellato,

Steven Weitzman

A complete list of books in the series is available from the publisher.

CHRISTIAN IMAGES AND THEIR JEWISH DESECRATORS

The History of an Allegation, 400–1700

Katherine Aron-Beller

PENN

UNIVERSITY OF PENNSYLVANIA PRESS

PHILADELPHIA

Published by
University of Pennsylvania Press
Philadelphia, Pennsylvania 19104-4112
www.pennpress.org

Printed in the United States of America on acid-free paper
10 9 8 7 6 5 4 3 2 1

Hardcover ISBN: 978-1-5128-2410-0
eBook ISBN: 978-1-5128-2411-7

A catalogue record for this book is available from the Library of Congress.

In memory of Brian S. Pullan
For Sam, Josh, and Naama

The true mystery of the world is the visible, not the invisible.

—Oscar Wilde, *The Picture of Dorian Gray* (1891)

Contents

Illustrations

Introduction

Where Christ-killers gather, the cross is ridiculed.
—John Chrysostom, Homily 1, Against the Jews

A group of five hooded and bearded medieval Jews sit at a long rectangular table, having gathered for an evening meal. In their identical dress, they are at ease with each other and celebrate their fraternity (Figure 1). Conversation is lively and energetic as they share a large flat loaf of bread and drink from carafes of wine. The second Jew on the left fingers his beard as he ponders a remark just addressed to him by his neighbor. Nevertheless, the Jew at the end of the table has been distracted and disturbed by a crucifix, larger than life size, which is positioned beside him on the floor on what seems to be a chiseled stone base. He calls out in shock, pointing to it in amazement that their host has tolerated or ignored it. Disturbed by the invasive presence of the image, which disrupts his sense of spiritual integration and cohesion, this Jew, as if he were bent on reenacting the murder of Jesus allegedly perpetrated by his ancestors, brandishes a sharp knife in his right hand and indicates with his left that he intends to attack the despicable crucifix.

This Flemish-style relief forms one panel of a large fifteenth-century *Passio Imaginis* stone altarpiece, now in the sanctuary of San Salvador in Felanitx in Majorca.[1] The altarpiece was created in the workshop of Guillem Sagrera, a renowned sculptor, commissioned by Jordi Sabet, a clergyman, and intended to be placed in a Passion chapel of the church.[2] Sagrera was dramatizing part of the legend of the "Christ of Beirut," a story Christians told about Jews that had first been composed several centuries earlier. In this tale, certain Jews are dining together in a private house when one of the company notices that their host is keeping on the premises an image of the Crucifixion left there by a previous occupant. Instead of merely removing this object, which is highly offensive to Jews, and perhaps returning it to the

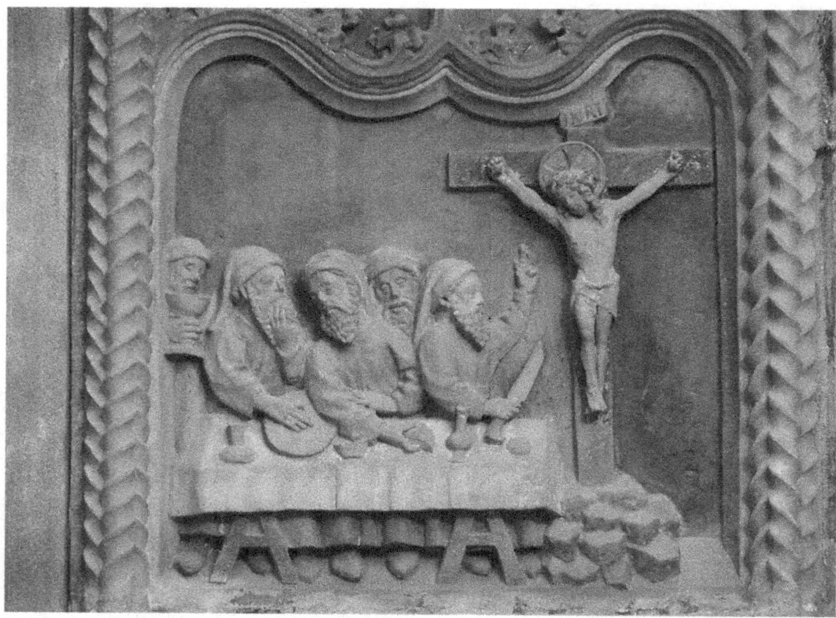

Figure 1. Desecration of the crucifix (detail) from the *Passio Imaginis* carved-stone altarpiece by Guillem Sagrera in 1442–1447, Shrine of the Holy Savior (Santuari de Sant Salvador), Felanitx, originally from the parish church of St. Michael (Sant Miquel), Felanitx. Photograph courtesy of Carlos Espí Forcén.

owner, they resolve to violate it by piercing the body of Christ, as did the soldier in Saint John's Gospel (John 19:34), as if reenacting an episode in the Crucifixion. Hence the actions of the Jew at one end of the table, who is threatening the crucified figure with a knife. In this Majorcan version of the story, the Jews, it seems, are not merely enjoying a convivial meal. The arrangement of figures at the table, and the presence of bread and wine upon it, are reminiscent of Christian representations of the Last Supper. But here the participants are a group of five Jews as opposed to thirteen, uniform and indistinguishable from one another, quite unlike the apostles of Jesus, and one of them is about to launch a physical attack on a hated Christian image. "Christ of Beirut" captures one classic version of the persistent allegation that medieval and early modern Jews were given to desecrating Christian images.[3]

Christian Images and Their Jewish Desecrators: The History of an Allegation, 400–1700 lays bare the longevity of Jews doing violence to images of Christ in Christian literature and nonliterary sources and examines how allegations, judicial accusations, as well as related charges launched within works of art affected Jewish individuals and communities. Ranging from the Byzantine Empire in the fifth century to early modern Europe at the end of the seventeenth, this book focuses on a particular aspect of late medieval anti-Judaism: how the Jews were portrayed by Christians as desecrators.

The book covers the persisting tales, myths, and fantasies about Jews that appear in historiography, literature, and art and explores the factors that shaped and sharpened this enduring allegation. It seeks to provide evidence concerning the longstanding popularity of the charge and the ways it changed over time. It also considers Jewish attitudes toward Christian imagery and Jewish responses to the Christian allegation. It shows how devotional images or objects fashioned to direct Christian worship of Jesus, Mary, or the saints acted as symbolic vehicles for the Christian majority's broader discourse with the Jewish minority. The degree of veneration of Christian images changed over time and space and intensified the animosity directed against Jews for this alleged offense. Finally, it analyzes the determining impact of doctrinal changes taking place within Christianity regarding the type of sacred images venerated, how this was expressed in the Christian allegation against Jews and attitudes toward them, and the Jews' different reactions to Christian images over time.

This study reconstructs the role of the *allegation* and the *accusation* in medieval and early modern European society. I define an "allegation" here as an assertion made without proof that an individual or a group of people has done something illegal or morally wrong. It can be very vague and may be founded on prejudice, such as a belief system that associates types of suspects (e.g., Jews) with a tendency to commit certain offenses. An example of an allegation is Pope Alexander IV's pronouncement in 1258: "the Jews, like ingrate enemies of the cross and the Christian faith . . . treat these pledges [Christian objects and images] with irreverence, to the disgrace of the Christian religion. And [they] act so nefariously towards them as is shameful to speak and horrible to hear."[4]

An allegation has the ability to travel globally through print and verbal transmission and endure especially if it is inspired by belief and fed by the needs of the varying societies that it serves. Allegations can be made outside of legal contexts through tales, myths, and fantasies about Jews. The congregations who heard these allegations in church sermons responded to powerful preachers who knew how to use "exempla" skillfully and persuasively.

In contrast, an "accusation" is a charge laid before a court of law and often changed people's lives, as they suffered punishment for specific offenses. An example of an accusation is that reported by Bartolomeo Malpio, a Modenese priest, to the Inquisition in July 1627: "The Jew [Simone Sasano] intended to remove the large figure of the Blessed Virgin in the house that he was renting . . . and you can get further information from Signor Annibal Mafioli."[5]

Almost all the legal cases discussed in this book date from the late thirteenth and early fourteenth century onward. They originated either in an accusation or denunciation laid before a court of law by an individual informing on another person or persons or in general reports or local rumors concerning crimes that court officials or inquisitors chose to investigate. As historians of the Inquisition will know, there was a distinction between "accusation," in which the accuser undertook to prove his case or suffer penalties if he failed to do so, and "denunciation" or "delation," in which a person merely submitted information to the court and the court decided whether or not to pursue it.[6] But for the purposes of this discussion, the word "accusation" will refer to any process by which a person was brought before a court on suspicion of committing a crime. The types of courts readers will encounter in this book include the court of the Knights of the Hospital of Saint John (Hospitallers), in Manosque, the court of the justices in eyre and the sheriff's court in Oxford, the medieval and early modern inquisitorial courts in Spain and Sicily, ducal/secular courts, episcopal courts, the medieval Inquisition in Italy and the Roman Inquisition, which was reconstituted in 1542 and asserted its claims to judge professing Jews after 1581.

It is true that, in some parts of Europe, and for part of the period covered by this study, conviction or acquittal did not depend on witness testimony or other evidence, but on trial by ordeal (such as being placed in a tank of water to see if the suspect could float). The submission of Rabbi Itzhak to ordeal by water was said to have occurred in a case of ritual murder in Blois in 1171, but trials by ordeal did not occur in cases of desecration.[7] Most of the trials discussed in this book depended on some version of Roman or canon law, whose particular rules of proof were set forth in legal textbooks and inquisitors' manuals.

Many of the trial records examined in this study contain evidence of the actual crime of image desecration. When the situation allowed, the defiled or damaged image might be produced in evidence as an exhibit; at other times, inquisitorial vicars went to visit the site of the image to inspect it in situ. Otherwise, all evidence in the investigative process was verbal. Accusers were expected to provide exact times and places of the occurrence of the offense and the names of two witnesses, usually Christians but sometimes Jews, to establish the authenticity of the charge. Some precautions were taken to ensure that hostile witnesses were not prejudiced against Jewish suspects. The key purpose of these trials was to obtain proof of an offense, either through confession by the suspect or by finding two respectable eyewitnesses.

This book then amasses evidence from stories told by moralist writers, from scenes presented by artists, and from records of formal legal proceedings, usually compiled by clerks, notaries, and judges. When a tale describes an act of desecration or an image depicts one, the story or the image is being offered by its maker as evidence that these things have happened in the past and may induce its audience to believe that they will happen again in the future.[8] In this respect images could be the objects of the crime of desecration, or they could provide evidence of the crime of desecration, by depicting, documenting, and fictionalizing it. And they could provide evidence of the offense by behaving miraculously, even traveling by themselves to new destinations. In twelfth-century Valencia it was reported that a wooden crucifix said to have been desecrated by the Jews of Beirut had miraculously swum almost the whole length of the Mediterranean and reached the city walls.[9] In desecration cases before the early modern Inquisition, the defiled or damaged image ought ideally to be produced in evidence; if this could not be done, for example, where flimsy prints (usually made from paper) had been removed from the Christian premises, the Jew would be accused of destroying them.[10]

If an image documented the allegation, then the audience may very well have assumed that, because the image was in a church and the preacher was repeating the story from the pulpit, it must be true.[11] There were no immediate consequences for any particular person, yet nonetheless the image symbolically punished the Jews for the alleged offense, and the public was encouraged to believe that Jews were capable of these wicked acts. This helped to confirm the truth of certain Christian beliefs such as the animating power of the cross, as representative of Jesus, to defend itself.

This study therefore tackles the subject on three different levels. First, there is that of the allegation in which artists and writers, mostly anonymous, manipulate fictive Jews (equally anonymous) to serve purposes that have little to do with Judaism but much to do with Christianity. Then there is a procedural level, in which Christianity is seeking to defend images it reveres against attacks by named Jews who are brought before courts of law, give evidence, and are the subject of criminal penalties. Between these two levels, I offer a discussion of the strategies used by Jews in order to survive in a world in which images are increasingly being thrust upon them and are increasingly difficult to evade.

Scholars have discussed the charges of ritual murder and host desecration leveled against Jews from the Middle Ages to the present day but there is no sufficiently wide-ranging study of the charge that Jews habitually violated Christian images.[12] By examining a panoply of sources from Byzantium, medieval England, France, Germany, Spain, and Italy, this study tracks this charge and sees it as parallel to those other anti-Jewish allegations, though it should be noted that charges of image desecration seldom led to such drastic consequences—there was no parallel, for example, to the trials for ritual murder of the Jews of Trento in 1475, when an entire Jewish community fell victim to execution or conversion.

The work follows the material pathways whereby the knowledge of Jewish image desecration was transmitted. The passage of the narrative brought by Greek clerics and pilgrims from Byzantium to western Europe enabled it to evolve, gaining new functions and appearing in new tales. These travelers repeated allegations of Jewish image desecration through their sermons and oral storytelling. Many factors shaped this persistent Christian conviction: Christian doctrinal and devotional developments; the circulation of various Christian moral tales and images that depicted Jews desecrating Christian imagery; the workings of various courts (secular and inquisitorial); Jewish-Christian polemics; and the behavior of Jews and suspected crypto-Jews (*conversos*) in Spain and Portugal.

The accusation of image desecration entailed not only attacking effigies of Christ but also reenacting the Crucifixion on Passion images and thereby causing them to bleed, a result that Christian accusers took as miraculous and that courts considered physical evidence of a crime. This understanding of image desecration sheds new light on the development of other medieval charges, in particular the emergence of the accusation of host desecration. I use the term "desecration" here to describe the crimes against images attributed to Jews, which include such offenses as "defilement" and "defacement." "Desecration" will refer to any form of vandalism—be it hammering, flogging, scourging, soiling, piercing, hitting, hiding, lancing, or stabbing a Christian image or object. According to Christians, Jews carried out such attacks to show contempt for an object and deprive it of the sacred qualities the Jews believed the Christians had mistakenly attributed to it. Desecration was not blasphemy (a verbal attack), though, of course, it could be accompanied by blasphemous words; it was an action one did with one's hands, feet, or even eyes, to objects and not human beings. Usually, it expressed hatred or contempt for the heavenly beings represented by the object if it were a statue or a picture, or embodied by it if it were a consecrated wafer. Christians understood desecration to be an intentional Jewish reaction—the inverted response to increasing Christian veneration. This could include covering or hiding the object, so that Christians would be prevented from venerating it. Veneration and violation thereupon become opposing actions: what the Christian venerates, the Jew is believed to violate. At times, desecration included showing disrespect to an image such as the careless handling of it by pawnbrokers, the failure to provide a key to a covered and locked image, letting a child empty a chamber pot upon a religious procession, or even the mere act of gazing upon an object that ought never to be seen by Jews. The last idea here was that a Jew could supposedly harm the image just by looking at it and not paying it due reverence, especially when it was borne through the streets in procession or passed under the windows and balconies of those who gazed upon it. This type of visual desecration scorned and mimicked the gratification that Christians received from images and hosts.

"Desecration" is defined in the *Oxford English Dictionary* as "the action of desecrating, deprivation of sacred or hallowed character, profanation."[13] But it is an expansive term, and it is useful here to define the distinct forms of desecration that will also appear in this study. The terms "defilement" and "pollution" describe attempts to make pure things disgusting, usually by sullying them (urinating or defecating on them, or throwing them on to dunghills or into latrines). With defilement or pollution, there was no mutilation—just the use of a filthy substance, readily available, to degrade something believed by Christians to be immaculate. Spitting on holy pictures also fell into this category. This was a form of superficial desecration because in most cases the image could be restored. Separately, an image could also be defaced, damaged, or mutilated (by stoning) without being either polluted or completely destroyed as a form of punishment or torture—sometimes as a reenactment of violence that Jews had inflicted or thought of inflicting on Christ himself or his followers as in Saint John's Gospel, 10:31–33, when Jews attempted to stone Jesus in the Temple for blasphemously claiming to be the Son of God.

Finally, "iconoclasm" is a form of desecration and shares its general intention to deny the sacred qualities of an image and to demonstrate that it has no power, to prevent it from being treated as an idol or a rival to God.[14] But not all forms of desecration constitute iconoclasm, though iconoclasm is always a form of desecration. For the purposes of this discussion, it will be useful to reserve the word "iconoclasm" for actions that seek to destroy images entirely or mutilate them irreparably, as did Christians at the time of the Iconoclastic Controversy in Byzantium or some Italian Philo-Protestants at the time of the Reformation. Jews, however, were commonly accused of merely defiling images—showing them profound disrespect and indecency, perhaps, but not putting them out of action. They did not eliminate the possibility that the defiled images might be cleansed or that they might, as a result of their mistreatment, begin to demonstrate miraculous powers and begin to undergo extraordinary physical changes. These were not acts of image-breaking, although they were acts of pollution. The implication of several of the stories discussed in this book is that the Jew did not have the power to destroy an image protected by the divine beings it depicted, although, as we shall see, there were lesser images that did not enjoy such protection—paintings that could be burned, statues that could be damaged, flimsy images that disintegrated as trial records demonstrate. In this area reality and fantasy occasionally overlapped, since Jews sometimes did what Christians accused them of doing (e.g., by stoning statues of the Madonna), although this action had completely different meanings for Christians and Jews. For Jews it was an attempt to spoil and eradicate an image they found offensive. For Christians it was proof that the Jew intended to test the image's miraculous powers.

An "image" was different from a "relic," which was an artifact surviving from an earlier time, or part of a deceased holy person's body that had come to be revered. In Byzantium, an "icon" was a two-dimensional image usually depicted on wood. But "image," or *imago*, refers to any kind of sacred representation in any medium—be it two or three dimensional (painting, sculpture, or print). The type of image and the materials used to make it—wood, wax, stone, marble, gold, silver, parchment, canvas, or paper—were not differentiated, nor did they affect the type of fictitious, real-life allegations or accusations that were made. Jews were shown to be capable of attacking anything, from tiny images on button boxes to drawings on broadsheets. Their targets supposedly included large, imposing stone statues, situated in prominent churches and public squares. These objects could be located in public or private, Christian or Jewish spaces.

The images allegedly and actually attacked by Jews fell into three categories: (1) crucifixes and images that depicted Christ's Passion (sometimes as small as pendants worn around the neck); (2) Madonnas and images of the Christ child and his mother; and (3) depictions of saints—intercessory figures who were not supposed to be worshipped as divine. Saints seldom appear as subjects in images desecrated by Jews either in Christian tales or real accusations. In most of our study, as will be shown, the images concerned belonged to the first two of these three categories.[15]

There are two different themes in the allegations of Jews violating images. The first theme is the rather more plausible idea that, since Judaism is a religion without images and Christianity venerates images, Jews must be tempted to attack any Christian image, especially if they are forced into unwelcome proximity to it. The second, less plausible, theme is the fantastical notion that Jews share the guilt of their ancestors for the murder of Jesus of Nazareth and that they are impelled to repeat this crime by violating images of Christ—those in categories 1 and 2 above. The implication is not only that the Jews of ancient Judea put Christ to death, but also that their descendants wish to go on attacking them in effigy, for example, by piercing Christ's side in an image of the Crucifixion, thereby mimicking the act that, according to Saint John's Gospel, is performed by a Roman soldier.[16]

Unlike "legends," which are stories handed down by tradition and regarded by ordinary folk as genuine, though unverified, history, Christian "tales" of image desecration were written by Christian authors (sometimes unknown) and were designed to make a point, teach a moral lesson—as was an exemplum (a moralizing tale). The moral was that images have miraculous powers and even Jews, the arch unbelievers, are compelled to recognize them. In Christian moral tales, Christian authors credit Jews with propaganda by act—actions that unintentionally confirm the truth of Christian beliefs about images because, by attacking it and making it bleed, they experience the "life" of the image. The reasoning went that, although Jews do not accept Jesus Christ as savior, they still are able to experience some of the powers latent in images of Christ. Their acts of aggression are a reenactment of the Crucifixion and form part of an ideological battle. By attacking Christian symbols, Jews mock or attack not only Christ but Christians as well. Desecration commonly has the opposite effect of that which Jews intend.

Their actions cause the picture or statue to demonstrate its miraculous powers, sometimes in such an awe-inspiring way that the Jews repent, convert, and are forgiven. In this way, Christianity achieves a great victory over its most obdurate enemies. If the Jew does not repent, he is usually sentenced to death. Often these tales, allegations, and accusations were ideological and part of a larger effort to convince Christians of the sanctity of images and to further anti-Jewish mythmaking in an increasingly intolerant medieval Europe.

This study will therefore scrutinize the relationship between the fictitious Jew accused in Christian desecration tales and the real Jew on trial for image desecration in England, France, Spain, and Italy. What determined the accusations were the interpersonal relationships between Jews and Christians, and on occasions the fears and interests of Christians who were influenced by the tales. It may sometimes, however, be possible to establish how Jews actually behaved and to explain when and why they really did desecrate images. Many records of proceedings against Jews in religious, secular, and inquisitorial courts will be explored. Punishment for violating images, even when the cases were not satisfactorily proved, ranged from heavy fines to galley service and occasionally Jewish "offenders" lost their lives because of these accusations.

Why did Christianity devise this allegation and why did it persist for so long? My claim at its simplest is that the allegation reflects contradictions in Catholic European society, revealing an uneasy equilibrium between fear of idolatry and eagerness to encourage popular practices of veneration. Anxiety about visual images developed in medieval Christian societies, fueled by religious authorities, theologians, and philosophers who were keen to encourage, shape, and monitor popular responses to these items. At the root of this anxiety was the fear of idolatry shared by both religions, although Christians and Jews approached their concerns from opposing sides, each attacking the other from different premises. Jews and Christians were aware of each other's beliefs and practices and often turned their understandings of the other into the stuff of polemics and allegations, especially in written texts.

The restrictions imposed on artistic creation in Judaism contrast sharply with the seemingly creative freedom that one finds in the Christian tradition. In scripture, Judaism absolutely rejects images as ways of encouraging devotion. The Jewish understanding of the Second Commandment in Exodus 20:3–5,

> You shall have no other gods before me.
>
> You shall not make for yourself a carved image, or any likeness of anything that is in heaven above, or that is in the earth beneath, or that is in the water under the earth.
>
> You shall not bow down to them or serve them, for I the Lord your God am a jealous God, visiting the iniquity of the fathers on the children to the third and the fourth generation of those who hate me,
>
> and repeated in Deuteronomy 5:8–9, prohibited Jews from idolatry. Idolatry was interpreted as a betrayal of God, as the error of worshipping other gods, as the worship of an intermediary rather than God himself, or as worshipping a mistaken idea of God.[17] Psalm 113:12–15 emphasizes the impotence of idols, with the hope that those who make them and worship them will become similarly impotent: "The idols of the nations are silver and gold; the workmanship of men's hands. They have a mouth but they cannot speak; they have eyes but they cannot see; they have ears but they cannot hear; they have noses but they cannot smell; they have hands but they cannot handle; they have feet but they cannot walk; they cannot speak through their throat. Let those that make them become like to them, and who trust in them."

But the wording of the Hebrew Bible prevented a simple understanding of this Second Commandment. Its meaning seemed to suggest a prohibition of all figurative art, because humans were made in "God's image" and images should never, in any way, compete with or distract from the admiration of God and his creation.[18] But in practice exceptions appeared to be made by virtue of divine commandments uttered at certain moments in the history of Israel. This in turn created an internal tension because it seemed that two extreme positions were being propagated: on the one hand, the Second Commandment prohibited man's creations; on the other, God commissioned man to create, in particular, two golden cherubim that were to be placed at either end of the Holy Ark cover in the Temple (Exod. 25:18–22) and the brass serpent that God ordered Moses to make—the sight of which would cure the mutinous Israelites bitten by snakes in the wilderness (Num. 21:4–9).[19] Jews were forced to live with the dichotomy of these two extremes. Rabbinic sources repeatedly tried to justify this peculiarity by claiming that these objects were not idols and the Jews who created them were responding directly to divine commandments.[20] The Jewish ban on images was more absolute in some periods than in others, as will be shown, and applied to sculptures and reliefs more than paintings, mosaics, and Hebrew illuminated manuscripts. Over time, Jews also found a substitute for images by focusing on the Word of God in their Torah scrolls, a divine symbol of God's presence. Unlike an image, this religious object was a handwritten copy of the Torah text on parchment, rather than a depiction of a divine being. These Torah scrolls were kept in synagogue arks and enshrined, adorned, and cared for, playing a far more central role in religious practice than any other ceremonial object.[21]

Christianity, on the other hand, increasingly encouraged image veneration and relied on images to inspire mass devotion. The Christian church was never in doubt that idolatry should always be condemned; but Christianity did not see idols and images as the same thing. The perennial debate was how to define and separate "correct" visual representations from improper idols and how to ensure veneration and not adoration/worship of these images.

"Adoration" (an approximate translation of *latria*, as defined by Saint Thomas Aquinas) was worship or reverence that Christians owe only to the Trinity or members of the Trinity, and Catholics owe to a consecrated wafer, which they hold to be the body of God.[22] "Veneration" was deep respect or honor that is owed primarily to a heavenly being and secondarily to a representation of that being—a crucifix, a picture of the Crucifixion, a statue or picture of the Virgin Mary or of a saint. Catholic authorities maintained in principle that pictures and statues could be valuable aids to devotion, that they helped pious people to concentrate their minds when praying. But in practice these things tended to become much more than aids to devotion and could take on a life of their own, so that they were always in danger of becoming idols or false gods. For that reason, Jews, Byzantine iconoclasts, and, later, Calvinists believed that pictures or statues of heavenly beings should be prohibited, partly because of the risk of creating idols, partly because spiritual things should not be turned into material objects, and partly because such an action violated a commandment in the Mosaic law.

By the early second century CE Christians had begun to use images in their devotional practices, but it was not until the fourth and fifth centuries that images of Christ and the saints appeared; the issue of their veneration and use for devotional and didactic purposes provoked both opposition and polemical support among churchmen.[23] The sacred image came to be venerated either for what it was or for its symbolic value, but never was it more than a concrete representation of some divine being.[24] Images became forms through which the individual could connect with God, and theologians were prepared to promote their veneration so long as the objects were not worshipped as divine. Christian art increasingly defined itself as an interpretation of spiritual doctrines and ideas, as a way of expressing a deeper truth and beauty inherent to redeem humanity, and as an expression of the divine spirit and the Lord's creation. The New Testament told Christians to be godly, to think godly—that is, to see the world as God sees it and to "bring every thought into captivity" (2 Cor. 10:5), to renew the mind (Rom. 12:1–2; 2 Cor. 3:18). The clergy permitted paintings, especially frescoes in churches, as they were used to communicate the Bible story to illiterate common people. Images were allowed to be a *means* of devotion but never the *object* of worship.

This powerful argument defined Christian art in accordance with the Second Commandment, until the Iconoclastic Controversy that shook Byzantium in the eighth and ninth centuries (730–787 and 815–843). It was the Christological teachings of the theologian John of Damascus (675–749) that identified the concept of the image of God and placed it into a sophisticated image theology based on the incarnation of Christ. In defending the usefulness of images in this crisis, he sanctioned the representation of Jesus in images because Jesus, unlike God the Father, had assumed flesh and lived as a human. Therefore, John argued, the Jewish aniconic requirement of the Second Commandment could be confidently rejected when depicting Christ.[25] Unlike God, Christ had made himself visible and therefore should be depicted in order that he might be venerated through visual devotion: "If we attempted to make an image of the invisible God, this would be sinful indeed. It is impossible to portray one who is without body; invisible, uncircumscribed, and without form. . . . But we are not mistaken if we make the image of God incarnate, who was seen on earth in the flesh, associated with men, and in His unspeakable goodness assumed the nature, feeling, form, and color of our flesh."[26]

Contrasting attitudes toward sacred images were a major source of tension between Jews and Christians. Christian tales alleged that Jews cannot entertain the idea of a god who is made flesh, much less the notion that Jesus of Nazareth was such a god. All the more emphatically, therefore, must they shun images of Jesus. Jews were critical of Christians for permitting sacred images, and Christians critical of Jews for rejecting them. As I will show, Christians and Jews formed their perspective of idolatry from the way in which its elements were deployed within the society to which they belonged.

It became the case that whatever was considered an exclusive characteristic of the *other* would become ipso facto against their own beliefs. Christians believed that Jews rejected images because they understood their power and were frightened that they would worship them as idols rather than guard them as ornaments.[27] Had not the Jews already shown their true idolatrous tendencies by worshipping the golden calf (Exod. 32:1–35) in the desert? In fact, when Christian apologists looked at Jewish practices, they perceived a marked contradiction between the prohibition contained in the Second Commandment, the biblical commands to destroy idols, and the Jews' failure to abide by them, committing the ultimate sin of idolatry by worshipping their own molded calf, which, in the Jews' minds, had morphed from an image into a god.[28] Neglect of the Second Commandment became, in Christian eyes, deeply characteristic of the Israelite religion.[29] The early Christian Epistle of Barnabas claimed that, because of Israel's idolatry, their covenant with God had been withdrawn from Israel and given to the church: "But in this way did they finally lose it [the covenant] when Moses had just received it. . . . But they turned to idols and lost it. For thus saith the Lord: 'Moses, Moses, go down quickly, for thy people whom thou broughtest forth out of the land of Egypt, have broken the Law.'"[30] Christians could and did continually exploit this dichotomy to its fullest.[31] As David Nirenberg writes: "On the question of images, for example, the Jews could provide Christians with examples of the most sublime rejection of the eye's attraction to the material object: 'Thou shalt have no graven image.' They could equally well model the most degraded submission to such objects, as in their worship of the golden calf. . . . So varied were these roles, so flexible this dialectic, that virtually any visual relationship to the object could be mapped onto the figure of the Jew."[32]

Jews argued against the accusation of being idolatrous in their worship of the golden calf.[33] But Christianity continued to condemn this Jewish failing, casting biblical Jews as being idolatrous rather than making any reference to the Jews' biblical commands to destroy idols.[34] The North African church father Tertullian of the early third century was one of the first theologians to refer to the story of the golden calf and the Jews' instinctive tendency to surrender to idolatry when they could and sin against God.[35] John Chrysostom in the late fourth century repeated this reasoning.[36] John of Damascus did not hesitate to attribute the practice of idolatry to the Jews, arguing that the greater maturity of Christians prevented them from falling into sin: "These precepts [concerning the idols] were issued to Jews because of their inclination for idolatry. We, on the contrary, we are no longer children."[37] By the early thirteenth century, the influential Franciscan and Dominican orders had made idolatry one of their main accusations against Jews living among Christians.[38]

Jews, on the other hand, argued that worshipping Jesus as a god was idolatrous, because he was a man, that Christians were descended from Edom—a biblical idolatrous nation from around Mount Seir whose ancestor was Esau[39]—and Christian images were idolatrous expressions.[40] In the words of Jeremy Cohen: "the crucifix and other icons in Christian churches and Christian homes . . . tainted Christianity with idolatry. Along with Jewish objections to the doctrine of the Trinity, the Christian veneration of icons led many rabbinic authorities to rule that Jews could under no circumstances enter a church."[41]

Jews continually alleged that crucifixes and images of Mary and the saints were idols and so Christianity was idolatry.[42] The commentary on Genesis, *Midrash Bereshit Rabbah*, written in the Land of Israel between the fourth and sixth centuries, described how the first Jewish patriarch, Abraham, shattered the idols in his father Terah's shop in order to show their impotence.[43] In his *Milkemet Mizvah* (The Obligatory War), probably written between 1230 and 1269, Rabbi Meir bar Simon of Narbonne condemned Christian worship of "sculptured and molten images" because it contravened biblical law.[44] "It is further written: 'You shall not make for yourself a sculptured image or any likeness [of what is in the heavens above or on the earth below or in the waters under the earth]. You shall not bow down to them or serve them' [Exod. 20:4]. It is further written: 'To whom, then, can you liken God, what form compares to him?' [Isa. 40:18]. However, they [the Christians] make sculptured and molten images in the likeness of the deity, even in public."[45]

Maimonides, in his *Guide for the Perplexed*, argued that the law against idolatry was the source of all other prohibitions and that the removal and complete destruction of idolatry was the principal reason behind Jewish law.[46] In late fifteenth-century Italy, in response to Franciscan friars' claims that Christians rigorously kept the Ten Commandments, Elijah Hayyim ben Benjamin of Genazzano had his Jewish interlocutor argue against the Christians: "you [Christians] nevertheless make all sorts of images (*tzurot*) for your houses of worship. And the worship of images belongs to the category of 'worshipping other gods.'"[47]

Thus, Jews and Christians accused each other of idolatry, despite their different approaches to the veneration of images.[48] When the Jews were expelled from Sicily in 1492, one of the reasons listed in the expulsion decree was that Jews were continually labeling Christians as idolaters and using the charge to justify the hostile action of lending money to them at exorbitant rates of interest: "To this should be added that we find that the said Jews, by their unrestful and perverse living, consume and absorb the property and substance of Christians with heavy and unsupportable usury, practicing loudly and pitilessly the pravity of usury on Christians, publicly and manifestly, as against enemies, considering them idolaters, of which grave complaints made by our subjects and natives have reached our ears; and we have understood and with much diligence recognized, that this could not be remedied as long as Jews lived among Christians."[49]

The aniconism of Judaism was one way for this culture and religion, based on the written word rather than the visual image, on the Torah scroll rather than the painting or the sculpture, to distinguish itself sharply and consciously from its neighbors. The persecution of Jews for image desecration was one among several Christian ways of isolating and stigmatizing Jews.[50] A recurrent theme in Christian polemics against Jews was the argument that Jews were blind to the power and beauty of Christian images because of their theological blindness in rejecting Christianity. As such Judaism was misguided and even sinful. The Jewish philosopher Philo Judaeus of Alexandria, circa 20 BCE to 50 CE, had already associated the idea of idolatry with blindness.[51] In his discussion "On the Contemplative Life," (*De vita contemplativa*), he had noted that idolaters were afflicted with spiritual blindness: "But since these men infect not only their fellow countrymen, but also all that come near them with folly, let them remain uncovered, being mutilated in that most indispensable of all the outward senses, namely, sight. I am speaking here not of the sight of the body, but of that of the soul, by which alone truth and falsehood are distinguished from one another."[52]

The concept of blindness preventing the recognition of falsehood would be adapted further in the language of the New Testament, and the distinctive quality of the idolater as a disbeliever came to represent a Jew. In John 9, Jesus is depicted healing a man born blind. Throughout the passage, John employs the dichotomies of literal versus metaphorical blindness, seeing the latter as the inability to understand or perceive and as a complete detachment from reality. Metaphorical blindness could then reflect a spiritual state of ignorance, which was applied to the Jews (1 Cor. 1:23). This was further explained in 2 Corinthians (4:3–4): "But if our gospel be hid, it is hid to those that are lost: In whom the god of this world hath blinded the minds of them which believe not, lest the light of the glorious gospel of Christ, who is the image of God, should shine unto them."

Israel's blindness is described as a collective failure, a moral error, and perhaps even an intellectual dimness and obstinacy that fails to visualize Christian redemption and salvation.[53] To Christians, Jews are metaphorically blind in that they cannot or will not see the spiritual truths contained in the scriptures entrusted to them. This kind of blindness does not stop them from allegedly harming images or consecrated wafers by "malevolent gazing"—they can see them but not beyond them and are blind to the things that lie behind or within them.[54] As Sara Lipton contends, Jewish vision was depicted as being restrained.[55] Or, in the words of Herbert Kessler, Jews remained "locked in [a] literal reading and seeing which prevented them from discerning the power and importance of sacred images."[56]

The Miraculous Powers of Images

In the Hellenistic and Roman periods, Plato and Aristotle had already theorized aspects of representation and emphasized the divine presence in images.[57] The Greco-Roman culture had attributed human powers to statues of the gods, for example, to move, to speak, to sweat, or to bleed. This notion was then applied to representations of Christ, which were believed to miraculously convert into Christ's flesh.[58] From the fourth century Christian imagination became sensitive to icons and relics, as though responding to the divine energy attributed to these items without worshipping them.[59] Since relics were needed for the consecration of churches, relics of Christ, the Virgin, or different saints were often actually inserted and stored in images, sculptures, and altarpieces.[60] Many of these objects were made specifically to house these relics, which established them as legitimate foci for veneration and prayer and confirmed their miraculous and healing powers.[61] Patricia Cox Miller sees certain Christian authors using discursive strategies she calls "corporeal imagination" to achieve "the conjunction of discourse, materiality, and meaning" that identified the Christian authors' turn toward material objects.[62] In her view: "The idea that a representation of a holy body might be animate was . . . a continuation, with a Christian hagiographical twist, of an ancient Mediterranean culture-pattern, in which immobility and animation were paradoxically linked."[63]

By the late sixth century, miraculous images were, according to Christians, appearing not only in churches but also in domestic spaces.[64] An image of Christ, the *Acheiropoieton* (ca. 600) was located at the Lateran, the icon of *Christ of Kamuliana* in Cappadocia, and similar icons were found in Constantinople and Edessa.[65] *Acheiropoieta* images were either those "not made by human hands" and considered venerable for that reason, or images reputed to have been painted by direct contemporaries of their subject and therefore inspired by divine intervention.[66] For example, Saint Luke began to be depicted as a painter as well as an evangelist and physician. Most of the works attributed to him were portraits of the Virgin, both sculpted and painted. In Spain he was believed to have been the creator of prestigious devotional images, such as the Virgins of Guadalupe, Montserrat, and Atocha. It was assumed that these images, whose origins were cloaked in mystery, had or would, at some point, perform some miraculous action. Other well-known *acheiropoieta* include the image of Christ's face impressed on Veronica's veil and an image of Mary in Rome attributed to Luke.[67]

Both western and eastern European Christians began to legitimate miraculous images in the eighth century. In the West, the Lateran Council of 769 approved the belief that holy images of Christ, Mary, and the saints could indeed work miracles, but warned that they should not be worshipped.[68] In the East, John of Damascus's definition of the image was based on the notion that the honor rendered to the images passes over to the beings they represent.[69] Stories of images' miraculous effects on believers and beholders recur in all literary genres in late antiquity and the Middle Ages, ranging from simple tales about the miraculous intervention of the Madonna, through numerous accounts of images of Christ growing nails and hair or exuding blood, tears, or sweat, to the highly intellectual scholastic treatise.[70] Many Christians regarded these images as powerful defenders of their churches or cities and venerated them accordingly. They gave rise to additional works of fiction in which the thaumaturgical images responded not only to those who venerated but also to those who violated them.[71] Any image—Christians believed—had the potential to be animate and it is hardly surprising that they would soon find a need for fictitious Jews to become quintessential desecrators, thereby confirming the miraculous qualities of the images.

The motivation for desecrating or destroying a Christian image probably arose from the practice of obliterating the memory of disgraced consuls or other magistrates (*damnatio memoriae*), which was legally sanctioned in the Roman period (in both the republic and empire). This concept was a highly sophisticated one, which implied that an attack on a statue of a past emperor represented an attack on that emperor himself.[72] Parallel to political iconoclasm was a persistent movement of religious iconoclasm in the early Byzantine period. Since the fourth century, Christians had desecrated pagan idols and sanctuaries.[73] By the sixth, Christians even destroyed their own statues of patriarchs of Constantinople, replacing them with those of their successors as a way of attributing power to these new representations.[74]

Christians, under pressure to affirm the ability of images to perform miracles, began to use images as evidence against Jews. The Jews' relationship with the Christian image was depicted as complex and variable and clearly appeared to Christians to be the gravest challenge to the power of the image.[75] If the Jew was metaphorically blinded to Christianity, what could he see when looking at the image? It seems this was never an issue for the authors of Byzantine and later high medieval tales. Sometimes the Jew is depicted as a curious desecrator, drawn to test whether the image is "real." This echoes the biblical story in chapter 5 of the first book of Samuel, which records how, after the Philistines had captured the ark from the Israelites, they placed it in the temple of Dagon (the god of crop fertility). The next day the Philistines saw Dagon bowing down to "the ark of the Lord." When they returned Dagon to his previous position the following day he bowed down again. But this time he had been decapitated and his hands broken off. Damage and destruction soon afflicted the people of Ashdod, and the message of the text was interpreted as follows in verse 7: "The ark of the god of Israel must not stay here with us because his hand is heavy on us and on Dagon our god." There was no point in the Philistines venerating the ark of the Jews because, if they did, they would be harmed. In the end the ark was sent back to the Israelites. Interestingly enough, Christianity does not depict the Jews as ever trying to venerate the Christian image. From the start, desecration is their only response to having ownership. But like the Philistines in the story of the temple of Dagon, in the Christian tale the Jew is forced to recognize the power of the object and to concede that its power cannot be defeated.

In general in Christian tales, the Jew appears to believe that the image is an idol—a mistaken substitute for God—and therefore tests the image's authenticity by subjecting it to tortures. The Jew in effect is shown as engaging in a dialectic inquiry into the truth of what Christians say, think, and propagate about sacred images. Any attempt by the Jew to destroy the image is always thwarted—he can never do more than graze or deface it, because of the sacred image's numinous and efficacious power. He is capable, however, of activating the image in such a way that it responds to his mistreatment, thereby bringing about a miraculous transformation or transfiguration, the process by which an image is harmed by a Jew and miraculously shows some sign of life. It may shed real blood and demonstrate the physical pain suffered by the sacred being whom it represents.

* * *

The possibility of images bleeding, crying out, responding to charges against them as well as prayers was a "fact" that Christians increasingly felt the need to authenticate. The Jew did not transform the image or work a miracle: God, Jesus, Mary, or the subject of the image performed that task in response to the Jew's treatment of it. These stories, like others, traveled well, widely and quickly in manuscript forms, being read, taught, or preached by traveling clerics. In early modern Spain and Italy they were disseminated through manuscripts. The tales adapted to new contexts and led on occasion to actual attacks on Jews.

As noted earlier, Jews were depicted as attacking crucifixes—those images that portrayed Christ's Passion, or Madonna images. In Christianity in Armenia and Syria in the pre-Constantine era the crucifix became a symbol of victory for liturgical purposes.[76] By the sixth century it was regarded as the defender of the Christian emperor. Later, in the Middle Ages, when the crucifix became more directly associated with the physical pain and suffering of Christ's Passion, it developed, in Christian eyes, into the main recipient of the Jews' aggression, sacrilege, irreverence, and violence. It was easy to merge the Christ killer with the image desecrator because the image was a direct conduit to the original. In general, the image violated by Jews would bleed if the image was one of Christ, or exude sweet-smelling oil or even blood if the image was one of Mary. Its seeping blood would confirm the Jews' violence against the bodies of Jesus and Mary and would sanctify the image, changing it to a sacred relic.[77] A Marian image that seeped oil would reflect the sort of activity that Mary performed in life—pouring and/or anointing with oil and exuding nourishing liquid from her body.[78] Oil seeping from an image of Mary would be interpreted as a sign that Christians had succeeded in healing the wounds inflicted on the image and on Mary herself by the Jews. None of the medieval tales of Jewish image desecration nor an actual court case against Jews in Spilamberto in 1632–1644 portray or describe images of the Virgin as producing breastmilk.

Images of Mary would become regular targets of alleged Jewish abuse in the twelfth and thirteenth centuries, as Mary gained more prominence through the dissemination of Marian tales in western Europe. As the Mother of God—a figure both maternal and human—Mary remained closer to Jesus than any other saint.[79] By the fifteenth century, representations of Mary inhabited many a street corner, becoming a constant reminder to Christians of the conventions of Christian life. She now appeared in public spaces, on most cathedral facades, inside parish churches and some domestic interiors.[80] From this time, too, Italian Jews began to encounter images of Mary that had been left behind in properties that they took over from Christians, an especially delicate matter because of the Catholic Church's growing interest in Marian shrines outside churches.[81] The Jews' complex relationship with the manifestations of what they considered ungodly and idolatrous in their intimate, domestic realm will be discussed in later chapters.

There was no corresponding Islamic allegation that Jews attacked Muslim art. Islam, like Judaism, is an aniconic religion, prohibiting figurative representations and therefore lacking images, symbols, and statues.[82] But at times Christian theologians did accuse Islam of idolatry, attacking Christian images, and despising Christians as idolaters.[83] In fact, on occasion Islam was actually accused by both Judaism and Christianity of being an idolatrous religion. One Jew who attacked the Muslims as idolaters in his work was the fourteenth-century Catalan kabbalist Joseph ben Shalom Ashkenazi.[84] Christian theologians argued this more regularly. As Muslim armies penetrated into regions of the Byzantine Empire, Muslim idolatry (worship of the Ka'ba stone at Mecca in particular, but also of Jupiter, Apollo, Priapus, and even the prophet Muhammad) played a major role in Christian polemics and even pictorial programs as early as the eighth and ninth centuries, justifying Christian aggression against these religionists.[85] These Christian ideas about Islam also permeated Christian Spain and other parts of Europe, where they remained popular until the nineteenth century.[86] In Christian tales, the Muslims were often described as destroying their own idols if they had failed to protect them from Christian attack.[87] Not only did Muslims worship their idols, but like Jews they might destroy them. This parallelism suggests how Muslims too were needed to play a role in Christian image theology.[88] Again the intention was to defend Christian image veneration and turn back Islamic accusations of Christian idolatrous practice and belief upon the accusers.[89] At the time of the Reformation in Europe, the Turk, as well as the Jew, would become a trope through which Protestant and Catholic apologists accused each other of idolatry to further their own beliefs against the Jews, the Muslims, and their Christian opponents.[90]

Jews were not alone then in being accused of desecrating religious images, particularly in the Byzantine era, during the first centuries after the Arab conquests, when Christianity was coming to terms with a new political, religious, and social situation. Here Byzantine Christians alleged that Muslims engaged in iconoclasm, developing similar responses to Jews to the temptations and opportunities offered by Christianity.

It is not surprising to see that, in Christian medieval tales, Muslims also made images bleed, but, unlike the Jew, would die as a result rather than convert, since the notion that the Jews would eventually convert to Christianity played a prominent part in Christian, and particularly in Augustinian, theology—the conversion of a Jew, as one of the most stubborn enemies of Christianity, was invaluable testimony of Christianity's truth.[91] Like Christian moral tales of Jewish image desecration, tales of Muslim desecration were intended to generate theological debates among Christians and to remind them where their loyalties should lie.[92]

As noted above, no single monograph has directly addressed the allegation of image desecration against Jews. When Joshua Trachtenberg wrote *The Devil and the Jews: The Medieval Conception of the Jew and Its Relation to Modern Antisemitism* in the early 1940s, he listed the charge of image desecration as one of a series of medieval allegations against Jews but did not discuss the matter at length.[93] In 1961, Jacob Katz contended that both Jews and Christians in the medieval period treated each other's symbols as "abominations," without developing "corresponding reactions."[94] Since then, two scholars—Christoph Cluse and Elliott Horowitz—have partly traced this allegation as a historical phenomenon and investigated its import. Whereas Cluse made a meticulous and groundbreaking study of the circumstances around the rare case of Jewish "iconoclasm" in Oxford in 1268, Elliott Horowitz made a sweeping declaration in his 2006 book, suggesting a collective, standardized, and uniform Jewish reaction to the cross/crucifix.[95] He argued that in diverse historical periods and geographical settings Jews displayed a strong attraction or "illicit desire" for crucifixes, and therefore deliberately acted to mock this Christian image.[96] Besides failing to give adequate consideration to the Christian tendency to disseminate the accusation of image desecration, Horowitz underestimated the number of differing attitudes of the Jews toward these objects through time, and it is unlikely that any one prevailed.[97] If a Jew urinated on a cross during the First Crusade in 1096, his motive and associations would have been different from those of an early modern Italian Jew tearing down a printed image of the Passion from the front of his market stall. The former may well have been a spontaneous outburst of defiance, but the latter was a careless moment of irritation against a Christian neighbor's invasion of his personal space.

Michele Luzzati has contributed a detailed inventory of Jewish image desecration trials he uncovered from the end of the fourteenth to the seventeenth centuries.[98] A bibliography on the late medieval artistic depictions and secondary sources documenting the development of the visual record of the allegation was collected by Eric Zafran.[99] Dana Katz has analyzed the effect of a number of fifteenth- and sixteenth-century paintings and inscriptions that commemorate this offense and other crimes attributed to Jews. Her intention is to uncover the nuances of meaning that paintings that showed Jewish abuse provided and how their iconographic import affected the level of tolerance toward Jews in northern Italy.[100]

In his recent monograph *Aesthetic Theology and Its Enemies*, David Nirenberg looks at three "modes of representation"—painting, poetry, and politics—to show how Christianity has *always* defined itself through the figures of Judaism that it produces.[101] In his section on painting, Nirenberg's thesis goes well beyond the topics of iconoclasm, idolatry, and image desecration, interpreting Judaism (as seen by Christians) as a dangerous, soul-destroying intellectual tendency toward the literal, the legalistic, and the materialistic, always ready to invade Christianity and needing to be resisted. Rather than confining Judaism to a people who profess the Jewish faith or are Jewish by genealogy, Nirenberg seems to see it as less specific, to the extent that almost anything one disapproved of could be considered Jewish.

In the following six chapters, my work will trace the chronological and geographical development of the image desecration allegation. Chapter 1 brings the first Byzantine tales of Jewish image desecration into sharper focus by mapping their constellation and their diachronic development and by discerning patterns in their social and cultural processes. These moral tales began to circulate during the Byzantine Iconoclastic Controversy, when Eastern Christianity attempted to return the religion to its purest form of devotion—a doctrine without images. Here I will uncover fictional tales that were constructed and disguised as polemics, causing the reader or listener to lose sense of whether the claims were fact or fiction. I will seek to understand and analyze these developing narratives, to consider the type of icons that were allegedly attacked, and to examine the changing roles attributed to the fictitious Jewish aggressor. On the one hand, the Jew was portrayed as one who attacked Christian images on the strength of the Second Commandment's prohibition of idolatry. On the other, he was reviled by the iconoclasts as an inveterate idolater himself. The fictitious Jew therefore became a valuable instrument for the formation of an orthodox Christian response to the Iconoclastic Controversy.

Chapter 2 follows the trail of Byzantine stories that were being borne westward both by traveling Greek clerics and by pilgrims returning from the Holy Land. It shows how they resurfaced in medieval England and France and how they and others were transformed into "Marian tales," primarily for the sake of their religious messages and moral lessons concerning Mary. In these countries, "Marian tales" evolved further from the twelfth century onward as the veneration of sacred images—particularly of the Passion—became increasingly popular. This was contemporaneous with a new way of thinking about Jews in Europe. Christians began to question the position of Jews in their society, particularly moneylenders who took these images as pawns. These Christians displayed a new interest in why Jews had killed Christ, rejecting the Augustinian view that they had killed him in ignorance, suspecting instead that they had acted maliciously, killing him in full knowledge of what they were doing, because of their fear of and malice toward the Son of God.[102] This sentiment intensified Christian suspicion and resentment of alleged Jewish acts of desecration. Some narratives and allegations of image desecration stemmed from the fear, as reported in trumped-up stories like that of the French chronicler Rigord in the early thirteenth century, that Jewish moneylenders would profane church images and objects that came into their hands as security for loans granted to impecunious clergy. As the clergy struggled to communicate religious meaning in an increasingly image-saturated society, one tale circulated more than the others. This tale described Eucharistic blood seeping from an image of the Crucifixion that a fictitious Jew had desecrated.[103] This basic but powerful narrative was open to multiple interpretations at every stage of its telling, and I will focus on its impact upon the host desecration allegation. Attention will also be given as to why in particular it was medieval Christian society in England and France that allowed the fictional allegation to become a real accusation and Jews to be tried before specific courts. This then set a precedent for later societies.

In Chapter 3, I explore to what extent the allegations against *conversos* that surfaced in fifteenth- and sixteenth-century Spain should be read as a continuation of the medieval narrative and discourse of Jewish image desecration or whether they reflected new developments in regard to Spain's own relationship with Christian images. Remarkably, before 1391, Spanish royal policies seem to have prevented charges of image desecration against Jews from being fully prosecuted in the courts. The attack on *conversos* or Marranos focused on secret desecration of the images and crucifixes these New Christians now kept in their own homes. "Marrano" was a disparaging term for a New Christian, implying that he or she was a heretic or apostate. It covered several situations and had several meanings: one who lived publicly as a Christian and privately as a Jew; one who amalgamated Christianity and Judaism and did not fully observe either religion (a syncretist); one who moved back and forth between Christianity and Judaism, especially when traveling or trading between countries where Judaism was suppressed and others in which it was tolerated; or one who turned away from Christianity altogether and became a professing Jew, for example, by being circumcised. Using thirteenth-century *adversus Judaeos* tracts (polemics against Jews) and church treatises that discuss the relevance of images in Spain, and also by following inquisitorial investigations of *conversos* for this offense, the chapter will show that an "alternative" image desecration narrative was actually created by inquisitors to promote their own agenda of controlling *conversos* and instructing the faithful how to behave toward their sacred images.

Chapter 4 turns aside from the fictitious Jew in Christian tales and the real Jew prosecuted by Christian courts to focus on what Jews themselves wrote about Christian images, allegations of Christian image desecration and how Jews were to fare with the ubiquity of Christian images in their daily lives. The chapter draws on rabbinic responsa, polemical arguments, chronicles, disputational literature, folktales, and Hebrew illuminated manuscripts. It reveals the social and structural perceptions held by medieval and early modern Jews with which they countered this allegation and uncovers the deep-seated hostility they harbored toward Christian images. As I will show, Jewish actions and reactions toward the Christian devotionalia that surrounded them were influenced by rabbinical teachings that allowed significant diversity of opinions and had no real strategy except to encourage Jews to show less sensitivity toward them.

Chapters 5 and 6 then shift to Italy, since inquisitorial archives there hold a large number of intriguing *processi* (records [or dossiers] of inquisitorial proceedings) in which Jews were accused of removing crucifixes from walls, stoning or damaging Christian statues and paintings, or failing to demonstrate the obligatory respect to images carried through the streets. These inquisitorial records contain no far-fetched accusations that Jews made crucifixes bleed but reveal how charges of image desecration were anticipated by the Jews themselves whenever they rented or occupied spaces that already housed Christian sacred images. Chapter 5 also compares these charges with those against Protestants and deviant Catholics in Italy, explores the frequency of the charges against Jews, particularly in the duchy of Modena (whose archives hold more complete inquisitorial records than do those of other Italian cities). It explores the type of prosecution the Jews faced for these offenses, the pivotal impact of doctrinal changes taking place within Christianity concerning their own images, and the likelihood of the Jews committing these offenses, and asks whether these objects did in fact have inherent meanings for Jews at this time. My decision to stop recording cases at the beginning of the eighteenth century was made due to the large amount of data uncovered up to that date.

My final chapter provides a microhistorical study of a series of incidents involving images that occurred in a small country town, Spilamberto, in the duchy of Modena, between 1632 and 1644, and were recorded in a lengthy trial dossier. Events took place mainly in a silk mill that was leased to Simon Sanguinetti and his four sons in 1632 after a severe slump in trade and industry that had set in throughout Italy following the 1630 plague. These Jewish tenants-cum-managers were accused of desecrating two types of Catholic visual representation. The first was a frescoed image or possibly a painted panel of a nursing Madonna (*Madonna Lactans*) suckling the child Jesus. The second consisted of a number of cheap prints of religious subjects. The conflicting demands of the two groups that occupied the work space—that of the Jewish bosses, who wanted images hidden, and that of the Christian workforce, who wanted them visible—had proved to be irreconcilable. During the investigations, three Jewish suspects were imprisoned for up to four months, and two of them were tortured. This trial dossier contains a wealth of detailed information on the extent to which an image served as the apparatus for defining spatial boundaries between Jews and Christians in the workplace in the seventeenth century.

This book is a culmination of a ten-year project attempting to catalog fictitious and real allegations made against Jews. While working in the Archivio di Stato of Modena on my first book, *Jews on Trial: The Papal Inquisi-*

tion in Modena, 1598–1638,[104] I uncovered a number of intriguing inquisitorial *processi* in which Jews were accused of image desecration. In one *processo* (for a full description see Chapter 5) a Jewish witness, Beatrice, is reported to have looked at the Madonna statue her son was accused of desecrating and said, "Bloody yourself, bloody yourself" (Vi sanguinite, vi sanguinite), an imperative, or possibly "You will bloody yourself" (Vi sanguinerete), which could be a prediction.[105] She later denied this and said: "Sir, never did I say such words. How can Your Lordship think that I said them, because if I had opened my mouth on that occasion, those Christians would have attacked me. Had I heard that one of them was claiming that I said something like that, I would have called witnesses to testify that I never said a word" (Signore, io non ho detto altrimenti quelle parole, e poi come VS vuole che io habbia detto simile cose, che si io havessi aperta la bocca in quella occasione, quei Christiani havrebbono bersagliata, et si io havesso sentito quelle d'uno di coloro, che havesso detto de haver mi sentito a dire simili parole io havrei chiamati testimonij del mio silentio).[106]

Beatrice's emotional reaction (*con lachrime*—with tears, as the notary recorded) struck me. One cannot know whether Beatrice actually said the words in question to the image. If she did, there is more than one possibility. She may have said them in mockery, as if she were challenging the assaulted image to behave as idolatrous Christians would expect it to behave and demonstrate its miraculous powers by bleeding. In that case, it was as if she knew about the Christian belief in transfigured Madonnas (probably no secret) and was making fun of it. Alternatively, she may have actually believed, or the witness thought she believed, that the statue really was going to react as if it were alive—in other words, that she was sharing a Christian belief and taking it seriously, as though an enemy of Christianity were authenticating, in spite of herself, something that Christians believed in and Jews generally did not.

What is clear is that Beatrice denied saying these words. If they were said in derision, they might be very provocative to Christians, and no sensible Jew would risk that. So it was probably true, as she claimed, that she did not utter these words, especially not loudly. Beatrice was not punished for her comment. Yet her statement made me wonder whether scholars were perhaps overlooking a recognized association and deep-seated fear held by early modern Jews that Christians would accuse them of desecration and causing Christian images to bleed. Was this fear that Jews would be accused of making images bleed a *secretum* known among Jews but hidden from

Christians, and if so, what role did it play in the Jews' relationship with the Christian majority?[107] Or was it a more general fear of being associated with Christian blood? Where did this idea of images bleeding come from? When I began my investigation, I used Beatrice's comment as a point of departure in tackling questions about the Jews' relationship with Christian images and the presence of Christian images in Jewish space.

The historical scope of my study is long, the geographical scope wide, but its intention is to confirm the breadth and length of the allegation's dissemination. It enables a long-range study of the relationship between Christian society, Christian images, and the Jews of Europe with the intention of deepening our understanding of Jewish-Christian relations. Each chapter addresses the same topics—the ideas, theories, and historical events surrounding the literary sources and/or judicial cases of image desecration. As will be seen, the developments of the moral tales, allegations, and real accusations are influenced by the historical circumstances and the ways that Christian images were defined and utilized in the various societies presented. My hope is that the tracing of this allegation will enable image desecration to be incorporated into the general history of Jewish-Christian relations, alongside the better-known themes of ritual murder, blood libel, and host desecration.

Chapter 1

The Creation of a Narrative
Byzantine Tales of Jews Desecrating Images

In the following pages, I will attempt to bring the first known legend and tales of Jewish image desecration into sharper focus by tracing their diachronic development, unraveling their intertwined strands, and discerning patterns in their social and cultural processes.[1] The chapter focuses on a literary-orientated comparative reading of the various Byzantine tales in an effort to draw the strands of the fictitious allegation together as it moves through time and place. It begins with the first known legend that described the Jews hiding the True Cross, and then follows the trail of allegorical tales of image desecration, considering two historical representations that strengthened the desecration narrative in Byzantine popular thought: first, the use of descriptions of alleged Jewish iconoclasm in Byzantine-Christian chronicles and, second, the propagation of rhetoric by Christian writers of the Jews' idolatry. The chapter finally suggests how the tale moves from an act of desecration by a single Jew to an act of crucifixion on an image by a group of Jews—who collectively convert as a result of the miracle brought about by their desecration. I will argue that the tale as it develops is concretized with Eucharistic implications, as Christian authors defend and vindicate Christian veneration of sacred images.

At the beginning of the fifth century, John Chrysostom, the bishop of Antioch, had already observed that Christian images of the local martyr Meletios were appearing everywhere in Antioch on fountains, on the walls of domestic spaces, and even on rings and seals.[2] From the sixth century, Christians are recorded as bowing and prostrating themselves before Christian images, including those of Christ and the saints. Holy portraits developed significantly over the next few centuries, and it was in the eighth century—the century that was dominated by the Iconoclastic Controversy—that the image began to be considered as an "intermediary between the viewer and the holy person represented."[3] As will be shown, both Christian iconoclasts' and Christian iconophiles' fears that their veneration of images might be misinterpreted as idolatry were the cause of the increasing complexity of the fictitious Jew's association with image desecration.

Our legend describes the discovery of the True Cross upon which Jesus had been crucified, but then our trail moves to the first tale that describes the desecration of a wooden portrait of "the living Jesus" (as distinct from the dead or dying Jesus on the cross) that is stolen by the Jew from the church in which it is situated and taken into his home. We then uncover a tale about a portrait of Mary, and finally move to another tale concerning a representation of Jesus's crucifixion found in a Jew's home. The creators of these tales not only use anti-Jewish polemics about idolatry but carefully craft the fictitious Jew to change his response to images as the narrative develops through time, from desecration out of rage to the actual reenactment of the crucifixion on the image.

For the purposes of this argument, "fictitious" Jews are those who appear only in Christian polemics and tales. These literary genres very rarely reflect historical reality or the real situation of the Jews in either the Byzantine Empire or western Europe. In polemics, the Jew becomes a rhetorical convention, sometimes a capable but defeated interlocutor, and it is most unlikely that the disputes written by Christian authors really occurred. On occasion, Christian tales blur reality and fiction by presenting the tale as a historical event in order to create a moralizing and illustrative lesson about Christian images and causing the reader or listener to lose sense of whether the claims were fictional or historical. Fictional Jews appear only in the work of imaginative writers who are seeking to instruct, to entertain, or to point out morals rather than to report events, and there is no independent recorded evidence of their existence—though aspects of them may be based on real people. "Historical" Jews are those who are commemorated by people such as chroniclers, notaries, or clerks whose intention, ostensibly at least, is not to teach or imagine, but simply to record and inform. Here, too, on occasions the chroniclers write with authority that the Jews themselves had been involved in iconoclastic acts against Christian churches and objects. As will be shown, the accuracy of these chronicles must be questioned, although it is clear that the Jews sometimes did commit some acts of desecration. One can recognize a Jew as fictitious in sources if he is like a puppet or a stereotype and his sole function is to prove a point being made by the writer or if he is a skeptic who accidentally provokes a miracle and is inspired to convert. In the Byzantine chronicles both the fictitious Jew and at times the historical Jew were intended to illustrate and promulgate the idea that Jews practiced and had tendencies toward committing image desecration.

The Foundational Legend: The *Inventio Crucis*

The earliest version of the allegation of image desecration was a Christian legend that arose at the end of the fourth century, developing a picturesque mixture of reality and fantasy. Around 340, Cyril (315–386), bishop of Jerusalem, had mentioned the presence of a relic of Christ's cross in Jerusalem, but it was John Chrysostom, who in his eighty-fifth homily on Saint John's Gospel (390), used the Gospel text for a tale in which three crosses were discovered and Christ's cross was identified by its headboard, or *titulus*.[4] Just a few years later, Ambrose, bishop of Milan, in his funeral oration for Emperor Theodosius I (d. 395), added the detail that Helena, the mother of Constantine the Great and a convert to Christianity (even before her son), had recovered the True Cross and nails on Golgotha.

In the fifth century, the Roman poet Paulinus of Nola (402) and Tyrannius Rufinus (403) wrote that Helena was helped not by pagans but by Jews and the local bishop of Jerusalem, Macarius.[5] These brief patristic references were aided, at the beginning of the sixth century, by an anonymous variant, probably of Syrian origin, known as the legend of Judas Cyriacus, who was in fact the last Christian bishop of Jerusalem with Jewish origins and who was killed in Jerusalem during the Bar Kochba Revolt. The legend told how Helena gathers together three thousand Jews (despite the fact that in the mid-fourth century, there was no Jewish community in Jerusalem). One particular Jew, Judas, who is singled out as knowing about the cross, refuses to cooperate with the queen and is placed in a dry well for seven days. When Judas is about to die of starvation, under pressure from Helena, he prays to God in Hebrew to reveal the location of the True Cross on Golgotha. When the earth shakes and a sweet-smelling perfume rises from Golgotha, Judas digs down to uncover three crosses. These crosses are then taken to the middle of Jerusalem where a dead youth is placed on each cross. The devil appears and tries to disrupt the events, but Judas crushes its power by uttering the name of Christ and condemning the devil to eternal fire. When the youth returns to life on the third cross, it is established that this is the True Cross. It is then venerated by being mounted in gold and precious stones and kept in a silver shrine inside a new church built on Golgotha.[6] Through the revelation of the truth, the Jew is then redeemed from Judaism and claimed by Christianity.[7] In addition, the happy ending of the legend confirmed that the Jew's genuine conversion to Christianity was a consequence of the miracle that he had witnessed. In the late fourth century Augustine's writing on miracles had argued that supernatural events were intended by God to arouse wonder in the faithful but terror in unbelievers who had the choice of conversion or damnation.[8] The story also touches on another theme, the idea that Jews were deliberately deceitful: Judas's father and grandfather knew very well that Jesus was really the Savior but refused to admit it. The name Judas linked the Jew to Judas Iscariot and, like him, stood for all treacherous Jews. But unlike Judas Iscariot, this Judas would have a chance to redeem himself.

The Latin version of the legend was known in Rome around 500 and made its way into European vernacular literature and the liturgies of both Greek and Latin churches.[9] Fragments of the True Cross, homilies, sermons, and feast days celebrating the legend's so-called discovery began to be transmitted across Europe, confirming its popularity and disseminating its anti-Judaic focus.[10] Its depiction in iconography came later.[11] Fragments of the cross could be found in almost every European town and were associated with sanctity and real presence, since they had been part of the object that had borne the body of Christ.[12] Pilgrims traveling to Jerusalem regularly bore witness to the presence of the True Cross there (except for the period between its temporary seizure by the Persian ruler Chosroes in 615 and its recapture by the Byzantine emperor Heraclius in 630) until its final loss to the Muslims in the Battle of Hattin in 1187 with the fall of the crusader city of Jerusalem.[13]

This legend allowed Christian authors to activate their own notions of Jewish abuse of sacred items. Although legends were not usually invented for a purpose, they clearly could be reformulated as they were circulated, especially if the message could be used to fulfill a need. As will be shown, the narrative of the *inventio crucis* had organized information on the Jew into a causal sequence that would influence and bolster moral tales that adapted themselves from it. As in many later desecration tales, there were three acts in this drama. In the first, the Jew conceals and therefore clearly misuses the sacred Christian object. Hiding is a form of desecration, because the

Christian is prevented from venerating it. In the second, the miraculous powers of the object unexpectedly compel him to acknowledge and proclaim the truth of Christianity. In the third, the Jew seeks baptism and becomes a convert. All this is done through the sacred power of the object. The legend combines the narrative of the Jew's manipulation and hiding of Christian materiality (the use of physical objects for spiritual ends), Judas's witnessing of Christian truth in the miraculous reaction of the relic, and his consequent desire to be baptized. The consequence here was restorative—conversion rather than retributive justice or death. The Jewish transgressor is afforded the opportunity to realize both the hurt that was caused by his action and also that he is not eternally defined by that transgression.

The subject of the Jew's relationship with miraculous images and the trope of Jews as actual "killers" of the animated holy bodies rather than mere desecrators of sacred images would be introduced next. It was in the fifth century in Byzantium that an allegation arose that Jews were reenacting the Passion on an effigy, "a form made to resemble the saint cross in contempt of the Christian faith." Christians believed that on the festival of Purim—when Jews celebrated the demise of Haman—they were equating him with Christ and crucifying him. In 408, the Theodosian Code of Emperor Honorius formally instructed his provincial governors to restrain the Jews from doing this, arguing that the Jews had the felonious intention of mocking the Christian faith.[14] It is unlikely, though, that our first author, Gregory of Tours, one of the most prolific writers of his age, knew about this allegation.

The Jew Who Stole an Image

The first surviving moral tale depicting Jews as image desecrators appeared in France in *De gloria martyrum* by Gregory of Tours (ca. 538–594).[15] This book contains a series of miracle tales about the lives and cult of martyrs, and it is here that the bishop of Tours confirms that he knew of the *inventio crucis* legend that told the story in Latin of a Jew desecrating an icon of Christ.[16] Monastic stories had started to flow between the East and the West from the fourth century. Some were written but others were delivered orally.[17] Their intention was to provide an idealized picture of Christian life and pious devotion. Gregory was clearly interested in tales that had been recorded by monks who, in the tales, were imagined to be living romanticized and ascetic lives; monasteries appeared earlier in Egypt and Syria than in Gaul and Italy. It seems likely that Gregory of Tours copied "The Jew Who Stole an Image of Christ," but the tale also stands as testimony to his support of images, their didactic purposes, and their miraculous potential.[18] It also confirms that, in sixth-century Gaul, Jews were one of the religious minorities that Gregory of Tours perceived as troublesome outsiders in Christian society.[19]

At the beginning of his tale, Gregory of Tours commends those Christians who are already hanging images of Christ in their homes and churches and using them to venerate Christ. The tale opens with these words: "For even now at this time Christ is cherished with such love through a perfect faith that believers who remember his law in the tables of their heart also hang a painted image of him in churches and houses to record his power in visible tablets."[20]

How widespread holy portraits were by this time is difficult to say. There had been no systematic theoretical explanation or defense of Christian images before this time, and scholars suggest that Christians were venerating images with no way of ensuring that veneration did not become or was not perceived as worship.[21] We know that during his tenure Gregory advocated the construction of monuments and image veneration by restoring murals on panels in his local church of Saint Martin, although in another of his works, *Life of the Father*—in which he discusses miracles—he makes no mention of his own belief in miraculous images.[22]

Gregory's text portrays an unnamed Jew, representative of "the eternal enemy of the human race," who "reveals himself to be envious" of the Christians. This jealous Jew had often noticed, on the wall of a church, a painting of Christ, a figure whom he accuses of degrading his people. "For after a Jew had often looked at an image of this sort that had been painted on a panel and attached to the wall of a church, he said: 'Behold the seducer who has humbled me and my people!' So, coming in at night, he stabbed the image with a dagger, pried it from the wall, concealed it under his clothes, carried it home, and prepared to burn it in a fire."[23]

In vengeance against Christ for degrading the Jews, he attacks the image of Christ, and removes it from the church. Gregory of Tours described the subsequent miracle: "But a marvelous event took place that without doubt was a result of the power of God."[24]

Immediately after the Jew had stabbed the painting, blood began to pour from it. However, the Jew, because he "was so obsessed with rage," failed to observe the blood.[25] It was only when he had returned home that he noticed it on his body: "But after he had made his way through the darkness of a cloudy night to his house, he brought a light and realized that he was completely covered with blood."[26] The Jew has initially not noticed the blood. At the moment when he sees it, he realizes that its presence signified not only his own guilt in attacking the image but also that his sin, like that of Cain in the Hebrew Bible, could not be concealed.[27] Frightened, but unsure of the power of the image, the Jew hid the painting in his home. The tale continues: "Fearing lest his crime became obvious, he hid the panel he had stolen in an obscure spot; nor did he dare any more to touch what he had wickedly presumed to carry away. At dawn the Christians came to the house of God. When they did not find the image, they were upset and asked what had happened. Then they noticed the trail of blood."[28]

The Jew had been unable to get rid of the bloody trail that began in the church and ended at his house. The Christians were able to successfully retrieve the image. Having restored the painting to the church, the Christians executed the Jewish image desecrator by "crush[ing] the thief beneath stones."[29]

Why did Gregory decide to cast a Jew as a desecrator? Was he elaborating on a theory that a historical Jew, plagued by his notorious iconophobic discomfort with images, would naturally want to desecrate or destroy them, more so than a pagan polytheist? As mentioned above, we know that Gregory knew the *inventio crucis*, since he made a brief reference to the role of Judas in it.[30] By the time Gregory of Tours wrote this tale, other writings had also emerged that had already connected Jews with the abuse of Christian images. For example, John Chrysostom had declared his own belief that Jews were guilty of mocking the cross in his *Adversus Judaeos Orationes*.[31] "Tell me, if demons dwell [in the synagogue], is it not a place of impiety even if there is not a statue of an idol standing there? Where Christ-killers gather, the cross is ridiculed, God blasphemed, the father unacknowledged, the son insulted, the grace of the Spirit rejected."

Augustine of Hippo (354–430) in his *Tractatus adversus Judaeos* had also depicted the Jews as a people who failed to recognize or understand the significance of Jesus's miracles and therefore were unable to respond to them.[32] In his tale, Gregory of Tours depicts the Jew as being initially blinded by the "darkness of a cloudy night" to the blood that seeped from the image or the trail of blood that would lead the Christians to him. This association of Jews with blindness had already been established in the New Testament, as noted in the introduction.[33] Jewish blindness would also become a major theme in *adversus Judaeos* literature—texts that lay the groundwork for the teaching of contempt toward Jews and are often formulated as dialogues between representatives of the two faiths. Perhaps Gregory of Tours had also seen the sixth-century *disputatio* between Gregentios, archbishop of Taphar, and Herban the Jew, probably written in Constantinople, with the intention that it might be used in a real dispute in the future. Here the miraculous appearance of Christ caused thousands of fictional Jews who, up until that moment, were blinded to his appearance to seek baptism and be healed from their maladies.[34]

In addition, the Jew calls Christ a seducer "who has humbled me and my people." This might well have been influenced by Augustine who had newly personified the hermeneutical Jew as a witness, there to benefit the church and retain some connection with the heavenly kingdom.[35] After all, the Jews' desecration had revealed the sanctity of the image and this benefited the Christians who witnessed its miracle and would continue to venerate it. However, there was no suggestion in the tale that the Jew was reenacting the Crucifixion on the image. The image is not described as a Passion painting or a crucifix but seems to be a portrait image representing Christ's corporeality (an image of Christ as a man). Gregory's tale portrays the Jew who attacked the body of the living Christ as a desecrator and not as a Christ-killer and his intention was to destroy the image by burning, not by crucifying. In his *Liber historiarum*, Gregory of Tours does not vilify the Jews nor blame them for Christ's death.[36] It seems that Gregory might well have tweaked the tale to present his own version that showed Jews attacking an image of the living Christ. The image responded to the Jew's violation by acting as a divine agency and a miraculous corporeal body. Once it was stabbed, the image came alive by bleeding.

Gregory's tale ends with the Jew failing to recognize (or acknowledge) the sanctity of Christ and the Christians exterminating the Jew. The damage the Jew would have liked to inflict on the painting was rendered ineffective by the presence of the divine being of Jesus in it, a kind of shield to which Gregory drew attention.[37] In addition, Gregory, by not setting the tale in a particular time or place, had enabled the Jewish desecrator to become a stock character.

Alleged Jewish Iconoclasm and Its Effect

Gregory's fictitious depiction of the Jewish desecrator was soon followed by hostile Byzantine-Christian chronicles, seemingly influenced either by the tale or by the fifth-century Theodosian Code of Emperor Honorius. These chronicles portrayed the alleged obliteration of images by historical Jews and not fictitious ones. Historical Jews were living in Byzantine territories, particularly in cities situated along the main waterways of the eastern Mediterranean and prominent land routes, and in political and administrative centers.[38] Their activities in Constantinople, Thessalonica, Thebes, Euripos/Negropont (modern Chalkis) in the island of Euboea, and Chandax/Candia (modern Iraklion) in Crete are well documented. Individual Jews were mobile and the flow of Jewish migration between Byzantium and Islamic countries, especially Egypt, would influence economic development between these regions. Despite some legal, administrative, and fiscal discrimination, they were able to engage in business activities of their choice, and they worked particularly in tanning, dyeing, and the manufacture of garments and silk textiles.[39] Descriptions of historical Jews committing crimes against Christian sacred images began to appear in Byzantine chronicles from the sixth century. John Malalas depicts them as a disobedient, disloyal people who deserve to be punished.[40] Seventh-century chroniclers, such as Sophronius and Antiochus Strategos describe them performing destructive acts against imperial and ecclesiastical authorities, participating in civil disturbances, and destroying Christian crosses and churches.[41] Jews appear as rebelling against imperial authority, rioting in Antioch in 608 or 609 and murdering the patriarch there. The chronicles also blamed Jews (as well as Christians) for the military crises created by the Persians in 614, and then the Islamic wars in 641 and 643. During the Persian siege of the Holy Land in 614, when the armies of Chosroes II, king of the Sassanids, occupied Jerusalem and captured the relic of the True Cross, descriptions of violent acts against Christians are ubiquitous, based on the assumption that Jews preferred to be ruled by Persians rather than Christians.[42] Jewish informers were reported to have assisted the Persian conquerors in entering the city, attacking local Christians, and burning and pillaging churches in their efforts to renew Temple services, as a quid pro quo with the Persians.[43] The author of the Khuzistan Chronicle (ca. 660–670) particularly stresses the Jewish attacks upon Jerusalem's churches, claiming that Jews had set fire to all of them.[44] These Christian texts constructed an image of the historical Jew that suited their need to categorize Jews in Christian theological formulations.[45] Recently, scholars have read these chronicles as sensational stories of historical Jews that intended to give a misrepresentation of Jewish treachery.[46] They argue that the loss of Jerusalem had a huge emotional and psychological impact on Byzantine Christians, who were unable to accept the idea that the holy city could be captured by a foreign and hostile enemy.[47] Some contend that Antiochus Strategos, a monk from the monastery of Sabas in the Judean desert, used his work to imply that the Jews were enemies of the Byzantines.[48] Strategos is now recognized as having exaggerated the Jews' role in the destruction of Jerusalem, the capture of the True Cross and the looting of sacred vessels from churches.[49] Although the Jews had welcomed the invaders, their involvement in Persian atrocities was inflated by these chroniclers to emphasize Jewish culpability.[50] Jews did not have the political structure to be recognized allies of the Persians or to exercise control over Jerusalem.[51]

In 641, Jewish rebels were again described as participating in a popular uprising to rid Constantinople of its patriarch, Pyrrhus. Rioters are recorded as breaking into Sancta Sophia, desecrating the church, and, in a display of mockery and triumph, carrying its keys through the city.[52] The *Chronicle of Theophanes* also reports that in the year 642/3 Caliph Umar was advised by the Jews of Jerusalem to take down the cross on the top of the Church of the Ascension on the Mount of Olives. The Jews, it was alleged, believed that this would enable the new al-Aqsa mosque to remain standing, since during its building it had continually collapsed.[53] Oddly, Theophanes concludes the summary of these events with the words: "For this reason Christ's enemies took down many crosses," although it makes no further mention of which crosses were in fact removed. It seems probable that the chronicler used poetic license here to show how the miraculous power of the cross on the Church of the Ascension had prevented the Muslims from building their mosque on the Temple Mount in Jerusalem. For when the "wicked" Jews brought about the destruction of the cross, they removed its miraculous power and caused not only the Christians' downfall at the hands of the Muslims, but prevented Christians from returning to the holy city.[54] Syriac and Greek sources record that the Jews also removed crosses from the roofs of churches in Damascus, including the Church of Saint John the Baptist.[55]

These records of supposed aggression against images, churches, and crosses, which are depicted in these chronicles with other forms of Jewish rebellion and civil protest against imperial authority, could certainly be used to associate the Jews with a tendency to attack Christian symbols and images. There is even some suggestion that the Byzantines might have been influenced in these beliefs by the Jews' actions against their own figural images in their Palestinian synagogues during the late sixth and seventh centuries.[56] For surely if Jews attack their own images, this confirms their wholehearted rejection of representations of figurative art. It is important to note that, from Theophanes onward, Byzantine chroniclers began to hold Jewish advisers responsible for the adoption of iconoclasm by Emperor Leo III in 727.[57] This alleged Jewish role in promoting iconoclasm would be repeated in all of the later Byzantine Jewish chronicles.

During the Iconoclastic Controversy, as crosses became increasingly central to the Christian faith, iconophiles (those who venerate icons) created cautionary tales based on historical Jews' alleged desecration of them in order to serve their own purposes.[58] As we shall see, to iconophiles the veneration of the cross authorized the legitimacy of images.[59]

Yet there had remained both a difference and a similarity between the fictional Jew of Gregory of Tours and the historical one of the Byzantine chronicles. In the chronicles, Jews are recorded as destroying crosses, whereas in the desecration tale, a painted image was violated, not obliterated. The similarity lay in the miraculous quality now being bestowed on crosses and Christian images. The *Chronicle of Theophanes* notes that, in 362/3, signs of the cross, which were appearing on altar cloths, church instruments, and clothes, were also miraculously appearing on the clothes of Jews.[60] Crosses, like Christian images were accepted as having transfigurational powers and were often worn by Christians either embroidered onto their clothes or as amulets around their necks.[61]

The Polemical Arguments

In the sixth and seventh centuries, portrayals of historical Jews and their alleged actions were becoming increasingly hostile not only in Byzantine Christian chronicles but in literary texts and anti-Jewish polemics, creating negative stereotypes that could easily be manipulated.[62] Byzantium had been profoundly affected by the Persian and then the Muslim invasions of 674–678 and 717. Coupled with a terrible plague and economic hardships, the empire had been reduced in size and its cities fractured and populations displaced.[63] Part of the Iconoclastic Controversy was connected with a reactive polemical outpouring as to who fitted into society and who did not, strengthening and defining the ideological boundaries and mindset of the Christian Byzantine mainly against the Jew, but also against the heretic and the Muslim.[64] There were many more Jews than Muslims living within the borders of the Byzantine Empire.

Although an allegation of the Jews' idolatry appears in the disputation literature of the beginning of the seventh century, there was as yet minimal discussion about the Jews' desecration or iconoclastic tendencies.[65] The disputation literature used the generic argument that the Hebrew Bible had prohibited icons being owned by Jews because Jews were prone to idolatry.[66] The fictional Jew would defend his aniconism and criticize the Christians for their usage of images.[67] Yet out of over thirty *adversus Judaeos* authors, Bishop Leontios of Neapolis, was the first to claim that images could work miracles. Around 630, he wrote a dialogue between a Jew and a Christian in order to refute Judaism and convert the Jews. Giving it the title "A Polemic Against the Jews," he provided a powerful critical defense of the Christian adoration of images against accusations by Jews of Christian idolatry: "If the Jews accuse the Christians of idolatry they should be covered with shame, for they did obeisance to their own kings and the kings of other nations. Everywhere the Christians have armed themselves against the idols. . . . Supposing that an idolater had come into your temple and seen the two sculpted cherubim and had blamed the Jews as being themselves idolaters, what could you reply? For the Christians, the cross and the icons are not gods; they remind us of Christ and His Saints that we should do them honor; they are there to beautify our churches."[68]

Here Leontios angrily contested the Jews' charge of idolatry by emphasizing, as many would after him, the memorial status of not only Old Testament kings but of the Jews' icons, which, he argued, like Christian icons, confirmed spiritual presence.[69] Leontios was also the first polemic writer to accuse Jews of desecrating Christian images, questioning why they were unable to "see" and love God, as Christians did. At one point the Christian interlocutor addresses the Jew with these words: "Tell me, is it not fitting to worship the saints, rather than to throw stones at them as you do? Is it not right to worship them, rather than to attack them, and to fling your benefactors into the mire? If you loved God, you would be ready to honor His servants also."[70]

Although Leontios does not mention the Jews' desecration in any other place in his dialogue, or give any specific examples of the Jews committing this offense (as Byzantine chronicles had), he still connected Jews and desecration. In referring to the fact that icons could perform miracles, he expressed his anger first against "fools" who misunderstand these reactions: "Often blood will gush forth from the icons and the relics of the martyrs, and foolish folk, though they see this, are not persuaded, they treat the miracles as myths and fables."[71] And then more so against the Jews:[72] "Let those who refuse to do obeisance to the cross and the icons explain how it is that the holy icons have often poured forth streams of myrrh by the power of the Lord and how it is that a lifeless stele when it has received a blow has miraculously given forth blood as though it were a living body."[73]

In effect Leontios was connecting two issues from Gregory of Tours's legend: the stubborn "blind" Jews on the one hand and the miraculous image that acted like a "living body" as a result of its violation.[74] What is never questioned by Leontios is how the Jews and the object related to each other, and why the object would react if it was violated by Jews. This suggests that his main focus is the ontological qualities of the image rather than the Jews as desecrators. Yet it confirms that the association between miraculous images and Jewish abuse was a recognized concept, and one might surmise that the Byzantine chronicles as well as tales of icons responding miraculously to Jewish desecration were spreading, although he does not refer to or include any historical event or tale in the polemical text.[75]

Another seventh-century *adversus Judaeos* text that focused on the issue of stubborn, blind Jews who show no respect to their own religious symbols was the *Dialogue of Papiscus and Philo* (which refers back to a much older second-century text, thus showing continuity). The participants are a monk (called Anastasius in one manuscript) and two wise Jews, Papiscus and Philo, and their discussion takes place before an assembly of Christians and Jews. Anastasius begins to blame the Jews for accusing Christians of committing idolatry when Jews themselves had worshipped the golden calf. Moreover, the monk asks: "Where are the tablets, the ark of the covenant, the tabernacle, the rod of Aaron, the burning bush, manna, the pillar of fire?"[76]

Why were the Jews so disrespectful to their most important religious relics? All these were holy objects that should have been preserved. But these, the monk continues, have all disappeared, but still the Jews remain blind to the power of Christian images.[77] Jews had come to represent image desecrators and idolaters who not only worshipped idols but had been unable to preserve their own most authentic symbols that legitimized their religious identity.

During the reign of Constantine V (741–775) who is considered the most "iconoclastic" emperor of the eighth and ninth centuries, iconophiles associated their iconoclast opponents and their position on idolatry with Jews, typically denouncing them as blasphemers and destroyers of images.[78] The iconoclasts' attack on images was interpreted as a strike at the sacred body depicted in the image. Of course, iconoclasts did not intend to attack Christ through his images, even though iconophiles argued that they did. What iconoclasts were attacking was the way that these images were used as cult objects and the way they had become sources of decadence for their owners. The iconophiles on the other hand selected the parts of the Jews' policies on idolatry most relevant to their own arguments.[79] It was the first internal debate in Christianity where Jews represented the enemy for both sides, the iconophiles and iconoclasts, concretizing the nature of a relationship between internal Christian developments regarding images and anti-Jewish accusations.

By the eighth century, as iconophiles strove for doctrinal unification, iconoclastic as well as desecrating Jews had become useful villains in cautionary tales both socially and theologically. The main message of the tales was that religious icons, with their miraculous qualities, were unquestionably to be understood as a fundamental component of Christian spirituality. It is with this background that we must turn to the next surviving tale.

A Traveler's Version

The next tale of Jewish desecration after that of Gregory of Tours was set in Constantinople and appears in a seventh-century travelogue *De locis sanctis*.[80] Composed by Adomnán, the hagiographer and abbot of Iona (627/8–704), the text describes the travels of Arculf, a Gallic bishop, who went on a pilgrimage to visit the holy sites in the Middle East and returned via Byzantium. Much has been written about Adomnán, his sources, and his relationship with Arculf.[81] Some scholars see the *De locis sanctis* as an authentic record of Arculf's travels, whereas others view it as Adomnán's sophisticated scriptural interpretation of the holy places Arculf visited.[82] Until now most scholars have analyzed book 1 of the travelogue, in which Adomnán describes the topography of Jerusalem. Book 2 describes Bethlehem. But book 3, which concentrates on Arculf's recollections of Constantinople and the island of Vulcano, is much shorter and has received far less attention.[83] Arculf's recollections are dominated by miraculous narratives that interchange theology with the topography of Byzantium.[84] Trying to set the story he describes within the landscape of the real city, Adomnán gives the description some authority and reliability by informing the reader that Arculf had heard the story from "well-informed citizens" of Constantinople. The Latin travelogue confirms that a prominent tale, now recorded as a "true story" of Jewish desecration of a specific image of Mary, was well known in Constantinople by this time. Adomnán relates the following:

> The oft-mentioned Arculf gave us an accurate rendering also of a true story about an ikon of the holy Mary, mother of the Lord, which he learned from some well-informed witnesses in the city of Constantinople. On the wall of a house in the metropolitan city, he said, a picture of the blessed Mary used to hang, painted on a short wooden tablet. A stupid and hardhearted man asked whose picture it was, and was told by someone that it was a likeness of the holy Mary ever virgin. When he heard this that Jewish unbeliever became very angry and, at the instigation of the devil, seized the picture from the wall and ran to a building nearby, where it is customary to dispose of the soil from human bodies by means of openings in long planks whereon people sit. There, in order to dishonor Christ, who was born of Mary, he cast the picture of His mother through the opening on the nuisance lying beneath. Then in his stupid folly he sat above himself and evacuated through the opening, pouring the nuisance of his own person on the ikon of the holy Mary which he had just deposited there. After that disgraceful action the hapless creature went away, and what he did subsequently, how he lived, or what sort of end he had, is unknown. After the scoundrel had gone, one of the Christian community came upon the scene, a fortunate man, zealous for the things of the Lord. Knowing what had happened, he searched for the picture of the holy Mary, found it hidden in the refuse and took it up. He wiped it carefully and cleaned it by washing it in the clearest water, and then set it up in honor by him in his house.

The painting then began to seep "wondrous oil." "Wonderful to relate . . . this wondrous oil proclaims the honor of Mary, the mother of the Lord Jesus of whom the Father says: 'With my oil I have anointed him.' Likewise the psalmist addresses the Son of God himself when he says: 'God thy God hath anointed thee with the oil of joy beyond thy companions.'"[85]

Gregory of Tours's trope had changed substantially by the seventh century into a "true story," or so it was disseminated in Byzantium. It propagated the idea of a historical Jewish desecrator rather than a fictitious one.

Here the legend involved an icon of the Virgin Mary rather than one of Christ. This change in the object of abuse reflects the growing variety of icons in the Byzantine world and the increasing prominence of the Virgin Mary in the Eastern church.[86] From this time, the Virgin was endowed with all the characteristics of a universal mother, and in our story in particular she is attacked by the Jew "in order to dishonor Christ," her son. Relics had already turned churches of Mary in Constantinople into cult centers, and there is some suggestion that miraculous images of Mary, or *acheiropoieta*, did so as well, in that these representations were supposedly not manufactured by human hands but had a miraculous origin, thereby bridging the gap of sanctity between a manufactured icon and a nonmanufactured relic.[87] The first "true" portrait of the Virgin and Child, and one of the few known about in Constantinople, was supposedly painted by Saint Luke and was discovered by Eudocia, the wife of Emperor Theodosius II (408–450). By the middle of the fifth century, it was reported that the painting was being kept in the former home for the blind.[88] Was this the image Adomnán was referring to when he wrote that the icon of Mary was exhibited in a "house"? It is possible that the use of the term house (*domus*) in this story as well as in other stories in Adomnán's travelogue could well have been due to the bishop's mistranslation of the Greek word for church.[89] Yet even if this was a church, the painting's ordeal ends with it being rescued by a Christian and kept in his house. So unlike Gregory of Tours's case, this "true story" involves three locations. The house/church in which the image was originally situated, the public latrines, and a new location—the home of the Christian who rescued it. While Adomnán recounts that Arculf saw not only this Marian icon but also its seeping oil, he makes no mention of the icon's exact location in the city, which in a travelogue would have been essential.[90]

The narrative also gives the Jewish desecrator a different, more aggressive role. The first time he is described, he is presented as "a stupid and hard-hearted man," but not as a Jew. The fact that the tale does not present him immediately as a Jew is interesting, allowing the reader to surmise that the desecrator could be a Byzantine iconoclast. But this assumption is quickly obliterated by the desecrator being shown as not knowing who Mary was. On being told, he flares up in anger and is moved to desecration at the "instigation of the devil." Functioning as a facilitator for the devil's magical actions, the Jew seems to be led not by his own desires but by the devil's own erroneous knowledge.

The Jews' association with the devil had originated in the New Testament and with the church fathers.[91] In the West, by the seventh century, Pope Gregory the Great had attacked the Jews for their alliance with the devil and the Antichrist—in particular alleging that Jews acted in the devil's interests and that the devil determined the Jews' past and future.[92] Devils who disseminated heretical ideas frequently appeared in seventh-century Byzantine tales depicting Jews.[93] The ecumenical council of Emperor Justinian II in 691, whose primary goal was the eradication of the remnants of pagan and Jewish malice, dealt with the devil who never ceased flinging arrows of evil and tormenting the believers with sorrow.[94] By the eighth century, the devil's connection with the Jews would be reemphasized through a particular tale, authors unknown, in which the devil together with the Jews and a Muslim caliph had initiated the iconoclasm of the Isaurian emperors in order to cause confusion regarding the prohibition and destruction of icons.[95] A "gigantic" Jewish adviser and magician Tessarakontapêchys (meaning "forty cubits"!) from Tiberias, had, under the influence of the devil, persuaded Yazid Ibn Abd al-Malik in c. 714, also known as Yazid II, a Syrian caliph who ruled from 720 until his death in 724, that if he destroyed all Christian images in Byzantium, he would reign for an additional thirty or even forty years.[96] Yazid had agreed to this plan in the second year of his caliphate and an edict was pronounced.[97] It seems that there really was some sort of iconoclastic movement under Yazid II almost as soon as he became caliph.[98] This Christian tale had actually cast the Muslim caliph's belief as Jewish, or at least Jewish inspired, and this became typical of Christian writings. On occasion Muslims were referred to as the "New Jews," since their arguments regarding the Christians' idolatry had been brought forward initially by the Jews.[99]

The abolition of images in the caliphate had apparently caused the Byzantine ruler, Emperor Constantine V, to enact the same measure in the empire. Christian iconophiles would argue that the Iconoclastic Controversy had been caused by the charge of idolatry against Christianity by the Muslims.[100] Greek sources were to promulgate the idea that, because Christians did not want to destroy their own images, Jews and Muslims had been employed to destroy them, and so iconoclasm, the full destruction of icons, spread through the empire at their hands.[101]

This tale clearly forged a false tradition, connecting the controversy's origin with the Jews' and Muslims' practice of iconoclasm. The Jew was being cast as devil-like with the capacity to cause colossal harm and shatter stability in the empire. For our purposes in particular, the recording of Adomnán's tale in the travelogue also confirmed that the Jew's association with the devil had, through the experiences of western pilgrim travelers to Byzantium, been brought back to western Europe.

In Adomnán's tale, the Jew's act of desecration has become the most outrageous possible violation of Christianity, that of defecating on the image. Was this extreme act of aggression influenced by Christian knowledge of Jewish writings in the Talmud and Midrash, which distorted the Latin form of Mary's name, Maria, to *haria* meaning feces?[102] The Jews' aggression seems to be directed at Mary herself rather than the image. This is emphasized by Adomnán's moralizing at the end of the tale, where he demands that his readers focus on the honor of the divine model, the Virgin Mary herself, rather than the miraculous image.

After his nauseating act, the Jew is forgotten—an important contrast with the Gregory of Tours tale, which concerned itself with the Jew's execution. Here the Jew's fate remains irrelevant to the tale since, as an infidel rather than a heretic, he cannot be saved by the Virgin's grace. In contrast to the Jew, the virtuous Christian iconophile is "zealous for the things of the Lord," rescues the painting, removes it from the privy, and meticulously cleans it "in the clearest water," thereby purifying it from the "dishonor" done by the Jew. The final message seems to rest with Mary as the divine model of the image. Her energies were invested not in retaliating against the Jew but in ensuring that, when treated appropriately, her images had the power to convey her favor upon her Christian venerators. By the end of the seventh century, it is clear that tales were circulating as if they described real events. At the same time Christian iconophiles in Constantinople were according images numinous attributes, including channeling access to divinity. Christians were expected to show suitable devotion and veneration to these Christian images that were now housed in private domestic realms to ensure that no devil or demon disguised as a Jew could lead them into temptation or inflict harm on Christianity.[103]

"Christ of Beirut" at Nicaea

The final stage of the chapter will trace one more desecration narrative as it developed through time and space. "Christ of Beirut," although an original tale, is built upon familiar tropes of the *inventio crucis* legend with the intention of bringing its message closer to the audience who would hear it or read it.[104] Like the *inventio crucis* and the tale of Tessarakontapêchys, "Christ of Beirut" (mentioned in the Introduction) is another tale that presents a moralizing and illustrative lesson about Christian images as a historical event, causing the reader or listener to lose sense of whether its claims were fact or fiction. By this time, iconodules were creating tales to promote the miraculous qualities of Christian images.[105] Their tales were not limited to using Jews as desecrators but included pagans, heretics, and Muslims, all committing various acts of sacrilege, since these groups shared an inability to recognize the divine presence in symbols and images. Muslims as well as Jews could make images bleed, reminding Christians to support the veneration of images.[106]

When "Christ of Beirut" was recorded there had been a significant shift in the development of Byzantine iconographic theology. John of Damascus had, as shown above, affirmed that Christ was present in images as true God and true man, but it was the Council of Hiereia in 754 that confirmed that both divinity and humanity existed in the iconic depiction of Christ.[107] "Christ of Beirut," recorded in Greek, contextualized this new reality, giving it explicit shape and form and portraying the possible complicated emotions that resulted from it. Moreover, in its depiction of the image's blood, the tale would incorporate Eucharistic elements, confirming how divine power could come to inhabit material objects.

The tale was recorded in the fourth session (October 1) of the Seventh Ecumenical Council at Nicaea in 787, which discussed the legitimacy of the worship of icons on the basis of the Holy Scripture and the fathers, as well as biblical and patristic texts.[108] Intimately connected with the broader issue of the church's authority and its ideological-political interests within the Christian-Roman world, the intention of ecumenical councils was to resolve the doctrinal differences not only on images but on the very nature of God. The acts of this council reinstated icons, proclaiming iconophile polemics rather than debating them and establishing a formal method of venerating images.[109] They also include extensive quotations from the anti-Jewish works of the seventh-century John of Salonica and the fifth discourse of the apology of Leontios, bishop of Neapolis, *On behalf of the Christians against the Jews and on the icons of the saints*.[110] One of the letters preserved in the same collection, purportedly from Pope Gregory II (715–731) to Emperor Leo III, justified and defended images and contained Christian polemics against Jewish accusations of idolatry, so it is not surprising that the following tale would be incorporated into its records.[111]

"Christ of Beirut" was one of the sixteen "reports" of miracle-working icons read at the council.[112] These stories, read as polemical texts, told of icons healing Constantine the Great and others and punishing Christians who had insulted them and affirmed their indestructible qualities as *acheiropoieta*. One particular miraculous image was the spurious "Christ of Beirut." It had originally appeared in a Greek theological anthology compiled in Rome in 774–775.[113] The "report" was publicly read by the iconophile bishop Peter of Nicomedia. He ascribed the story to the fourth-century saint Athanasius of Alexandria, clearly trying to validate its event by its association with an authoritative father of the church, and thereby rewriting the past.[114] The "Christ of Beirut" tale's crucial development has been meticulously traced by Michele Bacci, who argues that it created the most powerful exemplum of Jewish violence against images. Its concept also activated the trope of Jews as actual "killers" of the animated holy bodies rather than mere desecrators of sacred images. Its story is set in fourth-century Beirut, under Byzantine rule, where the Jews were integrated into the social structures and spaces of the town.[115] After a brief description of its geographical location, Peter recounted a complex narrative and sophisticated story of a devout Christian who prayed in his bedroom to a picture of Christ: "most definitely venerable since it reproduced the full figure of Christ the Lord."[116]

His dwelling was rather small and near the synagogue, so he decided to move to another part of town. In leaving his home, he forgot to take the portrait with him. The new owner, a Jew, is depicted as remaining oblivious or blind to the life-size Christian image hanging in his bedroom. One evening, the Jew invited some of his Jewish friends to dinner. Unlike the host, this group of Jews observed the image of Christ. One guest asked him: "How do you as a Jew have the nerve to have such an image in your house? . . . The host, who wanted to defend himself, stated with innocence that he had not noticed it before. Then the guest became silent."[117]

But the unnamed guest did not believe his host and, after dinner, before the whole company, he accused him of blasphemy. It is at this point that the story takes on narrative elements of Christ's crucifixion. The Jewish council was informed and decided that the image should be removed from the house, as Jesus had been removed from the Jewish community in Judea. The following morning the rabbis and other Jews broke into the Jew's home. Seeing the image, they began collectively to reenact the Crucifixion on the painting shouting out: "Whatever our fathers did to him, let us all do the same to this image."[118]

After spitting on and punching the image, they pierced its hands and feet with nails, applying a sponge soaked with vinegar and gall as if to slake Christ's thirst (John 19:29–30), and sticking a crown of thorns, one of the instruments of the Passion, on its head.[119] Then it was suggested that they whip the icon and one said: "It is common knowledge that they [our forefathers] pierced his side with a lance. Let us leave nothing out; let's do that too!"[120]

When they had pierced the side with a lance, they were shocked by the large volume of blood and water that seeped from the icon. This gushing of both blood and water attested to the Crucifixion story according to the fourth canonical Gospel of John, where a Roman soldier had pierced Jesus's side with a lance to check that he was dead, and from that place there had been "a sudden flow of blood and water."[121] Then in the tale, the Jews, wondering at this gushing and wanting to test the power of the image, decided to collect the liquids and test their potency on Jews who were afflicted with ailments: "Since Christian worshippers say that He was the author of many unprecedented miracles in the world, let us collect this blood and water and take them to our synagogue where we will gather everyone who is sick. We will sprinkle them with these liquids: if what is said about Christ is true, everybody will be immediately healed; otherwise we will use them as a proof against what his believers declare about him."[122] It is at this point that a new element is introduced. Many sick Jews, including the blind and paralytic were healed, and deceased Jews were brought back to life as a result of the miraculous power of the blood.[123]

The Jews then approached the local bishop and asked him to baptize them all. The bishop, keen to learn the details of the case before him, called for the first owner of the image. The owner explained that the image had been painted by Nicodemus, a Pharisee Jew who had shown kindness to Jesus.[124] Since, according to the Gospel of John, Nicodemus had been present at Jesus's crucifixion, the Beirut icon was noted as being an *acheiropoieton*—an original painting of Jesus's crucifixion, thereby attaining the authenticity of a New Testament relic.[125]

The Beirut synagogue was turned into a church and was consecrated to Christ, the Savior. Tarsasius, the patriarch present at the Nicaea council, confirmed the iconophilic message of the story for those present: "It is a sign that God has made through the image, that images should draw us closer to the Christian faith."[126]

This eighth-century tale/report of Jewish image desecration with its considerable shift in emphasis must be decoded. "Christ of Beirut" transformed the Jewish desecration narrative that depicted a single desecrator who, in previous tales, either died or vanished, into a meticulous and blatant reenactment of the Crucifixion played upon an image of Christ. This resulted in the miraculous blood confirming an authentic reaction of Christ through the painting, and its waters as symbolizing the redemptive waters of baptism that brought about the conversion of the Jews. Similar to the *inventio crucis* legend, the story is depicted in three acts. In the first, the Jew had attacked the icon (instead of hiding it); in the second, the icon had miraculously healed the sick; and in the third, the Jews voluntarily converted to Christianity. In both the *inventio crucis* and now "Christ of Beirut," the Jews converted, thereby accepting the religion of which they had previously been the greatest opponents.

There are other important developments in this tale, which, by its very telling, revealed that its Christian iconophile author/s were manipulating past knowledge and associations of Jewish image desecration as well as contemporaneous patterns of image veneration. Instead of stealing an image from a church or a Christian home, the Jew now has an icon of Christ in his own property. The fact that a Jew could find a Christian icon in his own domestic space confirms how ubiquitous these images had become in homes all over Byzantium, even being carelessly left when minorities rented these spaces, after Christian tenants had left. This first version of "Christ of Beirut" did not specify whether it was a Passion painting or merely "the full figure of Christ the Lord." This allowed it to be seen as either—an image of Christ as a divine man who bled or an image of his crucifixion whereby Jesus had already died and was God.[127]

The Jewish host who lived with the painting and was more in contact with the image than his guests, had failed to notice it. In fact, his blindness was only uncovered by a group of Jews who had come to his home. Like the *inventio crucis* legend, the Christian author/s here seemed to imply that Jews were a people who unconsciously preserved Christian sacred objects.[128] The Jewish guests who enter the host's home are the ones who attempted desecration in order to test the image's worth for themselves. This was a collective desecration, similar to the acts of historical Jews described in earlier Byzantine chronicles. Once these fictitious Jews had tested it and discovered the power of the image, they were granted a newly possible happy ending, signifying the ideal according to Paul's Epistle to the Romans, when all Jews would convert to Christianity.[129]

Adversus Judaeos dialogues had already propagated the idea that the way to convert Jews was to enlighten them.[130] It must be suggested that this tale was also connected to the experience of real Jews of Byzantium who, like Paulician heretics and pagans in the Peloponnese, had been subjected to forced conversion, first by an imperial edict of Heraclius, and then by similar rulings of Leo III and later by Basil I in 873–874.[131]

Moreover, from the late eighth-century Byzantium there had even existed an abjuration and conversion formula that Jews were expected to say when they chose to convert to Orthodox Christianity and were baptized. This was first mentioned in Evagrius's fifth-century *Altercatio inter Theophilum Christianum et Simonem Judaeum*. The formula read: "I next curse those [i.e., the Jews] who keep the festival of the so-called Mordecai on the first Sabbath of the Christian fasts (Lent) nailing Haman to wood and then mixing with him the emblem of a cross and burning them together, subjecting Christians to all kinds of imprecations and a curse."[132]

Imperial legislators clearly believed that, as mentioned earlier in this chapter, during the festival of Purim Jews burned the cross with an effigy of Haman—rather than Christ—affixed to it as a ritual derision of the Crucifixion.[133] By reciting this formula, new converts were seen to publicly denounce the Jewish practice of desecrating images.[134] The Jews' conversion in this tale clearly reflected not just the emperors' eschatological hopes but also the prevalence of this goal in contemporary hagiography, disputation literature, and other texts.[135] The Jews' conversion was encouraged in Byzantine by a promise of money, an exemption from heavy taxes and fiscal charges, the possibility of marrying a Christian and even achieving high office.[136]

Although the forced conversion of the Jews never became official Byzantine policy, their total integration was a more realistic goal than that of the Muslims who remained political as well as religious rivals and outsiders.[137] The 787 council had even sanctioned new guidelines advocating the sincere conversion of the Jews.[138]

A new feature of "Christ of Beirut" was that of Eucharistic symbolism, whereby the miraculous power of Christ's blood enabled the establishment of belief for the Jewish onlookers.[139] The iconophiles clearly intended to create a tale that directly connected Christ's Eucharist blood to an icon of Christ, confirming that the sacrificial death of Jesus could actually occur again in a Passion painting.[140] For whereas iconoclasts had argued that the concept of transfiguration should be reserved in the strict sense for the sacrament of the Eucharist alone, iconophiles were emphasizing in this council that even though the Eucharist was the superior sacramental image, it should also be associated with miraculous images.[141] The miraculous image had, like the Eucharist, become a material substitute for Christ's body. For it was reported at the end of the tale that Bishop Peter had ordered a great quantity of glass containers to be filled with the holy substance of the miraculous blood and water, which were then "dispatched throughout Asia, Africa, and Europe."[142] Here the miraculous liquid, the seeping Eucharistic blood, seemed to be as important as the icon. The bishop's legates were ordered to spread the "report" of the Beirut miracle and ensure that this miracle be commemorated annually on November 9.[143]

"Christ of Beirut" had morphed from a report at a council to a tale and now became a legend. An image appeared in Beirut that authenticated the tale with a relic.[144] In 872 the chief librarian of the Church of Rome, Anastasius (ca. 810–873), repeated and translated the legend from Greek to Latin. Given the increased attention, the Byzantine government subsequently ordered a real "image" to be transferred from the obscurity of Beirut to a proper home in Constantinople. Chroniclers report that in 975 "the image of Beirut" itself was brought to Constantinople by Emperor John Tsimiskes and placed in the chapel of the Chalkì of the imperial palace. Its Passion relics received official backing through the introduction of the new feast of "Christ of Beirut" and the inclusion of special liturgies.[145] Emphasis was placed not only on the Jews' abuse of Christian images but on the transfigurational power of the image that had caused the conversions of Jews to Christianity.[146] What the legend also achieved was the initiation of the idea that Jews would use Christ's blood for their own miraculous purposes.[147]

The "Christ of Beirut" tale's new emphasis on salvific blood that seeped from images seemed to give rise to new versions of its telling. Living under Muslim rule, Theodore Abū Qurrah, the Melkite bishop of Harran between the years 795 and 812 and one of the robust voices against Byzantine iconoclasm, in his "Treatise on the Veneration of Holy Icons" had noted how "Christ of Beirut" had become "famous and known in all the Christian churches." He recorded a Syriac tale where a blind Jew from Tiberias becomes a Christian after regaining his sight by placing the blood that had miraculously seeped from a desecrated image of a crucified Christ upon his eyes.[148] In this story two Jews—one blind and the other paralytic—who were cured by the miraculous blood and water seeping from the side of the image, convert to Christianity and become Christian heroes.[149] The tale itself is less about the bleeding image, which as a result of a divine earthquake "no man ever saw again," than its seeping blood and water, which continued to heal the sick. A similar story is recounted in Alexandria.[150] In all these examples, the Jews reenact the Crucifixion on a figure or icon, and the miraculous liquid that seeps from it heals those who touch it and brings about their abandonment of Judaism and their conversion to Christianity.[151] The central importance of the desecrated image has shifted to a secondary role after the Jews' reenactment of the Crucifixion on an image and that of its seeping miraculous Eucharistic blood.

A Final Tale

The final four Byzantine tales appear in the *Letter of the Three Patriarchs*, which purports to be an official letter written in Greek to the iconoclastic Byzantine emperor Theophilos (829–842). It was composed by the three oriental patriarchs—Christopher of Alexandria, Job of Antioch, and Basil of Jerusalem—who exercised control over the cult of icons in the East, at an apparently well-attended synod held at the Church of the Holy Sepulchre in Jerusalem in April 836.[152] This period was often known as "the second iconoclasm" and lasted from 815 until 842; the debate on images had moved to a more theoretical and theological ground, and churchmen and monks, even though complying with the official iconoclast line, vacillated between anti- and pro-image directives.[153] Many such letters survive from this period, and some are indeed theological tracts addressing major issues of practice and belief, and although the *Letter of the Three Patriarchs* seems to adopt this format, scholars tend to argue otherwise.[154] They claim that it is more likely that this *Letter* is a late ninth- or tenth-century anthology of an original document addressed to the emperor with a selection of other texts added. The *Letter* includes four stories about Jews and their attack on Christian images, which at that time were being disseminated in Constantinople.[155] The rewriting of the tales clearly served educational, religious, and ideological purposes, transmitting knowledge of miraculous icons and establishing dogma and certain religious ideologies regarding image veneration.

The *Letter* is a work of deliberate anti-iconoclastic propaganda demanding that the Byzantines view the eastern provinces, which continued to venerate religious images despite the pressure of Muslim criticism, as part of the Orthodox Church.[156] For our purposes, it confirms that the previous narratives and their oral traditions analyzed here had, by the late ninth and tenth centuries, been committed to writing in textual collections and were being transmitted through the empire. Two new, less aggressive tales were added.

The *Letter* consists of fifteen stories that bestow canonical authority on the restoration of images and give authenticity to twelve icons through which Christ, Mary, and Saint Andrew worked miracles. These images (including the Holy Face of Edessa, an image of Mary in the church in Lydda, and Luke's depiction of Mary) acted in favor of their supporters (such as historical figures—Constantine the Great and Pope Gregory II) or against their desecrators who included Muslims, Persians, Jews, and Christian heretics.[157] The message of these stories is mentioned toward the end of the *Letter*. Here iconoclasts, depicted as unbelievers who desecrate crosses or images of Christ, are again compared to Jews:

> Since whoever tramples upon or rejects the image and shape of the life-giving Cross in whatever material it may be depicted, though made by human hand, is a foul infidel and a denier of Christ and has made himself alien to the whole Christian faith because of the insult he is already levelling at the prototype, how much greater punishment and eternal condemnation do you think, will be deserved by anyone who sets aside the revered and honoured image of the crucified One, who sanctified the Cross, and how much more so if he tramples it underfoot and spits upon it? Such a person is similar and equivalent to those Jews who spat in His face, struck Him on the head with a rod and slapped Him.[158]

The text implies that the first type of iconoclast is the one who destroys the human-made crosses, which in effect is an attack upon Christ himself. The second type of iconoclast referred to is one who violates images of the Passion or crucifixes, since their desecration would be equal to the Jews' reenactment of the Crucifixion, an action already demonstrated in the previous "Christ of Beirut" legend and referred to again here. Jews were hereby recognized as standardized desecrators of Christ, to whom other iconoclasts were to be compared. Their pivotal role as desecrators suggests how successful the dissemination of such tales had been and that it continued to assist iconophiles in their polemical arguments.

If, as Jaś Elsner argues, iconoclasm had, by the ninth century, become a debate about "appropriate epistemology"—how the holy was to be "known, worshipped and approached"—it certainly made sense to disseminate further tales connected to real existing icons in the East with the intention of ensuring their veneration.[159] Images of the dead Christ on the cross, had actually become widespread only after the end of iconoclasm, from approximately the middle of the ninth century.[160] "Christ of Beirut" and the other three stories in the *Letter* now provided a mythical provenance to real images, which, according to Christians, were attacked by fictitious Jewish violators—in Beirut, Lydda, and one just outside Lydda and Constantinople. They all confirm the value of the icons in relation to their mediating functions. Stories about fictitious Jewish desecrators had clearly helped to disseminate the veneration of Passion paintings and crucifixes through Byzantium and the Holy Land.

In all of the four tales, the Jew's central position as the abuser is of less concern and there is no depiction of soiling or defecating on the image in any of the tales. In the *Letter*, the "Christ of Beirut" narrative merely describes how a Jew in Beirut (a wicked man), injured a sacred image of the Savior with a spear, "as did the Jews in the past" (a clear reference to the Passion itself). Immediately it caused an outpouring of blood that had healing qualities.[161] This version fails to mention the conversion and baptism of the Jewish community, giving the whole narrative a different emphasis. Perhaps "Christ of Beirut" was so well known that no further detail was necessary at this time.

The next story is an adaptation of the Arculf narrative from the seventh century, although here the image has changed back from that of the Virgin to an icon of Christ as it had been initially in Gregory of Tours's tale.[162] It is not clear that this was an image of the Passion, but its change to an image of Christ reflects the *Letter*'s intention of emphasizing that icons could also affirm the reality of Christ's incarnation. This icon was said to be situated next to a holy well at the Church of Sancta Sophia in Constantinople.[163] A Jew stabbed the icon through the heart, and blood covered the Jew's face and clothes. He quickly threw the icon into the well (no longer a latrine) and its water turned to blood. The blood on his clothes exposed his crime and the Jew was arrested as a murderer. When he admitted his guilt, the icon was removed from the well with a dagger plunged through the chest of Christ. Seeing the icon bleeding profusely, the witnesses were "gripped with amazement and terror." Here again as in the ending of "Christ of Beirut," the Jew and his family converted to Christianity and were baptized, "having believed in the Lord together with his entire household."[164] Arculf's tale had been significantly altered. Here the Jew is no longer despicable but plays a part as a compliant offender who admits his crime when he sees the Eucharistic blood and converts as the Beirut Jews had. The tale had incorporated the satisfactory ending, which involved not only the conversion of the desecrator but that of his family.

In the first two tales of the *Letter*, the Jews' attack resulted in the seeping of blood from the wounded image, which healed those who saw it and convinced Jews no longer to be enemies of the faith but to convert. In a period of continuing and bitter religious dispute, the depiction of the desecration act has become less unsavory—the Jew no longer puts the painting in a latrine nor does he defecate upon it. This did not necessarily reflect a less aggressive attitude toward Jews. But the emphasis of the tale has changed. Images were now legitimately venerated in Byzantium, and the Jews' role did not need to shock audiences as it had done in earlier centuries.[165] It was the favorable outcome of these stories—the seeping of Christ's blood from images and the open and willing conversion of the Jews—that needed to be emphasized. The Jews as converts were to be integrated into society—not killed, rejected, or seen as disgusting abusers. The *Letter* later confirmed: "with the shedding of the immaculate blood, flowing from God, the Church is revealed as sanctified, pure and unblemished, having no stain or wrinkle, through the waters of rebirth and the renewal of the Holy Spirit, and shown to be a chosen race, a holy nation, a royal priesthood, a unique nation."[166]

In the third and fourth tales, the Jews again play a far less aggressive role, being merely props to show the thaumaturgical power of Mary's images. Here, the Jews are not even able to physically desecrate a Marian image. One, called "Lydda," describes an *acheiropoieton* of Mary, which the Jews were unable to violate. It is set in the fourth century in a church originally built by the apostles Peter and John in Lydda (Lod/Diospolis), eighteen miles north of Jerusalem, and dedicated to the Virgin. It was a time when the Jews' presence in Palestine was considerably outnumbered by other religious and ethnic groups.[167] Mary's image had been miraculously imprinted on one of the columns of the church after the apostles had requested her presence at the church's consecration.[168] The emperor Julian the Apostate heard about this image and had a group of "Hebrew painters" investigate it.[169] When they tried to remove it, the image only became more radiant and luminous. Here the Jews' violation (an act officially sanctioned by the emperor himself) had no effect, nor were they punished for their indiscretion. The weakness shown by their inability to damage the painting is meant to contrast with the miraculous strength shown by Mary in keeping her image safe.[170] The tale reminded readers not only of the indestructible power of the *acheiropoieton* of Mary, but also the sanctification of Mary through her image. A recorded sermon from this time even "reported" the image's miraculous transportation to Constantinople, and its location in the Chalcoprateia church.[171]

Another very similar tale about a Marian image follows almost directly. The story describes how in a city near Lydda, the paralytic Aeneas, cured by Peter, had built with his own hands a house of prayer to Mary. Here the Jews share the stage with the Greeks who had taken recourse to the local governor because both parties wanted to gain possession of the holy site. The governor decided to have the site closed under guard for three days by which time an image of the Virgin had miraculously appeared on the western wall of the church, wearing purple, and with letters carved above her that read "Mary the Mother of Christ the King from Nazareth." The Jews and Greeks left humiliated, and the image continued to demonstrate its thaumaturgical qualities by healing the sick.[172]

* * *

Thus the first two tales had become far less aggressive, removing the evil Jewish desecrator from center stage. Icons of Christ were hereby confirmed as autonomous representations of Christ incarnate, defended by their divine model, who brought about the Jews' conversion. In the last two tales, potential Jewish desecrators remain powerless against Marian images, which in their *acheiropoeita* cannot be touched by unbelievers.[173]

Tales had become ways of confirming the miraculous qualities of real paintings in many places of the empire. For Christians this sanctified their use of paintings as icons but did so at the expense of their Jewish neighbors. Before finishing, some consideration should be given to the images of Jews in small Byzantine Psalters, books of psalms used by Christians as daily prayer books, which were produced in Constantinople at this time. The Khludov Psalter was created sometime between 843 and the end of the ninth century and was intended for private study by the patriarch himself.[174] Most of the polemical images in the Psalter, which were supposed to give context, clarity, and relevance to the flowery poetry of the psalms, depict Jews. Their portrayal as iconoclasts reflects not only the iconophiles' own refutation of iconoclasts but their own understanding of how closely the iconoclasts' arguments had corresponded with the thoughts and actions of Jews.[175]

Some of these images portray the Jews not only as crucifiers of Christ, but also as image desecrators. In the Psalter, Psalm 68—a psalm that beseeches God to save the psalmist from those attacking him—has line 22 illuminated: "They gave me also gall for my food and made me drink vinegar for my thirst." On the right side of the text, the artist paints the Passion (Figure 2). At the foot of the cross, two tormentors, identified as Jews by their "Jewish garments" (a barely visible knot of the cowl) and their facial features—a receding forehead, combined with an elongated jaw and nose to demonstrate their wickedness.[176] They attack and torment Jesus on the cross (the one on the right holds the lance with which he pierces Christ's side, and the one on the left pushes a sponge toward Jesus's mouth).[177] Below them stand two other bestial men (the one in the front has been identified as representing the patriarch of Constantinople himself, John VII the Grammarian, the "chief focus of Iconophile ire") who are whitewashing a medallion of Christ's portrait with a sponge dipped in lime.[178] The two large amphorae depicted below, there to catch the blood, connect both scenes and show that iconoclasts and fictitious Jews are identical in nature and behave in the same way toward images.[179] The medallion image is depicted as an authentic icon or image of Christ, which like Christ himself bleeds when stabbed or attacked. The juxtaposition of these two acts on the same page clearly merges the historical and allegorical depiction of the Crucifixion. But it also identifies Christian iconoclasts with not only fictitious Jews who desecrate Christian images but also historical Jews who crucify Christ.[180] This blurring of identity between Jews and iconoclasts is repeated in the Khludov Psalter's depiction of the iconoclastic Council of 815 in Constantinople, which shows the council "awash in blood," which had seeped from a crack in the wall next to the image of Christ. The blood flowed down the wall and covered Theodotus and Symbatios-Constantine (the iconoclasts) up to their shoulders. Just like fictitious Jews, iconoclasts could cause images to bleed and were therefore unbelievers themselves.

It is not surprising then that the fictitious Jews' association with iconoclasm and iconoclasts in these Byzantine tales would concretize the attitudes and ways of thinking of Byzantine chroniclers. The chroniclers' description of historical Jews as real desecrators continued unabated in the tenth century. Yahya ibn Sa'ib (Eutychius) reported that, in 937, Jews, together with Muslims, destroyed Saint Mary's Church in Ashkelon and thirty years later badly damaged three of Jerusalem's churches during anti-Christian riots during which the patriarch John VII was murdered.[181] Christian historians and apologists

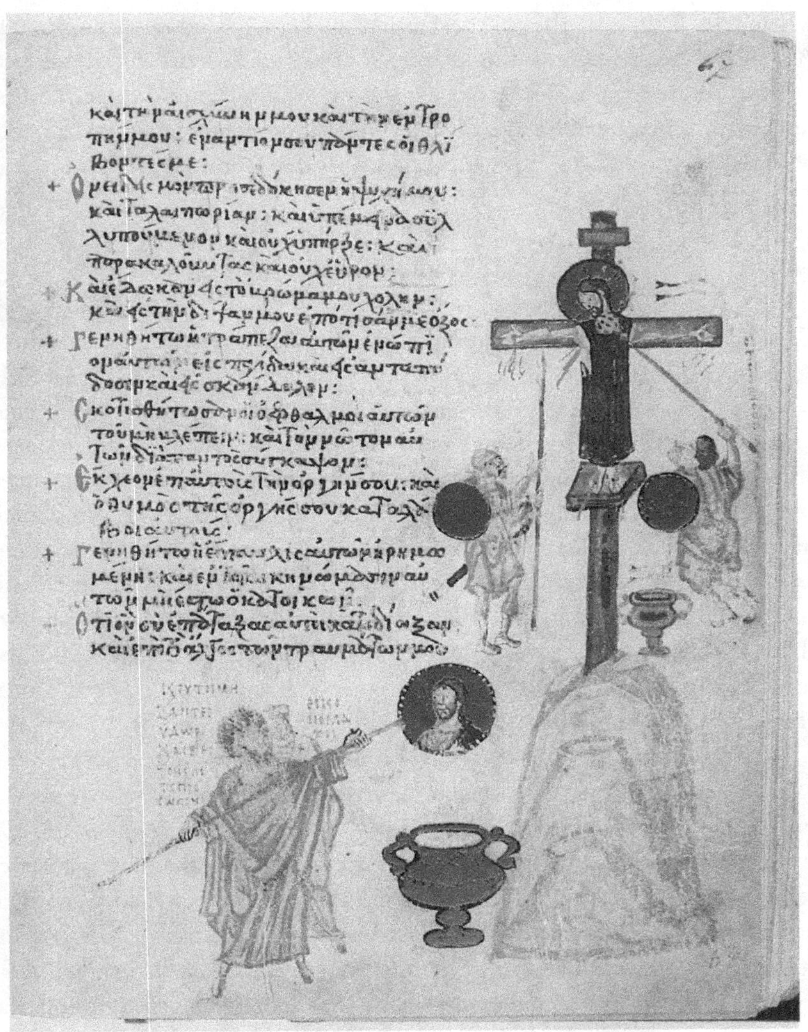

Figure 2. The Khludov Psalter, Cod. 129, fol. 67r, Psalm 68:22. © State Historical Museum, Moscow.

writing in Arabic in the tenth century, such as Theodore Abū Qurrah, Agapius of Manbij, Eutychius of Alexandria, and Severus ibn al-Muqafa, recorded numerous instances of clashes among Jews, Christians, and Muslims, often instigated by some alleged abuses of crosses or icons at the hands of Jews.[182]

Conclusion

This chapter began by showing how the *inventio crucis* legend of a church father triggered a narrative of Jewish desecration, which then appeared in polemical works, Byzantine chronicles, travelers' literature, records of ecumenical councils, an alleged *letter* to a Byzantine emperor, and the visual arts. The *inventio crucis* had initiated a sequential ordering of events, so that Christian authors, inspired by internal Christian developments regarding their images, could impute a motive to the Jews and shape the anti-Jewish accusation. Most of the tales by these anonymous authors were set in the Byzantine Empire and were held in high value. Like the *inventio crucis*, some of these tales would become legends—supposed records of truthful and historical events—so that for local Christians a miraculous painting in a specific location would become associated with Jewish desecration.

As the Byzantine tales traveled and developed against the background of an increasing imperial iconoclasm, the fictitious Jew's response to the images he tried to desecrate changed. It was a gradual, even opportunistic, layered development, manipulated and adapted by political and religious developments. In Gregory of Tours's tale the fictitious Jew had wanted to destroy the image of the living Christ but was killed. In Arculf's tale his attempt at destruction became the most outrageous and disgusting violation of Christianity enacted on an image of Mary. But by the later tales at the time of the Iconoclastic Controversy, the fictitious Jew is endowed with a knowledge of the painting—be it an image of Christ, Mary, or the Passion—which transforms him into a curious desecrator, drawn to test the image in a way he had not been credited with in previous tales. The variety of subjects in these paintings confirmed that images had become more ubiquitous. The Jew was equated with the hated iconoclast. Iconophile tales now empowered the Jew with the sort of knowledge of Christianity that the iconoclast had, since the two were interchangeable; the image now responded to the fictitious Jew in a way that it had not before. Christ caused his image to bleed and the miracle of the healing blood enabled the Jew to see him. In the heat of the Iconoclastic Controversy and its debate on the validity of images, "Christ of Beirut" was shown to seep Eucharistic blood miraculously so that the fictitious Jew could be converted to Christianity. This happy ending reflected policies concerning the conversion of Jews that were occurring in the empire. If the Jew could be converted, was there not hope that the iconoclast too could be redeemed?

Doctrinal issues regarding the types of images, representation, real presence, worship, and theological truth were integrated into these tales, resonating on different levels as has been shown. As we leave this chapter, Christian images have become agents of conversion. In addition, the fictitious Jew has assumed another characteristic in these Byzantine tales that he would carry with him as he traveled west again—his close affinity and association with the devil.

The Synod of 843 officially ended the image struggle by restoring the veneration of holy images, but as has been shown in our last source—the *Letter*—the promulgation of tales of Jewish image desecration did not cease in Byzantium. Moreover, the ampullae of blood and water that seeped from the violated image and the commemoration of a day in remembrance of the Jews' desecration would accompany our most prominent tale, the "Christ of Beirut" in all its force to the west; it would find its next home in Marian tales in England and France in the twelfth and thirteenth centuries.[183]

There was also a major polemical issue that had been left undefined in Byzantium. The Iconoclastic Controversy had never fully explained how an image could seep Eucharistic blood. The complex and eschatological Eucharist itself—hidden behind the communion screen—had always remained a mystery. This matter would need to be unraveled by western European theologians as they negotiated their own iconographic revolution in the thirteenth century. For surely it should not be left to fictitious Jews to claim that Christ's blood had healing qualities? How interesting then that by the middle of the thirteenth century real Jews would be accused of killing Christian children to collect their blood for these very healing qualities.

Chapter 2

Desecration Tales and Their Narrative Transformations in Twelfth- and Thirteenth-Century Western Europe

It was the monks of twelfth- and thirteenth-century France and England who took the compelling Byzantine tales of Jewish desecration and elaborated them into Marian tales that were disseminated, thus increasing their audience and furthering their polemical message. These miracle tales were sometimes presented as if they were real events, supplying nonspecialist audiences with a way of thinking about Jewish image desecration.

The present chapter will place these adapted tales among the religious, cultural, and social preoccupations of medieval Christian society. The prevalence of tales, as opposed to the few instances in which Christians actually leveled this charge against living Jews, continued to emphasize the literary topos already exhibited in Byzantium—that Jews were not merely attacking an image of Christ but reenacting the Crucifixion on Passion images and causing them to bleed. Other tales would play foundational roles in stereotyping Jews as impious and superstitious, thereby encouraging Christian fear of them; in one tale a Jewish moneylender is depicted as a vicious desecrator of Christian material objects. The question at the core of this chapter is how this topos against fictitious Jews contributed to the far more powerful, sophisticated, and dangerous allegations of host desecration and blood libel at the end of the thirteenth century. As will be shown, developments in Eucharistic theology led to the transition of key elements of image desecration narratives (Jewish attack, miraculous bleeding as a sign of Christian truth, Jewish conversion and punishment) into host desecration allegations.

When real accusations of cross desecration surfaced against Jews in Oxford in 1268 and Manosque in 1342, they failed to take hold or bring about the sorts of reactions that were prescribed in the tales or those provoked by accusations of blood libel or host desecration. In these cases, there was no convincing proof that real Jews had deliberately desecrated images, but they do suggest that the allegation had become credible enough to be legally investigated. At the same time, attention will be given to why it was medieval Christian society in England and France in particular that allowed for the fictional allegation to become a real accusation and for Jews to be tried before specific courts.

In order to explore the ways in which image desecration tales functioned, this chapter opens with the effects of the iconographic revolution in western Europe and the new veneration of images in the West. Arguments penned by theologians to defend Christian images against accusations of idolatry, particularly in *adversus Judaeos* tracts, will then be studied, as well as Christian allegations against Jewish moneylenders that highlight the deteriorating situation and increasing isolation of Jews in Christian society. We will then turn to the Christian perception of the Jews' economic activities in regard to sacred objects and images. The simultaneous appearance of Jewish image desecration tales in Marian collections will then be considered. Marian tales in which Jews were depicted as having attacked images of Mary are studied first, and then tales in which they were alleged to have attacked crucifixes and images of Christ's Passion, reenacting it and spilling Christ's blood. The connection between these tales and host desecration accusations and blood libel will be made at the end of the chapter, as will the study of real accusations of image desecration during this time.[1]

The Iconographic Revolution in Western Europe

Pope Gregory the Great may have had the Jews of Marseilles in mind when, in the sixth century, he famously warned Bishop Serenus not to destroy Christian images. Jews living in Provence, and those traveling on business from Italy, were known to have complained to the pope that they had been forcibly baptized by local bishops and compelled to acknowledge the sanctity of images. In fact, it was the pope's letter to the bishop that became the authoritative defense of images in the Latin West. Uneasily aware that Christians were seen as idolatrous, Pope Gregory set his Christian flock a clear code of behavior. They should look upon images rather than worship them and reject the idea that they had miraculous powers or that a relationship existed between the images and the beings they depicted. Images should not be destroyed, because they were useful for teaching.[2] In fact, until approximately 754, there was no breach in the relations between Rome and Constantinople regarding the use of religious images. When the Iconoclastic Controversy occurred, it was condemned in the West by the Carolingians.[3]

Charlemagne ordered a detailed review of the papal and Byzantine arguments, and this was compiled by the leading theologians at the Frankish court, becoming known as the *Book of King Charles* (*Opus Caroli Regis*, widely referred to as the *Libri Carolini*). Western theologians were concerned that belief in the divinity of images should not distract attention from the Eucharist as the central sacrament. Even though the *Opus Caroli Regis* presented a straightforward argument and reflected a new confidence and independence of mind among the theologians of the Frankish kingdom in the Carolingian period, its effect remained local, and issues regarding the divinity of images and the Eucharist would surface again as a result of the iconographic revolution a few centuries later.[4] Two types of images continued to proliferate in the West—those of Christ (hanging on a cross, either in the form of a crucifix or as a two-dimensional image of the Passion) and those of the Virgin (as a stone carving or a two-dimensional image) in churches and ecclesiastical institutions.[5]

Thereafter the West maintained its own tradition of polemics regarding the usage of Christian images, and the question never dominated theological debates. By the ninth century Archbishop Agobard of Lyons commented in his tractate on images that Jews were reproaching Christians for their idolatry, but Christian theologians such as Bishop Jonas of Orleans, Abbot Dungal of Saint-Denis, and Walafrid Strabo, the abbot of Reichenau, were not deterred and remained in favor of images.[6]

The consistent and firm rejection of Iconoclastic policies meant that images could be absorbed into written and oral culture. But it would only be a question of time before heretical groups within Christianity demonstrated their defiance by attacking Christian images. In 1025 at the Synod of Arras, Bishop Gerard of Cambrai condemned heretics who called into question doctrines of the church, including the worship of images. In the twelfth century, the Cathari—or people of Albi, Albigensians—carved deformed statues of the Virgin, placed them in their churches and mocked them. This practice continued until the Cathari were defeated by the Albigensian Crusade in 1229.[7]

From the Norman invasion of England, life-size crucifixes were erected to stand on the choir screen or hang from the chancel arch. These crucifixes sometimes stored relics, inspiring the contemplation of a realistic, suffering, but triumphant Christ on the cross.[8] These items confirmed the central truths of Christian belief and had a devotional purpose, playing an important part in the liturgy, whereby prayers asking for Christ's forgiveness were recited only in their presence.[9] Not only did crosses and, later, crucifixes proclaim the Passion in this medieval period but they also represented Christ's incarnation and salvation.[10] The French theologian Raoul Ardens (d. ca.1200) justified the viewing of such crucifixes in his homilies: "the image of the crucifix is now depicted in church so that we, seeing that our Redeemer voluntarily endured poverty, infirmity, taunts, spitting, beating [and] death for our salvation, may be more and more inflamed to live with Him in our hearts."[11]

Carolingian texts from the ninth century and Cistercian ones from the twelfth recorded worshippers kissing, embracing, and prostrating themselves before the images.[12] Miracles had become historically associated with crucifixes that were used in the office of holy mass, in liturgical blessings, and in religious processions and continued to be so in this period, where they were seen to offer spiritual consolation, redemption, and hope. By the time of Thomas Aquinas (ca. 1225–1274) the classic definition of a miracle (*miraculum*) had turned into a heavenly sign that bore "witness to the truth of some doctrine God wants accepted."[13] This would fit well with the miraculous happenings in tales of Jewish image desecration.

Impressive Romanesque cathedrals and churches were constructed (the Mainz Cathedral was completed in 1137 and Worms Cathedral in 1181); these acquired more and more sumptuous images, objects, and utensils that not only decorated and enhanced altars but were dispersed throughout these consecrated buildings and assumed the powers traditionally ascribed to relics. The cult of the Virgin had also been an important aspect of Anglo-Saxon spirituality. From the eleventh century there was a growing interest in Marian liturgical celebrations (in particular the feast of the Conception), and monasteries were established that were dedicated to her.[14] Her images appeared in different media, including manuscripts, ivory carvings, sculpture, wall paintings, wood carvings, and embroideries.[15] By the thirteenth century a newly founded confraternity in Rome put the figure of Mary on its flag in

Santa Maria Maggiore. From this time convents and confraternities—particularly those connected with the Franciscans and Dominicans, who were patrons of innovative Passion imagery among nuns and laypeople—also absorbed and popularized Marian icons, increasing their presence not only in religious spaces, but also outside. This was contemporaneous with the dissemination of collections of Marian tales, some of which clearly legitimated the new veneration of images in the West.

Scholars such as Jean-Claude Schmitt and Jean Wirth associate the twelfth century in the West with the initiation of its own iconographic revolution, a more elaborate religious appreciation of sacred art and figurative culture that came from the East in the form of precious exotic images and relics.[16] Constantinople had remained the home of most icon cults until it was besieged by crusaders in 1204, and it was these images, once they had reached western shores, that were copied and disseminated and believed to be able to avert all types of catastrophe.[17] These images emphasized the physical side of Christ and his incarnation, and relics purporting to be parts of his body, or the True Cross, encouraged devotion to him. Relics of the True Cross even continued their association with Jews. In early twelfth-century Cologne, Rupert of Deutz recorded in his *De divinis officiis* that a cloth covering the relic of the True Cross during Lent needed to be removed by Christians on Good Friday, since the cloth symbolized the blind Jews who had kept Christ hidden from Christians.[18]

Such a proliferation of images of Christ and Mary caused differing reactions among theologians, who remained unsure how to incorporate this new material representation of devotion into theology.[19] In a general treatise, *Apologia ad Guillelmum Abbatem* (ca. 1125), the Cistercian abbot Bernard of Clairvaux (1090–1153) denied the efficacy of any religious image as an agent, revealing a latent fear that such adoration would lead to spiritual distraction and, worse, idolatry.[20] Over a century later Thomas Aquinas's writings in his monumental *Summa theologica* (ca. 1265) suggested his own irresolution. On the one hand, he praised imageless piety as the highest level of devotion, but, on the other, he treated crucifixes and images of the Virgin as so holy that they should be venerated.[21] But he also put an end to controversy in western Europe by defining a hierarchy of images that were generally accepted. The most elevated forms were images of Christ, which attracted *latria* (the highest level of veneration); those of the Virgin, which called for *hyperdulia* (a high degree of veneration); and those of the saints, which deserved *dulia* (veneration).[22]

Not surprisingly then, one particular conduit through which churchmen voiced, explored, and articulated image veneration was the growing *adversus Judaeos* disputation literature in the West. Here Jews were portrayed as enemies of Christianity who accused it of advocating idolatry. Of the seventeen literary and philosophical disputational tracts that represented fictitious dialogues between Jews and Christians in the medieval West, four of them from the early twelfth century—those written by Petrus Alfonsi, Gilbert of Crispin, Guibert of Nogent, and Rupert of Deutz—have their participants debate the role of images, with the Christians reiterating that images were not idols but symbols.[23] Although Petrus Alfonsi did not discuss the Jews' aversion to images, he had his Jewish interlocutor reproach the Christian for having an anthropomorphic God. As a former Jew with a clear knowledge of both the Talmud and more contemporary Spanish rabbinic writings incorporating neo-Aristotelian ideas, Alfonsi argued that crosses/crucifixes were necessary reminders of the True Cross on which Christ had been crucified. These "copies" were therefore imitations. There could be no fear that they would become idols.[24]

The other three Western theologians unconditionally defended images against an alleged outpouring of the Jews' accusations of idolatry. Gilbert Crispin (d. 1117), in his *Disputatio Iudei et Cristiani*, probably written before the First Crusade, had his relatively peaceful Christian interlocutor in the debate deny the fictitious Jew's accusation that Christians committed idolatry in venerating graven images.[25] Was not, he argued, the verb *adorare* ambiguous, demanding a clear distinction between adoring or worshipping God himself and venerating representations of him?[26] Arguing against the same Jewish accusations, but this time specifically defending Passion images and crucifixes, another text—the *Tractatus de incarnatione contra Iudaeos* of the French Benedictine historian Guibert of Nogent (d. 1124) argued that the Christians did not venerate the wood of the cross they saw but the "substance" of God, which was invisible.[27] Writing after the massacre of approximately three thousand Jews in the Rhineland during the First Crusade, his tone is more aggressive, and his knowledge might well have been derived from conversations with Jewish converts who had entered his monastery. Seeing Christian images as "visible signs," he adds two other examples from the Old Testament that indicated that Jews, too, had shown devotion to "objects." The first was Joshua bowing down to the Holy Ark in Joshua 7:6 and the second Daniel turning toward the holy city of Jerusalem in Daniel 6:11. Both of these "objects," or "signs," he argued, were comparable with images.

The German Benedictine abbot Rupert of Deutz (d. 1130) in his *Anulus sive dialogus inter Christianum et Judaeum* put forward a similar argument, negating the Jew's accusation that Christians worshipped the crucifix. He denied that there was any virtue or grace inherent in a crucifix and said that the incarnate invisible Christ could be reached by its contemplation, not by its veneration.[28]

> We do not worship the image of a crucifix or of some such thing as the divine presence, as you [Jews] would accuse us, but through the form of the cross we represent in pious devotion, while adoring, the Passion of Christ for us, by which he was made accursed in the cross "for our sake," that he might snatch us away "from the curse of the law" [Gal. 3:13]. Insofar as while we imagine his death through the similitude of the cross on the outside, by it we might ascend to his love internally . . . how much we, covered with many and great sins, ought to endure for the sake of his love, we should carefully ponder always with devout meditation.[29]

Further arguments would be added by "Herman the former Jew," known earlier as Judas ben David Halevi, who was baptized in Cologne in 1128 and became Herman of Scheda, a Premonstratensian monk in the Cappenberg abbey. In his *Opusculum de conversione sua*, his own account of his long and difficult conversion, he described his disputation with Rupert of Deutz. Here he has Rupert argue that, just as the tribes of Reuben and Gad and the half-tribe of Manashe had built an altar in Transjordan as a sign that they belonged to the Children of Israel, so the Christians see and use the cross as a sign of their future salvation in the society of saints.[30] Herman, as a new convert, maintained the Jewish argument suggesting Christian idolatry, noting that Psalm 115 labeled idolaters as becoming "similar to their idols," so that Christians would become like the substance of their idols. Rupert rejects Herman's argument and contends that it is not the bodies of Christians that will become like idols, but their minds, and it is entirely proper that their minds should, through contemplation, be assimilated with Christ. To achieve this, the convert must recognize Jesus as the Messiah.[31]

In the dialogue Rupert also has an answer to Herman's unease at the "countless" images of saints that he was seeing in churches and in his abbey—male and female saints that were not gods. Referring to 1 Kings 6:29 and the multiplication of the cherubs and palm leaves in the Temple by Solomon, Herman makes Rupert speak as if he were a master sculptor, clarifying the difference between the images of saints and those of Christ: "It is why I legitimately carve the wood on all the walls of the church, multiplying not only the cherubs and the palm leaves, but also the different paintings that call to mind for me the deeds of the saints, the faith of the patriarchs, the truth of the prophets, the glory of the kings, the beatitude of the apostles, and the victories of the martyrs, while between the sacred images of them all, the lovely cross of the Lord dazzles me with its refulgence."[32]

One finds a similar argument in Paschalis Romanus's translation of an eighth-century Byzantine pamphlet called *Argument Against the Jews*, dated 1158.[33] In the dispute with his Jew, Paschalis has his Christian interlocutor confirm that sacred images were transient objects that eventually were destroyed and replaced: "When I worship an icon, it is not the nature of the wood but Christ or the saints whom I worship and honor. You can also understand that we worship neither wood nor image by the fact that we burn the old icons which have faded and make new ones, so that we may keep fresh in our minds [Christ and the saints]."[34]

Over a century later, and after the expulsion of the Jews from England, the French canonist, liturgical writer, and bishop of Mende William Durand the Elder (ca. 1230–1296) in his *Rationale divinorum officiorum* (ca. 1292–1296), which superseded all previous liturgical works within a few years of its publication, directed his attention at the Jews' "accusations" of idolatry and stressed that, despite the Jews' reprimand, sacred images were "venerated" because of what they represented rather than their "material stone": "The infidels direct strong accusations against us . . . but we do not worship images, nor do we call them gods, nor do we place our hope of salvation in them, because this would be idolatry, but we venerate them for the memory and remembrance of things done long ago."[35]

Moreover, regarding the dedication of a church, Durand emphasized how its cross-like shape represented the "replacement" of Jews by Christians:

> And this cross, which is drawn from one corner of the church to the other—namely, one section goes from the left corner in the eastern part to the right corner in the western part, and the other section goes from the right corner in the eastern part to the left corner in the western part—signifies that these people [the Jews], who were previously on the right, were moved to the left, and those who were

> at the head of the line were moved to the very back; and the ones on the left went right, and the ones in the back of the line went to its head, and this happened because of the power of the cross. Coming from the east, Christ left the Jews on His left side, since they were faithless, and He came to the Gentiles, to whom, though they were in the west, He gave the right to be on His right-hand side; and at last, having placed the Gentiles on the right in the east, He shall visit the Jews in the left corner in the west, who remain inferior to the Gentiles to whom He first came.[36]

These debates, contrived by Christian authors, in which Christians are pitted against fictitious Jewish interlocutors who persistently condemn Christians for idolatry, stressed how theologians had come to use Jews as a way of defending their own doctrinal and devotional reliance and usage of Christian images. Not only were these debates contemporaneous with the dissemination of Marian tales, but they also reveal a deep antagonism toward the real Jews remaining in France, particularly moneylenders, who began to be seen as scandalous violators of Christian objects, permeating society.

The Deteriorating Situation of Jews in Western Europe

The continuing depiction in the *adversus Judaeos* tracts of the Jew as condemning Christian idolatry, combined with familiarity of Byzantine tales and traditions, furthered Christianity's critical perceptions of the Jews' economic activities, especially in regard to sacred objects and images. The Jews' willingness to "buy" sacred items had been criticized by Pope Gregory I as early as 591, when the Jews of Campania had acquired sacred church vessels and ornaments from the clergy of Venafro.[37] Although no law existed in the late sixth century to prohibit such activity, Charlemagne, or one of his immediate successors, would find it necessary to promulgate a *capitularia* forbidding Jews from accepting sacred objects in settlement of a debt or as pawns. The punishment for a Jew committing either of these "sins" was to be confiscation of his property and amputation of his right hand.[38]

Western Europe's transition to a credit (coinage) economy in the twelfth century created commercial prosperity and rapid urban growth. As part of this economy, particularly in France and England, Jews became associated with moneylending and the charging of interest, provoking hostility for pursuing an activity that was regarded as morally reprehensible.[39] Since Western Christianity now sanctioned the use of opulent and grand sacred objects for pious devotion, the number of sacred articles being pawned by church officials in England, France, Sicily, and Germany increased significantly.[40] Sometimes, the Jewish moneylenders' premises for storing these items were even situated within the ecclesiastical institutions themselves, by arrangement with local churches or monasteries.[41] Bishop Nigel of Ely (1133–1169) is reported to have seized his cathedral's treasures, including the golden crucifix of King Edgar (959–973), and pledged them "to a Cambridge Jew."[42] Another church official, Abbot William de Waterville of Peterborough (1155–1175) handed over the most venerated objects from his churches, including the arm of Saint Oswald.[43]

Church thinkers quickly aired their views against the Jews' holding sacred objects; this often turned into unfounded allegations that the Jews abused them. Such allegations were even directed against the antipope Anaclete II, who ruled between 1130 and 1138 and was said to have Jewish ancestry. The Benedictine abbot Ernaldus (Arnaldus, Arnold), abbot of Bonneval accused him of increasing his wealth by removing gold chalices and crucifixes from the altars of Rome, and giving them to the Jews to be melted down. "He [Anaclete II] also removed from the altars the gifts of kings that had been offered as ecclesiastical ornaments. And since these profane Christians feared or blushed to break up the chalices or to tear apart limb from limb the gold crucifixes, they said that they sought out the Jews, who audaciously tore apart the sacred vessels and the images that were dedicated to God."[44] The eleventh-century Aquitanian Benedictine Adémar of Chabannes (d. 1034) in his sermon on the Eucharist attacked the Jews for continuing to destroy Christian symbols and blaspheming against the cross. He also reported that Pope Benedict VIII (1012–1024) was said to have "learnt" from a Jew that a recent earthquake had been caused by a group of Jews who were mocking the figure of a crucified Christ in their synagogue.[45] The Jews were supposedly decapitated and the fury of the elements subsided.[46] Behind this fantastical allegation was, I believe, an intrinsic fear that Jews now had uncontrolled access to Christian images and were likely to harm them. Desecration had become an intentional Jewish reaction—the inverted response to increasing Christian veneration. Veneration and violation were becoming mirror images coexisting in this state of conflict between Jews and Christians. For were not Jewish moneylenders really desecrating images in order to prove that the image was an unresponsive idol?

Church theologians soon began to condemn Jewish desecration in the West. In 1146, the reforming abbot Peter the Venerable of Cluny proclaimed that the greatest threat for crusading armies was not the distant Saracens, but "Jews long worse than Saracens, not far from us but in our very midst" who trampled and disfigured images of Christ and the Christian sacraments in their possession.[47] He was furious with his own clergy for borrowing considerable sums from Jewish moneylenders by pawning precious vessels from the cloisters, which, he said, now adorned the homes of local Jews. He intensified religious anxiety by warning King Louis VII that when these sacred objects were violated by Jews, Christ himself suffered: "In these objects which do not feel themselves to be consecrated vessels, Christ still feels Jewish insults completely because, as I have often heard from reliable people, to the shame of the same Christ and of ourselves, those wicked people employ these heavenly vessels for their own uses, which one should shudder to think and loathe to utter."[48]

Although Peter of Cluny insinuated that the Jews were committing some abhorrent act upon the objects, he failed to articulate what the actual abuse was. In the same century, Rigord of Saint-Denis (d. ca. 1207), King Philip Augustus's clerical biographer, actually blamed the expulsion of the Jews from the royal domain of France on the Jews' violation of sacred images taken as pledges for loans.[49] The Latin record reports that the king ordered the Jews to be seized in their synagogues and their precious objects confiscated from their homes.[50] A Hebrew source confirms that the king's guards (*shomrim*) ransacked Jewish houses and removed Christian holy objects from them; by way of reprisal, they also entered synagogues and seized ceremonial objects that belonged to Jews.[51] According to Rigord, these "mischievous Jews" had acquired so much wealth from their pledges that the king had already canceled all Christian debts to Jews.[52] Rigord then recorded one specific allegation against an anonymous Jewish moneylender in Paris who had supposedly desecrated images:

> one of them [the Jews] who lived in Paris, and who had received some church furniture in pledge, such as a golden cross enriched with jewels, a book of the gospel, adorned with an infinite art of the most precious stones, a few silver cups and other things, hid them all in a sack, and showed such impurity that he threw them down into the bottom of the pit where he unloaded his belly every day. Soon a divine revelation made this offense known to the Chris-

> tians who found them there. The objects were all returned to their own church with great joy and honor, and a fifth of the debt having been paid to the lord king of all that was owed.[53]

As will be shown below, Rigord was here trying to articulate a real accusation against French Jews by regurgitating the theme of Jews and latrines from the desecration tale composed by Adomnán in the seventh century and the Marian tale of "The Virgin's Image Insulted." It represents an important example of fiction being translated into fact.

Ecclesiastical prohibitions intended to stop Jewish moneylenders and church officials from exchanging sacred items were renewed by numerous ecclesiastical synods and, from the thirteenth century, sporadically by popes.[54] The Fourth Lateran Council of 1215 not only dealt with the growing anxiety about Jewish moneylending, urging princes to force Jews to abstain from excessive usury, but also (in canon 20) laid down rules for safeguarding sacred objects, ordering not only the Eucharist but also chrism and a church's relics to be kept locked in "properly protected places . . . to protect them from robbery or exposure for sale."[55] In 1229, a synod of Lord William of Bley, bishop of Worcester, pronounced that Jews who violated sacred objects should be "cut off from intercourse with Christians," which presumably meant that they would be unable to make a living.[56]

Other thirteenth-century assemblies repeated these interdictions. Again, when describing the acts that real Jewish moneylenders were supposed to commit against these objects, the papal letters merely repeated Peter the Venerable's vague accusation. In a 1205 letter to Philip Augustus of France, Pope Innocent III (ca. 1160–1216) suggested that Jews were liable to desecrate ecclesiastical goods in their keeping, and asserted that Jews performed "detestable and unheard of things against the Catholic faith."[57] In August 1258, Pope Alexander IV echoed these very ambiguous concerns to the archbishops and bishops of the kingdom of France, forbidding their clerics to pledge ecclesiastical objects to Jews, standardizing the often repeated phrases but failing yet again to give clarity to this allegation: "We heard and we speak of it not without bitterness of heart that some clergy make no distinction between the sacred and the profane and they dare leave such vestments, ornaments and vessels as loan-pledges with Jews. . . . And they, the Jews, like ingrate enemies of the cross and the Christian faith . . . treat these pledges with irreverence, to the disgrace of the Christian religion. And [they] act so nefariously towards them as is shameful to speak and horrible to hear."[58]

It would seem then that the increasing fear of the moneylenders' detestable treatment of Christian images stimulated the dissemination of the Marian tales of Jewish image desecration. The five tales discussed below confirm the permanence, range, and depth of the Byzantine tales and how over time their association with Marian miracles contributed to the widespread belief that Jews detested images and would seize opportunities to desecrate them. The tales portray the vicious and deliberate profanation of large, as well as small, portable Christian holy images by Jews. There is, not surprisingly, a tale of a Jewish moneylender in these new collections.

Western Marian Tales

Marian collections of exempla tales ("examples," or short didactic tales) featuring the Mother of God were gathered by monks from homiletic and chronicle sources, by word of mouth from Greek clerics traveling to France and England, and from pilgrims who had traveled to the Holy Land or participated in the First Crusade. The popularization and propagation of these tales were suitable tasks for the conscientious Christian clergy and replaced the collecting of contemporary personal miracle stories by earlier writers.[59] These were short, entertaining tales disseminated by priests and friars in their sermons, conveying the message that the Virgin (in direct contact with Christ) had the power to hear and respond to the petitions of her devoted followers.[60] In the thirteenth century, as a result of the increased importance attached to preaching to the people by Pope Innocent III (r. 1198–1216), the sermons that described these tales were even recorded in handbooks that were used by preachers throughout Europe. They confirm their widespread dissemination, their success at attracting the attention of audiences and keeping them interested.

The creation of Marian collections occurred almost concurrently on both sides of the Channel—initially in France with the writings of Guibert of Nogent, who recorded Marian miracles associated with relics in the Cathedral of Notre Dame of Laon in 1112–1113.[61] In the 1140s the canon Hermann of Tournai edited Guibert's writing, and several other versions appeared for the purpose of promoting Marian shrines in Chartres, Coutances, Rocamadour, Saint-Pierre-sur-Dive, and Soissons.[62] In England in the late 1120s, Dominic, prior of Evesham, is identified as the first author of a "little book" of Marian stories.[63] He was followed by Anselm of Bury St. Edmunds (d. 1148), who incorporated the liturgical practice of the Little Office and the Visigothic feast of the Virgin at his abbey, and then by the Benedictine monk William of Malmesbury (b. ca. 1090, d. ca. 1143), who composed his own volume of fifty-three miracles between 1125 and 1143, probably using the works of his two predecessors and a certain amount of information gathered by word of mouth.[64] William's work was less popular, although longer, than that of Dominic and Anselm.[65] He was keen to provide new information and historical settings for the tales that interested him.[66] These stories were to cross the Channel again and be translated into French by the Anglo-Norman poet Adgar circa 1165–1172.[67] Almost a century later, the Marian tales had their own version in Spain where they were illuminated in a sumptuous manuscript, the *Cantigas de Santa Maria* (Canticles of Holy Mary), produced for a royal patron by the court of the learned Alfonso X between 1260 and 1284 (the year of the king's death).[68] Exceptional for its age, in terms of the richness of its illustrations, its 427 narratives contain not only the standard Western Marian tales, but a rich harvest of local stories. Unusually, the king was involved in its production.[69] The *Cantigas*' vivid detailed tales and illustrations confirmed the ubiquitous intercessions of the Virgin, often as a savior in both spiritual and earthly concerns of the faithful. Important for our purposes, it also provides an intriguing visual rendition of the tales, where the holy images are depicted as being mediators that came alive in response to prayers of the faithful or desecration by their enemies.[70] It confirmed how Marian images, in particular, inherited sacred virtues from Mary herself that could and should be invoked by the faithful. The subjects of these illustrations, along with others depicting Jewish image desecration, will be used as a source of comparison to the tales originating in England and France.

At least sixteen stories in Marian collections focus on miraculous images.[71] These include both well-known miraculous icons, the basis of cults of Mary and Christ that existed in the East, and unspecified images and statues of the Virgin in both East and West.[72] Not surprisingly, in view of the Western theological debates about images discussed above, William of Malmesbury makes it clear in several of his tales that it was not the images that were miraculous, but their divine models—Jesus and the Virgin Mary—who gave them the power and capacity to act.[73] However, it was not just Jews who were desecrators in these tales. Both heretics and Muslims appear in this role. In the tales of desecration by fictitious deviant Christians and heretics, rather than Jews, the Virgin can be seen and heard by the offenders.[74] In desecration tales in which Muslims were the offenders, they attempted to desecrate the images but were unable to physically attack them, which suggests that they were considered worthier enemies of Christendom than Jews.[75] Around 10 percent of twelfth-century Marian collections depicted Jews. These tales were particularly popular and continually repeated and expanded.[76] Five tales in different Marian collections portray the Jews' relationship with Christian images; four of these are adaptations of earlier Byzantine tales discussed in Chapter 1.[77] In all of these five tales, the Jews' vulnerability is in stark contrast to the Christian image, which remains indestructible.

Two of the five tales, "Theodore and Abraham" and "Lydda," do not involve desecration by the Jews, although their disdain for Marian images is clear. They show Jews being affected by a miraculous response of a Marian image to their malevolent thoughts. In "Abraham and Theodore" the dishonest and avaricious Abraham, a Jewish moneylender, lends money to Theodore, a spendthrift Christian merchant, who accepts as surety a wooden image of the Virgin found at the Sancta Sophia in Constantinople.[78] After Theodore repays the loan, sending his payment by sea from Constantinople, Abraham (in Alexandria) hides the money under his bed, telling Theodore that he has never received it. In Adgar's version, the image calls out to Abraham:

> Abraham, Abraham, you lie!
> You have hidden the chest with the silver . . .
> Truly you have erred like a fool![79]

When the Jew witnesses the Virgin speaking through the image, he admits that he has lied and immediately converts to Christianity, giving away all his money.[80] The moral of the tale is that the cunning and duplicitous Jewish moneylender is saved by the beneficence and mercy of Mary, or, as William reminds his readers: "a convincing proof of how assiduously Mary works to convert the race she belonged to."[81]

This, however, was the only tale about Jews and a Marian image in which the Jew was converted by Mary's influence. The other tale, the "Lydda" story, describes how Mary was able to intimidate Jews in the Holy Land and prevent their plan to destroy her image in a church and reclaim it as a synagogue.[82] In its twelfth-century Marian version, the Jews take on a more active role than in the Byzantine tale and complain to Emperor Julian the Apostate, "the persecutor of churches," that they themselves had sold their synagogue to Christians who had converted it into a church and dedicated it to the Virgin.[83] The Jews regretted the sale and wanted to repossess the holy site. In order to decide whether the church should be returned to the Jews or not, the emperor ordered the site to be closed for forty days to reveal God's will. This story again changed from the Byzantine version where the closure of the church had been for three days and not forty. When it was reopened, the Jews saw that Mary had miraculously created a life-size image of herself dressed in purple robes on a marble western wall to confirm her continuing presence in the church. The Jews asked permission from the emperor to remove the image (instead of being ordered to do so as they had been in the earlier Byzantine version).[84] After a failed attempt to remove it, the Jews were overwhelmed by the power of the image, which struck terror in their hearts. They quickly withdrew and no longer demanded ownership of the building.

The choice of Lydda was not arbitrary. Lydda (Lod/Diospolis) at this time housed a church originally built by the apostles Peter and John and dedicated to the Virgin. It had become a crusader city, its church had been rebuilt in the twelfth century, and a new popular shrine to the skull of Saint George was established for Western pilgrims who traveled there.[85] The tale uses the Christianization of the Holy Land, which was occurring at this time and the sanctification of its landscape by the Virgin, to paint a picture of the Jews as frustrated outsiders, unable to attack the image or benefit from its miraculous glory.[86]

As we will see, like their Byzantine forerunners, the next three tales were dominated by male Jews, cast again in the role of aggressive desecrators. It was, after all, in reality, Jewish males who handled Jewish ceremonial objects in the synagogue and Christian ceremonial objects as pawns; they were certainly more active outside the home than Jewish women. Even though Marian tales depict Jewish women as often as men, their storylines are always different.[87] The Jewish male converts only after committing a heinous act or having malevolent thoughts and witnessing a miracle that thwarted or reversed his efforts. In contrast, the female Jew does not need to sin and be corrected in order to be saved. She is usually presented with a miracle, without herself doing anything, good or bad, to solicit one, though she may, on occasion have called upon the Virgin Mary. In response to this event, she converts and marries a Christian.

The fictitious Jewish woman is thus depicted as having a greater capacity for holiness and is able to convert easily without a second thought.[88] As will be shown below, Christian hermeneutics presented the fictitious Jewish desecrator as governed by the letter of the law, blinded to New Testament revelation, and a perverse and dangerous threat to Christian order and Christ's body and blood. He is portrayed as holding Christ and Mary in malicious disrespect, his desecration of images exemplifying his blasphemy and treachery. In fact, in the Marian tales, Jewish offenders were punished more violently than either heretics or Saracens.[89] The quintessential medieval tale describing an attack on the Virgin's image is "The Virgin's Image Insulted."

"The Virgin's Image Insulted"

This medieval tale is based on the story described by Adomnán in the seventh-century travelogue *De locis sanctis*.[90] In its Marian version, William of Malmesbury described how, in the church of Blachernai (one of the most important Marian shrines in Constantinople, which after the Latin invasion of 1204 was occupied by Latin clergy and placed directly under the pope), there was an image of the Virgin, supposedly an *acheiropoieton*, painted by Nicodemus, which captured her grace and beauty.[91] The story seems to describe an imaginary icon since no such icon was reported as being in Constantinople at this time.[92] William of Malmesbury describes the image as "beautifully painted on a panel"[93] A Jew "led by his fanaticism," entered the church, removed the painting, and threw it into a nearby public latrine.[94] In later thirteenth-century versions of this tale such as that in the *Cantigas* and that written by John of Garland, the Jew is following the devil's instructions as to what to do with the image once it was stolen.[95] By this time, in Western medieval tales, devils were known to haunt latrines, providing a locus of damnation that brought together the idea of moral and material impurity.[96] The Jew, already associated with offensive behavior, illness, and disease, now defecates on the image, implying his corruptive threat to Christianity's wellbeing.[97] William of Malmesbury writes: "Sitting there he disturbed the air, intending to bring disgrace to our faith by emptying his bowels on the image."[98] As in the Byzantine tale of Admonán, this action was intended to reflect the Jew's evil attack on Mary rather than her image.[99] Perhaps too these tales illustrated the rather inarticulate texts of the church theologians regarding the extent of the Jews' loathsome violation of the images. At this point in the tale, there is a further twist as the Jew is violently eliminated by his own act. William of Malmesbury continues: "Worthy punishment followed the sacrilegious man, for his innards went down into the pit in a horrid stream."[100] The violent extermination of the Jew in "The Virgin's Image Insulted" is reminiscent of Judas Iscariot's violent demise in the version given in the Acts of the Apostles.[101] This ending now becomes a crucial part of the Marian tale, described as the Jew's fittingly ignominious death, and a direct consequence of his shameful behavior toward Mary. In William's tale, the Christian who found the painting cleaned it, and it immediately began to exude a sweet-smelling oil, confirming that Mary's sanctity had been purified from the contaminating effects of its filthy association with the Jew. Christianity had washed away the filth of Judaism and even its disgusting Jewish smell.

The *Cantigas* holds the most meticulous and intricate visual depiction of the tale (see Figure 3). In the first image, the Jew triumphantly holds up a painting of Mary and Jesus, which he steals from the portico on the outside of an unidentified building, probably a church. His flamboyant gesture demonstrates his temerity. He wears a Jew's discriminatory pointed hat—reflecting a standard western European anti-Jewish topos that was developing at this time—and turns away from the image as he checks to ensure that no one is watching him. In the second miniature, a horned and rather comical looking devil approaches from behind the Jew as he places the image in the latrine, suggesting that the devil is his overlord or partner and has, in fact, ordered him to put it there. This confirms the visual correlation between the devil and the privy, and is confirmed by the *Cantigas* caption on top of the image, which reads "How the Jew Put the Image of Holy Mary in the Privy on the Advice of the Devil."[102] It should be noted that the initial act of desecration was carried out by the Jew before the devil's appearance in the second miniature, perhaps to show that the impulse to steal the image originated from the Jew himself.

An image of the Jew sitting on the latrine and defecating on the image was not added, probably because such a representation would have been inappropriate for a book that dealt with holy topics. In the third miniature, the Jew, already dead, is carried off on the back of the devil, trailed by a winged demon. Unlike the visual depiction of the devil in Cantiga 3, here the devil and the demon do not share similar physiognomy with the Jew to underscore a demonic relationship between the three of them, but the assumption is there of the devil and the Jew being joined together in their fight to destroy Christendom.[103] In the fourth miniature, the painting has been removed by the Christian and his wife from the latrine, and the woman pours water over the image as it is held up by her husband. In the fifth, the

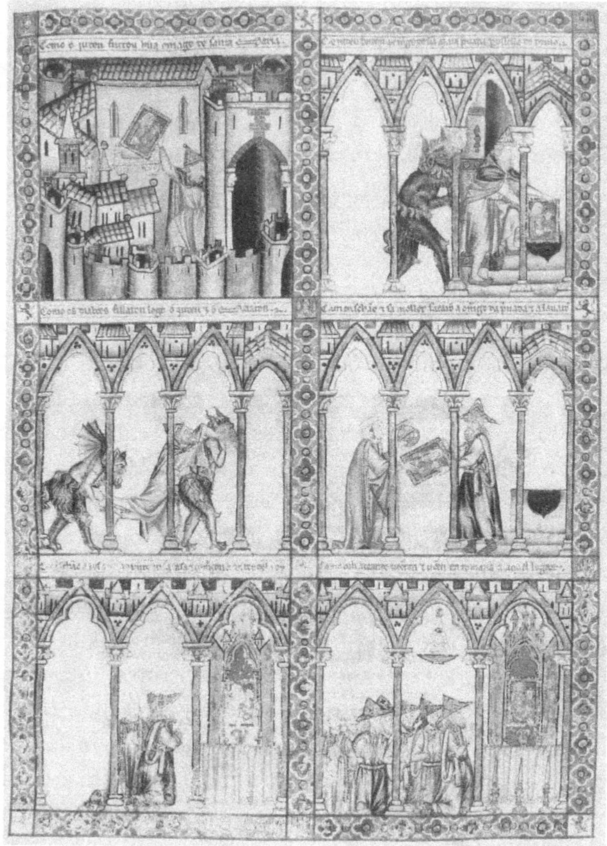

Figure 3. "The Virgin's Image Insulted," *Cantigas de Santa Maria* (T.I.1), fol. 50r. © Patrimonio Nacional.

Christian couple kneel before the painting, probably in some kind of tabernacle in a church, praying that the picture will regain its powers, after its unpleasant experience in the latrine. It is at this moment that the painting seeps oil, confirming that veneration has won over desecration. The final miniature portrays Christian worshippers surrounding the image and an incense burner hanging in front of it, as the image now regains its distinct and brightly colored character in comparison to its blurred state in the previous miniature.

This Marian tale quickly spawned alternative versions. While in the later twelfth century it circulated only in the devout monastic communities, by the thirteenth century collections of miracles of the Virgin and exempla compiled by Alfonso the Wise, Vincent of Beauvais, Gautier de Coinci, John of Garland, Caesarius of Heisterbach, and Joannes Herolt were widely available in various translations for the purposes of devotional reading and preaching.[104] The tale was even adopted by the inaccurate and devious English chronicler Matthew Paris (d. 1259), who wrote that, in order to publicize the Jews' "wickedness," he had decided to include it in his chronicle as the crime committed by Abraham of Berkhampstead.[105] He labeled it "Of the crime committed by a certain Jew."[106] But the story of a Jew who defiles a portrait of the Virgin had certainly been told before.

> There was a certain moderately rich Jew, Abraham by name, but not Abraham in faith, who had a house and resort at Berkhampstead and Wallingford, for he was, for some improper reason or other, as was said, intimate with Earl Richard. This man had a beautiful wife, and one who was faithful to him, named Floria; and in order to heap more insults on Jesus Christ, he purchased an image of the Blessed Virgin, handsomely carved and painted, as usual, and nursing her son in her bosom. This image the Jew placed in his privy, and what it is disgraceful and ignominious to mention, he, as if in blasphemy of the Virgin Mary, perpetrated a most filthy and unmentionable act upon it day and night and caused his wife to do the same. But when, after some days, his wife saw this, she, by reason of her sex, was touched with sorrow, and, secretly going to the place, washed the dirt from the face of the image, which was enormously defiled; but when the Jew, her husband, found this out, he secretly and impiously smothered his wife. When these crimes were detected, and he was clearly proved guilty of them, although there were not wanting other grounds for putting him to death, he was thrust into the foulest dungeon of the Tower of London. In order to obtain his release, he faithfully promised to prove all the Jews of England to be base traitors; whereupon a heavy accusation was made against him by almost all the other Jews of England, and as they endeavoured to cause him to be put to death, Earl Richard spoke for him. The Jews then accused him of money-clipping, and other heavy crimes, and offered the earl a thousand marks not to protect him, which, however, he refused, as the Jew was said to be a friend of his. The said Jew Abraham then gave the king seven hundred

> marks to free himself from perpetual imprisonment to which he had been condemned, and by the aid of Earl Richard he effected this.[107]

Although Abraham was indeed put on trial in England in 1250, there is no suggestion in the trial records that he was accused of image desecration.[108] Eventually Abraham was forced to pay a fine and freed on condition that he would not appear before the king for a year. Although this was perhaps a fitting punishment for image desecration, it was hardly appropriate for murder.[109]

"The Virgin's Image Insulted" tale gained buoyancy and was incorporated into longer vernacular poems. The abused image was sometimes described not as a painting on the wall of a church but as a privately owned one, kept in a Christian home, as in the original tale of Adomnán. The malicious and clever Jew of the story was now the Christian's neighbor, who contrived to enter the Christian's house. As such it explored a new theme—that of ubiquitous Jews who had dangerously infiltrated Christian society and populated Christian towns and cities. In a version written between 1223 and 1227 by Gautier de Coinci (1177–1236), the French abbot who was the most influential translator of Marian tales, the Jew is described as a blasphemer of the Virgin and an enemy of Christians:

> He [the Jew] was mischievous and clever.
> He despised Christians
> And slandered very willingly
> The powerful lady of Heaven.[110]

In Gautier de Coinci's popular manuscripts (tens of them have survived, many of them illuminated), the Jew had become a more powerful opponent, able to express his contempt and anger for Mary as well as for his neighboring Christians.[111]

A fourteenth-century miniature from a French collection of legends (Figure 4), depicts the tale in two pictures. In the first, a bearded Jew has removed the painting of the Virgin and Child and, holding it upside down, is about to place it in the latrine, but is restrained by a Christian who chastises him. In the second, the same Christian has restored the painting to its proper place on an altar where it can again command respect and is kneeling devoutly before it to pray. When it gushes holy oil, the Jew is nowhere to be seen. The Jew's devilish associations are suggested by the monstrous and gro-

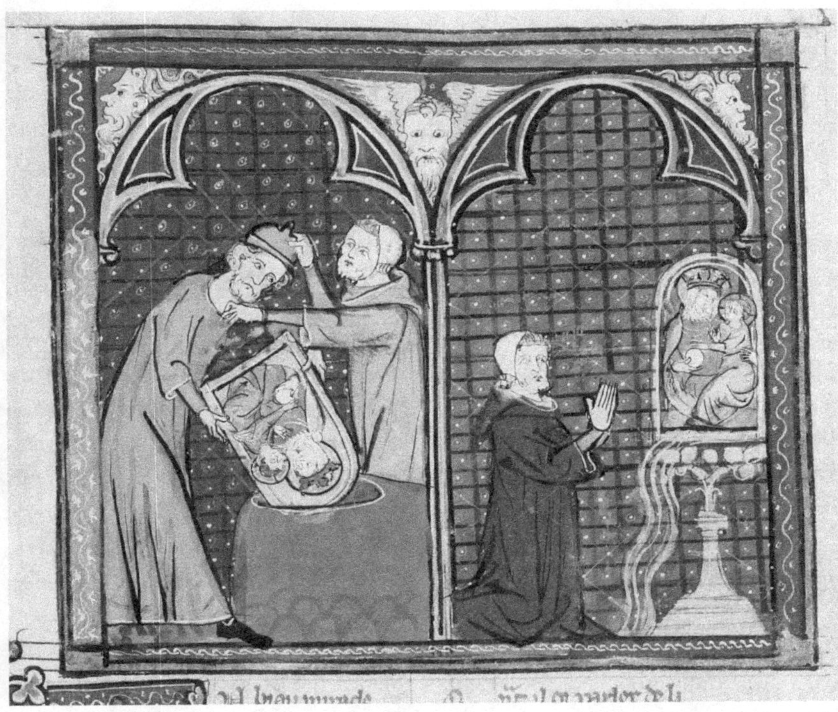

Figure 4. Miniature of "The Virgin's Image Insulted" in a fourteenth-century French collection of legends. Brussels, Bibliothèque royale de Belgique, MS 9229–30, fol. 12v.

tesque faces at the top, there to serve as evil signifiers and scare the viewer, suggesting the diabolical quality of the Jew who has been eliminated.

The Desecration of Crucifixes and Passion Images

In the Marian collections of the twelfth and thirteenth centuries, there are two tales, "Toledo," and "Christ of Beirut," in which Jews attacked not Marian images but crucifixes, and by desecrating them were seen to carry out a reenactment of the Passion.[112] "Toledo" was a new tale that had not appeared in Byzantine narratives and focused on the Jews' crucifixion of a waxen image they had molded themselves in their synagogue and their subsequent massacre at the hands of Christian knights. In "Christ of Beirut," as discussed in Chapter 1, an image of the Passion or a crucifix was desecrated by a Jew and the icon seeped blood as if it was the wounded Christ, confirming a more heinous act by the Jews. The message of these tales needs to be deciphered, as does their contribution in the thirteenth century to the host desecration libel and to legal proceedings in which Christians leveled formal charges against living Jews.

"Toledo"

"Toledo" was first recorded in Anselm's collection and was quickly absorbed into William of Malmesbury's tales.[113] It is a powerful and disturbing story without any literary precedent describing how, on the feast of the Assumption, the archbishop of Toledo and his congregation were celebrating mass and heard the voice of the Virgin from the heavens crying out that the Jews of the city were "recrucifying" Christ.

All Marian versions of "Toledo," except that of William of Malmesbury, appeared to be describing a recent event. According to the *Anales Toledanos*, a massacre of the Jewish community occurred on the eve of the Assumption in 1108, and most authors might have had this in mind.[114] Nevertheless, William of Malmesbury chose to set his "Toledo" in the Visigothic period during the reign of Reccared (586–601) and his successor King Sisebut (565–620), who finally rid Spain of its Jewish presence in 613. Perhaps his rationale for this time frame was the copious number of Jews living in Toledo in the seventh century and what he considered was a legitimate need to reduce their presence in the city.[115]

* * *

William of Malmesbury begins the tale by giving voice to Mary's lament against the Jews: "O the shame, O the pain, that the enemies of my son dwell amid His faithful! How shameful and disgusting it is that they are this day turning on His image with the same fury with which they once attacked Him in the flesh."[116]

At the end of mass and after consultation with the archbishop, the knights of the city rushed to the Jews' homes and to the synagogue. William of Malmesbury reports their invading the "Holy of Holies" in the synagogue (a reference to the most sacred part of the Temple in Jerusalem, whose destruction was seen as divine punishment, and not the Holy Ark of the Toledo synagogue).[117] Here they found the Jews reenacting the Crucifixion on a waxen image of Christ they had molded, by spitting at, slapping, and stabbing it.[118] The Jews of Toledo were immediately killed by the Christian soldiers.[119] Adgar narrated:

> When the Christians discovered this,
> they took the Jews, condemned them,
> they killed them with alacrity.
> They rendered to them their recompense according to law.
> Not a single one was assured of his life
> for their miserable treachery.[120]

This story incorporated new features into the narrative of Jewish desecration. In this tale, Mary was depicted as sanctifying the vengeance of the Christian soldiers against the large number of guilty Jews and even legitimizing extermination as a suitable punishment for their crime. When "Toledo" was originally written, Benedictine monks in northern France, in particular Robert the Monk (also known as Robert of St. Remy or Rheims), Guibert of Nogent, and Baldric Bourgueil, were formulating historical records of the First Crusade and the massacres of the Jews.[121] The anti-Jewish violence loomed large, and they appeared to feel a responsibility, as theologians, to give meaning to these outrages. Their works consistently connected crusading ideology with divine intervention and the belief that crusaders who killed infidels were carrying out the judgment of God in defense of the church.[122] For them, crusaders were obedient knights who followed divine orders to kill. William of Malmesbury seems to reflect this rationale and suggests divine reward for such killing in his rendering of "Toledo": "It was a fine exploit the Christians were engaged in; they could reckon up a laurel for themselves in heaven for each Jew they killed."[123]

Another new feature of "Toledo" was the Jews' creation of a wax effigy of Jesus—the *imago cerea*—molded by Jewish hands and providing a kind of plasticity on which they could easily and repeatedly reenact the Crucifixion. The Jews' use of a wax effigy in the tale may well have reflected the availability of tallow wax, which was now being molded into figurines. Wax as a creative medium had emerged in the eleventh century in western Europe, where ecclesiastical authorities in general approved of its use for votive offering at holy shrines.[124] The suggestion that Jews now molded their own images of Christ enabled readers and listeners to imagine that this blasphemous practice occurred more frequently.[125] An actual allegation of Jews reenacting the Passion on a painted or wooden effigy of Christ had surfaced already in fifth-century Byzantium, (see Chapter 1) where Christians believed that, on the festival of Purim when Jews celebrated the demise of Haman, they equated him with Christ and molded his form in order to destroy it. By the late twelfth century, the allegation had moved from Purim to Easter and the type of image had become one of wax. Arnold of Lübeck in his *Chronicle of the Slavs* even accuses real Jews of crucifying a waxen image of Christ every year on Good Friday.[126]

Again, it is the visual rendering of this tale in the *Cantigas* that best expresses the details of the narrative (Figure 5). The first miniature depicts Christians in a church, praying with the archbishop of Toledo, who is giving communion before an elevated and dominant statue of Mary. The cathedral in Toledo had actually been expanded during Alfonso's reign, so its importance as a place of worship and veneration of Mary is clear. The second miniature is of the same location, and at this point Mary's statue "speaks," revealing the Jews' crime to the archbishop. The two large candlesticks held before the statue by churchmen might well indicate the worshippers' gratitude for the miracle of the talking image. In the third miniature, the prelate stands outside the cathedral, reporting Mary's words to his congregants and ordering them to act. In the fourth miniature, Christian knights, in contemporary clothing, ride on horseback or march on foot toward the Jewish quarter, prepared for action, gazed at by the women of the city from high windows above the *cuadrados* (town squares). The fifth miniature depicts the Christian knights entering the door of the Jews' synagogue, as two Jews (with pointed hats) hold up the waxen figure, which is the size of a child. There is nothing to identify the building as a synagogue, even though the artists could have depicted some ceremonial object to show this. One of the Jews also holds up a crown of thorns above the figure's head; another absently pokes a stick of some sort toward the figure.[127] The portrayal of a wax image here shows a level of artistic sophistication. Its off-white color and shape suggests the figure of a child rather than an adult and has caused some scholars to argue that the artists might well have been referring to a ruling in Alfonso X's Castilian statutory code *Las Siete Partidas*, which listed together the offenses of ritual child murder and crucifying wax images:[128] "We have heard it said that in some places Jews celebrated, and still celebrate Good Friday, which commemorates the Passion of Our Lord Jesus

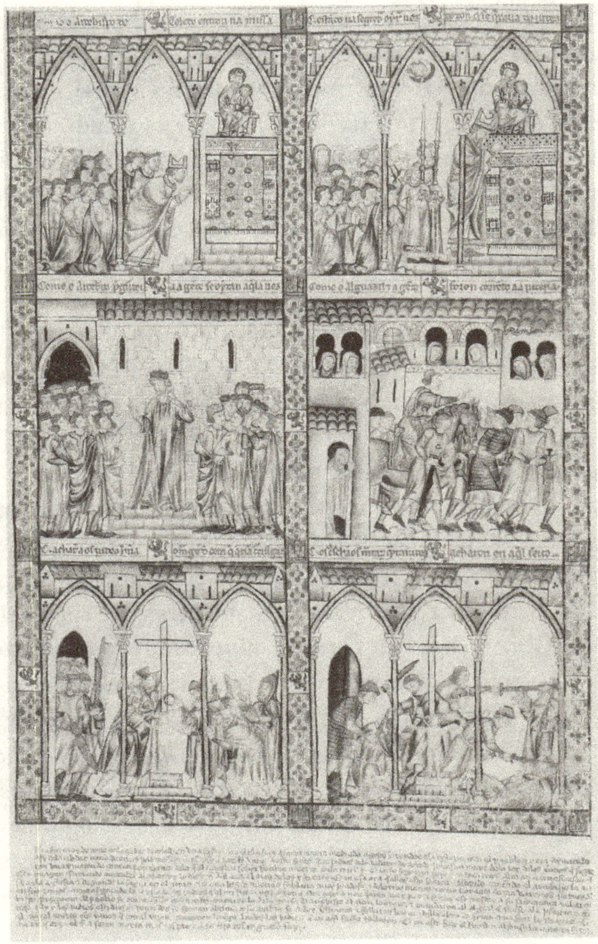

Figure 5. "Toledo," *Cantigas de Santa Maria* (T.I.1), fol. 20v. © Patrimonio Nacional.

Christ, by way of contempt: stealing children and fastening them to crosses, and making images of wax and crucifying them, when they cannot obtain children."[129] One might assume that the artists wished to point out the connection between the two crimes in the law, even though the king questioned the authenticity of both allegations.[130] Real accusations of ritual murder and image desecration were beginning to appear in Spain at this time (as will be discussed in the next chapter), and so it seems that Alfonso and his collaborators, or illuminators in court, felt the need to convey these rulings in the visual depictions.[131]

It is the sixth and final miniature that portrays a particular type of killing not mentioned in any literary version of the tale and not replicated in any other depiction of extermination of offenders, Jewish or otherwise, in this illustrated manuscript.[132] Here, as shown in Figure 6, the Jews are attacked with theatrical brutality by swords that strike them through their eyes, and no other part of their bodies. The soldiers even make awkward movements to achieve this, causing us to question why the artists wished to emphasize attacking the eyes of the Jews as the main thrust of their execution. Sara Lipton sees the visual rendering of Jews in the *Cantigas* as "symbols," Jewish men who become "a visible embodiment of the doctrine of 'Jewish witness,' which is usually attributed to Saint Augustine."[133] Augustine had disseminated the notion of the Jews' spiritual blindness to the truth of Christ and Christianity in literature and theology. Continuing Lipton's argument, I suggest that what is shown here is not foremost the killing of Jews, but rather a Christian response emphasizing the Jews' corporeality as opposed to the Christians' spirituality. As such they are spiritually blind to the sanctity of Christ, and their hermeneutical failure to recognize Christ as God is perhaps emphasized more powerfully since they had created the image themselves. In the process of their execution they therefore had to be physically blinded, which corresponds with their spiritual blindness, and punished in the part of the body that is most at fault—their eyes.

"Toledo" disseminated the idea that the Jews' increasing widespread desecration and mockery now included waxen images. Jews were seen as having the ability to create, attack, and then destroy these portable images with ease and in secret.

"Christ of Beirut"

An analysis of the remarkable proliferation of the Byzantine "Christ of Beirut" legend in medieval Europe and its appearance in Marian collections (although the text does not specifically include Mary herself) is fundamental to our understanding of the ways internal Christian developments influenced anti-Jewish accusations.[134] The Byzantine tale had already connected a Passion image with the Beirut Jews' abuse of the body of Christ and the resulting sacrificial symbolism of baptismal water and Eucharistic blood, which enables a group of Jews to convert. Christ of Beirut's blood was reportedly

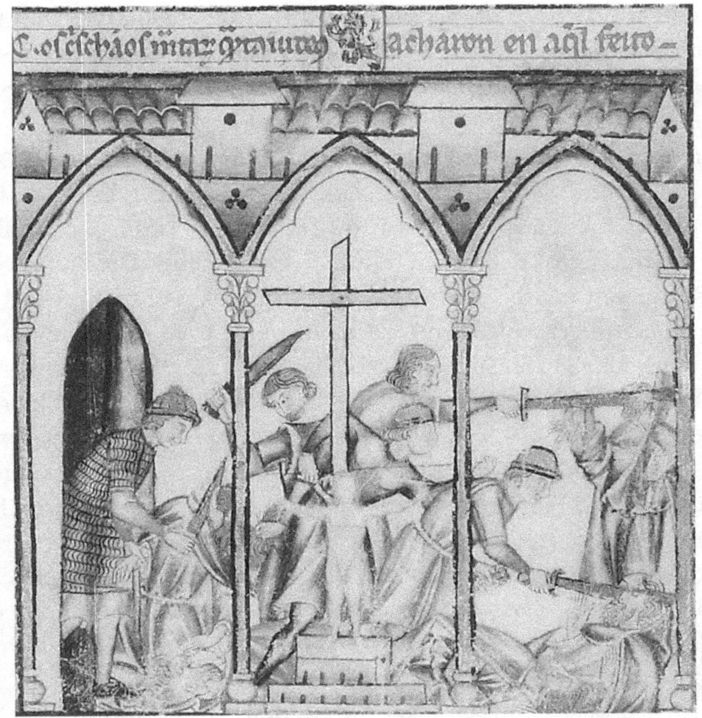

Figure 6. Sixth miniature, "Toledo," *Cantigas de Santa Maria* (T.I.1) 20v, © Patrimonio Nacional.

circulating from the tenth or eleventh century onward in western Europe.[135] Ampullae of its blood were housed in Oviedo, Spain, between the tenth and eleventh century, in the Cathedral of Pisa from the twelfth century, and in the thirteenth century it was recorded as being present in the church of San Pietro in Vinculis in Pisa, San Marco in Venice, and Sainte-Chapelle, Paris.

Eleventh- and twelfth-century texts confirmed that an actual Beirut image was now in the Church of All Saints in Constantinople, having been brought there by Nicephorus Phocas and not Giovanni Zimisce, substantiating the legend even further. Unfortunately the image itself was lost when Constantinople fell to the crusaders in 1204.[136] But in twelfth-century travelogues, Latin pilgrims revealed how local Beirut inhabitants used the legend to stress the importance of the exotic crusading city, worthy of a visit because of the alleged "memory of the miracle," particularly its Church of the Savior, previously a synagogue, where, they reported, the Jews had desecrated the image of Christ.[137] The legend linked the contemporary reader to the past artifact and also allowed for a hermeneutic leap to provide a common foundation for channeling religious thought about devotion through representational objects.

Since its first appearance in the Seventh Ecumenical Council at Nicaea in 787, its "miracle" was reiterated in numerous subsequent texts. As early as the tenth century a martyrology of the Cathedral of Girona, in Catalonia, testifies to the annual celebration of the "Passio ymaginis Domini Salvatoris quae crucifixa est in urbe Berito" (Passion of the image of the crucified Lord and Savior in the city of Beirut).[138]Also in Rome from this time, its story was commemorated annually on November 9 as a specific feast in honor of icons, being equivalent to the Byzantine Feast of Orthodoxy, and known as the Feast of the Savior.[139] The tale also appeared in visual representations on various altars, tomb reliefs, pulpits, and even Psalter manuscripts, but not, however, in the *Cantigas* manuscripts.[140] A limited number of French and English Marian collections of the twelfth and thirteenth centuries record the legend, but it appears widely in other twelfth-century exempla collections, including Sigebert of Gembloux (1112), Helinand of Froidmont (1211–1223), Caesarius of Heisterbach (1220–1235), Vincent of Beauvais (ca. 1244), and Jacobus de Voragine's famous collection of miracle tales—the *Legenda aurea* (Golden Legend, ca. 1255). This collection was one of the most influential books of the late Middle Ages and some one thousand extant manuscript copies of this document have survived, as well as hundreds of printed copies and translations in every European language, confirming the dissemination and popularity of this text, among clergy and laity alike.[141]

Representations of the Beirut tale also proliferated in illuminated texts. The image around the letter *S* in the twelfth-century passional in Figure 7 shows one Jew striking his lance into Jesus's side and another mocking Jesus by putting a sponge to his lips. Both these Jews have been depicted with the invidious pointed hats, which distinguishes them from the three neophytes below who have been cured of their wickedness by the seeping Eucharistic blood. One of these converts, who is collecting the blood from the image, is about to pour it over the paralytic Jew who is lying in the bed below. Another convert has received the blood from Jesus's wounded feet into his blind eyes, and his upturned hands show his amazement that he can now see.[142]

Another image of the tale appears in the same French collection of legends mentioned earlier (Figure 8). Here the scene on the left shows three Jews attacking a life-size crucifix—one sticking a lance into Christ's side,

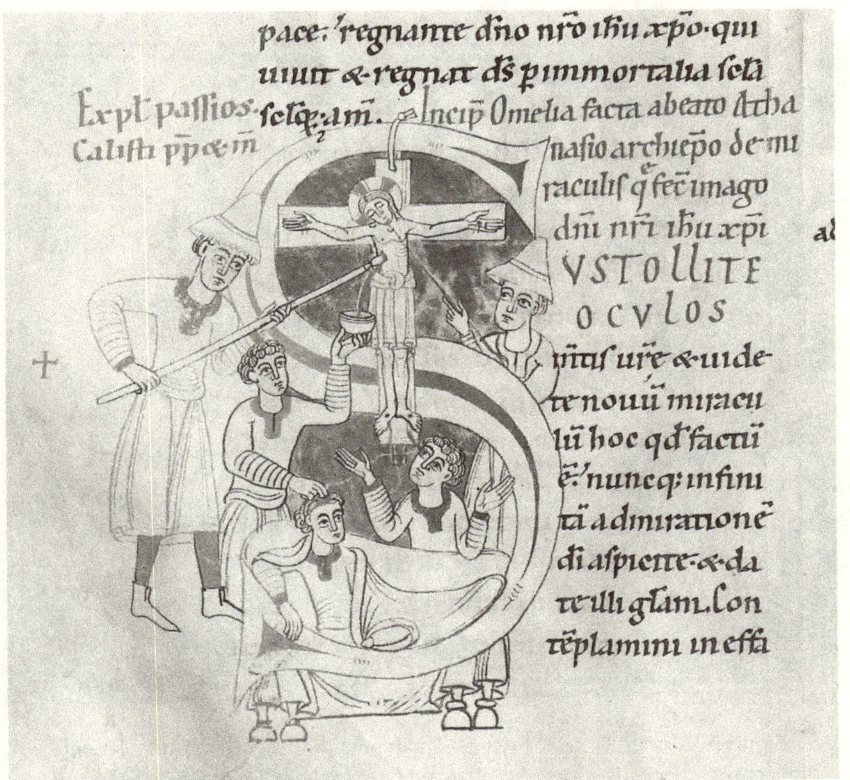

Figure 7. Miniature in a passional made in the Benedictine abbey of Zwiefalten, between 1160 and 1165. Stuttgart, Württembergische Landesbibliothek, Cod.bibl. fol.56, fol. 131v.

another collecting the blood, and a third raising a sponge to Jesus's face. In the second scene, one Jew is being baptized in a font by a haloed priest as another three look on. The grotesque Jewish faces in the top corners are similar to those in Figure 4 above.[143]

* * *

The "Christ of Beirut" tale had become a standard exempla legend of Jewish image desecration and the Jews' reenactment of the Crucifixion, circulating in theological, homiletic literature, hagiographic miscellanies, and church liturgy throughout Europe.[144] Whereas Byzantines had concentrated on

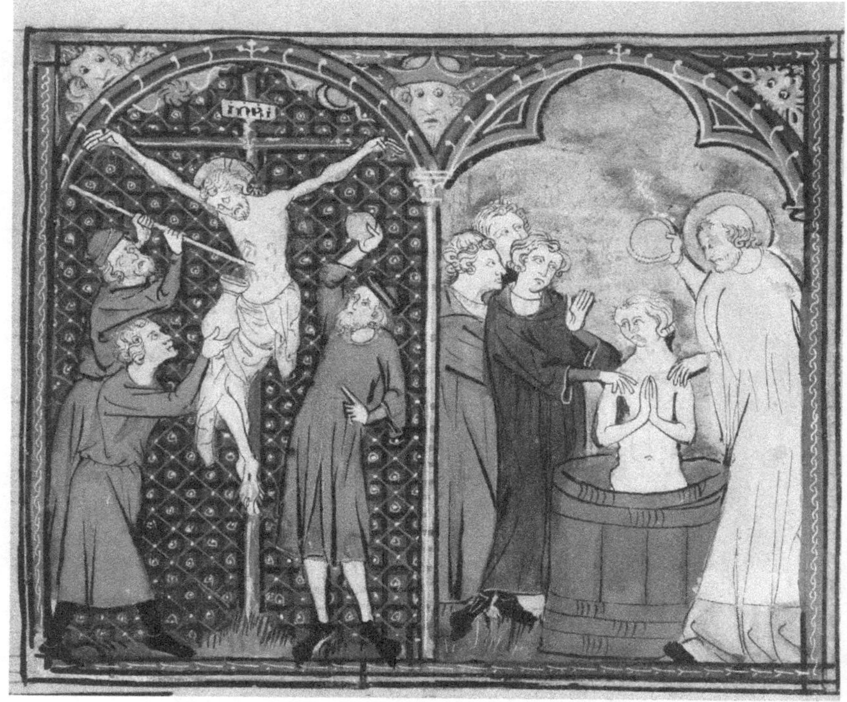

Figure 8. Miniature of "Christ of Beirut" in a fourteenth-century French collection of legends. Brussels, Bibliothèque royale de Belgique, MS 9229-30, fol. 88.

the deified and transfigured Christ, Western Christianity focused on the crucified body of Jesus.[145] "Christ of Beirut" was not so much a story of desecration as a meticulous and blatant reenactment of the Crucifixion upon an image of Christ, where Christ's blood is portrayed as seeping from it. The power and miracle of Christ's blood confirms the Jews' "authentic" killing of Jesus and persuades the obstinate, disbelieving Jews to convert.[146] In effect, the narrative had moved away from the centrality of the Jews' violation of an image and their conversion, to focusing on the sanctity of Christ's blood that seeped from it, and allowed a process of catechism to be associated with the "happy ending." It confirmed that only the physical touch of Christ's blood had the power to transform the Jewish male from a defiant and perverse enemy of Christian grace to a beneficiary of the miraculous Christ. At this point, though, the Jews were not imagined, seen, or reported as ingesting the blood of the image. What was being emphasized was that Christ's blood had the power, by touch alone, to persuade the Jews both to contemplate and to arrive at salvation, thereby separating these "converts" from the deficiencies of Judaism. Only those Jews cured of their "blindness" would be able to take their place among the sheep who are saved on the Day of Judgment. So two important points in the rendering of this tale in the medieval West need to be noted. The first is that Jews were still not seen as ingesting blood and the second is that only in this tale are the Jews saved by their encounter with Eucharistic blood.

A closer look at renditions of the tale will confirm how these two elements in "Christ of Beirut" contributed to the real allegations that Jews were guilty of desecrating hosts and committing a form of ritual murder that involved their ingestion of Christian blood. John of Garland (b. ca. 1185, d. ca. 1272) was the master of liberal arts who taught in the schools of thirteenth-century Paris and Toulouse. His *Stella Maris*, a collection of sixty-one Marian legends (ca. 1248), provided a shortened, popularized exemplum, using complicated Latin verse forms—as was typical of his work—to emphasize certain features of the "Christ of Beirut" legend. It read: "Blood seeped from the image of the Savior made by Nicodemus, as an everlasting memorial. The Jews pierced the image and collected large supplies of the blood in jars. Scarcely had the Jews believed, when they rushed to be baptized with joy in their hearts."[147] The focus has shifted to the image being painted by Nicodemus, its effusion of blood (the water is not even mentioned), the Jews' anxious and determined efforts to collect as much blood as they could, and their delight at what is recorded as genuine conversion, emphasizing a clear message of religious superiority of Christianity over Judaism. As can be seen, the story is short enough for its essentials to be easily understood and remembered.

This attention to the outcome of the legend and the miraculous effect of the image's blood would be highlighted by Bishop William Durand of Mende (ca. 1230–1296) in his *Rationale divinorum officiorum*. Although Durand does not mention any ingesting of the blood by the Jews, he records the legend as if it was a real event:

> In the city of Beirut, in Syria, when the Jews had defiled a certain image of the crucifix with their feet, and they pierced its side, blood and water immediately flowed from it. And seeing this, the Jews were amazed, and the sick among them, when smeared with this

> blood, were freed from all of their illnesses; on this account, all of them, receiving faith in Christ, were baptized and they consecrated all of their synagogues, making them churches. . . . And on account of this miracle, the church decreed that a commemoration of the Lord's Passion be celebrated the fifth day before the Calends of December and in Rome a church was consecrated in honor of the Savior where a vial with that blood is preserved and a solemn feast is celebrated for that event.[148]

Were Garland and later Durand emphasizing the seeping blood from the image because King Louis IX of France had recently acquired in Paris a blood relic from the Beirut source that had been placed in Sainte-Chapelle between 1231 and 1241?[149] It should be noted that in October 1247, a year before John of Garland wrote the *Stella Maris*, King Henry III of England had also received a precious relic of Christ's blood from Jerusalem; it was not from the Beirut image but was said to have been shed on Calvary and was sent under the seals of the patriarch of Jerusalem, the masters of the Templars and Hospitallers, and various bishops from the Holy Land.[150] In his meticulous study of this event, Nicholas Vincent has uncovered a deep skepticism that existed regarding this relic's authenticity. Vincent argues that, unlike the Beirut blood, there was an excessive amount of this holy blood in western Europe by the end of the twelfth century.[151] Vincent counted at least twenty churches that, by the beginning of the thirteenth century, claimed to possess ampullae of Christ's blood shed at the Crucifixion, and this number only increased once Constantinople fell in 1204 and the leaders of the Fourth Crusade returned home with more.[152] The principal aim of both John of Garland's and William Durand's texts could have been to authenticate the Paris Beirut blood relic that had been connected with the Jews' desecration and their rejection of holy blood, and that is why they chose to mention it.

There was clearly a contrast between the blood held in Paris, which was believed to be authentic, and the blood housed in England, whose authenticity was disputed. These doubts seem to have originated with a papal document, dated to the eleventh century (on historical grounds and evidence from the manuscript tradition), which had "verified" that the speech of Peter of Nicomedia regarding the Beirut image had not in fact been made at the eighth-century Second Council of Nicaea but in a recent eleventh-century synod of churches of Asia. This document had noted that the intention of the synod convened at Caesarea, "the largest of the cities of Cappadocia," was to "weed out a serious mistake that has arisen regarding the blood of Christ."[153] In this text, Bishop Peter of Nicomedia insisted that the blood that seeped from the image in Beirut was in fact the *only* true relic of Christ's blood in the world and needed to be understood as such, thereby denying the relic status of any other blood said to be connected to Christ's crucifixion:

> This is the true and absolutely believable story of the blood from our Lord and Saviour's side which was shed through His holy image crucified in Syria, in the town of Beirut. This is also that blood of the Lord many say they possess. True Catholics cannot believe differently from what we have written, that is, nothing of Christ's flesh and blood can be found in the world apart from that which is daily made spiritually on the altar, by hand of the priests. Aware, therefore, of this, beloved fathers and brothers, I have made haste to declare it to you for the edification of your souls and the deepening of our faith, so that you can know from this too how great are the power and goodness of our God and Lord Jesus Christ the Saviour.[154]

In contrast to the blood of the Beirut image, the authenticity of other types of blood relics was doubted both on historical and theological grounds by ecclesiastics. Guibert of Nogent (ca. 1055–1124) in his *De sanctis et eorum pigneribus* argued vehemently that not only were these relics not the true blood of Christ, but they were contrary to orthodox belief. The *Blutreliquien* (blood relic)—as it was known in Franconia—was clearly a sensitive and unresolved issue among theologians.[155] Thomas Aquinas only authenticated the blood derived from the Beirut image as blood relics, keen to redirect Christian devotion away from the belief that Christ's blood from the Crucifixion had remained on earth. Yet he clarified that the Beirut blood was not Christ's actual blood. He wrote: "All the blood which flowed from Christ's body, belonging as it does to the integrity of human nature, rose again with His body; and the same reason holds good for all the particles which belong to the truth and integrity of human nature. But the blood preserved as relics in some churches did not flow from Christ's side, but, it might be said, miraculously, from some maltreated image of Christ."[156]

These writings insisted that churchmen keep a firm separation in their minds between the Eucharistic body of Christ, the true body and blood of

Christ, and blood seeping from relics such as the Beirut image. In the papal document above, Bishop Peter of Nicomedia refuted the Eucharistic nature of the "Christ of Beirut" blood, differentiating it from the Eucharist, which was, as noted above, "daily made spiritually on the altar, by hand of the priests." Was this emphasis to prevent a literal interpretation of sacred embodiment in the Beirut image? The eleventh century was full of close debate and study by liturgists and theologians regarding the power of the Eucharist.[157] From the twelfth century, Gerhoh of Reichersberg, Peter Lombard, and members of the school of Peter Abelard and Gilbert of La Porrée consistently argued that the Eucharist was the only genuine "image" of Christian devotion and the symbol of unity of Christ and church. With the continuing contention regarding the veneration of images versus the Eucharistic claims, it certainly made sense to ensure that the Christian community understood the true identity and authenticity of Christ's blood. The blood that seeped from a crucifix could not be Christ's actual blood since the crucifix was a wooden object, so what counted as Christ's blood?

As is well known, belief in the presence of the real and historic body (flesh and blood) of Christ in the Eucharist was made binding by the Fourth Lateran Council in 1215, via the dogma of transubstantiation.[158] Christian doctrine now confirmed that salvation was to be reinforced through the sacramental meal of bread and wine, the ingestion of Christ's flesh and blood in the Eucharist. In other words, what was sanctioned here was that, through the miracle of the Eucharist, the very body of God and its historic suffering was present at every communion, in every church. (Even though the Lateran Council stipulated annual communion at Easter, synodal legislation suggested three times a year.)[159] Individual Christians were now allowed, through ingestion, to have contact with this transubstantiated material object. It became the tangible mystery of holiness, and it had the potential to live, bleed, and seep emotion through its prototype, as had the "Christ of Beirut" image.[160] But it was only Christians who were to be fortified by consuming the body and blood of Christ. They were doing this no longer metaphorically or as an act of commemoration but substantively.

So far this chapter has shown how fictitious Jews in "Christ of Beirut" were seen to attack a venerated image and cause it to bleed; on witnessing that blood they converted to Christianity. After the Lateran Council of 1215, a new allegation arose in which real Jews were accused of desecrating, by the same process, a consecrated host, now confirmed as the only true image of

Christ that contained his blood. In this narrative, whereas desecrating Jesus on the cross had been a symbolic reenactment of the Passion, the desecration of a host was a far more dangerous real "act" of slaughter, since each consecrated host, according to the Lateran canon, was Christ.[161]

With compelling insight, Miri Rubin has already meticulously connected the host desecration allegation to the long-standing tale of the Jewish boy who had swallowed a Eucharistic wafer.[162] Originally appearing in the *Historia ecclesiastica* of Evagrius Scholasticus of Antioch (ca. 536–600) and then in the tales of Gregory of Tours, this was adapted by Paschasius Radbert (ca. 785–ca. 860) around 831 to reinforce Eucharistic realism.[163] The tale authenticated the miraculous power of the consecrated bread that had been ingested by a Jewish boy in a church and saved him from the fires of the furnace in which his father placed him. The Jewish boy's survival was a miracle, convincing him and his mother to convert. But what was missing was a preliminary tale of the physical assault on the Eucharist and the spilling of its blood by the Jews.[164] It could be said that "Toledo," with its emphasis on the reenactment of the Passion on an image, and "Christ of Beirut," with its emphasis on the salvific blood, provided the motifs and themes to make this come about. This link between image desecration tales and host desecration accusations is fundamental to our understanding of the origins and nature of the host desecration accusation. Bleeding hosts indicated the "real presence" of Christ in the consecrated Eucharist. By contrast, bleeding images, not having undergone transubstantiation, did not contain the "real presence" of Christ; their miraculous bleeding had signified Christian truth through a lesser miracle—that of transfiguration.

In Paris in 1290, the first real accusation had been made to the effect that the Jew attacked the host, violating and abusing it and causing its miraculous bleeding. The host was believed to have been mutilated so that it would bleed profusely, and Jews were noted as using—as they had in "Christ of Beirut"—Christ's blood to heal their ailments.[165] Indeed, after the Jews were said to have attacked the host with knives and cast it into boiling water, it reportedly turned into a crucifix, which suggests that the literary topos of image desecration contributed to the construction of this allegation.[166] Scholars who have studied host desecration confirm that, in Europe, conversion frequently became a consequence of these accusations.[167] After the main Jewish suspects had been tried and executed, their family members were usually said to have accepted baptism, which continued to confirm, as the tales had, that they were now finally free to accept the true faith and be granted divine salvation.[168]

This overlap between tales and real accusations must be seen as the result of the power and influence of the tales, as well as the increasing focus and centrality of Eucharistic theology. The Jew remained the offender, but his aggression and the consequential bleeding of Christ's image was now a more heinous offense. In real accusations, the Jew begins to be considered not only as a desecrator of hosts but also as a killer of Christians and a user of their blood. As shown above, the image desecration tales never specified that the Jews ingested blood from the bleeding image. Yet, as scholars have argued, blood libels, in the form of accusations of killing a Christian child with the intention of using its blood to make unleavened bread and healing ointments, only began to surface in the later thirteenth century, postdating the Lateran Council.[169] The cases of Fulda in 1235 and of Valréas, Provence, in 1247 were the first to mention a blood accusation.[170] In Fulda, according to an account written the following year, two Jews had killed five sons of a miller and collected their blood in waxed sacks.[171] As in the "Christ of Beirut" tale, Jews were now seen to be using Christian blood for healing purposes and drinking it as Christians were expected to do at communion. A tale by Herman of Bologna in the *Viaticum narrationum* (ca. 1280–1290) describes the rather comical story of how a Jew of Cologne, having received communion, kept the host in his mouth; when he removed it, he discovered that it had turned into a tiny child. When he put it back in his mouth, it had become so hard he could not chew it or swallow it, and eventually, admitting the miracle, he was converted. This was in fact the first literary tale in which a Jew ingested the Eucharist. Many versions of this tale continued to be circulated in the later Middle Ages.[172] Blood then took on different meanings. For Jews blood was, allegedly, actual blood extracted from an innocent child martyr, whereas for Christians it was consecrated wine. Both Tobias and Samuel, two of the three prominent Jews accused of killing Simon of Trent in 1475, were forced to admit, after repeated torture, that they had drunk wine mixed with Simon's blood at Passover and sprinkled the blood over the dough to make the matzah.[173] The association of Eucharistic blood had been transferred from that of a bleeding image to that of real allegations against the Jews of Europe for host desecration and ritual murder. These damning accusations would cause the destruction of many Jewish communities in the later medieval period.

The Jews' association with miraculous images would also emerge in more sophisticated host desecration discourses toward the end of the medieval period. Mitchell Merback's detailed study of the "Man of Sorrows altar" (a statue of a suffering Christ holding the chalice or the host) in Pulkau, Lower Austria, shows how, in 1338, a statue was seen to bleed after a host desecration; this charge resulted in the massacre of its Jewish community.[174] These images seemed to connect a bleeding image with a Eucharistic wafer, in terms of both imagery and ideology. Here the bleeding occurred not only as confirmation of Jewish guilt but also as part of a purification process, turning the place of sacrilege into one of atonement and then to a hallowed and prosperous pilgrimage site that exhibited not only a desecrated host but also an image that seeped blood.[175]

The development and adaptation of real host desecration and blood libels did not stop the tale of crucifix desecration from being disseminated further. One "Christ of Beirut" version was penned in the late thirteenth century by the monk and chronicler Abbot Richer of Senones, who (in an attempt to present it as an actual event and miracle) chose to place his descriptive tale in Cologne and attributed the offense not only to Jewish men but also to Jewish women. He accused the Jews of stabbing a painting of the Passion and icons of the Virgin and Child, hidden on the interior walls of a house they were renting. In this version, the house had previously been rented by a Christian weaver, who was living too far from a church and had decided to compensate by hanging icons of the Crucifixion and Madonna and Child in his home, to define it as a Christian space. Again, when the knife struck a wound on Christ's body, the image gushed so much blood that neighboring Christians were able to witness the miracle. In this version, however, not all the Jews of Cologne were converted. Some were arrested and their goods confiscated, a few were baptized, others were executed, and some exiled. The synagogue was destroyed and a church in honor of the cross of Christ was erected on its site.[176] The literary topos of Jewish desecrators, miraculous images, and their blood relics had not ceased to be utilized in its own right and would continue.[177] The tale had come to serve as a message about the consequences of real accusations of host desecration and ritual murder. The expectation that Jews would always convert was unrealistic. For on many more occasions, Jews would be punished and killed for these offenses. Allegations disseminated through Byzantine tales had provoked Christians to level real charges against living Jews.

Real Accusations of Image Desecration

Finally, we need to turn from literary narratives, Marian tales of miracles, host desecration, and blood libels to real accusations of image desecration. Actual documented cases against Jews in the medieval period are unlike the tales appearing in manuscripts. They are both less dramatic and less violent.[178] Real accusations did not involve images located in churches or in the homes of Jews and Christians. Nor was there a miracle of bleeding or transfiguration associated with the accusation, and the Jew was neither killed nor did he convert.

The first real accusations against Jews for image desecration surfaced in Oxford (1268) and Manosque (1342). In neither of these cases was it proven that the Jews had committed the crime. They involved the desecration of crosses and not crucifixes or Passion paintings. The crosses said to have been attacked were situated outside the church in both places.[179] According to the fourteenth-century *Book of the Chancellor and Proctors of the University of Oxford*, the Oxford episode occurred on Ascension Day (May 17) 1268 when a local Jew was described as recklessly grabbing, breaking, and then trampling on a "certain small portable wooden cross" carried by a young clerk in a procession of the parish clergy, sacristans, choristers, townspeople of the city, and students.[180] The impact of this destruction was far greater because it was inflicted in public.

The annual procession had passed through Fish Street (St. Aldates) otherwise known as the "Great Jewry," the Jewish quarter, on the way to the churchyard of St. Frideswide's Priory, its final destination, where Master Nicholas of Ewelme, the chancellor of the university, was to give a public sermon before the townspeople, both lay and clerical.[181] The offense was said to have taken place near the churchyard, perpetrated by a single offender who then disappeared into one of the crowded main streets. It seems unlikely that a Jew would have risked openly desecrating a crucifix during a devotional procession, since the Jews' presence during such an event was in itself provocative and potentially volatile.[182] It is possible that a Jew was pushed against the crucifix accidentally causing a brawl between Jews and Christian university students in the narrow streets of the city.[183] In the crusading era when a cross represented a symbol not just of Christ's Passion but also of legitimate military action against infidels, Nicholas might well have been keen to promote such an allegation against the Jews.

The offense, recorded in the sources as a desecration, did not cause a hurling of insults or turn the neighborhood more antagonistic. Instead, the proceedings were carefully supervised by King Henry III himself, who waited three months while the chancellor and masters of the university set up an inquiry to see if the accusation was genuine. During this time the Jews, refusing to name any individual offender, were imprisoned until they could give security for the exorbitant amount the king ordered them to pay.[184] The Jews, by resolving to keep silent at this time, showed a common desire to avoid responsibility, keeping a collective distance from a crime with which any Jew or group of Jews could be charged. The only public protest the king made was to demand a disproportionate financial reimbursement. Whereas, as Christoph Cluse argues, Lord Edward (King Henry's son) might have been eager to exploit this accusation to fund the crusading expedition that he was to carry out in 1270, his father administered the fine so that only the university benefited. The Jews had to pay for two new sacred items, a portable gilded silver cross to replace the cross damaged by the Jew and a permanent sculpted marble crucifix (which on one side had a crucified Jesus and on the other the Virgin Mary) to stand in the place where the crime had been committed.[185] One crucifix desecrated by Jews was thus replaced by two crucifixes.

The inscription placed upon the permanent crucifix ran as follows:

> Who created me? Jews.
> In what way? With their money.
> Who ordered them to do this? The king.
> Who brought this about? Masters [of the university].
> Why? Because they broke a wooden cross.
> At what time? The feast of the Ascension of the Lord.
> Where was the place? Here where I stand.[186]

The inscription indicated that the Jews were instructed to erect a memorial in the exact place where they had physically violated the crucifix (although this was not in fact done).[187]

In September 1342 in Manosque, a town in Upper Provence in southeastern France, a Christian court, committed to rigid legal procedure, had no difficulty in acquitting the Jews of an accusation of image desecration. The accusation probably originated through the machinations of a priest, Rostagnus Obrerii, who accused the Jew Simon David of desecrating a wayside crucifix or cross that stood just outside the town.[188] David, who maintained his innocence throughout the trial, was protected by the cautious and painstaking procedures of the court of the Knights of Saint John (the Hospitallers, who were the feudal lords of the town of Manosque, with jurisdiction over it as a fief), foiling again any popular or ecclesiastical outburst against the Jewish community. Due to lack of evidence, the court absolved David of the crime of "purposefully and deliberately" violating (spitting at, stoning, and breaking) a public cross, which now stood without a left arm that had been broken off. No eyewitnesses could confirm the crime. In fact, the five Christian witnesses argued that the cross looked as if it had been broken, not on the day that Obrerii had described, but at a much earlier date. Nor was there any suggestion that the Jewish community was required to reimburse the damage done to the cross.

In Oxford, the accusation was dropped after the authorities imposed a heavy fine, and in Manosque, the accusation was described as an offense of *lèse-majesté*, that is, an act of material damage to the cross rather than a blasphemous violation against Christianity.[189] In Manosque, Simon David, the Jewish suspect, was released without prosecution or charge. Missing too from these two incidents was evidence or even a hint of a spontaneous, violent reaction on the part of local Christians. These accusations might have provoked volatile reactions, especially at a time of deep penetration of religious items into everyday life, but it seems that the governing authorities held the decisive role in preventing violence from escalating.[190] What should be conjectured from the two cases is that reactions to real accusations of Jewish desecration were by no means as extreme as those described in the Marian tales of the period. Nor did the legendary narrative spontaneously evoke the dangerous association with the Passion.[191] In the case of Manosque, a blood libel in 1296 had already caused mass hysteria, whereby approximately eight Jews were massacred and the homes of others attacked and robbed. The ritual murder allegation of Little Hugh of Lincoln had also caused an outcry resulting in eighteen Jews being hanged by Henry III in 1255 and their properties plundered by the crown.[192] The English and the French courts might well have been interested in preventing a public outbreak of violence for this type of offense. In England, Henry III bypassed clerical control to ensure that the investigation and its outcome were carefully managed and handled by his own officials; his intention might simply have been to extract additional income from the Jewish community. The secular authorities in both Oxford and Manosque publicly demonstrated that cross/crucifix desecration accusations—though familiar enough to warrant an official response—were to be efficiently controlled, preventing popular fervor or mass hysteria. The authorities, weary of anti-Jewish violence, considered image desecration less heinous than other anti-Jewish accusations.

Conclusion

The purpose of this chapter has been to trace in Marian tales of the twelfth and thirteenth centuries the essential narrative that associated the Jews with the desecration of images and examine how this reconfiguration of Byzantine tales developed this theme. The Byzantine allegation of Jewish image desecration had also traveled well and in western Europe was widely disseminated in disputation literature and aggressive *adversus Judaeos* treatises by church theologians.

It was the priests and friars who became the most important tellers of medieval Marian tales of image desecration. Once again, the fictitious Jew was given the task of dispelling Christian uncertainties regarding the status of images. The idea that the images were desecrated by Jews proved that they were worthy of veneration, and, if they were worthy of veneration, they could not be idols. Viewed together, these Marian tales permit several observations. They portray how fictitious Jews were compelled to acknowledge Mary's power through miracles brought about in response to their evil actions. The image sends a kind of distress signal to Mary, who then uses her image to take action against the Jew, legitimizing the Christian killing of Jewish offenders or triggering the Jews' genuine desire for conversion. The Jew is then permanently altered or destroyed by his own acts of violation. In "The Virgin's Image Insulted" and "Toledo" he was eliminated; in "Christ of Beirut," he became a Christian and was saved and absorbed by the power and glory of Christendom.

But in a period when holy images, wax effigies, and crucifixes were clearly understood as portable conduits of divinity, image desecration must be recognized as being more than just a repeating narrative trope.[193] The internal Christian development in Eucharistic theology influenced the anti-Jewish accusation and led to the translation of key elements of image desecration narratives into host desecration narratives and accusations. "Christ of Beirut" also contributed to the blood libel accusation by its focus on the Jews' use of Eucharistic blood to heal their ailments. For from this too could arise the pernicious idea that Jews, as enemies of Christ, chose to enact a kind of parody of the Mass using the physical blood of a martyred Christian child.

The importance of image desecration tales and real allegations must not be understated. For it was in the tales, rather than in the two real accusations of image desecration that have so far been uncovered, that the concept of the Jewish image desecrator had been established, and this would soon, as the next chapter will show, be disseminated into *converso* society in inquisitorial Iberia. For it is here that we will move away from the fictional convert encountered in the "Christ of Beirut" narrative to the real convert accused of desecrating images (among other offenses) in inquisitorial investigations.

Chapter 3

Jews, *Conversos,* and Image Desecration in Spain

Faith that has material taint
Is a magnet that lures to sin
And faith that has a heart of stone
Makes a corpse of him who owns it
The holy faith, the pure faith
Is the one the Hebrew observes
For he knows of only one God
As the light of understanding

—Antonio Enríquez Gómez, "Ballad in Honor of the Divine Martyr, Judah the Believer, Martyred in Vallodolid at the Hands of the Inquisition"

Literary tropes do not heed geographical boundaries, and it is not surprising to find that Iberia housed its own tradition and versions of image desecration stories about Jews. This chapter will study these narratives within their Christian frameworks together with real image desecration accusations against Jews before their expulsion in 1492 and against *conversos* after the establishment of the Spanish Inquisition in 1478. As will be shown, it is only once Catholic rulers and ecclesiastical authorities initiated their own iconographic revolution in the 1440s, with their demand that the Christian population venerate small objects in private devotion, that an allegation against *conversos* becomes widespread.[1] This confirms our thesis that allegations and accusations against Jews tend to reflect developments within the Christian religion rather than events in Jewish life. The late arrival of portable devotionalia—in particular of small-scale crucifixes adorning domestic spaces—was probably related to the slow Christianization of Spain as it moved from a multiconfessional state with Muslims and Jews, to one where mosques and synagogues had been eradicated.[2] Up to the fifteenth century, cult images had only been prevalent in churches as life-size sculptures of Christ, showing his divine or quasi-divine powers during his life, and Romanesque painted wooden panels of Mary the Virgin Mother, with Christ on her lap.[3] Moreover, in the Renaissance period, Spanish artists mainly worked on creating *retablos*—altarpieces for churches, monasteries, and occasionally nobles' residences, depicting common religious occupations.[4] In addition, images of the Passion and the suffering of Christ were too offensive and repugnant for medieval Iberian society, which preferred images to be, according to Felipe Pereda, "empathetically effective while preserving the decorum associated with sacred ancient icons."[5]

* * *

These factors need to be borne in mind when exploring the dissemination of medieval tales of image desecration and the allegation against Jews and later *conversos*. Obviously, if portable or easily accessible images were not part of the cultural landscape in medieval Spain, one could assume that there would be no cause for the dissemination of the belief that sections of society might desecrate them. In neither Rabbi Moses ben Nachman's *Sefer Ha-Vikuach* nor Pablo Cristiani's record of the Barcelona disputation of 1263 is there any mention of the polemical debate between Jews and Christians on images and idolatry, nor any reference to the Jews' association with image violation.[6] When the anonymous Christian author of the 1286 Majorca disputation addressed the Christian practice of using images and crosses in churches, the Christian interlocutor Inghetto Contardo, having been accused of idolatry by his Jewish opponent, put forward an unusual argument.[7] He rejected the accusation by suggesting that if there was a [humanitarian] need, he would destroy an image himself:

> We do not venerate idols and images but we venerate the God of heaven, the Father, and His only Son, our Lord Jesus Christ. . . .

And these images that you see in churches are not venerated by us, but our Mother the Holy Church has placed them there as mirrors and when the eyes of the flesh see them, the eyes of the heart also see them and recollect Christ's passion that he suffered for our salvation and for the redemption of mankind. . . . And indeed I say to you that if I had a wooden cross or image, and I had nothing with which to heat water for my Christian brother, or my Jewish friend were they to fall sick, I would put the cross and the image in the fire and burn them."[8]

There is nothing in this argument to suggest that Contardo associates Jews with image desecration. He belittles the sanctity of the images in order to convince the Jew that images were not idols but mirrors through which Christians may recall Christ's death in their hearts. The *Cantigas de Santa Maria* narratives also disseminate a similar attitude toward the way images were to be understood and venerated in the thirteenth century, with relatively little emphasis on their miracle-making potential. Cantiga 162 notes: "We should greatly revere the images of the Peerless Virgin, for it is fitting to honor them and render great devotion to them, not for their own sake, by my faith, but because of Her whom they represent. We should never attempt to bring harm to them nor defile them."[9] In this case, Marian images were to be venerated because the honor rendered to them is transferred to the beings they represent.

Different types of images play a pivotal role in 43 of the 427 tales and these include statues[10] and paintings of the Holy Mary and Child (always depicted in the form of a framed rectangular painting),[11] small devotional pendants, metal images of Mary,[12] *acheiropoieta* images (sacred images not made by human hands)[13] of the Virgin, a crucifix, a wax crucifix made by Jews, and a silver cross.[14] But in only 17 of the 43 stories are the images actually located in Iberia. The majority describe sacred images located elsewhere, seven in unnamed locations, six in France, six in Byzantium, four in the Holy Land, and three in Italy.[15]

This chapter begins by tracing image desecration tales in Spain, in particular "Christ of Beirut." The role of Christ's Eucharistic blood in desecration narratives will be examined and I will also ask whether the allegation in the tale was in any way associated with accusations that Jews in Spain committed host desecration and ritual murder. I will then turn to an analysis of the accusations of image desecration made against Jews before their expulsion in 1492. As will be shown, it is only in the fifteenth century, with the widespread activities of the mendicant orders and the dramatic increase in the production of small devotional objects, that internal Christian developments were able to influence and fully activate anti-Jewish accusations. Attention will finally turn to trials of *conversos* denounced to the post-1480 Spanish Inquisition for Judaizing. As will be suggested, the inquisitors actually constructed the reality they expected to see, absorbing ideas from desecration tales disseminated at that time, as well as an allegation of image desecration already made against Jewish apostates elsewhere.

Desecration Narratives

The quintessential widely circulated and influential medieval legend "Christ of Beirut," one of the most powerful anti-Judaic stories of the Christian tradition, was first found in Spain in a tenth-century martyrology at the Cathedral of Gerona in Catalonia, which testifies to the annual celebration of "Passio ymaginis Domini Salvatoris quae crucifixa est in urbe Berito."[16] How widely commemorated this day was is unclear. In the eleventh century, it was said that the cathedral of San Salvador at Oviedo had received some of the blood shed by Christ's image at Beirut.[17] By this time Oviedo housed a sizable relic collection and was a well-known station on the pilgrimage route to Santiago de Compostela.[18]

It is only from the thirteenth century that one finds actual narratives and artistic depictions of "Christ of Beirut." There appears to have been an altar dedicated to the Beirut image in Vic Cathedral, but no trace of it remains. One of the surviving visual representations of the *Passio Imaginis* is the 1442 altarpiece of Felanitx, Majorca, in the Shrine of the Holy Savior (Santuari de Sant Salvador), Felanitx (Figure 9), which I mentioned in the introduction.[19] This work implies a link between Jews crucifying the real Christ and the desecration of his image.[20] Six lateral panels surrounding the main cycle (of the Last Supper at the bottom, the Crucifixion in the center, and the Resurrection on top) depict this tale, and, as noted above, these six panels are the most accurate visual depictions of the legend.[21] The first panel on the top left, depicts the Christian owner of the image venerating the crucifix. The second panel below shows four Jews, distinguished by their beards and hoods, gathering for dinner as the guests of the new Jewish owner. Here,

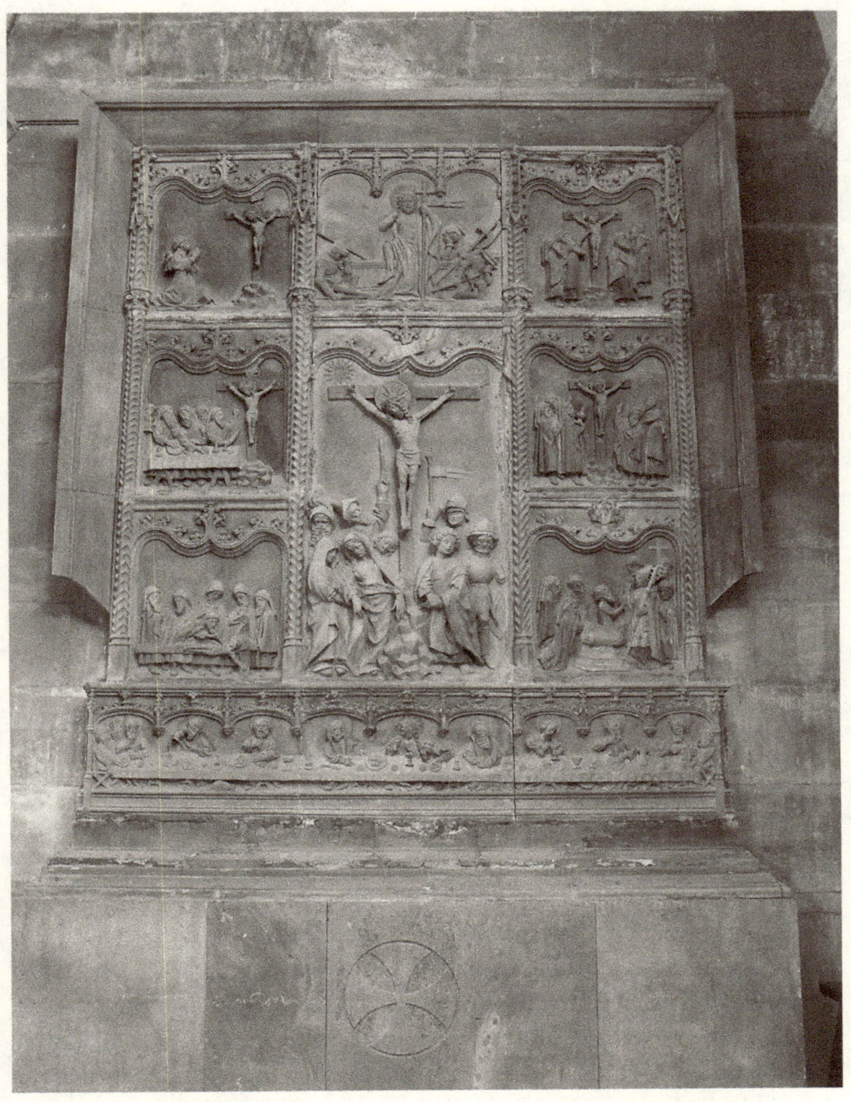

Figure 9. *Passio Imaginis* carved-stone altarpiece by Guillem Sagrera, 1442–1447, Shrine of the Holy Savior (Santuari de Sant Salvador), Felanitx, originally from the parish church of St. Michael (Sant Miquel), Felanitx. Photograph courtesy of Carlos Espí Forcén.

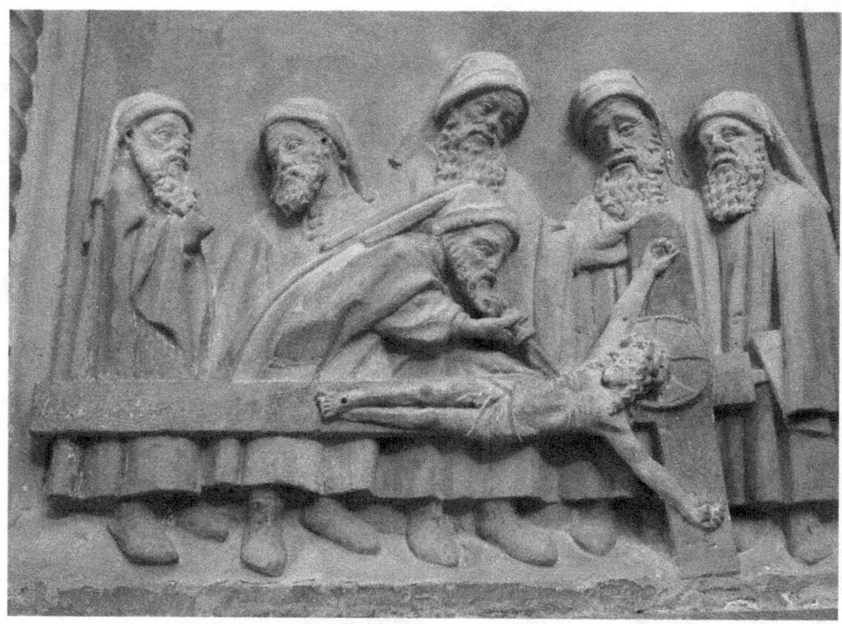

Figure 10. Desecration of the crucifix (detail), *Passio Imaginis* carved-stone altarpiece by Guillem Sagrera, 1442–1447, Shrine of the Holy Savior (Santuari de Sant Salvador), Felanitx, originally from the parish church of St. Michael (Sant Miquel), Felanitx. Photograph courtesy of Carlos Espí Forcén.

the Jew on the far right has discovered its crucifix, which the Jewish host had failed to notice.

In the third relief on the bottom left (Figure 10), six Jews (as opposed to five), now with capes wrapped around them, torture an image of Christ as it lies on its side, probably an artistic concession to simplify the portrayal of the puncturing of his skin. In the relief panels at the top right the six open-mouthed Jews have already lifted the crucifix up again to verbally attack the image, and the Jew nearest the image on the left stabs its side. In the middle image, the same Jew collects the image's blood as four Jews look on, while one Jew seems to reject defiantly its miraculous qualities. In the bottom panel, four Jews, convinced of the miracle, begin the process of conversion, with one naked Jew sitting in the font being baptized by the bishop, as three clerics behind him gaze upon the spectacle.[22]

These few and sporadic examples suggest a slower absorption and dissemination of the legend.[23] Its alleged acts and Eucharistic outpouring were not often included in literary texts or polemics. It is only the thirteenth-century Marian collection of exempla tales *Liber Mariae*, written by the Franciscan friar Juan Gil de Zamora (d. 1318), that included three image desecration tales—"Toledo," "The Virgin's Image Insulted," and "Christ of Beirut." The contemporaneous collection of Gonzalo de Berceo (d. 1264), *Milagros de Nuestra Señora*, which emerged at the same time as the *Cantigas*, only depicts "Toledo."[24] More important is the fact that "Christ of Beirut" did not appear in either Gonzalo de Berceo's work nor in the *Cantigas*. This suggests that the notion of Jews causing images or hosts to bleed was intentionally omitted from Spanish literary texts.[25] Juan Gil de Zamora was actually present in Alfonso X's court around 1278, collaborating with the king on the *Cantigas*. Knowing that the collectors of the cantigas made every effort to study anthologies of miracles past and present in Spain and beyond, one might surmise that the king himself made the political decision to omit "Christ of Beirut" and to reject certain notions, current elsewhere in Europe, that involved Jews, Christ's blood, and its miraculous Eucharistic elements.[26]

The Jews' position in Castile was fundamentally different from that of Jews in other parts of Europe. Jewish courtiers in the kings' courts held a degree of power, wealth, and influence—some acting as royal bailiffs—and these prominent aristocratic Jews expected to be given privileges and protection by Spanish kings.[27] It seems that the Jews' efficacy in Spanish society, especially in the thirteenth century, meant that Alfonso restricted the spreading of the notion that Jews needed the blood of desecrated images or crucified Christians for their own practices. Even though Alfonso's legal compendium *Siete Partidas* set punishments for abuse of images by Moors and Jews, these rulings seemed to have more relevance for Muslims, who, as political enemies, had removed crosses and altars, defiling and destroying churches during the period of Arab hegemony before Christian Spain was resurrected under Gothic kings.[28] Moreover, both ritual murder and image desecration were mentioned in the *Siete Partidas* as being rumored to be occurring in northern Europe, rather than actually happening in Spain.[29]

Protected Jews

In thirteenth-century Spain, Jews lived in self-governing communities—*aljamas*—which were owned by Spanish kings. As descendants of Andalusi Jews, who were profoundly influenced by Arabo-Islamic culture, and with a strong urban presence, these Jews proved useful to the powerful monarchs. Many of the Jews knew Arabic and used their economic expertise as financial advisers and diplomats.[30] The kings were largely dependent on the Jewish populations for credit, so they needed to provide them with support and patronage and to control any type of violence against them. The Muslims, more numerous in both Aragon and Valencia, were a greater cause of concern and attracted more attention.[31] Jews had extensive business relationships with their Christian neighbors. They might invest in Christian ventures in urban and rural projects or serve as moneylenders—a profession never challenged by the kings.[32] Unlike in France and England, Jews only took pawns for small loans to Muslim and Christian clients and continued to do so until the fifteenth century, providing financial liquidity.[33] There are only limited references to portable Christian devotionalia being pledged to Jews in return for cash, and it seems this was not as prevalent in Spain as it had been in France and England.[34] Jews in Spain were involved in a much wider range of economic pursuits including tax farming (particularly in the fifteenth century), agriculture, retail commerce, and a variety of crafts (as silversmiths, merchants, silk weavers, and shoemakers).[35] Unlike in England and France where Jewish silversmithing did not exist, Jewish silversmiths and artisans participated in the making of sacred reliquaries and altarpieces in Spain until their expulsion in 1492 without, it seems, exciting much adverse comment.[36] In fact, from the 1300s until 1492, the majority of Jewish artisans were silversmiths in Morvedre, and these Jews even had their own guild.[37] The kings' protection of the Jews explains why Jewish participation in crafting these religious objects did not seem to intensify Christian concerns about Jews desecrating them.

The mendicant orders' determination to stigmatize the Jews as an obstinate people adhering to a "literalist interpretation of the Old Testament" was tempered in the thirteenth century by the watchful Spanish kings, who were well aware of the increasing desire of the orders in Aragon, Catalonia, and Valencia to join with the bishops and clergy in promoting more fervent Eucharistic devotion and displays of religious piety.[38] By 1242 James I (Catalan, Jaume I; Spanish, Jaime I) the Conqueror of Aragon had yielded to the pressure to give permission for preachers, including apostates, to force Jews to attend conversionary sermons. In 1285, King Sancho IV of Castile granted Franciscan friars the privilege of preaching and hearing confessions freely throughout the whole kingdom.[39] King James II also granted the philosopher and theologian Ramon Llull (1232–1316) permission to preach on Saturdays and Sundays in synagogues and mosques, only demanding that the sermon be preached inside the Jewish quarter and with the number of Christians participating limited to ten.[40] The king even supported Jewish converts to Christianity, providing them with favors and protection, to enable their smoother integration into Christian society. Between 1263 and 1389, at least thirteen Jewish converts received preaching licenses from the kings, authorizing them to give sermons and ensure that royal officials compel Jews to attend them.[41]

Thirteenth-century churchmen resorted to attacking Jews in their writings. Although *adversus Judaeos* texts criticized Jews for committing idolatry, they did not mention the Jews' supposed desecration of Christian images.[42] In his *Pugio fidei* (1278) the Catalan Dominican friar Ramón Martí, present at the Barcelona Disputation of 1263 and censor of Jewish books in Aragon under James I, initiated the Spanish attack against Jews for being guilty of idolatry through their betrayal of the true God.[43] Other ecclesiastics also wrote of the Jews' idolatrous nature, in particular Pedro de Cuéllar, the bishop of Segovia from 1324–1350, in his 1323 catechism. Here he reiterated the Jews' own allegation that Christians were idolatrous but did not elaborate on the argument or refute it.[44] Whether he had had access to the writings of Maimonides, Nahmanides, Rabbi Solomon ben Avraham ibn Aderet (Rashba), or Rabbi Yom Tov ben Avraham Ishbili (Ritva), who all deemed Christianity a form of idolatry, is unclear.[45] He might well have absorbed this idea from Bernard Gui's *Practica inquisitionis*, which stated that the Jews, in their *Aleinu* prayer, daily petitioned God "to cause the idols to pass away from the earth," meaning "the images that Christians of the land adored in honor of Christ."[46]

If the proliferation of the "Christ of Beirut" legend and its Eucharistic blood was limited in Spain, as were any allegations of Jewish image desecration in *adversos Judaeos* texts, it is perhaps not surprising that simultaneous allegations of host desecration and ritual murder also seem to have been forestalled. The chimerical allegations that were associated with Eucharistic blood—the form of blood libel initiated in Fulda in 1235 and the host desecration that began in Paris in 1290—developed more slowly in Spain. When stories of host desecration reached Valencia in 1278 and inspired Bishop Jazpert de Botonach to forbid Christians to pledge church ornaments and chalices to Jewish moneylenders, the Jews remained protected by King Peter III.[47]

Ritual murder charges were also kept at bay. When, in 1301, the body of a child was found in a street in Barcelona, Jews were able to avert a full-scale accusation and investigation of the community.[48] When similar incidents occurred in Valencia in 1330, in Barcelona in 1367, in Huesca in 1377, and in Lérida in 1383, these accusations were also stalled.[49]

The medieval Inquisition, which conducted a campaign against any deviation from official Christian doctrine, was established by Dominican inquisitors in Aragon in 1265. Spanish kings believed that they had exclusive jurisdiction over Jews and that inquisitors were not responsible for disciplining them. Yet the Inquisition prosecuted Jews for perceived attacks against the Christian faith, and there were approximately seventy denunciations of Jews between its establishment and 1391 (when tens of thousands of Jews were forcibly converted—despite the efforts of municipal and royal officials to protect them). Five of these charges were against professing Jews for image violation. The objects involved were a pendant cross, a statue of the Virgin, a crucifix made out of bread, and a royal coin with a cross engraved on it. Royal officials were ordered by the king to protect the Jews from investigations, although it is unlikely that the Jewish suspects committed these offenses.[50] In 1266 the Jew Jahuda de la Caballería, favorite of James (Jaime) I the Conqueror and accountant general of the kingdom, was accused of storing in his home, between the pages of a book, a copper pendant crucifix that he had supposedly violated in contempt of Christianity. Only his immediate family, including his wife, daughter, and son-in-law, claimed to have seen the crucifix and when James I ordered his own investigation of the case it revealed nothing more than a family feud. The king quickly exonerated Jahuda.[51] In 1302 three Jews of Barcelona, Astrug, Sento de Forn, and Mosse Toros, were accused of blasphemous indecorum and desecration in front of the Greek church in Alexandria.[52] The incident came to be investigated in Barcelona. The Dominican Joan de Lotger, together with the bishop-elect of Barcelona, accused the Jews, on the testimony of Christian residents in Alexandria, of throwing stones at a statue of the Virgin and spitting on the ground. This accusation too proved to be false and a result of a conspiracy by local Catalan merchants who were jealous of these Jews and wished to stop their maritime commercial activities with the East.[53] The Aragonese king James (Jaime) II intervened, and, instead of investigating the case, he pardoned them but made them pay six thousand sous.[54] A third case was reported in 1321 in the Valencian town of Sogorb, where a Jew, Mosséhad, was accused of having made a Christ figure molded out of matzah and having burned it in a furnace; this seems to be an accusation of host desecration rather than of violation of a real image. The Jew fled without being prosecuted.[55] In 1327, Bonet Avincanes, employed as a wax-presser, was accused of flinging royal coins stamped with images of the king and the cross into the furnace. Although the king had his bailiff general investigate the crime, no official charges were laid.[56]

By the beginning of the fourteenth century the influence of the mendicant orders over the kings and the Christian population had strengthened, and it was a continuing battle for the monarchs to keep these passionate missionaries from attacking the Jews.[57] There were regular bouts of violence by local Christians who spread dangerous rumors and performed a ritual stoning of sorts against the walls of the *aljamas* every year during Holy Week.[58] The Jews were forced to endure forms of humiliation.[59] Another important change was the law set on September 11, 1314, by King James II who ordered that when a consecrated host was being carried through the city of Valencia, in order not to disturb the sanctity of the occasion, Jews and Muslims had to kneel before it or remove themselves quickly under threat of punishment of a fine or ten lashes.[60] The elevation of the host during mass had become a common practice from the early thirteenth century as a result of decisions taken at the Fourth Lateran Council. Eucharistic processions also became more widespread, especially with the institution of the Feast of Corpus Christi in 1264, which resulted in universal promulgation and acceptance by the early fourteenth century.[61] The 1314 law for Valencia demanded acts of deference from Jews, calling upon them to recognize the superiority of Christianity and convey the outward impression of conformity. Henceforth the Jews would do well to avoid encountering these public processions.

Jews were not always innocent of image desecration accusations, especially when they acted in retaliation for Christian aggression. On occasions, Jews vented their frustrations and committed the sacrilegious acts they were accused of. When, in 1308 during Holy Week, Jewish homes and property were attacked by a local Christian mob in Morvedre, Jews reacted to this annual ritual and stoned a church next to the Jewish quarter, shouting insults against Christians and their faith.[62] The Jews justified their defiance, seeing this attack on the outside of the church as equal to that on their own homes. In 1331, clerics of Girona accused the Jews of the city of bearing arms, opening their quarter, and even paying the bailiff to allow them to enter and attack the cathedral after the annual stoning.[63]

Converted Jews and Image Desecration

So far, we have evidence not only of accusations of Jewish image desecration but also of real Jews committing this offense. But before assuming that an allegation was able to be transferred to *conversos*, we should consider if there might be an additional prehistory of an allegation against Jewish converts to Christianity for the desecration of Christian images—an antecedent—that would allow us to come closer to a deeper understanding about what informed clerical beliefs of crypto-Jewish activity.

As noted in Chapter 1, in eighth-century Byzantium there was a conversion formula that Christians expected Jews to say when they were baptized—a formula that involved them denouncing the Jewish practice of desecrating images. Three centuries later, Western Christian literature actually portrays image violation as part of the imagined procedure for Muslims who wanted to convert to Christianity. In the late eleventh century, epic medieval poems—the chansons de geste—emerged in France and were quickly absorbed into other literary traditions. Imaginary epics glorifying Christian battles against Muslims depict them as polytheistic idolaters who worship their own graven images/idols of Mahum/Mahumet, Apolin, and Tervagan. The eleventh-century *Chanson de Roland* describes the Muslims destroying their own idols after a disastrous battle. In another part of the poem, the conversion of "over a hundred thousand" Muslims at Zaragoza by Charlemagne is reported as being accompanied simultaneously by the destruction of their own images/idols.[64]

> Holding iron hammers and axes,
> They smash the statues and all the idols.
> No sorcery or false cult will remain there.[65]

Whereas Jewish converts to Christianity supposedly abandoned their tendencies to desecrate Christian images as part of the procedure, here we see fictitious Muslims accepting the powerlessness of their own idols and then choosing to abandon and destroy them. What this clarified for the Christian reader/listener was the idea that both Jews and Muslims who converted to Christianity understood that Christian images were the only true images—all others should be reduced to nothingness. Thus the true medieval Christian was expected to venerate images. Whenever they took an oath in the name of Jesus Christ, they showed their allegiance by holding up a crucifix.[66]

Christian chronicles of the thirteenth century, however, propagated different ideas regarding Christian images. After the expulsion of French Jews in 1306, five major Christian chronicles in France and neighboring areas reported that historical Jews who had converted to Christianity and stayed in France were repudiating devotion to Christianity after their baptism by actually desecrating Christian images.[67] The five chronicles include: the chronicle of William of Nangis, the chronicle of Gerard of Frachet, the chronicle of William the Monk, John of Beka's chronicle of Utrecht and Holland, and John of Outremeuse's *Mirror of Histories*. French rulers had already been concerned about the sincerity of converted Jews after the Fourth Lateran Council in 1215, which had disseminated the fear that Jewish converts were not entirely genuine and that they continued with some of their former rites after baptism. By the latter half of the thirteenth century, the French kings explicitly supported the medieval inquisitors' jurisdiction over apostasy to Judaism and sought to promote the prosecution of Christian apostates and their Jewish abettors. In 1276, King Charles I of Sicily, Naples, and Albania, who was also Count of Anjou and Maine, Provence, and Forcalquier, ordered the seneschal and other officials of Provence to give support to the Dominican inquisitor Bertrand de Rocca on this matter. In 1284, King Philip III of France did the same with his own officials in Champagne and Brie, ordering them to assist the inquisitor Guillaume d'Auxerre.[68]

From the mid to the late fourteenth century, Christian chroniclers such as William of Egmond Abbey, writing in 1330, John of Beka in the 1350s, and John of Outremeuse, who wrote between 1395 and 1399, even argued that false converts sought baptism in order to gain access to holy images so that they could violate them.[69] Perhaps these ideas about Christian images were a distorted understanding of rabbinical rulings on the re-Judaization ceremonies or the unbaptism of Jews.[70] At the beginning of the fourteenth century in Barcelona, Rashba and Ritva had demanded that returning apostates perform a re-Judaization ceremony in particular to reinstate the Jews' trust in them.[71] One part of the process involved a Jew having the skin torn off his knees because he had kneeled before crucifixes.[72] This rite had developed in both northern Europe and Spain.[73]

Contemporaneous with these chronicles was the dissemination in 1322 of a well-known legend about a Jewish convert to Christianity, who had desecrated the painted image of the Virgin of Cambron in a Cistercian monastery in Hennegau (Hainaut), Flanders. The legend, which was based on a suspicion of an offense, became a place of pilgrimage.[74] Although there is no record of an accusation, investigation, or punishment for this offense, Philip VI of Valois, king of France (1328–1350), endorsed the allegation in a letter to Pope John XXII (1316–1334), who in response supported the cult of the image and helped to promote the abbey as a pilgrimage site.[75] The letter described how a local Jew, who had converted to Christianity and taken the name of William (since his godfather had been William the Good, Count of Hennegau), had attacked the image of the Virgin in the abbey. Documents prove not only the existence of William in Mons between 1310 and 1329 but also that the Jew had converted to Christianity around 1310. His death is reported around 1326. According to Philip VI's letter, John Flamens of Lessines, a local carpenter, took this case into his own hands and challenged William to a duel "without the authority of a court of law." John won the duel, and William admitted to the crime, although he seems to have remained unpunished. Soon the "event" was depicted in poetry, painting, and architecture, with significant embellishments of the bare facts.[76] There were soon accounts of the bleeding of the Marian image; of its loud screaming as soon as the Jew stabbed it; of five leering Jews rather than William alone desecrating the image; of Mary's appearance to a local carpenter in a dream (often a means of instruction and a guide for action), urging him to take justice into his own hands by killing William in a duel.[77] New chapels were dedicated to the cult near or on the site of the supposed combat between William and John in Mons. A crucifix was erected in 1387, and a chapel was built nearly two centuries later in 1550, which was demolished in 1798. When Emperor Maximilian I (1459–1519) visited the site in 1477, he ordered that an image of this story be painted in the Franciscan church of Colmar.[78] Another chapel was built in 1483 at Estinnes, at the home of the carpenter where he had the dream. It still stands today.

A visual memorial of this legend of William the Convert and his crime was even published by the Franciscan poet Thomas Murner and printed by Matthias Hüpfuff of Strasbourg in a large book probably published around 1513–1515, entitled *Entehrung und Schmach*. Its title page reads: "The Desecration and Shame [*Entehrung und Schmach*] of the Picture of Mary by the Jews erected for an eternal remembrance by Maximilian the Roman Emperor in the proud city of Colmar from which the Jews have been expelled forever."[79] Not long after the publication of *Entehrung und Schmach*, the narrative was adapted in a poem entitled "The Story of Five Shameful Jews."[80] Here the offending convert was reinvented as a professing Jew. Its subtext brings to the reader's attention the heinous crimes of a group of Jews and the consequences of their offenses. Particularly powerful are the twelve woodcuts that give the fullest surviving depiction of the image desecration legend from start to finish. In the first woodcut (Figure 11), William and four other Jews (identified by their badges and their hats, which they disrespectfully fail to remove in the church, but otherwise in standard dress for the period) are grotesquely depicted performing indecent acts and showing open insolence toward the image by mocking, spitting, and baring their backsides toward it. In the second woodcut (Figure 12), William can be more easily identified because of his ridiculous hat and the mock Hebrew letters depicted on the borders of his clothing. The Jews are discovered by two Christians, one, perhaps a Christian priest, appearing in the corner at the exact moment that the lance enters the face of the Virgin. He holds up his hands in shock as the image begins to bleed. The other Christian is making more of an attempt to stop the Jews by grabbing their lance and holding an ax in the other hand to threaten attack.[81]

In the last woodcut of the legend in the *Entehrung und Schmach* (Figure 13), William is finally killed in the most vicious and gory fashion. In front of the crowd, he was attached to a board dragged along the ground by a horse to the *Schnappgalgen*, a gallows constructed to hang the offender upside down. He was hanged between two wild and angry dogs suspended by their hind legs, with a fire burning beneath them to incite them to attack him. The text describes this punishment "as a terrifying example to the Jews who see these great miracles every day but are not moved by them." The Jews had seen the image of Mary bleed (as it does in some versions of the legend) but had not been moved to convert.[82]

Hanging by the feet over a fire was reserved for Jewish offenders, although there is no evidence that dogs were hanged alongside them.[83] The intention of these exceptionally cruel punishments was not only to encourage Jews to convert to Christianity before execution but to publicize the Jews' "stubborn" and "bad" nature. What we have here is, as Robert Mills terms it, "the medieval penal imaginary," or "spectacular justice," rather than real execution.[84] The Jewish desecrator, never having the foresight or ability to change, even if he had converted in the original legend, could still not "see" or witness the miracle of Christian grace through its images and was sentenced to the type of demeaning punishment that he was clearly thought to deserve.

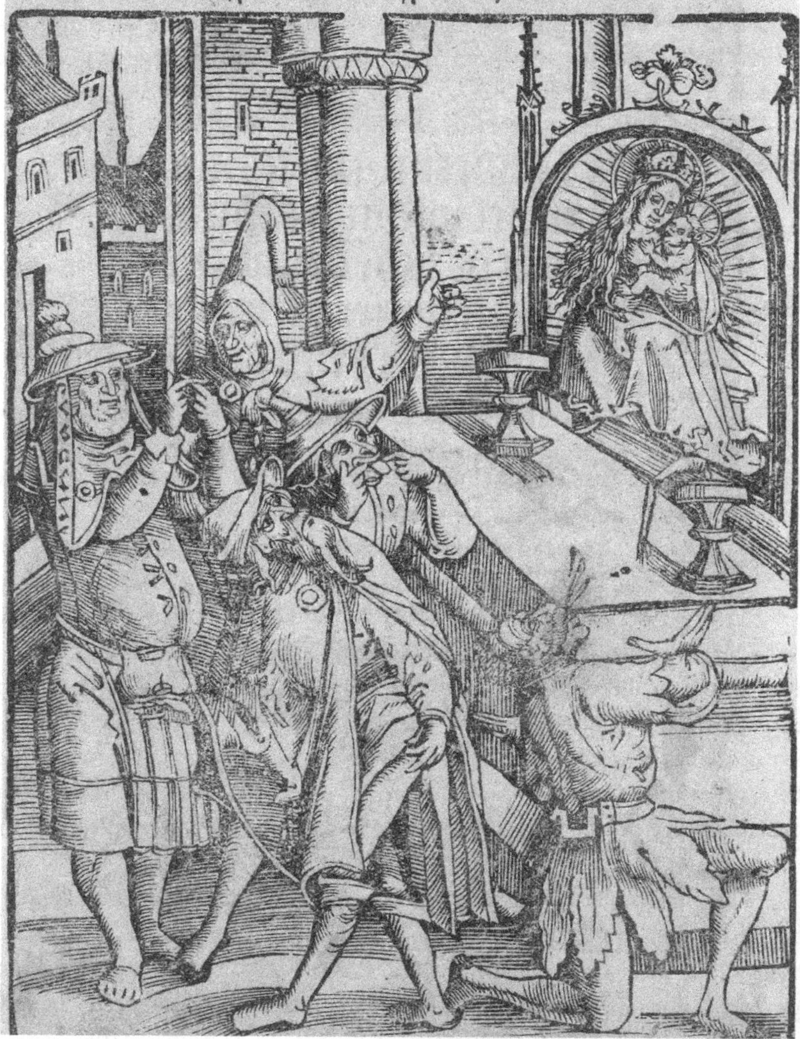

Figure 11. Woodcut illustration from the pamphlet *Entehrung und Schmach* (Desecration and Shame), attributed to Thomas Murner, printed by M. Hüpfuff, Strasbourg, 1515, page 1. Württembergische Landesbibliothek, Stuttgart HBK 119.

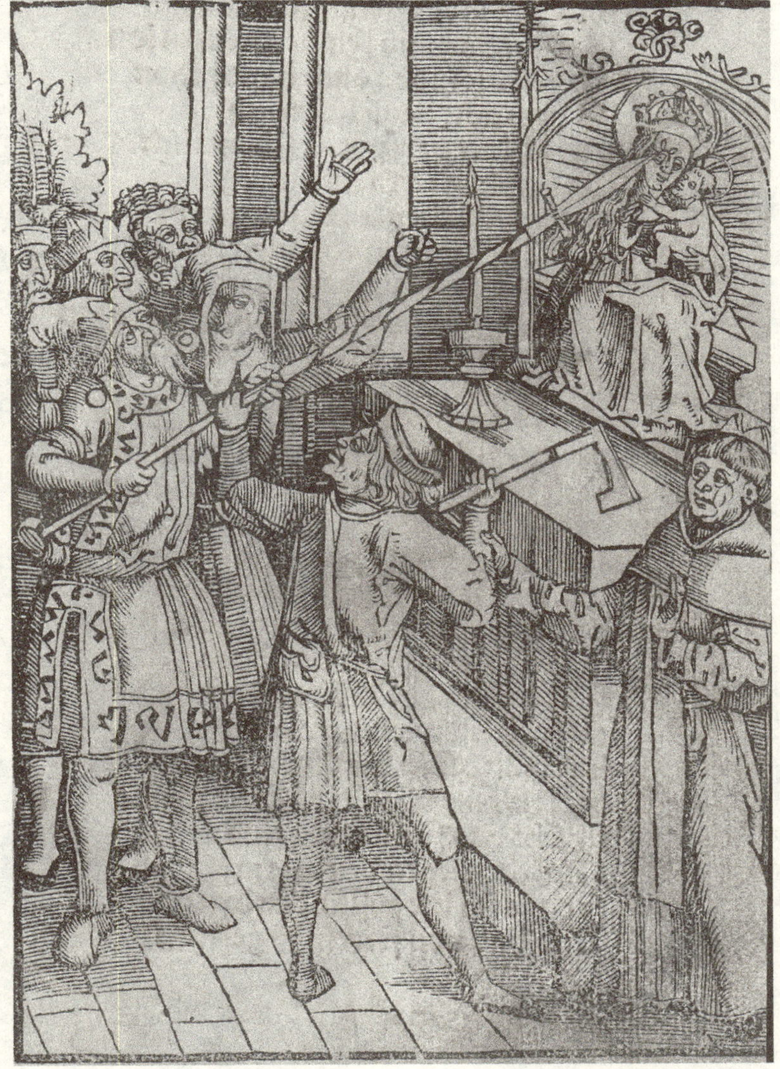

Figure 12. Woodcut illustration from the pamphlet *Entehrung und Schmach* (Desecration and Shame), attributed to Thomas Murner, printed by M. Hüpfuff, Strasbourg, 1515, page 2. Württembergische Landesbibliothek, Stuttgart HBK 119.

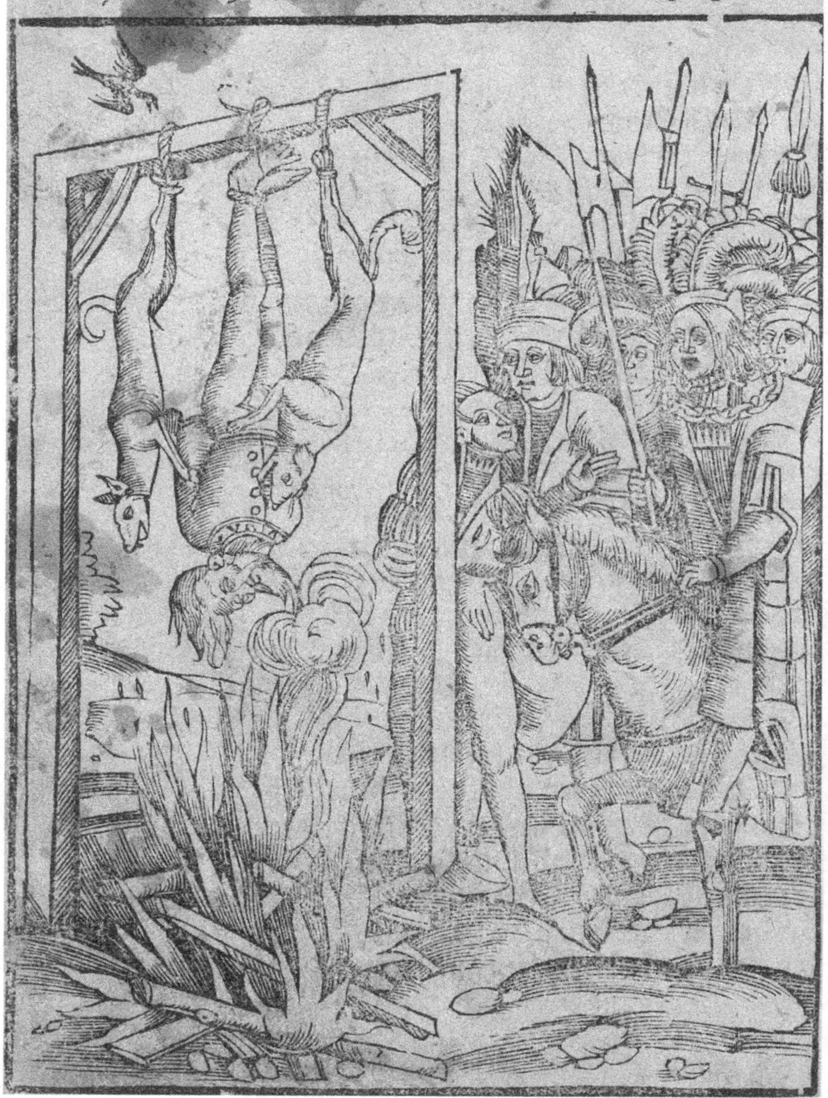

Figure 13. Woodcut illustration from the pamphlet *Entehrung und Schmach* (Desecration and Shame), attributed to Thomas Murner, printed by M. Hüpfuff, Strasbourg, 1515 page 6. Württembergische Landesbibliothek, Stuttgart HBK 119.

The widespread publicity of this legend reinforced the stereotype that the Jews would not only maintain their practices of image desecration but purposely go through the process of conversion in order to attack images from within, which would then authenticate their return to Judaism. It is obviously important in itself in that it seems to reverse the usual sequence of events. Usually, we start with a skeptical Jew who puts a Christian image to the test, and then, when it reacts, allows himself to be won over and converts to Christianity: he is redeemed by the image and escapes punishment for his act of sacrilege. In this case we begin with a Jew who appears to have converted but uses his new status to get access to a Marian image and damage it. The French chronicler William of Egmond Abbey even argued that, because of their desecration of images, neophytes were more dangerous than professing Jews.[85]

It must be suggested that these ways of thinking had penetrated Spain by 1391. Although Spanish suspicion of Jewish converts had existed since Visigothic times, the geographical proximity meant that these northern European ideas would easily pass down over the Pyrenees and penetrate into Spain. Hundreds of French Jews who had been baptized north of the mountains were known to have returned to Judaism in the Crown of Aragon. The medieval Inquisition investigated refugees from southern France who had escaped into Catalonia.[86] From 1313 to 1323, Dominican friars also investigated Jews in the *aljama* of Barcelona for aiding French Jewish converts to return to Judaism.[87]

The belief that converted Jews desecrated images as a way of demonstrating the insincerity of their conversion would certainly have prompted a drive toward an ever more zealous and strict application of the many canons that were intended to distinguish crypto-Jews from genuine converts. Was this at the root of the allegations of crypto-Judaism in Spain? In 1407, Peter Ganyier, a tailor from Lérida and a convert from Judaism serving in the local militia, was accused of secretly breaking into the local church in the village of Miralcamp, destroying the chest containing the Eucharist host, pulling down the crucifix and throwing it into a fire.[88] However, when a named witness denied knowledge of the case, Peter was acquitted. This additional prehistory needs to be kept in mind as we move to the fifteenth century.

The Mendicant Tales

By the fifteenth century, ideas on Jews and image desecration were again recirculated in Spain by Franciscans and Dominicans, who began to disseminate the medieval tales in their sermons. Friar Alonso de Espina (Alphonso de Spina) imported the tale of "Christ of Beirut" and that of a violated miraculous image of Christ in the Sancta Sophia in Constantinople from Jacobus de Voragine's *Legenda aurea* into the third book of his 1460 *Fortalitium Fidei*, the most detailed compendium on how to eradicate heresy.[89] Alonso de Espina had spent the early part of his life giving sermons on a regular basis in churches throughout Castile. His purpose in writing was to create an easily accessible resource book for preachers, since preaching had become a core mendicant activity and was making a strong impact on society.[90] Demanding that his Christian audiences do penance, he also propagated the forced baptism of Jews, believing this to be a morally positive activity especially if they refused to convert out of choice. Those who heard his sermons would easily remember the tales and the idea that Jews, as offenders against Christian images, were endangering Christendom.[91] *Fortalitium Fidei* was printed on at least nine different occasions between 1471 and 1525.[92] He placed the desecration narratives in the tenth chapter with other tales concerning miracles at which Jews had allegedly been present. He described the Constantine tale as a real event, and he told how a Jew entered the Sancta Sophia church, saw an image of Christ, and then:

> perceiving that he was alone, seized a sword, and approaching the image, dealt it a blow in the throat. Straightaway the blood gushed out, and sprinkled the Jew's face and head. Terror-stricken, he took the image, threw it into a well and fled. Then a Christian met him and said: "Whence comest thou, Jew? Thou hast slain a man!" "That is a lie!" responded the Jew. "In sooth thou hast done a murder," said the Christian, "for thou art spattered with blood!" "Verily the God of the Christians is mighty," said the Jew "and His faith is proven by all things. For I have not struck a man, but an image of Christ, and at once the blood gushed forth from its throat!" Then the Jew led the man to the well, and they drew out the sacred image; and it is said that the wound is still to be seen in the throat of Christ. As to the Jew, he became a Christian forthwith.[93]

The tale depicts a well rather than a latrine as the place where the image is immersed. By this time pilgrims to Constantinople had described in their travelogues a well at the southeast corner of the church.[94] When the Jew is confronted by the Christian, it is the Christian who is involved in the Jews' converting—setting an example perhaps as to how Christians were to behave in real life. Both this tale and "Christ of Beirut" describe images bleeding as a result of the Jews' violation, and Alonso de Espina drew attention to this with the comment: "Did not, more than once, an image of the Blessed Lord bleed when pierced by a Jew's weapon, or indeed was only struck by a Jew?"[95] Not only did these stories propagate the idea that Jews would convert to Christianity after seeing the miracle of an image bleed, but also that Christological images could contain sacramental grace. Christ could reveal himself through material representations such as Eucharist wafers, images, and even sculptures. In this new era of icons, Alonso de Espina was keen to reiterate the sanctity of images, particularly the crucifix, comparing its holiness to that of the Eucharist, while emphasizing the Jews' spiritual blindness toward both, and their refusal to accept their powers.[96] Many scholars argue that Espina's rhetorical attack was directed less at Jews and Judaism and more at the heretical position of false converts (whom he considered still to be Jews) since the danger posed by false converts was generally seen as much greater than the danger posed by the Jewish community.[97] But although he might be connecting this offense to crypto-Judaism, Espina's list of twenty-five possible Jewish transgressions that crypto-Jews might commit did not mention image violation but cited only "idol worship of strange images"—perhaps referring to the decorative motifs in former synagogues that were now consecrated as churches.[98] One cannot then argue that Alonso de Espina was already articulating image desecration as a crypto-Jewish offense. He was merely associating it with professing Jews.

"Christ of Beirut" was further broadcast in Castile at this time because of an increasing popularity of a local image that became associated with the legend. From 1465 an unusually realistic crucifix, called the *Cristo de Burgos*, kept in the monastery of San Agustin, gained attention and became the most important sacred image, authenticated as a miraculous image. The sculpture already existed in the early fourteenth century, but its origin (probably Rhenish) was based on two different legends, both recorded by Gabriel Tetzel, traveling with Leo von Rozmital, a Bohemian nobleman, through Spain in the fifteenth century.[99] From this time, writings began to comment on its striking realism, breathtaking presence, and miraculous powers. For the wooden cross with its body of Christ made from polychrome wood and leather looked particularly human, with real hair and false nails. Its skin was also covered with wounds and sores. Legends began to associate the image with the conversion of Jews who had encountered it, both in Spain and in

Beirut. The first told how the image had been found on a ship adrift on the ocean by Castilian sailors. It was then brought to land and deposited in a sanctuary, after a New Christian bishop (originally a Jew) confirmed that he himself had dreamed of the arrival of the crucifix. The cross then gained the reputation of being the work of Nicodemus, and it was said that it had persuaded four brothers of the bishop to convert. These men became bishops themselves and performed important and holy works in the church. As a reward for this, *Cristo de Burgos* had even leaned over and spoken to them on one occasion.[100]

The second legend associated this image with the "Christ of Beirut" legend, giving the *Cristo de Burgos* a provenance in Beirut, where it was believed to have brought about the conversion of several Jews in Spain.[101] But *Cristo de Burgos* was not reported as seeping blood until the eighteenth century. Instead it had merely moved its arms and grown hair and nails.[102] According to Tetzel, Solomon Ha-Levi (b. ca. 1350), the rabbi of Burgos, who converted with his brothers in the mass conversion of 1391, becoming Pablo de Santa María, or Paulus Burgensis, bishop of Cartagena, and subsequently the archbishop of Burgos, confirmed the miraculous nature of the *Cristo de Burgos*.[103]

When the Valencian Dominican Vincent Ferrer made a preaching tour of Castile in 1411–1412, he also managed to attract audiences of all socioeconomic levels. Using simple words that could be understood by all, his preaching would play a crucial part in the forced conversion of the Jews of Aragon, Castile, and Provence.[104] In his spirited sermons he carefully took pains to condemn any man for desecrating images: "Good people, it would be a great sin if a man were to strike or stab with ire or malice an image of God made from wood or stone or any other thing. I say that the greater sin is done by him who out of vengeance or out of ire injures or kills any man, because in doing so he kills or injures the very image of God."[105] Ferrer's first statement is clear and was directed against Christians in this new reality of sacred images. On no account may any faithful Christian desecrate an image of God made from any material. One who did so would be guilty of "great sin," and here in the historical context in which *conversos* were suspected of insincerity, "man" should be read as "true Christian," while simultaneously applying to any human being. Ferrer further stipulated the motivation for such an attack as ire or malice. This might have intentionally referred to crypto-Jews for, in his mind, it went without saying that a "good" Christian would never stoop to such an act. Nor, or so Ferrer hoped, would they injure or kill a man—a worse violation against God. In addition, the use of "image of God" to refer to both an image and a living man confirmed the increasing importance churchmen were bestowing on images and the conversion of Jews to Christianity.

These two tales of image desecration end "happily" with the conversion of Jews at a time when, in real life, many Jews were becoming Christians, either forcibly or willingly. As yet there was little to suggest that Jews converted falsely to Christianity and then, remaining Jews at heart, proceeded to desecrate Christian images. But as Christians, *conversos* were now expected to incorporate Christian images into their Christian practice and devotion at home, in church, and through the streets of the cities and towns where they lived. Would they really be able to do so, or would the Inquisition begin to suspect them of desecrating those images?

Conversos and the New Proliferation of Images

The proliferation of portable images in the mid-fifteenth century gave rise to much controversy among both Old and New Christians. It would seem that some converted Jews, who had welcomed baptism and were willing to become full-fledged Christians, could not be weaned from their old aniconic habits. Nor were Spanish theologians unanimous in their support of such devotion, and the appearance and power of sacred images were bitterly contested by ecclesiastical authorities, who were often New Christians themselves.[106] Even influential New Christian polemical dialogues between Jews and Christians, which included Pedro de Cavalleria's *Zelus Christi contra iudaeos* (1450) and Gonzalo García de Santa María's *Dialogus Ecclesiae et Synagoge* (1488), published in Zaragoza, displayed their authors' irresolution and discomfort when it came to the veneration of devotionalia.[107] Pablo de Santa María remained uncomfortable with this Christian practice and the new type of devotion that sacred images were expected to arouse. In 1434, he wrote his *Scrutinium scripturarum*, which included a polemical dialogue between a fictitious Jew, Saul, and a Christian, Paul. Interestingly here he reverted to the standardized Catholic argument originating from Pope Gregory the Great, that had appeared in theological texts in northern Europe from the sixth century: that Christians were not idolaters but merely using images as mediators for veneration, particularly for illiterate people.[108]

> The prohibition is not superfluous to the making of sculptures, because one who makes a sculpture and adores it is breaking two different precepts, but if he adores images already made, but he did not make them, then he is breaking only one command. Nevertheless, he who makes [an image], but does not adore it, nor makes it with the intention of being adored, is breaking no precept at all. And so you have here the clear sense of these prohibitions, so that you cannot accuse us any more of disobedience. Because we usually make figures and images in our oratories not for them to be adored or to venerate them like Gods, but only for the use of those, especially the unlettered, to remember the heroic deeds and virtuous actions of the saints, and be moved spiritually in the adoration of God, and the imitation of the Saints.[109]

An incendiary anonymous pamphlet was disseminated in Seville in the second half of the fifteenth century by a renegade *converso*, accusing Christians of being idolatrous in their veneration of images.[110] In response to this an edict of 1478, composed by Pedro Gonzalez de Mendoza, archbishop of Sigüenza, and Fray Hernando de Talavera, confessor to Queen Isabella, defended image veneration and urged that the "new style" of religious imagery now available should take a central place in Christian private devotion, together with emotionally engaged meditative or contemplative prayers. By 1493, Talavera had become archbishop of Granada and spearheaded a campaign of evangelization, part of which consisted of the semi-industrial production of religious statuary. As part of their missionary campaign, churchmen ordered that all the converted population of Castile keep religious images in their homes.[111] The edict, which applied to all Christians (New and Old), stated: "And because it is reasonable that the houses of faithful Christians should [honor] the memory of the passion of Our Lord Jesus Christ and of his blessed Mother, we desire and declare that every Christian should have at home the painted image of the cross where Christ was sacrificed and some painted images of the Virgin and other saints that would provoke the inhabitants, arousing them to devotion."[112]

The New Christian and rector of the University of Salamanca Alfonso de Madrigal Tostado (1400–1455) even publicly voiced his disapproval of certain manifestations of image piety in particular legends that suggested a supernatural element in an image's origin.[113] It seems clear that the reason that some *conversos* did not hold images of devotion in their homes or violated or insulted them in some way was that, even if they were genuine converts, they considered this new practice of Iberian Catholicism undesirable, "idolatrous," and inappropriate. The increasing role of images in devotion, the gruesome appearance of flagellated Christs in sacred art in Spanish and Portuguese churches, made them causes of concern. Had not Herman von Scheda already reacted with disgust when he, the quintessential medieval convert, first saw a crucifix in a church in Münster after his conversion, calling it "a monstrous idol"?[114]

With the sudden increase in the number of images in people's homes and in the importance of "image friendliness" as a test of good Christians, charges of "image hostility" would begin to multiply.[115] The presence and treatment of domestic images in Spanish homes would become a test of Christian orthodoxy according to the new Inquisition. It was in these private spaces that most *conversos* were accused of committing crimes of violation.[116] Inquisitors might well imagine these secret Jews defiantly acting against the images in their homes, as apostates had before. Two strong allegations were being carried forward. The first was that crypto-Jews showed their fidelity to Judaism by desecrating images. The second, that professing Jews had tendencies to desecrate Christian images to show their disgust of Christian practices and idolatrous habits.

Inquisitorial Sources

It is at this point that we must turn to the inquisitorial investigations of real flesh and blood *conversos* who were accused of image desecration. By 1480, the wheels of the new tribunal were in motion, and inquisitors were dedicating themselves to eradicating crypto-Judaism, condemning nearly one thousand converts to the stake between 1480 and 1530. When *conversos* were accused of image desecration, the offense was usually one in a list of many (observing Jewish laws in private, celebrating the Sabbath on Saturdays, celebrating Jewish festivals, refusing to eat pork, taking no notice of Lent, and so on)—the allegation rarely stood alone.[117] It was depicted as a crime against or scorn (*desprecio*) of the essence of Christianity, even though the abuse of a crucifix had nothing to do with the real practicing of Judaism by the *conversos*.

Conversos were accused of "offenses" that were not appropriate for Christians as well as "offenses" that suggested a hidden Jewish practice.

The inquisitorial narrative was therefore shaping an idea of Judaism that conformed to Catholic ideas about what constituted authentic crypto-Jewish activity. This new association provided a useful tool with which the Inquisition alleviated Christian anxieties over the mistreatment of sacred objects by nonbelievers. The most intense periods of accusations of crucifix desecration occurred in the late fifteenth century in the provinces of Cuenca, Ciudad Real, Zaragoza, Soria, and Valencia. Accusations came from townspeople who feared competition from former Jews and resented the part played by *conversos* in the king's service. This kind of anti-*converso* feeling, saying in effect that a Jew will always be a Jew and baptism did not wipe out his Jewishness, came to a head at about the same time as small images were becoming common. In the inquisitorial trials of *conversos* in Zaragoza between 1484 and 1515, the inquisitors' questions during an interrogation focused on the religious behavior of suspects, rather than considering whether their conversion had been authentic or not.[118] The inquisitors asked suspects whether they had images of Christ in their homes, where these images were located, and whether they were used regularly for prayer and devotion. María González, wife of the spice merchant Francisco de Toledo, was accused in Ciudad Real in January 1494 of having thrown an image of Mary into a sewer ditch. Item 5 of the arraignment stated: "it is said that María González, as an infidel and non-believer who shames our Sacred Catholic Faith, one time harmed a picture on which was painted an image of Our Mother the Virgin Mary, she seized it, and like a great wind, with joking and scoffing, threw it into a sewer-ditch that ran alongside the kitchen."[119] María was burned at the stake.[120] *Converso* offenses would soon include disrespect to, rather than actual desecration of, images—such as not caring for the image, not showing respect toward it, or even refusing to own images at all.[121] Thus this was seen as a form of desecration. In Zaragoza, another *converso*, Galcerán Fajol, testified that he had chosen not to keep crucifixes in his house in order not to mistreat them.[122] Witnesses testified that Berenguer de Torrellas had, on his deathbed, revealed his loathing of Christianity by refusing to say the name of Jesus, kiss the cross, or accept a candle in the shape of a cross.[123] Pedro de Santa Clara had even admitted to the Zaragoza inquisitor that he considered the images of the saints and the Holy Trinity that were depicted in the church a joke.[124] Almost a century later, in 1593, a public auto-da-fé was celebrated in Granada on the feast of the Ascension of Christ. The sentences of the crypto-Jews told how they had confessed to denying "in general the adoration of statues, saying it is only a matter of gold, silver or wood."[125] It is easy to imagine crypto-Jews choosing to keep as few images at home as they could. Sicilian inquisitorial inventories of secret Jews of the first generation after expulsion in 1493 confirm that these new converts had relatively few Christian cult objects in their domestic spaces, compared to Old Christians of the same social standing.[126] Before long, even Old Christians were accused of sacrilegious acts against images as a result of their discomfort with using them as part of their domestic devotion.[127] Protestant heretics on the Iberian Peninsula would also be charged by the Spanish Inquisition. Whereas *conversos* and Protestant heretics would face capital punishment, Old Christians would be given spiritual penances and a chance to repent publicly in a local church. The fact that Old Christians committed image desecration did not prevent the crime from being perceived as a quintessentially Jewish one. Crypto-Jews would commit image desecration because this was typical crypto-Jewish behavior.

Despite what inquisitors propagated, when these cases are decoded, it becomes clear that there was no uniform pattern to suggest that Christian images were causes of social discord, of lapsed practice, of backsliding, or even of defiance. Espina's dissemination in his *Fortalitium Fidei* of "Christ of Beirut" and the tale of the Jew who attacked the image in Constantinople occurred in the fifteenth century simultaneously with the translation of Jacobus de Voragine's *Golden Legend* into Castilian by Gonzalo de Ocaña, in the *Flos sanctorum*.[128] I would like to suggest that the allegations of image desecration against *conversos* were sometimes informed and influenced by the descriptions in these two tales and the inquisitors' view of how the images were treated. There are many examples. The accusations that *conversos* threw their images into latrines or urinated upon them might well have been reconfigurations of the Constantinople tale. Did Mari Sánchez really throw a "drawing of the crucifixion of Our Lord drawn on a piece of paper" into the latrine in Guadalupe in 1485 in the presence of two crypto-Jewish men, or was this something her daughter Inés had imagined from what she had heard in a sermon?[129]

A new form of desecration was, it seems, specifically labeled and associated with *converso* activity—a particular charge of "scourging," or flogging, crucifixes.[130] The 1484–1485 trial papers of the already deceased Juan Díaz recorded, among other crimes, how he would lash a crucifix every Friday before the commencement of his Sabbath.[131] In 1492 in the town of Canalejas, a professing Jew on the eve of expulsion was accused by the Inquisition at

Cuenca of scourging a crucifix.[132] Rather than a genuine offense, this might well have been a reconfiguration of the "Christ of Beirut" tale and the allegation that apostates desecrated images to show their affiliation with Judaism. Groups of crypto-Jews were now believed to be flogging a crucifix as if they were initiating a rite of re-Judaization.[133] In April 1487, Luis de Bardaxí was forced to confess to the inquisitorial court of Zaragoza that, as part of a select group of *conversos* in Lérida, he had joined others to whip and mistreat a crucifix.[134] He even testified to participating in the ritual on three different occasions in three different houses, where each time the crucifix was abused verbally as well as scourged. His testimony even sounds comical. The notary recorded: "He had a crucifix of Our Lord Jesus Christ in his house hung on the wall above a curtain, and because one of the arms of the crucifix became unnailed and it moved, he took it and gave it an enormous kick on the ground and he said to it 'If you are going to be dead, be dead for me now!' and he said that for hatred of Jesus Christ, and for the figure because he saw it move. And [. . .] that also he would whip it [. . .] but he did not have time as he was in a hurry."[135]

By the late 1490s, inquisitors more regularly accused *conversos* of scourging crucifixes, although there was no suggestion that the scourging released miraculous blood.[136] Scholars such as Felipe Pereda and Carlos Espí Forcén have argued to be fictitious the well-known Zaragoza accusation made against the powerful Cavallería family in the 1490s that, in 1484, a group of more than thirty prominent *conversos* of the city had, in the home of Gonçalvo Garcia de Santa María, scourged a wooden crucifix during a ritual parody of the Passion at Easter.[137] The sole testimony came from the priest Miguel de Almazán who had been twelve when the events had taken place. But his testimony was considered valid. He even asserted that the *conversos* had been assigned the roles of Pontius Pilate, Annas, and Judas in a Passion parody. This episode disseminated a deeper paranoia regarding the *conversos*' tendencies to desecrate sacred images. A similar ritual was recorded in the inquisitorial summary of witnesses regarding the prophetic movement "Innes Meharia" in the village of Simancas in 1499. According to these testimonies, more than one hundred people had congregated in the synagogue situated in the home of one Juardo Juan de Córdoba, not only to trample hosts but also to throw them into the latrine.[138] The allegations also involved the abuse of two images: "On the week after Easter . . . they brought a cross. . . . All the people wrapped ropes around the chest of the cross and dragged it on the floor of one empty hall, beat it and hammered nails into all parts of it."[139]

One Christmas, a Christ figure had also been "crucified": "Last Christmas eve, Chyler brought a large doll in the image of Christ with a crown upon its head. . . . They slapped the doll and ground it in to dust and then threw the debris into the latrine."[140] This seemed to involve the full destruction of a molded image—similar to that which fictitious Jews had executed in "Toledo."[141] In 1539–1540, a large group of *conversos* in Valencia and Alicante were arrested for partaking in a secret *converso* conventicle (meaning, in this case, a sect of Jews) in which a crucifix was scourged, but the retraction of more than forty of the accusers' denunciations stalled the investigation.[142]

By the sixteenth century, inquisitors such as Fray Jaime Bleda no longer differentiated the offense as either a crypto-Jewish or a Jewish offense. He would record categorically that *conversos* desecrated sacred images because this was an instinctive transgression, typical of them all.[143] Another case that came before the Inquisition between 1569 and 1582, this time in Naples, concerned *conversos* (often referred to in southern Italy as *neofiti*). Reports reached the Inquisition there and in Rome of "conventicles" living as Christians in the provinces of Calabria and Apulia, long after the official expulsion of professing Jews from the kingdom in 1541. The case against Antonino Vento of Catanzaro and his family and associates in 1577 was that "on Friday they put the crucifix in a corner and whipped it" (il di venerdi mettono lo crocifisso in uno cantaro et lo frustano).[144] They were also accused of burning crosses.[145]

But by the sixteenth century Christians were continually being reminded that Jews flogged crucifixes as they had once flogged Jesus. Statues of suffering, flagellated Christs were paraded through towns and cities during Holy Week processions by confraternities such as Real e Ilustre Hermandad y Cofradía de Nazarenos de la Sagrada Columna y Azotes de Nuestro Señor Jesucristo y María Santísima de la Victoria in Seville (1569) or the Cofradía del Santísimo Cristo de la Columna established in Ciudad Real from around 1575. These statues were being beaten by Christians dressed up as Jews.[146] The message given by these processions was that it was not Pontius Pilate who had ordered Jesus to be flogged but the Jewish mob itself, or so the Benedictine Agustín de Benavente would tell his readers in 1647.[147] It seems then that this accusation could well have been a perversion of the Christian penitential practice of self-flagellation. The practice was initiated by the eleventh-century church reformer Peter Damian, and an extensive movement surfaced in Italy in 1260, which began in Perugia and spread to Germany and France. The moving spirit was a hermit named Ranieri Fasani and some of the Scuole

Grandi in Venice traced their origins (accurately or not) to this well-known movement.[148] It surfaced in Spain with an extensive movement of flagellants in 1349 and later particularly with Vincent Ferrer, who made sure that he was accompanied by a group of flagellants on his preaching tours throughout the peninsula.[149] A more discreet practice, hidden within confraternities, persisted, and by the end of the fifteenth century the Franciscans were active in the propagation of several fraternities of penitents across the peninsula. Were not the persecutors of the *conversos* alleging that, where pious Christian penitents whipped themselves, crypto-Jews turned the practice around and flogged an image of the crucified Christ—not sharing Christ's suffering but inflicting it all over again? Scourging a crucifix was also something one could do in secret without leaving a mark on the image.

I would like to end with the *Cristo de la Paciencia* (the "patient" or "suffering" Christ) case of crucifix desecration, which was said to have occurred in Madrid in September 1630 in the home of Miguel Rodríguez among a group of poor illiterate Portuguese *conversos* including Beatriz Enríquez, Fernan Báez, Victoria Méndez, Violante Méndez, Isabel Núñez Álvarez, Elena Núñez, and Beatriz Rodrígez.[150] The accusation against these *conversos* was made by Andrés (Andresillo) Núñez, the seven- or nine-year-old son of the main suspects Miguel Rodríguez and Isabel Núñez Álvarez. When his parents were imprisoned for other Judaizing crimes, Andrés began to talk to neighbors about this particular offense, which caused the inquisitors, Pedro Diaz, Don Juan Dionisio Portocarrero Fernandez, and Don Cristobal de Ibarra to investigate it further. The image—a carved crucifix—was, according to Andrés, scourged and burned as a result of the group having organized a secret conventicle to reenact the crucifixion upon it.[151]

Andrés provided unreliable and contradictory testimony of the desecration, particularly about the physical characteristics of the image (supposedly life-size) that was violated, and this clearly concerned the inquisitors. Soon his twelve-year-old sister, Ana Rodríguez, was brought in for questioning and her testimony was equally unreliable, at first denying the activity and then confirming it a week later, implicating other siblings who had escaped, but rejecting the suggestion that she was personally involved. Some of their inquisitorial interrogations are recorded in a summary form, which prevents scholars from seeing the queries of the inquisitors and the extent to which these questions intimated to the children the kind of answers they were expected to give.[152] Six of the *conversos* were burned at the stake in the Plaza Mayor of Madrid in 1632, in the presence of King Philip IV, his ministers, and the assembled courtiers. The other seven were imprisoned for life.[153] Interestingly enough, two days after the auto-da-fé, the house in the Calle de las Infantas, where the desecration was said to have occurred, was destroyed, and Yosef Hayim Yerushalmi reports that "even the crowd, which had no tools, tore out stones and blocks from the foundations with their bare hands."[154] Neither the crucifix nor any trace of it were ever found in the homes of the *conversos*, but a Capuchin convent of La Paciencia was erected on the site of this alleged sacrilege.[155]

According to the unreliable testimony of the children, the *Cristo de la Paciencia* was said to have bled and spoken, asking why the *conversos* were attacking their Lord, whereupon the *conversos* had purportedly replied that it was merely a lump of wood.[156] This was the first case to configure blood into the image desecration accusation in Spain. But here the blood was not used for healing purposes as it had been in "Christ of Beirut." Rather its presence seemed to reflect the new dogmatic and disciplinary decrees of the Council of Trent, which initiated the cultural acceptance of such transfigurational images and accepted that images could miraculously bleed as a result of being attacked.[157] From the 1590s, "a bloodlike substance," indicating their miraculous qualities, was appearing on processional crucifixes carried by flagellant brotherhoods of Franciscans through Barcelona.[158]

The blood here was unlikely related to the crypto-Jews' specific action but was associated instead with the increasing popularity of transfigurational images and the tendency for Christians in Spain to dwell on Christ's sacrificial suffering in the flesh as a central tenet of orthodox devotion and to react to these miracles.[159] As we will see in Chapter 5, there are similar developments in Italy particularly with the bleeding crucifixes of the Bianchi movement which had occurred two centuries earlier at the end of the fourteenth century. A visual representation of this case appears in Francisco de Rojas Nieto's *Vespertinas de los opprobios de la Pasión de Cristo* (Sermons for the offenses to the Passion of Christ) (Figure 14), a pamphlet that publicized the case two years after the burning of the *conversos*. Here, instead of the large group of Jews indicted, two women and one man dressed as Spanish Christians without any features indicating that they might be Jews are shown holding whips above a large wooden crucifix. A second man holds a rope, which he pulls over his shoulders to drag the upside-down scourged but undamaged crucifix. There is no suggestion of blood or of the crucifix bleeding. The image merely publicizes the act to educate its readers that scourging crucifixes was a typical trait of Judaizing.

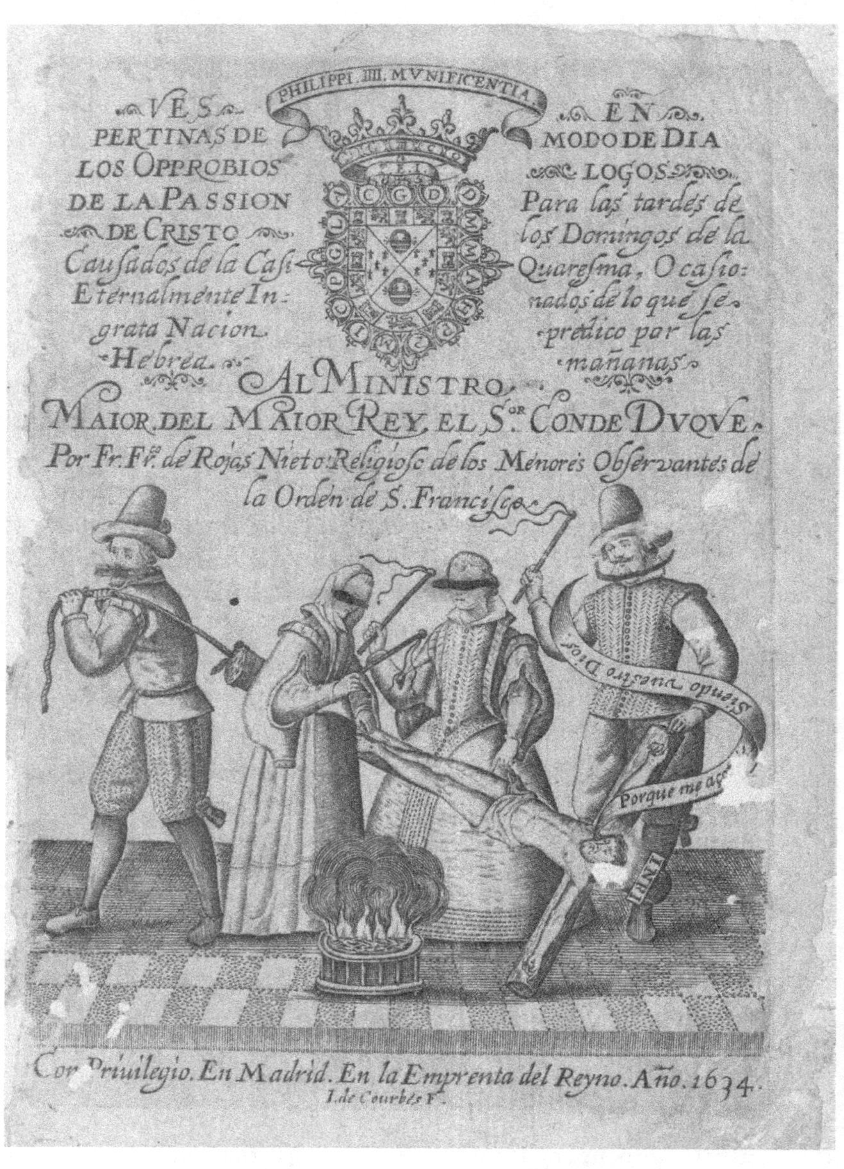

Figure 14. Portuguese *conversos* scourging a crucifix of Christ in Madrid. Francisco de Rojas Nieto, *Vespertinas de los opprobios de la Pasión de Cristo* (Madrid, 1634). By permission of Bibliotheca Sefarad and www.bibliotecasepharad.com.

To what extent should we consider as part of this narrative the case of the "miraculous" crucifix in the church of São Domingos that incited the massacre of at least one thousand converted Jews in Lisbon, just across the border, in 1506?[160] Did the blasphemous words of a Portuguese *converso*—well known for his rejection of Christian images and violent in his intent—really incite the crowd to finally punish the New Christians for their blasphemy? Riots initiated by the mendicant orders against these converts, forcibly and collectively baptized by order of King Manuel I in 1497, had already begun in 1504, and the riots were only aborted because of Queen Maria's intervention. The outbreak of the plague in October 1505 eventually caused the king to leave Lisbon in March 1506.[161] All extant chronicles of this event (in Portuguese, Spanish, German, and Hebrew) confirm that an occurrence at the Dominican convent had precipitated the massacre. One chronicler, Damião de Góis, stated that a crucifix above the altar in the church made a "sign," while Jerónymo Osorio noted that the crucifix had an inlaid crystal that seemed to light up as if a light emanated from it. The miraculous transformation caused a constant stream of visitors and an excitable crowd in the middle of Lisbon.[162] An anonymous German chronicler who, although present, had not witnessed the miracle personally, wondered if the friars had faked it.[163] A *converso* was then accused of blaspheming against the miraculous crucifix by saying: "How can a piece of wood work wonders?"[164] The German chronicler remains the only source to name the New Christian as João Rodrigues Mascarenhas, the king's *escudeiro* (shield-bearer), an extremely wealthy and hated tax farmer and one of the most prominent New Christians of the city.[165] It is unlikely that a New Christian would have risked saying anything so explosive, but having already been accused by the mendicant orders of a tendency to show disrespect and violate Christian images, both he and his brother were attacked and their bodies dismembered and finally burned in the Rossio square.[166]

Conclusion

It was the story of "Christ of Beirut" that first introduced an association of Jews and image desecration in Spain. When judicial accusations began to be made against Jews, these were prevented from erupting by Iberian kings who were keen to protect them. During the fourteenth century, a relevant prehistory—an antecedent—to the allegation that would be directed against *conversos* in Spain surfaced in France and probably penetrated into the peninsula from the north. Jewish converts to Christianity were depicted as seeking baptism solely for the purpose of accessing and desecrating Christian images. These accusations confirmed how a retained immutable "Jewishness" was understood by Christian society to linger after baptism. When the iconographic revolution erupted in Spain in the fifteenth century, the mendicant orders adapted the offense of image desecration to fit their needs. Here, as seen previously in our earlier chapters on Byzantium and medieval Europe, the increase in veneration of images coexisted with a rise of accusations against Jews, except this time Jews were replaced by crypto-Jews.

It seems, then, that accusations against baptized Jews in Spain eventually fell into two categories. The first consisted of accusations of lapsing or backsliding, or showing disrespect to images. These charges were extremely common and were quite enough to get a crypto-Jew or a genuine New Christian suspect charged with heresy, constituting in Catholic eyes a betrayal of baptism. The second category consisted of atrocity accusations against *conversos* of assaulting, breaking, defiling, flogging, or burning holy pictures, crucifixes, and statues. In these accusations there was a strong element of sheer fantasy related to ideas of re-Judaization ceremonies among secret conventicles of apostates. Later these apostates were also accused of causing the bleeding of an image. These categories may have derived from the kind of Catholic fiction the Inquisition came to propagate regarding *conversos*—that they were not really converts at all but apostates who converted in order to desecrate images.

By using image desecration accusations, the Inquisition also defined anew what Judaism meant, reaching back into the past to find appropriate legends to justify its threat; for when *conversos* were accused of image desecration, they could also be incriminated because the allegation that had originated in a legend and tale about fictitious Jews had become deep-rooted. The *converso*, like the fictitious Jew before him, would be accused of attacking images and crucifixes, putting them in latrines, scourging them—sometimes in deviant rituals—and reenacting the Crucifixion on an image of Christ. The mistrust of *conversos* and the idea that they would meet to desecrate a crucifix in secret conventicles continued into the eighteenth century and even traveled as far as the Americas.[167] The power of image desecration tales cannot be overstated.[168]

The resemblances to each other of allegations of scourging crucifixes and the frequency with which they were repeated might suggest that this sort of behavior was actually a pretext for crypto-Jews to gather in secret assemblies concealing themselves from the intimidating gaze of the Inquisition.[169] In these meetings they allegedly acted out their anger and imagined revenge upon a large crucifix probably handcrafted by them. As such it would read as a religious critique of inversion characteristic to crypto-Jews. The main problem here is that it is impossible to confirm what meaning this practice might have had for *conversos.* Would they have been provoked into desecrating an image just because this was what inquisitors imagined them doing? It is more likely that this allegation fitted how inquisitors imagined the subculture and behavior of crypto-Judaism. They repeated the allegation because it represented homogeneity of their beliefs and thoughts.

The trail of the allegation cannot be uncovered completely without considering those who were being attacked. We must now seek to understand how Jews responded to it. Their voices—in relation not only to the allegation but also to their own everyday encounter with Christian images—now need to be heard.

Chapter 4

Jewish Responses to Christian Images

> In the city where I was born, Riga, we Jews were in the habit of averting our gaze every time we passed a crucifix.
>
> —Amos Oz, *Judas*

No medieval or early modern European Jews could walk many steps in any direction in the streets and byways where they lived without encountering some representation of Christian sanctity in the form of a crucifix, a sacred image, a church, or a religious procession transporting a consecrated host, a painted image, or a statue. How did the Jews perceive, come to terms with, and respond to those encounters? Were they really, as Christian tales sought to imply, intrigued observers? Or rather were the actions or reactions of Jews tempered or even prohibited by rabbinic teachings that repeatedly through the centuries had encouraged certain desensitizing attitudes, as Shmuel's father seems to suggest in Amos Oz's *Judas*?

Although Jews were accustomed to the presence of Christian images, diverse Jewish sources including rabbinic responsa, polemic, chronicles, disputational literature, folktales, Hebrew illuminated manuscripts, and even texts on Jewish life written by early modern converts demonstrate that Jewish reactions to these images were complex. The texts, often functioning as foundations for faith, written to empower, support, and reassure the Jews, require reexamination since no scholar has so far inquired whether rabbis and community leaders in different periods advocated specific strategies and defense mechanisms enabling Jews to deal with Christian material culture and the charge of image desecration. This chapter will therefore attempt to provide a study of Judaic sources from early Christianity to the seventeenth century in order to establish how far these prescriptive texts were a reaction to this allegation and accusation.

This chapter also describes the long history of Jewish norms, writings, and practices condemning idols that suggests that it would have been natural for Jews to insult and on occasion physically harm Christian images. Christian accusations were not plucked out of thin air; rather they often reflected actual Jewish attitudes and behaviors, although they distorted them and invented many particular charges. I will demonstrate that Jewish suggestions that Christians attached exaggerated importance to images also sometimes drew on tales reflecting how fictitious Jews would behave. These tales should be read as a reflection of how Jews behaved—in particular how they reacted to the increasing number of icons around them. This overlap between Jewish behavior and Christian accusations and their nuances will be examined in each historical context.

This chapter will begin with an analysis of biblical and Talmudic rulings regarding the Jews' behavior toward images they perceived as idolatrous. Then it will show how Jewish sources directed not only the ways Jews were to control their contempt for Christian images but also how they were to react when they encountered these objects in public spaces. The chapter will also survey the types of abusive words that were used to describe these images, how the Torah scroll was depicted as a foil to these objects, and how the Jews, in their handbooks and early modern historical tales, responded to the allegation of image desecration.

Biblical Rulings

The Jews' rejection or at least suspicion of and discomfort with images had sprung from the Second Commandment in the Hebrew Bible regarding the sin of idolatry. Idol worship in its most primal sense was the deification of an object. Hence God had chosen not to reveal his physical form in order to ensure that the Jews would never be able to represent him. As noted in the introduction, God identified himself as a jealous God who acknowledged the existence of other deities but prohibited their worship in any form.[1] The Second Commandment prohibited idolatry, ordering Jews not to worship other gods, not to build their own carved idols, and not to create a divine image of God that would become an object of idolatrous worship.[2] The prohibition included any magical acts, which were also seen as a form of rebellion against God.[3] The majority of statements in the Hebrew Bible regarding idolatry constituted instructions to Jews not only to cease making idols themselves but also to destroy those of other religions. The first task undertaken by the Jews after seizing the Canaanites' territory in the Land of Israel was to desecrate and then destroy the statues created by their enemies. The rationale here was that the Israelites would be attracted to these idols, so the act of destruction was defensive rather than missionary. This ensured that the Jews quickly acquired a reputation for destroying idols and images. Exodus, Numbers, and Deuteronomy record a number of commandments to destroy images, as if the Israelites were being ordered to cleanse the land they had occupied of the idols that were polluting it. The Israelites were told:

> You shall not bow down to their gods nor serve them, nor do after their works: but thou shalt utterly overthrow them, and quite break down their images. (Exod. 23:24)

> Rather you shall break apart their altars, smash their pillars, and cut down their sacred trees. (Exod. 34:13)

> You shall destroy all their prostration stones; all their molten images shall you destroy. (Num. 33:52)

> Their altars shall you break apart; their pillars shall you smash; their sacred trees shall you cut down; and their carved images shall you burn in fire. (Deut. 7:5)

> The carved images of their gods you shall burn in the fire; you shall not covet and take for yourself the silver and gold that is on them, lest you be ensnared by it, for it is an abomination of Hashem, your God. And you shall not bring an abomination into your home and become banned like it; you shall surely loathe it and you shall surely abominate it, for it is banned. (Deut. 7:25–26)

> Tear down their altars, smash their pillars, put their sacred posts to the fire, and cut down the images of their gods, obliterating their name from that site. (Deut. 12:3)[4]

"Idols" was used here in a generic form and included altars associated with the gods of Canaan—effigies, statues, sculptures, stone pillars, and sacred trees—all of which, according to the biblical sanction, had to be destroyed.

Despite this biblical mandate, the Israelites in the Bible in the book of the Prophets (נביאים) and the book of the Writings (כתובים) were not always compliant.[5] Prophets rebuked the Israelites repeatedly for being decadent and even falling into idol worship themselves.[6] But in a society that clearly tolerated foreign cults and their idols more than it should have, there were rare moments when those idols were indeed destroyed as commanded. In 2 Kings 11:18, the priest Jehoiada, the brother-in-law of King Ahaziah, tore down the temple of Baal in "the land." In 2 Kings 23:4–20, King Josiah (640–609 BCE) went on a mission to "burn and smash" some of the Mesopotamian and Phoenician idolatrous shrines (*bamot*) and their idols.[7] God's accusation of idolatry against the Israelites in the book of Isaiah was particularly critical. In chapters 44–46, there is even discussion of the powers of God versus those of idols.[8]

This fight against idolatry, which was a central issue in biblical religion, lost importance as a national concern during the period of the Second Temple.[9] Only a few cases are described by Titus Flavius Josephus (37–100 CE), born Yoseph Ben Matitiyahu, in his works. In 5 BCE Judas, son of Saripheus, and Matthias, son of Margalothus, attempted to remove King Herod's golden eagle, which had graced the great gate of the Temple for some time.[10] Both Philo and Josephus described how, when serving as prefect or governor of Judea (26–36 CE), Pontius Pilate sent images of Caesar, known as "standards," into the city of Jerusalem at night.[11] Josephus reports: "This excited a great disturbance among the Jews when it was day; for those that were near them were astonished at the sight of them, as indications that their laws were trodden under foot, for those laws do not permit any sort of image to be brought into the city."[12] Josephus reported how Jews gathered from all over the countryside outside Pilate's headquarters in Caesarea, staging a passive demonstration by lying down on the ground for five days and nights. When Pilate finally agreed to hear their complaint in the marketplace, he took precautions and surrounded the protesters with armed soldiers: "Pilate also said to them that they would be cut into pieces, unless they would admit of Caesar's image, and gave instruction to the soldiers to draw their naked swords. Hereupon the Jews, as it were at one signal, fell down in vast numbers together, and exposed their necks bare, and cried out that they were sooner ready to be slain than that their law should be transgressed. Hereupon

Pilate was greatly surprised at their prodigious superstition, and gave order that the ensigns should be presently carried out of Jerusalem."[13]

Historical Jews seemed extremely determined to maintain an aniconic Jerusalem at all costs. In his *De Decalogo*, Philo Judaeus of Alexandria looked upon idol worshippers as being "in grievous error" and argued that painters and sculptors were creators of evil things.[14] In general in this period, the Jews are shown as being stubbornly intent on keeping their Temple and Jerusalem wholly free of idols and images and courageously protecting their land from any contaminating imagery being introduced by other powers.

Rabbinic Judaism: Advice to Look Away

In the Mishnah, the first compilation of the discussion of laws of the Hebrew Bible, revised in early third-century Palestine, an entire tractate, *Avodah Zarah* (*עבודה זרה*, which means "strange or foreign worship") was devoted to idol worship. Here the biblical laws of idolatry were newly contextualized.[15] The teachings of first- and second-century rabbis prohibited the Jews' involvement or participation in any aspect of idol worship as they tried to adjust to their minority position in pagan cultic society.[16] On the one hand, the Mishnah stated that these idols meant nothing, but, on the other, it showed an awareness that the Jews were living in a world where images were increasingly regarded as sacred by the dominant majority faith. In the long run, it was these Jewish laws that created a framework for the attitudes Jews were allowed to have toward sacred images. They were now told that they were powerless to remove the sacredness of these idols for the pagans and had no duty to nullify (i.e., deconsecrate) them unless they needed to use them. These were fundamental changes—destruction was no longer practicable and could not be encouraged in a Palestine that had ceased to be predominantly Jewish. The Jerusalem and Babylonian Talmuds (probably revised for the last time at the end of the eighth century) are digressive and lengthy commentaries on the Mishnah. Their rulings in *Avodah Zarah* depart from the biblical sanctions and create others of their own. These tannaitic rabbis (who lived between the first and third centuries CE under the aegis of Roman emperors) had been surrounded in both Babylonia and the Holy Land with the sacred images created by Romans, Christians, and the other ethnic and religious groups living among them.[17] The sacred images found in Palestinian cities included symbols of Roman imperial power and many idols associated with Roman and Greek cults, which were widely distributed throughout the Roman Empire[18]

When, in the first half of the fourth century, Palestine became increasingly Christianized, pagan idolatry was replaced by a large number of symbols of Christian sanctity; this was disconcerting for the Jews.[19] The Emperor Constantine (ca. 285–337) supported the building of large churches on sites associated with significant events in Jesus's life and death. Monastic orders followed suit, and by the sixth century more than five hundred churches had been built in the Holy Land, attracting thousands of Christian pilgrims to Jerusalem.

The Talmud unequivocally equates Jesus with the worship of idolatry, as if the rabbis hoped to keep Jews away from Christian devotional images, even at the cost of isolating them socially and restricting their commerce.[20] The ban on idolatry in *Avodah Zarah*, as Moshe Halbertal suggests, was "an attempt to dictate exclusivity, to map the unique territory of the one God."[21] This then was rabbinic Judaism's response to Christianity, taking place inside a Christian environment.[22] It reiterated the prohibition on practicing idolatry and commanded Jews to avoid all physical contact with idols and their accessories.[23] In the Babylonian Talmud Jews are commanded not to throw stones at or defecate on a gentile image.[24] The Talmud actually referred to the deity Markolis (the Roman god Mercurius, or Mercury), whose representation was not a formal statue in a house of worship but a simple pile of rocks built in the open air. Mercurius also paralleled the Greek god Hermes, although some suggest that the deity referred to in the Mishnah was Mercurius Helipolitanus, which was a local Syrian idol, influenced by Greek and Roman traditions. Mercurius Helipolitanus was viewed by its worshippers as the protector of travelers generally, and of traveling merchants specifically, which is why the representation of the deity appeared most often at crossroads. However, the method of worship was out of the ordinary. Travelers would add rocks to the pile, and these would become part of the idolatrous representation. Ironically, Jews were not allowed to throw stones at this idol. But a wider message was also clear: there was a danger and a concern that Jews might take it upon themselves to attack or defile idols, and they were being advised to do no such thing.

The new fluidity of the term "idol" in the Mishnah and its differing cultural and spiritual connotations would only add to the topic's complexity. A few texts in the Jerusalem Talmud seem to sanction a reaction to idols that involved imagining violent acts rather than actually performing them. In the following three cases, which appear together, rabbis are reported asking their respective seniors about what should be done when passing three different types of idols—an image, then a statue, and finally an idol. They all give the same response: "to put out its eyes" (*vesamme 'eneh*):

> Gamaliel Zuga supported himself on Rabbi Simeon son of Laqish [as they walked].
> When they reached an image (תבניתא—Aramaic), he (Gamaliel Zuga) said to him:
> "Should we pass before it?"
> He (Rabbi Simeon son of Laqish) said: "Pass before it and put its eyes out."
>
> Rabbi Isaac son of Matnah supported himself on Rabbi Johanan.
> When they reached the statue at the *boule* (the council building צלמה דבולי) he (Rabbi Isaac son of Matnah) said to him:
> "Should we pass before it?"
> He (Rabbi Johanan) said: "Pass before it and put its eyes out."
>
> Rabbi Jacob son of Idi supported himself on Rabbi Joshua son of Levi.
> They reached the image of *aduri* (or alternately, they came behind an image).
> He (Rabbi Joshua son of Levi) said to him:
> "Nahum of the Holy of Holies would pass, and you, you do not [wish to] pass?
> "Pass before it and put its eyes out."[25]

In another place in the Jerusalem Talmud, *Moed Qatan* 3:7, 83c, Rabbi Jacob, son of Idi, is also told by Rabbi Yohanan, that when he (Rabbi Jacob) walks up to and encounters an idol he is to "put out its eye "—*vesamme 'eneh.*

Where did this idea come from? In Roman society, rabbis writing the Mishnah would have witnessed the urban mob participating in *damnatio memoriae*—the symbolic destruction of statues, which involved decapitation and the replacement of heads.[26] This literal "blinding its eye" was an intrinsic part of an iconoclastic process. Eric Varner describes such an action as a form of "mutilation or execution in effigy," which denied these images the power to see and represented part of the *poena post mortem*, the desecration of corpses of capital offenders.[27] Yet Jewish scholars in general refuse to accept that the words "putting out the eye" or "blinding the eyes" in the Talmud literally approved the physical desecration of the idols of other religious cults.[28] Instead they believe that these words pointed to creative solutions that Jews were to adopt in response to living in an overwhelmingly non-Jewish physical space. Peter Schäfer describes *vesamme 'eneh* as shutting one's own eyes.[29] Gerald Blidstein argues that the rabbis were endorsing spitting.[30] More recently Rachel Neis suggests that Jews are being told to "look awry"—a looking away that involved a whispered cursing before the image.[31] According to the Talmud, the ideal treatment of images/idols by Jews was never to look at them. This is recorded in the Jerusalem Talmud as the method of Rabbi Nahum bar Simai, who never looked at an image in his life.[32] Hence Neis sees the rabbis as contriving various avoidance strategies, whereby Jews could eliminate the power of these idols without actually committing the act of physical desecration or destruction.[33] She also argues that, since images were accepted by tannaitic rabbis as having some kind of negative power or agency over the beholder, turning away would prevent this happening.[34] What these different theories seem to intimate is that the phrase *vesamme 'eneh* might well have been intentionally ambiguous, encouraging a form of discreet ridicule by rabbis and allowing Jews to only imagine what they would do to the image if they could. This actually becomes an act of desecration by proxy.

Desecration appears in another section of tractate *Avodah Zarah*, but as a deed performed by gentiles and not Jews. Here the Talmud provides a list of ways that the power of idols could be nullified by their gentile owners; one way was to desecrate them. This seemed to confirm that the rabbis attributed a certain sacredness to the gentiles' idols and the term "nullify" described the process of desacralizing them. The Tosefta, a supplement to the Mishnah written in the third century and containing the teachings of the tannaitic rabbis, gives various answers as to what desecration of an idol means, from hitting it with a hammer, pushing it, knocking it over, or possibly selling it or pledging it (though this is not stated).[35] However, nowhere in these sources is it suggested that a gentile could desecrate an image by destroying its eyes. This remained an action only a Jew could do.

Although there is a lack of clarity in the Jerusalem Talmud regarding the physical act of desecration, what is clear is that the sages did not sanction Jewish iconoclasm and attempted to keep Jews as far away as possible from idols/images of other religions.[36] In fact they argued that the Jews did not have the capacity to nullify the idol of a gentile once it had been worshipped.[37] Jews were permitted to mock the practice of idol worship rather than the idol itself. The Babylonian Talmud (Sanhedrin 7:6) has this to say: "Said Rabbi Nahman, any form of mockery is forbidden except for mockery of idolatry, which is permitted. For it is written 'Bel has bowed down, Nebo stoops over. Their images are consigned to the beasts and the cattle. The things that they carry are burdensome'" (Isa. 46:1). One senses the extent to which the Talmud demands that the Jews distance themselves from the images (in this case the idols Bel and Nebo—the supreme Babylonian deities), allowing the focus to be on the "sinner" who created them. According to both the Jerusalem and Babylonian Talmuds, it is God who will destroy the idols—not man. What Jews should do now is pray for their elimination not only in the Land of Israel but everywhere. In the Mishnah and Talmud, liturgical longing for divine iconoclasm comes with blessings to recite upon seeing idolatry and its hoped- and prayed-for erasure.[38]

This caused tension since, on the one hand, Jews were expected to disregard the idol's sacredness but, on the other, they were forced to acknowledge its presence by looking away. The lasting achievement of these Talmudic commandments was to modify the Jews' obligation, once imposed on them by the Bible, to destroy or damage the images or idols held sacred by other peoples and other religions. Yet Christian theologians seemed to remain oblivious to this rabbinic directive. In many premodern historical contexts, Christians had limited, if any, knowledge of postbiblical Jewish literature, and even when they did know, Christian theologians did not refer to the biblical commands to destroy idols when they accused Jews of being abusive to Christian images.

While these rulings were being absorbed, Jews sometimes strictly adhered to the Second Commandment in relation to their own artistic creations and at other times ignored it or ingeniously circumvented it. Floor mosaics in Palestinian synagogues, Jewish catacombs in Rome, and the synagogue decoration at Dura-Europas confirmed some Jews' acceptance of figural imagery even within religious spaces.[39] This flexible attitude needs to be noted. These artistic developments were the result of the Jews' acculturation to the societies around them, which they borrowed from a Christian or general Greco-Roman pattern book of cultic imagery.[40] Since paganism was waning, it is not clear whether the local rabbis' prohibition of this activity was overruled.[41] However, the tolerance for figurative imagery ended in the seventh century when these works were rejected by Jews.[42] Byzantine Jews intensified their opposition to the depiction of ornamental figurative works and destroyed their own mosaic images in the genuine belief that such representations were unsuitable for their sanctuaries.[43] The Jews' destruction of their figurative imagery needs to be read as their reaction to the Byzantine Christians' fear that their own images were cultic and focuses of devotion. Jews, conscious of what was happening in the Christian world, needed to reassure themselves that images in their synagogues played no part in their religious practice. At this time Mosaic floors in Palestinian synagogues, such as Beit Alpha, Ein Duk, and El Hammeh began to incorporate representations of inanimate objects only.[44]

Alternative Expressions of Disdain

From the late fifth and sixth centuries onward, Hebrew *piyyutim* (liturgical hymns) read during the synagogue service showed disdain for Christian images. These complex works confirmed the Jews' genuine abhorrence, on doctrinal grounds, and their discomfort with the increasing ubiquity of Christian images in the empire.[45] Rabbi Yannai, a sixth-century composer of liturgical poems, emphasized his contempt of Christian idolatry and condemned the Christians "who rejoice in statues of human figures" and "who prostrate and pray to a bush."[46] The "bush" in Judaic texts seems to have been the first insulting term for the cross. In the *Midrash Esther Rabbah* (an anthology of rabbinic interpretations of the book of Esther), written in Palestine around 500 CE, God is described as choosing a thorn bush as gallows to hang the villain Haman in the Purim story. Hanging upon a tree was commonly interpreted to denote crucifixion (which was a form of execution only used by Romans) since a tree and a cross both meant essentially the same in Roman law as well as in Targumic (Aramaic) translation.[47] As noted in Chapter 1, the execution of Haman (as the archenemy of the Jews in the biblical book of Esther) had become a crucifixion, and, as a result, Byzantine Jews were cursing and mocking Christ instead of Haman at their annual Purim festivities.[48] In an earlier section of *Midrash Esther Rabbah*, at the point in the book of Esther where they still believe that they are putting the Jew Mordechai to death, Haman's wife discusses with Haman and his counselors the form of killing that ensures that Jews don't survive. Haman's wife suggests hanging on the gallows, with a subtle allusion to the death of Jesus who was hanged on a wooden cross. "Hang him [Mordechai] therefore on a gallows, for we have not found one of his people who was delivered from that."[49] Perhaps there was another hidden message. The method of killing by hanging on a cross had in fact been successful and Jesus had died and had not been resurrected, as Christians believed. Further discomfort with Christian icons can be read in a polemical Hebrew text titled "The Apocalypse of Zerubbabel," or *Sefer Zerubbabel*, which was probably written in early seventh-century Palestine and described redemptive events in which Jerusalem is recaptured by the Jews who then destroy Christian idols so that they might live free of them.[50] The text offered Jews under the threat of a Persian invasion a longed-for eschatological revelation that would save them. The Jewish writers sublimated their abhorrence of the Byzantine emperors' oppressive policies, for which they hoped the emperors would be punished (according to Jewish eschatological traditions), by imagining violent attacks upon them.[51] At one point in the text the author describes the Roman emperor Armilos, a figure identified as the Antichrist and whose name is a cryptogram for the Byzantine emperor Heraclius, and his intention to build idols: "And he [Armilos] will begin to plant on the face of the land all the *asheroth* [idols] of the gentiles which the Lord hates, and he will take the stone from which he was born and transport it to [the valley of Arbael] and he will build seven altars from it, and it will be the chief object of idolatry, and all the peoples will come from all places and worship this stone and offer incense to it, and pour libations. . . . And Armilos angered the Lord with his evil deed."[52]

Although Asheroth was the name of a Canaanite goddess, the tale really implies the hoped-for destruction of Christian crosses in churches dedicated to the Virgin Mary in the Holy Land.[53] The text relates that, when God saves the Jews, "all the strange gods and every temple of images and wall and cliff" will fall to the ground.[54] Here the Jews portray themselves as waiting for divine intervention to destroy images rather than taking action themselves. The reference here to "all the strange gods" could also imply the increasing variety of Christian images and the increasing prominence of the Virgin image at this time.

Moneylending, Trade, and Christian Property

In the late tenth and eleventh centuries, Jews settled in medieval Ashkenaz (which included Franco-German Jewry with its smaller branches in England,

Bohemia, and Moravia), incentivized by growing commercial and economic opportunities and promises of protection by the political leadership. Here, Jews relied upon Christian society to provide their most basic needs, finding themselves in daily contact with Christian neighbors and their material culture.[55] When Jewish communities sprang up along the Rhine, the rabbis provided only cautious generalizations to direct the Jews' interaction with Christian images and sacred objects, and there were no uniform rulings regarding which types of objects could be taken from Christians as pledges.[56]

Judaism showed itself to be particularly permeable to the new social, cultural, and economic milieu, despite previous stringent Talmudic prohibitions. Some rabbis argued that the Talmud had given Jews a pretext, albeit a flimsy one, for accepting Christian items as pawns. Regarding the question of whether the act of pledging (or pawning) an idol could "nullify" it, the Mishnah *Avodah Zarah* (4:5) gives two opinions, one for it and one against it: "If an idol worshipper sold or pawned his idol it was nullified according to Rabbe [Yehudah Hanasi], but not according to the sages."[57] Nullification is again understood as the deconsecration of an object considered sacred and used by somebody else—in this case a follower of another religion—in order to free it from contamination and purify it in Jewish eyes. According to Talmudic sources, a Jew could buy a sacred object because, by selling it, the owner had deprived it of its power. But the Jew could not take it as security for a loan, because the object would recover its power if the owner redeemed it.[58] This loophole did not prevent concern among medieval rabbis regarding whether Jews should profit from these kinds of objects. Some rabbis were more liberal than others. In the tenth century, Gershom ben Judah of Mainz (also known as Rabbenu Gershom, ca. 1000) invoked the argument of *she'at ha-dehaq* (case of urgent necessity): because Jews needed an income, it might be permissible for them to receive sacred objects as pledges from Christians. Had Christians been considered idolaters, this would not have been allowed. But arguably Christians did not practice the kind of idol worship that had been condemned in the Talmud.[59] The opposite view was taken by Maimonides in his Mishnah Torah *Hilkhot Avodat Kohavim* (Laws of idol worship) compiled between 1170 and 1180 while he was living in Egypt. Here he set out the stringent Talmudic opinion that the idolatrous character of these types of objects could not be desacralized by non-Jews however they treated it. "If, however, one gave it as security for a loan, sold it to a gentile, [sold it] to a Jew who is not a jeweler, [left it] after it was covered by fallen articles without removing them, did not demand its return after it was stolen by thieves, spat in its face, urinated upon it, dragged it [in mud], or threw feces upon it, it is not nullified."[60] However, from the twelfth century, Christian devotional images were not just appearing on the exterior of churches and other buildings, but had become portable objects that could be pawned easily. Rabbinic texts increasingly referred to the Christian practice of pawning sacred objects with Jews. Rabbis quickly recognized the religious meaning of these objects to Christians, forbidding Jews under any circumstances to enter churches, but held differing opinions on which types of sacred objects might be accepted as pawns. Eliezer bar Nathan (Ra'avan), one of the Hebrew chroniclers of the First Crusade, a Jewish poet, and writer born around 1090, strictly prohibited Jews from receiving as pawns or selling Christian statues, icons, censers, and incense.[61] He was willing to tolerate the selling and bestowing of loans against clerical clothing and vessels such as chalices, since these were not considered sacred; the vessels were "there for the priests to drink from while praying."[62] Eliezer bar Nathan's sanctioning of the reception of chalices as pawns might suggest that he misunderstood their function as the vessel for the wine that was miraculously transmuted into the blood of Christ during mass. The words he uses may have been designed to belittle the chalice, by speaking of it as something that is just there for the priest's refreshment. Isaac of Dampierre (ca. 1120–1185) followed this doctrine.[63] But Isaac's uncle Jacob ben Meir Tam (d. 1171), who came from the northern French town of Ramerupt and was the leading French Tosafist in the twelfth century, contradicted Eliezer bar Nathan. He showed a far deeper level of concern and warned Jews not to accept clerical clothing or any church vessels as securities for debt. He demanded Jews "not to buy stolen things, such as images or a chalice or priestly vestments, and prayer books, or the vessels of worship because of the danger."[64] He was presuming that, since these things belonged to the churches and not individuals, the person trying to sell them must have stolen them. Jacob ben Meir Tam highlighted his fear that Jews might be charged with stealing and then desecrating these items, particularly sacred crucifixes and images. Eliezer ben Samuel of Metz (ca. 1115–1198) was stringent in his ruling against borrowing or acquiring church vestments. He also exhibited his knowledge of the new practice of Christian processions in which images or consecrated hosts were being carried around the city's streets and warned his coreligionists to stay away.[65] These texts reflect an important intersection between the Jews' fear of ritual contamination and anxiety regarding Christian accusations, prosecution, or persecution. According to Eliezer ben Joel Halevi, writing his *Sefer Ravi'ah* in the late twelfth century, the only crosses these rabbis permitted to be received as pledges were those worn by Christians around their necks: "We are not strict about the cross which they hang from their necks in remembrance of their mistaken beliefs, i.e. one may derive [economic] benefit from them."[66] The responsa of Isaac ben Moses of Vienna (ca. 1200–1270) in his thirteenth-century halachic guide *Or Zaru'a* (Light is sown [allusion to Ps. 97:11]) confirm that, despite these fears and dangers, Jews continued to receive these objects. Here the sermons of his son Rabbi Haim Eliezar ben Isaac (which were probably delivered in the town of Wiener Neustadt) bring up the Talmudic question as to what should be done to nullify the idolatrous character of the Christian religious objects when in Jews' hands. These might include pawned objects—for example, priestly vestments and even "a ciborium in which they carry abominable bread"—that were kept by Jews after loans were not repaid. If Jews had Christian ciboria, candles, or priestly clothing, these could now be reused. However, pans in which incense had been burned could not.[67] But Meir of Rothenburg (1215–1293), who sent his almost eight hundred responsa to the communities of Germany, Austria, Bohemia, and even France and was clearly more aware of what was occurring in the Christian world, forbade Jews either to sell any of these objects back to Christians or to use them for their own rituals.[68] The intention was that Jews should keep away completely from handling any religious objects belonging to Christians. It was not until the fifteenth century, when the iconographic revolution was occurring in Spain and images of Mary and Jesus were becoming ubiquitous, that the Radbaz, Rabbi David Ibn Abi Zimra (1479–1573), reiterated the prohibition there: "Images that we know are worshipped, like the image of the Virgin and Child or a cross, or the Crucifixion and others like these . . . are forbidden even if they appear on a mundane [vessel]. . . . Concerning images we know are worshipped, there is no distinction between those that are *intaglio*, those in relief, and those that are two-dimensional such as paintings, textiles or engravings. All are forbidden even if they appear on mundane utensils."[69]

Even though rabbis were suitably concerned about Jews handling objects used in Christian worship, historians have argued that in reality Jews did not curb their pawnbroking practices on account of rabbinic rulings. Jewish moneylenders in western Europe continued to pledge, repledge, or even acquire stolen sacred objects by accepting them as pledges—especially since these objects were almost certainly worth considerably more than the money loaned against them.[70] Jews needed collateral and, through holding these objects in the course of business transactions, became fully acquainted with Christian materiality, as did their counterparts in Spain who, as noted in Chapter 3, were often the painters and silversmiths of these very crucifixes and sacred objects.[71]

Invectives as an Act of Jewish Defiance

It was the Gospel parody *Toledot Yeshu* (History of Jesus), written around the fourth or fifth century, that first disseminated insulting and abusive ideas about Christianity. Anti-Christian invectives would become part of the Hebrew vocabulary and provided Jews with an arsenal of common emotive terms that they might employ to mock the images they encountered as they navigated Christian space.[72] In liturgical writings, medieval Jewish prayers, and even polemical works, a crucifix was repeatedly called "the abomination," (*to'evah*) or the "detestable idol" (*shikkutz*); Jesus, "the hanged one" (*ha' talui*) or "the son of whoredom" or "trampled corpse";[73] a church, "the house of idol worship" or "house of idolatry" (*bet to'evah*) or the "house of impurity" (*binyan ha-tum'ah*); and vessels used for Christian worship, "vessels of impurity" (*klei tum'ah*).[74] Certain versions of *Toledot Yeshu* also refer to Jesus's humiliation in being crucified not on a cross—since all the trees of the land had been enchanted by Jesus himself so that they could not bear his weight—but on a plant variously described as either a cabbage stalk or a carob bush.[75] The invective, which had originated in Yannai's poetry, was now clearly recognized as a derisive term for the cross.

In twelfth-century versions of the Purim story in the Aggadic midrash *Pirkei de Rabbi Eliezer* (which originated in the eighth or ninth century), Haman's clothing was described as being adorned with a cross. For this reason, Mordechai had refused to bow down to it or him: "so that everyone who prostrated before Haman also prostrated before the abomination [*to'evah*] that he made. Mordechai [the Jew] saw this and did not consent to bow down and prostrate himself before this detestable thing [*shikutso*], as it is said [in Megillat Esther 3:2] and Mordechai did not bow down and prostrate himself."[76]

Whereas Jews were forbidden to bow down to crosses, Christians were committing idolatry by prostrating themselves before idols. This tale was later copied by the fifteenth-century commentator Abraham Saba, who left Spain in 1492 for Portugal, where he stayed until 1496, and then fled to Morocco. Resetting the tale in his own times, he described Mordechai's discomfort when he saw the Spanish and Portuguese kings' clerks wearing crosses on their clothing: "First he [Haman] said that all the slaves of the king must bow before an idol that he had put on his chest and prostrate before Haman. . . . As do the kings of Edom, whose clerks have on their clothes [an image] of the cross, which is an abomination, and who looks at it bows down or prostrates himself; and Mordechai did not bow before the idol and did not prostrate himself before Haman."[77]

The refusal of Jews to bow down before Christian images is further reflected in the words of Herman von Scheda. In his *Opusculum de conversione sua*, mentioned in Chapter 2, he also describes how his first viewing of a crucifix in a church (in either Cologne or Deutz) had repulsed him by its brutal explicitness.[78]

> Examining all things with great care, I saw among the sculptured devices and variety of paintings a monstrous idol. I discerned one and the same man humiliated and exalted, abased and lifted up, ignominious and noble. He was hanging wretchedly from high to low on a cross, and from low to high, by the deceiving effects of the painting, he was sitting enthroned and as if deified. I admit I was stupefied, suspecting that effigies of this sort were likenesses of the kind common among the pagans. The doctrines of the Pharisees had, in the past, easily persuaded me that it was truly thus.[79]

Herman von Scheda's abhorrence of the crucifix indicates not only how his Jewish background had educated him to perceive Christian images as idols but also that he had trained himself to avert his eyes from all Christian images, never observing them properly. Crucifixes had become objects of hate and disgust for Jews who now had an armory of abusive words to describe them.

A Convincing Equivalent to the Crucifix: The Torah Scroll

The massacres of the Rhineland Jewish communities during the First and Second Crusades, in 1098 and 1145–1147, left a harrowing legacy for generations to come.[80] Surviving Jews or their descendants penned four Hebrew chronicles describing the massacres that became the first works of Jewish historical recording in medieval Europe.[81] There are three Hebrew chronicles of the First Crusade: the *Narrative of the Old Persecutions* (or *Mainz Anonymous*), written by an anonymous chronicler between 1097 and 1146; the *Chronicle of Solomon bar Simson*, compiled around the year 1140; and the *Chronicle of Rabbi Eliezer bar Nathan*, a well-known Ashkenazi rabbi, that was completed by 1146. The Hebrew chronicle of the Second Crusade is *Sefer Zekhira* written by Rabbi Ephraim of Bonn around the year 1171 or 1174.[82] These chroniclers described bands of crusaders making stops along the way at the towns of Ashkenaz to terrorize and cleanse the communities of those they saw as responsible for the demise of their savior. The chroniclers reported their own rage and pain at the severe persecution of their fellow religionists, recording case after case of suicide or the killings of unintended victims. It is here too that we find—for the first time in Jewish texts—descriptions of historical Jews desecrating crucifixes before they died. How should this phenomenon be understood and explained?

A new consciousness of the cross, as the distinctive symbol and badge of crusading vows, had been aroused by Urban II in his appeal to save the Byzantine Empire from the Muslims, at the Council of Clermont in 1095. Five Christian chroniclers reported his speech,[83] but it was Guibert of Nogent who wrote specifically about how the pope understood the cross as an emblem:

> He [Urban] instituted a sign well suited to so honorable a profession by making the figure of the Cross, the symbol of the Lord's Passion, the emblem of the soldiery, or rather, of what was to be the soldiery of God. This, made of any kind of cloth, he ordered to be sewed upon the shirts, cloaks, and *byrra* of those who were about to go. He commanded that if anyone, after receiving this emblem, or after taking openly this vow, should shrink from his good intent through base change of heart, or any affection for his parents, he should be regarded an outlaw forever, unless he repented and again undertook whatever of his pledge he had omitted.[84]

This new sartorial cross had become, according to Urban II, the symbol of Christ's soldiers and a sign of their oath and fidelity to the crusading cause. It was to be affixed to the clothing of Christians at formal public ceremonies.[85] Solomon bar Simson mentions the badge in the second paragraph of his Hebrew chronicle: "They [the crusaders] decorated themselves prominently with their signs, placing a profane symbol—a horizontal line over a vertical one—on the vestments of every man and woman whose heart yearned to go on the stray path to the grave of their Messiah."[86] The cross, as a visual sign of the crucified Christ ("the rotting corpse" as it is described repeatedly in these chronicles)[87] on the clothing of the crusaders evoked fear, contempt, and detestation among the Jews.[88] It became a symbol associated with religious violence against them, and thus a correlation should be drawn between its sartorial use by the crusaders and the new Jewish violence and sacrilege against the crucifix as depicted in these Hebrew chronicles. Most of these works were written and edited decades after the massacres, on occasion repeating the same narratives, so that their historical accuracy is dubious.[89] The use of particularly strong religious and biblical imagery, as well as a remarkable level of emotion, detail, and symbolism, has encouraged scholars to believe that the Jewish chroniclers' purpose lay elsewhere, in the messages of the narrative rather than the authenticity of the record. The intention here was to impress on future generations the need to be prepared for Christian violence.

There are no descriptions of crucifix desecration in the many Christian chronicles and contemporaneous works of the First Crusade, and one might argue that, if they had occurred, their authors would have used them as examples of the Jews' abominable offenses against Christianity. But the absence of references to these imputed actions in Christian chronicles does not strengthen this possibility. The Christian descriptions of the attacks do not go into any significant detail. They are a few sentences long, at most, and have entirely different aims, audiences, and agendas from the multichapter Jewish chronicles. Nevertheless the consensus among scholars is that the depictions of Jewish crucifix violation in the Jewish chronicles are fictitious and that these sources are literary adaptations of Jewish historical memory, rather than texts that described genuine events.[90] These texts serve to depict a counter-crusade in which the Jews of Ashkenaz present themselves as martyrs, just as the Christian crusaders who lost their lives in battle were celebrated as Christian martyrs.[91] Guibert of Nogent reported that Pope Urban had stated at Clermont: "We now hold out to you wars which contain the glorious reward of martyrdom, which will retain that title of praise now and forever."[92] Written after years of contemplation, these Hebrew chronicles depict the Jews not as helpless victims of a brutal and unjust assault but as those who saved the integrity of their own religion—taking an active role in their own deaths. By martyring each other, they died to sanctify God's name, thereby waging their own crusade.[93] Through their death by martyrdom, these Jews had become heroes of victorious counter-crusades. It is this message that gives the chronicles their true historical significance.

Hence, I would like to suggest that the Hebrew chroniclers' accounts of Jews violating crucifixes, the supreme symbol used in Christian worship, may have been consciously devised to offset their descriptions of crusaders destroying the Torah scrolls, the supreme symbol of Judaism. The idea that the Torah, as a divine object, had a preexistence in heaven had been developed in early rabbinic literature. Jews are not allowed to touch it with their hands, when it is carried before them in a procession in their synagogues. It is the only Jewish object Jews are expected to bow down before.[94]

Descriptions of crucifix violation by Jews are always depicted in the Hebrew chronicles as a reaction to the evil destruction of their Torah scrolls by the crusaders. During the First and Second Crusades, crusaders attacked the most holy object of the Jews, so the Jews in response are depicted as attacking the main symbol of Christianity and the crusading movement. In the First Crusade, the tearing of sacred Torah scrolls was part of almost every attack.[95] There are nine descriptions of Torah desecration in the four chronicles.[96] The Hebrew chroniclers first emphasized the holiness and beauty of the Torah, how it was honored by a particular Jewish community, and how terrible it was that the uncircumcised contaminated it. According to Eliezer bar Nathan, the crusaders trampled the Torah scrolls in the mud in Worms: "The enemies and oppressors set upon the Jews who were in their homes, pillaging, and murdering men, women, and children, young and old. They destroyed the houses and pulled down the stairways, looting and plundering; and they took the holy Torah, trampled it in the mud of the streets, and tore it and desecrated it amidst ridicule and laughter."[97] The *Mainz Anonymous* depicts the grief of the Jewish women who saw the Torah as it was torn in the Mainz synagogue in 1098: "There was also a Torah scroll in the room; the errant ones came into the room, found it, and tore it to shreds. When the holy and pure women, daughters of kings, saw that the Torah had been torn, they called in a loud voice to their husbands: 'Look, see, the Holy Torah—it is being torn by the enemy!' And they all said, men and women together: 'Alas, the Holy Torah, the perfection of beauty, the delight of our eyes, to which we used to bow in the synagogue, kissing and honoring it. How has it now fallen into the hands of the impure uncircumcised ones?'"[98] Furthermore, according to Solomon bar Simson, the Torah scrolls were trampled underfoot in Trier: "At that time the people of the community of Trier took their Torah scrolls and placed them in a sturdy building. When the enemy became aware of this, they went there while it was still day and broke the roof above; they took all the mantles and the silver adorning the rollers of the Torah, and threw the Torah Scrolls on the ground, and tore them and trod upon them with their feet."[99]

In these Hebrew chronicles, the narrative shows the desecration of large crucifixes usually just outside or inside churches (and, in one case, a portable one brought out of a church) occurring only after most of the Jews were massacred; it is depicted as a last act of defiance by individual Jewish men and women before dying. The chronicles describe for the benefit of their Jewish communities this dramatic public act that physically expressed the Jews' contempt for Christianity by desecrating the symbol that Christians held sacred. It also made a connection between the historical Jews' mocking of a Christian "idol" and suicide. The four chronicles record six cases of desecration. Three cases record Jewish men spitting on crucifixes and one a Jewish woman doing the same. Another two cases report Jewish men casting "a branch at the abomination," which scholars argue represents a type of mocking or actual urination on the image.[100] The first three cases are in Solomon bar Simson's chronicle. Of these the first relates how Isaac, son of Elyakim, when brought to a church, spat at the "object of their idolatry" and was slain.[101] In the second case, Natronai, son of Isaac, "threw a branch in their faces." He then slaughtered his brother and killed himself. The "branch" here, like that of a tree, a thorn bush, and a stalk already discussed, probably refers to a crucifix.[102] The third case relates to Asher, son of Joseph, the gabbai of Trier, who was escorted by crusaders to the door of the bishop's palace. When a crucifix was brought out of the palace, they (Asher and another Jew, Meir) "cast a branch at the abomination."[103] The fourth case is in the *Chronicle of Rabbi Eliezer bar Nathan*, which describes how Isaac of Cologne, when led to a church ("the house of idolatry"), "spat at them, reviled and ridiculed them." Here the spitting is at the Christians who brought him there rather than at the church itself or on a crucifix.[104] The fifth case is recorded in *Sefer Zehirah* and occurred during the Second Crusade. At the Stahleck Castle just outside Mainz, on the eve of Shavuot, three Jews of Bacharach left the castle where they were hiding in order to settle business matters. They were attacked by crusaders, and one of the Jews, Kalonymos, "openly spat on the image of the crucified one, and they slew him on the spot."[105] The sixth case again appears in *Sefer Zehirah*. Here the sister of Simeon bar Isaac of Würzburg was taken "to their place of idolatry so as to profane her, but she sanctified the Name and spat upon the abomination. They then struck her with stone and fist."[106]

Similar in many ways to the tale of "alleged" desecration in the Jerusalem Talmud, these chronicles, I believe, were not sanctioning a new way of acting toward Christian sacred images as much as representing an idealized Jewish response to the desecration of their Torah.[107] It would seem then that the crucifix is viewed in these sources as the intentional target of abuse and defiance by the Jews, just as the Torah scrolls had been the intentional target of attack by the crusaders. Crucifixes had become smaller, more portable objects that could be carried outside churches. The Jews' reverence for the Torah scroll clearly expressed the divinity they attributed to it. These observations cast valuable light on a statement made by Peter Cantor, the French theologian, who noted that when the city of Rheims was struck by severe drought in the mid-twelfth century, local Jews had offered to parade their Torah scrolls around the city after a three-day procession of Christian sacred icons had failed to produce rain.[108] Cantor records that the Jews' offer was accompanied by a promise that if they were unsuccessful they would convert to Christianity. It is highly unlikely that the Jews would have made such an offer to convert voluntarily.

Analogies between the cross and the scrolls are also suggested by the fourteenth-century writer Joseph Ibn Kaspi (1280–1345), who refers in his *Shulhan Kesef* to the Jews presenting the Torah to newly inaugurated popes, kings, and visiting dignitaries.[109] Here he has a Provençal bishop ask his Jewish interlocutor: "Why do you ask the kings, the popes and the bishops to honor and venerate the book of Moses' Torah when you take it before you on their entering the town, just as we do when we take out before them our icons?"[110]

From many angles, it would seem that medieval Jews did indeed see and parade their Torah as a counter-object to Christian images. By elevating the Torah scroll in this way, the Jews also had their own symbol to define and protect them.

Responding Through Polemics

The twelfth century was the time when meticulous Jewish polemical works were written in Western Christendom, particularly in southern France and northern Spain. These provided an outlet for Jewish thinkers who, familiar with parts of the New Testament, were ready to defend their religion against the dominant faith and its increasing missionizing tactics. In small handy guidebooks, rabbis penned their own fictitious disputational literature to counteract Christian works, offering support and advice to their followers, and it is here that one finds an attack against Christians for their increasing use of images. The Provençal biblical commentator Joseph Kimhi (1105–1170) had his Jewish interlocutor in *Sefer ha-Berit* remind Jews that since God spoke to Moses at Horeb without showing his face, Jews are forbidden to represent God in an image.[111] He then turns to the Christians. The fact that Christians make images and bow down to them means that they violate one of the seven Noahide commandments to which they, as gentiles, are beholden—that against worshipping idols.[112]

By the thirteenth century, more handbooks were needed to fight the increasing Christian attempts to convert Jews to Christianity, which included official disputations, Talmud burnings, and sermons delivered by friars that Jews were forced to attend. *Sefer Yosef HaMeqanne* (Book of Joseph ben Nathan Official, also known as Joseph the Zealot) from France and *Sefer Nizzahon Vetus* (Old Book of Contention) from Germany provided sophisticated retorts to any Christian arguments regarding the biblical texts.[113] These handbooks are full of defiant, mocking, humorous arguments Jews might advance to defend the Hebrew Bible against the many assertions Christian theologians made in regard to Christian doctrine and religious practice.[114]

In the introduction to his *Sefer Yosef HaMeqanne*, Joseph ben Nathan Official argues that he had written his handbook for two reasons; the first because many Jews seemed to be fascinated by the "foolishness" of Christianity and were converting, and the second because he was getting old and was anxious that the arguments of his forefathers should not be forgotten.[115] He portrayed his forefathers in his didactic tales as exemplary individuals, having defensive but fruitful conversations with different Christian clergy. At the same time, two of his tales confirm the Jews' contempt for crucifixes at the time when their ubiquity was felt through cities and towns. In one tale Joseph describes a conversation between a monk and Joseph's uncle, Rabbi Joseph of Chartres, who told the monk that God's own revelation took place in a "thorn bush" because there was no danger that this type of bush would be used to make a crucifix. Here the rabbi was ridiculing the fictitious Christian who would not have known of the *Midrash Esther Rabbah*'s usage of the thorn bush for a crucifix: "A monk once asked our uncle R. Joseph of Chartres: 'Why did the Holy One, blessed be He, reveal himself in a thorn bush, rather than in any other type of tree?'[116] He answered: 'It's because it is impossible to use it for making an image [= a crucifix].'"[117] There are also a number of rabbinic sources that ask why God appeared to Moses in a lowly thorn bush, the presumption being that appearing in a thorn bush was beneath God's dignity. A number of answers are given to this question, but the important point is that a Christian monk is the one to ask the question here. The rabbi answers by saying that the reason God appeared in the bush was because he thought it impossible for anyone to make a lowly bush into a holy image. This was a shrewd answer on the rabbi's part in light of the Christian interpretation of the burning bush as a metaphor for the Crucifixion. Christian exegesis argued that the angel of the burning bush was in fact Christ, who had "radiated his presence to bring salvation" in that bush.[118] The Hebrew Bible actually records that when Moses first approached the burning bush he saw an angel of God. Exodus 3:2 states: "And the angel of the Lord appeared unto him [Moses] in a flame of fire out of the midst of a bush: and he looked, and, behold, the bush burned with fire, and the bush was not consumed."

The *Sefer Nizzahon Vetus* noted: "And behold there was a bush all aflame, yet the bush was not consumed [Exod. 3:2]. They [the Christians] say that this refers to the one who was hanged."[119] Christian polemicists believed that, just as the bush was not burned up, so it was that Jesus, as God's eternal son, wasn't "consumed" in death but was resurrected. The rabbi was therefore telling the monk that God had appeared in a lowly bush because it could not be transformed into an image of God, and therefore the Christians were mistaken in turning the burning bush into a metaphor for Jesus's crucifixion. The message behind this short tale was a literary attack and a sly mockery of the crucifix. It was God who chose to appear in the "thorn bush," with a clear message that any images of God made from any type of wood—such as crucifixes—are idols.

A longer polemical folktale seems even more relevant for our purposes. Referring again to the thorn/burning bush, which here "radiated God's presence," Joseph describes his father, Rabbi Nathan, actually committing image desecration. He openly urinates on a cross in front of a Christian bishop, denying its sanctity and arguing that it should be considered putrid because it was the instrument that had caused the torture and death of Jesus:

> Once my lord and father, Rabbi Nathan, may he rest in Paradise, was riding alongside the bishop of Sens.[120] The bishop got off his horse opposite a bush in order to urinate. My lord and father saw this, and he got off his horse opposite an abomination [a cross] and urinated on it. The bishop saw this and was angry. He said to him, it is not proper to do that, to make the cross smell bad. My father replied, "On the contrary, it was a foolish thing for you to do [Gen. 31:28]. You urinated on a bush, on which the Holy One, blessed be He, radiated His presence in order to bring salvation [that is, at the burning bush, Exod. 3:1–3]. But this [cross], on which you [Christians] say that [the god] you fear was defeated, stank, and rotted, it is right that you should expose yourself and urinate all over it!"[121]

The Jew holds the trump cards. It would, Rabbi Nathan argues, make more sense for the Christian to desecrate the cross himself rather than venerate it. He first criticizes the bishop for urinating on a bush when, according to the Christian argument, Christ revealed himself in one. Second, he contends that it makes no sense for the bishop to venerate an object that caused the death of his savior. If the bishop saw the bush as a place of Christian divinity, the Jew argues, then he (the Jew) has shown more respect for Christ by not urinating on the bush than the bishop who did! It might well be argued then, that Joseph the Official was responding to the spreading allegations of Jews violating Christian images and offered in this polemic an allegorical retort.[122]

Another biblical fable appears in the anonymous *Sefer Nizzahon Hayeshun*—a slightly later handbook from Germany in the end of the thirteenth or early fourteenth century, which derived the bulk of its material from an earlier period. The purpose of this *Sefer* was to discipline the Jews, ridiculing Christianity in the hope of preventing Jews from converting.[123] More than the *Sefer Yosef HaMeqanne*, this work rejected, belittled, and mocked the Christian arguments that called attention to the presence of crucifixes and crosses in the Hebrew Bible text.[124] Genesis 47:31, the anonymous author argues, does not refer to the dying Jacob bowing his head to a staff or a cross at the head of his bed. (The word "bed" in Hebrew, *mitah*, is written without the Hebrew letter *yud* [י] and therefore can be read as the Hebrew word *mateh*, meaning "staff," or "rod.") The *Sefer Nizzahon Hayeshun* demands that Jews understand the text in this way: "One may answer them [the Christians] according to their foolishness and say that Jacob was distraught as a result of his illness, and he therefore bowed to the cross. But when he came to his senses, he changed his mind and regretted what he had done, as it is written, 'And he sat up on the bed (or staff)' [Gen. 48:2]. Thus, Jacob put it under his anus."[125] Here, presenting a clear message of humor and sly mockery, the anonymous author pretends to accept the illogical, anachronistic, but cherished Christian idea that a cross might have been on the wall in a Hebrew biblical story, in order that Jacob could retaliate by placing it under his backside. At this point, there is no suggestion of defecation as a form of desecration, but Jews were clearly channeling their contempt and disdain.[126] Unfortunately, the *Sefer Nizzahon* does not enlighten us further.[127]

At another point in *Sefer Nizzahon*, the cross on which Christ was crucified is referred to as the "stalk of cabbage," already labeled so in *Toldot Yeshu*.[128] Providing a paraphrase of Luke 23:32–43, in which two thieves hang on either side of Jesus, the *Nizzahon* provides a sly and derisive non sequitur text: "If he was divine, why did he allow himself to undergo such a peculiar shame of being hanged between thieves and on a stalk of cabbage?"[129] The continual reference to the cross as a stalk of cabbage indicates that this was a well-known term of humorous contempt, a form of derision that was to be understood only among Jews. The Jewish sources overwhelmingly refer to crosses/crucifixes as the Christian image that they particularly despise and ideally would like to mock—it was more central to their aggression than any image of the Virgin—contrary to the impression that Christian tales sought to convey. These sources bridged the gap between reality and fantasy by making it clear which objects the Jews would naturally choose to attack.

Withstanding the Christian Allegation

There are five extant mentions in Jewish sources of either fictitious or historical Jews being accused of image desecration, and it is remarkable how some of these texts show an overlap between Jewish behavior and the Christian tales of image desecration, suggesting that the Jews had some knowledge of these tales.

The first is a rabbinic document from eleventh-century France that reports that the Jews of Sens, a town on the southwestern border of Champagne, were accused of destroying a Christian cross, a sacred image, or a Christian ornament (the sources are not clear) and were supposedly punished by ruinous fines. The document did not indicate how the Jews responded to this allegation.[130] The second appears in the first half of the thirteenth century in a handbook, *Sefer Chasidim* (Book of Pietists), belonging to the Pietists of medieval Ashkenaz.[131] Unfortunately we have no way of knowing how many Jews associated themselves with this particular movement of Judaism. But *Sefer Chasidim* lists rigorous Pietistic rulings not only as exempla but also as innovative responses to the social and religious issues that Jews faced, particularly in their continuing navigation of Christian space.[132] Hasidic rabbis, unlike other Ashkenazic rabbis who proved to be less stringent, explicitly ordered Pietists to avoid all forms of Christian idolatry—the religious ceremonies, churches, and having any contact with their images. They were not to accept Christian objects as pawns and were reminded that they could not enter churches.[133] If they did, they would have to repent; and those who stayed away would be rewarded.[134] Pietists must not appear to show respect for any form of Christian ritual.[135] The good Jew had to avoid bowing down before a church, and if his home was built next to one, the windows had to be sealed off.[136] "When building his house, a person should not install windows facing a church, for when he bends down to open the windows it will seem as if he were bowing to the church. Furthermore, he will always be turning toward the church in violation of the scripture, "Do not turn to false gods [Lev. 19:4]."[137] If a Jew met a Christian on the way to church, he was not allowed to lend him money, as the Christian might use it to support the church. Although these rulings seem to reflect the growing intrusiveness of Christian materiality in the cities where the Jews lived, it should be noted that the Pietists' exemplary tales never appeared in other Jewish sources nor were they read aloud in synagogues.[138] Nevertheless, *Sefer Chasidim* contains one precise ruling regarding how Jews were to respond if they wanted to commit image desecration, written, like many others, as an exemplary tale, with signs of a literary imagination:

> A [Jew] wanted to eliminate [on or near a Christian image]. His companion said to him, They might kill you [if you do it there]. He said, It is for the sanctification of the Name [of God]! The other one replied, You will have no reward but only sin if you jeopardize your life. Moreover, don't endanger your children and the other [Jewish] residents of the town. That which is written, *I should be sanctified in the midst of the children of Israel* [Lev. 22:32] refers to when gentiles are oppressing one [by threatening]. If he doesn't do such

> and such they will kill him. It is also written, *It is for Your sake that we are killed all day long* [Ps. 44:23]. But if one causes himself to be killed, about him it is written, *But for your own life-blood, I will require a reckoning* [Gen. 9:5], and it is [also] written, *Preserve well your life* [Deut. 4:9].[139]

Here the fictitious Jew seemed to be audaciously copying the Jewish martyrs in the crusading chronicles, believing that their desecration represented an act of martyrdom—*kiddush hashem* (sanctification of God's name). The text then gives reasons why the Jew should not defile the image. He should only do so if there was nothing to lose and he was already on the point of being killed by Christians. If he was not in mortal danger, and he still fouled the image, his offense would probably be discovered, and then the Christians would kill him, as well as other Jews, for this blasphemous act. The story demands that Pietists do not violate Christian images, not from a conviction that desecration was wrong, but from a fear for the Jews' individual and collective safety.

This is the only proscriptive text to suggest that the Jews' actual desire to desecrate a Christian image was natural. The desecration act is defecation—a clear suggestion that there was an overlap between Jewish behavior and the Christian tale of "The Virgin's Image Insulted," which, by this time, had been disseminated in Christian literary texts and sermons. Did the Pietists know the tale with its ending in which the Jewish offender is killed or were the Pietist rabbis merely predicting that the Jews' desecration of Christian images could result in death? A record of the death of a convert to Judaism, Abraham ben Abraham of Augsburg, is listed in the *Memorbuch*, the memorial book of Nuremberg (a community prayer book that listed prayers, a necrology of distinguished persons, a list of martyrs, and bequests that Jews made for the sake of their souls). Recorded in 1296 by Isaac ben Samuel of Meiningen, it mentions one Rabbi Abraham son of Abraham, a convert to Judaism (since the name "son of Abraham" is given to every convert).[140] The entry relates how "Rabbi Abraham ben Abraham from Augsburg, who was disgusted with the god of the nations and cut off the heads of the images and trusted in the Eternal One, and underwent severe sufferings and was burnt for [the sake of the] Unity of the Name on Rosh Hodesh Kislev, which was a Friday, 'in the 25th year of the sixth millennium [i.e., 5025],' 21 November 1264."[141] Since Abraham is described as "the head of all the barefoot ones," he might well have been a prominent Franciscan before his conversion, as some mendicants did not wear shoes.[142] Two Hebrew liturgical poems (*piyyutim*) written in Rabbi Abraham's honor to commemorate his death as a martyr eulogized him.[143] One written by Rabbi Mordechai ben Hillel stated: "He walked in purity and broke images . . . he revealed the glory of the Creator to the nations, denying belief in the crucified one; to martyrdom he walked like a bridegroom to the bride."[144] The other, written by Moses ben Jacob, states clearly that Abraham attacked the images in order to show their powerlessness.

> [Abraham], the pure one, went and smashed images
> That [did not defend themselves but] were like mutes before him.[145]

It is more probable that Abraham was killed because of his decision to convert to Judaism, rather than purely for his destruction of images. Perhaps this desecration was done to prove that his conversion to Judaism was genuine, a similar act to that performed by converted Jews when they re-Judaized, as reported by French Christian chronicles, although Abraham was a cradle Christian. Whether the Pietists knew of his death is not known.

The fourth mention of an image desecration allegation in a Jewish source appears in a Hebrew anonymous narrative in a parchment preserved at Parma, whose first line describes it as an "epistle by the community of Lymonyys—a letter concerning God's deliverance," probably written in the thirteenth century to judge by its neat Ashkenazic semi-cursive script. It reports how, in around 992, the Jewish community of Lymonyys—the Hebrew makes it difficult to be sure where this was—escaped death by the hands of Sehok ben Esther, "a sprout of wickedness, the stock of a snake," who was a recent convert to Christianity.[146] According to Katelyn Mesler's reading, Sehok "went and worshipped the gods of the gentiles and the idols of the children of Esau that cannot see or hear or eat or smell, to these he clung, worshipping them, and bowing down to them. But he gave no heed to the God of fortresses, and he was worse than all who preceded him." He decided to seek vengeance: "he plotted to destroy, massacre and exterminate the remnant of Israel found, young and old, children and women on a single day and plunder them abundantly." After planting a wax effigy in the wooden Holy Ark of the synagogue, Sehok went to the local ruler, accusing the community of making an image of him and placing it in the synagogue, and then piercing it with a goad three times a year to (symbolically) destroy it, "as their ancestors had killed Jesus." As Sehok stood before the leader of the land, he associated the historical Jews' desecration of a waxen image of the ruler with the dangerous accusation of the Jews' reenactment of the Crucifixion: "Do you know what this nation has done? They have taken for themselves an image of wax in your likeness, and they suspend it, [sticking] a goad in it, at the three annual pilgrimage festivals, in order to wipe you off the face of the earth. This is just what their ancestors did to your god." Sehok demanded that the Jews be destroyed and their property confiscated. But the ruler remained hesitant, demanding proof of the Jews' crime and ordered that the synagogue be searched. Entering the synagogue on the Sabbath day during the reciting of psalms, the leader's men uncovered the waxen image. The condition of the image is described by the writer: "And this was its condition: its hands on its loins, nails between its knees, and both its feet were cut off." The Jews, terrified, swore that they were innocent, "that they had not had a hand in making an idol, which the Lord God of Israel abhorred," and accused Sehok of plotting against them. One line is particularly poignant. Here they stress their strict adherence to the Second Commandment: "We conceived of making neither the writings nor the image, and heaven forbid we should make any likeness other than our God, which he has not commanded us [to do]."

The ruler agreed to Sehok's proposal that a duel be fought between Sehok himself and a representative of the Jews. But the Jews pleaded that they were unaccustomed to such practices and asked to pay a substantial bribe instead. "Here we have great wealth, silver and gold. Please take it and do as you like, however do not change the law of our God for us." The text then reports that an investigation into this case proved that the Jews did not have any writings in their books that cursed the ruler. The "artisan" who had created the image, admitted that it was Sehok who had ordered him to make it and not the Jews: "And he [the leader] ordered that the writings be sought, but they did not find them. The searchers removed books from throughout the houses of the community on the Sabbath day. When they saw that it was not the case, they returned them to their owners. And the artisan who prepared the idol announced in the sight of the people that the enemy ordered him to make it."

The Jews' tale carefully discredits each part of the Christian allegation, showing the audience/reader that an accusation of this kind is unjust and does not fit the behavior or beliefs of the Jews. The Jews are also depicted as being powerless before the evil renegade and the whims of the secular ruler and decide on the following day to fast and don sackcloth. The conclusion of the story is not recorded, although it is clear that the Jewish community was miraculously saved. At the same time, the text confirms the Jews' awareness of the allegation, how it was perilous to rely on Christian rulers to defend them, and how the allegation's consequences were unpredictable and might cause the destruction of their community. It would seem too that, because the image was made of wax, the tale might well have been a Jewish parody of the contemporaneous "Toledo" tale, which depicted fictitious Jews trying to desecrate a wax image that they made in the synagogue. However, in the Jewish version given in the Parma manuscript, rather than being destroyed, the Jews were saved by God's miracle.

Our final source, a Hebrew tale, which seems to be associated with the one above, described the misfortunes of a Jewish community as a result of this allegation. It was said to have occurred in 1062 (though the evidence comes from a seventeenth-century text). The Jews of Pescara, Italy, were falsely accused of placing a wax image on a worm-eaten table and torturing it to death as if it were Christ, causing the image to bleed. The accused were tortured and the Jewish community was fined and lost its synagogue, which was transformed into a church.[147] This seventeenth-century work incorporated many earlier features of the desecration narrative, as well as the Christian idea that the image bled (which had never been included before in Jewish sources).

These five sources confirm that "Christ of Beirut," "Toledo," and "The Virgin's Image Insulted" were known among the Jewish communities of Ashkenaz and that the Jewish tales were manipulated as some sort of Jewish response. It was the Pietists' text that propagated the idea that Jews would naturally want to attack Christian images. One of the main features of Pietist theology was, of course, a desire to act *lifnim mi-shurat ha-din*—to go beyond what the Torah commanded—in order to show one's dedication to God. In this sense they were religious extremists who often made stringent demands on themselves beyond those required by Jewish law. The different endings of these Jewish tales reflect Jewish uncertainty as to what consequences they would face as a result of a false accusation. A description of blood seeping from an image was added only in the seventeenth century, perhaps when Jews were no longer so fearful of blood libel allegations and felt more free to reflect upon them.

A Jewish Response in Hebrew Illuminated Manuscripts

It is almost impossible to find any sort of depiction of Christian images in Hebrew illuminated manuscripts. In general, when Jews polemicized about the foolishness of what Christians believed, or the idolatry of the Christian religion, they usually referred broadly to worship, and not to image worship specifically.[148] On the other hand, one may suggest that the image of Israelites looting Egypt on the eve of the exodus in the 1320 Catalonian Golden Haggadah (Figure 15)[149] was in fact a comment on the Christians' excessive materiality.[150]

Ostensibly, this picture shows Israelites plundering the property of the Egyptians before their exodus from Egypt (Exod. 12:35).[151] But its depiction has not been set by the artists in the ancient Egyptian world; rather it has been recast in the fourteenth century, confirming the Israelites' need to contextualize their liberation within a more contemporaneous scene. It shows three slaves eagerly removing objects—in particular a chest, a chalice, and a ciborium (Eucharist container) from a Christian treasury, possibly within a church, as though they were retaliating against Christian domination and excessive materiality instead of the oppressive regime of slavery in ancient Egypt. A younger Israelite stands behind, holding in his hands two bags of coins. These Israelites, dressed in the short tunic of slaves, having gained

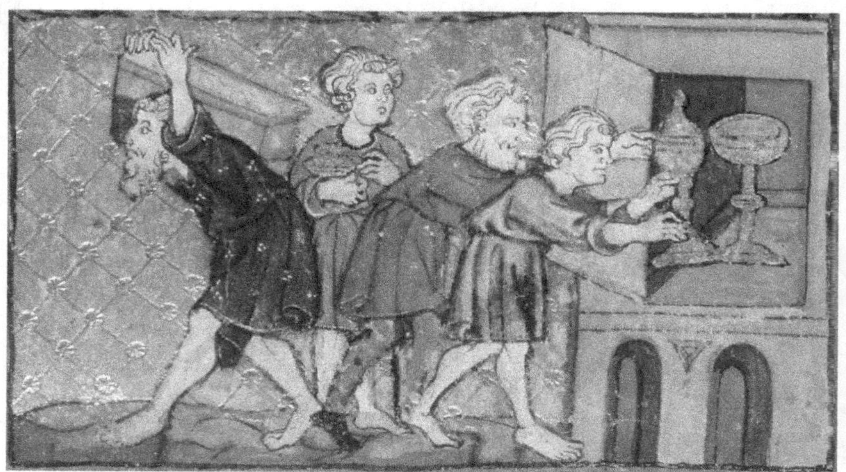

Figure 15. The Israelites despoiling the Egyptians. Image from folio 13 of the Golden Haggadah, 1325–1349. © The British Library Board.

access to unattended Christian liturgical vessels, are stealing them. In reality such action would have endangered the lives of medieval Jews.

The ciborium and chalice are also depicted as objects being carried away by the Israelites in the later Catalonian Rylands Haggadah (ca. 1330–1340; fol. 18) and the closely associated Catalonian Brother Haggadah (third quarter of the fourteenth century; fol. 6). But it is only the Golden Haggadah that depicts these other articles being removed from the inside of a building (a church).[152] The detailed knowledge of these church objects could be related to the fact that these objects were often crafted by Jewish silversmiths. It is possible, too, that the large number of affluent French Jews who had entered Catalonia after the expulsions in 1306 and 1320 had had such objects as pawns in France and this influenced the Golden Haggadah's iconography.[153]

There is no inclusion in any of these Haggadot of crucifixes or images of Mary or the saints, and therefore no comment on the image desecration narrative. Scholars argue that the illustrators of Hebrew manuscripts would have nothing to do with Christian attempts to introduce crucifixes into Old Testament stories.[154] In Christian Bible illustrations, the wood carried by Isaac to the Akedah is frequently arranged crosswise as a clear prefiguration of Jesus carrying his own cross to Calvary, whereas Jewish illustrations avoid representing this act (Gen. 22:6). In the Golden Haggadah, Isaac lies bound on the ground ready to be sacrificed, and there is no wood in the image.[155] In the same Golden Haggadah and other Sephardic Haggadot that depict Jacob blessing Joseph's sons, Jacob is sitting up in bed and, as Katrin Kogman-Appel argues, is "shown from the side. Although his arms are crossed, the position of the arms does not create a visual association with a cross with right angles. The focus on the crossed arms, which characterizes the Christian parallels, is avoided."[156] This reflects a firm resolution on the part of Jewish artists to avert all suggestions of crucifix imagery in Jewish art.[157]

In the thirteenth and fourteenth centuries, Hebrew illuminated manuscripts served as both functional ritual objects and status symbols.[158] These works confirm the frequent interaction between Jewish scribes and Christian artists who collaborated in urban workshops to produce valuable figurative codices that some medieval rabbis tried hard to prohibit. These Jewish works were very similar in design and layout to Christian liturgical books.[159] Yet the subtle differences need to be noted. For it is here that one notices the Jews' sensitivity to, and knowledge of, Christian ritual objects as well as their meticulous care not to depict any crucifix images in their art.

A Different Type of Response: The Early Modern Image Desecration Folktale

Descriptions of both image and crucifix desecration appear again in early modern Jewish historiographical texts that recorded different folk traditions without giving provenance or any comment. These sad tales, which at first traveled by word of mouth within and between communities, were later recorded by scholars in Spain and Italy for the educated elite of the various Jewish communities.[160] Once recorded, they were read out in synagogues, classrooms, and study halls, and their continual telling reflected their audiences' hunger for tales in which Jews survived, usually by the work of God's hidden hand, the most heinous acts against them. Storytelling conjured up a world of communal listening, of young and old sharing and shaping the collective memory of Jewish folklore. These Jewish storytellers used personal and collective experiences, as well as practical knowledge gained over centuries, to advise their fellow religionists how to behave. When these tales overlap with Christian ones, it is assumed that this is a reaction by the Jews.

In general, the authenticity of the events in these stories defies historical investigation, but their import for our purposes lies in the repeated tales of image desecration against Jews in medieval Ashkenaz and Sepharad (Iberia) and their effect on the interpersonal relationships between Jews and Christians. They illustrate the Jews' awareness at this time of how easily the accusation of image desecration might have been leveled at them and the expected consequences. The number of times image desecration tales appear in these works is noteworthy and demands detailed analysis.

The works include two sixteenth-century texts: Solomon Ibn Verga's *Shevet Yehudah* and Elijah Capsali's *Eliyahu Zuta*. Solomon Ibn Verga, a Jewish physician of Castile, who had some personal experience of defending his coreligionists before Christian authorities, wrote his popular *Shevet Yehudah* ("The Tribe of Judah" or "The Staff of Judah") some thirty years after the Jews' expulsion from Spain in 1492.[161] Having crossed over to Portugal, he and his fellow Jews faced forced conversion in 1497.[162] After the Lisbon massacre of 1506, during which he was outside the city, he left Portugal. He died en route to the Ottoman Empire, where his son completed, edited, and had his work published in Adrianople in 1554 and then in Sabbioneta in 1567.[163] This work, which became one of the most popular and influential Hebrew books of its kind, reaching Christian audiences as well as Jewish, was translated into Latin, Spanish, and Yiddish. It reflects his own traumatic experience of expulsion and focuses on the social and political realities of the Jews' misfortune and persecutions from ancient times until the 1506 massacre.[164] It includes three tales of image desecration, as well as a brief study of the 1506 slaughter, already discussed in Chapter 3, linking this devastating event to an insulting remark made against a crucifix by a crypto-Jew.[165] There are seventy-six tales in all, most of which discuss blood libel, so the three tales of image desecration represent only 4 percent of the total. The three desecration tales are repetitive and difficult to interpret, involving a skeptical Spanish king, popes (who usually defend the Jews and Judaism), a secular ruler, tribulations and threats of destruction against the Jews, exile (in all of them), and forced conversion (in one).[166] In all tales the accusation of image desecration is made by Christian churchmen (sometimes unnamed mendicants), whose baseless evil allegations were intent on harming the Jews. The churchmen create and disseminate the allegation and the mob respond to it unquestioningly, ready to act out their natural aggression against the Jews. In two of the tales, Jews are actually killed. Two of the three seem to be linked to real historical events as will be shown. The faceless and impassioned masses who fully support the ecclesiastics are there to enact their fury on the Jews, sometimes of their own accord and other times incited by churchmen. The Jews remain powerless to counter these allegations. Ibn Verga makes no comment about the image desecration allegation, refusing to descend into anti-Christian polemics, and remaining indifferent to its religious and theological implications.[167] He is perhaps the first Jewish writer to offer secular explanations of anti–Judaism. When non-Jewish authorities can be convinced that their interest lies in the protection of the Jews, they act accordingly; when they are convinced of the reverse, the Jews suffer.

The image desecration allegations were probably associated in Ibn Verga's mind with the social and economic tensions between Jews and Christians, expounded elsewhere in his text.[168] In chapter 14, Ibn Verga describes how a righteous pope in Rome was urged by his sister Sancha to expel the Jews from his domains because, she argued, Jews were "impure souls," ridden with guilt for committing the original sin in the Garden of Eden and then failing to accept Christ's salvation.[169] She alleged that, if the pope did this, it would encourage other rulers to do the same, and he would receive his reward in paradise. The pope refused to agree to her proposal, but she returned a few days later with a group of archbishops who testified that the Jews of Rome habitually mocked images of Jesus (צלם ישו) during public processions.[170]

No further evidence was offered and there was no further discussion of this allegation. The Jews—again powerless before the pope and his sister—are shown appealing to King Robert of Jerusalem, who "loved the pope" and was favorable to the Jews, to act as an intermediary. They offered to pay any sum that Robert might need in order to persuade the archbishops to hold back and therefore provide more time for them to leave the pope's domains with their worldly goods. The pope replied to Robert that he had made a vow to his sister to expel the Jews, and the only way to avoid this was by bribing her to change her mind. King Robert then offered her 100,000 florins from the Jews, which she accepted in appeasement. Sancha appears to have been a mercenary woman—the large financial grant placated her—and Ibn Verga concludes by stating that thereafter she favored the Jews and begged the pope not to expel them.[171] Here, image desecration is shown as a false charge that could potentially cause the Jews' expulsion. The pope was capable of being influenced by his family members and his toleration of the Jews in Rome could be withdrawn as a result. Even though another Christian leader was brought in to mediate, the situation came down to money that the Jews had to pay. The Jews could therefore stay in Rome—perhaps a reflection that they seemed to be able to maintain their footing there against all odds. But they had to be wary as to their presence during Christian processions.

Also in Ibn Verga's sixteenth-century work is a tale that, besides describing desecration of a crucifix (the Hebrew term is עץ ישו—"a tree of Jesus"), has similar features to the thirteenth-century Parma manuscript noted earlier. In chapter 19, Ibn Verga reports how, in Trani, Italy, a Christian enemy (in this tale a priest) had got into a disagreement with a Jew and hidden a crucifix in the refuse outside the Jew's house.[172] The priest then went to the "judges," saying that he had dreamt that a certain Jew had placed a crucifix in the rubbish.[173] When the crucifix was uncovered by a crowd, passions were inflamed, and the mob demanded that the Jewish community be violently attacked. But secular officials were skeptical, clearly more supportive of the Jews, and realized immediately that this was the priest's preposterous fabrication. Meanwhile a fractious mob began to attack the Jews and riots spread to Salerno and Naples. Although some Jews were able to hide in the officials' houses and then escape to "distant lands," most Jews of the area were forced to convert. Ibn Verga lamented the prominent and worthy Jews lost to the Jewish communities of southern Italy. The story ends with these words: "Later on, it became known to the king [of Naples] that the priest had made a false accusation, and the king commanded that the priest be hanged, but the people rebelled against this judgment, so the king decided to expel him to distant islands."[174] The tale has some historical foundation. Between 1288 and 1293, the Jewish communities in southern Italy, specifically in the areas mentioned by Ibn Verga—Naples, Trani, and Salerno—had been forced to convert, but not as a result of image desecration accusations.[175] Moreover, the Jews' quick decision to convert is described here without comment, assumed to be made under pain of death.[176] The trauma of forced conversion was clearly a central aspect of Ibn Verga's own personal experience, no matter how much he tried to play it down. The tale also implies that hiding a Christian object in Jews' possessions was a way of incriminating them. Secular officials might support the Jews against accusations by ecclesiastics but were powerless when these churchmen rallied a violent mob. It was these ecclesiastics who could orchestrate the destruction of Jewish communities and the conversion of their members. There was no justice for the Jews, and the priest who had laid the false allegation against them escaped unharmed. Yet Jews were able to escape and survive.

The last tale of Ibn Verga—in chapter 64—describes how, in another attempt to get Rome's Jews expelled, an archbishop falsely accused a Jew of stealing a sacred silver image (צלם אחד של כסף) from "their houses of idols" (מבת תועבותם) as Ibn-Verga calls Christian churches.[177] The accused Jew was hanged, and the pope, angry that the Jews had committed this offense, ordered them to be exiled; their wealth would go to their children, who would be forcibly converted. However, the night after the pope had ordered that the expulsion decree be written, the archbishop fell to the ground and died. The pope, convinced that his death was a punishment for the archbishop's threat to the Jews, decided not to make the expulsion decree public. In the meantime, the ministers and bishops, not realizing that the pope had changed his mind, were celebrating the forthcoming announcement. They were all killed when a powerful earthquake damaged the house they were in; miraculously, no other buildings were affected. When the pope heard about the disaster, he assumed that the churchmen had also been punished for intending to harm the Jews. He ordered that the Christian who had told the archbishop about the thieving Jew be arrested and tortured. The offender maintained that the story had been made up by the archbishop who had died. The pope said: "I suspect that it was on account of the Jews that the archbishop met his fate [that is, in the Jews' place]. I think that what has been said about them that they kill Jesus is untrue and whatever happens I keep seeing that God works on their behalf. And if this was not the case, he would not be doing anything because he is a god of righteousness and I love him. And my soul should die with the best of them."[178] The pope demanded that the decree be torn up and that the person who lied about the Jews' desecration should burn together with the decree. Ibn Verga reports a happy ending, almost worthy of a fairy tale: "From this moment on this pope respected the Jews and did what they wanted and cherished them. For the rest of his days, he sat with peace and contentment and nothing harmed him."[179] Here again the pope is shown as an unreliable ruler, inconsistent in his policies toward the Jews of Rome and affected by "miraculous" or supernatural incidents. As a result, Jewish existence hovered between residence and expulsion.

Was Ibn Verga hopeful that popes in Rome were more favorable to Jews than rulers elsewhere? Could this tale have been adapted from an earlier Christian story in which the Jews were depicted not only desecrating Christian symbols but causing the earthquake as well? The Jews had been killed and the fury of the elements subsided.[180] This tale had already been told by the Christian chronicler Adémar of Charbannes, an Aquitainian Benedictine (d. 1034).[181] Although Ibn Verga depicts the accusation as false, he makes no attempt to understand the basis of the image desecration allegation or why it is repeatedly directed against Jews. Even his report of the Lisbon massacre in 1506 with its mention of the verbal desecration/insult of a crucifix made by a Marrano fits this mold. Ibn Verga attributes the incident to the machinations of the Dominicans, otherwise known as the Friars Preachers.[182] He mentions, without much attention or discussion, a false miracle and a comment made on it by a crypto-Jew:

> And they concocted a ruse and made a hollow crucifix with an aperture in the rear, and its front of glass, and they would pass through there a lit candle, saying that the flame emerged from the crucifix, while the people would prostrate themselves and cry: "See the great miracle! This is a sign that God judges with fire all the Jewish seed!"
>
> A Marrano came there who had not heard these words, and he innocently remarked: "Would that there were a miracle of water instead of fire, for in view of the drought it is water that we should rather need!" The Christians, whose desire was evil, arose and said: "Behold, he mocks us!" That mob immediately took him out and killed him.[183]

Ibn Verga does not see the supposed insult as the sole reason for the massacre. He links the cause to both a secret Seder that had been conducted already in Lisbon and for which crypto-Jews were still imprisoned and the abuses attributed to a Jewish tax collector, Mascarenhas.[184] Yet again, he refuses either to blame the secular magistrates of Lisbon or the king himself.

Contemporaneous with Ibn Verga, Elijah Capsali, (b. ca. 1485, d. after 1550), who had studied in the Ashkenazic yeshiva of Rabbi Judah Mintz in Padua, in his miscellany *Seder Eliyahu Zuta* (The Little Order of Elia) written during the plague that broke out in Crete in 1523, gives a desecration allegation as one of the reasons why Jews were expelled from Ashkenaz.[185] He tells one of the longest and most complex desecration tales narrated in a Jewish source and invokes the authority of hallowed texts, particularly the book of Esther and other parts of the Hebrew Bible, to legitimate the tale's motifs. Capsali presents an allegory, which he states was told to him by "speakers of truth" in Padua.[186] "And now we will describe the abominable deeds that were committed against the Jewish people in the land of Ashkenaz, as was verified to us by speakers of truth, who related them to me when I was in Padua."[187] This is not history, but folklore.

> There was a Jew in the land of Ashkenaz [Esther 2:5], and he was very rich and great; "the One Who Blesses blessed his handiwork, and his livestock spread throughout the land" [Job 1:10]. "And it was a day of darkness and thick darkness, a day of cloud and thick cloud" [Joel 2:2]. One of the ministers[188] of the land was envious of him, of his considerable wealth and his many properties. For a long time he hated him, and planned to take his wealth and kill him and he took advice regarding what to do to him. "Perhaps he would be able to strike him." [Num. 22:6] He had evil thoughts in his heart. When the minister saw that the Jew enjoyed the favor of the ministers of the land and its barons, he desired to harm him and became filled with rage. The hostile minister turned and "went to his home sad and upset" [1 Kings 20:43],[189] and he desired to destroy and kill all the Jews who were in that land. He considered what he might do to this Jew because of his laws.
>
> That day was a troublesome and blasphemous day. The minister went to the home of a certain shoemaker who made shoes for this

Jew from *tachash* leather [Ezek. 16:10] and he said to the shoemaker: "Craftsman, I wish to tell you something in secret." The shoemaker stood before him in fear and said: "What is the reason that you have come before me, minister." The minister replied: "Listen to what I am going to command you to do in order to remove the Jews who hate us from the land, and I will pay you." The craftsman said, "Whatever you ask, I will do for you." The minister replied and seduced him, and said: "I will fulfill your needs, just listen to me. Take this image [הזה מלצה] and put it inside the Jew's shoe and sew it well. When the Jew comes to collect his shoes, put the shoe on him, and nobody will know anything about it." But the minister seduced him with his mouth; he lied to him with his tongue [Ps. 78:36].[190] He [the shoemaker] was persuaded and took the image and sewed it under the Jew's shoe. The Jew came to collect the shoes and put them on as usual, without noticing anything.

"It happened ten days after that the Lord struck Nabal" [1 Sam. 25:38] and the minister came in secret to the shoemaker and said to him, "Pretend to be sick, tell your household that you are about to die. The friar[191] will then come to see you, as is the custom, for you to confess your sins to him, and then tell him the secret. So the shoemaker carried out this evil plot. He deceived the household into believing that he was dying and lay on his bed for several days. The minister said, "See the shoemaker is dying; call the priest to come to him and take his confession, as is the tradition." So the friar came to the shoemaker's house and gave him the Eucharist, but the shoemaker began to act as if he were losing his mind. He gave a great and bitter cry and said: "Remove everyone from my presence." Everyone left so that no one else was there when he confessed to the priest. The shoemaker began to weep [Gen. 48:1–2] and said: "Save me, my lord the priest, 'shave me with the great razor' [Isa. 7:20] as I have behaved like a fool and I have done evil. 'Wash me thoroughly of my iniquity, and purify me of my sin'" [Ps. 51:4]. Then he became silent and mute "like a mute who does not open his mouth" [Ps. 38:14] as if he were ashamed and humiliated, and acted as if he were "awake but not awake, asleep but not asleep" [Babylonian Talmud, Pesachim 120a]. The friar grabbed him and said, "Do not be humiliated or ashamed before me. If you have sinned you can atone, it is the way of 'all sons of man, all mankind, both rich and poor'[Ps. 49:3] to sin and rebel against their king and their god for we are all 'formed from clay,' [Job 33:6] and 'there is no man so wholly righteous on earth that he [always] does good and never sins' [Eccles. 7:20] so do not try to hide anything from me." The shoemaker refused to speak to the priest, but the priest continued to try and persuade him, yet he was like someone who was dead and could not hear. When the priest saw this, he again tried to appeal to him, but the shoemaker did not listen. So the friar became angry and said, "Tell me your sin so that I can know what to do for you. If you do not, know that even your original sins will not be forgiven, and you will die as a villain, as 'one who conceals his sins will not succeed' [Prov. 28:14]." So when [the shoemaker] heard this, he continued to trick the friar, and began to "stagger like a drunkard, all his wisdom was destroyed" [Ps. 107:27]. He opened his eyes and looked behind him, and looked around his house, casting eyes in each room, lest he might see there a man or a woman, a child or an adult. He continued with this trickery so that the priest would believe him.

He then opened his mouth and "cursed the day he was born" [Job 3:2] and he told the priest the following:
"You know that this particular Jew is a regular client of mine, and he is very beloved by me and knows my inner thoughts and my dealings. I have not asked anything of him, nor have I hidden anything from him. I have trusted him, and he trusted me as one of his household, and so he has revealed to me his secrets and mysteries. Recently the Jew came to me and he had in his hand your god and his image [אלהיך וצלמו] and he said to me, "You have been aware of the love and friendship that was between yourself and me forever." And I said, "Yes, sir." And he said to me, "I have trusted you, my brother, do not disappoint me and do not turn me away empty-handed." I said to him, "I will fulfill your needs, my brother. Everything you say to me I will do." He quickly took out the image [צלם] from underneath his clothes and said to me: "Take this and sew it under the shoes that you make for me," and he promised me a sum of money to do his will. I did as he requested as I was enticed by his words. I held your god [באלהיך] and I sewed it under his shoes and

he gave me a sum of money for payment, 'behold, they are hidden . . . in the midst of my tent' [Josh. 7:21]. You must take the money from there and take it to the house of your god [i.e., church], as I have blasphemed. Forgive me for my sin.

He gave [the friar] his key and the priest angrily opened his chest and saw the gold pieces. When the priest saw the gold pieces that were found in the possession of the shoemaker and because he could not believe how the shoemaker had such money, the priest trembled and said, "This is what the Jew did with his image!" [זאת עשה היהודי בצלמו].[192] So he ran to the house of the king and the princes, and told them all these things. When they saw the gold pieces, they believed the shoemaker's tale.

Then the king sent for the ministers of the chariot and the officers and said to them. "Hurry and fetch this Jew." "The couriers went forth in haste" [Esther 3:15].[193] They turned toward the Jew's house and arrested him, binding his hands with new ropes, and brought him to the king and the ministers. They asked him, "Where are the shoes that this shoemaker made for you? Do not conceal anything from us lest we torture you." So the poor Jew, trusting in his innocence and his faith, immediately stated that he did not know what they were talking about. He removed his shoes and ripped them open. He then found inside them their god and his image [אלהיהם וצלמו].

The king and the princes trembled with fear. The evil minister who had been responsible for this series of events continued to accuse and slander the Jews. The king and his ministers all assembled, and the friar who had made known the incident summoned all his colleagues from one end of the city to the other, to see the Jew who had "kicked" the king of the land and their god. The priests spoke to the king and they accused [the Jew] and the king and the minister said: there is but one law for the Jews [based on Esther 4:11], to be burned, man and woman, from babe to suckling. They passed judgment by their laws against the Jew as said, and then they burned him, and he died sanctifying the Lord, our God and his Torah, and he gave up his life for his people.

Then they lit a fire and burned this splendid community, and they all died at God's word and in sanctification of our God. None of

> them escaped, except for one wealthy old woman and her two young great-grandchildren, a boy and a girl. She sheltered them and placed them under God's protection. They were not discovered, and she fled for her life and took with her great treasure. She brought them to Candia [Crete] and had them marry each other when they grew up, as they were cousins. The young boy who escaped was Reb Eliezer Ha-Cohen Tiroshlin the Elder[194] and his wife was called Hannah. They were the parents of Reb Ishpira and Mina, my grandmother, wife of my grandfather, the sage Reb Elkanah Dilmedigo, son of Reb Abba Ha-Cohen the Elder.[195]Aside from these, no one escaped. They were all put into the fire and consumed, due to my sins. "And God's fire burned against them" [Num. 11:1].[196]

This tale has no real foundation in recorded history, though it may have a tenuous connection with the expulsion of the Jews from France under Philip Augustus. As mentioned in Chapter 2, the French chronicler Rigord of Saint-Denis, King Philip Augustus's clerical biographer, reported that one of the reasons why the Jews were expelled from France was that an anonymous Jewish moneylender in Paris had defecated "on a golden cross enriched with jewels."[197] Had Capsali changed the allegation to a less disgusting violation—thereby "transforming an essentially non-Jewish story into one relevant for the Jewish perception of the self," as Robert Bonfil suggests?[198] Capsali had created a formula for depicting a complex image desecration allegation as the reason why Jews had been driven out of a medieval kingdom.

The anonymous but prominent Jew could hardly have been a powerful landowner in Ashkenaz—an area where Jews could not own land in the late medieval period. Capsali seemed instead to be imagining the status of a Jew in Sepharad, a member of the affluent Spanish Jewish courtier class. Yet the fictitious Jew is neither pious nor righteous. His wealth causes envy and enmity with one particular Christian minister, even though the Jews generally, it seemed, interact well with all the other ministers. This one minister—like Haman in the Esther story—decided that all the Jews must be killed because of his jealousy of one (Mordechai). The enmity though is not based on religious antagonism but on the jealousy of the Jew.

This minister is unable to bring about the Jew's destruction alone. He has to concoct a way to outsmart the Jew and so he employs the services of the Jew's shoemaker, who until this moment had been a loyal friend to his Jewish client. The minister uses his power and authority over the shoemaker to force him to agree to place a Christian image inside the sole of the Jew's new shoes. When the Jew wears his new shoes, he desecrates the image because he kicks "their god" without realizing it. This trick—namely, hiding something in the garments or the shoes that can cause later harm to their owner—was quite a common theme in Hebrew folklore stories.[199]

The tale continues with the second visit of the minister to the shoemaker ten days later. He has further precise orders. The shoemaker is now to pretend that he is about to die and during this subterfuge has to call a friar to whom he confesses his sins. The story goes to great lengths to dramatize the shoemaker's efforts to feign death. His pretense is acted out in an overdramatic way, with cunning gestures and rhetorical speech, whereby the shoemaker evokes the hope that he will be purified of his sins before Judgment Day. Eventually he shows himself willing to confess his "secret" to the friar. In order to be believed, the shoemaker overemphasizes his personal devotion, intimacy, and friendship with the Jew, and the hefty payment he had received from the Jew to fulfill the Jew's request—that he sew a Christian image into the soles of the Jew's shoes. To prove that this had occurred, he requests that the friar take the payment from his money chest (the money had been given to him by the minister) and donate it to the church. When the friar opens the chest and sees the money, his anger rises against the Jew and he rushes to report the misdeed to the king and his princes. In these final scenes, the friar urges the court to punish the Jew and condemns him and all the Jews of the land. The involvement of the friar and his colleagues is stressed here and seems to reflect the power of the mendicant orders over European secular rulers. It is they who demand an auto-da-fé and in the tale burn not just the individual Jew but the whole Jewish community. According to Capsali's reckoning, the destruction had supposedly taken place about six or seven generations before him—Elkanah Dilmedigo was Capsali's grandfather on his mother's side.[200]

What messages did this powerful cautionary tale intend to convey? The Jew is not a particularly worthy hero—he is wanting in experience and diplomacy. The first message seems to be that the Jews should not parade their wealth in front of Christians. The second, that Jews could not trust the judicial system of Ashkenaz because it could be manipulated by wicked Christians who would trick them. The third, that the mendicant orders had power to rally mobs against the Jews and cause their destruction. The fourth, that one cannot rely on "friends" who are not Jews. The Christian shoemaker needs little persuasion to betray his valued Jewish customer and goes so far as to blaspheme his own god out of hatred for the Jews. Perhaps last, the message was that everything bad that happened was a punishment for the Jews. There seemed to be no message about the actual accusation of image desecration. Instead the words used to describe "the god and his image," as if they were separate entities, highlight the Jewish belief that Christian images were idols rather than visual representatives of their god.

In these sixteenth-century postexilic texts, image desecration had become a recognized allegation and feature of the narrative of Jewish persecution in both Ashkenaz and Sepharad. Late medieval Jews were now copying the Christians by producing their own tale in which Jews are falsely accused of image desecration. This had less to do with reality than with Capsali's desire to fit chimerical allegations securely into early modern accounts of medieval Jewish survival. It seems to represent another baseless Christian allegation that only resulted in disproportionate persecution and suffering on the part of Jews. Perhaps it is not surprising that, in the seventeenth century, the Jewish philosopher, physician, and polemicist Isaac Cardoso should complain in his *Las excelencias de los Hebreos* of 1679 that Jews alone were continually accused of destroying miraculous images or hosts, because they had no power to dispute these false allegations: "when Calvinists or the Protestants or the Muslims drag Christs on the ground, trample hosts, destroy images or demolish altars, no miracles are invented claiming that the statues speak or the hosts leap or shed blood, but it is only when those [deeds] are attributed to the Jews, who are like shorn sheep and tame lambs. There is no one to protect or defend them, and they lack the power to defend themselves, and the voice with which to complain."[201]

In his defense of the "Hebraic truth," Cardoso listed ten calumnies against the Jews. The ninth of these asserted that Jews "desecrate images and are sacrilegious."[202] The allegation was baseless, he argued, because Jews regarded these objects as idols, and it was an abomination to interact with them. He also defended the Jews' position, reminding his readers that it was only in the Land of Israel that Jews had been allowed to destroy images and idols: "Only in the land of ours could we break the images, and destroy the idols, but God does not command that we will tear them down in strange lands."[203]

Cardoso argued that the allegation had terrible consequences for Jews and New Christians on both sides of the Atlantic: they were accused of attacking sacred objects—defiling crucifixes and statues of Jesus and the Virgin.[204] Cardoso was the first Jewish writer to mention statues of the Virgin.

The desecration of this image is linked to judicial accusations of real Jews, particularly in Italy in the early modern period, as will be seen in the next two chapters.[205]

Conclusion

Although the Hebrew Bible demanded that Jews should destroy the images and idols in the Holy Land, their changed circumstances soon made it impracticable to do so. Instead, ambiguous Talmudic rulings set up a code of law that enjoined the Jews to keep as far away as possible from the idols/images of non-Jews. It seems probable that these rulings were also enforced in the light of the Byzantine church's own discursive ideas about Jews and iconoclasm.

Medieval Jewish sources show how rabbis had to engage in a complex process of navigation and acculturation and develop a form of resistance adapted through time to deal with the increasing ubiquity of sacred images and the threat that members of Jewish communities would be accused of desecrating them. Not surprisingly, the sources urged the Jews to be passive—to avoid all contact and to keep away. In fact Victor of Carben (1423–1515) converted to Christianity in 1476 or 1477 and became a Dominican monk in Cologne; his work *Juden Büchlein* (1508), which described Jewish customs and rituals in early modern Germany, referred to several interesting actions performed by Jews to show their contempt for Christian crucifixes and crosses.[206] Victor records how Jews avoided walking near a church or a wayside shrine and, if this could not be helped, would utter a curse, such as "The Lord tears down the proud man's house" to demonstrate their disdain and the destruction they longed for.[207] This might well have been one of the utterances of early modern Germans Jews.

The avoidance of images was also disseminated through rabbinic responsa, which ordered Jews not to take these objects as security for loans and mocked the specific images, suggesting they were impure. They also alluded to Jews' tales of Jewish martyrs during the First and Second Crusades, which extolled the Torah as superior to crucifixes. The sources also developed a narrative about image desecration that both laughed at the allegation and warned Jews against committing it.

Jews compiled their own response not only in chronicles, poems, and tales but also, very occasionally, in their own figurative representations.

Through all these sources, it becomes clear that Jewish communities were fully aware and feared that they could be accused of image desecration and expected the repercussions to be harsh. But at the same time, they did not fear charges of image desecration as much as those of ritual murder and host desecration. Since charges of image desecration did not often come before courts of law, they responded with allegorical tales expressing abhorrence of these images rather than instructing Jews how to defend themselves against the allegation.

These texts also confirm a general contempt for crucifixes and crosses rather than for images of the Virgin or saints.[208] Because the cross and the crucifix were directly associated with Christ's body and his death, they received more varied responses from the Jews, and so we see certain derogatory terms repeatedly appearing in these texts, where the crucifix is miscalled a thorn bush or even a cabbage stalk. Allegations that Jews desecrated images of the Virgin are common in Christian sources; Jewish writings have very little to say about them. It confirms an overlap between fantasy and reality for, despite what Christianity propagated, it was crosses and crucifixes that disturbed Jews more than images or statues of the Virgin.

By the early modern period, the incorporation of the image desecration allegation into their post-exilic tales allowed them to disseminate a new version for their own purposes, defending their position. This transformed the allegation and its possible effect into an early modern appreciation and glorification of medieval Jewish survival. As a result, these writers seem to assign the allegation an unduly prominent role in their own accounts of medieval Jewish history, so that these writings could stand as another example of the Jews' ferocious tenacity in the face of the Christian majority.

Chapter 5

Image Desecration in Medieval and Early Modern Italy

> Because of the hatred of the Christian religion and the faith of the Redeemer that the Jews hold, which causes them to curse Jesus, without whom no one can live, these Jews will face the same penalties [as Christians] . . . if they dare to scoff at and mock the Christians or their rituals, the churches, the altars, the bells, the cemeteries of the dead, and the other sacred things, or if they attack the crosses and images of the saints or show signs of irreverence.
>
> —From the "Editto del Sant'Ufficio," September 8, 1667

This chapter traces the chronological development of the image desecration allegation in north-central Italy in the late medieval and early modern period. From the fifteenth century, Italian archives preserve many more judicial records, and it becomes possible to compare the Jew who was brought to court on charges of desecrating or showing disrespect for images with the fictive Jew of the medieval tales and legends. It may be that the Jew portrayed by court records is as much of an artificial construct as the Jew of the stories, but he is the result of different processes, which usually stem from denunciation by a Christian (occasionally by fellow Jews), investigation by a tribunal, the receipt of evidence that is often conflicting, and a decision to punish or release him. We have already seen in Chapter 3 something of the activities of the newly constituted Spanish Inquisition. In this chapter much use will be made of the records of the newly organized Roman Inquisition.

In the Italian states, religious offenses attributed to professing Jews, attacks both on religion and on public order supposedly launched by people outside the church, could be tried by lay magistrates or by ecclesiastical tribunals. Charges of ritual murder were judged by secular magistrates but, at least from the later sixteenth century, many charges against Jews of image desecration or disrespect were judged by branches of the Roman Inquisition. Arguably church courts should have no jurisdiction over unbaptized Jews, but in Italy the Roman Inquisition tried to assert its claims to defend the church and the things it held sacred against attacks from outsiders and misbelievers; these were summarized in *Antiqua iudaeorum improbitas*, a controversial bull of Pope Gregory XIII in 1581. Unbaptized Jews were disciplined not for heresy but for blasphemy and disrespect.

Inquisition records are particularly revealing on account of the dialogues between judges, witnesses, and prisoners, which they often preserve, together with denunciations and sentences. The archives of the Roman Inquisition in Modena are exceptionally complete, and I shall draw on them heavily for the purposes of this chapter, though not to the exclusion of other sources. It is obviously questionable whether inquisitorial sources can reveal what really happened, when those involved in the case were probably lying or working off personal scores. But inquisitorial rules and procedures demanded that denunciation be supported by eyewitness testimony, which meant that any accusation or evidence against the Jews was examined carefully. The Holy Office showed itself to be a court that focused on ascertaining the truth according to seventeenth-century standards; this meant distinguishing between innocence and guilt, differentiating between degrees of guilt, and punishing the Jews accordingly.

The total number of known judicial cases in which Jews were charged with desecrating images from the beginning of the fourteenth century to the end of the seventeenth is seventy-one.[1] It is hardly surprising that Italy, out of all Europe, should record such a large number of cases. This reflects the widespread presence of Jews throughout the peninsula in daily contact with Christians who frequently used these objects. Unlike other states in western Europe, several princely states of northern Italy and the mercantile republics of Florence and Venice had decided, because of the economic benefits the Jews provided, to continue to tolerate rather than expel them.

In thirteenth- and fourteenth-century Italy, the mendicant orders, particularly the Franciscans in their great churches, were already using sacred images to educate illiterate people and remind them of sacred stories and mysteries.[2] These orders supported their own image cults by housing images that had already shown their miraculous powers and taking charge of liturgical services dedicated to them.[3] Crucifixes and images of the Virgin and Child, the Passion, and saints were displayed in confraternity chapels, oratories, cathedrals, convents, monasteries, friaries, and parish churches across northern Italy.[4] Churches were lavishly furnished with fresco cycles often commissioned by wealthy laypersons as manifestations of their hopes for salvation, and the liturgy used a vast array of objects including sacred vestments, chalices, ciboria, patens, candles and candleholders, bells, and crosses.[5] Jacob Burckhardt argued that this materialism was a particularly Italian trait, since Italians had an eye for beauty and a genuine appreciation of the plastic arts.[6] The availability of affordable and diverse objects, furnishings, artworks, and religious texts grew especially with the streaming of Byzantine artifacts into Italy after the fall of Constantinople to the Turks in 1453. More than any other religion, Catholicism was a religion of objects.

Large portable statues, paintings, painted banners, diptychs or triptychs rich in ornament and artistic excellence were brought out of the church to function as objects of contemplation for the faithful during religious processions through the streets of the cities and towns. Their presence created an environment in which street violence was prevented and reverential behavior expected, celebrating communal piety, or *communitas*—the sense of belonging that was so much part of early modern civic existence.[7] Should Jews, who were outside the Christian community, fail to distance themselves from these processions, or to show proper respect (at least by removing their hats), their behavior would be noticed and brought to the attention of Christian authorities.

In the home, laypeople treasured their sacred objects and used them regularly. Domestic objects included Madonna images, large crucifixes or Passion paintings, rosaries, Agnus Deis, candles, candleholders, medals, holy water stoups, prints, and even small crucifixes to be worn as devotional jewelry on chains around the neck.[8] Marian paintings created areas in the home—particularly the bedchamber or *camera*—that enabled acts of devotion and a sense that the home was protected, both figuratively and literally.[9] Daily prayers would be said there, candles lit in front of them, and pious home dwellers would unveil, handle, and talk to these images, bowing their heads in prayers and kissing them.[10] Wealthy households would even create sumptuous altars generously furnished with images made from fashionable ebony and tortoiseshell.[11] During the sixteenth century, the three sessions of the Council of Trent (1545–1547, 1550–1551, and 1562–1563) tried to curtail the presence and use of altars and chapels in domestic spaces, restricting them to one place—an *oratorio*—to pray before an image of Christ, the Virgin, or other saints.[12] As we shall see, Italian Jews encountered these objects—in particular images of Mary—that were left behind or encased on walls in properties they rented from Christians.

Jews' homes also housed sacred objects for their own specific religious devotions, including Sabbath candles, goblets for the blessings over wine, religious texts, candles for the *Havdalah* service at the end of the Sabbath festival after nightfall on Saturdays, and sometimes circumcision instruments.[13] The Jews placed *mezuzot*—boxes holding a piece of parchment on which were inscribed specific Hebrew verses from the Hebrew Bible (Deut. 6:4–9 and 11:13–21)—on the right door frames of the internal and external doors of their homes.[14] The sixteenth-century Yiddish text *Meneket Rivkah* written by Rivkah Tiktiner in Prague suggests that Jewish homes, like Christian households, had certain spaces identified for study, private devotion, and prayer.[15] Some wealthy Italian Jews even housed synagogues in their own homes. There are no suggestions of complaints by Jews that their own objects of faith were desecrated by Christians.

The invention of the printing press and the distribution of paper as an inexpensive medium in the 1470s also modified practices of Christian devotion.[16] Pictorial religious placards were hung in homes, churches, taverns, and town halls throughout late medieval and Renaissance Europe and used by the clergy to educate illiterate people who would not have been able to read the lives of saints or of the Madonna.[17] By the late fifteenth century, thousands of these devotional images had been made and were displayed in both public and private spaces. By the first decades of the seventeenth century, cheap devotional objects, such as single-sheet woodcuts, could be easily acquired from street sellers at markets, fairs, or the church steps to be distributed in great numbers in urban and rural neighborhoods and households. As a result of their fragility, these objects were often the subject of desecration charges against Jews.[18]

This chapter is divided in the following way: after studying the infiltration of medieval tales of image desecration into Italy, the fictitious Jews' association with miraculous images, medieval judicial cases against Jews, and early modern judicial accusations against Philo-Protestants, the chapter will turn to early modern judicial cases that came before secular courts.[19] The latter part of the chapter will study the Roman inquisitorial *processi* (investigative processes) against Jews for this offense and analyze their types, testimonies, and details. The cases will be studied by focusing on the shift in the nature of the charges brought against Jews, from "fantastical" to "rational" and from "desecration" to "disrespect" regarding images both outside and inside the Jews' premises.

Byzantine Tales in Italy

The liturgy of the "Christ of Beirut" (*Passio Imaginis*) was widely known in the central peninsula from the eleventh century and confirms that Jews were already associated with this allegation. The Beirut miracle was commemorated on November 9 as one of the main feasts in episcopal churches dedicated to the Savior all over Italy (such as the major basilicas of Rome—San Salvatore al Laterano, Santa Maria Maggiore, and San Pietro). Wooden crucifixes in the Byzantine manner (representing Christ alive and clothed in a tunic) were also associated with this legend and appeared in various churches such as Bocca di Magra (near Sarzana) in the twelfth century and in Liguria and Tuscany from the thirteenth.[20]

There is also evidence of Franciscan preachers referring to the legend on the feast day of its commemoration. In 1304 Giordano da Rivalto, one of the most influential preachers of his day, in his sermon in front of Santa Maria Novella in Florence, referred to it and to the Jews' tendency to desecrate images.[21] Here he alludes to the allegation and compares it with the blood libel and charges of host desecration: "they also remake Christ's Passion not only in their hearts . . . but they remake it in their souls. . . . The other manner in which they remake it is in the sacrament of His body, doing cruel things to it. . . . Another manner in which they remake the Passion of Christ is in His image, and this in two ways, the one in the person of some man . . . and the other, in an image, such as the painted figures of Christ."[22] Over a century later, the prominent Pavian theologian Bernardino de Busti (ca. 1450–ca. 1515) took the legend of "Christ of Beirut" from Espina's *Fortalitium Fidei* and also incorporated it into his anti-Jewish sermons and writings, ensuring its further dissemination.[23]

"Christ of Beirut" was also transmitted in cult and relic form.[24] From the twelfth century, ampullae of blood spilled by the Jews' desecration were recorded as being present in Rome, Lucca, Sarzana, and Pisa (both in the church of San Pietro in Vinculis and on the main altar of Pisa cathedral).[25]

Another blood ampulla arrived in Siena in 1359.[26] Three popes in the fifteenth century—Nicholas V (1447–1455), Pius II (1458–1464), and Paul II (1464–1471)—shared a fascination with Christ's blood and supported the veneration of blood relics without questioning their provenance.[27] Nicholas V even repeated in a sermon Thomas Aquinas's argument that the blood from a crucifix violated by Jews somehow came from the body of Christ himself, which was capable of bleeding—a clear reference to "Christ of Beirut."[28]

Four extant series of paintings inside churches in Italy also depict the legend. The oldest series was portrayed on an altar retable in the church of the abbey of Berardenga in Siena, created in 1215 by the Master of Tressa (Figure 16).[29]

The retable is decorated on each side with three small side panels showing the two crucifix legends involving Jews. On the left side, the "Christ of Beirut" legend is depicted with Christ on a cross; the right shows the fourth-century legend of the *inventio crucis*. The placing of these two tales together allowed viewers to make connections between them and emphasized the Jews' destructive inclination toward Christian sacred symbols.[30] The Master of Tressa portrays the type of crucifix that was widespread in Italy by 1200, depicting a realistic figure of Christ, wearing a *perizoma* (loincloth), with eyes open and with feet.[31] In fact, the crucifix looks more like a real Christ on the cross than an image of Christ. On the top left side panel, the Jews are

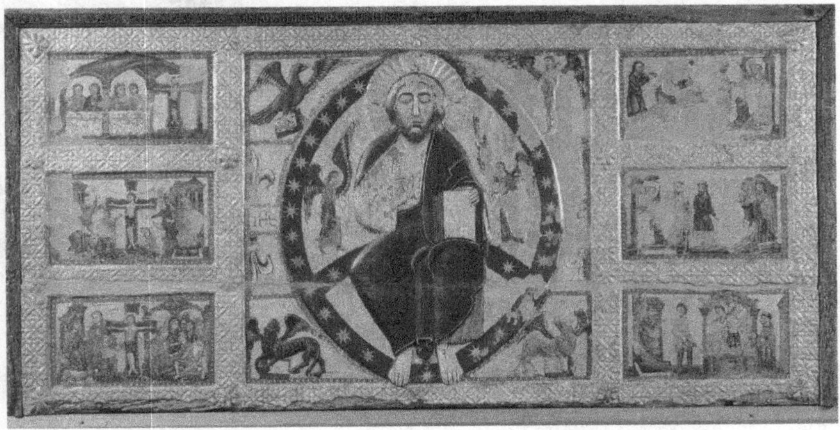

Figure 16. Master of Tressa, painted antependium, 1215, Siena. Foto Archivio Pinacoteca Nazionale.

gathered together to eat when they notice the image on the wall. In the middle panel, they attack the image and at the bottom, the seeping blood begins to work its miracles.

Other extant "Christ of Beirut" depictions are four anonymous wooden images (Figures 17, 18, 19, and 20), which were possibly part of another church altarpiece, painted during the first quarter of the sixteenth century. It is possible that this series was originally created to commemorate and celebrate the great "Crucifix" painted in the Church of San Petronio in Bologna at that time.[32]

The first (Figure 17) depicts a group of five Jews in Italian attire inside a room, looking at the crucifix hanging on the wall. A young man on the left looks as though he has just entered the room. His arms are slightly raised in surprise, showing bewilderment and confusion at the accusation by the man standing behind the table in the middle of the painting that he was keeping an image of Christ in his house.[33] The room gives the impression of a rather primitive, sparsely furnished interior of a Middle Eastern household in rustic sandy colors.

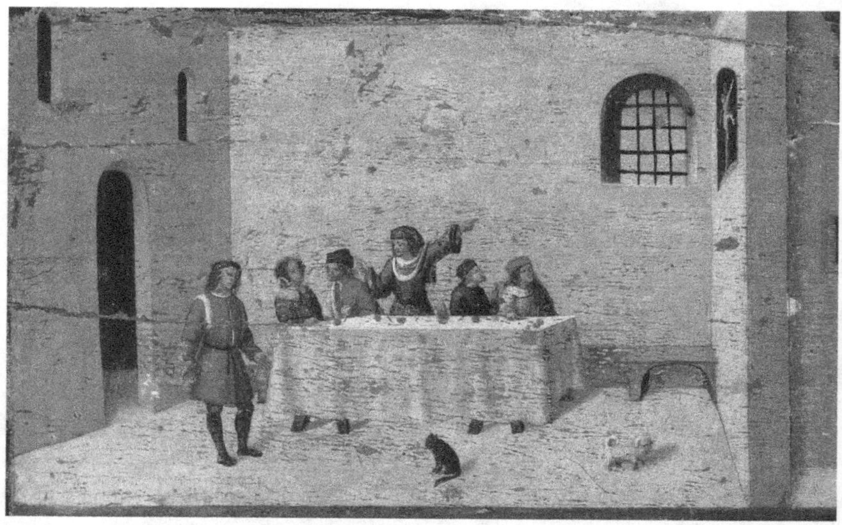

Figure 17. *Episode of the Legend of the Beirut Cross*, Bolognese School, first quarter of the sixteenth century, Federico Mason Perkins Collection, tempera on wood, 25×38.5 cm. Collection Fototeca Zeri no. 28886.

In the second (Figure 18) the action takes place before a building that resembles the outside of an Italian Renaissance mansion. The same five Jews are beating the Jewish householder with a spear for keeping the image of Christ in his home. This is a detail of the story not included in the original eighth-century text, but added in the version in Jacobus de Voragine's *Golden Legend*. Here it mentions the Jewish guests who "gathered and went to the house, saw the picture and belabored the householder with insults, manhandled him and expelled him half dead from the synagogue."[34]

In the third image (Figure 19) a smaller group of four Jews has surrounded the crucifix, which has changed from a two-dimensional fresco (in Figure 17) to a three-dimensional crucifix, perhaps for emphasis.[35] The Jews attack it with a stick and collect its blood in a basin below.

In the final painting in this series (Figure 20), three converting Jews kneel before a bishop, who, dressed in the pontifical vestments, stands at the portal of a cathedral. This was the location that was thought to separate the realm of the devil from that of God, and therefore it was fitting for it to be where the rite of exorcism, the first part of the sacrament of baptism for Jews and other adult catechumens, took place.[36] A priest stands by holding a basin from which the bishop pours holy oil over the Jews' heads. A group

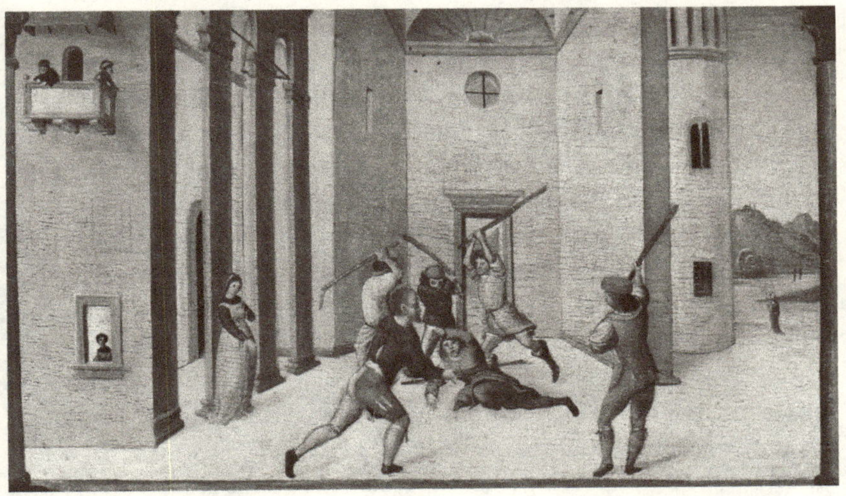

Figure 18. *The Jew of Beirut Punished by His Coreligionists* (attributed to the Bolognese School), ca. 1515–1520. Sold to private collector by Christie's in New York in 1981. Collection Fototeca Zeri no. 28888.

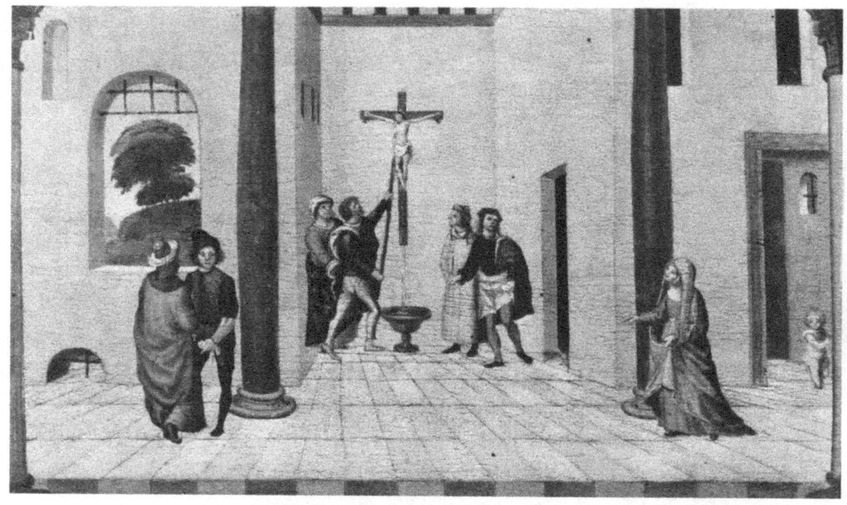

Figure 19. *The Jews Attack the Crucifix* (attributed to the Bolognese School), ca. 1515–1520, 24×40 cm. Last known in a private collection in Milan (1992). Collection Fototeca Zeri no. 28887.

of Christians standing nearby seem unaware of this ceremony. These three later images were probably painted by a different artist from the first.

In Bologna, between 1579 and 1622, another series of paintings, this time five large oil canvases, merely called *Quadri del Miracolo* (Paintings of the Miracle), suggesting that the miracle was well known, was painted by Jacopo Coppi, Giacomo Cavedone, Francesco Brizio, and two unidentified artists for the new church of San Salvatore. Four of the paintings are located on the lower wall of the choir, flanking the high altarpiece.

The first in the series was a painting of the tale by Jacopo Coppi (Figure 21), which depicted the Jews' violent attack on the crucifix. This had functioned as the main altarpiece of the old church before the new one was built in 1623. The painting is now located in the right transept of the new church. This painting, highly theatrical and full of figures, encapsulates the full story of the Beirut miracle from discovery of the image (in the back center) to the collective baptism of the Jews. The central focus is given to the miracle of the blood pouring from the crucifix as a large group of Jews, with rather unpleasant facial features, overshadowed by the centrality of the bleeding crucifix they have desecrated, look amazed and overwhelmed at the blood's miraculous power. The images made the local congregation aware of

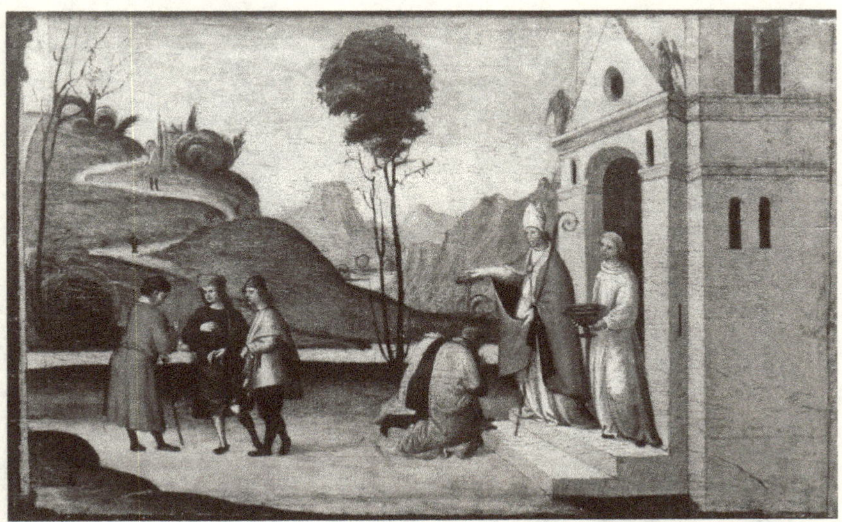

Figure 20. *The Baptism of the Jews* (attributed to the Bolognese School), ca. 1515–1520. Last provenance Brescia antique market (1985). Collection Fototeca Zeri no. 28889.

the "Christ of Beirut" tale and probably helped them to remember it. It is possible that the centrality of this painting, and the feelings of disgust it caused among churchgoers, might have contributed to the Jews' expulsion from Bologna in 1593. The expulsion signified the culmination of a long campaign to enforce Catholic orthodoxy after the Council of Trent. Jews were still absent from the city when the next series of paintings on this theme were created.

The four other miraculous crucifix scenes belong to an ensemble of eight canvases flanking the large high altarpiece and representing Christ as *Salvator Mundi*. This decoration communicated the indissoluble connection between the suffering body of Christ and the celebration of the Eucharist on the high altar.[37]

The main artist of the four paintings was Giacomo Cavedone, born in 1577 in Sassuolo, who had arrived in Bologna in 1593 as a student (*incamminato*) at the Carracci Academy. These baroque paintings divided the tale into four parts, locating it in sixteenth-century Italy rather than in the Levant. The Beirut crucifix has changed from a hanging crucifix to a two-dimensional framed image of the Passion, a far more likely object to hang inside the homes of premodern Italians.

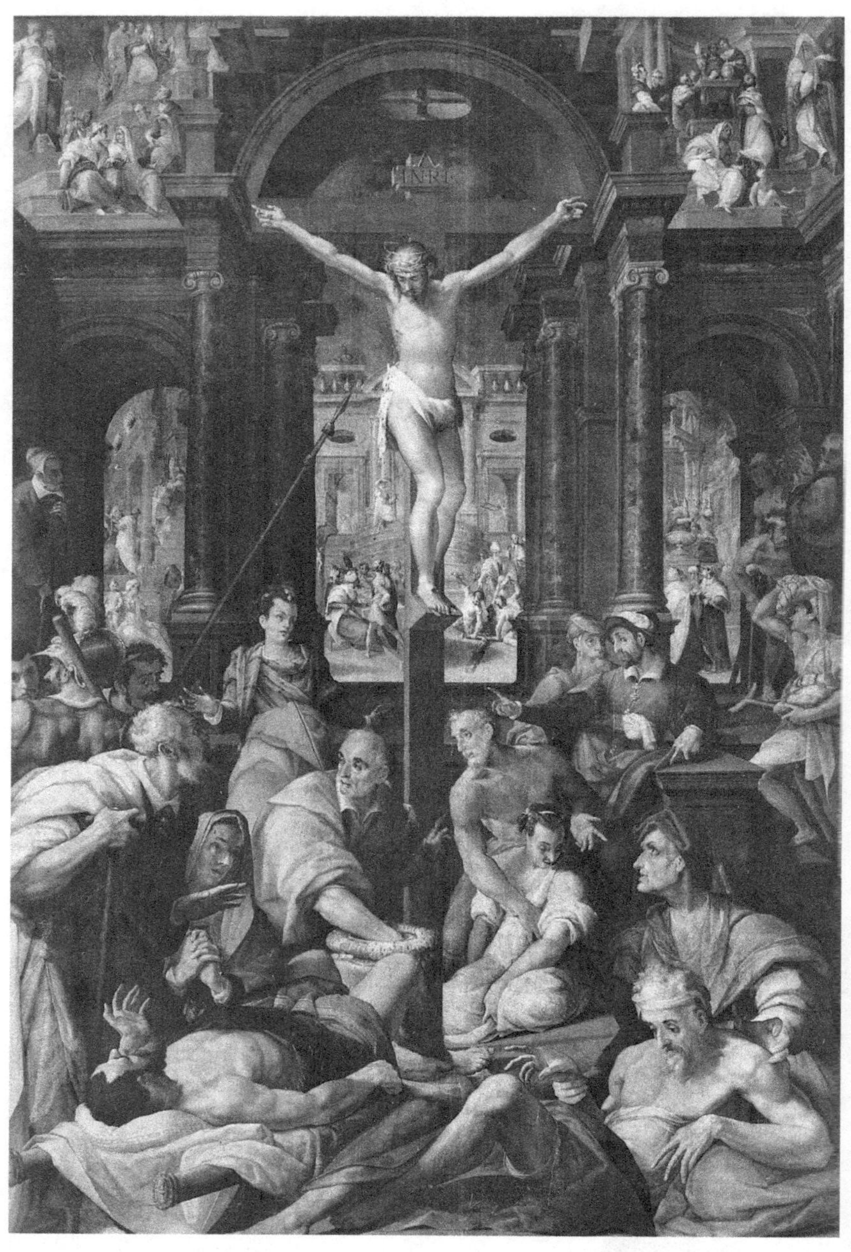

Figure 21. Jacopo Coppi, *Storia del Miracolo del Crocifisso di Beirut*, 1579. San Salvatore Church, Bologna. Alinari Archives.

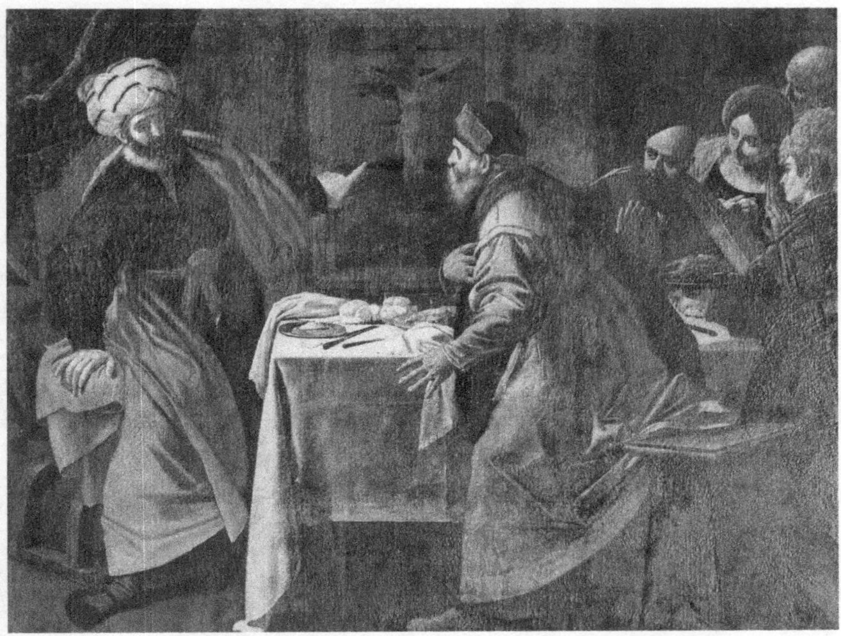

Figure 22. Giacomo Cavedone, *La scoperta della miracolosa immagine del crocifisso di Beirut*, (Discovery of the miraculous image of the crucifix of Beirut), ca. 1620–1622. Oil on canvas, 180×340 cm. San Salvatore, Bologna. Alinari Archives.

The first (Figure 22) depicts an alarmed turbaned Jewish rabbi (perhaps Cavedone had seen Levantine Jews in Italy), identifying the Jewish host and accusing him, before the other guests, of having the image in his home.[38] The sophisticated painting shows the influence of Renaissance painters such as Michelangelo Merisi da Caravaggio in its emphasis on the reactions of domestic figures—the host clasps his right hand to his chest in a gesture expressing disbelief and innocence. Cavedone gives equal attention to the accessories in the painting—the crumpled napkins, cutlery, crisply ironed tablecloth, the half-eaten bread, the glistening chicken, and barely touched red wine—so that the materialism of the Jews' household is given as much attention as the figures themselves.

The next two paintings are far less sophisticated and seem to lessen the power of the tale. Figure 23 shows the group of Jews on a shallow stage, shocked as the image spurts blood, which they collect in a large basin, similar to the ones in the Khludov Psalter (see Chapter 1). Here the Jews have

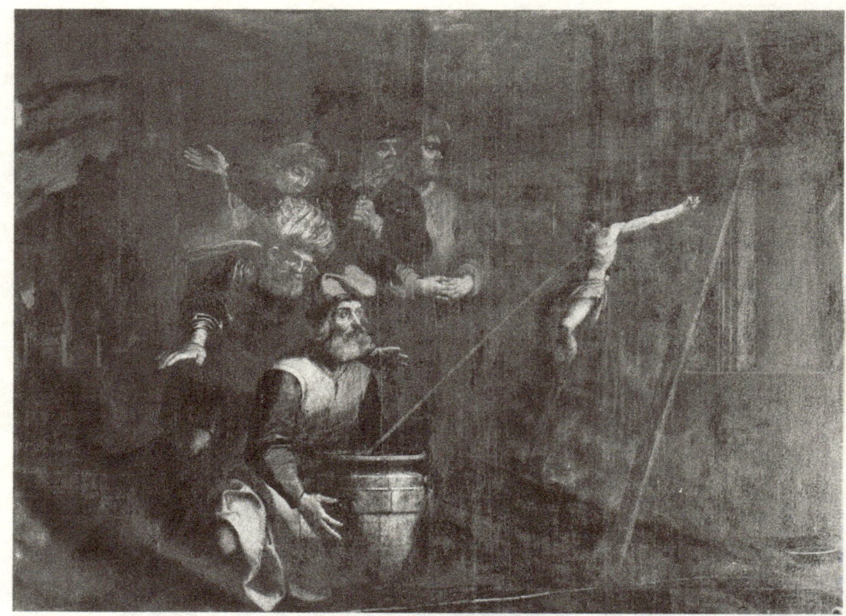

Figure 23. Studio of Cavedone (?), *La prova del sangue dell'immagine del crocifisso di Beirut* (The proof of the blood of the image of the Beirut crucifix), ca. 1620–1622. Oil on canvas, 180×340 cm. San Salvatore, Bologna. Alinari Archives.

lifeless facial features, barely recognizable as the same Jews from the painting before, and the composition and the background around the central bleeding of the image lack attention, imagination, and sophistication.[39]

The third image (Figure 24) portrays the "Orientalized" turbaned Jewish rabbi/accuser distributing the blood among the sick and crippled and watching it heal them. Although this painting is more sophisticated than the previous one, it still represents a type of folk painting. The cripple on the right is astounded as he contemplates his miraculous recovery. A few drops of blood spill over the filled basin and the redness of this blood contrasts sharply with the dull brown of the basin.

The last image (Figure 25), by Francesco Brizio (1574–1623), the Bolognese painter and engraver, is again more sophisticated and depicts the Jews being baptized by a bishop in the cathedral of Bologna, as well-dressed Catholics look on. The image of the mother protectively embracing her son could well have symbolized a young Jesus watching with Mary as Jews go through their process of "rebirth" and conversion to Christianity. However,

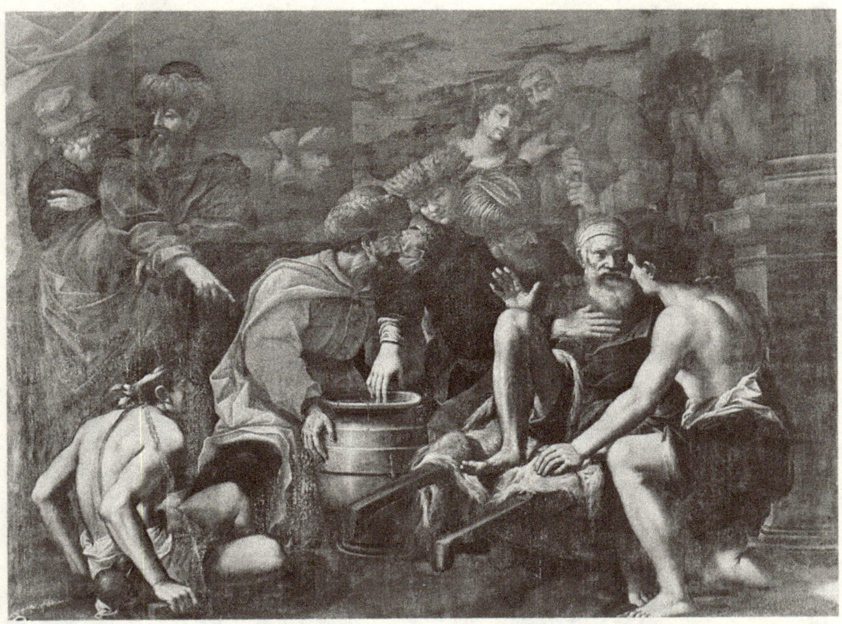

Figure 24. Studio of Cavedone (?), *La guarigione del paralitico* (The healing of the paralytic), ca. 1620–1622. Oil on canvas, 180 × 340 cm. San Salvatore, Bologna. Alinari Archives.

they appear as local Christians, without any identifying symbols, gazing at the scene. Here the emphasis falls less on the acts of ruthless desecration perpetrated by Jews and more on the increasingly systematic conversion policies that Rome had adopted in the middle and late sixteenth century and on the voluntary acknowledgment by Jews of Christ as the savior of the world. The papacy had rejected the policies adopted by Spain and Portugal of forcibly converting Jews, which it believed to be mistaken, and had chosen instead to bring them to baptism through ghettoization, regular preaching, and the censoring of Jewish books.

The continuous dissemination of "Christ of Beirut iconography," liturgy, and commemoration was clearly designed to ensure that this legend of Jewish hostility to Christ, followed by Jewish conversion to belief in him, was integrated and absorbed into Italian memory. The legend also appears in a fresco cycle in the apse of San Pietro in Vinculis in Rome, painted by Jacopo Coppi in 1577.

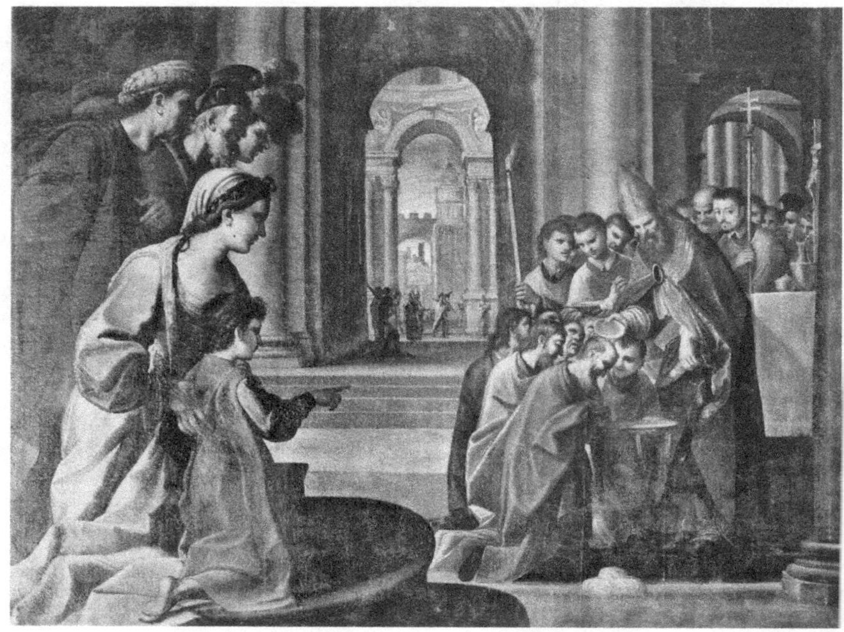

Figure 25. Francesco Brizio, *Battesimo degli ebrei* (Baptism of the Jews), ca. 1620–1622. Oil on canvas, 180 × 340 cm. San Salvatore, Bologna. Alinari Archives.

In the fifteenth century, the advent of the printing press altered and furthered the circulation of this allegation. Compilations of the medieval Marian tales, in particular "Christ of Beirut" and "The Virgin's Image Insulted," were printed by Italian presses from the 1470s.[40] These tales appear in printed editions of Vincent de Beauvais's *Speculum historiale*, composed in the thirteenth century, in some editions of Werner Rolevinck's *Fasciculus temporum*, written in the 1470s, and in Jacob Philip Foresti of Bergamo's *Supplementum chronicarum* of 1491. The last two Latin works were translated into Italian as well as French, German, and Dutch. Hartmann Schedel's 1493 *Liber chronicarum*, one of the most celebrated printed books of the fifteenth century, published in Nuremberg and narrating the history of the world from creation up to that time, included an illustration of "a Jew stabbing an image of Christ and blood flowing." The book was published in both Latin and German, and an estimated 2,500 printed copies soon spread through Europe. Copies of these books were affordable and accessible at bookstalls and bookshops and brought the Jew's alleged offense to a widespread audience.

The illustration (Figure 26) dominates the top left half of the page, with only a few lines (on the right side) describing the Jew stealing the image, making it bleed, and being punished by stoning. Rather than referring to "Christ of Beirut," this depiction seems to reflect the original narrative composed by Gregory of Tours in the late sixth century (which had, it seems, become a kind of cautionary tale in its own right and which included this punishment).

The proliferation of all these stories had probably led the Franciscan missionary Bernardino da Siena to include image desecration in his list of Jewish offenses when delivering a powerful sermon at Padua in 1423. He inveighed in particular against Jewish bankers who, he argued, violated the Christian sacred objects they received from Christian borrowers by sullying and defecation: "But what should I say of those who pawn sacramental vessels and chalices to the Jews? I believe that they urinate in [them as well] and do every kind of shameful act [upon them] in order to mock the Christian faith."[41] Was not Bernardino basing his assessment on "The Virgin's Image Insulted" tale? He was rebuking both the bad Christians who pledged these objects and the Jews who received them and were believed to defile them. In 1415, Benedict XIII (1394–1417), the last Avignonese pope, had issued *Etsi doctoribus gentium* in which he prohibited the Jews' engagement in the manufacture or selling of Christian liturgical and devotional objects. Even though Pope Martin V (1417–1431) repealed this oppressive legislation, it was to have a lasting effect on preachers and the policies adopted in central and northern Italy toward Jews and their relationship with these objects. Yet before we look at the prosecution of Jews for this crime in medieval times, a different association between Jews and the desecration of Christian images needs to be assessed. This association was based on how Christian society in Italy perceived miraculous images.

Jews and Miraculous Images

Even before "Christ of Beirut" reached Italy in the ninth century, the trope of the fictitious Jewish desecrator had become associated with certain miraculous images. These images were considered miraculous if they had in some way "transfigured"—that is, if the images had undergone changes that suggested that they were suffering as if they were human. The process was recognized by the Catholic Church as a correspondence or sympathy between

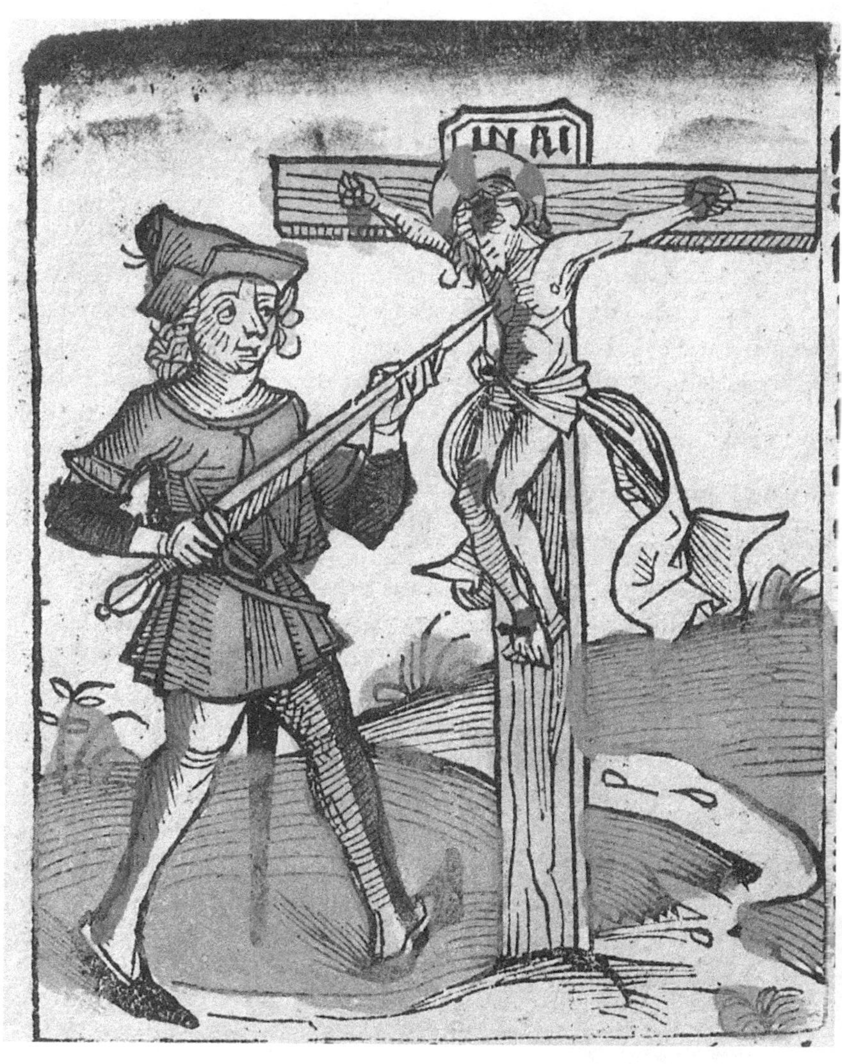

Figure 26. Illustration of a Jew desecrating a crucifix, from Hartmann Schedel's *Liber chronicarum. Das Buch der Croniken und Geschichten* (Nuremberg: Anton Koberger, 1493), fol. 149v. Württembergische Landesbibliothek, Stuttgart.

the image and the being it represented.[42] In Rome in the eighth century the "Lateran Christ," which was kept in the Santissimo Salvatore e Santi Giovanni Battista e Evangelista in Laterano, and probably dated from the seventh century, had been accepted as an *acheiropoieton* and during the reign of Pope Sergius I (687–701) began to be used in papal inauguration processions.[43] According to Census Camerarius (Cencio Savelli, the chamberlain of Pope Clement III [1187–1191] who wrote his *Liber Censuum* in 1192 and later became Pope Honorious III [1216–1227]), one such procession from St. Peter's in Rome to the Lateran basilica went past this image, which was said to have been struck on the forehead by a Jew causing it to bleed.[44] Papal processions in the seventeenth century still evoked bitter memories of this supposed misdeed.[45]

Three other cult images, in the cities of Venice, Rome, and Velletri, were also associated with Jewish desecration or attack. In San Marco, Venice, a crucifix just off the nave in a hexagonal stone tabernacle was thought to have been stabbed by a Jew and to have bled from its wounds.[46] In an abandoned prison in Rome, a fourteenth-century fresco of the Madonna and Child, called the *Madonna delle Carceri*, was even said to have miraculously stepped down from the wall on July 6, 1484, in response to offensive rituals being secretly performed by Jews somewhere nearby.[47] The image was subsequently said to have undergone other miraculous transfigurations such as weeping, opening and closing its eyes, bleeding and changing color; it was as if the Jews themselves had changed the status of the image. According to local tradition, a stone had been thrown by a Jew at an image of the Madonna in Velletri, leaving a mark on the hand of the Virgin's image.[48]

Jewish image desecration was also particularly associated with a prominent marble sculpture of the Madonna and Child, the *Madonna della Rosa*, erected in Florence in 1399.[49] The Madonna, which was located in the municipal grain market, had a strong association with Marian intercession. It was venerated as miraculous after a supposed act of Jewish desecration occurring on the feast of the Assumption of the Virgin in August 1493.[50] Contemporary sources record that a young destitute Sephardi Jew, Bartolomeo de Cases, attacked the eyes of the Child and the face of the Virgin with a knife before attacking other images.[51] But in reality it seems that Bartolomeo de Cases had quarreled with some Florentine youths, one of whom he attacked with a knife.[52] Perhaps the proximity of this brawl to the statue had caused it to be damaged. Once caught, the Jew was lynched by an enraged crowd before the Otto di Guardia e Balìa (a magistracy established in

1378 to have jurisdiction over crimes of state and threats to public order and crimes committed by Jews) could fully investigate the case.[53] At the base of the Madonna, the city council inscribed a Latin epigraph that outlined the event and the brutal punishment carried out by the people of Florence: "Hanc ferro effigiem petit iudaeus et index/ipse sui vulgo dilaniatus obit MCCCCLXXXXIII" (A Jew attacked this with a knife and died pulled to pieces by the crowd, in 1493).[54] This epigraph is still at the base of the image. The image henceforth became a site of powerful Marian intercession and was considered to be miraculous, although it did not bleed but was said to open and close its eyes. The image was encased within a tabernacle—a common form of architectural enshrinement used to protect and focus attention on an object—and at some stage it was covered with a shutter.[55] During the sixteenth century, the Guild of Doctors and Apothecaries (Arte dei Medici e Speziali), who cared for the image, arranged for an oil lamp to be kept alight before it and hymns of praise to be sung there.[56] Despite the account of the event provided in contemporary chronicles, there is no evidence of scratches on either the face of the Virgin or the eyes of Christ to confirm that this desecration really occurred.[57]

Hence, accounts of Jewish image desecration were disseminated in Italy through powerful legends, tales, and traditions—iconography, literature, and commemoration of "Christ of Beirut," and by a tendency to connect transfiguring miraculous images with Jewish assault. It is not surprising, then, to find one of the most prominent jurists of Roman and canon law in the fourteenth century, Petrus de Ancharano (ca. 1333–1416), asserting in his legal compendium that an offense typical of Jews was "hurling mud at a crucifix being carried in a procession through the town." As this was an offense against public order as well as religion, Petrus argued that Jewish suspects should be prosecuted by secular courts as well as church courts.[58] How often Jews were actually accused of image desecration in the medieval period will now be considered.

Late Medieval Judicial Accusations

Twenty-three cases in which professing Jews were charged with image desecration are known to have come before courts in the fourteenth and fifteenth centuries, from Vissio in the Marche to Livorno and farther north in the Modenese duchy. The chronological and geographical distribution of the cases is uneven. Cases were most numerous in the second half of the fifteenth century and concerned, in particular, images that were found in the Jews' domestic spaces. Omitting the isolated fourteenth-century case (1323), the distribution is as follows: 1401–1450, five; and 1451–1500, seventeen.

By the 1450s, Italian law courts had made image desecration a punishable offense. The number and spread of sacred images in cities and towns had increased—both inside and out of private spaces—and they demanded closer monitoring and policing to protect them. Around 1450, offenses against images began to be treated by Florentine laws as a form of transgressive blasphemy.[59] Jews came before different legal bodies whose punishments varied widely.[60] The courts involved in these twenty-three cases included ducal/secular courts (9); episcopal courts (4); the Otto di Guardia e Balìa (4); Apostolic Chamber in Rome (2); the podesta and ecclesiastical court (2); and the medieval Inquisition (2), even though it was not usual for the Inquisition to prosecute professing Jews before 1581, when a controversial bull of Pope Gregory XIII stated its right to do so in certain specified cases.

Ducal courts dealt with more cases than others and tried in particular to protect Jews from false and often perilous allegations. Where results of the cases are known, most ended either without punishment or with acquittal (9). Other punishments included fines (6); the obligation to provide, at considerable expense, a new work of art or tabernacle to replace one that had been violated (2); lynching (2); execution (1), and conversion of the Jew (1). In two cases, the punishments are unknown. The images involved included crosses/crucifixes (6); images of Mary (3); images of saints (2); image of Christ (1); and unknown (11). One case even dealt with images made from paper. In 1493 Davide di Dattilo from Tivoli was accused by the local podesta and the bishop of, among other offenses, destroying or damaging a number of sacred prints in the house that he was renting. He was eventually acquitted of this crime.

Outbreaks of popular fury against Jews for image desecration did occur, and in Italy Jews could be lynched for their association with these images. In 1456 an unnamed Jew allegedly entered the San Lorenzo church in Lodi and attacked the crucifix above the main altar with a sword; he was then lynched in his home. Unfortunately, it is unclear whether the Jew actually committed the offense because his case was never investigated by the Milanese ducal court, at that time under the authority of Duke Francesco I

Sforza.[61] The other case is that of Bartolomeo de Cases, which has already been discussed. Both cases demonstrate the Jews' political and judicial vulnerability at this time.[62]

In one case where Jews were executed as a result of judicial trials, image desecration was not the main offense. In 1470 in Milan, two Jews, Todeschino and Abraam Zudeo, who had pretended to be Christians, were put to death by the ducal court for murdering a Christian woman. In their list of crimes, they were said to have abused images.[63] Death sentences could be commuted, or executions made less painful, if the culprit sought baptism. In another case of image desecration, a Jew chose to convert to Christianity as a result of the accusation against him. In 1471, records confirm that a Jew, who faced a death sentence by the ducal court for damaging a statue of the Madonna on his way to Pavia, decided to convert in order to survive.[64] That the Jew was guilty seems likely. Embracing Christianity was clearly a means of evading further investigation and punishment, as the prominent Jewish goldsmith Salomone de Sesso discovered at the end of the fifteenth century.[65]

Other judicial accusations against Jews, particularly one in the fourteenth century and several in the fifteenth century, seem to have been fashioned after Byzantine tales and influenced by their narratives, rather than being based on facts. As in the "Toledo" tale, in 1323 in the duchy of Spoleto, Manuel of Vissio was accused by the Apostolic Chamber of taking a cross into a synagogue and desecrating it during Purim; he was fined three florins.[66] Sources do not show if he was found guilty, and the fine seems to represent a compromise made by the judicial authority to placate accusers rather than punish the suspect. The spiritual domain of the Jewish community—the synagogue—would again appear as the place of supposed desecration just over a century later. In a case even closer to the "Toledo" tale, in 1444 a Jew of Vigone in Piedmont was accused by the ducal court of making a wax crucifix and then damaging it. He was found guilty and sentenced to pay a fine of four hundred florins, after which no further action was taken against him.[67]

Although, as noted above, host desecration charges did not reach Italy, Jews could be accused, as they were in Sogorb in Spain, of molding crucifixes out of unleavened bread at Passover and then destroying them.[68] In 1441, Jews living in Savigliano, Piedmont, were accused of stamping the image of Christ on their unleavened bread, which they had then cooked in the oven. As a result, they were fined five hundred gold ducats by the ducal court.[69] In Lucca in 1471, Jews were accused of similar actions by a neophyte, Tommaso

Pacis, before the episcopal court. Here a Jewish servant, Salomone, together with another dependent, Angelo da Fermo, in the household of Guglielmo di Leone di Fano, was denounced for making "wafers" imprinted with crosses and destroying them by throwing them into the fire. The punishment is unrecorded.[70]

Several other cases reveal Jews being falsely charged with image desecration by Christian neophytes, converts from Judaism who had recently crossed over into Christian society. These cases hint at the existence of a group of disreputable converts, in the borderland between Judaism and Christianity, who were prepared to inform against professing Jews. Their hostility, deception, and the personal vendettas they appeared to be conducting were a perennial source of insecurity for Jewish communities, as they manipulated the charge of image desecration to serve their own needs. In 1414, the neophyte Marco de Manuele worked together with Manuele di Gaudio (also known as Manuele da Cento), a marginalized Roman Jew, and Antonio Mengarini di Pieve, a Christian, to bring before the court of the podesta in Bologna an accusation of image desecration against Salomone di Matassia of Perugia and five other wealthy and prominent Jewish bankers.[71] Marco falsely testified that the group of Jews had stolen a crucifix from a suburban church (when in fact the delators had stolen it themselves), accusing the Jews of subsequently burning the crucifix in their synagogue during the festival of Purim. It seems that Manuele and Antonio had their own grievances against the Jews and bribed Marco to denounce them. Both Manuele and Antonio believed that Marco, since he had passed from the Jewish world to that of the Christian, was more likely to be believed than either of them.[72] The allegation caused the torture and imprisonment of the Jews, but in the end Marco admitted, albeit under torture, that his allegation was false.

In 1470, Stefano Todesco, a neophyte, played a similar role and out of "malevolence and private enmity" falsely accused Falcone da Monza before the communal council of Milan of burning a painting of the Madonna in the fireplace of the house of Salomone da Monza (clearly a relative of Falcone). Falcone was tortured but maintained his innocence and was released.[73] In the end, Stefano confessed that he had accused Falcone from malevolence and personal animosity. Although he was sentenced to death, it was not clear if this punishment was carried out. Sometimes neophyte delators made more unlikely allegations. In Florence in 1481, an unnamed neophyte delated Bonaventura di Maestro Guglielmo da Genazzano for having, among other offenses, spat at the feet of an image of Saint Christopher.[74] This is one of the few known cases in which an image of a saint, rather than a crucifix or a Madonna, was said to be attacked.

In 1488, thirty-eight Jews were denounced by a neophyte, Vincentio de Galia, for showing contempt for Christianity. Ten of them were charged with desecrating images. At first these Jews were condemned to death. One of the many charges against these Milanese Jews was that they had assembled Christian images, which they then desecrated and destroyed.[75] Here the crime is described as acting "in vilipendium et contemptum vel" (in scorn or contempt) of Christian images. The prosecutors in the ducal court of Milan, including two Franciscan Observants, Bernardino de Busti and Cristoforo da Varese, even asked the Jews whether they had been paid to offend and destroy the images. Lazarro di Mandolino di San Colombano and another ten Jews (Simone di Giacobbe de Alamania di Monza; Giacobbe di Vita di Pavia; Giacobbe di Papia; Angelo di Novaria; Mosé di Israel da Rovigo di Parma; Samuele di Mosé di Cremona; Salomone di Angelo di Como; Isacco di Salomone da Parma di Castelnuovo; Giacobbe di Isacco di Castelleone Cremonese; and Giacobbe di Datteri di Vighizollo) were all asked the same question during their interrogations: "Did you make any images in the likeness of Jesus Christ or in the likeness of the Virgin Mary, and place the very image in the fire or in dung, or under your feet or treat it with contempt?"[76]

They all denied the suggestion, which seemed to echo two Marian tales, both "The Virgin's Image Insulted," where Jews not only desecrated and placed Christian images in a latrine, but also "Toledo" in that they made their own images in order to destroy them. On March 27, 1488, when Lazarro di Mandolino was interrogated about this practice, he tried to defend himself by arguing that Jews were forbidden to make images: "We have a commandment in our laws that prohibits us from making any kind of image."[77] The judges soon commuted the death sentence to a fine of 19,000 ducats.

It was the Christian images in the Jews' rented properties, situated on the outside walls or in antechambers, in bedrooms, or in niches under the stairs, that would cause increasing Jewish anxiety through the fifteenth century. At the root of this was the fear that they would be accused of tampering with and desecrating them. Jewish tenants could never be at ease with these images, while Christians remained convinced that Jews would damage or destroy them.[78] It is this aspect of "Jewish image desecration" that brings to mind its contested nature. Actions taken by Jews to make their homes suit their traditions and taste (e.g., whitewashing over a Christian religious painting on a wall) could be construed by Christians as an attack on Christianity. Here, more than in other cases, reality and fantasy overlap—since Jews were actually doing what Christians accused them of. Even though the intentions of the Jews were to fulfill their own needs, it points to the contingency of both the Jewish and Christian interpretations.

Of the twenty-three cases, twelve (52 percent) focused on images kept inside homes rented from Christians and left behind by previous occupants; these include not only trial proceedings against Jews for desecrating them, but also the Jews' official applications for licenses to remove or temporarily cover them. These will reveal not only the trouble the courts took to investigate these cases but the Jews' own efforts to be free of those images and forestall Christian accusations that they had violated them.

By looking particularly at the fifteenth-century cases of Isaaco di Vitale and Daniele da Norsa, Dana Katz and Michele Luzzati have demonstrated the type of retribution Jews in Italy could face when they tried to erase religious paintings in their homes.[79] In the fifteenth century, sacred images—often found on the premises of well-to-do Jewish moneylenders—were sometimes permanently obliterated, whitewashed over by the Jews themselves. Although Jews clearly preferred permanent erasure or whitewashing—so they had no visual reminder of the image in their homes—this method was quickly rejected after they became aware how hard it was to secure licenses from both the ecclesiastical and later secular authorities to permit this. There is only one case of a Jew acting without ecclesiastical permission: in 1439–1440, Benedetto di Calimano, a banker in Treviso, decided to whitewash four images (the Virgin and Child, Saint Christopher with a young Jesus on his shoulders, Saint Anthony, and Saint Catherine) in his home next to a church in the densely populated Jewish neighborhood of Sant' Andrea.[80] But Benedetto was in trouble already for two other offenses. He was therefore accused of three separate offenses: the first was whitewashing these four images; the second, improperly lending money on the security of a Psalter (which might well have included holy pictures); the third, not showing proper respect to a consecrated host. When this was discovered, Benedetto was brought before the inquisitor Fra Giuliano da Firenze and the episcopal vicar Antonio Ducci. The monetary penalty imposed on him had nothing to do with the whitewashed image, but related solely to the illicit loan. He had to forfeit his principal (fourteen ducats) and the accumulated interest (seven ducats). He might, however, have been in trouble for whitewashing the images without permission, because he was then ordered to leave his home within three months. He was not in lasting disgrace, though, to judge by the fact that his banking license was renewed two years later. Knowledge of his arrest and prosecution might have caused his fellow religionists to proceed more carefully.

There were three more cases of whitewashing in the late fifteenth century. In 1471 the Jewish moneylender Samuele di Consiglio of Gubbio, was granted full authorization by Antonio Severino, the episcopal vicar of Gubbio, and Angelo Cerreti da Camerino, the deputy bishop, to permanently erase an image on an exterior wall of the house by Jacopo Bedi, depicting the Virgin, the Child, Saint Anthony, and Saint Ubaldo of Gubbio. This was granted only after he had commissioned the artist to paint a similar painting in a newly constructed oratory.[81] This new work, in an area away from Jews where it would be venerated properly by Christians, fully compensated for the permanent destruction of the painting in his home. Within twenty years, there was another case of a request for permanent erasure. This one was made because an Italian Jewish banker needed to make structural repairs to his home. In 1491–1492, Isaaco di Vitale, who lived in the parish of Santa Margherita in the center of the Mezzo quarter in Pisa, had two paintings of Saint Christopher—one in a "lowly and vile location" and the other in the large room on the second floor of his home, which housed the synagogue.[82] It is probable that the images of Saint Christopher portrayed, as they usually did, the saint carrying the Christ child across a river; the Jews' concern was probably directed at the representation of Christ rather than that of the saint. Roberto Strozzi, the deputy bishop of Pisa, and a representative from the Otto di Guardia e Balìa, received confirmation from the Christian masons that it was necessary to completely erase the panels in order to do the structural repairs. The canons Antonio Perini da Cascina and Niccolo di Giovanni di Bergamo went to visit the site and confirmed in writing that Isaaco intended no harm to Christians or the Christian faith by these erasures.[83] How much money Isaaco had to pay for these licenses was unfortunately not recorded. To protect himself further, Isaaco also commissioned a new painting of Saint Christopher, probably in the local church of Santa Margherita.[84]

Ecclesiastical authorities were often reluctant to allow images to be obscured by whitewash and preferred other ways of solving the problem. Pressure could be placed on these judicial bodies not to provide licenses for Jews. In 1485, Giovanni Fortesa, the episcopal vicar of Cagliari in Sardinia, was reprimanded by the Apostolic Chamber for giving Jews a license to have an image of the Virgin permanently erased from a wall of their home. Fortesa was ordered to appear in Rome before the Apostolic Chamber to explain his actions, which had resulted in the complete obliteration of the image.[85]

Daniele da Norsa's lack of prudence and caution in gaining the necessary licenses resulted in violence. He permanently erased an image of the Madonna and Child accompanied by saints on the facade of his home in Mantua, when he only had an episcopal license and not a secular one. The situation was made worse since the erasure was on an outside wall and so could be readily seen by his neighbors, who were clearly sensitive to any suggestion of Jewish management of Christian images. Not only had Daniele failed to acquire a secular license, but he failed to state that he had no wish to offend Christianity and, unlike Isaaco di Vitale, he had not offered a substitute painting. On May 27, 1495, the eve of Ascension Day, the outside of his home was attacked by Christians during a procession. Paper prints of saints, annotated with inflammatory phrases that accused Daniele of blasphemy, were pasted on the outside of his home, and the Christian aggressors began to shout and throw stones, only stopping as a result of the intervention of Jacopo da Capua, the captain of the guard.[86] Daniele himself was absent from the city during this time, but when he returned, he appealed for protection to the Marchese Francesco Gonzaga. Francesco eventually decided that Daniele, as a penalty for whitewashing the image, would be hanged within three days unless he paid the large sum of 110 ducats for the construction of a more beautiful altarpiece to be dedicated to Our Lady of Victory in a local church.[87] In addition, his home was to be destroyed and replaced by a church dedicated to Santa Maria della Vittoria. It was as if the consecration of a new house of worship would compensate for Daniele's whitewashing.[88] In 1499 the Jew had to pay for an additional painting, which also hung in the Santa Maria della Vittoria complex and was probably commissioned by Fra Girolamo Redini, an Augustinian priest.[89] It was this carefully contrived painting (Figure 27), with its numerous iconographic messages, that for the first time included at the bottom of the painting the Jewish "image desecrators"—Daniele da Norsa, his son Isaac, and their wives—as miserable, guilt-ridden underlings. Above them to the left appears a small lion who looks disapprovingly down at the Jews. The central image of the painting is an enthroned Madonna and Child, both of whom raise their right arm as does Mary Magdalen (to their right) as if to approve the Jews' degradation. On the left side, Saint Jerome holds a model of the new church in his hands, to celebrate its consecration.

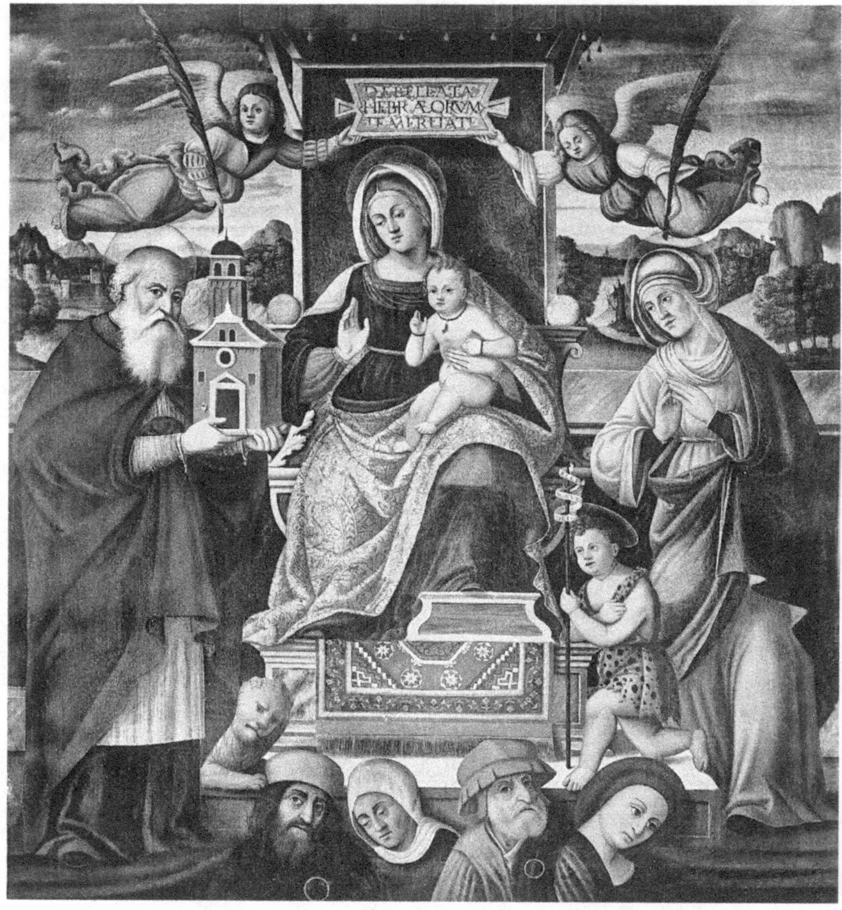

Figure 27. *Madonna and Child with Saints and Norsa Family* (Norsa Madonna), ca. 1499, Mantua, Sant'Andrea. Painting by an anonymous artist of the Mantegna school, now in the chapel of the Sant'Andrea basilica in Mantua. Alinari Archives.

In 1497, Daniele faced additional fines, being forced to pay for a new property adjacent to the church. After this payment, which probably bankrupted him, he was assured that no further action would be taken against him by a formal decree in August 1497.[90]

Hence, Jews began to survey new premises they intended to rent (whether they were houses, synagogues, professional work spaces, or shops) and register the subject matter and the precise condition of any images with local judicial authorities. They quickly learned from the experiences of their coreligionists what they had to do and the various agencies they needed to negotiate with to ensure that, before coverage, the actual physical condition of the image was meticulously recorded by the courts. Whitewashing was no longer a solution, but instead Jews requested permission to temporarily conceal the images. A notary would visit the Jew's home and record the exact condition of the image, which would then be covered and the cover locked with a key, and the key handed over to the court or to the landlord of the property. In theory at least, this would save the Jews having to look at the image and from being accused of its desecration or destruction.

The earliest license that I have found was recorded in 1449. David Consilio, a Jewish moneylender in the bank of Sabbioni of Ferrara, living in the district of San Gregorio, appeared before the episcopal vicar to report that, on a wall on the ground floor room of the house that he was renting from Giovanni Rubini, there was a niche with "painted figures"—a frescoed image of the resurrection of Christ, with Mary and Saint John the Baptist.[91] He reported that "humidity" had damaged the painting before he moved into the house; this was confirmed by the magistrate Guglielmo Scanaloca, who swore under oath that the condition of the painting had not changed.[92] David then made what was to become a common request: "that the image will be shut up in order that no one in the future will be able to accuse him or any members of his family of damaging it."[93] The niche was to be closed with two removable wooden planks that were held in place by means of a lock and key. The key was then handed over to the owner of the house, and the Jew was given a certified copy of the signed declaration of the state of the painting. Also in 1449, a license was given to a Jew from Bologna, Abraham, son of Leo, who was temporarily residing in Ferrara.[94] Before moving into the house he was renting from Bartholomeo de Salla in the district of San Giacomo, he acquired a license to have twenty-three hagiographical figures covered. The notary, Nicolò Cagnazzi, recorded the precise condition of the frescoed images and confirmed that Abraham's procurator, Peregrino Prisciano, had covered them with a "blue cloth" attached to the wall with nails.[95] This was done a day after the Jew had made the request, which shows how quickly the episcopal court was prepared to deal with these issues. In 1498 another case was listed before the medieval Inquisition. Here Beniamino, son of the late Josef da Reggio Emilia, the cashier of the bank of Ripa, verified that the house that he wanted to rent in the same district as Abraham also had various "damaged" images on the interior walls, including those of the Virgin, Saint Bartholomew, Saint Sebastian, and God the Father.[96] Here both the Christian owner and the Jewish tenant undertook to cover the images.

These procedures taken by the Jews were clearly effective in preventing them from getting into trouble. In November 1480 Emanuele de Buonaiuto da Camerino—one of the most important bankers in Florence—was immune from prosecution by both the Otto di Guardia e Balìa and the ecclesiastical authorities regarding the crucifix (it is unclear whether this was a painted panel or sculpted image) that was located in his San Giovanni Valdarno residence, since he had acquired licenses from both authorities to temporarily cover it.[97] Also, in June 1490, Isaaco, the banker of Badia Polesine, had ensured when signing a rental contract for five years with Alessandro Lanfranchi, the owner of the house, that the holy images were registered, that their damaged conditions were recorded, and that they were suitably covered.[98] Such acquisitions of licenses are numerous and continued well after the ghettoization of the Jews began in the sixteenth century.

The acquisition of licenses did not stop occasional visits of ecclesiastics to check on the state of the images and their coverings. In December 1485, Dattilo di Salomone da Camerino, a Jewish banker in Florence, who had already arranged for a *tabernacolo* of wood to cover two images in the inside of his home (which probably also housed the local synagogue), was ordered by the Otto di Guardia e Balìa to have the state of the *tabernacolo* assessed and to make sure it was worthy of the painting. After a visit by the captain of Cortona, the Jew was ordered to improve its condition.[99]

* * *

The Jews themselves, then, whenever they rented or occupied spaces that already housed Christian sacred images, had begun to anticipate charges of desecrating them. The image-saturated society had brought additional anxiety to Jewish home life in Italy. These anxieties would continue after the reconstitution of the Roman Inquisition in the 1540s, another body that would claim jurisdiction over Jews charged with image desecration. But, before examining later judicial cases, we need to note certain changes in the Catholic Church's attitude to miraculous images and also take account of Italian reactions to Protestant iconoclasm in the sixteenth century. Both of these developments influenced the character of the charges brought against Jews in Italy.

The Transfiguration of Sacred Images

By the early modern period, real Jews were no longer being accused of making images transfigure. Transfigurations were still widely reported, but they were attributed to other agents. The Catholic Church had always argued that images did not need to be attacked or desecrated in order for them to act miraculously, and from the late thirteenth century there had been a growth in cults associated with miraculous images, particularly those of the Madonna and Child. Images could transfigure on their own, and this process linked the Christian believer to a power beyond his or her own limited reality, promising protection from grief and sickness and the hope of a better existence. Between 1305 and 1378, when the papacy was absent from Rome and based in Avignon and pilgrimage to Rome no longer appealed, local miracle-working images grew in popularity, becoming associated not only with city's gates and bridges but also with disreputable areas notorious for prostitution, gambling, and heavy drinking.[100] At the end of the fourteenth century, crucifixes, most of them made of polychrome wood, were being placed by the Bianchi—a movement of popular devotion in northern and central Italy that concentrated on honoring the Corpus Christi—in parish churches and oratories.[101] Although this movement did not develop in Rome, many Bianchi crucifixes were reported to be miraculous because of their effusive bleeding, which was connected to the presence of the consecrated Corpus Christi in the church.[102] On occasion these objects would also sweat, cry, or bleed, and the miracle of seeping blood would be credited with providing divine cures or restoring harmony between quarreling parties.[103] By the late fifteenth century, image cults were promoted by the papal administrations of Innocent VIII (1484–1492) and Alexander VI (1492–1503) as miracles of transfiguration.[104] Vernacular literature, widely distributed in manuscript and print, promoted cults of miraculous images and told those who looked upon images how to address and behave personally toward them.[105] Ecclesiastical authorities began to see the need to intervene to legitimize and also control the delicate matter of miraculous Marian shrines that increasingly appeared in and out of churches during the fifteenth and sixteenth centuries.[106] There was a sharp increase in the number of sightings of miracles involving images in the decades immediately following the Council of Trent, especially in the territories subject to the Roman Church.[107] Hence the transfiguration of images was no longer associated primarily with Jewish attempts to test or otherwise abuse them. As images multiplied, it was the persons who venerated them who received the credit for their transfiguration.[108]

Christian images could also bleed if they were attacked by Catholics. However, these Catholics were attacking images from entirely different motives than Jews—chiefly out of frustration and resentment, because a saint or image had failed to give them the help they required.[109] Rather than seeing these images as wholly degenerate and as an idolatrous misconception of how to approach God, Catholics could be accused of testing the effectiveness of these images for themselves. In 1450, a painted Madonna in an arch of a building to the east of Naples, just north of Mount Vesuvius, was said to have bled when a boy threw a ball at it. Immediately, the Madonna dell'Arco became known for her miracles of healing.[110] By the sixteenth century a folktale had spread across Italy concerning a Christian gambler who attacked an image and made it bleed—whereupon the image killed him.[111]

Protestant Iconoclasm

During the sixteenth century, Jews were not the only enemies of sacred images. These objects were being attacked or disparaged by Christian heretics, though large-scale assaults on them, as in cities north of the Alps, were comparatively rare in Italy.[112] Yet Protestant doctrines had still been carried south through printed books promoting Lutheran, Calvinist, Anabaptist, and anti-Trinitarian ideas. In the late 1520s and early 1530s, Martin Luther's works confirmed that images were not required by God and sometimes argued that they should be removed from churches because they were not biblically mandated as necessary for worship or did not help to promote the faith by which alone human beings were justified. Luther moderated his position slightly when arguing against the Zwinglians in Zurich and Andreas Karlstadt in Wittenberg, saying that images should not be used in an idolatrous manner or be considered capable of being miraculous.[113] From 1523, Zwingli preached against the use of images, arguing that they inherently encouraged idolatry among those who viewed them. John Calvin was to go further in the late 1530s and early 1540s when he argued that all Catholic practices not laid down by God in the Bible were corrupt and offensive to God.[114]

The Jews' centrality in their alleged allegations against Christian idolatry was also overshadowed by Protestants' allegations of papal idolatry, which dominated the writings of both Catholics and Protestants. In fact, Luther labeled Catholics and Turks and sometimes Jews as idolaters, furthering his own religious position in light of all the faults of these other religionists.[115] But Luther's main adversaries remained the "Papists," and he ridiculed and mocked them for their blasphemous idolatry and excessive use of imagery. In return, Catholic apologists struck out at Luther, accusing him of being the real idolater.[116] But as is often the case, what was argued in print by Catholic antagonists was in fact the reverse of the truth.

The Catholic Church was thus forced to reformulate its response to sacred images and did so in a body of legislation created during the Council of Trent. Protestant iconoclasm was addressed in late 1562 during the last session. The council made no concession to Protestant opinion and was reasserting the doctrines it had preached in the Middle Ages. Reacting forcefully with its own understanding of the role of material objects in Catholic piety, it hastily defined, in light of the looming conclusion of the council, what constituted true miracle cults of images.[117] Whereas Protestants pointed to the falsity and diabolical origin of what local Catholics purported to be miracles, the papacy vigorously endorsed the value of venerating images and cult relics that dispensed favors, since these had enormous didactic and affective potency. After the close of the Council of Trent, Pope Gregory XIII appointed a four-person commission to carry out and administer the council's reforms; one member of that body was Cardinal Gabriele Paleotti, archbishop of Bologna, who published his *Discorso intorno alle imagini sacre e profane* in 1594.[118] He rebutted Protestant charges of idolatry and demanded that images should be honored and no longer thought to be superstitious, using the standard arguments that medieval theologians had used before him. In the aftermath of the Council of Trent, there was a spate of treatises on the question of decorum in religious art. Ecclesiastical authorities had imposed rules and guidelines where none had previously existed and a rigidly orthodox discipline over the use of these items to ensure their correct usage.[119] Religious images were to be revealed as merely material artifacts, products of artistic labor and individual talent.

* * *

It was the Roman Inquisition that became the important arbiter for the Catholic Church of religious conformity, watching over orthodoxy and purity within Catholicism and then outwardly—to repress heretical movements and to control those who were not Catholic. On July 21, 1542, Paul III (1534–1549), inspired by Cardinal Carafa's favorable impression of the efficiency of the Spanish Inquisition when serving as papal nuncio in Spain and concerned about the state of non-conformity particularly in Modena, Lucca, and Naples, issued the bull *Licet ab initio* reestablishing the Sacred Congregation of the Holy Office (the inquisitorial headquarters) in Italy. This time the Inquisition was to be an interstate institution with a mission to forcibly bring about religious unification and deal with Christian heretics throughout the Italian peninsula who tended to Protestantism. Inquisitorial tribunals were set up in local Franciscan and Dominican convents across the mosaic of separate states in northcentral Italy. Inquisitors had the power to prosecute offenses against the faith "in every single city, village, land and place in the Christian republic."[120] The irony was that inquisitorial authorities would be forced to control usage of the very materiality that Catholicism had made ubiquitous.[121]

The Inquisition invested much time in eradicating practices it considered superstitious, limiting the number of new miraculous cults and targeting, at first, the religious practices of Philo-Protestants. The term "Philo-Protestantism" implies that Protestantism was not highly organized or institutionalized in Italy—there were no Protestant churches, only conventicles, meeting places for people who read the scriptures and listened to sermons and shared the views of Protestant reformers on such matters as justification by faith alone and the nonexistence of saintly intercession, purgatory, and papal authority. There were no Protestant states or cities—just individuals or groups of people who sympathized with Protestant theology. Like the Jews, Philo-Protestants were hostile to images, but their concerns, it appeared, were rather different. Philo-Protestants were much more concerned about saintly intercession and images of saints, whereas Jews were thought to be more focused on images of Mary and Jesus. Jews were thought to see Jesus as a fraud, an ordinary man and a false messiah; Philo-Protestants were thought to object to the image of him on a crucifix. Some of the heretics were Nicodemites, people who observed Catholic rituals and practices while secretly disbelieving in them—rather like crypto-Jews, who outwardly abided by Catholic orthodoxy but followed their true beliefs in their private domestic spaces. The Nicodemites secretly criticized sacred art as a luxury and an economic waste detrimental to the needs of the poor, desecrating images with the intention of reducing them to the status of nonsymbolic objects (such as wood or stone).[122] Like those deeds of fictional Jews in medieval tales, the Philo-Protestants who destroyed images were committing this offense to confirm that they did not believe in the image's power. It was their religious beliefs, manifested through word or deed, that caused them to offend and their beliefs were now investigated.[123]

As mentioned above, even though there was an understandable fear that Protestant iconoclasm would penetrate into Italy, it did not happen on a large scale. Examples of cases in which these heretics actually attacked Christian images are limited. In Udine in 1543, a heretical Franciscan, Francesco Garzotto, led an attack on the church of Santa Maria delle Grazie in which the crowd desecrated all the images, including a statue of the Madonna reputed to perform miracles.[124] There was, at the same time, a rather tentative report to the effect that a woman called La Centa, might have damaged crucifixes and images of saints in her own home. In 1567 the walls of Ambrogio's apothecary in Cannaregio, near the ghetto of Venice, were found to have been stripped of sacred images, because it was a haven for Anabaptists.[125]

Philo-Protestants were denounced more often for disparaging images, for speaking ill of them rather than actually breaking or defiling them. In this way, their offenses, as will be shown, could resemble those attributed to Jews. Alessandro del Fornari was tried by the Inquisition in Modena in 1568 for screaming "Dio traditore!" ("False God" or "Betrayer of God") at a Christ image, and these actions were associated with his membership of a group of Modenese heretics known as the Fratelli.[126] In Venice in 1572, the artisan Battista Amai delle Bambine refused to go with his sister to visit an image of the Madonna at San Samuele in order to pray for a miracle ("He told me that it was very thick-headed [*gran pava di tonto*] to believe that a picture of wood could make miracles"). Battista had apparently decided that he did not believe in saintly intercession; he gave up making sculptures of saints, although that had once been his job.[127] Both Jews and Philo-Protestants were also accused of disrespect for the sacrament for not taking their hats off when they met it. Jews, as will be shown, were accused of being present when they should have been making themselves scarce.

Philo-Protestant iconoclasm remained a concern for the Roman Inquisition until the 1580s. From then, attention returned to the misdemeanors of professing Jews as well as deviant Catholics whose own activities involved suspicious or magical practices, often using sacred objects that may have been stolen. Inquisitorial tribunals made every effort to enforce religious and moral discipline and to obtain a level of cooperation and aid from the surrounding Christian community. In 1593, 1622, and 1637 Bolognese inquisitors dealt with the continual vandalizing of images of Jesus, the Virgin Mary, and the saints by deviant Catholics.[128] In 1622 the archbishop's court and the local Inquisition worked together to fight the heretical group of desecrators who had broken crucifixes and violated the images of the Madonna, offering two hundred scudi and a guarantee of anonymity for witnesses. For these Christian desecrators, inquisitorial procedure was didactic and corrective, providing spiritual penances and sanctions and a means to reenter the broader Christian society. In Modena, in 1623 a twenty-two-year-old Christian painter, Julio Cesare Mellato, admitted that he had soiled an image of San Sebastian that had recently been painted on the main door of the new church of that name. He told the inquisitor general Fra Giacomo Tinti di Lodi that he had intended only to soil the words written underneath the image rather than the image itself. He requested pardon for his actions and a series of penances were considered sufficient punishment for his misdeed.[129]

By the end of the century, the Jews, on various counts, came back into the frame—compulsory conversion sermons (from 1576), assertion of the Holy Office's jurisdiction over professing Jews (1581), perturbation over the protection extended to New Christian apostates in Venice and Livorno (1589, 1593), and eventually, after 1600, the return of some old-style charges of image desecration and the beginning of new-style disrespect. But before we study the inquisitorial trials, we need to consider the nine judicial cases that came before secular courts in the early modern period. How should we explain the continuing profusion of these charges?

Desecration Cases Before Secular Courts in Early Modern Italy

Surviving records show that nine cases of Jewish desecration came before secular courts in the sixteenth and seventeenth centuries, although it is not always clear which courts were involved. These include the ducal courts (5); the Otto di Guardia e Balìa in Florence (1); the Tribunale Criminale del Governatore di Roma (1); and two cases unknown (2).[130] As will become clear, secular courts were generally more hasty and less critical than the Inquisition and more inclined to believe medieval legends. Jews were tried and punished quickly, since the courts were less concerned with a deeper investigation and were influenced by popular feelings and prejudices.

In August 1602, the Duke of Mantua had seven Jews executed without trial for the crime of image desecration. Unfortunately, our knowledge of this case is limited and dependent on the writings of one chronicler, since a large section of the Jewish community archives of Mantua has been lost. An effective Franciscan preacher, Bartolomeo de Cambi (otherwise Bartolomeo Soluzio), had given a venomous sermon attacking the Jews and inciting a riot against them. The allegation was that Jews had made their own Christian image, a crucifix, and then destroyed it to reenact the Crucifixion.[131] This particular incident represents a strange throwback to the "Toledo" tale and to the late fifteenth and early sixteenth centuries when certain Franciscans (particularly Observants, the founders of the Monti di Pietà) had been vociferous critics of the Jews. At that time (in the late fifteenth and early sixteenth centuries) they had occasionally been restrained by governments, for example, in Florence and Venice, who objected to their rabble-rousing sermons, especially if they incited crowds to attack Jewish banks that were holding Christians' property as pledges.[132] The official record of the event—if this can be trusted—was published by Duke Vincenzo of Mantua on August 13, 1602, and distributed all over the city; it was transcribed by the lively Modenese diarist Giovan Battista Spaccini (who, between 1585 and 1636, recorded daily events including descriptions of court activities, daily stabbings, and weather reports). His account suggests that condemnation and punishment happened very quickly, within about six days and without the involvement of the local Inquisition.[133]

> Finding himself in the magnificent city of Mantua, Friar Bartolomeo Soluzio of the order of the Minorites, of Saint Francis, came to preach with great spirit and fervor. Since there was a large number of people, he had to preach in the main square of the city. In a discourse, he expatiated on the malevolence of the Jews, since there were many of them in attendance. Subsequently the preacher had words about it with His Highness, Duke Vincenzo. On another day, in the said piazza, and speaking likewise on the subject of the Jews, he said: "Go to their synagogue. Out of wickedness and evil intention against our Holy Faith and the servants of God, you will find

> that they have made a figure. And because they are unable to vent their wickedness against the servants of God, they direct it against the said figure." Then the most illustrious bishop went immediately to the synagogue, and found those wicked Jews had attached that figure to the rope, and tormented it, inflicting insults and scorn upon it. Finding that the allegation was true, the most illustrious bishop told the duke. He immediately closed the gates of the city, and took seven of the Jews, who were found to be the instigators of such a crime in contempt of the servants of God, and he had them hanged on Tuesday, the thirteenth of the present month. The names of the Jews were: Giacobe Sacerdote, Salamone de Meli, Salamone Forlani, Luzio Soavi, Gioseffe de Nati, Moise de Fano the son of Lazaro, and Rafaelle Franziosi. Apart from this [the duke] banished from his city and dominions the wives, children, brothers, and descendants [of those Jews].[134]

The document stated that the Jews had attached a rope to an image or effigy, tormenting and scorning it. Yet, Spaccini transformed the story of what the Jews did to the figure from being one of mockery to a tale of ritual murder by proxy, suggesting that rumors that Jews had desecrated images were capable of provoking not only the lynching of the culprits themselves but also mob violence against the entire Jewish community. In 1617, he made a rare comment on the prosecution of Jews for this offense. He wrote that he would expect such a reaction among Christians if the Jews were charged with image desecration: "If the Jews had been charged with the desecration of Christian images there would have been a general rising against all Jews, these Jews would have been killed and their possessions burned, and all other Jews would probably have been permanently banned from Modena."[135] Knowing Spaccini's dislike of Jews, whom he repeatedly referred to as *bestie* (beasts), one might speculate that his words reflected his hopes that this sort of treatment by the secular rulers would continue. A severe punishment was, it seems, imposed by a secular court in Siena on certain Jews from Livorno for defacing a number of sacred images. They were condemned to three *tratti* of the *corda* in public, followed by a stretch of galley.[136] I was, however, unable to find any record of this trial in the Archivio di Stato of Livorno.[137]

Spaccini also reported another case that reads like a desecration tale and may have come in 1610 before the governor of Sassuolo, a flourishing center of commerce in the diocese of Reggio Emilia. The item involved a cheap material object, which had been "revalued" speedily in order to blame the Jews for this crime:

> [Wednesday, August 11, 1610.] In Sassuolo, certain Jews went to live in a house belonging to Christians and found an image depicting the Virgin Mary. Not only did they violate and rip up the image—as they have done many times before—but they brought it to their synagogue, and these treacherous scoundrels together publicly abused and burned it and then threw the ashes to the wind. We know about this from a Jewish girl who escaped from her family to become a Christian and disclosed everything. So they [the Jews] were taken, around sixteen of these villainous men, and having been tortured, they all confessed. The word is that this was dealt with by the inquisitor, who conducted the trial, and so [the Jews] will probably receive the punishment they deserve.[138]

But Spaccini did not confirm that the Inquisition was involved.[139] The diocesan archives of Reggio Emilia house the actual correspondence between Cardinal Millino in Rome and the inquisitor Paolo Franco of Reggio from August 1610 to February 1611. It gives a more precise version of the story, suggesting that there were two images of the Blessed Virgin in the Jew's house and that the trial was held before the court of the governor of Sassuolo and not the Holy Inquisition.[140] The name of the Jew(s) and the outcome of the trial are not recorded, but one might presume that, because no other information exists about the trial, the accusation was found to be false and the trial discontinued.

Fanciful medieval allegations resurfaced on another two occasions, although it is not clear whether a secular court dealt with the case or whether the podesta took matters into his own hands. In his *Sefer emeq ha-bakha* the Jewish chronicler the Corrector of Joseph Ha-Kohen describes a riot that took place in 1558 in Recanati (where the Jewish community had existed since the thirteenth century). A neophyte, Fra Filippo Herrera (born Joseph Morro), had entered the synagogue on Yom Kippur and placed a Christian image in the Holy Ark. According to the Corrector, the Jewish community tried to remove Herrera, but it seems that a mob of his supporters had surrounded the synagogue and were ready to accuse the Jews of desecration. This seemed to be an attack on the presence of the synagogue rather than outrage at the Jews' supposed treatment of the image. Herrera's main concern was with the location of the synagogue outside the Jewish quarter; perhaps he was also trying to provoke the Jews into attacking the image, so that they could be charged with desecration.[141] Two Jews were arrested by the podesta of the city, and "they were whipped like burglars in the night in the government area," but no documentation records any court prosecution against them.[142]

There were also times when the secular court showed itself to be more concerned with quelling riots than inflicting harsh punishments on Jews. In 1518 in Empoli, Zaccaria di Isacco da San Minato, a Jewish moneylender, was charged because his small son Angelo had carelessly thrown excrement from his chamber pot onto the Corpus Domini procession from a window of their house.[143] To prevent a potential riot, the Jew was tried by the Otto di Guardia e Balìa and forced to pay ten florins for the creation of a *tabernacolo*—a canopy to cover the host, symbolic of offering protection to it in the future.[144]

There are also cases where the secular courts showed themselves to be more lenient. In 1600 an unnamed Jew of Ferrara was accused of slashing a sacred image placed on the facade of a house in Via Sabbioni.[145] It is unclear which court judged the case, but he was acquitted. On occasions, the leniency of the secular court was a result of ecclesiastical interference. In 1511, Bonaiuto, son of Manuele de Spello of Montefalco, Umbria, was accused of having damaged an image of Saint Nicholas on the external wall of the monastery of Santa Maria Magdalena. He was tried in the secular court, but the bishop of Spoleto, Francesco Ercoli, interceded in the Jew's favor, and the secular court responded to him.[146]

Inquisitorial tribunals found themselves competing with other courts for the right to judge Jews for image desecration. The cardinals of the Sacred Congregation repeatedly insisted upon the Inquisition's autonomy and immunity from secular control, especially when investigating Jews for this crime, but their ability to sentence Jews continued to be a matter of negotiation with other local courts. When, in 1605, they issued a decree claiming exclusive jurisdiction in the matter for themselves, it was not accepted by princely and republican governments.[147] Demands were made in Ancona in 1591, in Modena in 1617, in Rome in 1628, in Florence in 1638, in Reggio in 1650, in Ferrara in 1667, and finally in Livorno in 1671, but these demands were not met.[148] In July 1585, the Sacred Congregation wrote to the Duke of Ferrara demanding that the local Inquisition be given authority to judge Jews who had "spontaneously damaged an image of the Lord Jesus in the arms of the glorious Virgin Mary his mother and another image of the same Madonna"[149] in a house they were renting in Reggio. It seems that the duke did not heed the demands of the Inquisition, but continued to adjudicate on the matter, holding the Jews in lay prisons in Ferrara.[150]

Yet despite directives from Rome, peripheral tribunals were not always able to impose their jurisdiction because of the pressures of princes or secular governments and their own judicial bodies.[151] In 1585 unnamed Jews of Reggio were imprisoned in the secular jail for damaging two images (possibly statues, although the sources are not clear)—one of Jesus in the arms of his mother and the other of the Madonna.[152] The court documents describe a deliberate attack on the facial features: the eyes of Mary and Jesus were gouged out, and the nose of the Madonna was removed. Even though the inquisitor of Ferrara, Niccolo da Bertinova, made efforts to pursue the case and deal with the Jews, whether they committed the crimes and were punished is unclear.[153]

Secular courts were also occasionally involved in dealing with sacred images inside ghetto complexes. In 1580, a group of unnamed Jews requested licenses to remove all sacred images that were in the houses and on the walls of the ghetto in Cremona so that they would not be accused of image desecration.[154] The outcome is unclear. In Rome in 1625, an allegation came before the Tribunale Criminale del Governatore. In the course of some paving work being carried out in the area of the ghetto, the workers came across an "ancient" image of the Virgin and Child at the end of the Savelli alley, which they judged had been recently desecrated either by stones or metal implements.[155] In the related trial, the judge demanded a list of all the sacred representations that were in the ghetto.[156] One of the workers testified to seeing images of the Madonna both inside the houses and along the main roads of the enclosure.[157] The Jewish suspects in the trial who inhabited the building with the image of the Virgin and Child denied even having seen the fresco located on the door of their home, although this remains doubtful. One testified: "I do not know nor have I ever known that in that road of Savelli I live in there is an image depicted on any wall of the house."[158] Despite the Jews' testimony, the notary of the court went to visit the image and came back with the report that it had recently been damaged by "stones, irons, hammers or similar things."[159] It seems likely that the Jews had believed that they could get away with stoning and mutilating an image in their own enclosure. Had Jewish youths just picked up the weapon that was nearest to hand and used it or was there a special significance in the mode of desecration chosen? Perhaps they were retaliating for the occasions on which Christians had thrown stones at their houses during the fifteenth- and sixteenth-century Passiontide?[160] The investigation was eventually moved to the inquisitorial court at the Jews' request. Of the thirty-two Jews originally arrested, six were made to pay a surety of one hundred scudi, and the trial was discontinued. But Pope Urban VIII immediately ordered his cardinal vicar to remove all images from the ghetto to prevent further desecration.[161]

Quasi-medieval charges of image desecration continued to be made well into the seventeenth century. But a majority of desecration cases were now being claimed by the Roman Inquisition, which, as we shall see, looked on the evidence with a critical eye and proceeded with greater deliberation. Its records provide detailed information on the disciplining methods of Catholic orthodoxy regarding the widespread Jewish hostility to Christian representations, images, and symbols.

Inquisition and Jewish Desecration

Thirty-five cases of Jewish image desecration investigated by the Inquisition have so far been identified, as well as four that came before the episcopal court. The inquisitorial tribunals that investigated the cases included Modena (25); Rome (5); Livorno (1); Siena (1); Venice (1); Pisa (1); and Ancona (1). But the number is far from exhaustive. It is unlikely that the exact number of inquisitorial *processi* can ever be known due to the dispersion and the loss of inquisitorial material. The papal move to bring Jews within inquisitorial jurisdiction became an ancillary policy, claiming new responsibilities for the Papal Inquisition and attempting to ensure that professing Jews would be subjected to the system of social and religious discipline that was so important to the post-Tridentine church. In 1581, as noted above, Pope Gregory XIII attempted to define precisely the extent of inquisitorial jurisdiction over professing Jews. Another instrument of discipline was the ghetto, but by 1581 ghettos had been erected in only five Italian cities at this time: Venice (1516), Rome (1555), Bologna (1555), Florence (1571), and Siena (1571). All other cities that housed Jews (including Ancona, Ferrara, Genoa, Mantua, Reggio, Modena, and Savoy) had still not segregated them, despite Pope Paul IV's bull of 1555, *Cum nimis absurdum*, which had urged them to do so. Twenty-one of the thirty-nine cases were unresolved (in which the court dropped but did not formally close the trial). There were twelve convictions in which a penalty was imposed on a prisoner or he received a reprimand. Six of the cases resulted in acquittals.

If we add both the unresolved cases and the acquittals together (twenty-seven cases of the thirty-nine, or 69 percent) it is clear that the Holy Office dropped a fair proportion of cases, either because they did not meet its standards of proof, or because delators were shown to have been inspired by personal malice and no Christian witnesses supported the accusation. At this point the Inquisition would let the accused go and leave the case on file, to be resumed if more evidence turned up at some future date. Obviously, the Inquisition could not impose upon Jews the spiritual penances that were so prominent a feature of the sentences it passed on Christian heretics. Half of the number of Jews convicted were given fines. On four occasions Jews were whipped in the local piazza. Pecuniary punishments became almost a standardized form of punishment for the Italian Inquisition against Jews, which meant financial benefit for the court.[162] Jewish offenders were therefore transformed into debtors without the need for any costly sanctions to be applied or the involvement of other courts in the Jews' punishment. The types of penalties for convictions are listed in Table 1.

The location of the purported image desecration is known in thirty-three of the thirty-nine cases (see Table 2). Most of the Christian images

Table 1. Penalties for Jews convicted of image desecration as a result of judicial proceedings

Pecuniary punishments	6
Public whipping	4
Conversion of Jew (in order to mitigate his punishment)	1
Six months' imprisonment	1
Total	12

Table 2. Location of the purported desecration and number of trials

Images carried in a religious procession	12
Interior/exterior image in a house that Jews rented	6
Images in public spaces	5
Crosses/crucifixes held in banks/Jewish houses	3
Images inside the Jewish ghetto	2
Images inside a church or on the outside wall	2
Images in a prison	1
Images in a spinning mill	1
Images inside the workshop of a Christian artist	1

said to have been attacked were located outside buildings or were being carried in religious processions. But one Jew faced an accusation that he had offended images on the inside walls of a prison. In 1657 Daniele Gallichi was accused of desecrating an image of a crucifix and two saints while he was confined in the lay prison of Siena. In May 1658, after assuming jurisdiction over the case, the Sacred Congregation decided that the investigation should be discontinued due to lack of evidence.[163]

Of the cases in which the images were recorded, most were crucifixes or crosses (14) or statues, carvings, or paintings of the Madonna (11), probably often including the Christ child, since between the fourteenth and the seventeenth century they were frequently depicted together. Only one was a painting of a saint. The fact that crucifixes, crosses, statues of Mary, and Passion paintings were the most common subjects of attack is a reflection of their ubiquity in houses, at street corners, and on walls, as well as in churches and public buildings and in work spaces. The Madonna, as we shall see, was the subject of most of the paintings that were depicted on the interior of the houses in which Jews lived.[164] Perhaps it also echoes the belief, attributed to Jews, that Jesus and Mary were their principal enemies and that, compared with them, most saints were insignificant.

In the next sections, we will address the shift in the nature of charges brought against Jews from "desecration" to "disrespect" and also a shift from the "fantastical" to "rational." We will first study attacks on the Madonna and then move to charges against the Jews for disrespectful acts in their encounters with religious processions, images, and broadsheets. The final sections will consider cases that involved both disrespect and desecration regarding images on the outside and inside of the Jews' domestic spaces.

Attacks on the Madonna

When Jews were investigated for actual desecration by the Holy Office in Rome, the Inquisition, free from competing jurisdictions, was able to swiftly prosecute them and determine the punishments imposed upon the guilty.[165] In the spring of 1611, a group of nine Jews had dined in the tavern next to San Paolo in Rome outside the walls of the ghetto. Christians testified that the Jews, who were probably inebriated, had, on their way back to the ghetto, thrown stones at the effigy of a Madonna depicted on the gate of a vineyard in the vicinity of Monte Testaccio. They were guilty of a physical assault on the Madonna, not of mere disrespect for her, and their heavy sentences reflected the gravity of their crime; drunkenness was no excuse for a violent and blasphemous act. Six of the nine Jews were whipped "through Rome," and the older two were sent to the galleys for ten years—the most severe form of punishment short of death.[166] The Inquisition would not revoke this last punishment, despite the Jews' protestations.[167] Was this perhaps the favored punishment for this crime, imposed by an inquisitorial court undisturbed by competing jurisdictions?[168]

When in 1625, two neophytes, Ruben de Riperno and Leone da Cave, denounced Jews of the Roman ghetto for damaging an "ancient" image of the Virgin on the outside of a building within the confines of the enclosure, Riperno (who after his conversion was known as Angelo Brancaleone) even argued before the Inquisition that his own conversion enabled him to see the painting with clear eyes and notice that it had been desecrated. Six Jews lived in the building, but only four of them were arrested and imprisoned, since the other two were judged too old and short-sighted to have been involved in the desecration.[169] The case was passed to the Inquisition, but the outcome is not known.

Inquisitors interrogating Jews were inclined to put to them the proposition that Jews were naturally prone to insulting and damaging images of Christ and the Virgin. The inquisitor general Fra Michelangelo Lerri said to Simon de Camerino in 1614: "You are a Jew, and by your very nature derive a hatred of Christians and their own rites and ceremonies. You see yourselves above our nation, our Lord Jesus Christ and the Blessed Virgin his mother and consequently . . . it is likely that you uttered words to insult the images of the Blessed Virgin . . . It is unlikely that the deposition against you is not true."[170] In 1627, Domenico Greco, the vicar-general of the Inquisition in Modena, said these words to Emanuel Rava, a Jewish suspect accused of desecrating a painting of the Blessed Virgin on a street corner: "It is highly improbable that on such an occasion Christians would voluntarily throw stones [at a sacred image]. It is much more likely that Jews would throw stones at the Blessed Virgin, being enemies, you throw stones injuring the figure."[171] One senses not only the court's bias in the total rebuttal of Rava's statement, but also in the assumption that the Jews would commit this crime. These sources confirm the extent to which the Inquisition continued to propagate this narrative. The Jews' abuse was understood as their transgression of religious boundaries. If images were desecrated, the Inquisition expected Christians to denounce Jews for it.

* * *

A particularly intriguing case of 1627 was against five young Jewish men accused of throwing stones at an image of the Blessed Virgin in Carpi, Modena. The actual interrogations offer insight into the fear that some Jews had regarding Christian images. Two Christian witnesses in this case—Theodoro de Theodoro and Gio Batesto Soleri—testified that Beatrice, the mother of two of the young Jewish suspects, had, the following morning, while standing near the damaged Madonna image, mumbled: "What does it matter whether that statue bleeds or not? No harm will come of it!"[172] That Beatrice seemed to be referring disrespectfully to the transfiguration of the image worried Fra Domenico Greco, the vicar-general of the Holy Office in Modena. He decided to imprison her and conducted three interrogations in which Beatrice consistently denied that she had spoken such words. When Beatrice was interrogated on October 9 and 10, 1627, she reacted nervously when the inquisitor accused her of referring to the bleeding of an image. The notary recorded that she said while crying: "Sir, never did I say such words. How can Your Lordship think that I said them, because if I had opened my mouth on that occasion, those Christians would have attacked me."[173] It is unlikely that Beatrice would have risked making such a statement in front of Christians at a time when her sons were suspected of desecrating the image.[174] But in the minds of Christians, such comments triggered associations of Jews intentionally damaging images and causing them to bleed. At the end of the interrogation, Greco sent his vicar to examine the statue, who assured him that there was no evidence of bleeding.[175] The five Jews were ultimately found innocent.[176] It transpired that two poor Christians, Silvestro Bucchina and Vincenzo Stambacino, who had been sleeping under a portico, were suddenly awakened by having a lantern shone in their faces by Jews on their way to nocturnal prayers. Angered by this disturbance, the two Christians tried to stone the Jews and, missing their targets in the dark, had hit the image instead.[177] Thus Jews could even fall prey to fabricated accusations by their Christian neighbors, keen to absolve themselves of the blame of desecrating images. However, in regard to more substantial images on public streets and in piazzas, the inquisitorial *processi* confirm that Jews accused of harming these public images were not usually found guilty.

Encounters with Religious Processions

Between 1601 and 1670 charges of a different nature, involving disrespect for holy objects rather than violence or vandalism, began to be made before the Papal Inquisition. Fourteen cases involved the Holy Sacrament and religious images being escorted through the streets, or passing under the windows of houses on the outside edge of the ghetto, or Jews entering churches to see the duke's funeral.[178] Streets in Italian cities and towns were enhanced with entry facades, decorated doorways, and large piazzas that facilitated the flow of religious processions. Unlike the faithful who were to venerate the Eucharist and images by looking at them when they passed by and when they were displayed on temporary altars set along the streets in towns and cities, Jews were to remove their hats or take flight.

Jews had first been prohibited from attending processions of the consecrated host by the Council of Vienna in 1267, a year before their supposed desecration of the crucifix in the Oxford procession.[179] Once the festival of the Corpus Christi, a thanksgiving procession that venerated Christ's body, was celebrated all over Europe, any person present was expected to salute by removing their hats and reflecting upon the miraculous presence of the historic body of Christ in the monstrance passing before them.[180] The fear of Jewish proximity to the Eucharist in the Corpus Christi processions had intensified from the twelfth to the fifteenth century, mainly due to the proliferation of host desecration allegations.[181] The sight of Jews, with their hats securely and defiantly upon their heads, frustrated the Christians' sense of exclusive participation in the procession.[182] It confirmed and contributed to a sense of anti-structure—a failure to safeguard what was sacred—reminding Christians that occupants of their public space included followers of a different religion who might contaminate the event. This explains why, in the 1370s before the papal court of Avignon, fearful Christians accused Jews of failing to kneel during these processions and blaspheming in Hebrew when the displayed sacrament passed before them.[183] Jews were in fact forbidden by Jewish law to kneel before the Eucharist or any holy image. Any form of prostration was an act of worship.[184]

When the Modenese Inquisition promulgated its edict *Contra gli abusi del conversare de Christiani con Hebrei* against Jews in 1603, it demanded that no Jews should be present when religious processions passed through the duchy:[185] "They are not to meet in processions of Christians, and particularly when the most holy sacrament is being brought."[186] By 1667, the Inquisition of Ferrara under Inquisitor General Giacinto Maria Granara de Genoa had issued more specific directions on how Jews were to avoid encountering a Christian procession. The edict ordered:[187] "Jews found in a place where a procession passes, or a confraternity, with crosses or holy images, have to immediately retreat, not just turning away, but absenting themselves completely."[188]

Most of the twelve cases were initiated with delations by Christians, sometimes priests, who were irritated by the Jews' presence and their seeming contempt for processions and their participants. When, in 1639, a young friar of Santa Nicolai in Terra Finale was asked why he was denouncing Simone Donati Gentile (da Asolo) and Israel Rubiera, whom he accused of not withdrawing into their shop during a funeral carried out by the friars, he noted: "I have come to exonerate my conscience, but also because of the hatred that these Jews carry for Christians."[189] He clearly saw the Jews' presence at the procession as a defiant act of contempt. In 1636, Father Jacobo de Lauda came before the Inquisition in Modena to express his annoyance at seeing the Jewish banker Jacobo Donato, his wife Stella, and their Christian wet nurse standing at the window of their house (where most Italians gathered to perform tasks that needed daylight), while the Feast of the Holy Rosary procession passed by.[190] The priest admitted that he had looked up in the hope of catching some Jew out: "I looked at the window of the said Jacob to see if some Jew was there while the procession passed."[191] Witness testimony also suggests that these Christians expected the Jews to be aware of convenient escape routes, though these probably did not come to the Jews' minds in the heat of the moment.[192] Their close proximity to processions meant that accidents often happened. When Alessandro Formiggini was accused of failing to show reverence to the Holy Sacrament while he was walking through the streets of Terra Finale in Modena, he argued that he had been standing on the embankment of the Ponte Nuovo, and thus could not hide in time from the chaplain carrying the Eucharist to the sick.[193] Nor could he, he argued, enter one of the courtyards or houses in the vicinity because he did not know to which house the Eucharist was being taken.[194] On All Saints Day 1665, at a Christian funeral conducted by seven friars in Modena, Simon Levi and Samuel Sanguinetti were caught with their hats on their heads, in the presence of the Holy Cross. Both Jews argued that they had been inebriated, "having drunk some good wine," and apologized.[195]

What appeared to particularly annoy the Christian delators and witnesses was that the Jews, like defiant Philo-Protestants, refused to doff their hats toward the image. In Terra Finale in 1657, when Moysen Israel Meli was brought to the Inquisition for failing to absent himself from a procession carrying the Holy Sacrament, he stated that the Jews' failure to remove their hats was in fact done out of duty to Jewish law: "If I was contemptuous in not taking off my hat on this occasion, it is because, for us Jews, it is prohibited to remove our hats on such occasions."[196] In July 1639, the sixty-year-old Salomon de Moise de Castelfranco, when accused of standing firm with his hat upon his head when the Holy Cross passed him during a funeral, could only promise that in the future he would be more careful.[197]

Other Jews gave more imaginative excuses. In 1627 a group of unnamed Jews in Modena were denounced by the priest, Michael de Montilio, for encountering a procession on the corner of the street where they lived. They had failed to remove their hats, thereby showing contempt, when the Holy Eucharist was carried from the Duomo through the streets toward the home of a sick person.[198] One of the Jewish offenders, Gibertoni, told the inquisitor that, in Rome, he was used to the Holy Sacrament being carried under a canopy, and he had not identified its presence in the procession because it did not have a canopy above it.[199] The trial was discontinued.

In June 1631, Naphtali de Sermide of Finale was accused of a "certain contempt and irreverence for the most holy crucifix" by failing to move away from a procession of the Compagnia della Morte (a procession in Modena that accompanied criminals to execution, exhorting them to repent and bear their sufferings patiently) and in particular turning his back on the crucifix, which was carried on high so that all could see its approach.[200] When Naphtali was imprisoned and interrogated, his detailed knowledge of how the execution and burial was conducted suggested to the Inquisition that his fascination with the proceedings had actually caused him to linger unwisely. After being in prison and interrogated he was given a grave warning and released.[201]

Inquisitor General Giacomo Tinti of Modena had his notary draw a map of the intersection in Terra Finale where Emmanuel Castelfranco had stood without removing his hat at a funeral procession in 1645, when sacred images were carried past him. The Jew, in turn, used the map in order to testify to his exact location.[202] In this case, his reluctance to leave reflected his desire to show respect at the funeral of a friend. Emmanuel told the inquisitor: "Reverend Father, yes I knew the late Monsignor Domenico Ferrara. He was a great friend, whom I knew in Finale."[203] Although hints at friendship between Jew and Christian are rare in the cases that deal with the Jews' presence at processions, one can even find glimpses of tolerance and understanding on the part of Christian witnesses toward the unlucky Jew caught in the wrong place at the wrong time. In 1627 the priest Johannes Thomaso de Gibertoni showed compassion toward the predicament of Jews in these cases. He argued: "I believe that the most Holy Sacrament appeared suddenly before the Jews and therefore they were not able to retire in time. This action should not be attributed to malice but more to an oversight."[204] In 1657 the Dominican Reinaldini Vecchio—a citizen of Finale—had even gone to the criminal court in Terra Finale to state that he was with Moysen Israel Meli, the tobacco dealer, who was riding a donkey toward Modena when the procession carrying the Holy Sacrament to a sick woman had suddenly appeared. Despite Vecchio's testimony in his favor, Moysen was punished with the *tratto di corda* for a quarter of an hour in the public square.[205]

One of the reasons for enclosing Jews in ghettos in northern Italy during the late sixteenth and seventeenth century was to prevent them from seeing Christian processions. These areas were out of bounds for such activities, and their outward facing windows had to be covered to block the Jews' view. In 1579, the Jews in the ghetto of Rome were denounced for pelting stones at a procession carrying the Holy Sacrament to a sick person in his home (a practice done if they were too feeble to get to church). Nothing is known about the investigation of this crime or whether any punishment was imposed for it.[206]

The ghettoization of Jews (except those of Venice [1516] and Rome [1555]) would often involve specific policies to clear these areas of sacred images both outside and inside domestic spaces to control what Jews saw within their own enclosure.[207] Yet it has been argued that in Rome sacred images might have been left intentionally in order to persuade the Jews to convert to Christianity.[208] Most of the buildings surrounding the ghetto belonged to churches and confraternities, and representations of sacred subjects were found in both their interiors and exteriors.[209] Jews could be accused of irreverence and contempt for being physically present at processions or for being seen at their windows, which, at the time of the processions, were supposed to be closed. In 1625, Jews in Venice were charged with appearing at the windows of houses on the periphery of the ghetto, looking out over the Christian world, thereby offending Christians accompanying the sacrament.[210] This episode caused temporary unrest and stalled the negotiations over the renewal of the community's charter.[211]

In these cases, as noted above, the Inquisition intended to reprove and punish the Jews for disrespect for the Christian church rather than for more serious acts of sacrilege or blasphemy. But the intensity of investigations and the choice of punishments in these cases seem arbitrary. It depended on how much time the court had to spend on investigation and how important it was to individual inquisitors to punish the Jews. When in 1631 in Modena the inquisitor general, Fra Giacomo Tinti di Lodi, had sentenced Alessandro Formiggini to be whipped for not showing reverence when he encountered a religious procession, he did this without seeking permission in Duke Francesco I d'Este's name from the governor Tiburzio Madoni. Giovan Battista Laderchi, the ducal secretary, reprimanded Tinti for his unauthorized action and made him promise to observe ducal rules on the punishment of Jews in the future.[212]

Jews expressed in their testimonies their absolute respect for and sensitivity to the Christian icons and sacred objects that surrounded them and those that were carried in processions. Most understood that the ringing of the bell preceded the procession, and their best move was to retreat before it approached.[213]

Encounters with Images and Broadsheets

Jews also had to navigate the more permanent images displayed on external walls and niches, which offered protection to the surrounding location. These images were meant to expediate crowd movement and prevent street violence in the hope that people would be discouraged from rioting or quarreling by the need to show reverence for religious images.[214] The Jews were the only inhabitants of these towns and cities who were expected to look away and pass them without acknowledgment or reaction.[215] The Jews confirmed in their testimonies that their routes around town often took into account their desire to bypass these objects. This was borne out by their claim that they could not remember what was depicted in these images, suggesting that they conscientiously tried to ignore them. What they did not admit was that they had a defiant verse that they commonly uttered to protect themselves when they encountered these images. This was revealed by the neophyte Giacomo Grisoffi in 1605 in a trial against Donato Donati for dissuasion of baptism. He testified to the imprecation Jews uttered when Christians bowed down to a holy image during the Ave Maria:[216] "When they hear us singing the Ave Maria and the Christians kneel on the ground . . . they [the Jews] say the words of that verse of David, *Ipsi obligati sunt, et ceciderunt: nos autem surreximus et erecti sumus*,[217] which as the Jews understand it, means that those who kneel [the Christians] are small, unlike those others [the Jews] who stand on foot and are being raised in the grace of God. Their words are these: *ema caru, venafalu, vehanacnu camnu, vanit odad*."[218] By standing tall and failing to genuflect, Giacomo Grisoffi argued, the Jews believed themselves to remain closer to God than those Christians who had bowed down to worship him through the image.

However, one can also infer from these sources that some Jews did not always go out of their way to avoid Christian images and were capable of entering churches despite prohibitions against such actions.[219] In 1659, Josepho Daini and Abram Basilieri, two Jews of Reggio, caused a scandal because they entered the church of Sant' Agostino in Modena for the funeral of Duke Francesco I.[220] Knowing that their presence had caused some offense they came to denounce themselves before the Inquisition. Daini admitted to entering the church: "Out of curiosity, I was moved to enter the church to see the funeral of the most Serene Signor Duke but immediately I saw that church mass was being celebrated, so I left . . . I have come to ask pardon of the Holy Office, and assure you that we did not do this out of contempt, but out of inadvertence and that we are both foreigners. This is what I wanted to say to the Holy Office."[221] It seems that these Jews did not act particularly out of character. Their respect for the duke clearly overrode any discomfort they may have had with the ubiquity of Christian sacred images, crucifixes, and statues that surrounded them in that space. In 1663—a year after the next duke, Alfonso IV, had been buried—news reached the Inquisition that "a multitude of Jews" had voluntarily entered the church for the funeral and that they still wore their hats.[222] This caused a scuffle near the catafalque of the duke when local soldiers forced the Jews to remove them.[223] No Jew was called to defend himself. It can certainly be surmised that the discomfort Jews were supposed to feel with images outside their premises was, on occasion, exaggerated in the minds of Christians.

Other types of disrespect included verbal contempt of Christian images. In several cases, Jews were accused of verbally insulting Christian images. The concept of "insulting" a sacred image was included in definitions of blasphemy within religious discourse and codified within canon and secular law. Such a verbal attack in Rome in 1635 forced a whole family to choose conversion after being accused of blaspheming against a ciborium.[224] Whether this was an easy way out of a complicated accusation cannot be determined, due to lack of evidence. In Modena in 1539, an unnamed Jewish banker was accused of entering the workshop of the painter Niccolò dell'Abate, who, at that time, was painting a crucifix, and calling out, "What a beast that is!" The Jew was arrested by the episcopal vicar and heavily fined.[225]

Cheap paper prints were of no less importance to Christian authorities, who looked to what they represented rather than to the quality of the materials. But because they were fragile, they presented new problems. Inquisitorial courts sometimes considered the possibility that they had been accidentally rather than maliciously damaged. In Ancona in 1569, two Jews were indicted and investigated for burning a paper image of the Passion, but precise information on this case is not extant.[226] In 1609, in Modena, a fifty-five-year-old Christian carpenter, Fabio de Chiaveri, appeared before the inquisitorial vicar Hippolito Francesco de Mantua to report that an unknown Jew had urinated under a print of the Blessed Virgin glued to a wall on the small piazza by the city's main street.[227] He could give no indication as to who the Jew was or what he looked like, but he was quite certain that the offense had been committed by a Jew.[228]

* * *

In 1614, the sixty-two-year-old Simon de Camerino, accused of calling religious prints depicting the Blessed Mary and Saint Carlo Borromeo, hanging in a neighboring stall in the market of Piazzetta del Pallone, "bollocks" (*coglioni*), was able to argue his case more convincingly.[229] These prints had been hung by Adolpho Foraci de Bonania, who owned the stall next to the Jew, on the common wall between them and on the entrance to the Jew's stall. Adolpho had even left them up on Sundays when the stalls were shut, arguing that he did not have enough space to hang them in his own stall. He accused Simon of taking them down. When imprisoned and interrogated, Simon de Camerino naturally tried to defend himself, denying that he had in any way shown disrespect for the prints or their subjects.[230] But he did succeed in testifying to a more practical reason why he had demanded the removal of the sacred images: "I said that he [Adolpho] had to take those pictures away because they prevented me from opening and closing my door, and they were falling to the ground since they were attached only with a little nail. . . . I forbade him to put up those sacred images in order that they would not fall to the ground and then I would be investigated here by the Holy Office. But regarding the other images, there was no danger and I did not forbid him putting those up."[231] The Jew was given a warning and released without further punishment on November 10, 1614.

In 1620, Isacco de Sacerdote (the future rabbi of Finale), Giuseppe Melli, and Abramo Collorni were accused of showing contempt to a broadsheet sold by a local book vendor in a square in Terra Finale—in particular a drawing that depicted Jesus being crowned with thorns.[232] The three young men were accused of ridiculing the image with the following words: "These are fables they recount about history" (Queste sono favole che contano quelli del l'historia).[233] Isacco de Sacerdote argued that when he had been in a stall buying books, he had never seen nor mocked an image of the crucifixion, since "we [Jews] are not able to look at such images."[234] When interrogated further, Isacco de Sacerdote began to suggest that his mocking words might have been misinterpreted by the Christian delator: "It is possible that we said these words speaking of some other picture, but God is my guard, never have we said these words as the witnesses reported."[235] A sufficient number of Christian witnesses were able to testify that they had heard the derogatory words, and the Jews were convicted and sentenced to three years imprisonment. This however was commuted to a fine.[236]

When, in 1607, Abraam de Sacerdote had discovered that a broadsheet depicting the crucifixion with John the Evangelist at Jesus's feet had been attached to the entrance of the shop that he was renting in Modena, he went immediately to the inquisitor general Fra Serafino Borra.[237] Reading it as defacement of his property and a malicious, injurious insult, Abraam tried to protect himself against a potential accusation of disrespect. The inquisitor immediately sent one of his ministers to remove the image, and although there was no further investigation, the actual broadsheet was affixed to the back of the *processo* (Figure 28).

The print is a popular and rather primitive woodcut, strongly influenced by German Passion scenes that were fashionable throughout Reformation Europe, with a heavily wounded Christ, intended to arouse sympathy with his suffering, and a skull representing Golgotha resting at the bottom of the cross on the right. It was one of the most powerful devotional tools available to believers and suitable for a domestic setting.[238] Whoever had put it there

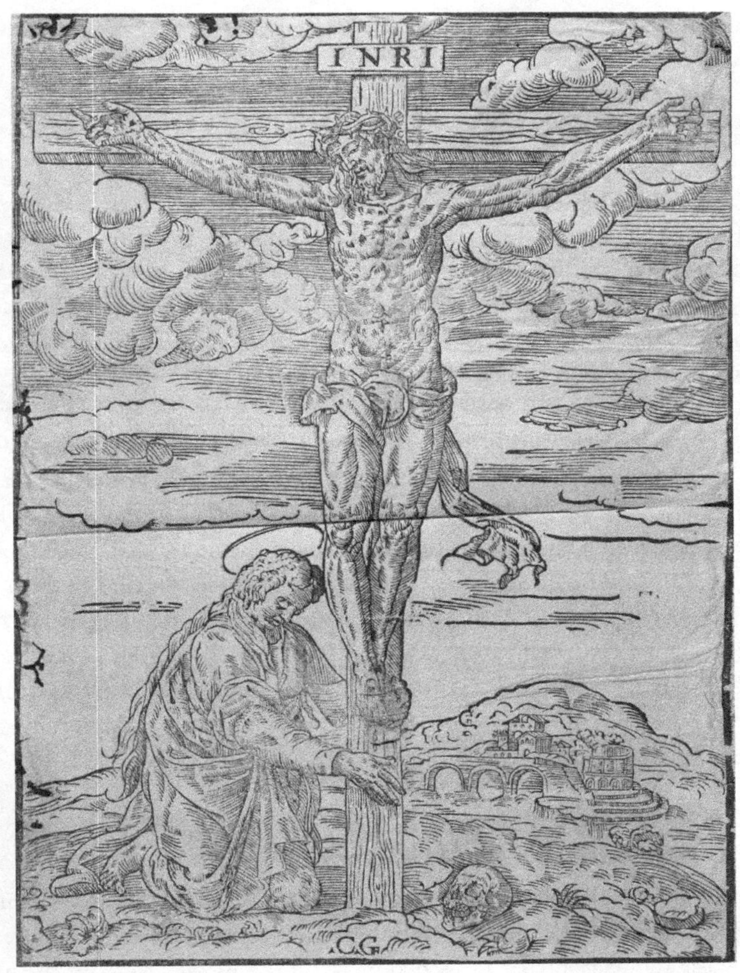

Figure 28. The broadsheet attached to the back of Abraam de Sacerdote's confession. Archivio di Stato di Modena, Fondo dell'Inquisizione, Processi 29, folio 19.

might have been trying to rid themselves of a sacred object they did not want or might have intended to get the Jew in trouble.

Images Inside and Outside Jewish Homes

Finally, in this last section we turn to domestic images inside the more affluent Jews' rented homes. These sacred images were frescoes or panel paintings incorporated into the woodwork (such as built-in devotional tabernacles, cupboards, wainscoting, or doors), sometimes many centuries old.[239] Whereas in earlier centuries Jews had struggled to acquire licenses to whitewash domestic images, in the seventeenth century Jews standing before the Holy Office showed that they had found that more temporary coverings were less likely to incur perilous charges of image desecration. In 1613 Raffaello Moreno, originally from Constantinople, was brought before the Holy Office in Pisa, accused of defacing an image of the Madonna in the house that he had rented for two years. He argued that he and his family had never lifted the cloth that covered the painting. He testified that this had been installed by the Christian landlord of the house, and he [Raffaello] would not have dared to deface a Christian image. He was probably able to use his license to confirm how the image had looked on the day he had moved in. As a result of his testimony, he was acquitted.[240]

* * *

Other Christian landlords also denounced their Jewish tenants. In 1619, a noble Christian landlord, Don Herculeo da Coccopani, testified before the Modenese Inquisition that a frescoed image of the Blessed Mary in the niche of a parapet around the stairs in the courtyard of a house that he owned in the district of San Nicolo in Carpi near the church of San Giovanni might be damaged.[241] The house had been occupied by a Jew, Salvatore de Modena, for twenty-five years. Coccopani said that, before Salvatore's time there, the painting had been covered by a board as specified in an episcopal license from the local vicar of the College of Priests, and he was anxious that the state of the image be rechecked.[242] However the investigation was not continued, and no record was made regarding the image's condition. Nor was Salvatore de Modena called to give evidence.

With this continuous anxiety regarding images in Jewish property, it is not surprising that Jews should, wherever possible, avoid renting premises that contained Christian images in any form. (This problem would generally only arise in places that had no ghetto). In 1613, Raffaello Moreno told the inquisitor in Pisa that Jews would no longer live in a house with a sacred image "because our law prohibits this absolutely."[243] But this answer probably reflected a well-rehearsed response rather than new rabbinical rulings on this. In 1627, Simone Camerino and his son-in-law Zaccharia Sassano—Jews of Modena—were investigated for wanting to rent a property that had depicted on its outside wall "a large figure of the Blessed Virgin facing the street."[244] It was revealed that the Jews had in fact wanted to remove not the image itself but the torch above it, since it provided illumination for members of a Christian confraternity who venerated the image by singing a litany before it every Saturday night.[245] The Jews' proposal to rent this apartment had clearly alarmed the Christian group. Zaccharia testified before Fra Domenico Greco: "Your Lordship should be assured that I absolutely did not say that the figure should be removed, but I only spoke of the danger of the lamp. I did not want to go and live in that house because of the danger. It would be much worse now to go and live there because these Christians are praying outside the house. They seem to be doing this to show their contempt of us."[246]

Because of this, Zaccharia testified, the Jews had decided not to rent the property.[247] It seems that by the middle of the seventeenth century certain cities such as Reggio had begun to authorize rulings that Jews could not live in properties that housed images of the Virgin or of Christ.[248] Pressure might have come equally from the Jews themselves and Christian authorities; whether this was part of an attempt to completely remove frescoes in ghetto apartments needs further research.

Crucifixes, Relics, and Pawnbrokers

In their domestic spaces, Jews not only lived but often ran their pawnbroking activities and stored, as we will see, small valuable pendant crucifixes made of gold or silver that had been pledged as security for loans.[249] Reliquary pendants (some of them very costly because of the sacred value of their contents) had become popular in the late fourteenth and early fifteenth centuries and had been worn to provide protection and remind the faithful of the sacred in their lives.[250] In mid-seventeenth-century Modena, pendant cross reliquaries, which contained tiny compartments filled with blessed wax or minute pieces of bone or fabric that had belonged to a saint, became the focus of three inquisitorial investigations. These pendants were worn around the neck on a chain or pinned to one's clothes and usually had their contents inscribed on the lid. Christians would open them and hold them in their hands during prayer, so that the relics could be gazed upon, venerated, and possibly extracted and kissed. The blessed wax, known as Agnus Dei—remains of the paschal candle of the previous year—had been blessed liturgically during Easter celebrations as a symbol of the body of the resurrected Christ.

Christians brought their little silver, gold, or pendant crosses as security for low-interest loans to Jewish bankers in Italy, just as they did to Monti di Pietà.[251] However, it is not clear whether the ducal charters expressly allowed Jews to accept religious objects that were personal possessions rather than church property, or merely did not forbid them doing so. The difference between "personal property" and "church property" was a complicated distinction when sacred images and devotional objects were involved. Movable sacred images utilized in churches could technically/legally be the property of the patrons who commissioned them. Families and confraternities with chapels/altars in churches could sell or repurchase their portable sacred images and could also restore or remove painted images, probably without obtaining a license. Jews obviously had every reason to keep these securities in a good state of preservation, ready to be handed back whenever the borrower could provide the funds. Yet, as we shall see, Jews could be prosecuted if they were suspected of trading in even the smallest crosses.

Sixteenth-century ecclesiastics often specified the items that must on no account be pawned with Jewish bankers.[252] In 1592, Girolamo Rusticucci, the cardinal vicar of Rome, had stated that Jews were not allowed to receive images of Christ, the Virgin, or the Saints, or any objects connected to sacred religious ceremonies.[253] This ruling was reissued in the middle of the seventeenth century, when the Holy Office in Rome was told that its rulings were being ignored.[254] Other edicts were propagated all over northern Italy in places where Jews served as pawnbrokers. In 1603, clause 7 of an edict of the newly established inquisitorial court in Modena stated: "We expressly prohibit and order that Jews do not sell or hold in their shops, nor take as pawns, objects of the church like goblets, patens, chalices, crosses, figures, images, relics and such things."[255]

From about 1600, there were four hundred to five hundred Jewish banks in northern and central Italy, but their number declined in some parts during the seventeenth century when banks were displaced by the Monti di Pietà and many of the more successful Jewish entrepreneurs turned to international trade in the ports of Ancona, Genoa, Livorno, and Venice. A common reason for the presence and survival of Jewish banks was the inability of many Monti di Pietà to meet the needs of local Christians. There were several reasons why Christians preferred to deal with Jews. Resorting to a self-proclaimed charity—even to one that did not give outright—could inflict a blow on a borrower's pride. Dealing with a Jew—the representative of a defeated religion—allowed Christians to retain a sense of moral superiority and regard the loan as a business transaction, not a form of almsgiving. The Jews were less hidebound than the Monti—freer to lend to outsiders, willing to accept pledges that a Monte would reject, able to lend on written undertakings alone, and, of course, less prone to perfunctory moral judgments. But from a religious standpoint—or at least from that of the Holy Office—even small crosses worn close to the body by individual Christians were especially cherished pieces of devotional jewelry and powerful religious symbols worthy of the utmost respect. These objects were associated with an aura of divinity and with private and religious everyday contemplation. By 1667, the Inquisition in Ferrara and Comacchio was more specific as to what Jewish pawnbrokers could receive on their premises.

* * *

An inquisitorial edict ruled: "We have renewed the prohibition at other times in the past, not allowing them to buy, nor to receive on their premises as pledges, jewels, gold, silver, fabric upon which are crosses, or other holy images, let alone chalices, or other consecrated things."[256] When Elia Teseo stood before Fra Laurentio de Parma, the inquisitorial vicar, on May 5, 1665, having been accused of holding crucifixes (some of them pendants designed to be worn around the neck) in his pawnshop, known as the "bank of the Spaniards" (*banco degli Spagnoli*) in Modena, he testified: "We Jews set up our bank according to the charter made by our Signor Duke and in this charter we can receive in pawn [Christian] crosses worn around the neck. I thought that it was not an error to take them as pawns, because in the charter there is a distinction between those things we are able and not able to pledge. If you want to see the charter, I will bring a copy."[257] Elia Teseo was not the first Modenese banker to be accused of holding such devotionalia. Investigations had already been conducted in 1617, 1641, and 1645.[258] None of these cases proved that Jews had actually abused the images and crucifixes in their care. The inquisitors seemed to be using these investigations to remind the Christians that it was improper to entrust such things to those followers of a religion who would at best treat them with indifference.

The 1617 case against Simone Sanguinetti seems to show how Jewish conspirators could play upon Christian beliefs that Jews were inclined to desecrate images. Michele Sanguinetti, a thirty-seven-year-old Jew, appeared before Fra Massimo Guazzone, the inquisitor general of Modena, with a fabricated charge against the wealthy Jewish banker Simone Sanguinetti (no relation).[259] In his denunciation, Michele testified to a fictitious meeting between him and the Jewish moneylender Simone Sanguinetti. He reported that when he had gone to pledge in Simone Sanguinetti's bank, the banker had "in a scornful fashion" blatantly broken open a crucifix filled with relics in front of him and tossed the relics out of the window: "It was five or six months earlier I went with Abramo Sanguinetti, son of Calmo, and Giuseppe Pontasso to see Simone Sanguinetti and pawn a sparrow hawk which belonged to Abramo. I then saw Simone break a cross bearing the figure of Christ, to which was attached a label [or ticket] and attempt to show contempt for it. The crucifix fell to the ground and some relics dropped out of it. Simone picked them up and threw them out of the window."[260] Even though within a few days the Inquisition had received two further delations from fellow conspirators Abramo Sanguinetti and Giuseppe Pontasso, which would have ensured the indictment of the wealthy Jewish banker, the court neither interrogated nor imprisoned him, clearly unwilling to risk wrongfully accusing a prominent member of the Jewish community. Michele Sanguinetti's accusation transpired to be the main component of a wide-scale fabricated plot against the wealthy Jewish bankers with the intention of irreparably damaging their reputation and prominent position, not only in Modenese society but also in the neighboring cities.[261] But in addition, the false testimony, which had to be credible in order for it to be acted upon, reflects the popular and common fear that Jews would handle crosses and relics contemptuously in their banks. The other delators coordinated their testimony. Abramo Sanguinetti elaborated further, giving evidence of Simone Sanguinetti's anger at having been observed while throwing a reliquary cross out of the window:

> I saw that he had a cross in his hand when he came to open the door [of the bank]. I then saw that he broke the cross, upon which an image of Christ was sculpted. I do not remember if the said cross with the Christ upon it was made of silver or gold. I saw also that when he broke the cross, relics fell out of it onto his desk, and then Simone took them in his hands, and threw them outside one of the windows of the bank, perhaps believing that we had not seen this. When he noticed that we had followed him into the bank, he became angry and said to us that he had told us to stand outside the bank and wait.[262]

Camillo Jaghel da Correggio (1554–ca. 1624), a neophyte who converted to Christianity in the early 1600s, a physician and corrector of Hebrew books, seems to have played an important role in conveying crucial information to the Inquisition.[263] He willingly agreed to act as the spokesperson for the *massari* (lay delegates) of the Jewish community. He appeared before the Inquisition after gaining the support of the duke's minister, Giambattista Laderchi de Imola. Jaghel stated:

> The lay delegates [*massari*] of the corporation of the Jews of Modena, i.e., David Diena, Samuel Sanguine, Moisè da Modena and Giuseppe Fiorentino, had heard tell of a plot hatched by Giuseppe Pontasso, Salomon Sacerdote, Michele Sanguinetti and Abramo Sanguinetti. They proposed to gather certain images of the Virgin and Christ our Lord, to defile and so profane them, and then hide them in the houses of several of the richer Jews—including those of the said Moisè da Modena, of a Jew at Carpi near Ravenna whose name I cannot remember, and of a number of others. The *massari* applied to His Highness the Duke, gave him a vociferous account of the conspiracy, and asked for a judge who would punish these criminals, pointing out the grave offense to God and the danger which all the Jews would incur if the plot were carried out.[264]

He continued, making it clear that his testimony was not to support the Jews on trial but for the sake of "simple truth": "They are utterly notorious, considered as evil spies throughout the whole city, more so by Jews than Christians and this I have testified for the sake of simple truth, and not for another interest."[265]

The neophyte confirmed that the conspirators' false accusation was being investigated by one Rondanelli, an ordinary judge of the Palazzo, who had accepted their request for action against these Jewish conspirators.[266] Although Michele Sanguinetti and Giuseppe Pontasso had fled in time, Abramo Sanguinetti was left standing trial alone and was tortured during one of his interrogations. Since he did not confess, Rondanelli accepted his story that he was not part of the conspiracy and released him. Jaghel's role here could not have been more different from neophytes in earlier cases who continued to falsely delate Jewish offenders. It confirms how an important neophyte could also mediate and protect the Jews from a false accusation.[267]

Inquisitorial edicts repeatedly prohibited Jewish bankers from holding relics, and those who accepted them, rather than the Christians who had pledged them, faced serious investigation. In 1645, Francesco Rabali, a fifty-five-year-old Christian, came to confess his friend's offense to the Inquisition.[268] He admitted that Giovanni Bacchino had asked him to entrust his wife's gold pendant cross—half a finger in length and "without any ornament or picture upon it"—to the Jewish banker Isaac Rovigo.[269] The pendant was a reliquary, although he had not known this at the time and, "out of a great need for money," Rabali had taken it to Rovigo to be pledged for his friend. Crosses, although sometimes of great sentimental value, were not essential to everyday life and so could be pawned when money was needed. Cash—not the full estimated value, but probably up to two-thirds of it—was lent against them and they were commonly accepted as security for the loan by Jewish and Christian pawnbrokers.[270] Francesco was lent sixteen lire by Rovigo who, he testified, had not opened the pendant to see if it was a reliquary after accepting it.[271] When called to the Inquisition a second time, he admitted that only afterward had he been told that it was a reliquary by his wife.[272] The inquisitor general, Giacomo Tinti, sent his notary to the Jewish bank to seize the cross. When Isaac Rovigo was called to the Inquisition, he again testified to his ignorance that the pendant contained relics.[273] If he had known that such a cross could be used as a reliquary, he stated, he would never have taken it as a pledge. Rovigo apologized and said that he would not take such objects again.

But whether these tiny crosses held relics or not, the Jews would still get into trouble for holding them. In 1641, Captain Camillo de Giosi reported to the Modenese Inquisition that, with the authority of the ducal treasury, he had gone to the house of Emanuel Casesso, a Jew, to make an inventory of the possessions of the late Angelo da Modena, a Jewish banker, as was the normal procedure after a wealthy Jew had died. Spotting a small chest, Camillo had asked for the key and found inside an empty brass cross reliquary (perhaps a costly one, which might explain the inquisitorial concern), which Emanuel told him was being kept among other things for Luccio, Emanuel's stepson who was also Angelo's heir.[274] The Inquisition was determined to prove that the Jews had held this cross out of contempt for Christianity. In the interrogation of Rabbi Natanel Trabotti on December 16, 1641, the vicar-general said to Trabotti: "The fact that the cross was treated as the property of the Jews, as part of the patrimony of the above said Luccio and that the cross was not to be retained by the Jews, suggests that this cross was held by the Jews in spite and contempt of Christian religious cult objects."[275] Emanuel was arrested and interrogated. He argued that the cross had originally been taken by his bank as a pledge from Angelo.[276] Further investigation confirmed that the cross had been in Emanuel's possession for about a year and had been passed to him by three important Modenese Jews—Michael de Modena, Rabbi Natanel Trabotti, and David Diena—who had been Luccio's guardians. Salomon de Modena, Luccio's uncle, argued that they had not known that the storing of such small sacred objects was prohibited.[277] Trabotti also testified that, since Jewish jewelers in Ferrara made and sold such crosses, he had no idea that storing them was forbidden.[278] These Jewish suspects did not react strongly to the accusation or have much to say about the cross reliquary. Their concern was to plead ignorance and behave in a way that might bring an end to their prosecution as soon as possible with limited damage to themselves.[279] When pressed further to admit that his intention was to harm the cross, Emanuel pleaded against this: "Your Reverence is imagining this, because I have never thought to harm the cross. We accept the prohibition against vilifying anything belonging to Christians, and to corroborate what I have said, Your Reverence should bear in mind, that I live in Carpi and the cross was being kept here in Modena, so how could I have contemplated this? God be my guard."[280] The trial was discontinued.

The Spagnoli bank, under the management of Elia Teseo, his son Salvatore Teseo, and Viviano Modena, was one of the three remaining Jewish banks that made small loans to Modenese Christians in the seventeenth century.[281] In 1665, this bank faced the most severe interrogation for holding such pawns: ten crosses, all of them reliquaries (each containing as many as eight tiny compartments), were uncovered, as well as a *ducatone* (a large ducat coin) or medallion with a portrait of Pope Innocent X. These devotional medals, usually bought as souvenirs from shrines, were molded in bronze, pewter, or lead, and either kept in homes or sometimes worn as a pendant or attached to clothing by a pin.[282] They were replicated in key production centers in Loreto and the Marche. The Jews' holdings had been disclosed by an auction that had been held in the Modenese ghetto in November 1664. Jacobus Mirandola declared: "It was around a month ago, that the Jews in the vicinity of the ghetto made an auction, of several things. I do not know the name of the Jew who did this, and it was held at about 22 hours. Among other things, a cross of silver was sold upon which was sculpted a Crucified Christ, and this I know because I held it in my own hands and saw it. . . . Many of us Christians were surprised that the Jews kept these types of things. And this was said aloud so that the Jews would have heard it."[283] It might well have looked to Mirandola as if Christ was being treated with profound disrespect, perhaps even sold again in effigy, but Teseo was probably obeying a regulation that obliged pawnbrokers to sell unredeemed pledges by auction and not dispose of them privately. Such regulations, found in several Jewish charters, were intended to get the best deal for the client. The Jewish pawnbroker was not allowed to make money by both charging interest and selling pledges at a profit. If, when the pledge was sold, it raised a sum that more than covered the amount lent plus the interest due upon it, then the surplus had to be handed over, wherever practicable, to the borrower or his heirs.

With regard to these pendants and the medallion, Elio Teseo, Salvatore Teseo and Viviano Modena argued that they had believed that there was a distinction between sacred items found in churches, which therefore had direct contact with the Eucharistic wafer and wine, and devotionalia which were personal possessions. They maintained that few of these crucifixes were worth a great deal. Viviano Modena stated: "When we take the pledges of gold and silver, we weigh them but we do not give all the money for the value of the said gold or silver according to its weight. We give only what conforms to the value of the object to remain as a security in the bank."[284]

So, the Jewish bankers argued, they were responding to Christian demand rather than plotting sacrilege. All of the three main bankers of the Spagnoli bank were interrogated, then imprisoned overnight, ensuring that they would not be able to collaborate or discuss their interrogations; they were released with a warning the following day. Each of the ten reliquaries held by the Inquisition was opened.[285]A notary speculated that the Jews might have forced the pendants open and scooped out the relics, since some of them were empty and their relics seemed to have been "recently removed."[286] Each of the Jewish bankers denied that they had even known about the crosses being reliquaries. Salvatore Teseo, the son of Elia Teseo, suggested that taking the pledge was simply a favor to the Christians needing the money: "I know for sure that they were not opened, nor did we look inside, because they are so small. They were noted as having the weight the Christians requested, and the bank always gave security on them."[287] Inquisitor General Giovanni Tommaso Visconti found it hard to believe that the Jewish bankers had not realized that these crosses were reliquaries. The suspects thought it wisest to apologize, place themselves at the mercy of the Inquisition, and accept its ruling. But the shocking realization that the Spagnoli bank had been holding crosses that were in fact reliquaries made the inquisitor general begin a sequestration of Christian sacred objects held by the other two Jewish banks of Modena and even further afield in the duchy. Recorded on 198 folios, this long investigation lasted from December 1664 to November 1665.[288] The other Jewish bankers who were interrogated included Isacco Benedetto de Modena, Benedetto de Arezzo, Raffaele Levi de Rovigo, Servadius de Rovigo, Avraham Rovigo, Salvatore Rovigo, Ventura Castelfrancho, and Simone Formiggini. The objective was to rid the Jews' pawn banks of such religious articles. One banker, Raffaele Levi de Rovigo, chose to forestall his own arrest by coming to the Inquisition and handing over the eight crosses he was keeping in his bank. Raffaele stated:

> I have presented myself here in this Holy Office because of a case against Elia Teseo and companions, who have a bank in this city, regarding a silver pendant cross, that they had sold by auction. I am a banker in another bank and I have come to admit some error. I have come to make it clear that in my bank too there are some small crosses of silver worn around the neck, which have been pledged as pawns by virtue of the privileges which we have in our charters, and if we did not have these privileges, we would not have taken them. . . . But if we had known that in regard to the Holy Office this was an error, we would not have accepted them.[289]

He claimed that he acted differently, opening pendants on receipt, and if he saw that they contained relics, would not accept them as pledges.[290]

When the pawns held by the banker of Terra Finale, Simone Formiggini, were sequestered, the Inquisition discovered "in total 16 crosses, gold and silver of which six were full of relics."[291] Formiggini was forced to admit that the ducal charter did not in fact allow him to accept relics and pleaded carelessness.[292] After choosing not to make a defense, the bankers requested the mercy of the court. Although they had suffered the humiliation and anxiety of being arrested and interrogated and then released on bail, they were not punished severely. They were given a grave warning and forbidden, on pain of a heavy fine, to accept "any type of cross" or "any type of object pertaining to the Christian religion."[293] All the reliquaries pawned were confiscated and deposited in the Holy Office.

Why had the Inquisition gone to such lengths to remove these trinkets or ornaments from Jewish premises? It seems that it wanted to be meticulously careful that no such object should be in the Jews' possession. On one occasion, marginal and disruptive Jews chose to denounce their coreligionists to the Inquisition, and a convert was called in to act as a mediator.

In 1640, Prospero Sforno and his wife Stella were called to Modena from Carpi to defend themselves.[294] They were accused of bringing young Christian girls into their homes to learn how to make buttons and also of using a small needle to disfigure the faces and hands of Christ, Mary Magdalene, and Saint John on a tiny reliquary chest (*scatola*); this had been left behind by Magdalena, daughter of Gio Antonio Cabassi, a Christian girl who had come to their house as a pupil. When interrogated, Magdalena stated that she had used this chest to store the buttons she made: "I know for sure, that when I brought it there, and left it there, there was not even a mark on the chest."[295]

Since another Christian witness was prepared to corroborate Magdalena's delation, both Prospero and Stella Sforno were imprisoned and tortured. When they refused to admit that they had damaged the box, they were fined one hundred scudi, a severe punishment for the desecration of an image on a tiny chest, thereby suggesting that even in the seventeenth century inquisitors were allowed considerable discretion in determining punishments. Charges of image desecration were increasingly concerned with small objects that had allegedly been violated or treated with contempt in private places. It was inevitable that Jews would again be caught handling these objects, especially since Christians so readily handed them over for cash.

Conclusion

Early modern Italian society had a way of thinking about Jewish image desecration that had certainly been built on "Christ of Beirut," other Byzantine narratives, miraculous images in Italy supposedly desecrated by Jews, and medieval judicial accusations. In the early modern period, secular courts hastily punished Jews, since they were less concerned with a deeper investigation and influenced by popular feelings and prejudices. Italian neophytes—those newly fashioned Christians living in Christian society, but still marginalized and looking for acceptance—were partly responsible for some of these false accusations. In many ways these neophytes can be construed as Jews-made-Christians who hated their former selves and their former coreligionists and were desirous of being considered worthy by the judicial court they approached. Philo-Protestant iconoclasm became a concern for the Roman Inquisition until the 1580s, when Jews returned into the frame of inquisitorial attention for this crime. When the Inquisition proceeded against Jews, they were not demonized or credited with nefarious conspiracies, save in one trial (1617) in which the accusation came from within the Jewish community and was exposed as false by a learned neophyte. On several occasions between 1611 and 1627 delators reported Jews for the traditional crime of stoning an effigy of the Madonna in a public place. In many other trials, however, the Inquisition appeared to be demanding respect for cheaper and more fragile objects, some of which were liable to be placed in the power of Jews in their capacity as pawnbrokers. The Inquisition was prepared to consider the possibility of accidental damage, mere carelessness, and ignorance of the rules. The Jews' crime often appeared to be disrespect rather than sacrilege. Much the same consideration would apply to the Jews' encounters with the Holy Sacrament in public places, in which their mere presence—usually inadvertent—was an act of disrespect rather than deliberate desecration, although it was sometimes believed that a Jew could contaminate the sacrament merely by looking at it. If inquisitors persisted in believing that Jews were naturally hostile to images, they did not hold that they would automatically seize every opportunity to do damage.

The "actual Jew" who comes to court or is forcibly brought to it differs from the fictive Jew of the Middle Ages. The "real" Jew did not test or experiment with images, but fully realized that Christians suspected him of damaging them—hence his need to protect himself when he found, to his embarrassment, that he had them on his premises (even though there were certain approved ways of doing this). To some extent the "real" Jew was the one who accidentally got himself into difficulties and tried to explain himself to Christian authorities—someone who accidentally came upon a religious procession, or whose embarrassing child had emptied a chamber pot from a balcony upon a religious procession passing underneath it.

The Roman Inquisition remained skeptical about the allegations of malicious image desecration but showed an interest in investigating the Christians' accusations and using them as an opportunity to monitor, judge, and discipline the Jews when expedient. The majority of accusations against the Jews of northern Italy were unproven. Jews did not usually engage in image desecration or readily risk removing Christian images from their immediate environment, whatever their Christian accusers might have said to the contrary.

As has been shown, most of the accusations in the seventeenth century related to less expensive images, prints, small crucifixes, medals, or reliquary pendants, made of wood, silver, gold, or bronze rather than the large crucifixes or panel paintings that had been the object of allegations in earlier periods. Images saturated society, and it is not surprising that accusations became more frequent. From the 1600s the Inquisition now concerned not only images on the walls but those in transit, in homes, in pawnbrokers' banks, and around people's necks. At the root of these accusations was suspicion among Christians, who were often uneasy when they saw a Christian image attached to or within a neighboring Jew's house. But at the same time, the Inquisition's flexibility and slowness to condemn and punish the Jews might well have relaxed tensions between Jews and Christians, thereby moderating potential acts of violence against the Jews of Italy.

In the crowded streets of Italy, Jews were under constant observation regarding their movements. Whenever they could, they escaped Christian processions in order to avoid witnessing the intense moments of public Christian piety in which they could not share. But how easy was it for them to escape and to what extent is their noncompliance exaggerated in the denunciations of their Christian delators, often churchmen who were themselves conducting the processions? Being in the wrong part of town at the wrong time seems to have been an inevitable consequence of daily life for Jews. The fact that they stubbornly refused to take off their hats shows a certain defiant rejection of Christian culture that clearly continually aggravated the Christians who surrounded them—especially when Modenese Jews invaded their sacred space by attending the state funeral of their duke inside the church. The seventy-one cases have, I believe, demonstrated a range of Jewish behaviors toward Christian images that were in turn self-protective, principled, respectful, pragmatic, legally circumscribed, professional, and regulated—a clear sign that it was better to desecrate an image through words under their breath than through physical violence. No case indicated that the Jewish bankers had destroyed the tiny crosses and crucifix pendants they stored in their banks.

Our last chapter turns to a micro-historical study of one particular case in which a Jewish entrepreneurial family was accused of image desecration in early modern Italy. It will allow us to access and analyze in detail a judicial proceeding and the critical interweaving of relations and attitudes toward images in an unusual space that they shared with Christians—a silk-spinning factory in Spilamberto in the duchy of Modena.

Chapter 6

Image Desecration in Spilamberto

A Case Study

A microhistorical study, with its emphasis on small-scale qualitative research, enables one to probe the nature of image desecration accusations and their Jewish-Christian tensions in new ways. It provides a sharper focus on the ideas and patterns that have been suggested in previous chapters, including the shifts from the fantastical to the rational accusation and from desecration to disrespect, and it attempts to show how socioeconomic and religious assumptions informed the Jews' and Christians' relationships with sacred images.[1] As Chapter 5 has shown, early modern Italy had a particularly large number of accusations against Jews for this crime, and it is not surprising to discover the complex and detailed case of Spilamberto (a small town in the Modenese duchy, about twenty-five kilometers west of Bologna and ten kilometers southeast of Modena) in the inquisitorial archives. In addition, the records of this case show how Jews reacted both to a traditional painting and to more fragile paper images within premises (a factory and an inn) not discussed in previous chapters. These were not private homes but semipublic places in which Christians and Jews regularly encountered and interacted with each other.

Trial proceedings of the specific case of 1632 are documented in a four-hundred-page dossier in the inquisitorial archive in Modena. Further material is contained in the archive of the Congregazione per la Dottrina della Fede in Rome, which holds communications between the inquisitorial *vicario* in Spilamberto, the Holy Office in Modena, and the Sacred Congregation of the Holy Office in Rome. It is the second longest case against professing Jews pursued by the Papal Inquisition in Modena.[2] The dossier itself holds a collection of documents, including the interrogations of Christian witnesses and Jewish suspects, interrogation summaries written to remind inquisitorial vicars of earlier interrogations, testimonials before the Giudici del Maleficio (the local criminal court) in Modena, and correspondence between the Sacred Congregation of the Holy Office in Rome and the Papal Inquisition in Modena and Reggio. During the investigations, three Jewish suspects were arrested and imprisoned for up to four months, and two were tortured.

In 1632, a year after a severe plague had ended, Simon Sanguinetti of Spilamberto and his four sons took on the lease of a flagging local mill ("un grosso edificio d'un filatoio di seta") as a kind of tenant-cum-manager.[3] It was an unusual move since Jews rarely acted as industrial entrepreneurs. In most of Catholic Italy, Jewish management of Christian workplaces was prohibited by both church and state, since it ran contrary to the papal principle that Christians should always be the superiors and Jews the subordinates.[4] Simon put much-needed capital of his own into the business, providing employment that brought significant economic benefit to the surrounding Christian community.

Within a few months, Simon's position was disclosed to the local Inquisition by Ludovico Marchesi, the notary of the Holy Office in Modena, who testified that Christian workers in the mill—in particular, Sanito Melloti, Benedeto Ludovico, and Stefano Carreta—had told him that the Jew had not only covered a sacred image but also prevented the Christians from praying before it. This large image was a depiction of the Virgin and Child, a frescoed image or a painted panel (*pittura* or *imagine*) already set within some kind of framing, molding, or tabernacle. In 1635, investigations were reopened, with two further accusations of image desecration: this time the destruction of cheap religious prints attached by Christian spinners to the walls of the mill and the removal of sacred prints stuck on wooden frames from a bedroom in an inn in Piumazzo, where one of Simon's sons, Alessandro, had stayed. The repetition of the type of accusation may, on the one hand, have resulted from a number of grievances held by these Christian workers who, inspired by malice against the Jews, had translated them into false delations. On the other hand, it could be that these Jews had in fact committed these offenses, although there was no conclusive evidence for this. The physical evidence was missing for two of the accusations. The images had disappeared from Piumazzo, and the cheap prints had allegedly been destroyed. Yet according to inquisitorial law, because suspicion was strong, the accusation of image desecration had been proven and the Jews were punished.

In this remote country town, a close network of Christian clergymen, including confessors, preachers, local friars, and priests, helped to keep Modena informed about irregularities. This was achieved mainly through investigations carried out by *vicari foranei* (local inquisitorial vicars) in response to specific orders of the Holy Office in Modena to seek out and report on nonconformity or heresy.[5] Although inquisitorial vicars did not have the authority to carry out formal proceedings or to arrest, charge, or pronounce sentence, they were expected to conduct initial interrogations and investigations and then pass on their findings to the tribunal in Modena, which they usually did efficiently.[6] Of the ninety-two interrogations in this case, thirty-nine (42 percent) were conducted in Spilamberto by these vicars, rather than at the Holy Office in Modena in the presence of the inquisitor general.

There was no ghetto in Spilamberto in the 1630s and 1640s, but there was none even in the capital, Modena, until 1638, and the government was much slower to introduce ghettos into small towns.[7] Yet the Sanguinetti family was permitted—as were a small number of Jewish families in other ducal towns—to remain in the peripheral town, a fief of the marquises Baldassare and Guilio Rangone.[8] This was because they had been contributing for many years to the development of the local economy, in particular, alleviating a shortage of cash by advancing loans against pledges deposited with them by the Rangone family.[9] Modenese towns such as Carpi, Soliera, Spilamberto, and Terra Finale offered Jewish banking families refuge from the political and religious oppression of the ghetto, but also exposed them to the economic and social context of their Christian counterparts and the inflexible rules of a distinctively Christian environment. Four Jewish families lived side by side with Christians in Spilamberto, attempting to integrate themselves while organizing their own religious community for worship and religious life.[10]

Since these Jewish bankers could no longer rely solely on high-interest pawnbroking for their livelihood, they had turned to other business opportunities, such as shopkeeping, importing wheat, and, in particular, manufacturing silk.[11] Silk had become a symbol of luxury and was usually one of the main fabrics included in a wealthy bride's trousseau. Silkworms were imported from the neighboring territories of San Felice to supply an increasing demand in local markets and for export to neighboring states.[12] Simon Sanguinetti's workforce consisted of approximately twenty-five to thirty Christian spinners, including men, women, and teenage boys and girls.

When Sanguinetti invested in the "Bolognese-style" technologically advanced mill, which used a hydraulic wheel for twisting fine filaments together into silk thread, he made his presence, and that of his sons, part of the daily routine, even though the labor force was efficiently supervised by a Christian *capo maestro*, or foreman.[13] Although Sanguinetti did not move into the mill, he closely supervised the building and its workforce for a period of two and a half years, initially instructing his sons to sleep there at night in order to open and close the mill for workers each day and to safeguard the silk thread against theft.[14] This constant observation was vital for the Jews' sense of authority and control in the workplace. Their rented home was next door. They could therefore move freely between the two.[15]

The Spilamberto mill produced *orsoglio alla Bolognese*, a high-quality silk yarn composed of multiple threads, twisted by water power, and used as the warp in organzine.[16] Production of this yarn represented a new industry in the early modern period—it was the first yarn to be mass-produced in factories.[17] According to Sanguinetti's testimony, from 1632–1634 his Christian workers were stationed at a series of machines through which the silk thread passed during its production.[18] Simon described the layout of the three-story mill and the production process.[19] Production began with reeling, or unwinding, the silk filaments from the cocoons. The strand was then doubled and twisted by the towering hydraulic machine. Three huge wooden wheels—placed one above the other—had dozens of spools attached to the sides. The younger Christian workers climbed up and down the stacked wheels, loading them with skeins of thread. They used their hands to guide the threads between sets of spindles. The warp threads then passed through large spinning wheels, which twisted them.[20] During the final stage, the female spinners, sitting in separate rooms in the shadow of noisy and complicated machinery, worked to double the thread by hand or as dryers.[21] Spinners worked a six-day week, with Sundays off.

The multitude of parts in these complex machines, the precision and speed of their functioning, and the interdependence of the moving parts demanded strong work discipline and meticulous concentration from the workers, who were themselves carefully watched by their Jewish employers. Furthermore, the work space was damp, dark, and dirty. Working hours were long, and the job was physically taxing. Despite these demands, the Christian spinners received low pay.[22] Most of the workers were poor, temporary unqualified laborers or craftsmen who had been disqualified from their skilled trades. Whole families, including children, often worked together.[23] Mortality and sickness were rampant—although this was never mentioned by either the Christian spinners or the Jewish managers in the trial records. Hence, it is difficult to gauge from the testimonies the amount of tension in the work space or any issues arising from different classes and cultures.

The main focus of this chapter is on the two types of Catholic images that were present in the mill (the painted panel on the wall and the prints), their religious and social significance to both religionists, the Jewish/Christian tensions that were created by them, and their supposed desecration. Christian evidence throws light on the motives and mentality of Christian employees and on their relations with their Jewish bosses. The inquisitorial responses confirm how the investigation into the offense was used not only to penetrate the daily interactions between Jews and Christians but also to assist inquisitorial efforts to remove the Jews from the mill. The Jews' testimonies show how they struggled with the intrusive presence of these images in their mill and tried to reduce not only the number of images but also the frequency with which Christians were allowed to visit the spaces where they were situated in order to pray before them.

This chapter has three sections revolving around the three accusations regarding Christian images—the Madonna and Child painting on the inside wall of the factory at the top of the main staircase, the cheap devotional prints scattered through various places in the factory, and the paintings in a bedroom in a Piumazzo inn. The fourth and last section will be concerned with the inquisitorial responses to the accusation, the Jews' methods of running the mill, and the reasons why they may have damaged images cherished by their workers.

The Covered Panel of the Madonna and Child, 1632

The first episode began in August 1632, when an *ex officio* report, probably prompted by a self-denunciation to a confessor, was made by Ludovico Marchesi, a thirty-four-year-old inquisitorial notary serving in Modena, to his inquisitor general, Fra Giacomo Tinti di Lodi.[24] Marchesi informed Tinti that Simon Sanguinetti, a fifty-year-old Jewish banker and businessman in the jurisdiction of Spilamberto, had for the previous six months leased a silk-spinning mill from Baldassare Rangone, an insolvent Marchigiano nobleman.[25] Acquiring a license from the archpriest of Spilamberto, the Jewish employer had initially nailed a board (*coperta*, or *una assa di legno*) across a painted panel of the Madonna and Child—a temporary closure, which he now controlled and which prevented the Christian workers from gazing upon it while praying and singing.[26] There is no suggestion that the Jew was concerned about getting a secular license, perhaps because he assumed that Baldassare Rangone would take care of that matter for him. Marchesi was able to name some of the Christian spinners, and Tinti immediately sent an inquisitorial notary, Geronimo de Ganatoni, to Spilamberto to interrogate them. The notary's interrogations—made in conjunction with Fra Michelangelo Cati de Modena, the inquisitorial vicar of Spilamberto—revealed that three Christian female dryers had submitted complaints to Filippo Mossa, the archpriest of the Cathedral of Modena, that they could not pray satisfactorily before a closed image. As a result of this, the archpriest of Spilamberto, Adriano Billari (alias Menozzi), was ordered to modify the board.[27] A central section was cut out with a saw (*la seghetta*) and made into a "window" (*fenestrella*) nailed to one side of the board with a hinge. The other side was closed with a lock and key, which was to be opened during Christian prayer so that the face of the Virgin and Child would be accessible and visible.[28] This modification was completed while Simon himself was out of town. It is unclear why the board was not removed entirely and a more workable door put over the whole painted panel to allow more visibility and full access for the Christians. Although it was never discussed, one assumes that to remove the whole board would have endangered the painting further, and it was easier to make a window in the existing board that was attached to the border of the painted panel. Nevertheless, the spinners were still unable to worship before the image, because the Jews, who kept the key, refused to unlock the flap (*una rebalta*) when the Christians requested them to do so.

The inquisitorial notary, on examining the image, found scratches—particularly on the hands of the Blessed Virgin where holes had been made for the flap. This evidence led to stronger allegations and accusations that the Jews had desecrated the image.[29] Tinti took no further action for several months, which suggests that the preliminary investigations had not warranted immediate action or he was too busy with other cases. During interrogations in October, Menozzi, the archpriest of Spilamberto, was ordered to appear before the Holy Office in Modena to excuse himself for his inaction. He tried to hide his shortcomings to the inquisitor, by arguing that, at the age of seventy, he was infirm and had not been able to climb the stairs of the mill to check the state of the painting and whether it was visible for prayer either before or after its coverage. He instead concentrated on his disappointment that Rangone had leased the mill to a Jew without consulting him.[30] Presenting himself as a mediator attempting to balance the demands of religious orthodoxy with the economic concerns of local nobles, Menozzi admitted that he had originally granted the Jews a license to cover the image, although he knew that this action was unacceptable. He was not authorized to do this without consultation with the Holy Office in Modena. However, he argued: "I believed that I should ensure that the image was preserved in great veneration, since images of devotion are usually covered."[31] Other Christian witnesses later admitted that Menozzi had allowed them to pray before a covered image. Sanito Melloti, a twenty-eight-year-old spinner in the mill, confirmed that he had said this in his testimony before the secular court on November 13, 1632. This section is underlined in the record: "The said Archpriest said to the supervisor [*capo maestro*] and other workers of the said mill that, wanting to say their prayers, *they should not look to check whether the image was closed. It was enough to have good intention and faith, and turn toward the image.*"[32] Menozzi clearly hoped that this compromise would be acceptable since it allowed him to satisfy Rangone, the Sanguinettis, and the Christian spinners. But what right did he have to determine that Christians could pray before a closed image? It is clear that these spinners felt that their worship was less effective and their religious freedom was being impaired.

Domenico Bonazzi, the thirty-two-year-old foreman in the mill, confirmed in his testimony that all the Christian workers continued to say their prayers before the window even when it was shut and the image was inaccessible.[33] It seems that at first the Christian spinners accepted the ruling of Menozzi and adjusted their devotional practice to try to convince themselves that the sacred presence of an image could still be felt even when the image was hidden.[34] Simon's testimony confirmed Menozzi's order to the Christians: "not to neglect recitation of their prayers, because although they could not see her [the Virgin], it was enough to have good intention and turn toward the image."[35]

On October 21, 1632, Simon was incarcerated in the inquisitorial prison in Modena; two of his sons soon followed—Raffaele (sixteen years old) on October 24 and Alessandro (twenty years old) on October 31.[36] Whereas the two young Jews denied all involvement in the violation of the painted panel of the Madonna and were only kept for a few days, Simon was imprisoned for a month. He admitted that, in discussion with Baldassare Rangone, Rangone had suggested that the painting be whitewashed as soon as Simon had taken possession of the mill. But Simon had failed to obtain permission from Archpriest Menozzi to obliterate the image.[37] Without permission he had sensibly not proceeded with permanent erasure. The inquisitorial vicar, Fra Michelangelo Cati, made it clear to Simon that he believed Jews were negligent, often covering images without obtaining all the required licenses.[38] Simon defended himself but at the same time showed his full understanding of the types of difficulties Jews had in Italy with images in their domestic spaces. He noted his genuine discomfort with the presence of the image as well as his nervousness that the image might be desecrated. Those, he argued, were the reasons why he wanted the image covered or removed as soon as he became manager of the mill. He testified: "I took the mill in Spilamberto, and because in that room I saw the image, that I believe is of the Madonna, . . . I attempted to remove the image, for all those who would be able to accuse me. I tried to address this but had little success. I resolved to discuss it with the Signor Archpriest, who said that he would have this image removed or erased [*ò cassari in qualchi modo*] in some way. . . . I did not want to make an affront by removing it, and then we be told that we had done something and then we would suffer in some way."[39]

The Jew had clearly proceeded with caution, knowing all too well the possible consequences of a serious accusation of erasing/whitewashing the image. Yet at the same time, he had remained hopeful that Rangone might be able to authorize this for him.[40] Had the position of tenant-cum-manager made him believe that he was entitled to special privileges? The Jews had quickly accepted that temporary concealment of the painting was clearly the most appropriate action. He had even paid for the materials and work this involved himself.

Simon eventually apologized for his carelessness in not unlocking the image when he should have and revealed under pressure that this practice signified not his family's disrespect for Christian prayer but their fear that the Christian workers would desecrate the image and then blame them. This confirmed the fundamental lack of trust between Jews and Christians. This fear of Christian desecration was echoed by his sons Raffaele and Alessandro, who admitted that the key for the image was often kept in the Jews' house, and so the flap could not be opened whenever the Christian workers wanted.[41] The physical covering of this image limited the Christians' view, rendering the image invisible on all but a few occasions. This situation was highly irregular. Christians were used to having access to these images—looking after them and kneeling before them whenever they wanted to pray to the Virgin. Ownership of the key controlled access to the image, reflecting the Jews' religious superiority over the Christian workplace.[42]

In November 1632, at the request of Rangone, several Christian witnesses gave written testimony to the Giudici del Maleficio of Modena. Rangone was probably keen to push for the civil authorities to verify that the Jews had not desecrated the image. The testimony of these Christian witnesses was less accusatory than previous ones, and the Sanguinettis were not recorded as having committed offenses of any kind. On November 13, the spinner Sanito Melloti gave a written statement that when the window or flap was made Sebastiano Martini, the carpenter and wall builder, had been the one to damage the painting, not the Jews.[43] The fact that these written testimonies appear in the inquisitorial file implies that the Holy Office was in no position to ignore the jurisdictional claims of the Giudici del Maleficio, the supreme criminal court of the duchy of Modena, and had actually accepted these testimonies as proof. This was despite the Sacred Congregation decreeing in 1628 that inquisitors should resist attempts by secular courts or princes to intervene in their proceedings.[44] During the investigation, Inquisitor Tinti made several complaints to the Sacred Congregation about the cost of the proceedings against the Sanguinettis and would probably have appreciated outside financial assistance.[45]

On November 16, 1632, Simon was released without punishment but ordered to take an oath that his family would no longer directly supervise the Christians in the mill. Here the Inquisition revealed its real concern and its intention to prevent a Jewish entrepreneur from employing a significant Christian labor force.[46] When he was asked by the inquisitor whether he knew that he was forbidden to employ Christians, Simon's answer was that he was aware that Christians were not able to serve him in the domestic space, but thought that the workplace was different.[47] When he complained that, if he were not permitted to direct the mill, he would be ruined financially, the Holy Office instructed him to address his plea directly to the Sacred Congregation in Rome.[48] When Simon appealed to the Sacred Congregation that he be allowed to retain his position in the mill if he hired a Christian supervisor, the Sacred Congregation rejected his petition.[49]

Despite Simon's oath that he and his sons would no longer directly supervise the Christians in the mill, he defiantly remained actively involved. When, at the beginning of 1633, the Inquisition summoned him to Modena to reprimand him, he pleaded with the inquisitor to give him more time to arrange his affairs: "I ask this consideration, because I cannot stop my work without the ultimate and total ruin of my household and my trade. I have large quantities of silk in my workshop and in my house—if they are not used, they will be spoiled. Therefore, I beg you to allow me some time to tend to my business. I do not control the Christians, nor do any of my sons. They are managed by a Christian supervisor, who takes care of the running of the workshop, and gives orders to the workers. I have reason to believe that the Sacred Congregation would not want to cause my ruin or destroy me.[50]

Simon defied the inquisitorial ruling and continued to run the mill, although significantly limiting his own presence and that of his sons by employing Leonardo Costantini as foreman in charge of the workers.[51] When, in February 1633, the Sacred Congregation summoned Rangone to explain himself, he argued that the Jews' business was alleviating the desperate situation of Christians who were destitute as a result of the plague.[52]

The Madonna Image on the Wall

Inquisitorial representatives who examined the image wrote the following description of its condition: "When the window was lifted, on the wall was a painting of an image of the Blessed Virgin Mary sitting on a throne with the infant in her arms, held tightly and suckling her breast. The image had lost much of its color [*perdebat ad colorem*], and was quite blackened [in places]. The golden dress [*aurem vestios*] of the Virgin could still be discerned, but recently marks appeared on the image here."[53]

The image of the child Jesus being suckled by his mother was very popular in early modern Italy. It affirmed the humanity of Jesus and served as a metaphor of the church feeding its faithful children.[54] In the mill this painting was located "at the entrance of the large workshop near the top end of the staircase"—a central position that was clearly visible to all Christian spinners who worked in that main area or frequently passed by during the day.[55] In the investigations conducted by the Holy Office, the inquisitors consistently referred to it as "sacred" (*sacra imago*).[56] This term did not imply that the image was miraculous, but rather that its subject matter consisted of a figure given sacred meaning.[57] Buonaiuto Sanguinetti, Simon's oldest son, who was interrogated on November 1, was the only Jew to demonstrate some knowledge of the subject of the image, describing it as "an ancient and old image."[58]

Such images were known to stir "emotion and empathy" and thoughts of "motherhood, conjugality, virginity, nurture, and bereavement."[59] Mary's bare breast highlighted her connection with other women through her simplicity and unassuming accessibility.[60] This might explain why the painting particularly spoke to the female spinners, who were the only ones to complain to Filippo Mossa that they could not access it for their prayers.[61]

The painting's presence inside a work space where Christian laborers were supervised by Jews created an extraordinary spatial dynamic. It brought Christians together and gave them a common identity and experience, for they alone could respond to what the object implied, its representation, symbolism, and value. These impecunious Christian laborers probably shared temporary living spaces with many others and were not able to create demarcated areas for prayer in their homes, so in order to fulfill their Christian duties it was important to make spaces of contemplation in their daily workplace. The spinners passed by the image when walking through the work space and sat or stood in front of it during their times of prayer. Through gazing, touching, and kissing the image, they would easily imagine a reciprocal exchange with Mary and her child.[62]

The Christian relationship with the painting stood in sharp contrast to the Jews' religious observance. The visible presentation also complicated the Jews' managerial role. The demands of the Jews, that the image be hidden, and those of the Christians, that it be visible while they were at work, were irreconcilable. If the Jews chose to cover it, this was interpreted as an attempt to control Christian prayer and piety. If the image was open, the Christians were exposing their prayer rituals and personal devotion in a space regulated by Jewish managers. The Sanguinettis' handling of the Madonna image paradoxically located it, in the mind of local Christians, within the sphere of Jewish negotiation and representation. Moreover, the act of covering an image in a Christian work space had a very different connotation from doing so in the Jews' own home. It gave them some authority over the Christians' worship and viewing of a Christian image; this had no known precedent in Italy.

Two Coverings of One Image

It was inevitable that the sacred image and its covering in the Spilamberto mill would be a source of religious tension. The image now had two coverings, representing the struggle between the religionists. The first was the board placed over the image by Simon. The second was the flap, lock, and key meant to give the Christians open access, although the key usually remained in the

Jews' possession. Testimonies highlight the Jews' and Christians' competing strategies to control its visibility in a space they both shared. Each side had an agenda that needs to be decoded from their testimonies.

It is not surprising that Simon and his sons Raffaele and Alessandro were determined to do what they could to keep the image covered.[63] The image's subject matter clearly disturbed these Jews who had to pass before it throughout the day. On the other hand, Christians were not used to their area of worship being manipulated and dominated by Jews, especially in a society and a duchy where Jews were prohibited from entering Christian churches. Ghettoization in Modena had been contemplated since 1618 but would not be instituted until 1638. No doubt the inquisitors and other clerics wished that the civil authorities would get on with the job. One effect of ghettoization was to allow Christians to maintain their power of negotiation over what the Jews could be permitted to see outside the space of the ghetto itself.[64]

For the first four months of the Jews' occupation, the Christians were unable to open the board and observe the painting in the mill, since Simon had secured a license from Menozzi to have it closed. When, in August 1632, the flap, lock, and single key were added, the full image's composition often remained locked away and hidden, further enforcing the idea for the Christians that this was a result of the Jews' presence. Moreover, from this time the Jews held the key to the new lock more often than Domenico Bonazzi, the Christian foreman. Alessandro Sanguinetti even admits that he had placed the key—not knowing its purpose, so he said—in his own home.[65] In his second interrogation in 1632, Domenico Bonazzi reported a clear lack of communication between himself and the Sanguinettis regarding the location of the key for the lock: "I therefore went to the house of the Jews, and I said that they had to give me the key, although I did not know who to ask. One of the Jews had the key but I did not know which one. I did not know then whether they had the key on them, or if it was in their home."[66]

The closure of the image and its one key increased the Jews' control over Christian time and space, encouraging the belief that, since the Sanguinettis were the only ones to have access to the image, they had desecrated it, causing the marks that were observed by Fra Michelangelo Cati, the inquisitorial vicar of Spilamberto, on October 29, 1632.[67] Simon, in contrast, continually argued rather unconvincingly that its closure would prevent his Christian spinners from desecrating the image and then blaming the Jews—an argument that was first propagated, as noted in Chapter 5, by David Consilio, the Jewish moneylender in the bank of Sabbioni of Ferrara in

1449—"because I knew from experience that Jews can be tricked, by someone or other damaging the painting and then blaming us [Jews]."[68] Simon's claim was difficult to prove. It seems unlikely that Christians would harm images that they needed and used themselves for Christian prayer, even to discredit the Jews.[69]

When the key was passed to the Christian foreman, Leonardo Costantini, in December 1633, the compromise for both Jews and Christians was to keep the image covered when not used for Christian prayer. Costantini argued that if the image was kept closed, he, as foreman, would feel more confident that the image was safe from Jewish violation. He testified: "During the day the said image was to remain open and in the evening after the workers left, I close the flap, always keeping the key near me."[70]

But even during the day, when the image was uncovered, it seems that the Christian dryers had veiled the image themselves. Did this move reflect their discomfort at seeing the Virgin's bared breasts or just that they did not want the Jews to be able to see them? Directives of the final session of the Council of Trent had ordered that those images with nudity remain covered.[71] The purpose of the veil was not discussed in the interrogations.

The ubiquity of images in Christian spaces clearly contributed to the subordination of Jews to Christian order and piety, but in spaces where Jews controlled Christian work the dynamic was different and the Christians' need for images of devotion was a cause of tension and altercation.[72] It is not surprising that the despondent spinners, whose ability to pray how and when they wished was at the mercy of poor communication between the Christian foreman and Jewish managers, began to hang their own printed images in more private spaces at the top of the mill as an alternative expression of religious autonomy and piety. These fragile images could hardly ignite the same amount of discomfort, controversy, or tension in this contested space. Or could they?

The Homemade Chapel and the Cheap Devotional Prints, 1635

> We boys agreed to buy some images of saints and the Madonna and to make a chapel in the top room of the said mill so that we could say our prayers, particularly the *laude* and the rosary. We therefore bought new images of saints and of the Madonna, and

> we made a chapel in the upper room of the mill, in a place where there was a window but in such a way that it was like a cupboard. At times we lit candles, hung up images of the saints, and put them on a table. I do not know for what reason we stopped going to the mill. But when we returned, we found that the images of the saints had been removed and torn from the wall, and scattered on the ground, particularly one image of the Madonna with child, which was torn in half. . . . In my judgment, I always believe that it must have been the Jews [who did this].
>
> —Testimony of Tommaso Caparelli, [20 July, 1635][73]

As has been shown in the previous chapter, small, portable devotionalia and paraphernalia were often allegedly or actually broken, damaged or verbally attacked as the result of altercations between Jews and Christians. The inquisitorial monitoring of flimsy devotionalia demonstrated the extreme measures that the Holy Office was prepared to take to discipline Jews and keep them away from all Christian representations. Investigations were reopened and recorded two years later in 1635. Francesco Mariano, a seventeen-year-old spinner in the mill, denounced the Sanguinettis for destroying printed images (*imagini*) of the Blessed Virgin and saints placed in a portable *altarino* covered with an altar cloth, candlesticks, and images nailed or glued to hard surfaces, which he and other Christian boys had set up on the upper floor of the workshop in 1633, intending to create an alternative space for prayer. The Madonna was again the main subject of these cheap prints, but others portrayed saints (whether they were local saints is not clear from the testimonies). It seems that by the seventeenth century, saints were often more popular as images of personal devotion than images of the Virgin.[74] In the Sanguinetti mill, the *altarino* represented a kind of homemade primitive chapel in a convenient but more private alcove on the top floor of the mill. Sacred figures and candles were placed on a flat surface—perhaps a table or windowsill—and cheap religious prints, particularly of saints and the Madonna, were stuck to the walls with soggy bread, which acted as an adhesive.[75] It is also clear that such prints were put up elsewhere across the work space of the mill.[76]

As has been shown, Jews could get themselves into trouble with these sorts of images and end up being prosecuted irrespective of the fragility or type of image supposedly attacked. In 1606 in Modena, Columbino, a twenty-year-old Jewish seller of secondhand goods, was accused of snatching and trampling on one of the fragile wax crucifixes that were being sold by Joannes Magnanini, a Christian teenager.[77] Columbino argued that he and his friend Jacob (who had died) were constantly attacked by poor Christian children, and the crucifix had been broken by them and not the Jews.[78] Although Columbino was probably exaggerating the extent of his victimization, one Christian witness, Antonio, the son of Domino Cristoforo, was able to give testimony that Columbino constantly remonstrated with Magnanini and threatened repeatedly to damage the wax crucifixes.[79] Probably on account of this one eyewitness, and as a disciplinary caution to a defiant lad, Columbino was sentenced to pay a fine of fifty scudi for irreverence.

In regard to the accusation of destroyed paper images in the mill, Menozzi, the local inquisitorial vicar in Spilamberto, acted with rigor, meticulously interrogating nine witnesses (seven of them more than once, for a total of eighteen sessions) regarding the running of the mill, the keeping of the keys of the mill, the involvement of the Jews in the daily administration of the factory, and the interaction between members of the two religions.[80] However, no one asked why these witnesses had waited a year and a half to report this allegation about the destruction of the prints. Again concerned that the Jews were still acting as managers of Christian spinners, it seems that the vicar was keen to investigate and uncover all aspects of Jewish-Christian interaction rather than be limited to the actual offense of desecration.

The spinners' testimony was contradictory, and each had difficulty in recalling precisely when the violation had occurred. Most mill work was done during the summer season, and only a few workers continued year round, weaving and dyeing rather than spinning.[81] Apart from the delator Francesco Mariano, who argued that the violation had occurred during Christmas 1633, none of the others could put a precise date to it.[82] Gio Baptista Bartholomeo, a thirty-year-old spinner, and Tommaso Caparelli, a fifteen-year-old spinner, asserted that it was during a Christian *festa* (which could refer either to a Sunday or to a religious festival), but could not be more specific.[83] Leonardo Costantini said it was during a Jewish festival and that, because the Jews were not working, the Christians could not either.[84] However, he could not remember whether the desecration had occurred when he was living in the mill or before he came. Domenico Bonazzi, another supervisor, reported that the violation occurred one night after the workers had left and before they returned the next morning.[85] Andrea Cavretti, a sixteen-year-old spinner, even depicted the desecration and violation as something that happened several times.[86] Desecration could not be proven categorically, and no flimsy or torn prints were brought as evidence.

Nevertheless, the Christian witnesses did testify to the Jews' repeated demands, prior to their being desecrated, that the Christian workers permanently remove the prints from the walls of the mill. In his second interrogation, which took place in Reggio, Francesco Mariano argued that Alessandro Sanguinetti's personal objection to the images and his threat to beat the spinners if they did not remove them surely linked him to the crime.[87] He told the inquisitor: "We put up these [images of] saints in the chapel. One morning Alessandro came into the workshop and he said, in the presence of all of the workers who had brought these [images of] saints, that he did not want them there, that we should take them away, and if not, said 'I will give you a beating [*se non vi darò delle bastonate*].'"[88]

Adriano Consini, another spinner, confirmed Francesco's words almost exactly.[89] Supervisor Leonardo Costantini testified that Alessandro had asked him to remove all the cheap prints across the mill, since the only authorized image was the painted panel of the Madonna and Child.[90] Costantini seems to have ignored this demand.[91] Faced with these new complaints not only of desecration but also of orders to remove the images, and angered that frequent and close interaction had continued despite inquisitorial prohibition, Fra Michelangelo Cati reincarcerated Raffaele in Modena and interrogated him on July 22. Despite some efforts by neighboring Holy Offices to track him down, his brother Alessandro had fled Spilamberto and only returned to the town nine years later on April 29, 1644.[92]

On July 30 while Raffaele was in prison, Sanito Melloti, a spinner in the mill, and Domenico Bonazzi, the foreman, were summoned to the city to confirm their testimony that the images and chapel had been destroyed when no Christians were in the mill. After further interrogations of five more Christian spinners, it became clear that Francesco Mariano—a spinner and the delator of this 1635 episode—had had an altercation with Simon and therefore harbored a personal grievance against the family. Perhaps the Christians' prime motive in bringing the accusations was not the desecration of the images, but rather resentment at their bad treatment and not being paid their final wages. Nothing had been done by the Christian workers about the desecration until they had stopped working at the mill and realized that the Jews were refusing to pay the money that they owed. They had then sought revenge in the inquisitorial court, which questioned whether the desecration had really happened or if it was just an excuse by which the Christian workers could denounce the Sanguinettis to the Inquisition.[93]

At this point, the file contains Christian written testimony delivered again before the Giudici del Maleficio notary in Spilamberto.[94] The written testimony of the Christian supervisor Leonardo Costantini, who appeared voluntarily on July 24, 1635 conveys much important information regarding his position as supervisor of the mill and offers evidence that contrasts with the testimony he provided a month later in the inquisitorial court.[95] Perhaps under pressure from Rangone not to indict the Jews directly for this crime, he stated that, although the printed images were ripped, they were found on the floor "wet and covered with mice droppings."[96] When Costantini appeared before Vicar Menozzi in Spilamberto in August 1635, he accused Alessandro of demanding that the printed images be removed from the mill but nothing more. He also stated that, when he had returned to the mill after a Christian festival, he discovered that the images had been destroyed. However, he was still unwilling to blame the Sanguinettis outright for this desecration, since he was unsure whether the Jews or the mice were responsible.

The testimony of the twenty-year-old Andrea Cavretti on August 6 in the inquisitorial court was more incriminating than that of the other spinners.[97] He argued three points succinctly. First, he asserted that only the Jews had been present in the mill when the chapel was destroyed.[98] Second, he stated that Leonardo had not been living in the mill when the desecration of the prints occurred; and, third, he said that Alessandro had shouted at the workers to be quiet when they were praying.[99] On the same day, an inquisitorial visitation was carried out to see where the main altar had been constructed in the mill.[100]

As he had been initially in 1632, Simon was once again the focus of inquisitorial investigation. On October 2, 1635, Menozzi was instructed to imprison him in Spilamberto and wait for orders to send him to the Holy Office in Modena.[101] Simon either had to pay five hundred gold ducats to travel alone to Modena, or he was to be bound by double fetters and sent in the custody of the constable (*bargello*), the agent of the secular arm.[102] Marquis Baldassare Rangone seems to have stepped in to grant the constable's assistance to the archpriest and the Inquisition.[103] On October 8, Simon was incarcerated in the prison of the Holy Office in Modena, where Menozzi subjected him to two long and grueling interrogations.[104] Here Simon showed a certain confidence as he stood before the inquisitor, determined to stand his ground and not be intimidated.[105] On November 20, he underwent a third interrogation but was released on the same day, giving surety that he would appear when summoned.

Apart from holding the key to the Madonna image, none of the Sanguinettis admitted to holding master keys to the mill that would have enabled them to enter whenever they wished. Instead, they testified that they had worked closely with Costantini, ensuring that if they needed access to the mill when he was not there, they could locate him and easily take the keys from him. Therefore, unquestionably, the Jews had had sufficient time and opportunity to desecrate the images and destroy the homemade chapel when their workers were not around. Domenico Bonazzi even testified to seeing the Jews in the mill in 1635, when he was no longer working there: "I saw them . . . when I was in the street, and they were in the mill. I saw them when they passed the window. Furthermore, we all know that they knocked things down inside the mill, and we heard them do so."[106]

Besides the more general allegations that Simon had hired Christians and desecrated Christian prints, he now faced charges of allowing his son Alessandro (now accused of having shouted at the workers while they were praying in the mill) to escape, to which he responded that his son had ignored his own demands and fled.[107] As proof, in December 1635 Simon submitted two letters to the Holy Office, which his son had apparently written from Bassano.[108] One of the letters read: "I say to you one thing for sure, that I do not want to come to the house, not because I have been at fault, but because I am certainly innocent of every sort of thing that they are able to charge me with. Also, I am unable to suffer the prison, and you know how much I was harmed the other times. I do not want to come home to suffer again, knowing the particular sacrifices and persecution that I would face."[109]

According to Simon, his son had been imprisoned shortly before this by the secular courts and feared further incarceration.[110] Simon described to the Inquisition his penultimate meeting with Alessandro in San Cesario sul Panaro at the home of a Christian farmer, Domenico Bastiani, and testified that he was unable to change his son's mind, despite his efforts: "I attempted to change his mind, saying that it was better to present himself, and that the Holy Office had long arms [*le mani longhe*], and that in the end, he would have to come at his own expense. . . . But he did not want to be calmed [*aquietare*] by my counsel."[111]

The Inquisition soon turned its attention to Simon's oldest son, Raffaele. On November 29, and subsequently on December 3 and 4, Raffaele was imprisoned and interrogated by Menozzi in Modena.[112] On December 14, the Jew declined the opportunity to make a formal defense and was released. His choice not to use legal counsel reflected the Jews' common practice of preferring to place themselves "at the mercy of the Inquisition," especially when they argued, as they usually did, that they had done nothing wrong.[113] Legal counsel was expensive and time-consuming. It made sense—or so the Jews had come to believe—to request pardon and pay the fine that the inquisitors usually demanded.

The Modenese Inquisition considered twenty-one-year-old Raffaele Sanguinetti to be the main suspect for the offense of demolishing the chapel and ripping the printed images. He was subjected to the longest periods of incarceration and the highest number of interrogations, often showing defiance and lack of respect.[114] It was clear that he played a bigger role in the running of the mill than his father or brothers.[115] Again, during these investigations the inquisitorial court never bothered asking why the Sanguinettis would have wished to desecrate sacred images. It neither interested the Inquisition nor was it thought relevant to its role in monitoring and disciplining Jews. Instead, the court's questioning concentrated on the interaction in the workplace between the followers of the two different religions, and the types of regulations and discipline that the Jews had imposed on their Christian spinners. Raffaele maintained his innocence throughout and continually depicted both himself and his family as victims of Christian hostility in the mill. He repeated his belief that the trial was dominated by the desire of his poor Christian workers for revenge.[116] He argued: "The people that have said this against me are evil people, and my enemies, as you will see in time."[117] An interesting document, probably drafted by Annibale de Barnardi, the defense advocate in the Holy Office, between December 10 and 14, 1635, when Raffaele was contemplating his defense, hints at the arguments that would have been used had he requested legal counsel:

> On two important charges Raffaele Sanguinetti, who is now held in the court of the Holy Office, is being prosecuted and charged by the Holy Office. The first is that he tore down sacred images attached to a wall and threw them onto the ground. The second is that he was in contempt of the Christian religion by tearing and disfiguring them according as witnesses examined by the court were seen to testify. But on neither of these charges should he be punished, nor can he be, neither ordinarily nor extraordinarily, nor can

he even be prosecuted on either of them, nor held in detention. Granted that the witnesses testified that they had seen the images torn from a wall, and in their own words ripped and on the ground, further saying that they believed that this had been done by those Jews, because on festival days the keys of the building where the images had been affixed were held by them, nevertheless this reason is not sufficient, neither can it affect those Jews, nor is the argument against them conclusive, since even though they may have had the keys, and kept them on festival days, it cannot be assumed from such slight presumption and conjecture that they were guilty, since this is against legal rules and any assumption must be included as part of the indictment. Nor does the reasoning necessarily lead to this conclusion, since while it is granted that the crime was committed on the day of a festival, it does not necessarily follow that it was the said Jews who committed it, since it could have been Christians who were responsible, in order that those Jews should be charged with an assumed crime for which they were not responsible. Indeed it could even have been that it happened by accident, either because mice did it, or the force of the wind, or of a storm, or of water raining down from the sky or by someone else's fault or trick, indeed it is credible that it really happened because of mice, since the images were said by boys and witnesses to be attached to the wall with bread, and the informer testified that most of the images thrown on the ground were wet and soaked in mouse droppings, as can be clearly seen from their testimony. Therefore, no valid charge can be brought against this Raffaele, who has been held in custody and threatened with prison, to justify condemning him, nor detaining nor subjecting him to an investigation.

But, without ever agreeing that this was actually the case, it could be that the said images were torn down by Raffaele himself or by other members of his family, but even then it certainly does not follow that the said images were torn down or ripped up in contempt for the Christian religion, and he cannot in any way be pursued in criminal proceedings, since even if the Jew had taken the images into his house or removed them from the wall thereof, he would have committed no crime, since to do so is not forbidden in law: whether it be done in fraud or in contempt as a cause for fraud, or contempt, it is an attempt to prove a crime which is not in itself

> a crime but has the nature of fraud, but since the element of fraud or contempt was not proven, he cannot in any way be persecuted or punished, since Jews did not keep sacred Christian images on their walls, nor is it forbidden them to take them down from walls, or their own dwellings, or to take them away, provided that it was not done in contempt or fraud.
>
> Furthermore, since almost two years have passed, and the images which were taken from that wall and ripped up are not present nor can they be seen, it is not fair that he should be accused of any crime, since proof of the crime must actually be shown before anyone can be prosecuted or punished, and especially in our case where the crime concerns a permanent and not a temporary fact, as can be clearly seen.
>
> Wherefore since all the things already mentioned are true, from the foregoing renunciation of all his defenses since he cannot believe that any other defense is necessary, where the substance of the crime is not apparent, the said Annibale de Barnardi deservedly petitions and urges that the Advocate and Procurator of prisons of this Holy Office [rule] that the same Raffaele Sanguinetti be released from prison, and freed.[118]

This document reveals some intriguing points about image desecration and the Jews' defense. Annibale echoes the Jews' belief that if they were in close proximity to images, they would be accused of desecrating them. Annibale also argued that what was important was not the crime itself but the reason why the Jew would have wanted to remove the image. (This document gives no references to legal texts to back his claim, possibly because it was preliminary notes, never formalized into a defense document). If contempt or deceit were found to have been a motive, then the Jew was guilty. Yet, it argued, the inquisitors never questioned the Jews' motive for this offense, either in this trial or in others for image desecration, which seemed to question what legal right the Inquisition had to prosecute Jews for this crime. Other important points were that, since no one saw the Jews actually commit this crime and no evidence of the desecration had been found because the prints had disappeared, then Raffaele could not be blamed. Again, Annibale offered no legal references here. Finally, he argued that it was not an offense for Jews to remove fragile images from their dwellings as long as this was not done in contempt. Whether the Inquisition would have accepted this point is doubtful. This was not an official Jewish dwelling. Nor did the Holy Office consider the desecration of prints a lesser crime than that of desecrating an ancient painting that had a special rank or claim to sacrality. Had not the Twenty-Fifth Session of the Council of Trent promulgated resolutions demanding that equal reverence be paid to all types of images?[119]

Due to a heavy workload and lack of funds, the Holy Office did not imprison Raffaele or his father again until March 5, 1636. In Tinti's letter of February 1636 to the Sacred Congregation in Rome, he complained of the poverty of the Holy Office and the cost of continuing to investigate Simon's case.[120] The Sacred Congregation responded by ordering that Raffaele be tortured.[121] On March 16, Raffaele was stripped and tortured for half an hour on the *strappado* (whereby the suspect's hands were bound behind his back and he was lifted by a rope tied to the wrists, which was then attached to a beam on the ceiling), in the presence of Inquisitor General Tinti.[122] He suffered dislocation of his arms, and the notary recorded that his screams included: "The truth, I have said the truth. I have said it. Let me down from here so that I can die. I am a respectable man [*che io morto, sono huomo da bene*]."[123]

After his torture failed to bring any confession, he and Simon were released. The Jews were prohibited from being tenants of the mill in the future and forced to pay a substantial fine of three hundred scudi (one of the heaviest fines ever imposed on Jews in the duchy of Modena) for their repeated insolence in defying the Inquisition's instructions to withdraw from the management of the mill.[124] Correspondence between Tinti and the Sacred Congregation in Rome reveals Tinti's wish that the Jew be whipped instead of being fined.[125] He wrote: "If I had authority to determine the punishment, I would impose a public whipping which the offense seems to deserve but I do not want any other wrongdoing."[126] As Tinti saw it, the offense of the Jews being tenants of the mill was of much greater importance and needed a more severe punishment. Preoccupied with other offenders, understaffed, and clearly curbed by the power over the Jews of the ducal courts, the Holy Office was not able to discipline the Jewish communities as much as it would have liked.[127]

The Prints and Their Meaning

Hindered by the painting's inaccessibility and central position in the mill, the Christian spinners had transferred their devotion to cheap prints stuck with chewed bread to various locations in the mill, including a makeshift *altarino* on the top floor of the building. Treated as devotional images or even ritual objects that could only be enjoyed close-up, these prints provided a framework for prayer and contemplation for small groups in the workplace.[128] Domenico Bonazzi gave the most vivid description of the chapel: "There was a chapel in the said mill on high, where we worked the silk, toward the street. . . . [It was] in a niche [*un nichio*], where at one time there had been a window with certain doors. On the windowsill was a small table, with the image of the Blessed Virgin and other images of various figures."[129] Here the Christian spinners added their own atmosphere to the interior of the mill with their visible religious imagery, light (of candles), and sounds of prayer.[130] But this one chapel was not sufficient for the number of spinners, and an alternative chapel and images of devotion were placed in another area. Leonardo Costantini testified in 1635: "Because not all the workers had the comfort of saying their prayers before the images at the top of the mill, the boys or other workers erected a chapel at another table where the boys worked. There they placed many images of saints and the Madonna, and in the evenings, they lit two candles. On Saturday and the other days, they said their prayers."[131]

When Christian festivals removed all the spinners from the mill, their sacred spaces—which clearly meant more to them than the Jews realized—were exposed to Jewish violation. The Christians believed that, because they were not present to protect the images, it was inevitable that they would be desecrated by the Jews, because this was what Jews did. The spinner Francisco Mariano added: "I am sure that the Jews, that is, members of the family of Simon Sanguinetti, are the ones who are doing the damage in the mill. One day, Alessandro, son of Simon, was outside the mill, and he called Master Domenico [Bonazzi], the capo maestro of the mill. He asked Master Domenico if he had seen who had broken the chapel, and Master Domenico replied that no one would ever want to damage it, because it would distress [*per non disgustare*] the other workers."[132]

Moreover, according to Leonardo Costantini, Alessandro Sanguinetti, before his escape, had wanted the cheap images removed and had asked him repeatedly to do so.[133] Simon had, according to Leonardo, removed one of the Madonna images from the door of the cellar.[134] Interestingly, all Christian witnesses unanimously testified to the prints' desecration and argued too that they had all been destroyed by the time they returned to work after their break.

These images were flimsy, printed on cheap paper, and could easily be destroyed (possibly by mice, as Raffaele argued). Yet it is unlikely that all these images would have been destroyed in this way, and therefore it must be suggested that the young Jewish lads—in particular, Alessandro or Raffaele or both—were responsible for their destruction and committed image desecration as accused. But the Inquisition did not concern itself with proving that Raffaele had committed this crime. Its attention now focused on the Jews' continued illegal tenancy of the mill since 1633 and the fact that Alessandro was still at bay, unpunished.

The Case of the Pictures in the Bedroom at the Inn of Piumazzo, 1635

A third report, also in 1635, was again submitted by the inquisitorial notary Ludovico Marchesi on August 10.[135] He informed Tinti of an act supposedly committed by Alessandro on his hurried escape from inquisitorial arrest in Spilamberto, after staying over a weekend in an inn in Piumazzo in the diocese of Bologna.[136] Alessandro was suspected of defacing and removing three printed images of the Madonna of the Rosary, Saint Luke, and angels and saints that were glued to wood and hanging in the three rooms where he stayed.[137] Hostel rooms were expected to be decorated with prints of holy subjects in order to provide guests with an area of contemplation and prayer like that they had at home. These particular images had been put up by the innkeeper at the request of a local archpriest, Bonensi, who had instructed all innkeepers in Modena to have images of the saints in each of their bedrooms, subject to a fine of twenty-five scudi if they were not visible.[138]

Apparently, after Alessandro had left the inn, the images could not be found, and, because he had been the last to occupy the room, the innkeeper Thomaso Garagnane, who gave testimony on August 16, felt he had sufficient evidence that the Jew had committed the offense.[139] Again, just like the prints in the mill, these images had disappeared and the assumption was that Alessandro had destroyed them. No suggestion was made as to what Alessandro might have done with them. On August 20, Menozzi interrogated Thomaso's wife Caterina, who provided the same information, which suggests that husband and wife had agreed on their stories.[140] When Thomaso was interviewed again at home, he also blamed Simon for attempting to bribe him not to report his son's transgressions to the Inquisition when the Jew had come to visit him at the inn after his son had left. Simon himself later admitted to trying to convince the innkeeper not to press charges, with the argument that members of his family had stayed in Christian inns many times, but had never been accused of such an offense.[141]

It is doubtful that Thomaso fabricated the accusation. He displayed no personal grievance against Alessandro, although he referred to the Jew as a "beast" three times.[142] Surely if Thomaso had intended to wrongfully incriminate the Jew, it would have made more sense for him to leave proof of broken or damaged images on the floor. Thomaso argued: "It can't be anyone else except the Jew, because a Christian would not have done this. . . . If the wind had blown down [the images], they would have been found in the room when it was swept, but nothing was found. As I already said, there were three rooms [in which he stayed], but nothing was found in any of them, while [the images] disappeared at the time that the said Jew was there. Nothing like this has ever happened throughout the seven years while I have been the innkeeper."[143] Moreover, he argued, the images themselves were not worth stealing: "As these images were printed on wood, they were not valued at more than four to six pennies [*quattrini*]. No one would steal them for their value."[144]

His argument implied that, since a Christian would not steal them because they were not valuable, it was likely that the Jew had destroyed them. Yet the inquisitorial investigation revealed two discrepancies in Thomaso's testimony. In his first appearance he had stated that he had discovered the burglary on Sunday afternoon. When he was interviewed again he said that it was in fact on Sunday morning, putting the blame on the carelessness of the notary who, he said, had previously failed to record his testimony correctly.[145] Another inconsistency is that Thomaso was adamant that Alessandro was the only guest staying in the inn for the weekend, but his wife contradicted his testimony by naming Betiga Magnano Milanese as another traveler staying in the inn at the same time (on his way to Bologna).[146] Alessandro also named a fellow Jew, Josephino, who was staying in his room: "I say that this [Thomaso's] testimony is false, because when I lodged in this inn at Piumazzo, there was with me one Josephino who stayed there at the same time as me. All the time that I stayed in the inn, he lodged in one room, nor do I know if others were staying there. . . . Therefore, one cannot conclude that it was I who had removed these images. It is possible that it was one of the others who were also lodging there."[147] But neither Betiga nor

Josephino was summoned to give evidence. To support his testimony, Thomaso showed the inquisitor the marks on the walls where the images had hung in the three rooms. Had not, he argued, Jews always removed images while they stayed in Christian inns? He told the inquisitor he knew this from an acquaintance:[148] "After this happened, I was discussing it with Monsignor Francesco, son of Mastro Gaspareo of Spilamberto, in a shop in Spilamberto. . . . Monsignor Francesco said to me that he had stayed in inns at other times, I don't know where, in the company of Jews. He said that the Jews, whose names he did not know, detached an image of the saints in the evening, and placed it under the bed, and in the morning returned it [to the wall] and reattached it."[149] Testimonies in this dossier of both Jews and Christians bear witness to the Jews' overpowering discomfort in the presence of Christian images in the inns where they stayed. According to Thomaso's friend, Jews would not sleep in a hostel room with a Christian image hanging on the wall. They would temporarily remove the image and return it to its place the following morning. The problem here was that the images had disappeared; Thomaso's testimony seemed to suggest that Alessandro had gone one step further than other Jews and chosen to destroy the images.

If Alessandro had indeed desecrated the cheap images in both the mill and in Piumazzo, his aggressive tendencies reflect both a juvenile rashness and a restrained assault on Christianity through a violation of its images, which he probably believed he would be able to get away with. His flight, then, may signify his sudden realization and consequent fear that he might in fact have been in more trouble than he had previously thought.

Naturally, the Inquisition considered Alessandro a more serious offender once the allegation was made that he had perpetrated this second crime in Piumazzo in mid-July 1635—a few weeks after the accusation surfaced that he and his brother had demolished the chapel and images in the mill. The Inquisition waited patiently for nine years for his return and then arrested him.[150] Why Alessandro decided to surrender himself at this particular time is unclear but in 1644, then thirty-two years old, he replaced Raffaele as the main suspect before an Inquisition keen to conclude its investigation. The Inquisition indicted Alessandro for fleeing inquisitorial arrest and prosecution, for hiring Christians in the mill, and for showing irreverence by desecrating images of devotion both in the mill and in Piumazzo.

Tinti himself interrogated Alessandro on three occasions, on May 6, 9, and 14.[151] He was temporarily released, only to be ordered back to prison on June 28 to face further interrogation and torture. Four months later, after recovering from an illness that led Baldassare Rangone to transfer him from the inquisitorial prison to the Spilamberto hospital, he was tortured on the *strappado* on October 27, even though the left side of his body was crippled and the torturer could only attach the cords to his right arm.[152]

Alessandro maintained his innocence regarding all the allegations and, as usual, chose to forgo the right to a formal defense, placing himself at the mercy of the Inquisition.[153] Tinti clearly remained confident that Alessandro was guilty. He sentenced him to an extraordinary punishment, a *poena extraordinaria* of exile or imprisonment, which the Inquisition resorted to when guilt could not be formally established but strong suspicion was attached to the accused in the eyes of the court. Alessandro appealed the punishment since exile would, he was reported as saying, "cause the total ruin of his family, bearing in mind his poverty."[154]

In a show of flexibility, the court imposed instead a fine of one hundred Modenese pounds, a considerable sum that reflected the inquisitors' determination to discourage the Jews from again taking control of the mill and its workers.[155] The case provides the clearest evidence of a judicial case of image desecration, where the Jew is indeed shown and proven—according to inquisitorial law—to be a desecrator.

The Running of the Spilamberto Mill, 1632–1635

Instead of uncovering the reasons why the Sanguinettis might choose to desecrate images and prints, the Inquisition had spent considerable time questioning both Jewish suspects and Christian spinners regarding the details of the working relationship in the mill between Jews and Christians. The testimonies give us some indication of the tensions that existed in the workplace, but these were not limited to the Christian images themselves. In its efforts to assert jurisdiction over Jews who lived outside the Modenese ghetto, the Holy Office had gone beyond the jurisdiction set by Pope Gregory XIII's bull *Antiqua iudaeorum improbitas* in its prosecution of these Jews.[156] Perhaps they might have been angry that no plans were being made either to force the Jews of Spilamberto to return to Modena and live in the ghetto there, or to introduce a mini-ghetto into Spilamberto itself. The Holy Office tried to circumscribe the Jews' economic activities and especially to stop them from renting, acquiring, or owning landed property.[157] Moreover, Simon was ignoring the church's official ban on Jews employing Christians.

Outside Modena, away from the watchful eyes of city dwellers and inquisitorial spies, these Jews had repeatedly flouted regulations regarding the hiring of Christians.[158]

Although Tinti wanted to destroy the influence of the Sanguinetti family and much of his persistent, time-consuming, and expensive investigation tried to achieve this, he failed. This was because of the machinations of the prominent Rangone nobles, who used the Giudici del Maleficio as an alternative forum for Christian witnesses to provide evidence confirming the innocence of the Sanguinettis regarding the main desecration of the Madonna image. Baldassare Rangone also argued in letters to the Inquisition that the mill business had been badly affected by the 1629–1631 plague, and that he needed the Sanguinettis' financial contribution and tenancy of the mill to alleviate his insolvency.[159] Moreover, Duke Francesco I d'Este had authorized the Jews to hold landed property, and the duke alone was entitled to revoke this privilege.[160] Despite inquisitorial pressure. the Sanguinettis remained involved until the mill was no longer financially viable, or, as Leonardo Costantini testified in 1635, until the "money had run out." It is significant that Baldassare Rangone then transferred the lease to other Jews, two brothers—Biondi and Salomone (their surname is not specified).[161] Clearly the marchese was not inclined to defer to the Inquisition's demands and its objection to Jewish tenants running the mill.

There were clearly issues of social class and tensions of learned versus popular culture at play here too. In 1632 Simon was able to give an exact account of the names and ages of his male spinners to the inquisitors. He seemed to know all his workers and feel that he was in charge of them. He had also taken control of the one image in the mill and determined the times at which these Christians were able to see it and pray before it. When he was interrogated in 1635, he was no longer able to name the Christian spinners who had worked for him, because, first, he was far less involved in the daily running of the mill, and, second, the number of foreigners and itinerant workers who came to work but then left the next day made it impossible to control, interact with, or identify them.[162] Social tensions were probably far greater, and the Christians' own creations of different altars around the work space confirmed the Jews' lack of control over their workers and these workers' own desire to create private space away from them. Simon revealed the tensions that existed between him, his sons, and Francesco Mariano, describing the delator as a lad of "no intelligence," who had been placed in the Spilamberto prison since he performed shoddy work, spoiled (or wasted) materials owned by the Sanguinettis, and never came to work on time.[163] Now Simon even testified that he had to fire some workers because "their work was not to his liking."[164] Mariano, for his part, described Simon as "that son of a bitch with a buggered mouth."[165] Other Christian spinners—in particular the young lads Adriano Consini (sixteen years old) and Gio Baptista Cagarelli (thirteen years old)—in 1635 condemned the Jews for not paying them the salaries they had agreed upon.[166] It is probable that the 1629–1631 plague, which led to population losses and then labor shortages in the countryside, forced Simon to surrender the mill after December 1634.

* * *

Christian witnesses also gave contradictory testimony about the tensions between Jewish managers and Christian spinners and this was exacerbated by the presence of Christian imagery in the mill. Some, such as Gio Baptista Cagarelli, said that the Jews shouted at them for saying their prayers in front of the images, while others, such as Leonardo Costantini (who, perhaps, as the foreman felt more loyalty to the managers), denied this.[167] These unhappy incidents might have occurred because the Jews disregarded the needs of Christian spinners for space in which to pray and time in which to do it. The Christians expected the Jews to allow them this religious freedom, to be attentive to their prayer times and to keep their distance, but, due to the noise in the mill and the pressures of production, these expectations were clearly not met. One therefore witnesses a clear case of Jewish intolerance toward Christian piety, prayer, and imagery, indicating that, when they had the upper hand, they would show the same intolerance as they were subjected to by Christians.

In 1635 other Christian spinners argued that the Jews had often shouted at them to pray silently, although the Jews denied this categorically.[168] Spinners Francesco Mariano (seventeen years old), Adriano Consini (sixteen years old), and floss silker Gio Baptista Bartholomeo (thirty years old) testified that Simon had insulted and cursed one particular floss silker, Andrea Cavretti (twenty years old), telling him to lower his voice when reciting the rosary of the Blessed Virgin.[169] They also said that he shouted at and cursed a group of Christians one night when they were singing the same prayers.[170] Gio Baptista Bartholomeo describes the Jew as "exploding with rage" and said that Simon ordered that Cavretti be fired the next day for making a disturbance.[171] When Simon was interrogated about this, he denied the allegation. He asserted instead that the noise of the prayer had disturbed not him but the local governor, Paulo Falaschi, who had complained to Simon that he could not bear the noise that penetrated his neighboring house.[172] Simon argued that it was Falaschi, and not he, who had shouted at Andrea, adding that he believed Cavretti had intended to disturb others rather than truly pray.[173] Falaschi was not summoned by the Inquisition to be cross-examined nor asked why he would have found Christian prayer disturbing. But when Cavretti was interrogated for the second time, he changed his story, arguing instead that the Jews mainly kept away during Christian prayer and it was Alessandro who had shouted at the Christian spinners several times, although never directly at him.[174] Since at that particular time he was working for Baldassare Rangone, Cavretti may have been told to temper his aggression against the Jews.

But ordering the Christians to pray more quietly was not the same as telling them to stop. Foreman Leonardo Costantini again confirmed that the Jews had never used force to stop the Christians from praying.[175] Further, even if Francesco's delation was exaggerated, it seems clear that the Jews' intention here was to enforce factory discipline rather than to interfere with Christian piety. Francesco reported:

> One evening, some of the floss silkers, that is, Steffano de Sassuolo who is here at Reggio, a certain Giovanni Battista Genoese, and Mister Giovanni Battista of Spilamberto, were reciting the rosary while they proceeded with their work. While they were reciting the rosary, Raffaele the Jew arrived in the workshop. His task was to inspect everyone's work for flaws. On that occasion, he hit with a stick [*un legno*] the three men who were reciting the rosary and also another fellow who wasn't reciting it, though I don't remember who he was. As he struck them, he said, "Look what a mess you've made of this job!" At other times, he attacked me and the others. He once hit me and injured both my arms, because I hadn't appeared for work [*che mi ruino tutti i bracci, perche non era andaro in botega*].[176]

Again, confusion existed among the Christian witnesses as to whether Raffaele had hit the Christians because they were saying Christian prayers or because they were not doing their work correctly. But the fact that he had hit them confirmed his intolerance and exasperation. Eventually Francesco even retracted the above statement about being hit, testifying that during prayer time the Jews "just went away . . . because they did not want to hear us saying them."[177] Supervisors armed with sticks were a standard feature of early modern mills, where the work of unqualified spinners was closely monitored.[178] But when the sticks belonged to Jewish managers who had assumed a position of authority over Christians and threatened to beat them, the Christian spinners could use this against them in an inquisitorial court, arousing the suspicion of the Holy Office.

With all these differing accusations often being retracted, Alessandro Sanguinetti still appears throughout the dossier as a belligerent, ruthless, and selfish character, fleeing from inquisitorial jurisdiction and leaving his father Simon and his brother Raffaele to suffer prolonged imprisonment and interrogation for allegations that were directed at him as much as at them.[179] Many of the testimonials confirm that, of all the family, it was Alessandro who was most aggressive toward the Christian workers. Moreover, in his own interrogation on November 2, 1632, he admitted that he had removed the key from the flap of the Madonna and Child image, placing it in one of the storerooms, effectively leaving the image shut for approximately two months.[180] Spinners Francesco Mariano and Adriano Consini testified that when the cheap images were put up around the mill, it was Alessandro who again threatened that, unless the images were removed, the Christian spinners would receive a beating.[181] Francesco Mariano accused Alessandro of forbidding the Christians to report the desecration of their cheap images to the local archpriest and said that Alessandro had called the spinners "ugly brutes." At least three spinners confirmed that Alessandro had repeatedly threatened to beat them.[182] It seems clear that such belligerent tendencies could well have caused him to desecrate religious images, choosing in particular to destroy and dispose of the wooden images in Piumazzo. In both the mill and the hostel room, he seemed to exercise a certain defiance that is comparable to that described by Samuel Nachmias, who converted to Christianity as Giulio Morosini in 1649. He reported how wealthy Venetian patricians often deposited the keys of their *palazzi* with Jewish merchants in the city state, allowing them to use their homes while they were away. Morosini then described how he and other Jewish merchants had been able to behave aggressively to religious images in the rooms of the palazzi: "we acted with as much disrespect as we could, with physical gestures, with shouting and spitting."[183] Like many neophytes, Morosini may be a fairly tendentious writer. Nor should we place too much trust in the anecdotes of a neophyte bent on making new converts. But his comments do indicate the basic understanding among Jews that to do any real damage to paintings and sculpture remained unwise. The fact that Alessandro's actions were confined to prints suggests that he believed he could escape retribution. Yet not only was he tortured, but he was also punished by the Inquisition for this offense. The Inquisition had hoped to terminate the Jewish tenancy of the mill but in the end was limited to fining the Sanguinettis for their supposed infringement and preventing their daily interactions with the Christian spinners.

Conclusion

The Spilamberto case has faint echoes of the "Christ of Beirut" legend discussed in earlier chapters. In the narrative, the host of the Beirut party was greatly embarrassed by the presence of a Christian Crucifixion picture left behind on his premises and by his guests' suggestion that he was blaspheming against Judaism by holding on to it. In a way that is superficially similar, the Sanguinettis were embarrassed by the Madonna on their premises (as other Jews had been in various episodes since the fifteenth century). When Christians entered the Jews' space, the assumption was, as in the legend, that Jews would desecrate their images. In our real case in the seventeenth century, the ubiquity of images only complicated matters. Images were now in factories and inns as well as domestic and public spaces. It was also getting easier and easier to damage the flimsier items or be accused of desecrating or removing them. But unlike "Christ of Beirut," there was no suggestion of any miracles. No image had come alive and reacted to being ill-treated, and no Jews suddenly saw the error of their ways and converted.[184] This remained the stuff of tales and legends, and was not part of real cases against Jews in early modern Italy, that concentrated more on cases of disrespect rather than desecration.

Inquisitors seemed to assume that, because Judaism was a religion which eschewed images and did not believe in the special powers of Jesus, the Madonna or the saints, Jews were uncomfortable with Christian images and would ideally like to be without them. They had a motive for attacking them which was taken for granted. But that did not mean that they would seize every opportunity to destroy them. Yet the Holy Office handled this accusation soberly. Both disrespect and desecration were prominent in these proceedings, and they were conducted in a very rational manner. The court took note of the contradictions in the evidence, observed its own law on proof, did not jump to hasty conclusions, though it did use brutal methods, such as the application of torture to prisoners deemed to have given rise to reasonable suspicion.

Alternative explanations for damage to images were considered (such as mice being responsible). The Jews were not charged, as they once were, with creating images in order to defile or destroy them. Rather, they were reacting to images which had been thrust upon them. Jews were not actually convicted of maliciously damaging the prints in the mill, though Alessandro Sanguinetti was fined for removing prints from the inn where he stayed. The Sanguinetti were not seen as malevolent, conspiratorial Jews who spent their lives reviling and plotting against Jesus and the Madonna. They were not hobgoblins or fiends in human shape, but bullying bosses striving to enforce factory discipline. There is a very strong contrast between the handling of the Spilamberto affair and the case in Mantua described in the previous chapter.

Nor were the Sanguinettis charged with desecrating the suckling Madonna. Simon had taken reasonable steps to fend off such accusations and there was little damage to the painting. The complaint against the Sanguinettis was a subtler one: disrespect for the religious sensibilities of their Christian workers, and perhaps for the Madonna herself, by presuming to control access to her image. The images served a purpose in facilitating Christian prayer and devotional trends and Inquisitorial scrutiny was directed, not at preserving the sanctity of the images, but at the issue of how and when Christians used them for worship in the Jewish space. And there was evidence (no doubt some of it tainted) of the Sanguinettis showing disrespect towards workers who wanted to say their prayers or sing the rosary with the assistance of Christian images which helped them to concentrate their minds. Clearly, of course, charges of actual desecration were also present, and they related to cheap and fragile images. It is evident that the act of ripping up or making off with a cheap devotional print is, at least in theory, just as reprehensible as vandalizing or defiling an old master or spitting on an oil painting.

This case study also confirms how, in real cases, arguments over images often interacted with other issues. What concerned Tinti far more than Jewish desecration was the Sanguinettis' tenancy of the mill. Jews were to be stopped from exerting any authority or discipline over Christians, either inside or outside the home, since social, economic and especially sexual relationships contaminated Christian purity.[185]

By the mid-seventeenth century, the Jews of Modena had experienced nearly half a century of close inquisitorial monitoring and knew well how to take advantage of the limited political power of the Holy Office: Alessandro by fleeing Spilamberto and escaping prison for a limited period, and Simon by continuing to operate the mill until it was no longer financially viable. Simon's testimony in particular confirms not only his calculated, rational thinking but his refusal to be manipulated by the flagging tribunal. It was the dukes of Modena who still controlled the Jews and had the ability to curb the power of the Inquisition. Furthermore, the Giudici del Maleficio provided an alternative and more favorable forum for Christian testimony that helped prove the Jews' innocence, at least concerning the painting of the Madonna and Child. The spinners' tendency to give more detailed testimony to the Giudici del Maleficio might also indicate their fear that giving the Inquisition too much information might imperil themselves unnecessarily.

The insistence of the complainants on their need to pray and their reliance on these images reveal much about the level of religious fervor these destitute Christians wished to maintain and the importance of these visual aids. Was this an expression of the centrality of sacred images to their devotional life, or were these visible markers being used, almost as talismans, to define their sense of separation from the Jews' mill? If the latter is the case, we may comprehend how the religious prints aggravated the Jews and became the target for Raffaele's and Alessandro's aggression; perhaps a lack of caution that was rarely exhibited by mature, older Jews.

Finally, I would like to suggest two Jewish attitudes to Christian images that resonate through these sources. First, intriguingly, it is clear that the Sanguinettis believed initially and rather naively that they would be able to control and manipulate the spinners' devotion and usage of images when they became tenants-cum-managers. Second, these Italian Jews were sufficiently troubled by visible symbols of Christian devotion in the mill where they spent a considerable amount of time, and they openly demonstrated their distaste and discomfort. The mill, at night and during Jewish and Christian festivals, became their private space, where they might act out their disdain and disrespect for Christian images that in general they had to temper. This represented a breaking of boundaries or an erasing of lines that Christian society in early modern Italy had drawn for them. Within closed quarters these Jews had acted as though their power over the Christians was not confined to the mill. And if Alessandro also desecrated images in Piumazzo, it should be read as a demonstration of Jewish violence—juvenile rashness, radicalism, inexperience, and the actualization of emotions against the very images themselves. Were not the Jews' actions a throwback to the types of iconoclasm that the Hebrews had been commanded to execute on their return to the Land of Israel? But Alessandro—like the fictitious Jew in Gregory of Tours's initial tale—had failed to hide his attack. Could such actions ever be hidden in a Christian society preoccupied with monitoring its sacred images?

Conclusion

This book has attempted to describe the long history of the allegation that Jews made a practice of desecrating religious images revered by Christians, from the fifth to the seventeenth century of the Christian era. It has presented four main arguments, of which the first is that the Jews' principal targets were generally said to be Jesus of Nazareth, Christ's Passion, and the Virgin Mary (either on her own or with her child) as they were represented by a wide range of objects, which included relics, crosses, crucifixes, paintings, drawings, and statues. Only rarely were Jews charged with attacking images of saints. The second argument is that the stereotype of the Jew as image desecrator was created and spread by many different media, which included tales, legends and fables, dramatic paintings and illustrations, and accusations or denunciations laid before secular and ecclesiastical tribunals (both episcopal courts and branches of the Inquisition).

The third argument is that many factors shaped the persistent Christian conviction that Jews were prone to desecrating Christian imagery; these included Christian doctrinal developments, Christian devotional developments, Jewish-Christian polemics (Christian accusations that biblical Jews were idolatrous and Jewish accusations that Christians were idolatrous), the circulation of various kinds of texts, actual Jewish and *converso* behavior, and the viewing of images that depicted Jews as image desecrators.

The fourth argument is that the balance between these various factors and how they related to each other proved to be different in each historical context examined—Byzantium, high medieval Europe, medieval and early modern Spain and Italy—depending on the extent of image saturation in society, the political, social, and economic position of the Jews, and the level of antagonism against them.

Chapters 1, 2, 3, and 5 considered the actual material pathways whereby the knowledge of the allegation or accusation against Jews was transmitted and its context—that of the increasing proliferation and sophistication of Christian art and iconography. Because of the Christian tendency to use Jews (or *conversos*) as foils for their own beliefs and practices, the Jews' violation was seen as an inverted response to Christian veneration. Although at times Christians disagreed with Muslims, much as they did with Jews, Christians did not find it necessary to defend themselves against Muslims in the same way.

It was fiction, above all, that enabled Christians, collectively, to imagine Jews desecrating images. Tales and legends instilled common ideas and beliefs in the minds of large numbers of people. The fifth-century *inventio crucis* first accused Jewish men of hiding or burying the archetypal Christian relic—the True Cross. This relic had supposedly been unearthed by Helena, the mother of Constantine the Great, on her trip to Jerusalem. The Judas of the story was understood to be the guardian of the cross, secretly knowing that Christ was the Savior, but only capable of revealing the object and its miraculous qualities under the direction of Christians. By the sixth century, Christians had begun to bow down or prostrate themselves before images of Christ and the saints, and it was then that Gregory of Tours connected a Jew with the abuse of a sacred image. He described the fictitious Jew as violent and delinquent, having the capacity to make an image bleed as a result of his efforts to harm it. At the same time, it was believed that God had turned the Christian image into a miraculous and salvific object by virtue of the transfigured bleeding of the being it represented.

The legend and tale moved across Europe, where their listeners shaped and shared knowledge, especially when Christian images began to define who fitted into society and who did not. At the time of the Byzantine Controversy, iconodules shaped and expanded desecration tales to support the veneration of images. Jewish desecrators became the prime examples of iconoclasts whose blasphemous acts—sometimes in their own homes where Christian images were occasionally present—struck at the sacred being whom the image represented. In fact, when the Byzantines told themselves stories about Jews and images, they told two kinds of stories. According to the first of these, Jews are moved primarily by the commandments in Mosaic law forbidding the creation of images, which may become objects of worship. Fictitious Jews were assumed to object to Christianity as an idolatrous religion and to believe that Jesus and Mary had become rivals to the true God. They therefore targeted their images, which were now ubiquitous in Christian society, above all others. In the second kind of story, this hatred for Jesus and

Mary is the motive for physical attacks on images—sometimes by trying to whitewash them (as they did at Lydda) and at other times by defecation or mutilation. These stories started differently—the Jew could be in his own home or inside a church—but ended up, with the same "happy ending," the conversion of the Jewish desecrator. Sometimes the whole Jewish community converted—now convinced of the truth of Christianity because an image, tested and provoked by them, had demonstrated its power. Christian images had become powerful transmitters of holy presence and were rapidly reestablished as central to the Orthodox religion. This policy affected not only the administration of the empire, common public events, and the interests of the body of Byzantine citizens but also every citizen's domestic space. Moreover, during the Iconoclastic Controversy there had been no need to define where the seeping blood, purported to be from the miraculous image, actually came from.

Our Byzantine tales would then travel westward to shape Marian tales in medieval Europe. These stories were newly adapted in light of the increasing isolation and violence that the Jews faced in England and northern France, reflecting the Christian anxieties toward them. Here, more so than in Byzantium, the stories would end with the punishment of the Jew. It was only when western Europe went through its own iconographic revolution that "Christ of Beirut"—its blood and its liturgy—began to increase in importance and attract more attention, especially in light of other types of flowing holy blood. The notion that Jews would attack images gave rise to the belief that—as a deicidal people—they would do something even worse than that: by attacking images, they were attacking and attempting to kill the live holy bodies these images represented. In this way image desecration would be similar to ritual murder and host desecration. Once the Fourth Lateran Council had pronounced that only the Eucharist was capable of exuding Eucharistic blood, ecclesiastical anxiety turned to the fear that real Jews were committing both blood libel and host desecration, a far more explosive and dangerous allegation than image desecration. Accusations were fabricated and embellished to conform to the negative Christian stereotypes of Jews and to arouse Christian loathing and horror.

The Marian tales also led to real accusations and judicial prosecution of Jews for the desecration of images. The accusation's staying power had less to do with real offenses than with the proliferation of Christian images in society, the increase in the number of allegations against Jews, the expansion of judicial control over them, and the rise of record keeping.

Spain was much slower than other European countries to bring charges of image desecration against professing Jews. Here the proliferation of sacred objects occurred relatively late, and they entered domestic spaces only from the mid-fifteenth century. Charges only became common after this and were brought predominantly against *conversos*, as it was thought that these crypto-Jews were still secretly practicing Judaism and were therefore apostates or heretics. The combination of more domestic images and more converts, some of whom were thought to have insincerely converted under pressure, meant more charges of image desecration. In Spain, the prosecution was at its bloodiest, and *conversos* accused of attacking images were often burned at the stake.

In Spain, we also witnessed the development of a new type of desecration accusation—that of scourging crucifixes, usually in collective and deviant rituals. There may even be a parallel between the accusation of cannibalistic ritual murder—consuming the blood of children—and that of flogging crucifixes in the late fifteenth century. In both there were two elements, "projection" and "perversion." Christians projected their own actions onto *conversos*, considered to be Jews, but charged the Jews with doing them in a perverted way. Whereas Christian flagellants punished themselves in memory of Christ's Passion, Jews supposedly wielded scourges, not on their own bodies, but on images of the suffering Christ. Judaism had become a distorting mirror of Christian practices.

To assume that Jews were silent would be wrong. As soon as Jews were confronted by Christian images, they were forced to apply Judaic law to these objects in public spaces and refute charges of materialism and image desecration. Christian theologians could openly condemn Judaism, but rabbis had to be more circumspect about Christianity. Jewish texts began to reflect the fact that they were a minority group living in the midst of an idolatrous host nation—Edom. As images proliferated and became ubiquitous, the rabbis increasingly adopted tactics to avoid looking at them and minimize contact with them. Desecration might be considered in an extreme situation where there was nothing to lose, as at the time of the Crusades, but even then the accounts by Jewish chroniclers of Jewish attacks on crosses were probably not authentic. In their own prescriptive sources, Jews were warned that they could expect to be framed by unscrupulous Christians who were determined to discredit them and who contrived to accuse them of treating Christian images with gross disrespect. By the late fifteenth and sixteenth century, when Jewish scholars, strongly influenced by Renaissance humanism, began to write history, they depicted the allegation as a medieval one—a falsity—that had fueled hatred against communities and could even cause their expulsion. Even though Jews and Christians represented their tales in a similar way, their intentions were always opposite. The Jews glorified their own resistance to the pressures of an image-saturated society. The Christians repeatedly rejected the Jews' contention that Christians were idolaters and continued to demonize Jews by accusing them of sacrilegious acts.

It was always safer for Jews to curse Christian images quietly and discreetly under their breath. Jews in early modern Italy were accustomed to mutter a certain imprecation as they passed Christian images, and those who stayed at inns probably temporarily removed Christian pictures from the walls of their chambers, so as not to have to sleep under their gaze. In many ways the accusations against Jews in Italy were an amalgamation of tales, except that now Jews were no longer seen as agents of transfiguration. As Christian images became ubiquitous in both public and private spaces, accusations against Jews involved images on walls, in transit, in homes, in pawnbrokers' banks, and around people's necks. The Papal Inquisition investigated charges of both desecration and disrespect with some care and some regard for the laws of proof, as opposed to the case in Mantua in the early seventeenth century—one not investigated by the Inquisition—that led to the execution of Jews after agitation by a Franciscan preacher. More common by far were accusations of disrespect for images in private homes or for the Holy Sacrament when it was being carried through public places to the sick or the dying.

Court records show that flesh and blood Jews, well aware of Christian prejudices, were forced to devise strategies for defending themselves against charges of image desecration. This was one of the many hazards of living as a minority in a Christian country. It seems clear that although Jews were believed by Christians to be moved by hatred of anthropomorphic images of sacred things in general (including saintly intercessors), they were only roused by hatred of Jesus of Nazareth and the Virgin Mary, the God incarnate and the super saint. Ordinary saints worried them less. Jews led their lives trying to defend themselves against these types of accusations, as yet another form of discrimination that they had to cope with. What for a Christian participating in a procession was a moment of euphoric veneration was for a Jew a moment of concern, fright, fear of surveillance, and an overwhelming need to escape. These different reactions explain why the Jews were unable to maintain their authority over Christian spinners in the mill of Spilamberto. The presence of Christian images complicated their daily interactions, intruded into the close proximity of their work space, and thus threatened their own interreligious boundaries.

In exploring the relationship between the fictitious Jew constructed by Christian writers and the real Jew, this book has identified a recurring pattern of anti-Judaism. Christianity attributed to Jews a mentality involving idolatry, materialism, legalism, and literal-mindedness, which acted as a foil for everything that true, spiritually minded Christians were supposed to believe in.[1] Jews became the "other" against which Christianity defined itself, and here their main function was to demonstrate the truth of Christianity. In many of the tales, Jews "obliged" by attacking images, which then demonstrated their miraculous power; sometimes this caused the Jew to convert, acknowledging the truth of Christianity, and possibly escaping punishment. These were not real Jews, but marionettes invented by Christian puppeteers according to their own needs.

To be sure, the Jews' supposed relationship with Christian images and their transfiguration was framed within the two most important periods of suppression and destruction of images in European Christianity: the Byzantine Controversy between 730 and 843 and the Protestant attacks, especially from the 1530s onward. Both of these monumental events were caused by disagreement over the religious functions that images fulfilled. Over the centuries between them, allegations, collections of moral tales, Christian polemics, imagery, iconography, hagiography, judicial accusations, conversion theories, street talk, village gossip, institutional developments, woodcuts, broadsheets, and prints all fed the belief that Jews were desecrators. By the time of the Reformation, the violent iconoclasm of Protestant reformers meant that attention was switched from the "offending" Jew and refocused temporarily on heretical Philo-Protestant iconoclasts. Moreover, after the 1580s the Jews' desecration was often considered to be more a case of simple disrespect for Christianity than an indication of more complex theological grievances. The defense document in the trial against Simon Sanguinetti's son Alessandro completely ignored the ideological foundations of the image desecration discourse and inclined toward jurisprudence and practicality.

Yet assertions and ways of thinking die hard, and the belief that Jews were inclined to damage images persisted well after the close of the seventeenth century.[2] In 1736, when the neophyte preacher Paolo Sebastiano Medici published his *Riti e costume degli ebrei confutati*, he recorded a long list of examples of the Jews' hatred for Christianity. His list still included offenses against Christian images.[3] In addition, the Dominican Lorenzo Filippo Virgulti, who preached conversionary sermons to the Jews in Rome, repeated the claim that Jews "violently" profaned images of Christ.[4] In Pisa in 1787 crowds attempted to lynch three Jews who were falsely accused of spitting on sacred images in the cathedral. Unusually, two Muslims were also involved. A North African Jew was killed after the forces of law and order failed to protect him, for which dereliction of duty they were later punished by Grand Duke Pietro Leopoldo.[5] Even though the nineteenth century was to bring a secularization of art and society, making the allegation less common, it seems that, as late as 1903, Jews in Faro, Portugal, were accused of passing their time in the synagogue by breaking up wooden crosses with hammers.[6] Even today, a crucifix known as El Señor del Tambo de Montero, which was supposed to have been scourged by Portuguese *conversos* in the 1630s, is preserved in the Mercedarian church of Cuzco in Peru and remains an object of popular veneration. This famous case is commemorated in Peruvian poetry, folklore, and iconography.[7]

Knowing something of the allegation's foundation narrative, sampling the key episodes in the development of its Christian lore, and exploring some of the many reports of this offense being committed has, I hope, allowed readers to experience the allegation's fundamental anti-Judaism, its widespread dissemination and prosecution. There is much still to do. I would suggest three areas of further study. First, research should be extended to the Holy Roman Empire where, from the mid-fourteenth century, a number of expulsions and massacres of Jews had brought about the destruction of synagogues and their appropriation as miraculous Christian shrines; this was prevalent in the southern areas between 1349 and 1520. Most of the images of Mary and/or Christ in these shrines were at this time associated with Jewish desecration, although the Reformation probably put an end to such beliefs.[8] Second, more research should be done on the connection of Voragine's tale of Saint Nicholas of Myra, otherwise known as St. Nicholas of Bari, to the image desecration narrative, and how its iconography compared and contrasted with that of the desecration of images of Jesus and Mary.[9] Third, there seems to be a tendency in certain cases in Italy for Christian judicial authorities to force Jews to commission Christian art as a form of punishment for offenses against Christianity. For example, in 1453, a Jewish innkeeper in Treviso was forced, as a punishment for giving meat to Jewish converts to Christianity on Fridays, to pay for a new crucifix in the church of San Francesco.[10] How common was this in early modern society and how should it be connected with how the church understood the Jews' relationship to Christian art?

Measuring the effects of the allegation must continue, and I know I have only begun the task of tracing its historical journey, its progressive articulation, meaning, and significance. It remains for me to surmise—perhaps as a last thought—that this long-standing allegation contributed significantly to the creation of the modern antisemitic perception of Jews in some art historical surveys as lacking their own identity and cultural and artistic ability, and continually preying upon the art of their host nation. This perception, which was reiterated in 1849 by Richard Wagner in his *Das Kunstwerk der Zukunft* (The Art-Work of the Future), would last until the 1980s when finally Jewish art began to be regarded as a subject worthy of its own study at Israeli universities.[11]

Notes

INTRODUCTION

Epigraph: John Chrysostom, *Adversus Judaeos Orationes* 1.6, *Patrologiae cursus completus, series Graeca,* ed. Jacques Paul Migne (Paris, 1857) (*PG* from here on) vol. 48:852. Translation taken from John Chrysostom, "Homily 1 Against the Jews," in Wayne A. Meeks and Robert L. Wilken, *Jews and Christians in Antioch in the First Four Centuries of the Common Era* (Missoula, MT: Scholars Press, 1978), 97. All translations are mine unless specified.

1. The term *passio imaginis* first refers to the feast devoted to the desecrated image held on November 9 according to tenth- and eleventh-century Catalan passionals. See Michele Bacci, "The Berardenga Antependium and the *Passio Ymaginis* Office," *Journal of the Warburg and Courtauld Institutes* 61 (1998): 1–16, 10. On this altarpiece, see Carlos Espí Forcén, "Jews Desecrating a Crucifix: A *Passio Imaginis* Altarpiece from Mallorca," in *Iconographica: Rivista di iconografia medievale e moderna* 8 (2009): 83–97, 84, 87.

2. A Passion chapel was a medieval chapel dedicated either to the *Passio Imaginis* or the *Passio Domini.* See Espí Forcén, "Jews Desecrating a Crucifix," 94 n. 1.

3. See Chapter 1.

4. Shlomo Simonsohn, ed., *The Apostolic See and the Jews*, 7 vols. (Toronto: Pontifical Institute of Mediaeval Studies, 1988–1991), 2:62–64 (doc. 6), Alexander IV, August 23, 1258.

5. Archivio di Stato di Modena (hereafter ASMo.), Fondo dell'Inquisizione (hereafter FI), Processi, busta 85, fasc. 11, fol. 1r. (1r is the folio page within the fascicle.).

6. Brian S. Pullan, *The Jews of Europe and the Inquisition of Venice, 1550–1670* (Oxford: Basil Blackwell, 1983), 92–93.

7. See H. L. Ho (Ho Hock Lai), "The Legitimacy of Medieval Proof," *Journal of Law and Religion* 19, no. 2 (2003): 259–298; esp. 274 n. 96, which notes how the process of ordeal could be manipulated, abused, and used as weapon against the Jews. On this case, see Jacob Rader Marcus, *The Jew in the Medieval World: A Source Book, 315–1791* (Cincinnati: Hebrew Union College Press, 1999) 142–146, 143. See also Magda Teter, *Blood Libel: On the Trail of an Antisemitic Myth* (Cambridge, MA: Harvard University Press, 2019), 29–30, who points out that the ordeal should not have been contemplated in the Blois case, because "Jews were exempted from ordeals by royal or imperial privileges."

8. Scholars are beginning to appreciate how visual material within different disciplines might be used as evidence. This is presently being researched by a group of scholars led by Klaus Krüger of Freie Universität. See "Bildevidenz: Geschichte und Ästhetik," Freie Universität, Berlin, accessed July 17, 2022, http://bildevidenz.de/en/team/klaus-krueger/. An example of this is how a representation might indicate the existence of a belief system and its position within it.

9. Espí Forcén, "Jews Desecrating a Crucifix," 90.

10. See Chapters 5 and 6.

11. This idea is suggested by Dana E. Katz, *The Jew in the Art of the Italian Renaissance* (Philadelphia: University of Pennsylvania Press, 2008), 12.

12. On ritual murder and blood libel, see Teter, *Blood Libel.* On host desecration, see Miri Rubin, *Gentile Tales: The Narrative Assault on Late Medieval Jews* (Philadelphia: University of Pennsylvania Press, 2004); and Mitchell B. Merback, *Pilgrimage and Pogrom: Violence, Memory and Visual Culture at the Host-Miracle Shrines of Germany and Austria* (Chicago: University of Chicago Press, 2013).

13. *Oxford English Dictionary*, s.v. "desecration," last accessed July 14, 2022, https://www.oed.com/view/Entry/50762?redirectedFrom=desecration#eid.

14. Leslie Brubaker has convincingly demonstrated that the word "iconoclasm" (derived from *eikon* [image] and *klastes* [breaker] and meaning "image breaker") was not used either during the Iconoclastic Controversy in Byzantium or in early modern Europe. By the 1950s it had become, in English publications, a "modern hybrid word." Stacy Boldrick expands the meaning of "iconoclasm" to include "burial or hiding as well as additive acts, such as covering, marking and the relocating or reframing art objects." Stacy Boldrick, Leslie Brubaker, and Richard Clay, eds., *Striking Images, Iconoclasms Past and Present* (Burlington, VT: Ashgate, 2013), 13–24 (Brubaker), 2 (Boldrick).

15. There is one Christian tale that appears in thirteenth-century collections (see Chapter 2) about an image of Saint Nicholas, but in real accusations, saints (for example, Saint Christopher) appeared only when they were portrayed with Christ or the Virgin.

16. John 19:33–37.

17. Moshe Halbertal and Avishai Margalit, *Idolatry*, trans. Naomi Goldblum (Cambridge, MA: Harvard University Press, 1992), 238–240.

18. Rachel Neis, *The Sense of Sight in Rabbinic Culture: Jewish Ways of Seeing in Late Antiquity* (Cambridge: Cambridge University Press, 2013), 170.

19. Eric Lawee, "Graven Images, Astromagical Cherubs, and Mosaic Miracles: A Fifteenth-Century Curial-Rabbinic Exchange," *Speculum* 18, no. 2 (2006): 754–795. Lawee shows how continuous references were made to the Jews' reliance on the cherubs by Christian scholars such as Stephen of Bostra, Leontios, Theodulf of Orléans, Nicholas of Lyre, Thomas Aquinas, Gilbert Crispin, and Rupert of Deutz. Henry N. Claman, *Jewish Images in the Christian Church: Art as the Mirror of the Jewish-Christian Conflict, 200–1250 C.E.* (Macon, GA: Mercer University Press, 2000), 23ff.

20. Rabbi Aron ben Gerson Abulrabi of Catania presented a fascinating argument in the fifteenth century, noting in his commentary on Rashi how, when he met Pope Martin V in 1418 in the presence of the cardinals, he argued that the cherubim in the Temple were not covered by the biblical prohibition against the Jews making graven images. J. Perles, "Ahron ben Gerson Aboulrabi," *Revue des Études Juives* 21 (1890): 246–269. The anonymous *Sefer Nizzahon Hayeshun*—a handbook from the end of the thirteenth- or early fourteenth-century Germany, attempts to explain the biblical passages: Exodus 20:4 (the Second Commandment), Numbers 21:9 (the bronze serpent), and Exodus 25:18–22 (the cherubim of the Temple). David Berger, *The Jewish-Christian Debate in the High Middle Ages: A Critical Edition of the Nizzahon Vetus with an Introduction, Translation, and Commentary* (Philadelphia: Jewish Publication Society of America, 1979), 261.

21. Karel Van der Toorn, "The Iconic Book: Analogies Between the Babylonian Cult of Images and the Veneration of the Torah," in *The Image and the Book: Iconic Cults, Aniconism,*

and the Rise of Book Religion in Israel and the Ancient Near East, ed. Karel Van der Toorn (Leuven: Peeters, 1998), 229–250.

22. Thomas Aquinas, *Summa Theologiae*, ed. Thomas Gilby (Garden City, NY: Doubleday, 1969), pt. 3, q. 25, art. 3 (on the image of Christ), art. 4 (on the cross of Christ), art. 5 (on the Mother of God).

23. Ernst Kitzinger, "The Cult of Images in the Age Before Iconoclasm," *Dumbarton Oaks Papers* 8 (1954): 83–150, 92ff.; Leslie Barnard, "The Theology of Images," in *Iconoclasm*, ed. Anthony Bryer and Judith Herrin (Birmingham: University of Birmingham Press, 1977), 7–15; Norman H. Baynes, "Idolatry and the Early Church" in *Byzantine Studies and Other Essays* (London: Athlone Press, 1960), 116–143. Christian thinkers who wrote on images and their uses include Epiphanius of Salamis, and Jerome in his letter to Bishop Neopotian in 394 (Frederick Adam Wright, trans., *Jerome: Select Letters*, Loeb Classical Library 262 [Cambridge, MA: Harvard University Press, 1933], 215–17). Also the early fifth-century Philostorgius (Joseph Bidez, *Philostorgius Kirchengeschichte*, GCS 21 [Leipzig, 1913], 78) and the late fifth-century Neoplatonic mystical writer Pseudo-Dionysius in *Pseudo-Dionysius Areopagita: De Coelesti Hierarchia, De Ecclesiastica Hierarchia, De Mystica Theologia, Epistulae* (Berlin: De Gruyter, 2012), 1.2; and in *PG* vol. 3, col. 373a–b.

24. Herbert L. Kessler, "'Pictures Fertile with Truth': How Christians Managed to Make Images of God Without Violating the Second Commandment," *Journal of the Walters Art Gallery* 49/50 (1991/1992): 53–65, 64.

25. Bernard Hamilton, "The Jews and the Byzantine Iconoclastic Controversy," *Eastern Churches Review* 5, no. 2 (Autumn 1973): 125–135, 133.

26. Translation taken from Herbert L. Kessler, *Spiritual Seeing: Picturing God's Invisibility in Medieval Art* (Philadelphia: University of Pennsylvania Press, 2000), 35. See also "St. John of Damascus: Apologia Against Those Who Decry Holy Images," Fordham University, Internet History Sourcebooks Project, accessed July 14, 2022, https://sourcebooks.fordham.edu/basis/johndamascus-images.asp.

27. Kessler, "'Pictures Fertile with Truth,'" 59; and Christopher S. Wood, "In Defense of Images: Two Local Rejoinders to the Zwinglian Iconoclasm," *Sixteenth Century Journal* 19, no. 1 (1988): 25–44.

28. Pier Cesare Bori, *The Golden Calf and the Origins of the Anti-Jewish Controversy*, trans. David Ward (Atlanta: Scholars Press, 1990), 80.

29. Reinhard Hoeps, *Aus dem Schatten des goldenen Kalbes: Skulptur in theologischer Perspektive*, Ikon Bild + Theologie (Paderborn: F. Schöningh, 1999), 10–11.

30. Kirsopp Lake, *The Apostolic Fathers with an English Translation*, 2 vols. (London: Heinemann, 1965), 1:351.

31. Medieval Jews also saw their own sin of idolatry as something to be atoned for and this sin was used to account for Jewish hardship and persecution through the Middle Ages. The Babylonian Talmud, Sanhedrin 102a, 694; the Babylonian Talmud, Nezikin 111. The *Midrash Rabbah: Exodus*, ed. H. Freedman and Maurice Simon (London: Soncino Press, 1981), noted "for there is no generation . . . that does not receive a particle of punishment for the sin of the calf-worship" (43.2). Rashi too commented on the sin as "a disgrace in the mouth of all that rise up against them." *The Pentateuch and Rashi's Commentary: A Linear Translation into English*, vol. 2, *Exodus*, ed. Abraham Ben Isaiah and Benjamin Sharfman (Brooklyn: S. S. & R., 1950), 410. Kenneth Bland, *The Artless Jew: Medieval and Modern Affirmations and Denial of the Visual* (Princeton, NJ: Princeton University Press, 2001), 123–124, notes how Samuel ben Meir (Troyes, ca. 1085–ca. 1158), the Rashbam, described how Christians continually used the episode of the golden calf.

32. David Nirenberg, *Aesthetic Theology and Its Enemies: Judaism in Christian Painting, Poetry, and Politics* (Waltham, MA: Brandeis University Press, 2015), 24.

33. Michael Camille, *The Gothic Idol: Ideology and Image-Making in Medieval Art*, Cambridge Studies in New Art History and Criticism (Cambridge: Cambridge University Press, 1991), 171 and 193; Bland, *The Artless Jew*, 118; Rosemary Radford Ruether, "The *Adversus Judaeos* Tradition in the Church Fathers: The Exegesis of Christian Anti-Judaism," in *Essential Papers on Judaism and Christianity in Conflict: From Late Antiquity to the Reformation*, ed. Jeremy Cohen (New York: New York University Press, 1991), 174–189, 177.

34. On the biblical commands to destroy the idols of nations in the Land of Israel, see Chapter 4.

35. Moshe Barasch, *Icon: Study in the History of an Idea* (New York: New York University Press, 1993), 108.

36. "John Chrysostom: Against the Jews, Homily 1," Tertullian Project, ed. Roger Pearse, accessed July 14, 2022, http://www.tertullian.org/fathers/chrysostom_adversus_judaeos_01_homily1.htm.

37. "St. John of Damascus: Apologia Against Those Who Decry Holy Images," Fordham University, Internet History Sourcebooks Project, accessed July 14, 2022, https://sourcebooks.fordham.edu/basis/johndamascus-images.asp.

38. Hyam Maccoby, ed. and trans., *Judaism on Trial: Jewish-Christian Disputations in the Middle Ages* (London: Littman Library of Jewish Civilization, 1993), 54–55.

39. For example, Kimchi, Ibn-Ezra, the Ramban, and Abarbanel say that Edom was Christianity. See Halbertal and Margalit, *Idolatry*, 210. Yehuda Halevi calls Christian Spain *hevel Edom* in his poem "My Heart Is in the East," writing "How keep my vows and pledges—with Zion / In the boundary of Edom, and I in Arabia bound?" See Joseph Yahalom, *Yehuda Halevi: Poetry and Pilgrimage* (Jerusalem: Hebrew University Magnes Press, 2009), 85–86. For some further discussion of the term in Byzantine Jewish writing, see Joshua Holo, "Byzantine-Jewish Ethnography: A Consideration of the *Sefer Yosippon* in Light of Gerson Cohen's 'Esau as Symbol in Early Medieval Thought,'" in *Jews in Byzantium: Dialectics of Minority and Majority Cultures*, ed. Robert Bonfil et al. (Leiden: Brill, 2012), 923–949, 942–949.

40. Bland, *Artless Jew*, 121, 123–124, 139, 143; Maimonides, *Commentary on the Mishnah, Avodah Zarah*, in the Ryzman Edition Hebrew Mishnah Avodah Zara (Rahway, NJ: Artscroll Mesorah, 2012), 1:3; and *Mishneh Torah, Hilkhot Avodat Kohavim* 9:4 (Jerusalem, 1922); Solomon ben Avraham ibn Aderet (Rashba), *Sheelot u-teshuvot (Responsa)*, 7 vols. (Bnei Brak, 1957–1959), vol. 5, no. 66; and Yom Tov ben Avraham Ishbili (Ritva), *Sheelot u-teshuvot (Responsa)*, ed. Yoseph Kapah (Jerusalem, 1959), no. 159.

41. Jeremy Cohen, *Christ Killers: The Jews and the Passion from the Bible to the Big Screen* (Oxford: Oxford University Press, 2007), 144.

42. Sidney H. Griffith, "Theodore Abū Qurrah's Arabic Tract on the Christian Practice of Venerating Images," *Journal of the American Oriental Society* 105, no. 1 (1985): 53–73. Theodore Abū Qurrah, who served as the Melkite bishop of Harran between the years 795 and 812, even argued that the Jews' (and Muslims') open mockery of and objection to Christian images and their accusations of the Christians' blasphemous idolatry was actually forcing Christians to stop using them when living under *dar al-Islam*. Eventually the Jews' disgust with Christian images would be expressed with more defiance. During the Majorca disputation in 1286, one Jew stated: "I wonder at you Christians . . . [for you] fashion and adore idols and images that neither feel nor hear, and you [thereby] act against God!" Ora Limor, ed.,

Die Disputationen zu Ceuta (1179) und Mallorca (1286): Zwei antijüdische Schriften aus dem mittelalterlichen Genua (Munich: Monumenta Germaniae Historica, 1994), 289--90.

43. *Midrash Rabbah: Genesis*, trans. and ed. Harry Freedman and Maurice Simon (London: Soncino Press, 1983), 38:28; Joseph Gutmann, "Abraham in the Fire of the Chaldeans: A Jewish Legend in Jewish, Christian, and Islamic Art," *Frühmittelalterliche Studien* 7, no. 1 (1973): 342–352.

44. Robert Chazan, *Fashioning Jewish Identity in Medieval Western Christendom* (Cambridge: Cambridge University Press, 2004), x.

45. This is Chazan's translation (ibid., 308), from *Milhemet Mizvah*, in *Shitat ha-Kadmonim 'al Masekhet Nazir*, ed. Moshe Y. Blau (New York, 1974), 305–357, 309–310.

46. Moses Maimonides, *The Guide for the Perplexed*, trans. M. Friedländer (New York: Dover, 1956), chap. 55.

47. Bland, *The Artless Jew*, 142.

48. When Ciro da Correggio censored Jewish *mahzorim* for the seventeenth-century Modenese Inquisition in order to eliminate offenses against Christianity, he had to check to see if the Jews had defined Christianity as an idolatrous religion. ASMo. FI, Processi, busta 69, fasc. 8, October 10, 1624, unpaginated documents; reported by Ciro da Correggio, October 12, 1624.

49. Shlomo Simonsohn, *Between Scylla and Charybdis: The Jews in Sicily* (Leiden: Brill, 2011), 506.

50. For the ways in which the Catholic Church stigmatized its Christian enemies, such as Hussites and Anabaptists, by accusing them of destroying images, see Martin Warnke, *Bildersturm: Die Zerstörung des Kunstwerks* (Munich: Carl Hanser, 1973); and Horst Bredekamp, *Kunst als Medium sozialer Konflikte: Bilderkämpfe von der Spätantike bis zur Hussitenrevolution* (Frankfurt: Suhrkamp Verlag, 1975).

51. *The Works of Philo: Complete and Unabridged*, trans. C. D. Yonge (Peabody: Hendrickson, 1993).

52. Ibid., 699.

53. Moshe Barasch argues that blindness in Christianity was related to a punishment for offending God. Moshe Barasch, *Blindness: The History of a Mental Image in Western Thought* (New York: Routledge, 2001), 26, 45. In the third century, Eusebius, the bishop of Caesarea, wrote of the Jews' blindness to their own scriptures. Eusebius of Caesarea, *De Vita Constantini*, introd. Bruno Bleckmann, trans. into German and commentary Horst Schneider (Turnhout: Brepols, 2007), 333 (book 3, chap. 18). See also Eric R. Varner, *Mutilation and Transformation: Damnatio Memoriae and Roman Imperial Portraiture* (Leiden: Brill, 2004), 60–61.

54. Kessler, "'Pictures Fertile with Truth,'" 61.

55. Sara Lipton, *Dark Mirror: The Medieval Origins of Anti-Jewish Iconography* (New York: Metropolitan Books, 2014), 3–4.

56. Kessler, *Spiritual Seeing*, 92.

57. Jaś Elsner, "Iconoclasm as Discourse: From Antiquity to Byzantium," *Art Bulletin* 94, no. 3 (September 2012): 368–394, 369.

58. Patricia Cox Miller, *The Corporeal Imagination: Signifying the Holy in Late Ancient Christianity* (Philadelphia: University of Pennsylvania Press, 2016), 137; Hans Belting, *Likeness and Presence: A History of the Image Before the Era of Art*, trans. Edmund Jephcott (Chicago: University of Chicago Press, 1994), 40; Kessler, "'Pictures Fertile with Truth,'" 64–65.

59. Megan Holmes, *The Miraculous Image in Renaissance Florence* (New Haven, CT: Yale University Press: 2013), 20.

60. David Freedberg, *The Power of Images: Studies in the History and Theory of Response* (Chicago: University of Chicago Press, 1991), 93.

61. Peter Brown argued that the reason for the rise of the veneration of images lay in the desire to maintain piety toward saints and holy men, whereas Ernst Kitzinger believes it was due to the continual influence of the Roman cult of the imperial portrait after the acceptance of Christianity by Christian emperors. Peter Brown, "Society and the Supernatural: A Medieval Change," in "Wisdom, Revelation, and Doubt: Perspectives on the First Millennium B.C.," special issue, *Daedalus* 104, no. 2 (Spring 1975): 133–151; and Ernst Kitzinger, *The Art of Byzantium and the Medieval West: Selected Studies* (Bloomington: Indiana University Press, 1976).

62. Miller, *The Corporeal Imagination*, 7.

63. Ibid., 136.

64. Ibid., 165.

65. Belting, *Likeness and Presence*, 106.

66. Camille, *The Gothic Idol*, 30.

67. Averil Cameron, "The History of the Image of Edessa: The Telling of a Story," *Harvard Ukrainian Studies* 7 (1983): 80–94.

68. Celia M. Chazelle, "Images, Scripture, the Church, and the Libri Carolini," *Proceedings of the PMR Conference* 16–17 (1993): 53–76, 54.

69. "St. John of Damascus: Apologia Against Those Who Decry Holy Images," Fordham University, Internet History Sourcebooks Project, accessed July 14, 2022, https://sourcebooks.fordham.edu/basis/johndamascus-images.asp.

70. Hans Belting, *The Image and Its Public in the Middle Ages: Form and Function of Early Paintings of the Passion*, trans. Mark Bartusis and Raymond Meyer (New Rochelle, NY: Aristide D. Caratzas, 1990), 14.

71. Freedberg, *The Power of Images*, 378ff.

72. Elsner, "Iconoclasm as Discourse," 370 and 377.

73. Ibid., 373.

74. Ibid., 370. Elsner notes that the sixth-century Syriac historian John of Ephesus recorded this process. As a result he believes that John of Ephesus saw this iconoclastic strategy as a normal procedure.

75. It is surprising to me that the Jew as an attacker of images is not discussed in Leopold Kretzenbacher, *Das verletzte Kultbild: Voraussetzungen, Zeitschichten und Aussagewandel eines abendländischen Legendentypus* (Munich: Bayerischen Akademie der Wissenschaften, 1977).

76. Barbara Baert, *A Heritage of Holy Wood: The Legend of the True Cross in Text and Image* (Leiden: Brill, 2004), 20.

77. Piero Camporesi, *Juice of Life: The Symbolic and Magic Significance of Blood*, trans. Robert R. Barr (New York: Continuum, 1995), 54.

78. For example, John 12:3 and Mark 16:1. For a discussion of such Marian qualities, see Miri Rubin, *Mother of God: A History of the Virgin Mary* (New Haven, CT: Yale University Press, 2009), 42, 64.

79. Miri Rubin, *Emotion and Devotion: The Meaning of Mary in Medieval Religious Cultures* (Budapest: Central European University Press, 2009).

80. Ibid., 58.

81. David Gentilcore, "Methods and Approaches in the Social History of the Counter-Reformation in Italy," *Social History* 17, no. 1 (1992):73–98, 82; Megan Holmes, "Disrobing

the Virgin: The Madonna Lactans," in *Picturing Women in Renaissance and Baroque Italy*, ed. Geraldine A. Johnson and Sara F. Matthews Grieco (Cambridge: Cambridge University Press, 2012), 167–195, 191.

82. There is no mention of images in the Qur'an but only in the Hadith, where Islam forbids any representations of humans or animals.

83. Peter Schadler, *John of Damascus and Islam: Christian Heresiology and the Intellectual Background to Earliest Christian-Muslim Relations* (Leiden: Brill, 2018), 227; Daniel J. Sahas, *John of Damascus on Islam* (Leiden: Brill, 1972), 137.

84. Georges Vajda, "Un chapitre de l'histoire du conflit entre la kabbale et la philosophie: La polémique anti-intellectualiste de Joseph ben Shalom Ashkenazi de Catalogne," *Archives d'histoire doctrinale et littéraire du Moyen Age* 23 (1956): 45–144, 135.

85. Suzanne Conklin Akbari, *Idols in the East: European Representations of Islam and the Orient, 1100–1450* (Ithaca, NY: Cornell University Press, 2009), 5, 157, 203–206; John V. Tolan, *Saracens: Islam in the Medieval European Imagination* (New York: Columbia University Press, 2002), 276. Jerome had actually been the first to portray Muslims as idolaters devoted to Venus. John V. Tolan, *Faces of Muhammad: Western Perceptions of the Prophet of Islam from the Middle Ages to Today* (Princeton, NJ: Princeton University Press, 2019), 24.

86. Tolan, *Faces of Muhammad*, 22.

87. Akbari, *Idols in the East*, 206.

88. Tolan, *Faces of Muhammad*, 36, shows how Muslim idolatry served as a foil to Christian devotion in fourteenth- and fifteenth-century English mystery plays.

89. Ibid., 22.

90. Maya Corry, Marco Faini, and Alessia Meneghin, eds., *Domestic Devotions in Early Modern Italy* (Brill: Leiden, 2018), 421.

91. Arietta Papaconstantinou, "Saints and Saracens: On Some Miracle Accounts of the Early Arab Period," in *Byzantine Religious Culture: Studies in Honor of Alice-Mary Talbot*, ed. Denis Sullivan, Elizabeth Fisher, and Stratis Papaioannou (Leiden: Brill, 2012), 323–339, 329. Papaconstantinou notes that around 690, Anastasios of Sinai in his treatise against demons wrote a story about how a portrait of Saint Theodore in a church outside Damascus was attacked by a Muslim. It then bled and twenty-nine Muslims died.

92. Ibid., 334; Kathleen Corrigan, *Visual Polemics in the Ninth-Century Byzantine Psalters* (Cambridge: Cambridge University Press, 1992), 78.

93. Joshua Trachtenberg, *The Devil and the Jews: The Medieval Conception of the Jew and Its Relation to Modern Antisemitism* (Philadelphia: Jewish Publication Society of America, 1943).

94. Jacob Katz, *Exclusiveness and Tolerance: Studies in Jewish-Gentile Relations in Medieval and Modern Times* (Oxford: Oxford University Press, 1961), 11.

95. Christoph Cluse, "Stories of Breaking and Taking the Cross: A Possible Context for the Oxford Incident of 1268," *Revue d'Histoire Ecclésiastique* 90 (1995): 396–442; and Elliott Horowitz, *Reckless Rites: Purim and the Legacy of Jewish Violence* (Princeton, NJ: Princeton University Press, 2006).

96. Horowitz, *Reckless Rites*, 150.

97. Gavin Langmuir also argues that the meaning of the crucifix changed for successive generations of Christians. Gavin I. Langmuir, *History, Religion, and Antisemitism* (Berkeley: University of California Press, 1990), 164.

98. Michele Luzzati, "Sulle tentazioni iconoclaste ebraiche in Italia fra tardo Medioevo e prima età moderna," in *"Conosco un ottimo storico dell'arte . . .": Per Enrico Castelnuovo; Scritti*

di allievi e amici pisani, ed. Maria Monica Donato and Massimo Ferretti (Pisa: Edizioni della normale, Scuola Normale Superiore, 2010), 227–234.

99. Eric Zafran, "The Iconography of Antisemitism: A Study of the Representation of the Jews in the Visual Arts of Europe, 1400–1600" (PhD diss., New York University, 1973), 195–216.

100. Dana Katz, *The Jew in the Art of the Italian Renaissance*.

101. Nirenberg, *Aesthetic Theology and Its Enemies*, 7.

102. Cohen, *Christ Killers*, 86.

103. Jeanne Halgren Kilde, *Sacred Power, Sacred Space: An Introduction to Christian Architecture and Worship* (Oxford: Oxford University Press, 2008), 67–68.

104. Katherine Aron-Beller, *Jews on Trial: The Papal Inquisition in Modena, 1598–1638* (Manchester: Manchester University Press, 2011).

105. ASMo. FI, Causae Hebreorum (from here CH) 245, fasc. 38, fol. 3r.

106. Ibid., fol. 21v.

107. Daniel Jütte, *The Age of Secrecy: Jews, Christians, and the Economy of Secrets, 1400–1800* trans. Jeremiah Riemer (New Haven, CT: Yale University Press, 2015), 3.

CHAPTER 1

1. For a previous article in which I discuss some of the ideas presented in this chapter, see Katherine Aron-Beller, "Byzantine Tales of Jewish Image Desecration: Tracing a Narrative," *Jewish Culture and History* 18, no. 2 (2017): 209–235.

2. Michele Bacci, "Devotional Panels as Sites of Intercultural Exchange," in Corry, Faini, and Meneghin, *Domestic Devotions in Early Modern Italy*, 272–292, 275.

3. Leslie Brubaker and John Haldon, *Byzantium in the Iconoclastic Era, c. 680–850: A History* (Cambridge: Cambridge University Press, 2011), 51.

4. Baert, *A Heritage of Holy Wood*, 24.

5. Ibid., 36.

6. Ibid., 44.

7. Other developing legends about important Christian relics at this time, including the Virgin's cloak and belt and Jesus's shroud, also credited a Jew with possessing and hiding them. See Ora Limor, "Christian Sacred Space and the Jew," in *From Witness to Witchcraft: Jews and Judaism in Medieval Christian Thought*, Wolfenbütteler Mittelalter-Studien 11, ed. Jeremy Cohen (Wiesbaden: Harrassowitz, 1996), 55–77, 57–61.

8. Augustine, *City of God* 22.8–10. See "Medieval Sourcebook: Augustine: City of God: Book 22:8–10. On Miracles," Fordham University, Internet History Sourcebooks Project, accessed July 14, 2022, https://sourcebooks.fordham.edu/source/augustine-cityofgod-22-9-10.asp.

9. Stephan Borgehammar, *How the Holy Cross Was Found: From Event to Medieval Legend*, Bibliotheca Theologiae Practicae, Kyrkovetenskapliga Studier 47 (Stockholm: Almquist & Wiksell International, 1991) 203.

10. Baert, *A Heritage of Holy Wood*, 2–5.

11. The legend of the True Cross had a strong iconographic presence, being found, as Giuseppe Capriotti and Barbara Baert have revealed, in the wall paintings in Franciscan churches, including the church in Montegiorgio in the province of Fermo and the churches dedicated to the Holy Cross, one in Sassoferrato, in the province of Ancona, and the other in Matelica, in the province of Macerata. See Giuseppe Capriotti, "L'iconografia di S. Elena nella leggenda della 'vera croce' e il problema ebraico nelle Marche del XV secolo," in *L'Abbazia di*

S. Elena nella valle dell'Esino: Storia, arte e architettura, ed. Marta Paraventi (Jesi: Tipografia Stampanova, 2008), 221–262, 233.

12. Merback, *Pilgrimage and Pogrom*, 16.

13. F. E. Peters, *Jerusalem: The Holy City in the Eyes of Chroniclers, Visitors, Pilgrims, and Prophets from the Days of Abraham to the Beginnings of Modern Times* (Princeton, NJ: Princeton University Press, 1985), 342.

14. This was repeated in the Justinian Code (529–534); see Amnon Linder, *The Jews in Roman Imperial Legislation* (Detroit: Wayne State University Press, 1987), 236–237.

15. Gregory of Tours, *Liber in gloria martyrum*, no. 21, ed. Bruno Krusch, Monumenta Germaniae Historica, Scriptores rerum Merovingicarum (Deutsches Institut für Erforschung des Mittelalters) vol. 1.2 (Hannover, 1885), 857–72. For the English translation, see *Gregory of Tours: Glory of the Martyrs*, trans. with introd. Raymond Van Dam (Liverpool: Liverpool University Press, 1988).

16. Baert, *A Heritage of Holy Wood*, 59; see also Alexander C. Murray, ed., *A Companion to Gregory of Tours* (Leiden: Brill, 2016).

17. Robert Wiśniewski, "Relate and Retell: Eastern Monastic Stories and the Beginnings of Latin Hagiography," in *Metaphrasis: A Byzantine Concept of Rewriting and Its Hagiographical Products*, ed. Stavroula Constantinou and Christian Høgel (Leiden: Brill, 2021), 63–82, 64.

18. Six of Gregory of Tours's tales in *De gloria martyrum* have been confirmed as originating in the East. In his introduction to the work, Van Dam discusses the influence of the East on Gregory's martyr stories; see *Glory of the Martyrs*, 8–10.

19. Avril Keely, "Arians and Jews in the 'Histories' of Gregory of Tours," *Journal of Medieval History* 23 (1997): 103–115, 111; Brian Brennan, "The Conversion of the Jews of Clermont in AD 576," *Journal of Theological Studies*, n.s., 36, pt. 2 (October 1985): 321–337.

20. *Glory of the Martyrs*, no. 21 ("The Jew Who Stole an Image of Christ").

21. Peter Brown, "Images as a Substitute for Writing," in *East and West: Modes of Communication; Proceedings of the First Plenary Conference at Merida*, ed. Evangelos Chrysos and Ian Wood (Leiden: Brill, 1999), 15–34, 24.

22. *Gregory of Tours: Life of the Fathers*, trans. with introd. Edward James, 2nd ed. (Liverpool: Liverpool University Press, 1991). When he rebuilt the cathedral in Tours, he commissioned a new set of Saint Martin murals to be exhibited there.

23. *Glory of the Martyrs*, no. 21.

24. Ibid.

25. Ibid.

26. Ibid.

27. Cain's guilt after killing his brother could not be hidden, since "the voice of thy brother's blood crieth unto me from the ground" (Gen. 4:10).

28. *Glory of the Martyrs*, no. 21.

29. Ibid.

30. Baert, *A Heritage of Holy Wood*, 59.

31. "John Chrysostom: Against the Jews, Homily 1," "Tertullian Project," ed. Roger Pearse, last accessed July 14, 2022, http://www.tertullian.org/fathers/chrysostom_adversus_judaeos_01_homily1.htm. John Chrysostom, *Logoi kata Ioudaiōn* 1.6 PG 48 ;852. Translation taken from Meeks and Wilken, *Jews and Christians in Antioch*, 97.

32. "Augustinus, Tractatus Adversus Judaeos," Documenta Catholica Omnia, Cooperatorum Veritatis Societas, accessed July 14, 2022, https://www.documentacatholicaomnia.eu/02m/0354-0430,_Augustinus,_Tractatus_Adversus_Judaeos,_MLT.pdf.

33. Rom. 11:25–28; 2 Cor. 4.4; 2 Cor. 3:15–18; see also John 9 and 12.

34. Albrecht Berger, ed., *Life and Works of Saint Gregentios, Archbishop of Taphar: Introduction, Critical Edition and Translation*, Millennium-Studien 7 (Berlin: De Gruyter, 2006), 780–796; Vincent Déroche, "Forms and Functions of Anti-Jewish Polemics: Polymorphy, Polysémy," in Bonfil et al., *Jews in Byzantium*, 535–548, 544.

35. "Augustinus, Tractatus Adversus Judaeos," Documenta Catholica Omnia, Cooperatorum Veritatis Societas, accessed July 14, 2022, https://www.documentacatholicaomnia.eu/02m/0354-0430,_Augustinus,_Tractatus_Adversus_Judaeos,_MLT.pdf.

36. Gregory of Tours, *Libri historiarum X* 5.11, ed. Bruno Krusch and Wilhelm Levison, Monumenta Germaniae Historica, Scriptores rerum Merovingicarum 1.1 (Hanover, 1951).

37. In *Glory of the Martyrs*, Gregory of Tours includes another tale of a Jewish violator. In "The Boy Who Was Thrown into the Fire," a Jewish glazier in Constantinople threw his son into his furnace for ingesting the Eucharist. As in our tale, the Jewish glazier was not killed by divine retribution but was burned to death in the furnace, the same place where he had attempted to kill his son. On this tale, see *Glory of the Martyrs*, no. 9, "The Boy Who Was Thrown into the Fire"; Rubin, *Gentile Tales*, 8–9. Like the image in Gregory's tale, the host remains indestructible.

38. David Jacoby, "The Jews in the Byzantine Economy," in Bonfil et al., *Jews in Byzantium*, 219–255.

39. Ibid., 229.

40. Ra'anan S. Boustan, "Immolating Emperors: Spectacles of Imperial Suffering and the Making of a Jewish Minority Culture in Late Antiquity," in *Violence, Scripture, and Textual Practices in Early Judaism and Christianity*, ed. Ra'anan S. Boustan, Alex P. Jassen, and Calvin J. Roetzel (Leiden: Brill, 2010), 204–234, 225.

41. Averil V. Cameron, "Byzantines and Jews: Some Recent Work on Early Byzantium," *Byzantine and Modern Greek Studies* 26 (1996): 249–274, 255.

42. On the Jews' iconoclasm in Jerusalem, see *The Chronicle of Theophanes Confessor: Byzantine and Near Eastern History, AD 284–813*, trans. Cyril Mango and Roger Scott (Oxford: Clarendon Press, 1997), 301; and Frederick C. Conybeare, "Antiochus Strategos' Account of the Sack of Jerusalem in A.D. 614," *English Historical Review* 25 (1910): 502–517, esp. 507–508.

43. The evidence for the attempted renewal of Temple sacrifices is very slim. Stefan Leder has drawn attention to the distortions in the sources in his useful article "The Attitude of the Population, Especially the Jews, Towards the Arab-Islamic Conquest of Bilad al-Sham and the Question of Their Role Therein," *Die Welt des Orients* 18 (1987): 64–71. See also *Chronicon Paschale, 284–628 AD*, trans. Michael Whitby and Mary Whitby (Liverpool: Liverpool University Press, 1990), 183.

44. *Chronicon anonymum*, ed. and trans. Ignazio Guidi, in *Chronica Minora* 1 (Paris: L. Durbecq, 1903), 26 (text), 23 (trans.), cited in Robert Schick, *The Christian Communities of Palestine from Byzantine to Islamic Rule: A Historical and Archaeological Study* (Princeton, NJ: Darwin Press, 1995), 33–39; Elliott Horowitz, "'The Vengeance of the Jews Was Stronger Than Their Avarice': Modern Historians and the Persian Conquest of Jerusalem in 614," *Jewish Social Studies* 4 (1998): 1–39, 9.

45. Averil Cameron, "Blaming the Jews: The Seventh-Century Invasions of Palestine in Context," *Travaux et Mémoires* 14 (2002): 57–78.

46. For example, in 609 the chroniclers Theophanes and Michael the Syrian blamed the Jews for the murder of Anastasis II, the patriarch of Antioch. *The Chronicle of Theophanes*

Confessor, 425–426. But Joseph D. Frendo succinctly proves that the patriarch was not murdered by the Jews of Antioch but killed by soldiers. Joseph D. Frendo, "Who Killed Anastasius II?" *Jewish Quarterly Review* 72 (1982): 202–204.

47. Robert Louis Wilken, *The Land Called Holy: Palestine in Christian History and Thought* (New Haven, CT: Yale University Press, 1992) 192ff.; Cameron, "Byzantines and Jews," 253.

48. David M. Olster, *Roman Defeat, Christian Response, and the Literary Construction of the Jew* (Philadelphia: University of Pennsylvania Press, 1994), 206

49. Wilken, *The Land Called Holy*, 219.

50. Rivkah Fishman-Duker, "Anti-Jewish Arguments in the Chronicon Paschale," in *Contra Iudaeos: Ancient and Medieval Polemics Between Christians and Jews*, ed. Ora Limor and Guy G. Stroumsa (Tübingen: J. C. B. Mohr, 1996) 105–118, 116. Moreover, there are chronicles that do not mention Jewish rebellion. The seventh-century *Chronicon Paschale* does not name the Jews as rioters in Antioch or as collaborators with the Persians in the massacre of Christians in Jerusalem in 614. Rivkah Fishman-Duker, "Images of Jews in Byzantine Chronicles: A General Survey," in Bonfil et al., *Jews in Byzantium*, 777–798, 790.

51. Wilken, *The Land Called Holy*, 213.

52. Jean-Baptiste Chabot, ed., *Anonymi auctoris Chronicon ad annum Christi 1234 pertinens I: Praemissum est Chronicon anonymum ad A.D. 819 pertinens; interpretatus est* (Louvain: Imprimerie Orientaliste, L. Durbecq, 1952), 262–263.

53. *The Chronicle of Theophanes: Anni mundi 6095–6305 (A.D. 602–813)*, ed. and trans. Harry Turtledove (Philadelphia: University of Pennsylvania Press, 1982), 476.

54. Limor, "Christian Sacred Space and the Jew," 55–77, 73–74.

55. *Anonymi auctoris Chronicon ad annum Christi*, 262–263. The anonymous Syriac chronicle records the Jewish measures taken against Christians in the time of Caliph Uthman (644–656).

56. This is discussed in Chapter 4. See also Charles Barber, "The Truth in Painting: Iconoclasm and Identity in Early-Medieval Art," *Speculum* 72 (1997):1019–1039, 1026.

57. Fishman-Duker, "Images of Jews in Byzantine Chronicles," 790.

58. Leslie Brubaker, *Inventing Byzantine Iconoclasm* (London: Bristol Classical Press, 2012), 4; Erik Thunø, *Image and Relic: Mediating the Sacred in Early Medieval Rome* (Rome: "L'Erma" di Bretschneider, 2002), 151–152. Note how John of Damascus in his *Contra imaginum* subtly legitimates the veneration of the crucifix because of the Christians' veneration of the cross: "If we bow down before the Cross, no matter what substance it is made from, shall we not bow down before the image of Him who was crucified upon it?" *Contra imaginum calumniatores orationes tres*, vol. 3 of *Die Schriften Des Johannes von Damaskos*, ed. Bonifatius Kotter (Berlin: De Gruyter, 1975), 54, 156; Brubaker and Haldon, *Byzantium*, 45.

59. Thunø, *Image and Relic*, 151.

60. *The Chronicle of Theophanes*, 82.

61. On the wearing of crosses and their uses, see Henry Maguire, "Garments Pleasing to God: The Significance of Domestic Textile Designs in the Early Byzantine Period," *Dumbarton Oak Papers* 44 (1990): 215–224, 218.

62. Boustan, "Immolating Emperors," 209.

63. Averil Cameron, "Disputations, Polemical Literature and the Formation of Opinion in the Early Byzantine Period," in *Dispute Poems and Dialogues in the Ancient and Mediaeval Near East: Forms and Types of Literary Debate in Semitic and Related Literatures*, ed. G. J. Reinink and H. L. J. Vanstiphout (Louvain: Peeters, 1991), 91–108, 106.

64. Ibid.; Averil Cameron, "How to Read Heresiology," in *The Cultural Turn in Late Ancient Studies: Gender, Asceticism, and Historiography*, ed. Dale B. Martin and Patricia Cox Miller (Durham, NC: Duke University Press, 2005), 193–212, 204.

65. Vincent Déroche, "La polémique anti-judaïque au VIe et au VIIe siècle: Un mémento inédit, les *Képhalaia*," *Travaux et Mémoires* 11 (1991): 275–311, 290ff. The *Kephalaiae paporetika* published by Vincent Déroche, a collection of questions for Christians to use in arguments with Jews, does not mention desecration. Other disputation literary works include *The Disputation of Sergius the Stylite Against a Jew*, ed. and trans. A. P. Hayman, CSCO 338–339, Scriptores Syri 152–153 (Louvain: Secrétariat du Corpus Scriptorum Christianorum Orientalum, 1973); the fragments of Stephen of Bostra, *Against the Jews*, in Giovanni Mercati, *Opere minori*, vol. 1, Studi e Testi 76 (Vatican City: Biblioteca apostolica vaticiana, 1937), 202–206. These works do not discuss the Jews' desecration of images. On Stephen of Bostra, see also Alexander Alexakis, "Some Remarks on the Colophon of the Codex *Parisinus Graecus* 115," *Revue d'Histoire des Textes* 2 (1992): 131–143; and Alexander Alexakis, "Stephen of Bostra: Fragmenta Contra Iudaeos (CPG 7790)," *Jahrbuch der Österreichischen Byzantinistik* 43 (1993): 45–60, 51–55. Averil Cameron, "Byzantines and Jews," 262–263, also notes the treatise written by Anastasius of Sinai (see Anna D. Kartsonis, *Anastasis: The Making of an Icon* [Princeton, NJ: Princeton University Press, 1986], 40–63), as well as an extant dialogue on the Trinity between a Jew and a Christian by Jerome of Jerusalem (*Quaestiones ad Antiochum ducem*, ed. Hans Georg Thümmel, *Die Frühgeschichte der ostkirchlichen Bilderlehre: Texte und Untersuchungenzur Zeitvordem Bilderstreit*, Texte und Untersuchungenzur Geschichte der altchristlichen Literatur 139 [Berlin: Akademie-Verlag, 1992], 246–247). On eighth-century works, see John of Damascus, *Contra imaginum*, ed. Kotter, 123–126. *Objections to the Hebrews*, probably composed shortly after the Council of Nicaea in 787, has hardly any discussion on Jews and images. Patrick Andrist, "Les *Objections des Hébreux*: Un document du premier iconoclasme?," *Revue des Études Byzantines* 57 (1999): 99–140.

66. Vincent Déroche, "L'*Apologie contre les juifs* de Léontios de Néapolis," *Travaux et Mémoires* 12 (1994): 45–104.

67. Rina Talgam, "Constructing Identity Through Art: Jewish Art as a Minority Culture in Byzantium," in Bonfil et al., *Jews in Byzantium*, 399–454, 417.

68. Déroche, "L'*Apologie contre les juifs* de Léontios de Néapolis," 77.

69. Ibid., 75; Hoeps, *Aus dem Schatten des goldenen Kalbes*, 21.

70. Déroche, "L'*Apologie contre les juifs* de Léontios de Néapolis," 75.

71. Ibid.

72. Kitzinger, "Cult of Images," 147.

73. The translation is Norman H. Baynes's, in "The Icons Before Iconoclasm," *Harvard Theological Review* 44 (1951): 93–106, 101.

74. Déroche, "L'*Apologie*," 75; and Déroche, "Forms and Functions of Anti-Jewish Polemics," in Bonfil et al., *Jews in Byzantium*, 546.

75. Nor did later anti-Judaic tracts by iconophiles disseminate desecration tales or discuss Jewish desecration.

76. Quoted from Herbert R. Kessler, "Judaism and the Development of Byzantine Art," in Bonfil et al., *Jews in Byzantium*, 490. See Arthur Cushman McGiffert, *Dialogue Between a Christian and a Jew: The Greek Text, Edited with Introduction and Notes, Together with a Discussion of Christian Polemics Against the Jews* (Marburg, 1889), 75ff., incorporating the *Dialogue of Papiscus and Philo.*

77. Cushman McGiffert, *Dialogue Between a Christian and a Jew*, 76.

78. *Objections to the Hebrews*, in Andrist, "Les *Objections des Hébreux*."

79. Corrigan, *Visual Polemics*, 30–31.

80. *Adamnan's De Locis Sanctis*, ed. Denis Meehan, Scriptores Latini Hiberniae 3 (Dublin: Dublin Institute for Advanced Studies, 1958), 112–113.

81. Rodney Aist, "Adomnán, Arculf and the Source Material of *De locis sanctis*," in *Adomnán of Iona: Theologian, Lawmaker, Peacemaker*, ed. Jonathan M. Wooding et al. (Dublin: Four Courts Press, 2010), 162–180.

82. Thomas O'Loughlin, "The Exegetical Purpose of Adomnán's *De Locis Sanctis*," *Cambridge Medieval Celtic Studies* 24 (Winter 1992): 37–53.

83. See Rodney Aist's discussion in "Adomnán, Arculf," 162–180.

84. Rodney Aist, *From Topography to Text: The Image of Jerusalem in the Writings of Eucharius, Abomnán and Bede* (Turnhout: Brepols, 2018), 63–67.

85. *Adamnan's De Locis Sanctis*, 119–120; see also Evelyn Faye Wilson, ed., *The "Stella Maris" of John Garland* (Cambridge, MA: Mediaeval Academy of America, 1946), 115, no. 18, "De Iudeo Rapto a Demonibus."

86. See John of Damascus's classification of six types of images, in *Contra imaginum*, ed. Kotter, 123–126. On the increase of the cult of the Virgin, see Belting, *Likeness and Presence*, 34. At the Council of Ephesus (431), the title of Theotokos ("Mother of God") was officially bestowed upon Mary, and this set in motion her autonomous and general veneration and her position in the Christian liturgical calendar where various festivals were created to mark events in her life. Ora Limor, "Mary and the Jews: Story, Controversy and Testimony," *Historein* 6 (2006): 55–71, 56.

87. Such objects had begun to appear after the death of Emperor Justinian but before the Iconoclastic Controversy. Averil Cameron, "The Language of Images: The Rise of Icons and Christian Representation," in *The Church and the Arts*, Studies in Church History 28, ed. Diane Wood (Oxford: Oxford University Press, 1992), 1–42, 31.

88. Belting, *Likeness and Presence*, 75.

89. David Woods, "Arculf's Luggage: The Sources for Adomnán's *De locis sanctis*," *Ériu* 52 (2002): 25–52, 37–38. Unfortunately this does not help us to locate the actual image.

90. By the time this tale is circulated in medieval England and France, the location of the image is the church of the Blachernai in Constantinople, although no such miraculous image was reported as being seen there (see Chapter 2).

91. See, e.g., John 8:44. John Chrysostom had elaborated the idea that Jews worshipped the devil but that their synagogues were also "the homes of the devil." See "St. John of Damascus: Apologia Against Those Who Decry Holy Images," https://sourcebooks.fordham.edu/basis/johndamascus-images.asp.

92. Jeremy Cohen, *Living Letters of the Law: Ideas of the Jew in Medieval Christianity* (Berkeley: University of California Press, 1999), 85.

93. Spyros N. Troianos, "Christians and Jews in Byzantium," in Bonfil et al., *Jews in Byzantium*, 133–148, 146.

94. Ibid.

95. Vera von Falkenhausen, "In Search of the Jews in Byzantine Literature," in Bonfil et al., *Jews in Byzantium*, 871–892, 888.

96. The original version of the tale has been lost. But it appears among the lists of approved quotations in the second session of the Seventh Ecumenical Council at Nicaea in 787, on September 26, in one of the council's many false citations—the *narratio* of John of Jerusalem (who represented the Eastern patriarchates). Ambrosios Giakalis, *Images of the Divine:*

The Theology of Icons at the Seventh Ecumenical Council, rev. ed. (Leiden: Brill, 2005), 5–6. On this decree, see Alexander A. Vasiliev, "The Iconoclastic Edict of the Caliph Yazid II, A.D. 721," *Dumbarton Oaks Papers* 9/10 (1956): 23–47.

97. Vasiliev, "Iconoclastic Edict," 47.

98. Ibid., 45.

99. Corrigan, *Visual Polemics*, 94.

100. Ibid., 91; Paul Speck, *Ich bin's nicht, Kaiser Konstantin ist es gewesen: Die Legenden vom Einfluß des Teufels, des Juden und des Moslem auf den Ikonoklasmus* (Bonn: R. Habelt, 1990), 55.

101. Vasiliev, "Iconoclastic Edict," 30–31, 34.

102. Limor, "Mary and the Jews," 64. The Talmud tells of Jesus being condemned to be tortured in hell in boiling feces (Babylonian Talmud, Gittin 57a).

103. Bacci, "Devotional Panels as Sites of Intercultural Exchange," in Corry, Faini, and Meneghin, *Domestic Devotions in Early Modern Italy*, 273.

104. Stavroula Constantinou, "Metaphrasis: Mapping Premodern Writing," in Constantinou and Høgel, *Metaphrasis*, 3–60, 6–7.

105. Espí Forcén, "Jews Desecrating a Crucifix."

106. Papaconstantinou "Saints and Saracens," 328ff.

107. Belting, *Likeness and Presence*, 107 and 139; Charles Barber, *Figure and Likeness: On the Limits of Representation in Byzantine Iconoclasm* (Princeton, NJ: Princeton University Press, 2002), 41–42.

108. Marcella Forlin Patrucco, "Il 'miracolo del sangue' nella tarda antichità: Tipologia e valenze politico-teologiche," in *Sangue e antropologia biblica nella Patristica: Atti della settimana, Roma, 23–28 novembre 1981*, ed. Francesco Vattioni (Rome: Pia Unione Preziosissimo Sangue, 1982), 2:693–712, 710–11.

109. Cameron, "Byzantines and Jews," 269.

110. Giakalis, *Images of the Divine*, 39 and 41.

111. Brubaker and Haldon, *Byzantium*, 91.

112. Giakalis, *Images of the Divine*, 18, 48.

113. *PG* 28:797–812. "De Miraculo Beryti Edito."

114. Giakalis, *Images of the Divine*, 47.

115. Michele Bacci, "'Quel bello miracolo onde si fa la festa del santo Salvatore': Studio sulla metamorfosi di una leggenda," in *Santa Croce e Santo Volto: Contributi allo studio dell'origine e della fortuna del culto del Salvatore (secoli IX–XV)*, ed. Gabriella Rossetti (Pisa: GISEM–Edizione ETS, 2002), 1–86; Bacci, "The Berardenga Antependium," 4.

116. *PG* 28:799. English translations adapted, with minor changes, from Bacci.

117. *PG* 28:799; Bacci, "The Berardenga Antependium," 4.

118. *PG* 28:799.

119. See Matt. 27:29; Mark 15:17; John 19:2, 5.

120. *PG* 28:799; Bacci, "The Berardenga Antependium," 5–6.

121. John 19:33–37. In addition, according to the fourth/fifth-century Acts of [Pontius] Pilate, also known as the Gospel of Nicodemus, the Roman centurion was called Longinus. The Greeks connected this name with the Greek word *longsche*, meaning lance, lancer, and commander of a troop of lancers. Montague Rhodes James, trans., *The Apocryphal New Testament: Being the Apocryphal Gospels, Acts, Epistles, and Apocalypses, with Other Narratives and Fragments*, corrected ed. (Oxford: Clarendon Press, 1953), 113, 155. The patristic poet Venantius Fortunatus (ca. 530–609) noted this idea with the words "From the wound opened by a

cruel lance poured forth water and blood, to cleanse us from the stain of our sins." A. S. Walpole, *Early Latin Hymns* (Cambridge: Cambridge University Press, 1922), 174.

122. *PG* 28: 802.

123. The presence of blind Jews who regain their sight in this tale reiterates perhaps what Tertullian, an important thinker of the early Latin Church, calls in his short treatise *On Baptism*, the "happy sacrament of baptism" whereby the water washes away "the faults of former blindness." Barasch, *Blindness*, 55.

124. John 3:1–20; Bacci, "'Quel bello miracolo,'" 17–18, doc. 3.

125. Kitzinger, "Cult of Images," 113. In discussion with Carlos Espí Forcén, he argued that, according to tradition, the image was painted by Nicodemus but it was finished by angels, so this turned it into an *acheiropoieton*.

126. *PG* 28: 802.

127. In the tale the image is described as a full-length image of Christ, so that Jews were imagined attacking the whole body depicted in the painting. Michele Bacci argues that it is only later texts that refer to "Christ of Beirut" interchangeably as an image, a painted board, or a crucifix ("The Berardenga Antependium," 4; "'Quel bello miracolo,'" 43).

128. Limor noted in "Christian Sacred Space," 77, that the Jew "is the one who guards their secret, brings them to light voluntarily or under coercion and confirms their sanctity. . . . The Jew is the constitutor of Christian identity."

129. Ibid., 76; Rom. 11:25–26.

130. Von Falkenhausen, "In Search of the Jews in Byzantine Literature," in Bonfil et al., *Jews in Byzantium*, 878.

131. Cameron, "Byzantines and Jews," 257. On the topic of the forced baptism of Jews, see also L. W. Barnard, "The Jews and the Byzantine Iconoclastic Controversy," *Eastern Churches Review* 5 (1973): 125–135, for various cases of baptism by force carried out against the Jews in the Byzantine Empire, including in 721–722 by Emperor Leo III, and in 873–874 by Emperor Basil I.

132. Evagrius, "Altercatio inter Theophilum Christianum et Simonem Judaem," in *Patrologia cursus completus, series latina*, ed. Jacques Paul Migne (hereafter *PL*), vol. 20 (Paris, 1845), cols. 1165–1180; see also a Byzantine conversion oath/text found in the appendix of *PG* 1:1457–1458; T. C. G. Thornton, "The Crucifixion of Haman and the Scandal of the Cross," *Journal of Theological Studies* 37, no. 2 (1986): 419–426, 426; and David W. Chapman, *Ancient Jewish and Christian Perceptions of Crucifixion* (Tübingen: Baker Academic, 2008), 238–239. 238.

133. Socrates Scholasticus, *Ecclesiastical History* 7.16, trans. A. C. Zenos, in *A Select Library of Nicene and Post-Nicene Fathers of the Christian Church*, 2nd ser., ed. Henry Wace and Philip Schaff, vol. 2, *Socrates, Sozomenus: Church Histories* (Oxford, 1891), 161; and the Latin translation by Cassiodorus-Epiphanius, *Historia ecclesiastica tripartita* 11.13, ed. Walter Jacob and Rudolf Hanslik (Vienna, 1952), 644–645.

134. Brown, "Images as a Substitute for Writing," 19; Déroche, "*L'Apologie contre les juifs*," 112.

135. Cameron, "Byzantines and Jews," 257.

136. Amnon Linder, "The Legal Status of Jews in the Byzantine Empire," in Bonfil et al., *Jews in Byzantium*, 149–217, 216.

137. Robert Bonfil, "Continuity and Discontinuity (641–1204)," in Bonfil et al., *Jews in Byzantium*, 65–100, 96; and Youval Rotman, "Converts in Byzantine Italy," in Bonfil et al., *Jews in Byzantium*, 893–921, 920.

138. Carlos Espí Forcén, *Recrucificando a Cristo: Los judíos de la "Passio Imaginis" en la isla de Mallorca* (Palma de Mallorca: Objeto Perdido, 2009), 47–49.

139. Forlin Patrucco, "Il "miracolo del sangue,"" 697.

140. Giakalis, *Images of the Divine*, 39.

141. Reinhard Hoeps, "Gottes Gegenwart im Bild? Vom Streit zwischen Bild und Sakrament," in Peter Hofmann and Andreas Matena (eds.) *Christusbild: Icon + Ikone; Wege zu Theorie und Theologie des Bildes*, ed. Peter Hofmann and Andreas Matena (Paderborn: Ferdinand Schöningh, 2010), 101–116, 101.

142. *PG* 28: 819 "Sancti Patris Nostri Athanasii," "Denique ampullas praecepit fierivitreas, in quibus portiones misit singulas de sanguine et aqua, quæ de imagine Domini Salvatoris nostril decurrerunt: quasetiam per Asiam, Africam, Europam"; Bacci, ""Quel bello miracolo,"" 55–58, docs. 6, 7, 8, 10.

143. *PG* 28: 819.

144. Maria Vassilaki, "Bleeding Icons," in *Icon and Word: The Power of Images in Byzantium*, ed. Antony Eastmond and Liz James (Aldershot: Ashgate, 2003), 121–129.

145. Bacci, ""Quel bello miracolo,"" 13.

146. Camporesi, *Juice of Life*, 54.

147. The Christian idea of the Jews' demonic sacrilege, based on a supposed fixation on Christian blood, had not as yet developed as it would from the twelfth century. On the Jews association with Christian blood, see Caroline Walker Bynum, *Wonderful Blood: Theology and Practice in Late Medieval Northern Germany and Beyond* (Philadelphia: University of Pennsylvania, 2007), 180–185.

148. Griffith, "Theodore Abū Qurrah's Arabic Tract," 61. Sadly, this Syriac tale has no provenance and one cannot identify the exact period in which its narrative arose.

149. According to the tale, the Jews of Tiberias had deceived a Christian painter into believing that they were genuine worshippers of Christ. They commissioned him to paint an image that would "multiply" Christ's praise among men. The converts in our story had to struggle with and deceive the Jews in order to have access to the image. Could the Jews in fact be Jewish Christians as Simon C. Mimouni suggests in his article "Pour une définition nouvelle du judéo-christianisme ancien," *New Testament Studies* 38, no. 2 (1992): 161–186? According to Rivka Fishman-Duker, this is a typical feature in Byzantine chronicles whereby potential converts are portrayed as saintly even before their conversion ("Images of Jews in Byzantine Chronicles," in Bonfil et al., *Jews in Byzantium*, 793).

150. Bacci, ""Quel bello miracolo,"" 10; Agapius of Manbij, *Kitab al-'unvan: Histoire universelle* 2.2, ed. and trans. Alexandre Vasiliev, *Patrologia Orientalis* 38 (8.3) (Turnhout: Brepols, 1971), 408.

151. The end result was also the foundation of several monasteries in Syria. Agapius, *Kitab al'unvan,* 408 and Bacci "Quel bello miracolo," 10.

152. Joseph A. Munitiz et al., eds., *The Letter of the Three Patriarchs to Emperor Theophilos and Related Texts* (Camberley, Surrey: Porphyrogenitus, 1997), 158–160, xiii.

153. Brubaker and Haldon, *Byzantium*, 6; Brubaker, *Inventing Byzantine Iconoclasm*, 90–93.

154. Brubaker, *Inventing Byzantine Iconoclasm,* 277.

155. Belting, *Likeness and Presence*, 185, 192.

156. Corrigan, *Visual Polemics*, 102.

157. Munitiz et al., *The Letter*; for Constantine the Great, see 18 (5a); Pope Gregory II, 48 (7.14a); a Muslim who had caused a mosaic icon of Christ to continually bleed, 40 (7.7); Persians, 42 (7.8a); and Christian desecrators, 44 (7.9–11).

158. Ibid., 60 (9.d).

159. Elsner, "Iconoclasm as Discourse," 382.

160. Brubaker and Haldon, *Byzantium*, 220.

161. Munitiz et al., *The Letter*, 34 (7.2).

162. Bacci, "'Quel bello miracolo,'" 15–16; Bacci shows how the texts of the icon at Beirut and the icon at Constantinople were often read together in church services, propagating some confusion between the stories (ibid., p. 65, doc. 22).

163. Christopher Walker, "Iconographical Considerations," in Munitiz et al., *The Letter*, lx. On this as well, see George P. Galavaris, "The Mother of God, Stabbed with a Knife," *Dumbarton Oak Papers* 13 (1959): 229–233, 231.

164. Munitiz et al., *The Letter*, 46 (7.13).

165. On the position of Jews between 641 and 1204, see Robert Bonfil, "Continuity and Discontinuity (641–1204)," in Bonfil et al., *Jews in Byzantium*, 65–101.

166. Munitiz et al., *The Letter*, 10–11 (2b).

167. Oded Irshai, "Confronting a Christian Empire: Jewish Life and Culture in the World of Early Byzantium," in Bonfil et al., *Jews in Byzantium*, 17–64, 29.

168. Munitiz et al., *The Letter*, 36–39 (7.4). The story of Lydda is possibly derived from Acts 9:32 where Peter had gone to preach to the people (ibid., 150 [4b]). The same story appears in a shortened form of *The Letter*, the "Letter to Emperor Theophilus on the Holy and Venerated Icons," in the same volume, attributed erroneously to the Syrian priest John Damascene (6.75/6.79).

169. Fishman-Duker points out in "Images of Jews," Bonfil et al., *Jews in Byzantium*, 782–783, that Byzantine chronicles are not fastidious about the terms "Jews" and "Hebrews" and use these terms interchangeably.

170. Munitiz et al., *The Letter*, 36 (7:3).

171. Belting, *Likeness and Presence*, 190.

172. Munitiz et al., *The Letter*, 38–41 (7.6).

173. Ibid., 44 (7.9–10).

174. Helen C. Evans and William D. Wixom, eds., *The Glory of Byzantium: Art and Culture of the Middle Byzantine Era, A.D. 843–1261* (New York: Metropolitan Museum of Art, 1997), 98.

175. The Psalters show other images in which Jewish prophets of the Old Testament are even venerating Christian images. The message of these images was to confirm that the events of Christ's life had been foretold by the prophets. This was not a new phenomenon in the ninth century, as the Rossano and Sinope Gospels had already done this. Corrigan, *Visual Polemics*, 44, 118.

176. Corrigan, *Visual Polemics*, 47, 48.

177. Glenn Peers, *Sacred Shock: Framing Visual Experience in Byzantium* (University Park: Pennsylvania State University Press, 2004), 35–58; Elisabeth Revel-Neher, *The Image of the Jew in Byzantine Art*, trans. David Maizel (Oxford: Pergamon Press, 1992), 32. These insulting and humiliating depictions of Jews are also unusual in Byzantine art, which, as Revel-Neher has shown, until this time depicted Jews with simple undistorted accuracy.

178. Evans and Wixom, *The Glory of Byzantium*, 98.

179. Corrigan, *Visual Polemics*, 48. Note too how Psalm 21 is depicted in both the Khludov and Pantokrator Psalters. Here Jews again attack an image of Christ rather than Christ himself.

180. Ibid., 30.

181. Shelomo Dov Goitein, *Palestinian Jewry in Early Islamic and Crusader Times* [in Hebrew], ed. J. Hacker (Jerusalem: Magnes Press, 1980), 17.

182. Ibid.

183. Bacci, "'Quel bello miracolo,'" 14–15, 24–25, 39. As Bacci points out, from the tenth and eleventh centuries, the sermon of the pseudo-Athanasius read out at Nicaea, which reported the tale of "Christ of Beirut" was included in the homiletic collections, theological and exegetical texts from the tenth century. It was incorporated into lectionaries and passionals of the Benedictine abbeys and canonical colleges of the great cathedrals.

CHAPTER 2

1. An earlier article on this topic is Katherine Aron-Beller, "Fictional Tales and Their Narrative Transformations: Accusations of Image Desecration Against Jews in 12th and 13th Century Europe," *Antisemitism Studies Journal* 1 (Spring 2017): 38–81.

2. Brown, "Images as a Substitute for Writing," 19ff.

3. Brubaker and Haldon, *Byzantium*, 85.

4. Thomas M. Izbiki, *The Eucharist in Medieval Canon Law* (Cambridge: Cambridge University Press, 2015), 21.

5. Barbara Raw, *Anglo-Saxon Crucifixion Iconography and the Art of the Monastic Revival* (Cambridge: Cambridge University Press, 1990), 41.

6. Agobardo, *De picturis et imaginibus* 19, ed. Lievan van Acker, Agobardus *Opera omnia,* (Turnhout: Brepols, 1981), 168; Egon Boshoff, *Erzbischof Agobard von Lyon: Leben und Werk* (Cologne: Böhlau, 1969); and Jean-Claude Schmitt, *The Conversion of Herman the Jew: Autobiography, History, and Fiction in the Twelfth Century*, trans. Alex J. Novikoff (Philadelphia: University of Pennsylvania Press, 2010), 122ff.

7. Alejandro García Avilés, "Imágenes 'vivientes': Idolatría y herejía en las Cantigas de Alfonso X el Sabio," *Goya* 321 (2007): 324–342, 326.

8. Jean-Claude Schmitt, "De Nicée II à Thomas d'Aquin: L'émancipation de l'image religieuse en occident," in *Le corps des images: Essais sur la culture visuelle au Moyen Âge* (Paris: Éditions Gallimard, 2002), 63–127, 80–81.

9. Raw, *Anglo-Saxon Crucifixion*, 41, 62, 65, 162.

10. Merback, *Pilgrimage and Pogrom*, 83.

11. Giles Constable, *Three Studies in Medieval Religious and Social Thought* (Cambridge: Cambridge University Press, 1995), 197.

12. Thomas F. X. Noble, *Images, Iconoclasm, and the Carolingians* (Philadelphia: University of Pennsylvania Press, 2009), 276–277 and 369.

13. Merback, *Pilgrimage and Pogrom*, 8.

14. Mary Clayton, *The Cult of the Virgin Mary in Anglo-Saxon England* (Cambridge: Cambridge University Press, 1990).

15. Ibid, 143–178; Belting, *Likeness and Presence*, 300.

16. Schmitt, "De Nicée II," 63–127; Jean-Claude Schmitt, "La question des images dans les debates entre juifs et chrétiens au xii siècle," in *Spannungen und Widersprüche: Gedenkschrift für František Graus*, ed. Susanna Burghartz et al. (Sigmaringen: Jan Thorbecke, 1992), 245–254.

17. The most comprehensive work on images in both the East and West is Belting, *Likeness and Presence*; and Belting, *The Image and Its Public.*

18. Baert, *A Heritage of Holy Wood*, 121. Note also later in this chapter how Jacobus de Voragine developed the True Cross legend and the role of the Jews.

19. Bynum, *Wonderful Blood*, 8.

20. Conrad Rudolph's translation of the *Apologia* in Conrad Rudolph, *The "Things of Greater Importance": Bernard of Clairvaux's "Apologia" and the Medieval Attitude Toward Art* (Philadelphia: University of Pennsylvania Press, 1990), 281.

21. Thomas Aquinas, *Summa Theologiae*, pt. 3, q. 25, art. 3 (on the image of Christ), art. 4 (on the cross of Christ), art. 5 (on the Mother of God).

22. Ibid.; Felipe Pereda, "Through a Glass Darkly: Paths to Salvation in Spanish Painting at the Outset of the Inquisition," in *Judaism and Christian Art: Aesthetic Anxieties from Catacombs to Colonialism*, ed. Herbert Kessler and David Nirenberg (Philadelphia: University of Pennsylvania Press, 2001), 263–290, 278.

23. Johan Del Plato, "On Jews and the Old Testament Precedent for Sacred Art Production: The Views of Some Twelfth-Century Abbots," *Comitatus: A Journal of Medieval and Renaissance Studies* 18 (1987): 34–44.

24. Schmitt, *The Conversion of Herman the Jew*, 28–29.

25. Anna Sapir Abulafia and G. R. Evans, eds., *The Works of Gilbert Crispin, Abbot of Westminster* (London: Oxford University Press, 1986), 50–53, nos. 153–161.

26. Schmitt, *The Conversion of Herman the Jew*, 123.

27. Heinz Schreckenberg, *Die christlichen Adversus-Judaeos-Texte (11.–13. Jh.): Mit einer Ikonographie des Judenthemas bis zum 4. Laterankonzil*, 3rd ed., rev. (Frankfurt am Main: Lang, 1997), 93.

28. Rupert of Deutz, *Anulus sive dialogus inter Christianum et Judaeum*, ed. Rhabanus Haacke, in Maria Lodovica Arduini, *Ruperto di Deutz e la controversia tra Cristiani ed Ebrei nel secolo XII: Con testo critico dell'"Anulus seu dialogus inter Christianum et Iudaeum," a cura di Rhabanus Haacke* (Rome: Istituto Storico Italiano per il Medio Evo, 1979), fasc.119-121.

29. Ibid.

30. Anna Sapir Abulafia, "The Ideology of Reform and Changing Ideas Concerning Jews in the Works of Rupert of Deutz and Hermannus Quondam Iudeus," *Jewish History* 7, no. 1 (Spring 1993): 43–63, 53.

31. Schmitt, *The Conversion of Herman the Jew*, 132–133.

32. Ibid., 134.

33. Gilbert Dahan, *The Christian Polemic Against the Jews in the Middle Ages*, trans. Jody Gladding (Notre Dame, IN: University of Notre Dame Press, 1998), 59.

34. Ibid., 60.

35. *Guillelmi Duranti Rationale divinorum officiorum*, Corpus Christianorum Series Latina, Continuatio Mediaevalis, ed. Anselme Davril and T. M. Thibodeau (Turnhout: Brepols, 1995–2000), book 1 (3:1). See the new English translation by Timothy M. Thibodeau, based on this text, *The Rationale divinorum officiorum of William Durand of Mende: A New Translation of the Prologue and Book One* (New York: Columbia University Press, 2007), 32–33.

36. *Rationale divinorum officiorum of William Durand*, trans. Thibodeau, 67.

37. Simonsohn, *The Apostolic See and the Jews*, 7:185–186; and vol. 1, doc. 6.

38. Ibid., 7:186.

39. Julie L. Mell, *The Myth of the Medieval Jewish Moneylender* (New York: Palgrave Macmillan, 2017).

40. See the first three chapters of Joseph Shatzmiller, *Cultural Exchange: Jews, Christians, and Art in the Medieval Marketplace* (Princeton, NJ: Princeton University Press, 2013); see also my review of this work in *Jewish History* 28, no. 2 (2014): 221–223.

41. Shatzmiller, *Cultural Exchange*, 42–43.

42. Ibid., 34.

43. Joe Hillaby, "The London Jewry: William I to John," *Transactions of the Jewish Historical Society of England* 33 (1992–1994): 1–44, 9.

44. Arnold of Bonneval, *Sancti Bernardi abbatis Clarae-Vallensis vita et res gestae, Liber secundus,* in *PL* 185:267–302, 269: "Quibus erogatis, donaria regum in ornamentis ecclesiae ab ipsis evulsit altaribus. Et cum calices frangere, et crucifixos aureos membratim dividere ipsi profani Christiani vel timerent, vel erubescerent; Judaeos aiunt esse quaesitos, qui sacra vasa et imagines Deo dicatas audacter comminuerent."

45. Michael Frassetto, "Heretics and Jews in the Early Eleventh Century: The Writings of Rodulfus Glaber and Ademar of Chabannes," in *Christian Attitudes Toward the Jews in the Middle Ages: A Casebook*, ed. Michael Frassetto (London: Taylor and Francis, 2007), 43–60, 51.

46. Adémar de Chabannes, *Chronique*, ed. Jules Chavanon (Paris: A. Picard, 1897), 52, 175.

47. *The Letters of Peter the Venerable*, ed. Giles Constable (Cambridge, MA: Harvard University Press, 1967), vol. 1, 327–330, 328.

48. Ibid., 329.

49. H. François Delaborde, ed., *Oeuvres de Rigord et de Guillaume le Breton*, vol. 1 (Paris: Librairie Renouard, 1882), 25–27.

50. William Chester Jordan, *The French Monarchy and the Jews: From Philip Augustus to the Last Capetians* (Philadelphia: University of Pennsylvania Press, 1989), 30.

51. Ephraim Urbach, *Ba'alei Ha-Tosafot* (Jerusalem: Mosad Bialik, 1955), 108.

52. Rigord, *Vie de Philippe-Auguste*, in *Collection des memoires relatifs à l'histoire de France*, ed. François Guizot, vol. 11 (Paris: Brière, 1825), 9–179, 22.

53. Ibid., 24–25.

54. Resolutions prohibiting this practice were passed by church councils in Paris (about 1200), Worcester (constitution of Bishop William Bley, 1229), Gnesen (1285), Tarragona (1329), Lavaur (1368), and Basel (1434). Shatzmiller, *Cultural Exchange*, 33.

55. Solomon Grayzel, "Jews and the Ecumenical Councils," *Jewish Quarterly Review* 57 (1967): 287–311.

56. Solomon Grayzel, *The Church and the Jews in the XIIIth Century: A Study of Their Relations During the Years 1198–1254, Based on the Papal Letters and the Conciliar Decrees of the Period* (Philadelphia: Dropsie College for Hebrew and Cognate Learning, 1933), vol. 1, 321 (doc. 23).

57. Simonsohn, *Apostolic See*, 1:82–83, Innocent III, January 16, 1205 (doc. 147).

58. Grayzel, *The Church and the Jews*, vol. 2, 62–64, Alexander IV, August 23, 1258 (doc. 6).

59. These personal miracle stories have been meticulously studied in Rachel Koopmans, *Wonderful to Relate: Miracle Stories and Miracle Collecting in High Medieval England* (Philadelphia: University of Pennsylvania Press, 2010).

60. Ibid., 204.

61. Kati Ihnat, *Mother of Mercy, Bane of the Jews: Devotion to the Virgin Mary in Anglo-Norman England* (Princeton, NJ: Princeton University Press, 2016), 102.

62. Benedicta Ward, *Miracles and the Medieval Mind* (Philadelphia: University of Pennsylvania Press, 1982), 142–155.

63. Richard Southern, "The English Origins of the 'Miracles of the Virgin,'" *Medieval and Renaissance Studies* 4 (1958): 176–216, 182.

64. Peter Carter, "The Historical Content of William of Malmesbury's Miracles of the Virgin Mary," in *Writing the History of the Middle Ages: Essays Presented to Richard William Southern*, ed. R. H. C. Davis and J. M. Wallace-Hadrill (Oxford: Clarendon Press, 1981), 127–165.

65. Ihnat, *Mother of Mercy*, 103.

66. William of Malmesbury, *The Miracles of the Blessed Virgin Mary*, ed. and trans. R. M. Thomson and M. Winterbottom (Woodbridge: Boydell Press, 2015), xx.

67. Jennifer Shea, "Adgar's *Gracial* and Christian Images of Jews in Twelfth-Century Vernacular Literature," *Journal of Medieval History* 33, no. 2 (2007): 181–196.

68. Alfonso X El Sabio, *Las Cantigas de Santa María: Códice Rico, Ms. T-I-1 Real Biblioteca del Monasterio de San Lorenzo de El Escorial*, 2 vols., facsimile ed. (Madrid: Patrimonio Nacional; Testimonio, 2011).

69. The manuscript was written in Galician-Portuguese—the language considered most suitable for the composition of lyric poetry—and was modeled on the Marian tales of the French abbot Gautier de Coincy (1177–1236) and the prolific Dominican friar Vincent of Beauvais (1190–ca. 1264). On the individual tales, see John Esten Keller, "Daily Living as Presented in the *Canticles* of Alfonso the Learned," *Speculum* 33, no. 4 (1958): 484–489; and John Esten Keller and Annette Grant Cash, *Daily Life Depicted in the "Cantigas de Santa Maria"* (Lexington: University of Kentucky Press, 1998).

70. Maria Dolores Bollo-Panadero "Heretics and Infidels: The *Cantigas de Santa María* as Ideological Instrument of Cultural Codification," *Romance Quarterly* 55, no. 3 (2008): 163–173; and Pamela A. Patton, *Art of Estrangement: Redefining Jews in Reconquest Spain* (University Park: Pennsylvania State University Press, 2012), 87ff., 170.

71. Such Marian tales include "Gethsemane," "Saturday," "The Bleeding Christ-Child," "Mary-Image at Cologne Robbed of Its Golden Crown." William of Malmesbury includes six tales about images of the Virgin; see William of Malmesbury, *Miracles*, 99 (bk. 2, no. 34), "Bread Offered to the Christ-Child"; 108 (bk. 2, no. 40), "St. Mary of Egypt"; 125 (bk. 2, no. 49), "Fire at Mont St. Michel"; 126 (bk. 2, no. 50), "Saracens Cannot Deface Mary-Image"; 129 (bk. 2, no. 52), "Constantinople"; and 130 (bk. 2, no. 53), "Purification."

72. Belting, *Likeness and Presence*, 192.

73. William of Malmesbury, *Miracles*, 125 (bk. 2, no. 49), "Fire at Mont St. Michel." Here it is Mary who prevents her images in the church from being burned in a fire.

74. For tales in which deviant Christians and heretics violated images, see the catalog of Marian tales in H. L. D. Ward, *Catalogue of Romances in the Department of Manuscripts in the British Museum*, vol. 2 (1893; reprint, London: British Museum, 1962). The tales recorded here are in Additional 18, "The Bleeding Christ Child" and "Mary-Image at Cologne Robbed of Its Golden Crown."

75. For tales in which Saracens attack images, see ibid., Additional 19, Egerton 612, Harley 4401, and Royal 20B, "Saracens Cannot Deface Mary-Image"; and William of Malmesbury, *Miracles*, 126 (bk. 2, no. 50), "Saracens Cannot Deface Mary-Image."

76. Ihnat, *Mother of Mercy*, 139 n. 4, 239.

77. Themes of the Jews' abuse of sacred items and their eventual conversion appear in other tales. One such is that of Mary's Dormition (*dormitio*) which was probably of Syro-Palestinian or Egyptian origin dating from the fifth or sixth century. Limor, "Mary and the Jews," 59.

78. "Abraham and Theodore" is based on a seventh-century Byzantine tale. For the Greek and Latin history of the story, see Benjamin Nelson and Joshua Starr, "The Divine Surety and the Jewish Moneylender," *Annuaire de l'Institut de Philologie et d'Histoire Orientales et Slaves* 7 (1939–1944): 289–338. The tale appears in William of Malmesbury, *Miracles*, 92ff. (bk. 2, no. 32); here the story is also called "Jew Lends to a Christian." For other versions, see Ward, *Catalogue of Romances*, where it appears in Royal 6 B, Arundel 407, Additional 17,

Additional 33, Royal 8 C, Egerton 612, and Royal 20. See also Wilson, *The "Stella Maris" of John of Garland*, 115, no. 19.

79. Shea, "Adgar's *Gracial*," 192–193 (Shea's translation).

80. William of Malmesbury, *Miracles*, 95.

81. Ibid., 96.

82. "Lydda" is derived from a ninth-century Byzantine tale; see Chapter 1. The "Lydda" tale also appears in a number of Marian miracle collections from the twelfth century; see Ward, *Catalogue of Romances*, Cotton, Cleopatra C X, here called *Libia* (a mistake for Lydda); Wilson, *The "Stella Maris" of John of Garland*, p. 114, no. 17, and p. 172.

83. Note that the rabbis in the Babylonian Talmud, Megillah 3:2, forbid the selling of synagogues for improper uses.

84. See Chapter 1.

85. On the church in Lydda, see Denys Pringle, *The Churches of the Crusader Kingdom of Jerusalem: A Corpus* (Cambridge: Cambridge University Press, 2009), 2:25–27.

86. Ora Limor, "'Holy Journey': Pilgrimage and Christian Sacred Landscape," in *Christians and Christianity in the Holy Land: From the Origins to the Latin Kingdoms*, ed. Ora Limor and Guy G. Stroumsa (Turnhout: Brepols, 2006), 321–355.

87. Jacob Lackner, "Violent Men and Malleable Women: Gender and Jewish Conversion to Christianity in Medieval Sermon Exempla," *Nashim: A Journal of Jewish Women's Studies & Gender Issues* 30 (2016): 24–47, 25.

88. Ibid., 40.

89. Wilson, *The "Stella Maris" of John of Garland*, 106, no. 7; Patton, *Art of Estrangement*, 124. On the more favorable treatment of Saracens by Christians, see Irven M. Resnick, *Marks of Distinction: Christian Perceptions of Jews in the High Middle Ages* (Washington, DC: Catholic University of America Press, 2012).

90. See Chapter 1.

91. On Blachernai, see Norman Baynes, "The Finding of the Virgin's Robe," *Annuaire de l'institut de philologie et d'histoire orientales et slaves* 9 (1949): 87–95; and Averil Cameron, "The Virgin's Robe: An Episode in the History of Early Seventh-Century Constantinople," *Byzantion* 49 (1979): 42–56. In different versions of "The Virgin's Image Insulted," sometimes the image is described as being just of Mary and sometimes she is with the Christ child. William of Malmesbury, *Miracles*, 127 n. 1.

92. It seems that a cult of the desecrated image existed in Beirut at this time too. Espí Forcén, "Jews Desecrating a Crucifix," 89.

93. William of Malmesbury, *Miracles*, 127 (bk. 2, no. 51).

94. See Chapter 1, note 102. The original association in Jewish texts of Jesus and latrines is found in the Babylonian Talmud, Gittin 57a, where Jesus is described as being punished with having to crawl through boiling hot excrement.

95. Shea, "Adgar's *Gracial*," 194. In his version, Adgar associated his Jewish desecrator more directly with the devil. For other versions of "The Virgin's Image Insulted," see Ward, *Catalogue of Romances*, where the tale appears in Egerton 612, fols. 1–75. On the *Cantigas* version, see Vikki Hatton and Angus MacKay, "Anti-Semitism in the *Cantigas de Santa Maria*," *Bulletin of Hispanic Studies* 60 (1983): 189–199, which develops the idea of the Jew being the "devil's disciple." See also Albert I. Bagby Jr., "The Jew in the *Cántigas* of Alfonso X, El Sabio," *Speculum* 46, no. 4 (1971): 670–688, 674; and Patton, *Art of Estrangement*, 160.

96. Martha Bayless, *Sin and Filth in Medieval Culture: The Devil in the Latrine* (London: Routledge, 2011), 2.

97. Resnick, *Marks of Distinction*, 2ff.

98. William of Malmesbury, *Miracles*, 127.

99. Alexandra Cuffel, *Gendering Disgust in Medieval Religious Polemic* (Notre Dame, IN: University of Notre Dame Press, 2007), 5–6.

100. William of Malmesbury, *Miracles*, 125.

101. Judas Iscariot's death is recorded in the New Testament: see Matt. 27:3–10, in which he commits suicide out of remorse; Acts 1:18–19.

102. On this topic, see, for example, Hatton and MacKay, "Anti-Semitism in the *Cantigas de Santa Maria*," 192, where they mention the idea of the Jew being the "devil's disciple."

103. Patton, *Art of Estrangement*, 80; Keller and Cash, *Daily Life Depicted*, 49.

104. For a list of the works of these authors, see Ward, *Catalogue of Romances.*

105. *Matthew Paris's English History: From the Year 1235 to 1273*, trans. J. A. Giles (London: Henry G. Bohn, 1852–1854), 2:340.

106. Ibid.

107. Ibid., 340–341.

108. Sophia Menache, "Matthew Paris's Attitudes Toward Anglo-Jewry," *Journal of Medieval History* 23 (1997): 139–162, 146 for another defecation story of the Jew of Tewkesbury.

109. Gavin I. Langmuir, *Toward a Definition of Antisemitism* (Berkeley: University of California Press, 1990), 242.

110. Gilbert Dahan, "Les Juifs dans les Miracles de Gautier de Coincy," *Archives Juives* 16 (1980): 41–49, 59–68, at 47: "Malicïeus estoit et cointes, / Crestienté mout despisoit / Et mout volentiers mesdisoit. / De la puissante dame celestre" (lines 12–15).

111. Ibid.; Gautier de Coinci, *Les Miracles de Nostre Dame*, ed. V. Frédéric Koenig, vol. 2 (Geneva: Droz, 1961), 101–104, lines 17–25; Ward, *Catalogue of Romances*, Gautier de Coincy, tale 4, and Royal 20 B.xiv, fols. 102b–170, 73, tale 54 (bk. 3, miracle 23), "Insulted Mary-Image"; Wilson, *The "Stella Maris" of John of Garland*, 115, no. 18, "De Iudeo rapto a demonibus."

112. Richard Landes, "The Terrible Hopes of the Millennial Generation and the Weeping Crucifix," in *Relics, Apocalypse, and the Deceits of History: Ademar of Chabannes, 989–1034* (Cambridge, MA: Harvard University Press, 1995), 285–308, 301.

113. Ward, *Catalogue of Romances*, Cotton, Cleopatra C X; Additional 33; Additional 17; Royal 8 C; Egerton 612; Royal 20 B; Harley 2277; Cotton, Cleopatra D and Additional 10; Wilson, *The "Stella Maris" of John of Garland*, 107, no. 9, "De querela beate virginis de Iudeis." Other versions appear in Gonzalo de Berceo, *Miracles of Our Lady*, ed. and trans. Richard Mount and Annette Grant Cash (Lexington: University Press of Kentucky, 1998), 137; Vincent of Beauvais's *Speculum historiale* (1266–1283), ed. Michel Tarayre, *La vierge et le miracle: Le "Speculum historiale" de Vincent de Beauvais* (Paris: Honoré Champion, 1999), 38–39; and the *Cantigas of Santa Maria*, no. 34, in *Songs of Holy Mary of Alfonso X, the Wise: A Translation of the "Cantigas de Santa Maria,"* trans. Kathleen Kulp-Hill (Tempe: Arizona Center for Medieval and Renaissance Studies, 2000), 45; and Joseph F. O'Callaghan, *Alfonso X and the "Cantigas de Santa Maria": A Poetic Biography* (Leiden: Brill, 1998), 31.

114. Norman Roth, "New Light on the Jews of Mozarabic Toledo,"*Association of Jewish Studies Review* 11, no. 2 (1986): 189–220, 198.

115. Fritz Baer, *Die Juden im christlichen Spanien* (Berlin: Academie Verlag, 1929), 18. What is missing from the records of this event either during Reccared's reign or in 1109 is

any suggestion that these Jews were killed for desecration or the reenactment of the Passion.

116. William of Malmesbury, *Miracles*, 27.

117. Perhaps the usage here of the "Holy of Holies" reflected Jesus's explicit prophecy of the destruction of the Temple, which had been transmitted in the Synoptic Gospels; see Mark 13:1–3.

118. William of Malmesbury, *Miracles*, 27.

119. Ibid.

120. Shea, "Adgar's *Gracial*," 187 (Shea's translation).

121. Jonathan Riley-Smith, *The First Crusade and the Idea of Crusading* (Philadelphia: University of Pennsylvania Press, 2009), 135–141.

122. Ibid., 139; Susanna A. Throop, *Crusading as an Act of Vengeance, 1095–1216* (Burlington, VT: Ashgate, 2011) 71.

123. William of Malmesbury, *Miracles*, 27.

124. Churches were using more and more candles at this time, and the wax could be collected after candles burned down and turned the wax into figurines. Pierre-André Sigal, "L'ex-voto au moyen âge dans les régions du nord-ouest de la Méditerranée (XIIe–XVe siècles)," *Provence historique* 33 (1983): 13–31, 19.

125. For another tale associated with Jews and waxen images according to Christian sources, see Sarah Zartman, "The Jewish Tale in the Middle Ages: Between Ashkenaz and Sepharad" (PhD diss., Hebrew University, Jerusalem, 1993), 78.

126. Monumenta Germaniae Historica, Scriptores rerum Merovingicarum (Deutsches Institut für Erforschung des Mittelalters) vol. 21,190–191. He suggests that this ritual was carried out in Cologne during the archiepiscopate of Philipp von Heinsberg (1167–1191). Ihnat, *Mother of Mercy*, 162–167, also mentions another case of 1123, where, according to the *Chronicle of Maillezais*, written in the 1140s, the Jews of Rouen are described as doing "something detestable to a waxen image," although it was not certain that it was an effigy of Christ.

127. Patton, *Art of Estrangement*, 151.

128. Paulino Rodríguez Barral, "La dialéctica texto-imagen: A propósito de la representación del judío en las *Cantigas de Santa María* de Alfonso X," *Anuario de Estudios Medievales* 37, no. 1 (2007): 213–244, 223.

129. Dwayne E. Carpenter, *Alfonso X and the Jews: An Edition of and Commentary on "Siete Partides" 7.24 "De los judíos"* (Berkeley: University of California Press, 1986), 63–66.

130. Ibid., 65.

131. Rodríguez Barral, "La dialéctica texto-imagen," 222–223. Note, too, that according to Thomas of Monmouth, *The Life and Passion of William of Norwich*, ed. and trans. Miri Rubin (London: Penguin, 2014), 61, it was "the leaders and rabbis of the Jews who dwell in Spain, at Narbonne," who annually decided where ritual murder should be committed.

132. See *Songs of Holy Mary of Alfonso X, The Wise*, 6, 45. For example in, Cantiga 4 ("The Murdered Jewish Boy"), the story of "how Holy Mary saved from burning the son of the Jew [who] had thrown him into the furnace" the father is then thrown into the fiery furnace and in Cantiga 6, "The Story of the Boy Who Sang 'Gaude Virgo Maria,'" the Jewish murderer is also burned, in the same square where the murdered choirboy had sung. In Cantiga 34 the Jew was killed by the devil. I have not found reference in literary works of Spain, contemporaneous with the *Cantigas*, of this type of killing. For a view of other versions of the "Toledo" tale, see "The Oxford University *Cantigas de Santa Maria*

Database," accessed July 14, 2022, http://csm.mml.ox.ac.uk/index.php?p=poemdata_view&rec=12.

133. Sara Lipton, "Where Are the Gothic Jewish Women? On the Non-Iconography of the Jewess in the *Cantigas de Santa Maria*," *Jewish History* 22 (2008): 139–177, 155. See also her more recent book *Dark Mirror*, 5ff. Jewish blindness in Christian art was often depicted by a blindfolded *synagoga*. See the most recent work on *synagoga* by Nina Rowe, *The Jew, the Cathedral, and the Medieval City: Synagoga and Ecclesia in the Thirteenth Century* (Cambridge: Cambridge University Press, 2015).

134. It is perhaps intriguing why these collections would include a tale that did not mention the Virgin at all, but it is not surprising. Marian miracle collections did sometimes feature miracles that were not, strictly speaking, Marian in content.

135. Bacci, "'Quel bello miracolo,'" 20ff..

136. See Chapter 1; Bacci, "'Quel bello miracolo,'" 13.

137. See Bacci, "'Quel bello miracolo,'" 40, where Bacci cites the Russian pilgrim Daniel Igumeno who saw the image when he was in the Lebanese city in 1106.

138. Ibid., 27.

139. Ibid., 17ff.

140. Belting, *Likeness and Presence*, 356.

141. The tale had first been recorded in the West by Sigebert of Gembloux in his *Chronicon* of 1112, Monumenta Germaniae Historica, Scriptores rerum Merovingicarum (Deutsches Institut für Erforschung des Mittelalters) vol. 6, 333. The Chronicle of Helinand of Froidmont (ca. 1160–ca. 1237), written at the beginning of the thirteenth century, was almost identical in its narration of the tale as was that of the Dominican Vincent of Beauvais (ca. 1190–ca. 1264) in his *Speculum historiale* (Douai, 1624), 955 (bk. 23, chap. 160). See Jacobus de Voragine, *The Golden Legend: Readings on the Saints*, trans. William Granger Ryan (Princeton, NJ: Princeton University Press, 1995), 1:xiii. In fact, there are three desecration tales here as well as the *inventio crucis* legend which he expanded and readapted to show greater hostility toward Jews. Writing at a time when rigorous anti-Judaic legislation was being launched in Europe, Jacobus recorded three tales of Jewish image desecration. The first was Adomnán's tale of the Jews' desecration of a miraculous image of Christ located now in Santa Sophia (the largest Christian church in the Byzantine Empire, which became temporarily the city's Latin Catholic cathedral from 1204 until 1261). This tale had been continually narrated in codices from the eleventh to the thirteenth centuries (Jacobus de Voragine, *The Golden Legend*, 2:170–171). The second was "Christ of Beirut" (*The Golden Legend*, 1:25–27). It is the third tale that was actually created by Jacobus himself and related to an image of a saint, Saint Nicholas, which, like that of "Christ of Beirut" was located in the home of the Jew. Here the Jew, capable of seeing the image, defaces it in frustration that the image had not protected him from a recent burglary. The slight deviation from the traditional narrative here allows the Jew to become an offender who chooses to desecrate because the image fails to protect his home. The Jew's thinking has been influenced by pseudo-Christian tendencies, whereby he is seen as acknowledging the protective powers of a Christian image—perhaps because, by the thirteenth century, images of saints had now entered some domestic spaces. The story backfired for the Jew, because only at the moment of desecration did the image's powers begin to work: Saint Nicholas appeared before the robbers in a vision, calling himself the servant of Jesus, and informing them that he was being beaten by the Jew. There is a "happy ending" as the robbers returned the stolen goods to the Jew, chastised themselves, and the Jew, amazed by the powers of Saint Nicholas, embraced Christianity. Eric Zafran

("Iconography of Antisemitism," 207ff.) notes that this tale was often represented in stained glass: at the Münster of Freiburg im Breisgau; a French one, previously at Auxerre Cathedral; and an English one at Hillesden. In a Flemish book of hours of circa 1500, now at the Bodleian Library (Oxford, Douce MS 112, fol. 160), the story forms the decoration of one page. In Italy, there is a fresco cycle by a follower of Giotto in the lower church of S. Francesco, Assisi.

142. Heinz Schreckenberg, *The Jews in Christian Art: An Illustrated History* (New York: Continuum, 1996), 259.

143. Franz Delitzsch-Vorlesungen and Bernhard Blumenkranz, *Juden und Judenturm in der mittelalterlichen Kunst* (Stuttgart: W. Kohlhammer Verlag, 1965), 54–55.

144. Alexander Alexakis, *Codex Parisinus Graecus 1115 and Its Archetype* (Washington, DC: Dumbarton Oaks Research Library and Collection, 1996), 170–172. Between the tenth and thirteenth centuries, the text circulated throughout Europe. There are three fundamental texts recorded by the Bollandist Fathers. As an example, see Albertus Poncelet, "Catalogus codicum hagiographicorum latinorum: Bibliothecae nationalis Taurinensis," *Analecta Bollandiana* 28 (1909): 417–478, 418 (no. 7).

145. David Nirenberg, "The Historical Body of Christ," in James Clifton, *The Body of Christ in the Art of Europe and New Spain, 1150–1800* (Munich: Prestel, 1997), 17–26, 17.

146. Espí Forcén, *Recrucificando a Cristo*, 55–77, 60–61.

147. For John of Garland's version, see Wilson, *The "Stella Maris" of John of Garland*, 117 no. 21, "De Ymagine que sanguine fudit," which begins "Formam fecit salvatoris." See Ward, *Catalogue of Romances*, for its appearance in Royal 8 C.

148. *Rationale divinorum officiorum of William Durand*, trans. Thibodeau, 61.

149. Bacci, "'Quel bello miracolo,'" 63, doc. 18.

150. Nicholas Vincent, *Holy Blood: King Henry III and the Westminster Blood Relic* (Cambridge: Cambridge University Press, 2001), 13.

151. Ibid.

152. Ibid., 65–67.

153. Bacci, "'Quel bello miracolo,'" p. 51, doc. 3, and p. 54, doc. 4; *PG* 28:811–820, "Relatio miraculorum Domini nostri Jesu Christi quae per imaginem ipsius facta sunt in Beryto, Syriæ civitate, quinto Idus Novembris."

154. I have used Bacci's translation here. Bacci, "The Berardenga Antependium," 8.

155. Guibert of Nogent, *De sanctis et eorum pigneribus*, in *Guitbertus abbas Sanctae Mariae Novigenti: Quo ordine sermo fieri debeat; De bucella iudae data et de veritate dominici corporis; De sanctis et eorum pigneribus*, ed. R. B. C. Huygens, Corpus Christianorum, Continuatio Mediaevalis 127 (Turnhout: Brepols, 1993), 79–175. The question remained a challenge to theological orthodoxy due to its denials by the Cathars and the thesis of Berenger of Tours, as well as developing church doctrine on the incarnation and resurrection of Christ. Even Pope Innocent III (r. 1198–1216) in his important manual on Eucharistic practice, questioned from a theological point of view whether Christ after being resurrected had removed his blood that had "poured out on the cross." Innocent III, *De sacro altaris mysterio* 4.30, in *PL* 217:876d–877b, "Utrum Christus resurgens sanguinem resumpsit quem effudit in cruce."

156. Thomas Aquinas, *Summa Theologiae*, pt. 3, q. 54, art. 3; Bynum, *Wonderful Blood*, 96–111; Caroline Walker Bynum, *Christian Materiality: An Essay on Religion in Late Medival Europe* (New York: Zone Books, 2011), 155.

157. Miri Rubin, "Imagining the Jew: The Late Medieval Eucharistic Discourse," in *In and Out of the Ghetto: Jewish-Gentile Relations in Late Medieval and Early Modern Germany*,

ed. R. Po-chia Hsia and Hartmut Lehmann (Cambridge: Cambridge University Press, 1995), 177–208, 178.

158. Henry Joseph Schroeder, *Disciplinary Decrees of the General Councils: Text, Translation and Commentary* (St. Louis: B. Herder, 1937), 236–296, canon 1.

159. Miri Rubin, *Corpus Christi: The Eucharist in Late Medieval Culture* (Cambridge: Cambridge University Press, 1992), 70.

160. García Avilés, "Imagenes 'vivientes,'" 331; Sylvie Barnay, *El cielo en la tierra: Las apariciones de la Virgen en la Edad Media* (Madrid: Encuentro, 1999).

161. Robert Stacey, "From Ritual Crucifixion to Host Desecration: Jews and the Body of Christ," *Jewish History* 12, no. 1 (1998): 11–28, 12.

162. Rubin, *Gentile Tales*, 8ff.

163. Rubin, "Imagining the Jew," 179.

164. Rubin, *Corpus Christi*, 116–124.

165. Miri Rubin, "Desecration of the Host: The Birth of an Accusation," in *Christianity and Judaism*, ed. Diana Wood (Oxford: Blackwell, 1992), 169–185.

166. This is according to the anonymous *De miraculo hostiae* (On the miracle of the host, ca. 1299), which notes that when the Jewish desecrator threw the host into a cauldron of boiling water, the water became bloody and the host was transformed into a crucifix that poised itself over the cauldron.

167. Rubin, *Gentile Tales*, 84, 85, 87; one even sees the Jews being accused of placing consecrated hosts in latrines (ibid., 91).

168. Merback, *Pilgrimage and Pogrom*, 23, 29.

169. Alan Dundes, "The Ritual Murder or Blood Libel Legend: A Study of Anti-Semitic Victimization Through Projective Inversion," in *The Blood Libel Legend: A Casebook in Anti-Semitic Folklore*, ed. Alan Dundes (Madison: University of Wisconsin Press, 1991), 336–378, 356.

170. Teter, *Blood Libel*, 5, 32

171. Ibid., 33.

172. Rubin, *Gentile Tales*, 35.

173. Guiseppe Divina, *Storia del beato Simone de Trento*, 2 vols. (Trento: Artigianelli, 1902), 302.

174. Mitchell B. Merback, "Fount of Mercy, City of Blood: Cultic Anti-Judaism and the Pulkau Passion Alterpiece," *Art Bulletin* 87, no. 4 (2005): 589–642, 603.

175. Ibid., 631; Merback, *Pilgrimage and Pogrom*, 50, 61.

176. "Richeri Gesta Senoniensis Ecclesiae," in Monumenta Germaniae Historica, Scriptores rerum Merovingicarum (Deutsches Institut für Erforschung des Mittelalters) vol. 25, 322–323.

177. In John Mirk's *Festial*, an early fifteenth-century collection of exempla, a Jew sneaks into a church, stabs a crucifix, and converts after he sees it bleed. John Mirk, *Mirk's Festial: A Collection of Homilies*, ed. Theodor Erbe (London: Kegan Paul, Trench, Trübner, 1905), no. 58, p. 252.

178. There is a suggestion of an incident in eleventh-century Sens, a town on the southwestern border of Champagne, where the Jewish community was reportedly ruined by fines imposed for their supposed destruction of a cross or a church (the Hebrew text just calls the cross a *to'evah*, an "abomination") in the locality. See Chapter 4 for a discussion of *to'evah* and other invectives. There are no legal documents to confirm this, and the only contemporary source is the rabbinical responsum of Rabbi Joseph Tov-Elem (Bonfils) recorded to approve

the Sens Jews' exemption from paying dues to the Jews of Troyes. Avraham Grossman, *The Early Sages of Ashkenaz: Their Lives, Leadership, and Works* [in Hebrew] (Jerusalem: Magnes Press, 1981), 6–8. It is possible that the destruction in Sens was caused not by the Jews but by King Henry I who, following a seven-day siege, pillaged and burned parts of the town and its environs, in particular the Jewish quarter. A fine was levied on the Jews by the local count, Eudes II, to pay for the restoration of the town. The very limited sources available suggest that the Jews did not face any further retaliation or violence as a result of this "desecration."

179. Emily Taitz, *The Jews of Medieval France: The Community of Champagne* (Westport, CT: Greenwood Press, 1994), 73.

180. Henry Anstey, ed., *Munimenta Academica, or Documents Illustrative of Academical Life and Studies at Oxford*, Roll Series 50, 2 vols. (London: Longmans, Green, Reader, and Dyer, 1868), 1:36–37; and Cluse, "Stories of Breaking and Taking the Cross."

181. Cluse, "Stories of Breaking and Taking," 397.

182. Ibid., 429–430.

183. Ibid., 398.

184. There is a suggestion of one Jewish name, Jacob, son of Master Mosey, but the king orders that neither he nor his sons be molested. Ibid., 400.

185. Ibid., 400–402. There is some confusion as to where the marble cross was actually erected. Pressure was placed upon the Jews to ensure that the two crosses would be completed by the feast day of Saint Edward in January 1269. But on February 11, 1269, the king issued new instructions to his sheriff, Thomas de Sancto Vigore, changing the place where the permanent cross was to be erected, since the churchyard was inconvenient for some of the townspeople. It was decided to erect the cross near the church of St. John the Baptist and give the portable cross to the masters of Merton College. The order was changed again in April when the sheriff was told to deliver the portable cross to the university and the treasury of St. Frideswide. Anstey, *Munimenta Academica*, 1:37.

186. Ibid.

187. Pam Manix, a project historian of the Oxford Jewish Heritage Committee, argues that the replacement cross was actually located outside the Jewish quarter (and definitely not in front of the synagogue, but hidden eighty yards from any public thoroughfare). As such it hardly represented a permanent "public humiliation" for the Jews. She also believes that the base of the permanent 1268 cross is actually extant and is the one that was housed in the basement of the old Museum of Oxford. This stone base was identified as a thirteenth-century one that had been removed from one of the Saxon-era cloisters at Christ Church, when they were excavating there in search of the Saxon monastic cemetery of St. Frideswide's Priory. This base has four sides, each with Old Testament figures carved upon it.

188. Joseph Shatzmiller, "Desecrating the Cross: A Rare Medieval Accusation" [in Hebrew], *Mehqarim be-Toledot 'Am Yisrael ve-Erez Yisrael* 5 (1980): 159–173.

189. Cluse, "Stories of Breaking and Taking the Cross," 408.

190. On popular reactions to anti-Judaic charges, see Hans Liebeschitz, "The Crusading Movement and Its Bearing on the Christian Attitude Towards Jewry," *Journal of Jewish Studies* 10 (1959): 97–111.

191. Bynum, *Christian Materiality*, 21–24; and Cluse "Stories of Breaking and Taking," 414.

192. Joseph Jacobs, "Little St. Hugh of Lincoln: Researches in History, Archaeology, and Legend," in Dundes, *The Blood Libel Legend*, 41–71, 53.

193. Hoeps, *Aus dem Schatten des goldenen Kalbes*, 35.

CHAPTER 3

Epigraph: Poem by the New Christian or Marrano poet Antonio Enríquez Gómez (1600–1663), in honor of the martyr Lope de Vera y Alarcón, also called Judah the Believer, who was burned by the Inquisition in Valladolid in 1644, in which the poet writes a speech for the martyr, professing the Jewish faith, in praise of the one God and the one Law, and in the course of it makes his case against Christian images. Timothy Oelman, ed. and trans., *Marrano Poets of the Seventeenth Century* (London: Littman Library, 1982), 185–187.

1. Pereda, "Through a Glass Darkly," in Kessler and Nirenberg, *Judaism and Christian Art*, 263–290; Felipe Pereda, "El debate sobre la imagen en la España del siglo XV: Judíos, cristianos y conversos," *Anuario del Departamento de Historia y Teoría del Arte* 14 (2002): 59–79, particularly the appendixes at the end of the article.

2. Jerrilynn D. Dodds, María Rosa Menocal, and Abigail Krasner Balbale, *The Arts of Intimacy: Christians, Jews, and Muslims in the Making of Castilian Culture* (New Haven, CT: Yale University Press, 2008).

3. José Gudiol, *The Arts of Spain* (London: Thames and Hudson, 1964), 98; Cynthia Robinson, *Imagining the Passion in a Multiconfessional Castile: The Virgin, Christ, Devotions, and Images in the Fourteenth and Fifteenth Centuries* (University Park: Pennsylvania State University Press, 2013), 6.

4. Robinson, *Imagining the Passion*, 48, 213, 224.

5. Pereda, "Through a Glass Darkly," 284. Devotions to the Passion began later in the fifteenth century with the great catechetical display of narrative golden *retablos mayor* (main altarpieces) such as that in Seville Cathedral created by the Flemish craftsman Pierre Dancart in 1482. Cynthia Robinson argues that its purpose was didactic rather than devotional. Cynthia Robinson, "Preaching to the Converted: Valladolid's *Cristianos nuevos* and the *Retablo de don Sancho de Rojas* (1415)," *Speculum* 83 (2008): 112–163, 112–113, 121.

6. Robert Chazan, *Barcelona and Beyond: The Disputation of 1263 and Its Aftermath* (Berkeley: University of California Press, 1992).

7. Ora Limor, "Polemical Varieties: Religious Disputations in 13th Century Spain," *Iberia Judaica* 2 (2010): 55–79.

8. Ibid., 75.

9. *Songs of Holy Mary*, trans. Kulp-Hill, 197.

10. Marian statues in churches appear in Cantigas 25, 139, 162, 164, 185, 196, 207, 215, 272, 282, 292, 294, and 405. Statues in monasteries appear in Cantigas 38, 39, 312, and 353; statues in a cathedral in Cantiga 324; statues in a convent in Cantigas 251, 303, 332, and 361; a statue in a king's chapel in Cantiga 349; statues on a gate of a city in Cantigas 51 and 293; a statue in a Christian city in Cantiga 99; a statue in the Holy Land in Cantiga 46; a statue in a fortress in Portugal in Cantiga 183; and statues whose provenance is not clear appear in Cantigas 121 and 312.

11. Cantiga 9, Damascus; Cantigas 34 and 342, Constantinople.

12. Four tales focus on small devotional pendants or metal images of Mary; Cantiga 161 is set in Morella, Spain, 188 has no provenance, 256 involves a metal image and is set in Capilla, Spain, and 299 has no provenance, but depicts an emblem worn around the neck.

13. Cantiga 27, Lydda; Cantiga 29, Gethsemane; Cantiga 264, Constantinople.

14. Crucifix (in the Fontevrault-l'Abbaye Nunnery in Maine-et-Loire, France) in Cantiga 59; wax crucifix (in Toledo), Cantiga 12; cross (in Hita, Spain), Cantiga 318.

15. Patton, *Art of Estrangement*, 146. Tales set in unnamed destinations include Cantigas 99, 139, 188, 207, 297, 349, and 353; in France, Cantigas 38, 39, 51, 59, 121, and 251; in Byzan-

tium, Cantigas 25, 34, 196, 264, 342, and 405; in the Holy Land (I include Damascus here), Cantigas 9, 27, 29, and 46; in Italy, Cantigas 272, 293, and 294. Tales set in Iberia include Cantigas 12, 161, 162, 164, 183, 185, 215, 256, 282, 292, 299, 303, 312, 318, 324, 332, and 361.

16. Bacci, "'Quel bello miracolo,'" 27. On the festival of the *Passio Imaginis* in Catalonia, see also Juan B. Ferreres, *Historia del misal romano: Su origen (sacramentarios, antifonarios, epistolarios, etc.), el misal plenario, el misal de curia, su variadísimo desarrollo en la edad media, su unidad desde San Pío V, su brillante coronación con la fiesta de Cristo Rey* (Barcelona: Eugenio Subirana, 1929), 310–312.

17. Bacci, "The Berardenga Antependium and the *Passio Ymaginis* Office," 8. It was included with other precious relics in the so-called Arca Santa, a sculpted reliquary commonly said to be the work of the twelve apostles, whose cult was promoted by King Alfonso VI of León (1065–1109). Joan Molina Figueras, "La imagen y su contexto: Perfiles de la iconografía antijudía en la España medieval," in *Els jueus a la Girona medieval (XII ciclo de conferencias Girona a l'Abast)* (Girona: Bell-lloc, 2008), 33–85, 53.

18. Sara Lipton, "Images and Their Uses," in *The Cambridge History of Christianity*, vol. 4, *Christianity in Western Europe, c. 1000–c. 1500*, ed. Miri Rubin and Walter Simons (Cambridge: Cambridge University Press, 2009), 254–283, 257–258.

19. For other altarpieces in Aragon, see Carlos Espí Forcén, "De Oriente a Occidente: La leyenda Bizantina de la *Passio Imaginis* en el siglio XV en la corona de Aragón," *Estudios bizantinos* 2 (2014): 205–229.

20. Espí Forcén, *Recrucificando a Cristo*, 18. A letter of Father Villanueva from 1802 seems to suggest the existence of an actual wooden crucifix in the Cathedral of Valencia believed to be the original Beirut image that had arrived there miraculously in 1250, having been discovered by the bishop Fray Andrés Albalat (Espí Forcén, "Jews Desecrating a Crucifix," 90). Paulino Rodríguez Barral, *La imagen del judío en la España medieval: El conflicto entre cristianismo y judaísmo en las artes visuales góticas*, Memoria artium 8 (Bellaterra: Universitat Autònoma de Barcelona, Servei de Publicacions; Barcelona: Publicacions i Ediciones de la Universitat Barcelona, 2008), 95ff., describes a painting of the fifteenth-century altarpiece by Juan de la Abadía with the iconography of the *Passio Imaginis*.

21. Espí Forcén, "Jews Desecrating a Crucifix," 83–84, 90.

22. Ibid., 90–92.

23. In terms of illuminated manuscripts, Pamela Patton discusses a fourteenth-century Crucifixion miniature added to the twelfth-century manuscript of the *Fuero de Estella* now in Salamanca, which shows a connection to this tale (*Art of Estrangement*, 75). Even artistic representations of the *inventio crucis* legend are difficult to find. There is one visual depiction in a Catalan embroidery of Genesis (1050–1100) now in the museum of Girona Cathedral. Another example of its appearance is the mid-fourteenth-century fresco cycle of the discovery of the True Cross in Tarragona Cathedral, which defines the Jew's hooded figure in two depictions with a badge.

24. E. Michael Gerli, "Poet and Pilgrim: Discourse, Language, Imagery, and Audience in Berceo's *Milagros de Nuestra Señora*," in *Hispanic Medieval Studies in Honor of Samuel G. Armistead*, ed. E. Michael Gerli and Harvey L. Sharrer (Madison, WI: Hispanic Seminary of Medieval Studies, 1992), 139–151. For the version of Gonzalo de Berceo, see *Los Milagros de Nuestra Señora*, Biblioteca Gonzalo de Berceo, accessed July 14, 2022, http://www.bibliotecagonzalodeberceo.com/tesis/milagros.pdf, p. 76 (tale 18). For Juan Gil de Zamora's version, see Fidel Fita, "Cincuenta leyendas por Juan Gil de Zamora combinadas con las *Cantigas* de Alfonso el Sabio," *Boletín de la Real Academia de la Historia* 7 (1885): 54–144, 96 (tale 19); and

for his *Officium almiflue Virginis*, see Juan Gil de Zamora, *Obra Poética: Ymago, ymitago; Quid uigoris, quid amoris; Officium almiflue Virginis*, ed. and trans. Estrella Pérez Rodríguez (Madrid: Instituto de Estudios Zamoranos "Florián de Ocampo," 2018), 74ff.

25. Katherine Aron-Beller, "The Jewish Image Desecrator in the *Cantigas de Santa Maria*," *Ars Judaica* 14 (2018): 27–45. Cantiga 104 is loosely based on Caesarius of Heisterbach's early thirteenth-century tale "Bleeding Host" in the *Dialogus Miraculorum*. It tells of a Christian concubine, encouraged by her neighbor to try to win back the affection of a recently wed squire by stealing a host to use as a love charm.

26. Pamela A. Patton, "Constructing the Inimical Jew in the *Cantigas de Santa Maria*: Theophilus's Magician in Text and Image," in *Beyond the Yellow Badge: Anti-Judaism and Antisemitism in Medieval and Early Modern Visual Culture*, ed. Mitchell Merback (Leiden: Brill, 2010), 233–256, 248; Patton, *Art of Estrangement*, 140. This has already been suggested by Keller and Cash (*Daily Life*, 2) and Patton (*Art of Estrangement*, 13 and 62).

27. Mark D. Meyerson, *Jews in an Iberian Frontier Kingdom: Society, Economy, and Politics in Morvedre, 1248–1391* (Leiden: Brill, 2004), 19.

28. Joseph F. O'Callaghan, *Alfonso X, the Justinian of His Age: Law and Justice in Thirteenth-Century Castile* (Ithaca, NY: Cornell University Press, 2019), 238. Verbal insults were prohibited, as were spitting on crosses, altars, or images, striking holy objects, and throwing stones at churches. If Jews or Moors offended in this way, they would lose a quarter of their goods for the first offense, a third for the second, half for the third, and if they did it another time they would be banished. If the offender was a propertyless minor, his hand would be amputated. Tolan, *Saracens*, 188.

29. *Siete Partidas* 7.24.2.

30. David Nirenberg, *Communities of Violence: Persecution of Minorities in the Middle Ages* (Princeton, NJ: Princeton University Press, 1995), 28, 37.

31. Ibid., 37, 48.

32. Meyerson, *Jews in an Iberian Frontier Kingdom*, 34.

33. Ibid., 184, 275.

34. Yom Tov Assis, *Jewish Economy in the Medieval Crown of Aragon, 1213–1327* (Leiden: Brill, 1997), 85. The only document I have found is in Simonsohn, *The Apostolic See and the Jews*, doc. 538, Valencia, May 11, 1415. By 1454, Pope Nicholas V included Christian punishment in the Valencian prohibition, threatening Christians with excommunication if they pawned their objects with Jews. Simonsohn, *Apostolic See*, 7:187.

35. Mark D. Meyerson, *A Jewish Renaissance in Fifteenth-Century Spain* (Princeton, NJ: Princeton University Press, 2004), 110, 128.

36. Cesare Colafemmina, *Per la storia degli ebrei in Calabria: Saggi e documenti* (Messina: Rubbettino, 1996) 27 n. 36; Shatzmiller, *Cultural Exchange*, 141, 151; and Vivian B. Mann, "Jews and Altarpieces in Medieval Spain," in *Uneasy Communion: Jews, Christians, and the Altarpieces of Medieval Spain*, ed. Vivian B. Mann (New York: Museum of Biblical Art, 2010), 106–118.

37. Meyerson, *A Jewish Renaissance in Fifteenth-Century Spain*, 93, 129.

38. Jeremy Cohen, *The Friars and the Jews: The Evolution of Medieval Anti-Judaism* (Ithaca, NY: Cornell University Press, 1982), 41, 76.

39. Francisco Javier Rojo Alique, "Fifteenth-Century Franciscan Preachers in Castile: The Example of Valladolid," in *Franciscans and Preaching: Every Miracle from the Beginning of the World Came About Through Words*, ed. Timothy J. Johnson (Leiden: Brill, 2002), 353–379, 354.

40. Yom Tov Assis, *The Golden Age of Aragonese Jewry: Community and Society in the Crown of Aragon, 1213–1327* (Oxford: Littman Library of Jewish Civilization, 1997), 53–54.

41. Paola Tartakoff, *Between Christian and Jew: Conversion and Inquisition in the Crown of Aragon, 1250–1391* (Philadelphia: University of Pennsylvania Press, 2013), 88.

42. Kessler and Nirenberg, *Judaism and Christian Art.*

43. Ramón Martí, *Pugio fidei adversus mauros et iudaeos* (Paris, 1651), part 2, chap. 8, "Qualiter Dominus noster, Iesus Christus destruxerit statuam Danielis, & idolatriam per miracula," p. 286; there are two copies in the Biblioteca de la Universidad de Comilas (2689 and 2585). See Robert Chazan, *From Anti-Judaism to Anti-Semitism: Ancient and Medieval Christian Constructions of Jewish History* (Cambridge: Cambridge University Press, 2016), 160; and Cohen, *The Friars and the Jews*, 203. Likewise, Ramon Llull in his *Libre de doctrina pueril* argues that the Jews were not idolaters but they had been punished with servitude because they had rejected Christ (see *Obres de Ramón Llull*, vol. 1, *Doctrina pueril; Libre del orde de cavalleria; Libre de clerecia; Art de confessió*, ed. Mateu Obrador, facsimile ed. [Palma de Mallorca: Miquel Font, 1986]).

44. José-Luis Martín and Antonio Linage Conde, *Religión y sociedad medieval: El catecismo de Pedro de Cuéllar (1325)* (Valladolid: Junta, 1987), 174.

45. Maimonides, *Commentary on the Mishnah, Avodah Zarah* 1:3; *Mishneh Torah, Hilkhot Avodat Kohavim* 9:4; see also Solomon ben Avraham ibn Aderet, *Sheelot u-teshuvot (Responsa)*, vol. 5, no. 66; Yom Tov ben Avraham Ishbili, *Sheelot u-teshuvot (Responsa)*, no. 159. Nachmanides argued at the Barcelona Disputation of 1263 that worship of the Messiah or any other man as if he were a god clearly indicated idolatry; see Maccoby, *Judaism on Trial*, 131.

46. At the beginning of the fourteenth century Bernard Gui translated, with some degree of accuracy, extracts from Jewish prayer books in his manual for inquisitors. See Bernardus Guidonis, *Practica inquisitionis heretice pravitatis*, ed. Célestin Douais (Paris: Picard, 1886), 290–292; Tartakoff, *Between Christian and Jew*, 107; Meyerson, *Jews in an Iberian Frontier Kingdom*, 85.

47. Meyerson, *Jews in an Iberian Frontier Kingdom*, 90; Elka Klein, *Jews, Christian Society, and Royal Power in Medieval Barcelona* (Ann Arbor: University of Michigan Press, 2006), 161.

48. Klein, *Jews, Christian Society, and Royal Power*, 195.

49. Meyerson, *Jews in an Iberian Frontier Kingdom*, 90. For a description of the depiction of the allegation in the retable frontal ensemble made for the Catalan monastery of Vallbona des Monges in 1348, see Pamela Patton, *The Art of Estrangement*, 63.

50. Assis, *The Golden Age of Aragonese Jewry*, 60; Tartakoff, *Between Christian and Jew*, 18. A fifth case is reported by Jean Régné, where Abraham Cofen supposedly broke a cross. Jean Régné, "Rapports entre l'inquisition et les juifs d'après le mémorial de l'inquisiteur d'Aragon (fin du XIVe siècle)," *Revue des Études Juives* 53 (1906): 224–233, 226.

51. Jean Régné, *History of the Jews in Aragon: Regesta and Documents, 1213–1327*, ed. Yom Tov Assis, Hispania Judaica 1 (Jerusalem: Magnes Press, 1978), 24; Horowitz, *Reckless Rites*, 177.

52. Yom Tov Assis, "The Jews of Barcelona in Maritime Trade with the East," in *The Jew in Medieval Iberia, 1100–1500*, ed. Jonathan Ray (Boston: Academic Studies Press, 2011), 180–226, 203.

53. Ibid.

54. Ibid.

55. Nirenberg, *Communities of Violence*, 220; Tartakoff, *Between Christian and Jew*, 7.

56. Meyerson, *Jews in an Iberian Frontier Kingdom*, 91–92.

57. Assis, *The Golden Age of Aragonese Jewry*, 62–63.

58. Nirenberg, *Communities of Violence*, 202–204.

59. Tartakoff, *Between Christian and Jew*, 94.

60. Meyerson, *Jews in an Iberian Frontier Kingdom*, 85.

61. Rubin, *Corpus Christi.*

62. Meyerson, *Jews in an Iberian Frontier Kingdom*, 89.

63. Nirenberg, *Communities of Violence*, 221.

64. Akbari, *Idols in the East*, 5, 157, 203–206.

65. Ibid., 209; Tolan, *Faces of Muhammad*, 31.

66. Tartakoff, *Between Christian and Jew*, 13.

67. Jessica Marin Elliott, "Jews 'Feigning Devotion': Christian Representations of Converted Jews in French Chronicles Before and After the Expulsion of 1306," in *Jews and Christians in Thirteenth-Century France*, ed. Elisheva Baumgarten and Judah D. Galinsky (New York: Palgrave Macmillan, 2015), 169–182. For an actual description of the Jews' return to Judaism according to Bernard Gui, inquisitor in Toulouse, see Yosef Hayim Yerushalmi, "The Inquisition and the Jews of France in the Time of Bernard Gui," *Harvard Theological Review* 63, no. 3 (1970): 317–376, 363–364.

68. Paola Tartakoff, *Conversion, Circumcision, and Ritual Murder in Medieval Europe* (Philadelphia: University of Pennsylvania Press, 2020), 40.

69. Elliott, "Jews 'Feigning Devotion,'" 177.

70. Tartakoff, *Between Christian and Jew*, 48.

71. Ibid., 125.

72. Ibid., 104

73. For a full discussion on this, see Ephraim Kanarfogel, *Brothers from Afar: Rabbinic Approaches to Apostasy and Reversion in Medieval Europe* (Detroit: Wayne State University Press, 2020).

74. Eric M. Zafran, "An Alleged Case of Image Desecration by the Jews and Its Representation in Art: The Virgin of Cambron," *Journal of Jewish Art* 2 (1974): 62–71; see also Gérard Waelput, "Les Juifs à Mons au Moyen Âge," part 2, *Le Moyen Age* 107, nos. 3–4 (2001): 503–508, under "Le Sacrilège de Cambron"; Théophile Lejeune, "La vierge miraculeuse de Cambron," *Annales du cercle archéologique de Mons* 7 (1867): 66–95; Félix Hachez, "La littérature du sacrilège de Cambron," *Annales du cercle archéologique de Mons* 27 (1897): 97–152.

75. A summary of the papal letter is found in Solomon Grayzel, "References to the Jews in the Correspondence of John XXII," *Hebrew Union College Annual* 23, no. 2 (1950–1951): 37–80, no. 35, 75–77; Heinrich Loewe, *Die Juden in der katholischen Legende* (Berlin: Jüdischer Verlag, 1912), 66ff.

76. Hachez, "La littérature du sacrilège de Cambron," 115ff.

77. Zafran, "The Iconography of Antisemitism," 210ff.

78. This church was subsequently destroyed in 1792.

79. Loewe, *Die Juden in der katholischen Legende*, 71ff.

80. The text is given in Karl Goedeke, *Pamphilus Gengenbach* (Hanover: Rümpler, 1856), 39–53, and discussed at 557–558.

81. Thomas Murner], *Enderung und Schmach der bildung Marie von den Juden* [. . .] ([Strasbourg]: [Hüpfuff], [ca. 1515]). The model for these woodcuts was provided by a cycle of pictures commissioned in 1477 by the emperor Maximilian I for the Franciscan church in Colmar.

82. Written on top of the image are the words: "Wie der Graue den juden ließ erhenckē mit zweyē rüden und verbrenē und dem galgē," which means "Gray lets the Jew hang on the

gallows and burn between two male dogs." Gray is the magistrate on horseback looking on at the execution.

83. Maria R. Boes, "Jews in the Criminal-Justice System of Early Modern Germany," *Journal of Interdisciplinary History* 30, no. 3 (Winter 1999): 407–435, 430–431.

84. Robert Mills, *Suspended Animation: Pain, Pleasure and Punishment in Medieval Culture* (London: Reaktion Books, 2005), 16.

85. Elliott, "Jews 'Feigning Devotion,'" 176.

86. Tartakoff, *Between Christian and Jew*, 26.

87. Ibid., 29–30. These Jews felt it was their religious duty to help re-Judaize French Jewish converts.

88. David Nirenberg, *Anti-Judaism: The History of a Way of Thinking* (New York: W. W. Norton, 2013), 228–229.

89. The tale appears in a chapter titled "The Willfulness and Wickedness of the Jews Who Do Not Accept the Christian Faith Despite Several Miracles." Alphonsus de Spina, *Fortalitium Fidei*, accessed July 14, 2022, https://archive.org/details/ita-bnc-in1-00000788-001. José Amador de los Ríos, *Historia social, política y religiosa de los judíos de España y Portugal*, vol. 3 (Madrid: Ediciones Turner, 1984): 134–135; Klaus Reinhardt and Horacio Santiago-Otero, *Biblioteca bíblica ibérica medieval* (Madrid: Editorial CSIC–CSIC Press, 1986), 63–64.

90. Rojo Alique, "Fifteenth-Century Franciscan Preachers in Castile," 353.

91. Steven J. McMichael, *Was Jesus of Nazareth the Messiah? Alphonso de Espina's Argument Against the Jews in the "Fortalitium Fidei" (c. 1464)* (Atlanta, GA: Scholars Press, 1994), 22.

92. Rojo Alique, "Fifteenth-Century Franciscan Preachers in Castile," 357.

93. Alonso de Espina, "Fortalitium fidel contra saracenos aliosque Christiane fidei inimicos," incunabulum edition of Antonius Koberger, prepared and completed in Nuremburg on February 25 1494, Friedenwald collection, Edelstein Library, National Library of Jerusalem, folio 170, "The Willfulness and Wickedness of the Jews." On this tale in Juan Gil de Zamora's writings, see Fita, "Cincuenta leyendas por Juan Gil de Zamora," 96 (tale 19).

94. Christopher Walker, "Iconographical Considerations" in *The Letter of the Three Patriarchs*, lx.

95. A. Lukyn Williams, *Adversus Judaeos: A Bird's-Eye View of Christian Apologiae Until the Renaissance* (Cambridge: Cambridge University Press, 1935), 278–279; McMichael, *Was Jesus of Nazareth the Messiah?*, 6.

96. Felipe Pereda, *Las imágenes de la discordia: Política y poética de la imagen sagrada en la España del 400* (Madrid: Marcial Pons Historia, 2007), 126.

97. Chazan, *From Anti-Judaism to Antisemitism*, 185.

98. Haim Beinart, *Conversos on Trial: The Inquisition in Ciudad Real* (Jerusalem: Magnes Press, 1981), 12–13. There are a few decorative remains of medieval synagogues in Castile—particularly those of Cordoba built in 1315 and El Transito synagogue in Toledo built in 1357.

99. Malcolm Letts (ed.), *The Travels of Leo of Rozmital through Germany, Flanders, England, France, Spain, Portugal and Italy 1465–1467* (Abingdon, Oxon: Routledge, 2016) 79–80.

100. María José Martínez Martínez, "El Santo Cristo de Burgos y los cristos dolorosos articulados," *Boletín del Seminario de Estudios de Arte y Arqueología* 69–70 (2003–2004): 207–246, 232.

101. Felipe Pereda, "La conversión por la imagen y la imagen de la conversión: Notas sobre la cultura figurativa castellana en el umbral de la edad moderna," in *Cartografías visuales y arquitectónicas de la modernidad: Siglos XV–XVIII*, ed. Sílvia Canalda, Carme Narváez, and Joan Sureda (Barcelona: Publicacions i Edicions de la Universitat de Barcelona, 2011), 227–241.

102. Pereda, "Through a Glass Darkly," 282.

103. Letts (ed.), *The Travels of Leo of Rozmital through Germany*, 79. He would later become lord chancellor of Castile and León and tutor of the Crown Prince Juan II as well as executor of King Enrique III's last will and testament.

104. Rojo Alique, "Fifteenth-Century Franciscan Preachers in Castile," 379.

105. Pedro M. Cátedra, *Sermón, sociedad y literatura en la Edad Media: San Vicente Ferrer en Castilla (1411–1412)* (Valladolid: Junta de Castilla y León, 1994), 411: "Buena gente, grand peccado sería si un omne con yra o con malicia diesse una bofetada o una cochillada a una ymagen de Dios fecha de madero o de piedra o de otra cosa. Digo que mayor peccado faze aquel que por venganza o por yra fiere o mata algún omne, porque aquel tal mata o fiere la propia ymagen de Dios."

106. Robinson, *Imagining the Passion*, 7; Pereda, "Through a Glass Darkly," 264–265.

107. Pereda, "Through a Glass Darkly," 283.

108. On this, see Pereda, "El debate sobre la imagen en la España," 65–66; Pereda, *Las imágenes de la discordia*, 113.

109. Pereda, "Through a Glass Darkly," 282 (Pereda's translation).

110. Robinson, *Imagining the Passion*, 8.

111. Pereda, *Las imágenes de la discordia*, 60.

112. Pereda, "Through a Glass Darkly," 264.

113. Pereda, "El debate sobre la imagen en la España," 63; see also Pereda, *Las imágenes de la discordia*, 84–85 and 423–424, where Pereda provides the text of Alfonso de Madrigal's *Confessional del Tostado* (Alcalá de Henares: Arnao Guillén de Brocar, 1517), which was concerned with the growing number of superstitions coming to light regarding the lifelike qualities recently associated with images. This, Tostado complained, smacked of paganism.

114. Karl F. Morrison, *Conversion and Text: The Cases of Augustine of Hippo, Herman-Judah, and Constantine Tsatsos* (Charlottesville: University Press of Virginia, 1992), 80.

115. François Soyer, *Antisemitic Conspiracy Theories in the Early Modern Iberian World: Narratives of Fear and Hatred* (Leiden: Brill, 2020), shows how antisemitic conspiracy theories in both polemical works and sermons in Catholic Spain saw the *conversos*' desecration of images as part of a plot against the Iberian church; see in particular pp. 95–96.

116. This space would become the location for crypto-Jewish women in particular to practice their Judaism in secret. See Debra Kaplan, "Living Spaces, Communal Places: Early Modern Jewish Homes and Religious Devotions," in *Domestic Devotions in the Early Modern World*, ed. Marco Faini and Alessia Meneghin (Leiden: Brill, 2002), 315–333, 321; and Reneé Levine Melammed, *Heretics or Daughters of Israel? The Crypto-Jewish Women of Castile* (New York: Oxford University Press, 1999).

117. David M. Gitlitz, *Secrecy and Deceit: The Religion of Crypto-Jews* (Philadelphia: Jewish Publishing Society, 1996), 160–167; David M. Gitlitz, "Las presuntas profanaciones judías del ritual cristiano en el decreto de expulsión," in *Judíos, sefarditas, conversos: La expulsion de 1492 y sus consecuencias*, ed. Angel Alcalá Galve (Valladolid: Ambito Ediciones, 1995), 150–169; Michael Alpert, "Did Spanish Crypto-Jews Desecrate Christian Images and Why? The Case

of the *Cristo de la Paciencia* (1629–32), the *Romance* of 1717 and the Events of November 1714 in the *Calle del Lobo*," in *Faith and Fanaticism: Religious Fervour in Early Modern Spain*, ed. Lesley K. Twomey (Aldershot: Ashgate, 1997), 85–94.

118. Anna Ysabel d'Abrera, *The Tribunal of Zaragoza and Crypto-Judaism, 1484–1515* (Turnhout: Brepols, 2008), 51.

119. Lu Ann Homza, ed. and trans., *The Spanish Inquisition, 1478–1614: An Anthology of Sources* (Indianapolis: Hackett, 2006), 27; Jessica Weiss, "Inquisitive Objects: Material Culture and Conversos in Early Modern Ciudad Real," University of New Mexico UNM Digital Repository Research Papers, no. 55 (2011), accessed July 14, 2022, https://digitalrepository.unm.edu/cgi/viewcontent.cgi?referer=https://www.google.com/&httpsredir=1&article=1049&context=laii_research, quote at p. 11.

120. Weiss, "Inquisitive Objects."

121. Pereda, "Through a Glass Darkly," 274. Obviously I have mainly restricted my research to actual cases of desecration by crypto-Jews and do not include many examples of negative attitudes such as praying toward a wall in the house where no images were hanging or taking flight rather than kneeling before a public image. On *conversos* carrying the cross disrespectfully, see Albert A. Sicroff, "Spanish Anti-Judaism: A Case of Religious Racism," in *Encuentros and Desencuentros: Spanish Jewish Cultural Interaction Throughout History*, ed. Carlos Carrete Parrondo et al. (Tel Aviv: Tel Aviv University Press, 2000), 589–613.

122. D'Abrera, *The Tribunal of Zaragoza*, 186.

123. Ibid., 180.

124. Ibid., 184.

125. Homza, *The Spanish Inquisition*, 258.

126. Nadia Zeldes, *"The Former Jews of This Kingdom": Sicilian Converts After the Expulsion, 1492–1516* (Leiden: Brill, 2003), 284.

127. Soyer, *Antisemitic Conspiracy Theories*, 121, 123.

128. Pereda, *Las imágenes de la discordia*, 133.

129. Gretchen Starr-LeBeau, "Mari Sánchez and Inés González: Conflict and Cooperation Among Crypto-Jews," in *Women in the Inquisition: Spain and the New World*, ed. Mary E. Giles (Baltimore: Johns Hopkins University Press, 1999), 19–41, 34–36.

130. Espí Forcén, "Jews Desecrating a Crucifix," 91. Here he believes that it might have been the popularity of the Christ of Beirut legend that induced Christians to believe that Jews flogged crucifixes.

131. Haim Beinart, ed., *Records of the Trials of the Spanish Inquisition in Ciudad Real* (Jerusalem: Magnes Press, 1974), 1:85–86; Weiss, "Inquisitive Objects."

132. William A. Christian Jr., *Moving Crucifixes in Modern Spain* (Princeton, NJ: Princeton University Press, 1992), 192.

133. Yitzhak Baer, *A History of the Jews in Christian Spain*, vol. 2 (Philadelphia: Jewish Publication Society of America, 1961), 362. Pereda, *Las imágenes de la discordia*, 107–109, discusses the similarity between this allegation and the "Christ of Beirut" tale. On this trial, see also d'Abrera, *The Tribunal of Zaragoza*, 185–187.

134. D'Abrera, *The Tribunal of Zaragoza*, 186.

135. Ibid.

136. Baer, *A History of the Jews*, 362–363. Baer records a case of a woman who was asked if she had, or knew of anyone who had, ever whipped a crucifix. Baer thinks that this question may have originated from the 1487 Zaragoza trial.

137. D'Abrera, *The Tribunal of Zaragoza*, 186–187; Pereda, *Las imágenes de la discordia*, 104–105; Espí Forcén, *Recrucificando a Cristo*, 106.

138. Haim Beinart, "A Prophesying Movement in Cordova in 1499–1502" [in Hebrew], in *Yitzhak F. Baer Memorial Volume, 1888–1980*, ed. H. Beinart, S. Ettinger, and M. Stern (Jerusalem: Historical Society of Israel, 1980), 190–200.

139. Ibid., 195–196.

140. Ibid., 196.

141. Aron-Beller, "The Jewish Image Desecrator in the *Cantigas de Santa Maria*," 12ff.

142. Soyer, *Antisemitic Conspiracy Theories*, 132–133.

143. Fray Jaime Bleda's treatise printed in Valencia in 1600 that discusses this offense. Jaime Bleda, *Quatroçientos Milagros y muchas alabanzas de la Santa Cruz con unos tratados de las cosas mas notables desta divina señal* (Valencia: Patricio Mey, 1600), chap. 77 (269), chap. 106 (301–304), chap. 110 (309–310), chap. 119 (322–324), chap. 158 (389–390), chap. 159 (390–3911), chap. 278 (444); chap. 318 (461).

144. Pierroberto Scaramello, "La campagna contro i giudaizzanti nel Regno di Napoli (1569–1582): Antecedenti e risvolti di un'azione inquisitoriale," in *Le Inquisizioni cristiane e gli ebrei: Tavola rotonda nell'ambito della Conferenza annuale di ricerca, Roma, 20–21 Dicembre 2001*, ed. Giuseppe Galasso (Rome: Accademia Nazionale dei Lincei, 2003), 357–373, 367.

145. The scourging of crucifixes even reached inquisitorial cases in Venice. See Pier Cesare Ioly Zorattini, ed., *Processi del S. Uffizio di Venezia contro ebrei e giudazzanti (1548–60)* (Florence: Olschki, 1980), 4:93–94.

146. Soyer, *Antisemitic Conspiracy Theories*, 124.

147. Ibid., 125; Agustín de Benavente, *Segunda parte de las Luzes de Dios, resplandor de las llagas de Cristo Señor Nuestro empleo del pensamiento cristiano en la vida del mismo Señor, y su santissima Madre* (Valladolid: Antonio de Ruenda, 1647), 62. All the Gospel accounts of Christ's passion suggest that on the orders of Pontius Pilate Jesus was scourged or "chastised" before he was crucified (Matt. 27:26; Mark 15:15; Luke 23:22; John 19:1).

148. Many medieval penitents wished to share some of Christ's pain and to help expiate the sins of the world (or of their own city). They could hardly crucify themselves, but they could flog themselves with a scourge or discipline and draw their own blood. On the Scuole Grandi in Venice, see Brian S. Pullan, *Rich and Poor in Renaissance Venice: The Social Institutions of a Catholic State to 1620* (Oxford: Oxford University Press, 1971), 35–37.

149. Patrick Vandermeersch, "Self-Flagellation in the Early Modern Era," in *The Sense of Suffering: Constructions of Physical Pain in Early Modern Culture*, ed. Jan Frans van Dijkhuizen and Karl A. E. Enenkel (Leiden: Brill, 2008), 253–265, 262.

150. Yosef Hayim Yerushalmi, *From Spanish Court to Italian Ghetto: Isaac Cardoso; A Study in Seventeenth-Century Marranism and Jewish Apologetics* (New York: Columbia University Press, 1971), 114ff.

151. Soyer, *Antisemitic Conspiracy Theories*, 125.

152. Yerushalmi, *From Spanish Court to Italian Ghetto*, 119.

153. Juan Ignacio Pulido Serrano, *Injurias a Cristo: Religión, política y antijudaísmo en el siglo XVII (análisis de las corrientes antijudías durante la Edad Moderna)* (Alcalá de Henares: Instituto Internacional de Estudios Sefardés y Andalusíes, Universidad de Alcalá, Servicio de Publicaciones, 2002), 124–153, 136–137; Alpert, "Did Spanish Crypto-Jews Desecrate Christian Sacred Images," 84–96. On other cases of scourging crucifixes in the seventeenth century, see Julio Caro Baroja, ed., *Los judíos en la España moderna y contemporánea*, vol. 2 (Madrid:

Ediciones Arion, 1961), 165; and Gitlitz, *Secrecy and Deceit*, 164, for the cases of the merchant Diego Rodríguez, Ventura Binimelis, and Pedro Carretero.

154. Yerushalmi, *From Spanish Court to Italian Ghetto*, 118–119.

155. Pulido Serrano, *Injurias a Cristo*, 146; Alfonso Rodríguez G. de Ceballos, "Image and Counter-Reformation in Spain and Spanish America," in *Sacred Spain: Art and Belief in the Spanish World*, ed. Ronda Kasl (Indianapolis: Indianapolis Museum of Art, 2009), 15–36, 29.

156. Alpert, "Did Spanish Crypto-Jews Desecrate Christian Sacred Images," 84.

157. William A. Christian Jr., *Local Religion in Sixteenth-Century Spain* (Princeton, NJ: Princeton University Press, 1981), 190–194. María José del Río Barredo, in her "Imágenes callejeras y rituales públicos en el Madrid del siglo XVII," in *La imagen religiosa en la Monarquía hispánica: Usos y espacios*, ed. María Cruz de Carlos et al. (Madrid: Casa de Velázquez, 2008), 197–218, brings to light extensive archival discoveries that document the abundance of religious images on the streets of seventeenth-century Madrid. See also Pulido Serrano, *Injurias a Cristo*, 138–139.

158. Susan Verdi Webster, *Art and Ritual in Golden-Age Spain: Sevillian Confraternities and the Processional Sculpture of Holy Week* (Princeton, NJ: Princeton University Press, 1998), 14; Christian, *Moving Crucifixes*, 196; Vandermeersch, "Self-Flagellation in the Early Modern Era," 262.

159. Rodríguez G. de Ceballos, "Image and Counter-Reformation," 29; Margaret R. Miles, *A Complex Delight: The Secularization of the Breast, 1350–1750* (Oakland: University of California Press, 2008), 70; Nirenberg, "The Historical Body of Christ," 17.

160. Maria José Pimenta Ferro Tavares, *Judaísmo e Inquisição: Estudos* (Lisbon: Presença, 1987), 124; François Soyer, "The Massacre of the New Christians of Lisbon in 1506: A New Eyewitness Account," *Cadernos de Estudos Sefarditas* 7 (2007): 221–243, 235. Soyer notes that the Portuguese chronicler Damião de Góis, who wrote over fifty years later, had put the number killed at over a thousand, while Solomon Ibn Verga provides a much higher figure of three thousand.

161. See Yosef Hayim Yerushalmi, *The Lisbon Massacre of 1506 and the Royal Image in the Shebet Yehudah*, Hebrew Union College Annual Supplements 1 (Cincinnati: Hebrew Union College, 1976), for Ibn Verga's and the anonymous chronicler's version of the event.

162. Soyer, "The Massacre of the New Christians," 226–227.

163. Yerushalmi, *The Lisbon Massacre of 1506*, 4–5.

164. Ibid., 10.

165. Ibid., 11.

166. Further research will, I believe, reveal that the destruction of a statue of Our Lady in Gouveia in 1528 created the climate for the establishment of the Inquisition in Portugal. See Tavares, *Judaísmo e Inquisição*, 124.

167. Soyer, *Antisemitic Conspiracy Theories*, 131. Another example, this time in Pisa and Milan in 1618–1626, can be found in Ioly Zorattini, *Processi del S. Uffizio di Venezia contro ebrei e giudaizzanti*, 10:203–213.

168. Soyer, *Antisemitic Conspiracy Theories*, 134; here Soyer shows how these accusations entered local folklore.

169. James C. Scott, *Domination and the Arts of Resistance: Hidden Transcripts* (New Haven, CT: Yale University Press, 1990).

CHAPTER 4

Epigraph: Amos Oz, *Judas*, trans. Nicholas de Lange (London: Chatto & Windus, 1988).

1. Exod. 20:3–5; also Exod. 34:14 and Deut. 5:7–9.

2. Exod. 20:3–5; Deut. 5:7–9; Halbertal and Margalit, *Idolatry*; Neis, *The Sense of Sight in Rabbinic Culture*, 170.

3. Halbertal and Margalit, *Idolatry*, 105–106, 238–240; Sarah Pearce, ed., *The Image and Its Prohibition in Jewish Antiquity* (Oxford: Journal of Jewish Studies, 2013), in particular Philip Alexander's article, "Reflections on Word Versus Image as Ways of Mediating the Divine Presence in Judaism," 10–27.

4. Many verses in Deuteronomy warn the Israelites of foreign worship in the land of Canaan and make a correlation between intermarriage with Canaanite women and worshipping their gods. This is also mentioned in Exodus 34:10–17.

5. Van der Toorn, "The Iconic Book," 239.

6. See Judges 2:2 for the command that idols be destroyed. The prophet who speaks about idolatry the most is Jeremiah (10:3–9). Ezekiel (8:5–12) also meticulously describes the pictorial reliefs at the northern city gate of Jerusalem and does so with eloquent disapproval.

7. This took place in 622/621 BCE. See Joseph Gutmann, "Deuteronomy: Religious Reformation or Iconoclastic Revolution?" in *The Image and the Word: Confrontations in Judaism, Christianity and Islam* (Missoula, MT: Scholars Press, 1977), 5–25, 7–8.

8. Although Isaiah is a mid-First Temple prophet, the second half of his book is believed by scholars to have been framed in the Persian period.

9. Halbertal and Margalit, *Idolatry*, 2; and also Rivka Raviv, "The End of Idolatry in Israel During the Persian Period" [in Hebrew], *Bekhol Derakhekha Daehu—Journal of Torah and Scholarship* 25 (2011): 83–92.

10. Josephus, *Antiquities* 17.6, in *The Genuine Works of Flavius Josephus, the Jewish Historian*, accessed July 14, 2022, https://penelope.uchicago.edu/josephus/ant-17.html; Albert I Baumgarten, "Herod's Eagle," in *"Go Out and Study the Land" (Judges 18:2): Archaeological, Historical and Textual Studies in Honor of Hanan Eshel*, ed. Aren M. Maeir, Jodi Magness, and Lawrence H. Schiffman (Leiden: Brill, 2011), 7–21; Steven Fine, *Art and Judaism in the Greco-Roman World: Toward a New Jewish Archaeology* (Cambridge: Cambridge University Press, 2005), 72–81.

11. Daniel R. Schwartz, "Josephus and Philo on Pontius Pilate," in *The Jerusalem Cathedra: Studies in the History, Archaeology, Geography, and Ethnography of the Land of Israel*, vol. 3, ed. Lee I. Levine (Jerusalem: Yad Izhak Ben-Zvi Institute, 1983), 26–45.

12. Josephus, *The Jewish War* 2.9.2, in *The Genuine Works of Flavius Josephus*, accessed July 14, 2022, https://penelope.uchicago.edu/josephus/war-2.html. Here and below I have quoted with minor changes to the translation of William Whiston.

13. Ibid., 2.9.3.

14. *The Works of Philo*, 524 and 531.

15. The term *Avodah Zarah* is not a biblical one. See Rachel Neis, "Religious Lives of Image-Things, *Avodah Zarah*, and Rabbis in Late Antique Palestine,"*Archivfür Religions-Geschichte* 17, no. 1 (2016): 91–121, 95; and Halbertal and Margalit, *Idolatry*, 5. See also Ishay Rosen-Zvi, "The Polemic on the Obligation to Destroy Idolatry in Tannaitic Literature" [in Hebrew], *Reshit: The Shalom Hartman Institute Academic Annual* 1 (2009): 91–116, which ar-

gues that Mishnaic passages show how the obligation to destroy images is transformed into the obligation of excluding them and prohibiting their enjoyment; and Yair Furstenberg, "Idolatry Annulment: Rabbinic Dialogue with Paganism Under the Roman Empire" [in Hebrew], *Reshit: The Shalom Hartman Institute Academic Annual* 1 (2009): 117–144, which argues that the exclusion of iconoclastic laws in the Mishnah is intended to prevent Israel from making secondary use of surrounding idols. This enabled the Jews to cope with the changing theological-political framework in which they lived.

16. Seth Schwartz, "The Rabbi in Aphrodite's Bath: Palestinian Society and Jewish Identity in the High Roman Empire," in *Being Greek Under Rome: Cultural Identity, the Second Sophistic and the Development of Empire*, ed. Simon Goldhill (Cambridge: Cambridge University Press, 2007), 335–361, 337.

17. Fine, *Art and Judaism*, 110.

18. Gerald J. Blidstein, "R. Yohanan, Idolatry, and Public Privilege," *Journal for the Study of Judaism in the Persian, Hellenistic, and Roman Period* 5, no. 2 (1974): 154–161, 154.

19. Neis, "Religious Lives of Image-Things," 105.

20. Ephraim Urbach, "The Rabbinical Laws of Idolatry in the Second and Third Centuries in Light of Archaeological and Historical Facts," *Eretz Israel* 5 (1958): 189–205. Note that in the Talmud, the rabbis depicted Jesus as being a pupil of Rabbi Joshua ben Perahia, expelled by his master because of his lewdness and his subsequent idolatry. See Babylonian Talmud, *Sotah* 47a; and Babylonian Talmud, Sanhedrin 107a.

21. Halbertal and Margalit, *Idolatry*, 5.

22. Daniel Boyarin, *Border Lines: The Partition of Judaeo-Christianity* (Philadelphia: University of Pennsylvania Press, 2004), 56, 85–86.

23. Blidstein, "R. Yohanan, Idolatry," 154.

24. Babylonian Talmud, Avodah Zarah 49a–b.

25. Jerusalem Talmud, Avodah Zarah 3:8, 43b. This translation is taken from Fine, *Art and Judaism*, 113. See also Rachel Neis, "Eyeing Idols: Rabbinic Viewing Practices in Late Antiquity," *Jewish Quarterly Review* 102, no. 4 (Fall 2012): 533–560, 551.

26. Peter Stewart, "The Destruction of Statues in Late Antiquity," in *Constructing Identities in Late Antiquity*, ed. Richard Miles (London: Routledge, 1999), 159–189, 161–165.

27. Varner, *Mutilation and Transformation*, 2–3, 217; see also Neis, "Eying Idols," 554, who notes that eyes were "among the most often struck organs"; and Jaś Elsner, *Roman Eyes: Visuality and Subjectivity in Art and Text* (Princeton, NJ: Princeton University Press, 2007), 21–22.

28. Neis, *The Sense of Sight in Rabbinic Culture*, 188 n.89.

29. Peter Schäfer, "Jews and Gentiles in Yerushalmi Avodah Zarah," in *The Talmud Yerushalmi and Graeco-Roman Culture*, vol. 3, ed. Peter Schäfer (Tübingen: Mohr Siebeck, 2002), 335–352, 348.

30. Blidstein, "R. Yohanan, Idolatry," 158 ("spit in its eye").

31. Neis, *The Sense of Sight in Rabbinic Culture*, 174, 186ff.; see also Christine Elizabeth Hayes, *Between the Babylonian and Palestinian Talmuds: Accounting for Halakhic Difference in Selected Sugyot from Tractate Avodah Zarah* (Oxford: Oxford University Press, 1997), 214–215 n. 34.

32. Blidstein, "R. Yohanan, Idolatry," 159.

33. Neis, "Religious Lives of Image-Things," 108; Neis, *The Sense of Sight in Rabbinic Culture*, 192.

34. Neis, "Eyeing Idols," 541; Neis, *The Sense of Sight in Rabbinic Culture*, 171; Neis, "Religious Lives of Image-Things," 117. Neis cites Judaic texts that suggest that a time will come when idols will themselves bow down to God.

35. Tosefta, Avodah Zarah 6:2. See Urbach, "The Rabbinical Laws of Idolatry," 149–165, 229–245, 231–232. Discussion of desecration uses the example of a Jew purchasing a scrapheap from a non-Jew. If the Jew found idolatrous objects in the scrapheap he could require the non-Jew to nullify them.

36. The Jerusalem Talmud, Avodah Zarah 4:4, 43d. Scholars agree that the iconoclastic injunction by R. Yohanan to Bar Derosay to break "images" (*tsalmayya*) in the bathhouse should not be compared to images in other settings. Since it is situated in a bathhouse, and non-Jews urinate before it, it cannot be held in the same respect as other images. See Neis, *The Sense of Sight in Rabbinic Culture*, 190; Schäfer, "Jews and Gentiles," 350.

37. Mishnah, Avodah Zarah 3:3; Neis, *The Sense of Sight in Rabbinic Culture*, 192 n. 103.

38. Mishnah, Berakhot 9:1–2; Tosefta, Berakhot, 6:2, both Talmuds, Berakhot 6:2–6; Jerusalem Talmud, Berakhot 9:1. See Neis, "Eyeing Idols," 558, for a discussion of these blessings; and Rachel Neis, "Pilgrimage Itineraries: Seeing the Past Through Rabbinic Eyes," *Jewish Studies Quarterly* 20 (2013): 224–256, 229 and 230. These ideas are also reflected in Psalm 97:7.

39. Barber, "The Truth in Painting," 1036; Bianca Kühnel, "Jewish and Christian Art in the Middle Ages: The Dynamics of a Relationship," in *Juden und Christen zur Zeit der Kreuzzüge*, ed. Alfred Haverkamp (Sigmaringen: Jan Thorbecke, 1999), 1–16.

40. Ze'ev Weiss, "Decorating the Sacred Realm: Biblical Depictions in Synagogues and Churches of Ancient Palestine," in *Jewish Art in Its Late Antique Context*, ed. Uzi Leibner and Catherine Hezser (Tübingern: Mohr Siebeck, 2016), 121–138; Bianca Kühnel, "The Synagogue Floor Mosaic in Sepphoris: Between Paganism and Christianity," in *From Dura to Sepphoris: Studies in Jewish Art and Society in Late Antiquity*, ed. Lee I. Levine and Zeev Weiss (Portsmouth, RI: Journal of Roman Archaeology, 2000), 31–43.

41. Rina Talgam, "Constructing Identity through Art," in Robert Bonfil et al., *Jews in Byzantium*, 398–454, 410–411.

42. Steven Fine, "Iconoclasm and the Art of Late-Antique Palestinian Synagogues," in Levine and Weiss *From Dura to Sepphoris*, 183–193; Sacha Stern, "Pagan Images in Late Antique Palestinian Synagogues," in *Ethnicity and Culture in Late Antiquity*, ed. Stephen Mitchell and Geoffrey Greatrex (London: Duckworth and Classical Press of Wales, 2000), 241–252.

43. Steven Fine, "Iconoclasm: Who Defaced This Jewish Art?," *Bible Review* 16, no. 5 (2000), Center for Online Judaic Studies, accessed July 14, 2022, http:cojs.org/category/greco-roman-period/Judaism-under-christian-rome, for his references to the *miqdasheikhon*; see also Noa Yuval-Hacham "'You Shall Not Make for Yourself Any Graven Image . . .': On Jewish Iconoclasm in Late Antiquity," *Ars Judaica* 6 (2010): 7–22.

44. Fine, "Iconoclasm: Who Defaced This Jewish Art?,"

45. Oded Irshai, "Confronting a Christian Empire: Jewish Life and Culture in the World of Early Byzantium," in Bonfil et al., *Jews in Byzantium*, 17–64, 48.

46. Steven Fine, *Art and Judaism*, 117; Zvi M. Rabinowitz, ed., *The Liturgical Poetry of Rabbi Yannai* (Jerusalem: Bialik Institute, 1985–1987), 2:221–222; Hagith Sivan, "From Byzantine to Persian Jerusalem: Jewish Perspectives and Jewish/Christian Polemics," *Greek, Roman and Byzantine Studies* 41 (2000): 277–306.

47. Katrin Kogman-Appel, "The Tree of Death and the Tree of Life: The Hanging of Haman in Medieval Jewish Manuscript Painting," in *Between the Image and the Word: Essays in Honor of John Plummer*, ed. Colum Hourihane (University Park: Pennsylvania State University Press, 2005), 187–208, 199.

48. Thornton, "The Crucifixion of Haman and the Scandal of the Cross," 421, 425.

49. *Midrash Rabbah*, ed. H. Freedman and Maurice Simon, 13 vols. in 10 (London: Soncino Press, 1939), 9:110–112; Kogman-Appel, "The Tree of Death," 198–199, who argues that in illuminated manuscripts, Jews confidently equated Haman with Jesus.

50. Israel Lévi, "L'Apocalypse de Zorobabel et le roi de Perse Siroès," *Revue des Études Juives* 68 (1914): 126–160. Paul Speck, "The Apocalypse of Zerubbabel and Christian Icons," *Jewish Studies Quarterly* 4, no. 2 (1997): 183–190, argues against Déroche for a later seventh-century date for the tale.

51. Boustan, "Immolating Emperors" 231ff.

52. Lévi, "L'Apocalypse de Zorobabel," 158–159.

53. Wilken, *The Land Called Holy*, 210.

54. Lévi, "L'Apocalypse de Zorobabel," 139 (Hebrew) and 155 (French).

55. Jacob Katz, *Exclusiveness and Tolerance*, 28–30, 162, 212.

56. Daniel J. Lasker, "Jewish Knowledge of Christianity in the Twelfth and Thirteenth Centuries," in *Studies in Medieval Jewish Intellectual and Social History: Festschrift in Honor of Robert Chazan*, ed. David Engel, Lawrence H. Schiffmann, and Elliot R. Wolfson (Leiden: Brill, 2012), 97–109, 99.

57. It is further discussed in the Babylonian Talmud, Avodah Zarah 53a–b.

58. Ibid.; Magda Teter, *Sinners on Trial: Jews and Sacrilege After the Reformation* (Cambridge, MA: Harvard University Press, 2011), 55.

59. Katz, *Exclusiveness and Tolerance*, 32; Katz calls this "halakhic casuistry." See also David Novak, "The Status of Christianity in Medieval European Halakhah," in *Jewish-Christian Dialogue: A Jewish Justification* (New York: Oxford University Press, 1989), 42–56.

60. *Maimonides Mishneh Torah: Hilchot Avodat Kochavim V'Chukkoteihem The Law of the Worship of Stars and their Statutes,* a new translation with commentaries and notes by Rabbi Eliyahu Touger (New York: Moznaim Publishing, 1990), 162–164, Chapter 8 verse10.

61. Eliezer bar Nathan, *Sefer Ra'avan: Hu Sefer Even ha-Ezer* (Jerusalem: H. Vagshal, 1984), response nos. 288–289.

62. Shatzmiller, *Cultural Exchange*, 32. On the type of priestly vestments and the most ornate one used during mass, which clearly contributed to the dignity of the sacrament, see Christa C. Mayer-Thurman, *Raiment for the Lord's Service: A Thousand Years of Western Vestments* (Chicago: Art Institute of Chicago, 1975), 13.

63. Shatzmiller, *Cultural Exchange*, 32–33. On Isaac of Dampierre, see Ephraim E. Urbach, *The Tosaphists: Their History, Writings and Methods* [in Hebrew], 4th ed., enl. (Jerusalem: Bialik Institute, 1980), 1:226–260; and José Faur, "The Legal Thinking of Tosafot: An Historical Approach," *Dine Israel* 6 (1975): xliii–lxxii, esp. lxviii (English section).

64. Shatzmiller, *Cultural Exchange*, 27; and Louis Finkelstein, *Jewish Self-Government in the Middle Ages* (New York: Philipp Feldheim, 1964), 201.

65. Eliezer of Metz, *Sefer Yereim ha-Shalem: Issurim she-Ra la-Shamayim Vela-Beriot* (Jerusalem, 1973), 37a, 36a.

66. Eliezer ben Joel Halevi, *SeferRav'iah*, ed. Avigdor Aptowitzer (Jerusalem: Mekize Nirdamim, 1938), no. 1049; translation here from Vivian Mann, *Jewish Texts on the Visual Arts* (Cambridge: Cambridge University Press, 2000), 57.

67. Haim ben Isaac, *Sefer Teshuvot m. ha-R. H. Or Zaru'a* (Jerusalem: Avitan, 2002) in the section that discusses sermons (דרשות), art. 11, pp. 14–16.

68. Meir of Rothenburg, *Responsa Maharam II. Pesakim u-Minhagim*, ed. I. Z. Kahan (Jerusalem: Mosad HaRav Kook, 1960), nos. 123–125; translated in Mann, *Jewish Texts*, 42–46.

69. Mann, *Jewish Texts*, 56–57.

70. Haym Soloveitchik, "Pawnbroking: A Study in *Ribbit* and of the Halakah in Exile," *Proceedings of American Academy for Jewish Research* 38–39 (1970–1971): 203–268. Examples of Jews not abiding by rabbinic rulings include examples of Jews in Norwich, England, cooperating with Christians in the theft of church objects. Zefira Entin Rokéah, "The Jewish Church-Robbers and Host-Desecrators of Norwich (ca. 1285)," *Revue des Études Juives* 141 (1982): 331–362.

71. Ephraim Shoham-Steiner has even proved that some Jews made pilgrimages to Christian shrines, confirming the strong attraction of cults of healing saints in medieval European societies. Ephraim Shoham-Steiner, "Jews and Healing at Medieval Saints' Shrines: Participation, Polemics, and Shared Cultures," *Harvard Theological Review* 103, no. 1 (2010): 111–129.

72. Anna Sapir Abulafia, *Christians and Jews in the Twelfth-Century Renaissance* (London: Routledge, 1995), 70; Avraham Grossman, "Rashi's Commentary on the Psalms and the Jewish-Christian Disputation," in *Studies in Bible and Education Presented to Professor Moshe Ahrend*, ed. Dov Rappel (Jerusalem: Touro College, 1996), 59–74.

73. For references to Jesus as a "stinking corpse" or "rotting corpse," see Abraham Meir Habermann, ed., *Sefer Gezerot Ashkenaz Ve-Tsarfat: Divre Zikhronot Mi-Bene Ha-Dorot Shebi-Tekufat Mas'e Ha-Tselav U-Mivhar Piyutehem* (Jerusalem: Mosad HaRav Kook, 1945), 34, 43. Shoham-Steiner, "Jews and Healing at Medieval Saints' Shrines," 119, notes how frequently Jews in Ashkenaz referred to the dead Jesus so that they could contrast him to the "living, eternal Jewish God."

74. For the consistent use of the term *bet to'evah* in the polemical *Sefer Nizzahon Vetus*, see Berger, *The Jewish-Christian Debate*, 99, 175, 213. See the mid-eleventh-century Italian scroll of Ahimaaz who refers to the Hagia Sofia in Constantinople as the "house of impurity."

75. Hugh J. Schonfield, *According to the Hebrews* (London: Duckworth, 1937); G. W. Foote and J. M. Wheeler, ed. and trans., *The Jewish Life of Christ, Being the Sepher Toldoth Jeshu, or Book of the Generation of Jesus* (1885; repr., London: Pioneer Press, 1919), 30–32 (verses 43–49). This could also be an oblique allusion to Jesus cursing the barren fig tree in Matthew 21:18–20.

76. Katrin Kogman-Appel, "The Tree of Death and the Tree of Life," 196–197.

77. Ibid., 197.

78. On the biography of Herman von Scheda, see Schmitt, *The Conversion of Herman the Jew*, 115–145.

79. This English translation comes from ibid., 115.

80. There is no agreement regarding the actual number of Jews killed during the First Crusade when the communities of Cologne, Mainz, Metz, Mörs, Neuss, Regensburg, Speyer, Trier, Worms, and Xanten were attacked. The attacks on the Jews in the Second Crusade in 1147 were less severe, and the one chronicle we will be looking at here, that of Ephraim bar Jacob of Bonn, describes smaller attacks on Jews in Rameru, France, and Cologne and the surrounding fortresses in Mainz, Worms, Würzburg, and a place called Ham whose identity is unclear.

81. Yosef Hayim Yerushalmi, *Zakhor: Jewish History and Jewish Memory* (Seattle: University of Washington Press, 1982), 31.

82. All of these chronicles have been translated into English by Shlomo Eidelberg in *The Jews and the Crusaders: The Hebrew Chronicles of the First and Second Crusades* (Madison: University of Wisconsin Press, 1977). See also Eva Haverkamp, ed., *Hebräische Berichte über die Judenverfolgungen während des Ersten Kreuzzugs* (Hannover: Hahnsche Buchhandlung, 2005).

83. These chroniclers were Fulcher of Chartres, Robert the Monk, the anonymous author of the *Gesta Francorum*, Balderic of Dol, and Guibert of Nogent. For their versions of the speech, see "Medieval Sourcebook: Urban II (1088–1099): Speech at Council of Clermont, 1095," Fordham University, Internet History Sourcebooks Project, accessed July 14, 2022, https://sourcebooks.fordham.edu/source/urban2-5vers.html.

84. Ibid.

85. Rebecca Rist, *Popes and Jews, 1095–1291* (Oxford: Oxford University Press, 2015), 107.

86. Eidelberg, *The Jews and the Crusaders*, 21. *The Narrative of the Old Persecutions*, or the *Mainz Anonymous*, also mentions the emblem (Eidelberg, *The Jews and the Crusaders*, 99).

87. Eidelberg, *The Jews and the Crusaders*, 60 and 111 ("putrid corpse").

88. Cohen, *Christ Killers*, 144.

89. For example, the story of Rachel of Mainz and her four children appears in *The Chronicle of Solomon bar Simson*, in Eidelberg, *The Jews and the Crusaders*, 35; and also the *Mainz Anonymous* in Eidelberg, *The Jews and the Crusaders*, 111.

90. Robert Chazan, *European Jewry and the First Crusade* (Berkeley: University of California Press, 1987), 40–49; Ivan G. Marcus, "From Politics to Martyrdom: Paradigms in the Hebrew Narratives of the 1096 Crusade Riots," *Prooftexts* 2, no. 1 (January 1982): 40–52; and Jeremy Cohen, "*Gezerot Tatnu*: Martyrdom and Martyrology in the Hebrew Chronicles of 1096" [in Hebrew], *Zion* 59 (1994): 169–208.

91. Guibert of Nogent's version of Urban's speech, "Medieval Sourcebook: Urban II (1088–1099): Speech at Council of Clermont, 1095," https://sourcebooks.fordham.edu/source/urban2-5vers.html.

92. Ibid.

93. Avraham Grossman, "The Cultural and Social Background of Jewish Martyrdom in Germany in 1096," in *Juden und Christen zur Zeit der Kreuzzüge*, ed. Alfred Haverkamp, Konstanzer Arbeitkreis für mittelalterliche Geschichte, Vorträge und Forschungen 47 (Sigmaringen: Jan Thorbecke, 1999), 77–79; and Simha Goldin, "The Socialisation for *Kiddush ha-Shem* Among Medieval Jews," *Journal of Medieval History* 23, no. 2 (1997): 117–138.

94. On the Torah scroll being the most holy object in Jewish ritual, see Mishnah Megillah 3:1; and Joseph Karo, *Shulhan Aruch*, Orah Hayyim 154:6, with commentary by Moses Isserles. Van der Toorn, "The Iconic Book," 243–244.

95. Eidelberg, *The Jews and the Crusaders*, 41, 50, 85. The Hebrew chronicle from the Second Crusade mentions only once that a Torah scroll was destroyed (ibid., 130).

96. Eidelberg, *The Jews and the Crusaders*, 23 (for the *Chronicle of Solomon bar Simson* in Worms), 37 (in Mainz), 41 (for the Mainz synagogue destruction), 50 (for the Cologne synagogue destruction), 62 (Trier); 81 (for the *Chronicle of Rabbi Eliezer bar Nathan* in Worms), 85 (for Mainz); 112–113 (*Mainz Anonymous* for Mainz); 130 (*Sefer Zekhirah* for Rameru).

97. Ibid., 81

98. Ibid., 112–113.

99. Ibid., 62–63.

100. Horowitz, *Reckless Rites*, 165. Horowitz interprets this formulation as evidence that the Jews urinated on the cross or simply exposed themselves in vulgar hostility. Perhaps there were those who argued that Rabban Gamliel had actually sanctioned the act of urination in the Mishnah Avodah Zarah 3:4 by urinating on a statue of Aphrodite in a bathhouse, as a standardized method of showing insult and contempt for idols. See note 36 above.

101. Eidelberg, *The Jews and the Crusaders*, 50.

102. Ibid., 57–58.

103. Ibid., 65.

104. Ibid., 85.

105. Ibid., 125.

106. Ibid., 127.

107. Robert Chazan, "The Hebrew First-Crusade Chronicles," *Revue des Études Juives* 133 (1974): 235–254.

108. John W. Baldwin, *Masters, Princes, and Merchants: The Social Views of Peter the Chanter and His Circle* (Princeton, NJ: Princeton University Press, 1970), 1:153 and 328.

109. See Amnon Linder, "'The Jews Too Were Not Absent . . . Carrying Moses's Law on Their Shoulders': The Ritual Encounter of Pope and Jews from the Middle Ages to Modern Times," *Jewish Quarterly Review* 99, no. 3 (2009): 323–395, 353. Here he observes that such a ceremony was a type of exchange "essentially interpersonal, establishing an unmediated nexus between ruler and subjects."

110. Joseph ibn Kaspi, *Shulhan Kesef*, ed. Hanna Kasher (Jerusalem: Ben Zvi Institute, 1996), 58–59. I use the translation of Amnon Linder in "'The Jews Too Were Not Absent," 336; Linder argues how the analogy between the two symbols could cause moments of real tension (335–336).

111. Lasker, "Jewish Knowledge of Christianity," 101; Joseph Kimhi, *Sefer ha-Berit*, ed. Frank Talmage (Jerusalem: Bialik Institute, 1974); Joseph Kimhi, *The Book of the Covenant*, trans. Frank Talmage (Toronto: PIMS, 1972), 72; and Chazan, *Fashioning Jewish Identity*, 98.

112. The seven Noahide commandments were Hebrew Bible rulings that enabled non-Jews who observed them to be numbered among the "pious of the Gentile peoples" (Babylonian Talmud, Sanhedrin 59a).

113. Joseph Official, *Sefer Yosef HaMeqanne*, ed. Judah Rosenthal (Jerusalem: Mekize Nirdamim, 1970); subsequent references to *Sefer Yosef HaMeqanne* are to this edition. The *Sefer Nizzahon Vetus* also deals with a review of the New Testament. See Lasker, "Jewish Knowledge of Christianity," 103–106.

114. Berger, *The Jewish-Christian Debate*, 3; see also p. 68 (no. 41), where the anonymous author of *Sefer Nizzahon Vetus* argues through the mouth of Rabbi Kalonymus of Speyer that the Christians' cathedrals are ugly, filthy, and incomparable to the Temple of Solomon. The Christian king Henry, discussing this with the rabbinic scholar, then challenges him by asking in what way Solomon's Temple was greater than the cathedral. Kalonymus defiantly replies (after he has full permission to speak without facing consequences) by quoting Kings 8:11, that in the Temple, the glory of God was so formidable that the priests were unable to minister. In contrast to the overwhelmingly powerful presence of God in the Temple, Kalonymus declared: "if one were to load a donkey with vomit and filth and lead him through the church, he would remain unharmed."

115. *Sefer Yosef HaMeqanne*, 3–6; see also Harvey J. Hames, "Urinating on the Cross: Christianity as seen in the *Sefer Yoseph ha-Mekaneh* (ca. 1260) and in Light of Paris 1240," in *Ritus Infidelium: Miradas interconfesionales sobre las prácticas religiosas en la Edad Media*, ed.

José Martínez Gázquez and John Victor Tolan, Collection de la Casa de Velázquez 138 (Madrid: Casa Velazquez, 2013), 209–220, 210.

116. Why the bush is thorny is actually a question discussed in the Midrash; see *Midrash Rabbah*, ed. Freedman and Simon, 9:110–112.

117. *Sefer Yosef HaMeqanne*, 45, no. 24 (כד). I have used Christoph Cluse's translation here. Cluse, "Stories of Breaking and Taking the Cross," 405.

118. For example, in the illustrated *Bibles moralisées* of the late twelfth or early thirteenth century. See *Bible moralisée*, Codex Vindobonensis 2554, Vienna, Osterreichische Nationalbibliothek, fol. 17v, discussed by Sara Lipton in her *Images of Intolerance: The Representation of Jews and Judaism in the "Bible moralisée"* (Berkeley: University of California Press, 1999), 5. This idea is also expanded in the *Sefer Nizzahon Vetus*; see Berger, *The Jewish-Christian Debate*, 63 (no. 30).

119. Berger, *The Jewish-Christian Debate*, 63 (no. 30). The *Sefer Nizzahon Vetus*, discussed below, looks at this biblical text slightly differently connecting the angel not to Christ but to Joseph. See Berger, *The Jewish-Christian Debate*, 63 (no. 41).

120. Hames, "Urinating on the Cross," 209, who notes that the family of Rabbi Nathan was originally from Narbonne but had moved to the north where they seem to have been in the employ of the bishop of Sens.

121. *Sefer Yosef HaMeqanne*, 14. My translation is based on Ivan G. Marcus, "A Jewish-Christian Symbiosis: The Culture of Early Ashkenaz," in *Cultures of the Jews: A New History*, ed. David Biale (New York: Schocken Books, 2002), 449–516, 483.

122. Marcus, "A Jewish-Christian Symbiosis," 483. Marcus contends that Jews did in fact commit latrine blasphemy themselves, but I am not convinced that this is the suggestion behind the polemic here.

123. John Sewell, "The Son Rebelled and So the Father Made Man Alone: Ridicule and Boundary Maintenance in the *Nizzahon Vetus*," in *Laughter in the Middle Ages and Early Modern Times: Epistemology of a Fundamental Human Behavior, Its Meaning and Consequences*, ed. Albert Classen (Berlin: De Gruyter, 2010), 295–324, 296.

124. See Berger, *The Jewish-Christian Debate*, 59 (no. 27), where the crossing of Jacob's hands on the heads of his two grandsons is seen as a symbol of the cross (Gen. 48:14); see also p. 64 (no. 33), where the anonymous author rejects the notion that the sign the Israelites put on their doorpost to protect them from the Angel of Death was a cross; a third example, p. 65 (no. 36), which repeats the Jewish argument from *Sefer Yosef HaMeqanne* regarding whether the piece of wood the Israelites put in the water so that the water turned sweet in Exodus 15:23–25 was a cross; and the last two examples, at p. 72 (nos. 45 and 48), where the striking of the rock and the copper serpent used by Moses are seen by Christians as symbols of the cross.

125. Berger, *The Jewish-Christian Debate*, 59 (no. 26).

126. Another example of the Jews knowing full well how Christianity depicted them was the Bird's Head Haggadah of the early fourteenth century, where human faces have been replaced with animal heads that reflect antisemitic iconography in Christian illuminated manuscripts. See Marc Michael Epstein, *The Medieval Haggadah: Art, Narrative, and Religious Imagination* (New Haven, CT: Yale University Press, 2011), 45–63.

127. In its discussion of Christian practices and doctrine, the *Sefer Nizzahon Hayeshun* turns not only to a short discussion of Christian idols but also to the Christian accusation of ritual murder and the blood libel. Berger, *The Jewish-Christian Debate*, 229 (no. 244). Image desecration accusations were clearly not threatening enough to demand more specific attention in these handbooks.

128. Berger, *The Jewish-Christian Debate*, 202 (no. 202).

129. Ibid., 229 (no. 244).

130. See Chapter 2; Grossman, *The Early Sages of Ashkenaz*, 6–8; Irving Agus, "Democracy in the Communities of the Early Middle Ages," *Jewish Quarterly Review*, n.s., 43 (1952–1953): 153–176, 167; David Malkiel, *Reconstructing Ashkenaz: The Human Face of Franco-German Jewry, 1000–1250* (Stanford, CA: Stanford University Press, 2008), 52; and Lipton, *Dark Mirror*, 41.

131. On this sect, see Peter Schäfer, "Jews and Christians in the High Middle Ages: The *Book of the Pious*," in *The Jews of Europe in the Middle Ages (Tenth to Fifteenth Centuries): Proceedings of the International Symposium Held at Speyer, 20–25 October 2002*, ed. Christoph Cluse (Turnhout: Brepols, 2004), 29; and Ivan G. Marcus, *Piety and Society: The Jewish Pietists of Medieval Germany* (Leiden: Brill, 1981).

132. *Sefer Chasidim*, ed. Reuven Margaliot (Jerusalem: Mosad HaRav Kook, 1957); the English translation is taken from *Sefer Chasidim: The Book of the Pious by Rabbi Yehudah HeChasid*, trans. Avraham Yaakov Finkel (Northvale, NJ: Aronson, 1997).

133. Katz, *Exclusiveness and Tolerance*, 99, 101; Katz confirms that Rabbi Moses of Coucy in his *Sefer Miswoth Gadol*, wrote similarly on this matter (102).

134. Finkel, *Sefer Chasidim: The Book of the Pious*, docs. 432, 660. A tale reports how a Jew who never went into a church was rewarded after his death by his hearse avoiding the road where a crucifix was located.

135. Jews were forbidden to wear crosses if they were attempting to disguise themselves in front of Christians. Schäfer, "Jews and Christians in the High Middle Ages," 34.

136. Finekl, *Sefer Chasidim: The Book of the Pious*, doc. 431.

137. Ibid., docs. 1353 and 1364. Jews could not put their books on a windowsill that looked out onto a church. If a Jew had a door that faced a church and it was so low that he had to bow his head when going through the door, he had to turn his head or exit backward in order not to arouse suspicion of idolatry. Ibid., see doc 1354.

138. Eli Yassif, *The Hebrew Folktale: History, Genre, Meaning*, trans. Jacqueline S. Teitelbaum (Bloomington: Indiana University Press, 1999), 284.

139. Marcus, "A Jewish-Christian Symbiosis," 483–484.

140. Paola Tartakoff, "Martyrdom, Conversion, and Shared Cultural Repertoires in Late Medieval Europe," *Jewish Quarterly Review* 109 (Fall 2019): 500–533, 529; Tartakoff, *Conversion, Circumcision, and Ritual Murder*, 13 and 77.

141. Siegmund Salfeld, *Das Martyrologium des Nürnberger Memorbuches* (Berlin: Simion, 1898), 22. Translation of the text is adapted from Simha Goldin, *Apostasy and Jewish Identity in High Middle Ages Northern Europe: "Are You Still My Brother?"* trans. Jonathan Chipman (Manchester: Manchester University Press, 2014), 107.

142. Tartakoff, *Conversion, Circumcision, and Ritual Murder*, 77.

143. Israel Davidson, *Thesaurus of Medieval Hebrew Poetry* [in Hebrew], 4 vols. (New York: Ktav, 1970), 3:69 (no. 604); and Goldin, *Apostasy and Jewish Identity*, 107.

144. Davidson, *Thesaurus of Medieval Hebrew Poetry*, 3:69 (no. 604).

145. Tartakoff, "Martyrdom, Conversion, and Shared Cultural Repertoires," 501.

146. The Hebrew text has been dated as 992 by Robert Chazan, "The Persecution of 992," *Revue des Études Juives* 129 (1970): 217–221; and Israel Lévi, "Le Juif de la légende," *Revue des Études Juives* 22 (1891): 233–235. See also Malkiel, *Reconstructing Ashkenaz*, 57. Recently Katelyn Mesler has been preparing a new edition and translation as a prelude to an eventual reassessment of the text's dating and context. Quotations here are taken, by permission, from

the draft of her translation, dated September 26, 2019. I thank her for sharing this with me before publication. The Parma document is Parma, Biblioteca Palatina, Parm. 2342, fols. 286r–782v. Kati Ihnat and Katelyn Mesler, "From Christian Devotion to Jewish Sorcery: The Curious History of Wax Figurines in Medieval Europe," in *Entangled Histories: Knowledge, Authority, and Jewish Culture in the Thirteenth Century*, ed. Elisheva Baumgarten, Ruth Mazo Karras, and Katelyn Mesler (Philadelphia: University of Pennsylvania Press, 2017), 134–159. All subsequent quotations are from Mesler's draft.

147. Jean-Marie Sansterre, "L'image blessée, l'image souffrante: Quelques récits de miracles entre Orient et Occident (VIe–XIIe siècle)," *Bulletin de l'Institut historique Belge de Rome* 69 (1999): 113–130, 123–124.

148. There is some contemplation in Jewish illuminated manuscripts regarding the golden calf and how the Jews should understand this biblical episode. For this, see Sarit Shalev-Eyni, *Jews Among Christians: Hebrew Book Illumination from Lake Constance* (Turnhout: Harvey Miller, 2010), 76–77.

149. The Haggadah is the Jewish text that sets forth the order of the Passover Seder.

150. This was connected to the understanding of the text and the *Midrash Shmot Rabbah* (chap. 14), which describes the Israelites entering the homes of the Egyptians and seeing there vessels made of gold and silver.

151. Shatzmiller, *Cultural Exchange*, 40.

152. Julie Harris, "Polemical Images in the Golden Haggadah (British Library, Add. MS 27210)," *Medieval Encounters* 8 (2002): 105–122, 111 and 113; and Michael Batterman, "Bread of Affliction, Emblem of Power: The Passover Matzah in Haggadah Manuscripts from Christian Spain," in *Imagining the Self, Imagining the Other: Visual Representation and Jewish-Christian Dynamics in the Middle Ages and Early Modern Period*, ed. Eva Frojmovic (Leiden: Brill, 2002), 53–89.

153. Harris, "Polemical Images in the Golden Haggadah," 118.

154. Katrin Kogman-Appel, "Coping with Christian Pictorial Sources: What Did Jewish Miniaturists Not Paint?," *Speculum* 75 (2000): 816–858, 836, 840, 858.

155. Ibid, 840.

156. Ibid., 849.

157. Kogman-Appel, "The Tree of Death and the Tree of Life," 187–208. Kogman-Appel suggests that the Jewish images of the hanging of Haman from a Tree of Life or Tree of Jesse in thirteenth- and fourteenth-century southern German *mahzorim* crafted their own "anti-Christian cultural polemic," although this was directed at Christ's death rather than the crucifix itself.

158. Shalev-Eyni, *Jews Among Christians*, 16–17.

159. Ibid., 51. For later examples of this collaboration, see Shalom Sabar, "Messianic Aspirations and Renaissance Urban Ideals: The Image of Jerusalem in the Venice Haggadah, 1609," *Jewish Art* 23 (1998): 294–312. Even the *aron kodesh* in the Levantine synagogue in Venice was inspired by a Christian altarpiece. Shalom Sabar, "'The Right Path for an Artist': The Approach of Leone da Modena to Visual Art," in *Hebraica Hereditas: Studi in onore di Cesare Colofemmina*, ed. Giancarlo Lacerenza (Naples: Instituto Univesitario orientale, Seminario di studiasiatici, 2005), 1–36, 3.

160. Yassif, *The Hebrew Folktale*, 265, 298.

161. Solomon Ibn Verga, *Shevet Yehudah*, ed. Azriel Shochat and Yitzhak Baer (Jerusalem: Bialik Institute, 1947).

162. Jeremy Cohen, *A Historian in Exile: Solomon ibn Verga, "Shevet Yehudah," and the Jewish-Christian Encounter* (Philadelphia: University of Pennsylvania Press, 2017), 2.

163. Ibid., 2, 132–133.

164. Jeremy Cohen, "From Solomon bar Samson to Solomon Ibn Verga: Tales and Ideas of Jewish Martyrdom in *Shevet Yehudah*," in Engel, Schiffman, and Wolfson, *Studies in Medieval Jewish Intellectual and Social History*, 279–297, 297; Teter, *Blood Libel*, 226.

165. For a full analysis of the tales, see Jeremy Cohen, "The Blood Libel in Solomon ibn Verga's *Shevet Yehudah*," in *Jewish Blood: Reality and Metaphor in History, Religion, and Culture*, ed. Mitchell B. Hart (London: Routledge, 2009), 116–135, 116.

166. On the enigmatic aspect of Ibn Verga's work, see Joseph Dan, "*Shevet Yehuda*: Past and Future History," in *Jewish Mysticism*, vol. 4, *General Characteristics and Comparative Studies* (Northvale, NJ: Jason Aronson, 1999), 25–56, 27.

167. Ibid., 31; Cohen, "The Blood Libel," 116.

168. Dan, "*Shevet Yehuda*," 55.

169. Ibn Verga, *Shevet Yehudah*, 60–61.

170. Ibid.

171. Ibid.

172. Ibn Verga, *Shevet Yehudah*, 66–67.

173. Umberto Cassuto, "Un ignoto capitolo di storia ebraica," in *Judaica: Festschrift zu Hermann Cohens siebzigstem Geburtstage*, ed. Ismar Elbogen, Benzion Kellermann, and Eugen Mittwoch (Berlin: B. Cassirer 1912), 389–404, 398.

174. Ibid.

175. In Samuel Usque's major work the *Consolaçãoás Tribulações de Israel*, which was published in Ferrara, 1553, he makes no mention of image desecration being an act Jews performed or were accused of in Trani or Naples. *Samuel Usque's Consolation for the Tribulations of Israel (Consolaçam as tribulaçoens de Israel)*, trans. Martin A. Cohen (Philadelphia: Jewish Publication Society of America, 1965), 178–180.

176. Note that Yerushalmi, *The Lisbon Massacre of 1506*, 62, argues that Ibn Verga preferred not to address the topic of forced conversion even in his description of the Lisbon massacre.

177. Ibn Verga, *Shevet Yehudah*, 151–152.

178. Ibid.

179. Ibid.

180. Adémar de Chabannes, *Chronique*, 52, 175. See Daniel F. Callahan, "Ademar of Chabannes, Millennial Fears and the Development of Western Anti-Judaism," *Journal of Ecclesiastical History* 46, no. 1 (1995): 19–35; Daniel F. Callahan, "The Cross, the Jews and the Destruction of the Church of the Holy Sepulcher in the Writings of Ademar of Chabannes," in Frasseto, *Christian Attitudes*, 15–59, 15; and Frasseto, "Heretics and Jews in the Early Eleventh Century," in *Christian Attitudes*, 51.

181. Frasseto, "Heretics and Jews in the Early Eleventh Century," 51; see Chapter 2 above.

182. Yerushalmi, *The Lisbon Massacre of 1506*, 1.

183. Ibid., 1–2.

184. Ibid., 2.

185. On Capsali, see Martin Jacobs, *Islamische Geschichte in jüdischen Chroniken: Hebräische Historiographie des 16. und 17. Jahrhunderts* (Tübingen: Mohr Siebeck, 2004); and

Aleida Paudice, *Between Several Worlds: The Life and Writings of Elia Capsali; The Historical Works of a 16th-Century Cretan Rabbi* (Munich: Peter Lang, 2010).

186. Eliyahu Capsali, *Seder Eliyahu Zuta*, ed. Aryeh Shmuelevitz, Shlomo Simonsohn, and Meir Benayahu, vol. 2 (Jerusalem: Ben-Zvi Institute, 1977), 230–232.

187. Ibid., 230.

188. This word could also be translated as "prince/aristocrat."

189. This biblical reference was not cited in Shmuelevitz, Simonsohn, and Benayahu's edition of *Seder Eliyahu Zuta*.

190. Here there is a slight emendation—the biblical verse is plural, here singular.

191. Even though the Hebrew word here is for "monk," a monk is someone who normally lives in a cloister and devotes much of his time to reciting the office in choir (e.g., a Benedictine, Cistercian, Carthusian), whereas a friar is a missionary and a preacher, active in the community, a Franciscan, Dominican, Augustinian, or Carmelite.

192. *Seder Eliyahu Zuta*, 232.

193. This biblical reference was not cited in Shmuelevitz, Simonsohn, and Benayahu's *Seder Eliyahu Zuta*.

194. The Candia decrees, "Takkanot Kandiyah," in Elias S. Artom and Humbertus [Umberto] M. D. Cassuto, eds., *Statuta Iudaeorum Candiae eorumque memorabilia*, vol. 1 (Jerusalem: Mekize Nirdamim, 1943), 71, mention Eliezer Cohen Tiroshlin, son of Avraham, one of the signatories of the decree of 1489. The tale is not mentioned in Capsali's *Takkanot Kandiyah* (Candia Decrees), which record the communal legislation and legal history of the Cretan community from 1228 to 1363. On the *Takkanot*, see Martin Borýsek, "The Jews of Venetian Candia: The Challenges of External Influences and Internal Diversity as Reflected in *Takkanot Kandiyah*," in *Al-Masāq: Journal of the Medieval Mediterranean* 26, no. 3 (2014): 241–266.

195. Elkanah son of Abba Delmegiddo was *condo-shtebalo* (chief representative) of the Jews of Candia in 1435. Arton and Cassuto, *Takkanot Kandiyah*, vol. 1, 57ff.

196. This biblical reference was not cited in Shmuelevitz, Simonsohn, and Benayahu's *Seder Eliyahu Zuta*.

197. Robert Bonfil, "Jewish Attitudes Toward History and Historical Writing in Pre-Modern Times," *Jewish History* 11, no. 1 (1997): 7–40, 24–25.

198. Another example of Capsali's imagination is the invention of the story of Abarbanel who, with Abraham Seneor and other "sages of Israel," went to the king in order to annul the decree of the expulsion of the Jews; see Norman Roth, *Conversos, Inquisition, and the Expulsion of the Jews from Spain* (Madison: University of Wisconsin Press, 1995), 298. Nor do the scholars Aryeh Shmuelevitz, Shlomo Simonsohn, and Meir Benayahu, in their scientific edition of *Seder Eliyahu Zuta*, refer to any actual event of expulsion of the Jews connected to this tale.

199. See Admiel Kosman, *Women's Tractate: Wisdom, Love, Faithfulness, Passion, Beauty, Sex, Holiness* [in Hebrew] (Jerusalem: Keter, 2007), 190–199, where the same trick is used by a tailor.

200. The tale is obviously not mentioned in Capsali's *Takkanot Kandiyah*, which only records the communal legislation and legal history of the Cretan community from 1228 to 1363.

201. Yerushalmi, *From Spanish Court to Italian Ghetto*, 454–455. For the original, see *Las excelencias de los Hebreos: Por el Doctor Yshac Cardoso; Impresso en Amsterdam en casa de David de Castro Tartas, El Año de 1679*, Rosetta Digital Object, National Library of Israel,

accessed April 20, 2018, http://rosetta.nli.org.il/delivery/DeliveryManagerServlet?dps_pid=IE48164038.

Rosetta Digital Object, National Library of Israel, accessed April 20, 2018, http://rosetta.nli.org.il/delivery/DeliveryManagerServlet?dps_pid=IE48164038

202. The other nine were false adorations, the Jews' bad smell, their color and blood, their praying three times a day, their persuading people to Judaize, their infidelity to princes, their impiety and cruelty, their corruption of sacred books, and killing Christian children to use their blood for their rites. Yerushalmi, *From Spanish Court to Italian Ghetto*, 399–408.

203. Ibid., 402.

204. Within this section, Jews are also accused of debasing the sacraments, particularly the Eucharist.

205. Cardoso described in detail only one episode of image desecration, known as the *Cristo de la Paciencia*, which took place while he was still in Spain in 1630 and is discussed in Chapter 3.

206. Maria Diemling, "Navigating Christian Space: Jewish Responses to Christian Imagery in Early Modern German Lands," in *Visualizing Jews Through the Ages*, ed. Hannah Ewence and Helen Spurling (London: Routledge, 2015), 181–198; Shalev-Eyni, *Jews Among Christians* 16–17.

207. Diemling, "Navigating Christian Space," 187.

208. On the role of Mary in Jewish thought, see Ephraim Shoham-Steiner, "The Virgin Mary, Miriam, and Jewish Reactions to Marian Devotion in the High Middle Ages," *AJS Review* 37, no. 1 (2013): 75–91.

CHAPTER 5

Epigraph: Biblioteca dell'Archiginnasio di Bologna, B-1892, "Editto del Sant' Ufficio in ordine a gli Hebrei, Noi Fr. Giacinto Maria Granara dà Genova dell Ord. de Predicatorì Maestro in Sacra Teologia, e nelle Città di Ferrara, e Comacchio, Terre, e Luoghi annessi & contro l'heretica pravità Generale Inquisitore dalla Santa Sede Apostolica specialmente Delegato." This edict is also mentioned in a document in the central archives of the Holy Office in Rome, the Archivio della Congregazione per la Dottrina della Fede (hereafter ACDF), Sant Officio, Stanza Storica, AA la, sulla copertina, "Si manda per manus dell SS VV Ill. Me l'inclusa scrittura concernenti le ragioni del S. Officio in conoscere le cause delle percussioni dell'imagini sacre, essendo già stata riverduta dagl'altri signori consultori. Per manus dell'ill. Mi monsignori Emerix e Pallavicino, che è supplicate rimandarla al S. Officio" (Attached notes concerning the rights of the Holy Office to prosecute cases, regarding the desecration of sacred images; which has already been reviewed by the other consultants), 375. This document will be referred to in footnotes from now on as ACDF, "Si manda per manus."

1. Thirteen of these cases were recorded in the late seventeenth-century Roman Inquisition *memoria* involving Jews across northern Italy from 1567 to 1693 (ACDF, "Si manda per manus"). The *memoria* was put together by Cardinal Jacob Emerix de Matthijs (1626–1696), the "administrator" of the German national church of Santa Maria dell' Anima, and Cardinal Pietro Sforza Pallavicino (1607–1667), who had become a member of the Sacred Congregation of the Inquisition in 1661. See Irene Fosi, *Convertire lo straniero* (Rome: Viella, 2011), 199 and 205 n. 59; and Joseph Schmidlin, *Geschichte der Deutschen Nationalkirche in Rom S. Maria dell'Anima* (Freiburg im Breisgau: Herder, 1906), 479, 483, 502; Friedrich Noack, *Das*

Deutschtum in Rom seit dem Ausgang des Mittelalters, vol. 1 (Stuttgart: Deutsche Verlags-Anstalt, 1927). Emerix de Matthijs served on the Sacred Rota (as, it seems, did other members of his family). He was the author of *Tractatus seu Notitia S. Rotae Romanae*, and he was appointed to a congregation of legal representatives in 1692 to reform or suppress many lesser courts. It seems that this *memoria* was designed to lay the foundation for an archival file in which would be collected all correspondence with peripheral branches of the Inquisition concerning Jews charged with these offenses. But this intention was not realized. There were many cases against Jews not listed here, and its information was not updated or corrected. Such inconsistencies reveal not only the limited reliability of the *memoria* but that the inquisitorial headquarters had insufficient manpower to update its own records. In 2012, Michele Luzzati identified twenty-six additional cases not included in the *memoria*. See Luzzati, "Sulle tentazioni iconoclaste ebraiche," 227–234. To these I have added a further thirty-two cases, of which twenty-three have been drawn from my own research on the well-ordered archives of the Roman Inquisition in the duchy of Modena and nine from a variety of other sources.

2. Schmitt, "De Nicée II," 91–92.

3. Holmes, *The Miraculous Image*, 80.

4. Ibid., 63–127; and Lipton, "Images and Their Uses," 277.

5. Corry, Faini, and Meneghin, *Domestic Devotions in Early Modern Italy*, 12–13.

6. See Jacob Burckhardt, *The Civilization of the Renaissance in Italy* (London: Penguin Classics, 1990), 299.

7. See Edward Muir, "The Virgin on the Street Corner: The Place of the Sacred in Italian Cities," in *Religion and Culture in the Renaissance and Reformation*, ed. Steven Ozment (Kirksville, MO: Sixteenth Century Journal Publishers, 1989), 25–40, 28.

8. On domestic furniture, see Maria Vittoria D'Addario, "La casa," in *Vita privata a Firenze nei secoli XIV e XV* (Florence: Leo Olschki, 1966), 53–73.

9. See Sabrina Corbellini, "Creating Domestic Sacred Space: Religious Reading in Late Medieval and Early Modern Italy," in Corry, Faini, and Meneghin, *Domestic Devotions in Early Modern Italy*, 295–309. In the same volume, see Jane Garnett and Gervase Rosser, "The Ex Voto Between Domestic and Public Space: From Personal Testimony to Collective Memory," 45–62.

10. Maya Corry, Deborah Howard, and Mary Laven, eds., *Madonnas and Miracles: The Holy Home in Renaissance Italy* (London: Philip Wilson, in association with the Fitzwilliam Museum, 2017), 3, 10.

11. Ibid., 157.

12. Ibid., 160.

13. Ibid., 41; here one sees how a seventeenth-century tower-shape Jewish spice box used for the *Havdalah* ceremony actually resembles a Catholic reliquary, showing that Jews and Christians shared similar styles of articles.

14. It is interesting that Jewish *mezuzot* are not discussed in *processi*. It seems that these objects posted on the doorposts of Jewish houses did not in general cause distress or anxiety for the Jews or their Christian landlords.

15. Rivkah bat Meir [Tiktiner], *The Meneket Rivkah: A Manual of Wisdom and Piety for Jewish Women*, ed. Frauke von Rohden, *Meneket Rivkah*, trans. Samuel Spinner, introd. and commentary trans. Maurice Tszorf (Philadelphia: Jewish Publication Society, 2009), 107; and Debra Kaplan, "Living Spaces, Communal Places: Early Modern Jewish Homes and Religious Devotions," in Faini and Meneghin, *Domestic Devotions in the Early Modern World*, 315–333, 316–318.

16. Roger Chartier, ed., *The Culture of Print: Power and the Uses of Print in Early Modern Europe*, trans. Lydia G. Cochrane (Princeton, NJ: Princeton University Press, 1987), 1–6.

17. David S. Areford, *The Viewer and the Printed Image in Late Medieval Europe* (London: Routledge, 2010); Jan Nicolaisen, "Einige Beobachtungen zur 'Privatisierung' des gedruckten Bildes im 15. Jahrhundert: Publikum und Gebrauch des Kupferstichs," in *Spiegel der Seligkeit: Privates Bild und Frömmigkeit im Spätmittelalter*, ed. Frank Matthias Kammel (Nuremberg: Verlag des Germanischen Nationalmuseums, 2000), 84–96.

18. Patron saints increasingly took more substantial roles as subjects in printed images from the fifteenth century. These prints might depict patron saints of cities, professions, or brotherhoods. These images were intended to protect their venerators from all sorts of ailments, from a toothache to sudden death. See Nicolaisen, "Einige Beobachtungen zur 'Privatisierung,'" 85–86.

19. Jane K. Wickersham, *Rituals of Prosecution: The Roman Inquisition and the Prosecution of Philo-Protestants in Sixteenth-Century Italy* (Toronto: University of Toronto Press, 2012), 26 and 50, uses the term "Philo-Protestants" to define the various individuals labeled as "Lutheran" by the Papal Inquisition.

20. Holmes, *The Miraculous Image*, 9.

21. Giordano da Rivalto, *Prediche del beato Giordano da Rivalto dell'ordine dei Predicatori recitate in Firenze dal MCCCIII al MCCCVI*, ed. Domenico Moreni (Florence: Magheri, 1831), 2:231–232 (no. 61); and Cohen, *The Friars and the Jews*, 240.

22. The translation comes from Rubin, *Gentile Tales*, 141.

23. Francisco Javier Rojo Alique, "Fifteenth-Century Franciscan Preachers in Castile," in Johnson, *Franciscans and Preaching*, 353–379.

24. Holmes, *The Miraculous Image*, 50.

25. Ibid., 38–39. Jacobo de Voragine confirms circa 1250 that the miracle was the origin of the November 9 liturgical memorial of the "Passion of the Lord," which is why "a church was consecrated in Rome in honor of the Savior, and there a phial of that blood is preserved and a solemn feast observed" (*The Golden Legend: Readings on the Saints* vol. 2, 171); see also Bacci, "'Quel bello miracolo,'" 66 (doc. 26). William Durand the Elder, bishop of Mende, reported on the Beirut origin of the ampullae in the Roman basilica in his *Rationale divinorum officiorum* (1286). See Bacci, "'Quel bello miracolo,'" 64 (doc. 28). On Pisa, see Giuseppe Scalia, "La consecrazione della cattedrale pisana 26 Settembre 1118," *Bollettino Storico Pisana* 61 (1992): 1–31, 12.

26. Bacci, "'Quel bello miracolo,'" 9.

27. Caroline Walker Bynum, "The Blood of Christ in the Later Middle Ages," *Church History* 71, no. 1 (2002): 685–714, 698–699.

28. Ibid., 694, 698–699.

29. Bacci, "The Berardenga Antependium," 4; Barbara Baert, "The Retable of the Master of Tressa (Siena, 1215): Iconography and Function," *Pantheon* 57 (1999):14–21; and Raffaele Argenziano, *Agliinizi dell'iconografia sacra a Siena* (Florence: Sismel-Edizioni del Galluzzo, 2000), 147–170.

30. In Italy, the Invention of the *inventio crucis* had its feast day on May 5; and the Exaltation of the Cross, on September 14. During the fourteenth and fifteenth centuries, the theme of the *inventio crucis* was also depicted in wall paintings in the Franciscan churches in Florence (Agnolo Gaddi, Santa Croce, from 1388 to 1393), Volterra (Cenni di Francesco di Ser, San Francesco, 1410), Empoli (Masolino da Panicale, Santo Stefano, 1424), and Arezzo (Piero della Francesca, San Francesco, before 1466).

31. Baert, "The Retable." Sara Lipton, "Images and Their Uses," 259, sees these types of images and tales becoming increasingly common on retables.

32. Federico Zeri, *La collezione Federico Mason Perkins (Sala Alitalia, Museo-Tesoro della Basilica di S. Francesco)* (Assisi: Casa Editrice Francescana Assisi, 1988), 134–136.

33. Giuseppe Palumbo, *Collezione Federico Mason Perkins: Sacro Convento di S. Francesco, Assisi* (Rome: Tip. Staderini, 1973).

34. Jacobus de Voragine. *The Golden Legend: Readings on the Saints,* vol. 2, 171.

35. Zeri, *La collezione Federico Mason Perkins*, 135–136. See "Fondazione Federico Zeri," Università di Bologna, accessed July 16, 2020, http://catalogo.fondazionezeri.unibo.it/entry/work/30789/Anonimo%20bolognese%20sec.%20XVI%2C%20Gli%20ebrei%20oltraggiano%20il%20Crocifisso.

36. Tamar Herzig, *A Convert's Tale: Art, Crime, and Jewish Apostasy in Renaissance Italy* (Cambridge, MA: Harvard University Press, 2019), 101–102.

37. Laura M. Giles, "Picturing Absence: The Jewish Presence in Giacomo Cavedone's *Discovery of the Miraculous Crucifix of Beirut*," lecture delivered at the Renaissance Quarterly Conference, Berlin, 2015.

38. Stephen Campbell, "The Conflicted Representation of Judaism in Italian Renaissance Images," in *The Passion Story: From Visual Representation to Social Drama*, ed. Marcia Kupfer (University Park: Pennsylvania State University Press, 2008), 67–90, 86.

39. Giles, "Picturing Absence,"

40. Corry, Howard, and Laven, *Madonnas and Miracles*, 140.

41. Franco Mormando, *The Preacher's Demons: Bernardino of Siena and the Social Underworld of Early Renaissance Italy* (Chicago: University of Chicago Press, 1999), 176–177.

42. Richard C. Trexler, "Being and Non-Being: Parameters of the Miraculous in the Traditional Religious Image," in *The Miraculous Image in the Late Middle Ages and Renaissance*, ed. Erik Thunø and Gerhard Wolf (Rome: "L'Erma" di Bretschneider, 2004), 15–27, 15.

43. Holmes, *The Miraculous Image*, 23.

44. Cencius Camerarius, *Le liber censuum de l'église romaine*, ed. Paul Fabre and Louis Duchesne (Paris, 1905), vol. 1:290–316; and 2:123–135, where the ceremony is discussed by Albino in 1189: "Ubi vero [papa] ventum fuerit ante basilicam sancti Silvestri super cuius arcum qui sustentatur duabus columpnis porfireticis est ymago Salvatoris que a quodam iudeo percussa in fronte emanavit sanguinem, sicut hodie cernitur, ad quam iudices electrum ducunt."

45. Adriano Prosperi, "Incontri rituali: Il papa e gli ebrei," *Storia d'Italia* 11 (1996): 495–520, 497–498.

46. Ferdinando Ongania, *Documenti per la storia dell'augusta ducale basilica di San Marco in Venezia* (Venice, 1886) docs. 87 and 822; Michele Bacci, *Il pennello dell'Evangelista: Storia delle imagini sacre attribuite a san Luca* (Pisa: GISEM, 1998), 316–317.

47. Holmes, *The Miraculous Image*, 116.

48. Giuseppe Capriotti, "L'infamante accusa di deicidio. Propaganda antiebraica nella pittura italiana del Quattrocento: Zanino di Pietro, Giovanni Boccati, Luca di Paolo e Carlo Crivelli," in *Antigiudaismo, Antisemitismo, Memoria: Un approccio pluridisciplinare*, ed. Giuseppe Capriotti (Macareta: EUM, 2009), 51–97, 53; and Bonaventura Theuli, *Teatro Historico di Velletri,* (Bologna: Alfonso dell' Isola, 1644), 306.

49. Holmes, *The Miraculous Image*, 70–72.

50. Ibid.

51. Pereda, "La conversión por la imagen," 228.

52. Umberto Cassuto, *Gli Ebrei a Firenze nell'età del Rinascimento* (Florence: Tipografia Gallettie cocci, 1918), 64–65.

53. Tribaldo de Rossi reported in Gene A. Brucker, *Firenze nel Rinascimento* (Florence: La Nuova Italia, 1980), 387; and see Cassuto, *Gli Ebrei a Firenze*, 64–65; and Dana Katz's discussion of this offense in *The Jew in the Art*, 107–117, and particularly the Otto at pp. 112–113.

54. Katz, *The Jew in the Art*, 109.

55. Holmes, *The Miraculous Image*, 73–74.

56. Ibid. The statue was relocated to the interior of Orsanmichele in the seventeenth century where it remained until 1925, when it was reinstalled in the exterior niche.

57. Ibid., 189. Diane Zervas's two-volume monograph on Orsanmichele, *Orsanmichele a Firenze / Orsanmichele Florence* (with Italian and English text) (Modena: Franco Cosimo Panini, 1996), 1:460, notes: "The fact that there are no visible traces of his knifed attack, reputed to have scratched the Virgin's face and Christ's eye (Rossi 1786), is disquieting, unless the work was completely polychromed, which is by no means impossible."

58. Petrus de Ancharano, *Consilia sive iuris responsa* (Venice: Apud Nicolaum Bevilaquam, 1568), consilium 15, fols. 8–9.

59. Katz, *The Jew in the Art*, 107.

60. David S. Chambers and Trevor Dean, eds., *Clean Hands and Rough Justice: An Investigating Magistrate in Renaissance Italy* (Ann Arbor: University of Michigan Press, 1981), 14.

61. Michele Luzzati, "Ebrei, chiesa locale, 'principe' e popolo: Due episodi di distruzione di immagini sacre alla fine del Quattrocento," in *La casa dell'ebreo* (Pisa: Nistri-Lischi, 1985), 208; Luzzati, "Sulle tentazioni iconoclaste ebraiche," 228; Ariel Toaff, *Il vino e la carne. Una comunità ebraica nel Medievo* (Bologna: Il Mulino, 1989), 156–158.

62. Katz, *The Jew in the Art*, 117.

63. Shlomo Simonsohn, ed., *The Jews in the Duchy of Milan*, 4 vols. (Jerusalem: Israel Academy of Sciences and Humanities, 1982–1986), 1:513, doc. 1212, January 25–27, 1470 (Archivio di Stato di Milan, Carteggio Sforzesco 892).

64. Ibid., 1:552–554 (docs. 1315, 1317, 1318).

65. Herzig, *A Convert's Tale.*

66. Luzzati, "Sulle tentazioni iconoclaste ebraiche," 228; Ariel Toaff, *The Jews in Umbria*, vol. 1, *1245–1435* (Leiden: Brill, 1993), 76–77 (doc. 104); Archivio Vaticano Camera Apostolica, Registri del Ducator di Spolato, Entrate e Uscite 22, fol. 133b.

67. Toaff, *Il vino e la carne*, 176; Luzzati, "Sulle tentazioni iconoclaste ebraiche," 227; Renata Segre, ed., *The Jews of Piedmont*, 3 vols. (Jerusalem: Israel Academy of Sciences and Humanities, 1986–1990), 1:171; and Ariel Toaff, *Pasque di Sangue: Ebrei d'Europa e omicidi rituali*, 2nd ed. (Bologna: Il Mulino, 2007), 139 and 292.

68. See Chapter 3.

69. Luzzati, "Sulle tentazioni iconoclaste ebraiche," 227; Segre, *The Jews of Piedmont*, 1:146–147 (docs. 326 and 327); Toaff, *Il vino e la carne*, 176. This was similar to the Sogorb case in Spain. See Chapter 3.

70. Luzzati, "Sulle tentazioni iconoclaste ebraiche," 227; Luzzati, "Ebrei, chiesa locale," 225 n. 25; Archivio Arcivescovile di Lucca, Libri Antichi, 99/A c.48. See also Michele Luzzati, "'Satis est quod tecum dormivit': Vero, verosimile e falso nelle incriminazioni di ebrei; Un caso di presunta sodomia (Lucca, 1471–1472)," in *Una manna buona per Mantova: Man Tov le-Man Tovah; Studi in onore di Vittore Colorni per il suo 92° compleanno*, ed. Mauro Perani (Florence: Olschki, 2004), 261–280.

71. Luzzati, "Sulle tentazioni iconoclaste ebraiche," 228; Maria Giuseppina Muzzarelli, "Ebrei a Cento in epoca medievale," in *Gli ebrei a Cento e Pieve di Cento fra medioevo ed età moderna: Atti del convegno di studi storici, Cento, 22 aprile 1993*, ed. Maria Giuseppina Muzzarelli, Antonio Samaritani, and Paolo Ravenna (Cento: Fondazione Cassa di Risparmio di Cento, 1994), 13–28, 19–22.

72. Muzzarelli, "Ebrei a Cento," 19–22.

73. Angela Möschter, "*Et Verbum caro factum est*: Begegnungen und Differenzen von Juden und Christen beim Fleischmahl," in *Campana pulsante convocati: Festschrift anlässlich der Emeritierung von Prof. Alfred Haverkamp*, ed. Frank G. Hirschmann and Gerd Mentgen (Trier: Kliomedia, 2005), 361–362 and 386–388.

74. Luzzati, "Sulle tentazioni iconoclaste ebraiche," 227; Archivio di Stato di Firenze, Otto di Guardia e di Balia, n. 57 cc. 85rv, February 26, 1481.

75. Luzzati, "Sulle tentazini iconoclaste ebraiche," 231; Anna Antoniazzi Villa, *Un processo contro gli ebrei nella Milano del 1488: Crescita e decline della comunità ebraica lombarda alla fine del Medioevo* (Bologna: Cappelli, 1985), 10, 56, 86, 93, 95, 97, 112, 114, 115.

76. Antoniazzi Villa, *Un processo contro gli ebrei*, 86–115.

77. Ibid., 112.

78. On the increased number of painted Madonnas in homes, see Andrea Menzione, *Preghiera e diletto: Immagini domestiche a Pisa nel Seicento* (Pisa: Edizione Plus, 2010), 17–20. On the Christian anxiety regarding the Jews living in these houses, see Bernardino of Siena's angry reproof of Christians who rented houses to Jewish usurers in Mormando, *The Preacher's Demons*, 177.

79. Luzzati, "Ebrei, chiesa locale." On the Daniele da Norsa episode, see Dana Katz, "Painting and the Politics of Persecution: Representing the Jew in Fifteenth-Century Mantua," *Art History* 23, no. 4 (2000): 475–495; and Katz, *The Jew in the Art*, 40–68. Luzzati in general is more concerned with the type of judicial courts that were adjudicating in these cases. See also Michele Luzzati, "Vescovi ed ebrei nell'Italia tardomedievale," in *Vescovi e diocese in Italia dal XIV alla metà del XVI secolo*, ed. Giuseppina De Sandre Gasparini (Rome: Herder, 1990), 1099–1123, 1115–1117.

80. Möschter, "*Et Verbum caro factum est*," 361–362 and 386–388.

81. Luzzati, "Vescovi ed ebrei nell'Italia tardomedievale," 1114; Katz, *The Jew in the Art*, 53; Katz, "Painting and the Politics of Persecution," 482.

82. Luzzati, "Vescovi ed ebrei nell'Italia tardomedievale," 1115; Katz, *The Jew in the Art*, 53–55; Luzzati, "Ebrei, chiesa locale, " 203–234; Luzzati, "Sulle tentazioni iconoclaste ebraiche," 229–230; Michele Luzzati, "Alla ricerca delle sinagoghe medievali di Pisa," in *La sinagoga di Pisa dalle origini al restauro ottocentesco di Marco Treves* (Florence: Edifir, 1997), 11–21.

83. Katz, *The Jew in the Art*, 54.

84. Ibid., 54 and 179 n. 43; Luzzati, "Vescovi ed ebrei nell'Italia tardomedievale," 1115.

85. Luzzati, "Sulle tentazioni iconoclaste ebraiche," 228; Simonsohn, *The Apostolic See and the Jews*, vol. 2, doc. 1056.

86. Luzzati, "Ebrei, chiesa locale"; Katz, *The Jew in the Art*, 40–68, 174 n. 5; Daniele da Norsa, Jew, to Marquis Francesco, May 29, 1495, Archivio Gonzaga, busta 2447, carta 137. On the episode, see also Katz, "Painting and the Politics of Persecution"; and Giovanni Agosti, "Intorno alla Madonna della Vittoria," in *Mantegna, 1431–1506*, exhibition catalog, ed. Giovanni Agosti and Dominque Thiébaut (Milan: Officina Libraria, 2008), 297–305, 310–312, esp. 299, 302, 304, 312.

87. See Katz, *The Jew in the Art*, 179 n. 48. Francesco wrote to Sigismondo Gonzaga on August 18, 1495.

88. The removal of the Jew's home is similar to the tendency in Spain to replace synagogues with churches after the Jews' expulsion in 1492. See Yom Tov Assis, "Synagogues in Medieval Spain," *Jewish Art* 18 (1992): 6–29.

89. Katz, *The Jew in the Art*, 56.

90. Katz, "Painting and the Politics of Persecution," 475–495; Katz, *The Jew in the Art*, 40–68.

91. Luzzati, "Sulle tentazioni iconoclaste ebraiche," 228; and Adriano Franceschini, *Artisti a Ferrara in età umanistica e rinascimentale: Testimonianze archivistiche*, part 2, vol. 2, *Dal 1493 al 1516* (Ferrara: Gabriele Corbo, 1997), 325–328 (docs. 637–638).

92. Franceschini, *Artisti a Ferrara*, 325–328 (docs. 637–638).

93. Ibid.

94. Ibid.; Luzzati, "Sulle tentazioni iconoclaste ebraiche," 228.

95. Franceschini, *Artisti a Ferrara*, 327–328 (doc. 638).

96. Ibid.

97. Luzzati, "Sulle tentazioni iconoclaste ebraiche," 230. His house also contained a library. See Roberto G. Salvadori and Giorgio Sacchetti, *Presenze ebraiche nell' Aretino dal XIV al XX secolo* (Florence: L. S. Olschki, 1990), 43. See also Luzzati, "Ebrei, Chiesa locale," 847–77, and Katz, *The Jew in the Art of the Italian Renaissance*, 44–68.

98. Luzzati, "Sulle tentazioni iconoclaste ebraiche," 229–230; and Elisabetta Traniello, "Presenze ebraiche nel Polesine di Rovigo nel XV secolo," *Materia giudaica* 7, no. 1 (2002): 118–119.

99. Luzzati, "Sulle tentazioni iconoclaste ebraiche," 229.

100. Holmes, *The Miraculous Image*, 45–46.

101. Ibid., 48, 153–154.

102. Ibid., 174.

103. Daniel E. Bornstein, *The Bianchi of 1399: Popular Devotion in Late Medieval Italy* (Ithaca, NY: Cornell University Press, 1993), 98, 158.

104. Holmes, *The Miraculous Image*, 115.

105. Ibid., 166.

106. Gentilcore, "Methods and Approaches," 82; and Holmes, "Disrobing the Virgin," in Johnson and Matthews, *Picturing Women*, 191.

107. Chiara Franceschini counts thirty cases in the peninsula that were investigated by the Congregation of the Holy Office in Rome from 1607 to 1723, particularly between 1637 and 1639, in Assisi, Pesaro, Cagli, and Rome, concerning at least eight wooden sculpted crucifixes that had miraculous tendencies. None of these images were reported as having transfigured as a result of Jewish abuse. Chiara Franceschini, "Arti figurative: La rappresentazione," in *Dizionario storico dell'Inquisizione*, vol. 1, ed. Adriano Prosperi (Pisa: Scuola Normale Superiore, 2010), 105–107.

108. It was, after all, the Catholics who were taught the miraculous qualities of paintings. Note the texts from the Council of Trent. Norman P. Tanner, ed., *Decrees of the Ecumenical Councils*, 2 vols. (Washington, DC: Georgetown University Press, 2016), vol. 2, 774–776.

109. Ibid.

110. Corry, Howard, and Laven, *Madonnas and Miracles*, 137.

111. Michael P. Carroll, *Veiled Threats: The Logic of Popular Catholicism in Italy* (Baltimore: Johns Hopkins University Press, 1996), 46–47.

112. Robert Scribner, "Incombustible Luther: The Image of the Reformer in Early Modern Germany," *Past & Present* 110, no. 1 (1986): 38–68; and Caroline Bynum, "Are Things 'Indifferent'? How Objects Change Our Understanding of Religious History," *German History* 34, no. 1 (2016): 88–112.

113. Wickersham, *Rituals of Prosecution*, 111.

114. Carlos Eire, *War Against the Idols: The Reformation of Worship from Erasmus to Calvin* (New York: Cambridge University Press, 1986), 78.

115. Thomas Kaufmann, *Luther's Jews: A Journey into Anti-Semitism*, trans. Lesley Sharpe and Jeremy Noakes (Oxford: Oxford University Press, 2017), 79.

116. Tolan, *Faces of Muhammad*, 108.

117. Tanner, *Decrees of the Ecumenical Councils*, 2:774–776.

118. Paolo Prodi, "Ricerche sulla teorica delle arti figurative nella riforma cattolica," *Archivio italiano per la storia della pieta* 4 (1962): 124–212.

119. Irene Galandra Cooper, "Investigating the 'Case' of the Agnus Dei in Sixteenth-Century Italian Homes," in Corry, Faini, and Meneghin, *Domestic Devotions in Early Modern Italy*, 220–243.

120. The papal bull *Licet ab initio* is transcribed by Romano Canosa, *Storia dell'Inquisizione in Italia dalla metà del Cinquecento alla fine del Settecento*, 5 vols. (Rome: Sapere 2000, 1986–1990), 1:151–153.

121. Elena Bonora, "The Takeover of the Roman Inquisition," in *A Companion to Heresy Inquisitions*, ed. Donald S. Prudlo (Leiden: Brill, 2019), 249–279, 275.

122. Dario Gamboni, *The Destruction of Art: Iconoclasm and Vandalism Since the French Revolution* (New Haven, CT: Yale University Press, 1997), 28–29.

123. Wickersham, *Rituals of Prosecution*, 66; and Joanna Kostylo "Contested Devotions: Space, Identities and Religious Dissent in the Apothecary's Home," in Corry, Faini, and Meneghin, *Domestic Devotions in Early Modern Italy*, 408–435, 417.

124. Wickersham, *Rituals of Prosecution*, 114–115, 212–217, 324 n. 71.

125. Kostylo, "Contested Devotions," 408.

126. Wickersham, *Rituals of Prosecution*, 24 and 118.

127. Ibid., 188–190, 361 n. 122.

128. Biblioteca dell'Archiginnasio di Bologna, B-1891, fol. 71. Concerning this case, a 1622 edict was signed by Fra Paolo, the inquisitor of Bologna, and Arcilles Gonzado, the archbishop of Bologna. In 1637, the Inquisition of Bologna was sent instructions on how to interrogate potential offenders who had committed acts of sacrilege against the statues of the Virgin. Biblioteca dell'Archiginnasio di Bologna, B-1892, fol. 34r. Francisco Bethencourt, *The Inquisition: A Global History, 1478–1834* (Cambridge: Cambridge University Press, 2009), 208–209.

129. ASMo. FI, Processi busta 67, fasc. 2.

130. In Rome, the papacy had exclusive legal authority over Jews, and the latter were subject to the papal vicar, the Tribunale Criminale del Governatore, and the Senatore. Although Jews were summoned before the Holy Office the loss of *processi* makes it impossible to quantify the number of trials prosecuted by this court. See Antje Bräcker, "The Series 'Stanza Storica' of the Sanctum Officium in the Archive of the Congregation for the Doctrine of the Faith as a Source for the History of the Jews," in *The Roman Inquisition, the Index and the Jews: Contexts, Sources and Perspectives*, ed. Stephan Wendehorst (Leiden: Brill, 2004), 169–176.

131. Luzzati, "Sulle tentazioni iconoclaste ebraiche," 229.

132. Germano Maifreda has shown in his *Italya: Storie di ebrei, storia italiana* (Bari: Gius. Laterza & Figli, 2021), 152–153, how the Massari of the Jewish community in Mantua would complain to the duke twenty-three years later because the painter Vincenzo Sanniti had painted anti-Jewish images, including the 1602 hanging of these seven Jews and the case of Simonino di Trento. The Jews' offer to reimburse the paintings' value was successful in having these paintings destroyed, even though Sanniti tried to appeal. It shows a rare case of Jewish political agency concerning sacred images.

133. The ACDF *memoria* does not even mention this case.

134. Giovan Battista Spaccini, *Cronaca di Modena*, ed. Albano Biondi, Rolando Bussi, and Carlo Giovannini, 6 vols. (Modena: Franco Cosimo Panini, 1993–2008), 1:584–585.

135. Ibid., 4:342.

136. The punishment in Siena seems out of place. An explanation could be that the Jews had escaped from Livorno and were arrested in Siena. But I have found no documentation to confirm this.

137. ACDF, "Si manda per manus," 387, records: "The Jew confessed that he had done this in disgrace of the Christian faith to show that Judaism was better." In the Archivio di Stato di Livorno, there was no information either in the Capitano poi Governatore Auditore Vicario (1505–1808), where it is possible to trace documents related to both trials of the years 1550–1808 of the civil cases, nor in the Fondo Governatore e Auditore 2603-1, 2603-2, Atti Civili Repertori, 1633–1700, or Spezzati Atti Criminali dal 1617 al 1672, which relate to these years.

138. Spaccini, *Cronaca di Modena*, 2:487.

139. ACDF, "Si manda per manus," 386–387. Although no information survives in the Archivio di Stato of Modena, there is reference to the case in the Vatican archives. However, there are no details regarding the court that investigated the offense, the torture of the unnamed Jew(s), or any punishment they may have received. It is merely noted here as "the case of the Jew[s] in the town of Sassuolo who had damaged and ruined an image of the Blessed Virgin and possibly burned it" (ibid.).

140. Archivio Diocesano di Reggio Emilia, Litterarum trasmissarum a supremo tribunali ab anno 1598 usque ad 1611, Tomus I, cc. 201, 207, 208, 209, 211. See document 207, in which Cardinal Millino asks the inquisitor to secretly find out about the previous trial in Reggio in 1585, and which court had had jurisdiction over the Jews.

141. *Joseph Ha-Kohen: Sefer 'Emeq Ha-Bakha (The Vale of Tears) with the Chronicle of the Anonymous Corrector*, ed. Karin Almbladh (Uppsala: Almqvist & Wiksell, 1981), 80. On Fra Filippo Herrera, see Shlomo Simonsohn, "Some Well-Known Jewish Converts During the Renaissance," *Revue des Études juives* 148, nos. 1–2 (1989): 17–52, 31 n. 58.

142. *Sefer 'Emeq Ha-Bakha (The Vale of Tears)*, 80.

143. Luzzati, "Sulle tentazioni iconoclaste ebraiche," 230; Louis Waldman, "A Late Work by Andrea della Robbia Rediscovered: The Jews' Tabernacle at Empoli," *Apollo* 150 (September 1999): 13–20.

144. Holmes, *The Miraculous Image*, 212–215.

145. Abramo Pesaro, *Memorie storiche sulla Comunità Israelitica ferrarese* (Ferrara, 1878–1880; repr., Bologna: Forni, 1967), 1:45.

146. Luzzati, "Sulle tentazioni iconoclaste ebraiche," 228.

147. ACDF, "Si manda per manus," 373.

148. Ibid., 373, 376.

149. Ibid., 368–379. The archive of the Holy Office of Ferrara, run by Dominicans, is lost except for part of the documentation of administrative character conserved in the Vescovile Archivio.

150. Ibid., 369. The *memoria* recorded the letter sent by the Sacred Congregation to the local inquisitor of Ferrara, demanding that "the Jews of Reggio who have committed such a sacrilege should not be in the power of lay judges who want to investigate the case together with Your Reverence, since the details of this and similar cases should be dealt with only by the Office of the Holy Inquisition."

151. Katherine Aron-Beller and Christopher Black, eds., *The Roman Inquisition: Centre Versus Peripheries* (Leiden: Brill, 2018).

152. ACDF, "Si manda per manus," 368–369.

153. Ibid. Until 1598 when an inquisitorial tribunal was established in Reggio, the court was under the authority of the inquisitor of Ferrara, and its records are scant. Luca Al Sabbagh, "L'Inquisizione di Reggio Emilia fra centro e periferia tra XVII e XVIII secolo: Il repertorio dei carteggi" (master's thesis, University of Bologna, 2013).

154. Luzzati, "Sulle tentazioni iconoclaste ebraiche," 229.

155. Simona Feci, "Guardare e vedere al di là del muro: Immagini sacre e iconoclastia ebraica a Roma in età moderna," in *Le Inquisizioni cristiane e gli ebrei: Tavola rotonda nell'ambito della Conferenza annuale della ricerca (Roma, 20–21 dicembre 2001)*, ed. Giuseppe Galasso (Rome: Accademia Nazionale dei Lincei, 2003), 407–429.

156. Ibid., 413.

157. Ibid.

158. Ibid., 414.

159. Ibid., 415.

160. Ibid. Feci remains doubtful that the Jews had committed the offense, suggesting that, given the position of the image, the damage might have been caused by stones thrown at the ghetto by Christians outside it.

161. Ibid., 424.

162. Aron-Beller, *Jews on Trial*, 66.

163. ACDF, "Si manda per manus," 374.

164. See Menzione, *Preghiera e diletto*, about the prevalence of Madonna images in domestic devotion in Italy in the early modern period.

165. The papal state comprised the tribunals of Rome, Ancona, Avignon (France), Bologna, Faenza, Fermo, Ferrara (after 1598), Gubbio, Perugia, Rimini, and Spoleto, all run by Dominicans.

166. ACDF, "Si manda per manus," 426; Feci, "Guardare e vedere," 421ff.

167. Feci, "Guardare e vedere," 423. See ACDF, Sant'Officio, Decreta 1612, c. 55, regarding the reduction of the punishment; and Decreta 1613, c. 195.

168. Feci, "Guardare e vedere," 426, confirms that, according to the edicts of the Tribunale Criminale del Governatore, the punishment for image desecration was ten years galley service.

169. Feci, "Guardere e vedere," 410ff.

170. ASMo. FI, Causae Hebreorum (from here CH) busta244, fasc. 16, folio 14.

171. ASMo. FI, CH busta 245, fasc. 38, folio 9.

172. Ibid., folio 21.

173. Ibid.

174. No real investigation was made into the meaning of Beatrice's purported expression about the bleeding of the image.

175. ASMo. FI, CH busta 245, fasc. 38, folio 21.

176. Ibid.

177. Ibid. Here we see the ducal court helping the Inquisition find the real culprits.

178. For a specific role of Jews in the investiture processions of new popes (from the investiture of Gregory XII [1406] to Leo X's election in 1513), see Linder, "'The Jews Too Were Not Absent.'" Adriano Prosperi demands that we see the Jews' role here as relating to the political power of the pope as a successor to the Roman emperors, rather than as a spiritual overlord ("Incontri rituali," 497–498).

179. Rubin, *Corpus Christi*, 289.

180. Ibid., 302, 334; Daniel Jütte, "'They Shall Not Keep Their Doors or Windows Open': Urban Space and the Dynamics of Conflict and Contact in Premodern Jewish-Christian Relations," *European History Quarterly* 46, no. 2 (2016): 209–236, 219.

181. Note also that in the fifteenth century, the noted rabbi Seligman Bing reprimanded a Jew who had followed a procession on the day when a priest was ordained. Arye Maimon, Mordechai Breuer, and Yacov Guggenheim, eds., *Germania Judaica*, vol. 3, *1350–1519*, part 3 (Tübingen: Mohr Siebeck, 2003), 119 n. 47.

182. Victor Turner, *Dramas, Fields, and Metaphors: Symbolic Action in Human Society* (Ithaca, NY: Cornell University Press, 1974), 262–270.

183. Rubin, *Corpus Christi*, 289.

184. Halbertal and Margalit, *Idolatry*, 207.

185. Albano Biondi, "Gli ebrei e l'Inquisizione negli Stati estensi," in *L'Inquisizione e gli ebrei in Italia*, ed. Michele Luzzati (Rome: Laterza, 1994), 265–285, 270.

186. Ibid.

187. ASMo. FI, busta 270, Editti e Decreti VII, "Editto del Sant Ufficio in ordine à gli hebrei."

188. ASMo. FI, busta 288, Carteggi Diversi, 1600–1769, Fra Nicola Bolognese, vicar of the Holy Office of Terra Finale, letter, June 4, 1671. He also noted the bad behavior of Jews, when they spoiled a Christian procession by hanging out offensive and indecent materials from their homes while Christians welcomed it by hanging their best carpets out of the windows. The actual material hung by the Jews is unclear. Spaccini also mentions a case in his diary that highlights the tension when Jews appeared during a procession on Saturday, April 20, 1630. In the morning the chaplain Don Giovanni Selingardi went to give communion to several sick people in the district of the Jews, and encountered one Pellegrino Levi who, Spaccini remarks, "brazenly pulled his hat over his eyes, without withdrawing." Those who accompanied the most holy sacrament wanted to punch him for his insolence. Spaccini, *Cronaca di Modena*, 6:56. There was no subsequent trial investigation.

189. ASMo. FI, Processi busta 111, fasc. 12, folio 3.

190. ASMo. FI, CH busta 247, fasc. 24; Jütte, "'They Shall Not Keep Their Doors or Windows Open,'" 220.

191. See ASMo. FI, CH busta 247, fasc. 24, folio 1, for the testimony of Father Jacobo de Lauda.

192. For example, ASMo. FI, Processi busta 111, fasc. 12, folio 15–16, the testimony of Father Joannes Augustini on June 8, 1639. He noted: "There is a small street that runs behind the Canaletto, into which they could have turned, those Jews. Also they could have turned into two streets, one of them by the Canaletto, and the other from there, they were able to turn behind by the street where one comes without meeting us, and they were able also to return into the shop."

193. ASMo. FI, CH busta 245, fasc. 53.

194. Ibid., folio 23.

195. ASMo. FI, CH busta 250, fasc. 28.

196. ASMo. FI, CH busta 250, fasc. 84.

197. Ibid., 1r–53v; this fascicle contains several cases together.

198. ASMo. FI, CH busta 245, fasc. 37.

199. ASMo. FI, CH busta 250, fasc. 84.

200. ASMo. FI, CH busta 245, fasc. 58. On the Compagnia della Morte, see Adriano Prosperi, "Il condannato a morte: Santo o criminale?," in *Il delitto narrato al popolo: Immagini di giustizia e stereotipi di criminalità in età moderna*, ed. Roberto de Romanis and Rosamaria Loretelli (Palermo: Sellerio, 1999), 219–227; and Nicholas Terpstra, *The Art of Executing Well: Rituals of Execution in Renaissance Italy*, Early Modern Studies 1 (Kirksville, MO: Truman State University Press, 2008).

201. ASMo. FI, CH busta 245, fasc. 58. Note the description of his offense that was read out to him by the inquisitor at the end of his interrogation: "We have deduced and presumed that this was done in contempt of the most holy image of the crucifix, that he irreverently turned his back to the most holy image of the crucifix. He did not give offense in turning his back before the arrival of the crucifix but only after, since he had remained there until the holy image had passed."

202. ASMo. FI, CH busta 247, fasc. 55.

203. ASMo. FI, CH busta 245, fasc. 55, folio 10.

204. ASMo. FI, CH busta 245, fasc. 38, folio 7–8.

205. ASMo. FI, CH busta 250, fasc. 84.

206. ACDF, "Si manda per manus," 367.

207. Dana E. Katz, "'Clamber Not You up to the Casements': On Ghetto Views and Viewing," *Jewish History* 24 (2010): 127–153, 137; Dana E. Katz, *The Jewish Ghetto and the Visual Imagination of Early Modern Venice* (Cambridge: Cambridge University Press, 2017), 67–83.

208. Feci, "Guardare e vedere," 416.

209. Ibid.

210. ACDF, "Si manda per manus," 382. On the spatial politics of the window in early modern Italy and England, see Katz, *The Jewish Ghetto*, 67–83.

211. Benjamin Ravid, "An Introduction to the Charters of the Jewish Merchants of Venice," in *The Mediterranean and the Jews*, ed. Elliott Horowitz and Moises Orfali (Jerusalem: Bar-Ilan University Press, 2002), 203–246, 219.

212. ASMo. FI, CH busta 245, fasc. 53, letter of Tinti to the duke on the last day of February, 1631.

213. Pullan, *The Jews of Europe*, 124.

214. Richard Trexler, "Florentine Religious Experience: The Sacred Image," *Studies in the Renaissance* 19 (1972): 7–41, 17.

215. Katz, *The Jew in the Art*, 160. Katz sees the Jews as being repelled by the "corporeal sacredness" of Christian communal images.

216. ASMo. FI, Processi busta 26, fasc. 9. The *processo* remained a preliminary investigation.

217. The Latin passage, "Ipsi obligati sunt," is actually a quotation from the Vulgate, Psalm 20:8. It appears in the seventeenth-century King James Bible as "They are brought down and fallen: but we are risen and stand upright" (likewise, Ps. 20:8).

218. ASMo. FI, CH busta 244, fasc. 16. The Hebrew is transliterated in the trial transcript as shown above.

219. It is important to note that, when in 1584 Pope Gregory XIII ordered Jews to attend forced sermons, the sermons were to take place not in churches (unless portable sacred objects could be removed) but in unconsecrated spaces such as church oratories. Emily Michelson, "How to Write a Conversionary Sermon: Rhetorical Influences and Religious Identity," in *Religious Orders and Religious Identity Formation, ca. 1420–1620: Discourses and Strategies of Observance and Pastoral Engagement*, ed. Bert Roest and Johanneke Uphoff (Leiden: Brill, 2016), 235–251.

220. ASMo. FI, CH busta 250, fasc. 89.

221. Ibid., folio 1.

222. ASMo. FI, CH busta 250, fasc. 32.

223. Ibid., folio 14.

224. ACDF, "Si manda per manus," 372; Feci, "Guardare e vedere," 410ff.

225. Luzzati, "Ebrei, chiesa locale," 208.

226. ACDF, "Si manda per manus," 367.

227. ASMo. FI, Processi busta 35, fasc. 10.

228. Ibid., folio 3.

229. ASMo. FI, CH busta 244, fasc. 16.

230. ASMo. FI, Processi busta 26, fasc. 9, 11r, October 15, 1614. He noted: "It is not true that I would have said those words. God be my guard. Your Reverence has such an opinion of me that I would say such things? Do I not know what is important? Do you think that I would prejudice myself in such a way? For what reason would you think that I would say such words?" Later he pleads, "I would renounce my life, my possessions and my children and what I have if I had ever said such words. It is possible that someone out of malevolence has said such a thing against me. But I have never said such words" (12r).

231. Ibid., folio 17.

232. ASMo. FI, CH busta 244, fasc. 26; Rosa M. Salzberg, "'Selling Stories and Many Other Things In and Through the City': Peddling Print in Renaissance Florence and Venice," *Sixteenth Century Journal* 42, no. 3 (2011): 737–759, 738.

233. ASMo. FI, CH busta 244, fasc. 29, folio 21.

234. Ibid., folio 8.

235. Ibid., folio 9.

236. On the 1635 case against Jews of Spilamberto and the prints the Jews were accused of desecrating, see my article "Image Desecration in Spilamberto: Jews and Christian Images in Seventeenth-Century Italy," *English Historical Review* 132 (August 2017): 823–862; and the next chapter in this work.

237. ASMo. FI, Processi busta 29, fasc. 19.

238. Corry, Howard, and Laven, *Madonnas and Miracles*, 52.

239. The interior of Jewish homes would look somewhat different from Christian homes, as Rabbi Leon de Modena pointed out in his *Historia de' riti hebraici*: "They [the Jews] do not have [painted] figures, images, or statues in the home and certainly not on the synagogues and in their holy places. . . . Notwithstanding, in Italy, many take the liberty of having pictures and images in their houses; especially if they be not with relief, or embossed work, nor the bodies at large." Quoted here, with adaptation, from Leone Modena, *The History of the Rites, Customes, and Manner of Life, of the Present Jews, Throughout the World*, trans.

Edmund Chilmead (London, 1650), part 1, chap. 2.3; and Sabar, "'The Right Path for an Artist,'" 268. But the rabbinical responsa of Joseph Karo, Rabbi Shmuel Archivolti, Leon de Modena, Avraham Graziano, and Shmuel ben Avraham Aboab never argued for a ban on figurative art.

240. ACDF, "Si manda per manus," 373, 385; ACDF, Sant'Officio, Decreta 1610–1611, fol. 344v; Feci, "Guardare e vedere," 421ff.

241. ASMo., FI, CH busta 244, fasc. 23.

242. Ibid., folio 1–2.

243. Luzzati, "Ebrei, chiesa locale," 216.

244. ASMo. FI, Processi busta 85, fasc. 11.

245. Ibid., folio 8–9.

246. Ibid.

247. Ibid.; ACDF, Sant'Officio, Decreta 1650, fol. 85v.

248. Stephan Wendehorst, "The Roman Inquisition, the Index and the Jews: Sources and Perspectives for Research," *Jewish History* 17 (2003): 55–76, 55.

249. Ariel Toaff, *Love, Work and Death: Jewish Life in Medieval Umbria*, trans. Judith Landry (London: Littman Library of Jewish Civilization, 1996), 167–171; Giovanni Ciappelli, "La devozione domestica nelle ricordanze fiorentine (fine XIII–inizio XVI secolo) in religione domestica," *Quaderni di storia religiosa* 8 (2001): 79–115, 82–83; Danielle Menozzi, *La Chiesa e le immagini: I testi fondamentali sulle arti figurativi dale origini ai nostri giorni* (Milan: San Paolo Edizioni, 1995) 133–134; and Lina Bolzoni, *La rete delle immagini: Predicazione in volgare dalle origini a Bernardino da Siena* (Turin: Einaudi, 2002), xvi.

250. Corry, Howard, and Laven, *Madonnas and Miracles*, 128.

251. Ibid., 82.

252. ACDF, Sant'Officio, Decreta 1653, fol. 37v. Here Jewish pawn banks were banned, as well as Jews buying or selling books containing sacred images.

253. Feci, "Guardare e vedere," 415–416.

254. Ibid.

255. ASMo. FI, busta 270, Editti e Decreti, 1550–1670.

256. Given in the chancellery of the Holy Office of Ferrara on September 8, 1667. There is a copy in the ASMo FI, busta 270, Editti e Decreti VII, "Editto del Sant Ufficio in ordine à gli hebrei"; and also in the Biblioteca dell'Archiginnasio di Bologna, B-1892. Note also the copy of the letter from Cardinal Millino of the Sacred Congregation in ASMo. FI, CH busta 250, fasc. 25. The letter of May 29, 1614, already spoke about holding any sacred object. "It is understood that these Jews are taking jewels as pledges, and gold in crosses or crucifixes or other sacred images, we do not allow this, being that it is prohibited to Jews to hold any sacred thing. And so this my Most Illustrious Signore have ordered that your Reverend be vigilant about this and not permit any Jew to receive in pledge, any of these things, and so this be conserved."

257. ASMo. FI CH busta 250 fasc. 25, folio 49.

258. See ACDF, "Si manda per manus," 387; also ASMo, FI CH busta 244, fasc. 18; and CH busta 250, fasc. 48 and fasc. 53.

259. This is not the same Jew as discussed in Chapter 6.

260. ASMo, FI CH busta 244, fasc. 18, folio 1. I think it is relevant that the inquisitor did not ask any of the three delators what sort of relics were in the crucifix. Instead, he asked them what they thought of the banker Simone Sanguinetti whom they were denouncing. This suggests that even at this stage their testimonies were not taken seriously by the inquisitor.

261. These conspirators tried hard to convince neighboring Christians of the Jews' infamy.

262. ASMo. FI, CH busta 244, fasc. 18, folio 4–5.

263. ACDF, "Si manda per manus," 368–369. Some information about this case can be garnered from the Archivio Diocesano di Reggio Emilia, Litterarum trasmissarum a supremo tribunali ab anno 1598 usque ad 1611, Tomus I, cc. 201, 207, 208, 209, and 211, since letters between Cardinal Millino and the inquisitor of Reggio, Paolo Franco, in 1610–1611 refer back to this case of 1585 in Reggio. See Federica Francesconi, *Invisible Enlighteners: Modenese Jewry from Renaissance to Emancipation* (Philadephia: University of Pennsylvania Press, 2021), 75–81. Jaghel was nicknamed *doctor hebreorum* by the inquisitors.

264. ASMo. FI, CH busta 244 fasc. 18, folio 6.

265. ASMo. FI, CH busta 244 fasc. 18, folio 7r.

266. ASMo FI. CH busta 244 fasc. 18, folio 6–7. Jaghel mentions a fourth conspirator—Salomon Sacerdote who did not give a delation to the Inquisition. The case is also reported in ACDF, "Si manda per manus," 387, where the Sacred Congregation demands that the Inquisition of Modena adjudicate this case rather than the ducal ministers. Also see the correspondence on this case between the Inquisition and the Congregation of the Holy Office. ASMo. FI, Modena: Lettere della Sacra Congregazione di Roma 1609–1621, busta 252, letters of October 7, 14, 29, November 25, December 15, 1617, January 1618, and April 12, 1618. There is also an incomplete letter written to Duke Cesare d'Este dated 1618, probably from the ordinary judge about this matter, also discussing what should be the appropriate action for Jews who had falsely delated fellow Jews and tampered with Christian images. Also see the Central Archives of the History of the Jewish People, Jerusalem, files on Modena, A.S.E. Archivi per Materie "ebrei" busta 4 Processi 1-LXXXIII 1600–1629 pezzi n. 83, HM 5407 microfilm c, 113–116, March 29, 1617.

267. ASMo. FI, Modena: Lettere della Sacra Congregazione di Roma 1609–1621, busta 252, letter from Cardinal Millino in Rome, June 29, 1617. The Jewish Università had previously petitioned Inquisitor Guazzoni for a copy of the trial formulated against them by these denouncers. Here in a letter Cardinal Millino forbids Inquisitor Guazzoni to give the Jews such evidence. In the same file is a letter of March 30, 1618, in which Cardinal Millino authorizes the Inquisitor Guazzoni to hand the case over to the ducal court since he realizes that the offense is not related to image desecration.

268. ASMo. FI, CH busta 250, fasc. 53.

269. Ibid., folio 1–2.

270. Some Monti di Pietà followed the same rule that the Jews of Modena were observing. The Monti were not supposed to accept items belonging to churches without the permission of the bishop or his vicar-general. But there are examples from the seventeenth and eighteenth centuries of Monti accepting crosses and other privately owned religious properties such as coral rosaries.

271. ASMo. FI, CH busta 250, fasc. 53.

272. Ibid., folio 7–8, April 27, 1645.

273. Ibid., folio 10–11, September 25, 1645.

274. ASMo. FI, CH 250, fasc. 48.

275. Ibid., folio 27.

276. Ibid., folio 5–6.

277. Ibid., folio 12–13.

278. Ibid., folio 5–6, 27, 5–6. Emanuel also argued that he was from Mantua, where he said Jews actually made such crosses, since they were goldsmiths. They stored them and sold

them in public. But Jews in Modena were also involved in jewelry, and there is a strong likelihood that they too made crosses. On the Formiggini family in Modena and the making of jewelry, see Federica Francesconi and Luisa Levi D'Ancona, *Vita e società ebraica di Modena e Reggio Emilia: L'età dei ghetto* (Modena: Edizioni Panini, 2007), 32–33.

279. ASMo. FI, CH busta 250 fasc. 48, folio 27. Note Emanuel's testimony: "I am not able to say that at times we did not see the cross. I needed to get into that chest and did so many times, but even though this happened, I can promise that I never touched the cross, even though I saw it many times."

280. Ibid., folio 9.

281. The other two banks belonged to Avraham Rovigo and Raffaele Rovigo, his nephew. When Salvadore Rovigo, the brother of Avraham Rovigo, was interrogated, he stated that his brother and he had split their banks three years previously in 1661, and that his son Raffaele now ran the bank. Ibid., folio 118. There were also two Monti di Pietà in Modena.

282. ASMo. FI, CH busta 250, fasc. 25. The full inventory of the objects, with the name of the Christians who deposited them, the date they were deposited, and how much money was put against them can be found on folio 44–46. Each of the crosses was opened. See Corry, Howard, and Laven, *Madonnas and Miracles*, 83.

283. ASMo. FI, CH busta 250, fasc. 25, folio 28.

284. Ibid., folio 57.

285. Ibid., folio 44–46.

286. Ibid., folio 81–83. This was carried out in the Holy Office on May 11, 1665.

287. Ibid., folio 65.

288. ASMo. FI, CH busta 250, fasc. 25.

289. Ibid., folio 90–91, May 12, 1665.

290. Ibid., folio 90; the crosses in the bank of Avraham Rovigo are described on folio 93.

291. Ibid., folio 169 and the following.

292. Ibid., folio 172r.

293. Ibid., folio 184–198, for the sentencing of the Jewish bankers.

294. ASMo. FI, Processi busta 111, fasc. 10.

295. ASMo. FI, Processi busta 111, fasc. 11, folio 14.

CHAPTER 6

1. On the advantages of microhistorical research, see Sigurdur Magnússon, "The Singularization of History: Social History and Microhistory Within the Postmodern State of Knowledge," *Journal of Social History* 36, no. 3 (Spring 2003): 701–735.

2. On the Jews and the Inquisition in Modena, see my monograph *Jews on Trial*, where I mention the Spilamberto case on a few occasions (see 74, 80 n. 66, 124 n. 187), but I had not yet had the chance to analyze the trial in detail. I did this more recently in my article "Image Desecration in Spilamberto," 823–862. The longest case in the archives is against Lazarro Norsia for sodomy in 1670. See Katherine Aron-Beller, "*Sopra l'imputatione del delitto di sodomia con christiano*: The Proceedings Against Lazarro de Norsa (Modena, 1670)," *Genesis* 20, no. 1 (2021): 53–91, 166–167, at 65–93.

3. There is correspondence on this case in the ACDF, St. St. CC 1c, titled "Gli ebrei di Roma e Dello Stato Pontifico"; it is recorded that Fra Giacomo da Lodi, inquisitor general of Modena, had informed the Sacred Congregation that Baldassar Rangone had leased his mill

to the Jews (fol. 150rv). For the inquisitorial trial itself, see ASMo. FI, CH busta 256, fasc. 17. Unfortunately, the file in the archive is not in order, nor is it paginated. The page numbers in this chapter refer to my pagination. From now on the trial will be abbreviated to ASMo. FI CH busta 256 fasc. 17. This Simon Sanguinetti is not the same Jew as discussed in Chapter 5.

4. ASMo. FI CH busta 256 fasc. 17, folio 1. This unusual situation was echoed by Ludovico Marchesi. He stated: "The house of the mill is at the top end of the main street, and in the past there were always Christians who lived there."

5. There were initially forty *vicari foranei* across the Estensi region, and each had at least two staff members: a notary and an agent or nuncio of the inquisitor. See Katherine Aron-Beller, "Outside the Ghetto: Jews and Christians in the Duchy of Modena," *Journal of Early Modern History* 17 (2013): 245–271, 249.

6. In the seventeenth century, the network of these delegates—many of whom held other ecclesiastical offices, for example, as archpriests—exercised a particularly well-defined strategy in these areas, instigating inquisitorial action against both Christians and professing Jews, and increasing the Inquisition's investigative capability on a local level.

7. Aron-Beller, *Jews on Trial*, 244–245. There is a reduction in the Inquisitorial monitoring of Jews once they are ghettoized in 1638.

8. One prominent member of the Rangone family was Alessandro Rangone, bishop of Modena between 1628 and 1640. Interestingly, the bishop was personally involved in the establishment of the ghetto in Modena. He blamed the Jews for the plague in 1630 and was uncomfortable with the existence of profitable bankers in the duchy. In a previous inquisitorial *processo* of 1624 in which Simon was accused of hiring Christians in his home, Simon had called himself the financial agent of the Rangone family and testified that he had already been working for the family for eighteen years, managing rental properties worth four thousand scudi. See ASMo. FI, Processi busta 70, fasc. 13.

9. Simon Sanguinetti was not forced to sell his bank in 1631, as were his fellow religionists in the ducal capital. See ASMo. FI CH busta 256 fasc. 17, folio 23.

10. Aron-Beller, "Outside the Ghetto." In the trial against Simon Sanguinetti in 1624, Simon lists the four Jewish families living in Spilamberto. See ASMo. FI, Processi busta 70, fasc. Folio 3 Such activity and interaction of small Jewish groups has been termed "communitarian cosmopolitanism" by Francesca Trivellato. See Francesca Trivellato, *The Familiarity of Strangers: The Sephardic Diaspora, Livorno, and Cross-Cultural Trade in the Early Modern Period* (New Haven, CT: Yale University Press, 2009), 18.

11. Maria Pia Balboni, *Gli Ebrei del Finale Emilia nel Cinquecento e nel Seicento* (Florence: Giuntina, 2005), 36 and 137, where she lists the Jewish bankers involved in the silk trade in Finale Emilia.

12. Ibid., 138. See Dora L. Bemporad, "Jewish Ceremonial Art in the Era of the Ghettos," in *Gardens and Ghettos: The Art of Jewish Life in Italy*, ed. Vivian Mann (Berkeley: University of California Press, 1989), 111–135, 124, which documents significant activity among the Jews in the silk trade in Italy.

13. For an excellent analysis of the Bolognese style of spinning and its initiation in Italy, see Carlo Poni, "All'origine del sistema di fabbrica: Tecnologia e organizzazione produttiva dei mulini da seta nell' Italia settentrionale (sec. XVII–XVIII)," *Rivista Storica Italiana* 88, no. 3 (1976): 444–497, 446–447; Carlo Poni, "Archéologie de la fabrique: La diffusion des moulins à soie 'alla bolognese' dans les États vénitiens du XVIe au XVIIIe siècle," *Annales: Économies, Sociétés, Civilisations* 27, no. 6 (1972): 1475–1496.

14. See ASMo. FI CH busta 256 fasc. 17, folios 35, 36, and 39. See also ACDF, St. St. CC 1c, fols. 160r and 161v. Inquisitor General Tinti notes in March 1633 that both men and women worked there under a Christian foreman. See ASMo. FI CH busta 256 fasc. 17, folio 134; also 12v. Petri di Monlis, a dryer in the mill, stated that the Sanguinettis "made sure that one of them [the Jews] was there all the time." This changed with the arrival of Leonardo Costantini, the foreman who was appointed on December 14, 1633. He was removed from the mill on November 24, 1634, by one of the Rangones to be employed elsewhere.

15. In his interrogation on Monday, November 19, 1635, Simon suggests this ease of movement. See ASMo. FI CH busta 256 fasc. 17, folio 49. "The mill adjoins my house, which I rent from Signor Marchese. One [of my family] stays for one hour in the mill, and then another for the next hour, to keep watch on the mill."

16. It is unclear from the proceedings how water entered the mill to facilitate the hydraulic wheel. But the Po Valley has abundant waterways with assured seasonal flows.

17. See Nicholas Terpstra, "Working the Cocoon: Gendered Charitable Enclosures and the Silk Industry in Early Modern Europe," in *Worth and Repute: Valuing Gender in Late Medieval and Early Modern Europe; Essays in Honour of Barbara Todd*, ed. Kim Kippen and Lori Woods (Toronto: Centre for Reformation and Renaissance Studies, 2011), 39–72, 64. Terpstra notes that the ones who benefited most from the factory work were the silk merchants and investors. See also Nicholas Terpstra, *Lost Girls: Sex and Death in Renaissance Florence* (Baltimore: Johns Hopkins University Press, 2012), 76ff.

18. ASMo. FI CH busta 256 fasc. 17, folio 24. Simon testified: "These workers are in different places. They work in different rooms, according to their duties."

19. Ibid., folio 48.

20. See Terpstra, "Working the Cocoon," 39–72.

21. ASMo. FI CH busta 256 fasc. 17, folio 10.

22. Terpstra, "Working the Cocoon," 47ff., notes that silk produced far less income per pound than wool.

23. ASMo. FI CH busta 256 fasc. 17, folio 59–61. For example, Francesco de Bartholomeo reports that his whole family worked in the mill. After they stopped their work in Spilamberto, they moved on to Reggio to work.

24. See Christopher Black, "The Trials and Tribulations of a Local Roman Inquisitor: Giacomo Tinti in Modena, 1626–1647," *Giornale di Storia* 9 (2012), www.giornaledistoria.net. Black makes an important study of Giacomo Tinti da Lodi, who served as inquisitor general of Modena from 1626 until his death in 1647. As Black notes, 44 out of 933 cases carried out during the generalship of Tinti prosecuted Jews. *Ex officio* indicates a process that is initiated by the Inquisition itself, usually on the strength of "common report," or self-denunciation, rather than that of a denunciation by a particular person.

25. ASMo. FI CH busta 256 fasc. 17, folio 23, 36; ACDF, St. St. CC 1c, fol. 158rv. Rangone had written to the Sacred Congregation to explain that, because of plague, the factory was in difficulties and Christians were in danger of starving.

26. Marta Ajmar-Wollheim and Flora Dennis, *At Home in Renaissance Italy* (London: V&A Publishing, 2010), 191. Ajmar-Wollheim and Dennis report numerous references to shutters and veils over paintings in domestic spaces in contemporary inventories. See Megan Holmes, "Miraculous Images in Renaissance Florence," *Art History* 34, no. 3 (2011): 432–465, at 439–441, where Holmes notes that miraculous images would be covered with a veil that was drawn back only on feast days, with all the liturgical implications of such a revelation.

This meant, incidentally, that images would not have opportunities to perform before onlookers new miracles of transfiguration by being seen to bleed or sweat.

27. It is interesting that the Christian women did not overtly blame the Jews for keeping the image shut. They saw it as Archpriest Menozzi's fault and not the Jews'. See ASMo. FI CH busta 256 fasc. 17, folio 24, 92, and 109.

28. Ibid., folio 28. Although Sebastiano Martini, the carpenter who made the window, testified that this was not what the Jew wanted, Simon had still financed this alteration.

29. Ibid., folio 92.

30. Inquisitor Michelangelo's own disappointment regarding Menozzi's lack of attention to this case is evident from his questioning on October 2. For example, Michelangelo asked Menozzi, "Why did you not discuss this very important case with the Reverend Father Inquisitor General?" Ibid., folio 22.

31. Ibid.; see also folio 23. He also argued that lack of funds had prevented him from traveling to Modena from Spilamberto to discuss the matter with the inquisitor.

32. Ibid., folio 188. Domenico Bonazzi also reported this. See ibid., folio 18 ff.

33. Ibid., folio 20. "I never saw any of the workers omit to say their prayers before the image when it was shut."

34. Holmes, *The Miraculous Image*, 177.

35. ASMo. FI CH busta 256 fasc. 17, folio 38.

36. In general, Jews who lived outside the city were summoned to appear at the Holy Office in Modena, rather than being interrogated locally. This served to emphasize the centrality and authority of the tribunal in the city and the Holy Office's preference for coming face-to-face with individual Jewish suspects. Two other Sanguinetti brothers were Buonaiuto (age twenty-four) and Angelo (age fifteen). Angelo was not indicted or called to give testimony.

37. Ibid., folio 24; see also folio 22. Menozzi reported Simon's thwarted attempts to address this: "One time also before he began to run the mill, Simon Sanguinetti asked me if I would be willing to whiten this image of the Madonna, and I said that I did not want him to do this."

38. Ibid., folio 25.

39. Ibid., folio 37–38.

40. Ibid., folio 24.

41. Ibid., folio 39. Alessandro admitted: "One day, one of the boys who works in the mill found a key on the ground under the place where he works. He gave it to me and I put it in the dressing room [*camerino*] at the bottom of the mill, where other things which are found, are kept": and later, "For two reasons did I keep the key. The first because I was never asked for it. The other reason is that if the Christians did not have the key, they would not be able to do any damage to the painting. Otherwise, they would damage it and blame us for this evil act."

42. Daniel Jütte, *The Strait Gate: Thresholds of Power in Western History* (New Haven, CT: Yale University Press, 2015), 14, 108, 123.

43. ASMo. FI. CH busta 256 fasc. 17, folio 188.

44. See Black, "The Trials and Tribulations," 26. It was difficult for Tinti to obey those orders of the Sacred Congregation, as he felt pressure to comply with the demands of the Modenese duke. See also ASMo. FI, Modena: Lettere della Sacra Congregazione di Roma 1621–1628, busta 253, dated March 1, 1628.

45. See, for example, ACDF, St. St. CC 1c.

46. See the letter of December 18, 1632, in ASMo. FI, Modena: Lettere della Sacra Congregazione di Roma, 1629–1638, busta 254, where Antonio Barberini, cardinal of Sant'Onofrio, displayed his disgust that Christians were serving Jews, and demanded that the inquisitor should "prohibit the said Jews from using the spinning mill."

47. ASMo. FI CH busta 256 fasc. 17, folio 24. Simon had already been prosecuted and fined for hiring Christian servants in his home in 1624 and 1629, a practice also followed by the three other Jewish families living in the same town. No reference is made by the inquisitor to these cases. For these two previous cases, see ASMo. FI, Processi busta 70, fasc. 13, and busta 88, fasc. 10.

48. ASMo. FI CH busta 256 fasc. 17, folio 184.

49. See ASMo. FI, Modena: Lettere della Sacra Congregazione di Roma, 1629–1638, busta 254. See the letter of Cardinal Antonio Barberini to Tinti, December 18, 1632.

50. ASMo. FI CH busta 256 fasc. 17, folio 184, February 7, 1633.

51. Ibid. See Simon's testimony, folio 49. See also testimony of Buonaiuto, folio 63.

52. ACDF, St. St. CC 1c, February 23, 1633.

53. ASMo. FI CH busta 256 fasc. 17, folio 17. and 91. See also ACDF, St. St. CC 1c. Here there is a letter from Tinti dated December 14, 1632, where he gives the same report.

54. John T. Paoletti and Gary M. Radke, *Art in Renaissance Italy*, 3rd ed. (Upper Saddle River, NJ: Pearson/Prentice Hall, 2005), 16.

55. See ASMo. FI CH busta 256 fasc. 17, folio 119. Tinti's notes mention that the image was of "Mary nursing her child." On typical poses of the Madonna and Child, see Freedberg, *The Power of Images*, 112ff. *Madonna lactans* images had increased in popularity in the fourteenth and fifteenth century; on this iconography in the Western tradition, see the work of Beth Williamson, *The Madonna of Humility: Development, Dissemination and Reception, c. 1340–1400* (Woodbridge: Boydell Press, 2010). But by the sixteenth century, they had lost their importance as devotional symbols and been replaced by images of the Immaculate Conception, Assumption, and Coronation, which stressed Mary's unique integrity and purity—rather than maternal themes of nurturing and nourishing Christ. But the nursing Madonna was still often represented not only in churches and among religious cults but also in domestic spaces. See Menzione, *Preghiera e diletto*, 20; and Naomi Yavneh, "To Bare or Not to Bare: Sofonisba Anguissola's Nursing Madonna and the Womanly Art of Breastfeeding," in *Maternal Measures: Figuring Caregiving in the Early Modern Period*, ed. Naomi J. Miller and Naomi Yavneh (Aldershot: Ashgate, 2000), 65–81, 65.

56. The image is referred to as sacred ninety-six times in this file, most of the time by the inquisitors in their questioning. There is no reason to believe that the image was sacred as a result of consecration.

57. See Holmes, "Miraculous Images in Renaissance Florence," 437–438.

58. ASMo. FI CH busta 256 fasc. 17, folio 32. In an unusual move, Michelangelo summoned Buonaiuto Sanguinetti to appear before him in the Church of the Annunciation on November 1, 1632, which was the Jewish Sabbath. It was rare for the Inquisition to interrogate a Jew on their sabbath. Yet Buonaiuto did not exploit his legal right to defer attendance, but instead made it clear in his two interrogations that he would not be able to sign his name on the written record of his testimony.

59. Rubin, *Emotion and Devotion*, 82.

60. See Margaret R. Miles, *A Complex Delight: The Secularization of the Breast, 1350–1570* (Berkeley: University of California Press, 2008), 41 and 45. Caroline Walker Bynum,

Fragmentation and Redemption: Essays on Gender and the Human Body in Medieval Religion (New York: Zone Books, 1991), 102, describes this lactating image of the Virgin as "one of the most common iconographic themes in all of Christian art."

61. Having said this, Caroline Walker Bynum has successfully shown how it is problematic to assume that images of the Virgin Mary, even the nursing Madonna in the High Middle Ages, appealed predominantly to women. See Caroline Walker Bynum, *Jesus as Mother: Studies in the Spirituality of the High Middle Ages* (Berkeley: University of California Press, 1982), 110–169.

62. Rubin, *Emotion and Devotion*, 82ff.

63. As Daniel Jütte has argued, any open door or flap could be seen as an invitation for others to approach (*The Strait Gate*, 5).

64. Katz, "'Clamber Not You Up,'" 133, 139.

65. ASMo. FI CH busta 256 fasc. 17, folio 36. See also folio 29. The Christian blacksmith Francesco Casalgrande even admits that after he made the lock on the board, he too had given its keys to Alessandro and not left them in the lock.

66. Ibid., folio 28.

67. See ibid., folio 27, October 29, 1632, for the observations of Michelangelo. Elsewhere, the inquisitor accuses Simon with these words: "These marks that were seen on the said sacred image, and have been identified by the Christians who have seen it, could not have been made by the Christians, since you had the key and could freely open this sacred image and damage it" (ibid., 40b–41a).

68. Ibid., folio 24 and folio 182, July 24, 1635.

69. Ibid., folio 73.

70. Ibid., folio 135.

71. See Yavneh, "To Bare or Not to Bare," 75.

72. See Muir, "The Virgin on the Street Corner," 25–40,

73. Testimony of Tommaso Caparelli, ASMo. FI CH busta 256 fasc. 17, folio 116.

74. Menzione, *Preghiera e diletto*, 19. On the Virgin's decreasing importance, see Geraldine A. Johnson, "Idol or Ideal? The Power and Potency of Female Public Sculpture," in Johnson and Grieco, *Picturing Women*, 222–245, 235.

75. See Lisa Pon, *A Printed Icon in Early Modern Italy: Forlì's Madonna of the Fire* (Cambridge: Cambridge University Press, 2015) 20, 102. See also Ajmar-Wollheim and Dennis, *At Home in Renaissance Italy*, 201–202.

76. ASMo. FI. CH busta 256 fasc. 17 folio 119. In his interrogation on July 24, 1635, Raffaele stated, "The boys who worked in the mill attached figures wherever they were positioned." As Lisa Pon has shown, a domestic chapel was usually situated in a multipurpose room containing a table upon which a Eucharist would be placed during mass. In 1562, the Council of Trent ordered that a domestic chapel should be separated from the house's main room, or *sala*. Religious images could be placed here as well as being scattered throughout the home. Pon, *A Printed Icon*, 102.

77. ASMo. FI, CH 244, fasc. 8.

78. Ibid., folio 18v.

79. Ibid., folio 7v.

80. ASMo. FI CH busta 256 fasc. 17. The nine witnesses (with the number of times they were interrogated in parentheses) were Francesco Mathioli (3), Gio Baptista Bartholomeo (1), Domenico Bonazzi (2), Andrea Cavretti (2), Gio Battista Cagarelli (2), Tommaso Caparelli (2),

Adriano Consini (3), Leonardo Costantini (2), and Sanito Melloti (1). Some of these witnesses had already given testimony in 1632. According to Black, Tinti's busiest year was 1635 ("The Trials and Tribulations," 14).

81. Terpstra, "Working the Cocoon," 52.

82. ASMo. FI. CH busta 256 fasc. 17, folio 130.

83. See ibid., folio 126 and folio 127.

84. Ibid. See Leonardo's first testimony in 1635, folio 135–136.

85. Ibid., folio 4.

86. Ibid., folio 111.

87. Ibid., folio 59. Francesco Mariano's interrogation by the inquisitor general Petro took place in Reggio because he had moved there after he left the mill.

88. Ibid., folio 60.

89. Ibid., folio 115.

90. Ibid., folio 135.

91. Ibid., folio 182. In his later written testimony before the criminal court, Costantini also described Simon physically removing a cheap religious print of the Madonna that was on the door of a cellar in the mill.

92. Ibid., folio 96. Here there is a note, dated August 29, 1635, from the inquisitor of Bologna, who was trying to trace him.

93. Ibid., folio 69.

94. Ibid., folio 182 ff.

95. Ibid., folio 183.

96. Ibid;, see also the inquisitor's notes on folio 173.

97. Ibid., folio 140 ff.

98. Ibid., folio 55. Although many of the Christian spinners argued this, it was clear from Raffaele's testimony on November 14, 1635, that he sometimes went into the mill on Sundays to allow the floss silkers (*bavellini*) to carry out their work of folding and weighing the floss silk. They only came to the mill on Sundays.

99. Ibid.

100. Ibid., folio 113v.

101. Ibid., 175r. During these proceedings, Simon was imprisoned for three periods and interrogated seven times. From October 21 to November 30, 1632 (five weeks), during which he was interrogated three times (October 21 and twice on November 2); from October 8 to November 20, 1635 (almost eight weeks), during which he was interrogated twice on November 19 and once on November 20; and finally from March 5 to April 14, 1636 (one month) with one interrogation on March 16.

102. The problem of security could be partly resolved for the Inquisition by making the wealthier escorted prisoners put up large sums of money as bonds.

103. Ibid.

104. Ibid., folio 47 ff.

105. Ibid., folio 38. Note how he argued back about his sons sleeping in the mill: "I did not know that it was forbidden for us to sleep in a place where Christians pass through [to go to work]. All the more so as the archpriest came several times to the mill and saw the beds, and he did not say anything about this."

106. Ibid., folio 126.

107. Ibid., folio 53.

108. Ibid., folio 77. After Alessandro's later arrest in 1644, he had some discussion with the inquisitors about Bassano's geographic location. Alessandro explained: "there are two as I remember, one in the mountains above Trent, and the other in Turkey toward Salonika."

109. There were two copies made of each letter in the dossier. Ibid., folio 152, folio 190, and folio 191.

110. Ibid., folio 52.

111. Ibid.

112. Ibid., folio 65 ff.

113. See Aron-Beller, *Jews on Trial*, 62–63.

114. ASMo. FI CH busta 256 fasc. 17; Raffaele was interrogated nine times between the years 1632 and 1644, and imprisoned during three periods, from October 24, 1632 to November 3, 1632 (ten days); July 22, 1635, to December 14, 1635 (almost five months), and March 5–16, 1636 (eleven days), when he was tortured. Regarding his defiance, Raffaele in his interrogation on November 29, 1635, states, "I did not say this to deny what is true when I said no. But now I say yes because only now do I remember," and later, "I said that I was not there because I figured it was so. But having thought about it, I remember now that I was there, so now I confess it. Although I did not confess this the first time. I did not do this to keep the truth quiet" (folio 65).

115. Ibid., folio 28. On October 29, 1632, he had testified, "Now I am running the mill. I live there and at times in my house, I come and go. I give orders to the supervisor who carries them out."

116. Ibid., folio 75.

117. Ibid., folio 121.

118. Ibid., folio 173–174.

119. See Tanner, *Decrees of the Ecumenical Councils*, 2:774–776.

120. ACDF, St. St. CC 1c. He also reports on his arguments with Simon about how much he should be fined.

121. ASMo. FI CH busta 256 fasc. 17, folio 72.

122. Ibid., folio 73 ff.

123. Ibid. The notary hints at the pressure and stress in the torture room by his untidy writing, which deteriorates as he rushes to record every word uttered by Raffaele.

124. Ibid., folio 97. Simon managed to negotiate and reduce his fine from 550 scudi to 300. Part of this payment went to the Inquisition in Reggio. See ASMo. FI, Modena: Lettere della Sacra Congregazione di Roma, 1629–1638, busta 254, February 23, March 29, and April 12, 1636. See also Black "The Trials and Tribulations," where he notes that Giacomo Tinti was later warned that using large fines to punish Jews risked causing scandal. In ACDF, St. St. CC 1c, fol. 195r, Fra Gialcomo Lodi writes that on April 19, 1636, he has released Simon from prison. He had so far paid out seven hundred lire and given suitable security to cover the rest, which was eight hundred lire, within eight months. Tinti asks the Sacred Congregation to reduce the fine (196r); Tinti resolved on April 9 that he should pay three hundred scudi.

125. ACDF, St. St. CC 1c, fol. 194.

126. Ibid.

127. Other cases under prosecution by the Modenese court at this time included ongoing problems with foreigners—in particular, Swiss merchants and their heretical ideas, Modenese soldiers who denied the true faith, and Clarissa nuns who were poorly disciplined

and failed to conform to post-Tridentine rules. See Jeffrey R. Watt, *The Scourge of Demons: Possession, Lust, and Witchcraft in a Seventeenth-Century Italian Convent* (Rochester, NY: University of Rochester Press, 2009), who discusses the cases of the Clarissa nuns.

128. Chartier, *The Culture of Print.*

129. See ASMo. FI CH busta 256, fasc. 17, folio 4.

130. See Areford, *The Viewer and the Printed Image*, 15. The act of viewing prints could include "a variety of manipulations, from cutting away parts of the print to adding painted details, titles, prayers and interpretive inscriptions . . . a range of devotional practices and communal rituals."

131. See ASMo. FI CH busta 256, fasc. 17, folio 135.

132. Ibid., folio 3.

133. Ibid., folio 135.

134. Ibid., folio 182.

135. Ibid., folio 144. Marchesi begins his testimony with the words "There is more." Marchesi also reported that Ricca, Simon Sanguinetti's wife, had blasphemed in her home, using the words "Puttana della nostra donna," and "Putta di Dio". How Marchesi knew what blasphemies the Jewish woman said in her own home is not explained. The inquisitors seemed to ignore these blasphemy allegations completely and never called Ricca for interrogation.

136. ACDF, St. St. CC 1c. Here, under August 1635, the damage to the primitive chapel is noted, as well as damage to the prints and the images in the inn. Alessandro is at once targeted as a culprit.

137. ASMo. FI CH busta 256, fasc. 17, folio 145. The innkeeper Thomaso Garagnane testified, "I say to your Reverence, that this Jew was in the middle room above the inn in the part that faces Bologna. Not only in the room where he slept were there images of the saints and the Madonna, but also in two other rooms adjacent to it, which he was able to use and pass through." And later, Thomaso notes "in the room where he stayed there was an image of the Madonna and saints, but I do not remember well which saints they were" (45r).

138. Ibid., folio 42.

139. Ibid., folio 42 ff.

140. Ibid., folio 45 ff.

141. Ibid., folio 45. Thomaso Garagnane's testimony confirms this. See also ACDF, St. St. CC 1c, fols. 171v–172r.

142. For the use of this term in Thomaso's testimonies, see ASMo. FI CH busta 256, fasc. 17, folio 46 and 145.

143. Ibid., folio 44.

144. Ibid., folio 45.

145. For the discrepancy about the time of discovery of the images, see ibid., folio 81–82.

146. See also ACDF, St. St. CC 1c, fol. 169v. Here it is noted that Caterina had testified that Betiga could not have done it since he was "a good man and had been a thousand other times to stay and no trouble had arisen. No Christian would have done this."

147. See ASMo. FI CH busta 256, fasc. 17, folio 45, regarding Bernardo Betiga; and Alessandro's testimony at folio 81–82.

148. Ibid., folio 145.

149. Ibid., folio 45.

150. See ASMo. FI, Miscellanea, busta 295, "Modo et ordine che omnia il Reverendo Padre Inquisitore nelle essercitare il suo officio nella città di Modena," which records in-

quisitorial procedure when a suspect flees the Inquisition: that he is to be treated as a disobedient suspect, and if he does not appear after three summons by the Inquisition or give a reasonable excuse for his absence or flight, he will be excommunicated.

151. ASMo. FI CH busta 256 fasc. 17, folio 76.

152. The inquisitorial records use the word *appestato* ("infected" or "tainted") to describe Alessandro's right side. Romano Canosa seems to suggest that he had a withered right arm, but it is difficult to identify the exact nature of the problem. See Canosa, *Storia dell'Inquisizione,* 1:45ff. In the text of the trial, ASMo. FI CH busta 256, fasc. 17 folio 88, it is difficult to decipher the handwriting.

153. A rare case where a Jew, Moise de Modena, in 1622 sought legal counsel in Modena is mentioned in Aron-Beller, *Jews on Trial*, 221ff.

154. ASMo. FI CH busta 256, fasc. 17, folio 154.

155. Ibid.

156. *Bullarum diplomatum et privilegiorum sanctorum romanorum pontificum*, vol. 8 (Turin, 1863), 378–379.

157. ASMo. FI CH busta 256 fasc. 17, folio 23. See Simon's testimony.

158. See Aron-Beller, "Outside the Ghetto"; on inquisitorial action in Ferrara, see Guido Dall'Olio, "L'inquisizione romana e gli ebrei nella Ferrara del Seicento: Prime indagini," in Galasso, *Le Inquisizione cristiane e gli ebrei*, 297–321, 320. Not until 1742 were Italian Jews permitted to establish their own silk manufacturing facilities. Economic historians even argue that in seventeenth- and eighteenth-century Italy, it was in the country districts and small towns, away from the conservative influence of the corporations in the old-established centers, that industries could flourish.

159. ASMo. FI, Modena: Lettere della sacra congregazione di Roma, 1629–1638, busta 254, fol. 181r, February 26, 1633, with copy of memorial from Rangone.

160. Despite papal pressure, the Jews continued possessing immovable goods until 1670. At that point, during the regency of Duchess Laura Martinozzi—corresponding to the recent establishment of the Reggio ghetto in the duchy—Jews were finally forbidden to hold immovable goods and were forced to sell their lands. Duchess Laura Martinozzi was the regent between 1662 and 1674 for her son Francesco II who was Duke of Modena from 1662 to 1694.

161. ASMo. FI CH busta 256, fasc. 17, folio 118.

162. Ibid., folio 48.

163. Ibid., folio 58.

164. Ibid., folio 54.

165. ACDF, St. St. CC 1c, fol. 172v.

166. ASMo. FI CH busta 256, fasc. 17, Adriano Consini's testimony on folio 116 and Gio Baptista Cagarelli's testimony on folio 118.

167. Ibid., folio 129.

168. Ibid., folio 65. Raffaele in his interrogation on November 29, 1635, noted, "I have never shouted nor given a beating to anyone for singing their prayers, but at times I have indeed shouted and given slaps if the silk was torn."

169. Ibid., folio 59.

170. Ibid., folio 129, 131, 132.

171. Ibid., folio 132. Gio Baptista Bartholomeo says that Simon lost control when one evening the Christians sang together. The noise was too much for him.

172. Ibid., folio 55.

173. Ibid.

174. Ibid., folio 140.

175. Ibid., folio 182. Leonardo recorded in his written testimony: "If at times the Jews were there, they never impeded the workforce in their work or in their prayers. In faith I say this in truth, and written by my own hand, by me Leonardo as above."

176. Ibid., folio 60.

177. Ibid. He replied: "No, Father, I was never attacked while I was saying the prayer of Sant' Elena, or just before or just after saying it. One or another of the Jews sometimes happened to come in while I was saying prayers, but they just went away. Usually, they never entered the workshop except to see if there was something wrong. . . . Father, I have spoken the truth. It is true that he never did anything to me for saying these prayers. On the occasions that we said them, the Jews would go away because they did not want to hear us saying them."

178. See Poni, "Archéologie de la fabrique," 1476.

179. ASMo. FI CH busta 256, fasc.17, folio 36.

180. Ibid.

181. See testimony of Francesco Mariano (ibid., folio 60) and Adriano Consini (ibid., folio 131); also testimony of Leonardo Costantini (ibid., folio 135) and Domenico Bonazzi (ibid., folio 124 ff.). Bonazzi testified that Alessandro had complained about the images, demanding that they be removed.

182. Ibid., folio 129. See, for example, testimony of Andrea Cavretti (ibid., folio 140) and Tommaso Caparelli (ibid., folio 116).

183. Pier Cesare Ioly Zorattini, "*Derekh Teshuvah*: La via del ritorno," in *L'Identità dissimulata: Giudaizzanti iberici nell'Europa cristiana dell'età moderna*, ed. Pier Cesare Ioly Zorattini (Florence: Olschki, 2000), 195–248, 243. See also Michela Andreatta, "The Persuasive Path: Giulio Morosini's *Derek Emunah* as a Conversion Narrative," in *Bastards and Believers: Jewish Converts and Conversion from the Bible to the Present*, ed. Theodor Dunkelgrün and Paweł Maciejko (Philadelphia: University of Pennsylvania Press, 2020), 156–181, 177.

184. In fact, I have not come across any genuine examples of early modern Jews converting in response to the behavior of a miracle-working image.

185. ASMo. FI CH busta 256, fasc. 17, folio 110–111. Ludovico Marchesi reported on October 7, 1632, in Spilamberto that "Gio Maria said to me that someone had seen with his own eyes one of those Jews who wanted to take hold of one of those girls who went to the mill." This hearsay accusation was not confirmed by anyone else.

CONCLUSION

1. See Nirenberg, *Anti-Judaism*.

2. A sculpted crucifix on the Charles Bridge in Prague was, according to its inscription, erected in September 1696 with funds from the Jewish community, after a Jew was accused of mocking a crucifix. See Kamil Novotný and Emanuel Poche, *The Charles Bridge of Prague* (Prague: V. Poláček, 1947), 29. For other cases in seventeenth-century Poland, see Teter, *Sinners on Trial*, 78–79.

3. Marina Caffiero, *Forced Baptisms: Histories of Jews, Christians, and Converts in Papal Rome* (Berkeley: University of California Press, 2011), 23–25; Caffiero notes that in 1697 the Università of the Jews of Rome, already having experienced Medici's blatantly aggressive

beliefs preached in his sermons, denounced him formally to the Inquisition in a document written by Tranquillo Vita Corcos. See ACDF, Sant'Officio, Stanza Storica, UV 24, fols. 137–153, "Alla Sacra Congregatione del S. Offizio Per l'Università degl' Ebrei. Memoriale. Romae, Typis Rev. Cam. Apost. 1697."

4. Caffiero, *Forced Baptisms*, 28.

5. Lucia Frattarelli Fischer, "Ebrei a Pisa e Livorno nel Sei e Settecento tra inquisizioni e garanzie granducali," in Galasso, *Le Inquisizioni cristiane e gli ebrei*, 288.

6. Cardozo de Bethencourt, "The Jews in Portugal from 1773 to 1902," *Jewish Quarterly Review* 15, no. 2 (1903): 251–274, 273.

7. François Soyer, "The Passion of Christ in the Church of San Cristóbal de Rapaz: An Example of Medieval Anti-Jewish Iconography in Colonial Peru?," *eHumanista/Conversos* 5 (2017): 392–416.

8. See Allyson F. Creasman, "The Virgin Mary Against the Jews: Anti-Jewish Polemic in the Pilgrimage to the Schöne Maria of Regensburg, 1519–25," *Sixteenth Century Journal* 33, no. 4 (2002): 963–980, 968–973, where an allegation of ritual murder in 1476 brought about the imprisonment of Jews until their release in 1480. The Jewish community (approximately eight hundred Jews) were then expelled in 1516. See also Annette Weber, "New Attitudes Towards the Jews in the Era of Reformation and Counter-Reformation: The Patronage of Bishop Echter von Mespelbrunn," in Merback, *Beyond the Yellow Badge*, 347–369, 358–359.

9. "Medieval Sourcebook: The Golden Legend: St. Nicholas," Fordham University, Internet History Sourcebooks Project, accessed July 17, 2022, https://sourcebooks.fordham.edu/basis/goldenlegend/GL-vol2-nicholas.asp.

10. See Möschter, "*Et Verbum caro factum est*," 362 and 388–393. This fits into the more widespread Italian tradition of forcing Jews, through fines or taxes, to finance artistic projects. See Andrea Bruscino, "Una presenza ebraica di lungo periodo: La famiglia da San Miniato ad Empoli (secc. XIV–XVI)" (PhD diss., Università di Pisa, 2006), 92–94 and 428–444.

11. Richard Wagner, *"The Art-Work of the Future" and Other Works,* trans. William Ashton Ellis (Lincoln: University of Nebraska Press, 1993), 177.

Bibliography

MANUSCRIPT SOURCES

Bologna, Archivio di Stato di Bologna

Podesta, Libri, Inquisitionum 303 (1413–1414)
Sententiae 35 (1413–1417)

Bologna, Biblioteca dell'Archiginnasio di Bologna

B-1891
B-1892

Florence, Archivio di Stato di Firenze

Otto di Guardia e di Balia, n. 57
Otto di Guardia e di Balìa, n. 72

Jerusalem, Central Archives of the History of the Jewish People

A.S.E. archivi per Materie "ebrei" busta 4 Processi 1-LXXXIII 1600–1629 pezzi n. 83, 5407 microfilm c, 113–116, March 29, 1617

Livorno, Archivio di Stato di Livorno

Capitano poi Governatore Auditore Vicario (1505–1808)
Fondo Governatore e Auditore 2603-1, 2603-2
Atti Civili Repertori, 1633–1700
Spezzati Atti Criminali dal 1617 al 1672

Lucca, Archivio Arcivescovile di Lucca

Libri Antichi, 99/A c.48

Mantua, Archivio Gonzaga di Mantova

Busta 2447, carta 137

Modena, Archivio di Stato di Modena (ASMo.)

Fondo dell' Inquisizione, Processi 26
Fondo dell' Inquisizione, Processi 35
Fondo dell' Inquisizione, Processi 67
Fondo dell' Inquisizione, Processi 69
Fondo dell' Inquisizione, Processi 70
Fondo dell' Inquisizione, Processi 85
Fondo dell' Inquisizione, Processi 111
Fondo dell' Inquisizione, Causae Hebreorum 244
Fondo dell' Inquisizione, Causae Hebreorum 245
Fondo dell' Inquisizione, Causae Hebreorum 246
Fondo dell' Inquisizione, Causae Hebreorum 247
Fondo dell' Inquisizione, Causae Hebreorum 250
Fondo dell' Inquisizione, Causae Hebreorum 256
Fondo dell' Inquisizione, Modena: Lettere della Sacra Congregazione di Roma, 1609–1621, busta 252
Fondo dell' Inquisizione, Modena: Lettere della Sacra Congregazione di Roma, 1621–1628, busta 253
Fondo dell' Inquisizione, Modena. Lettere della Sacra Congregazione di Roma, 1629–1638, busta 254
Fondo dell' Inquisizione, busta 270, Editti e Decreti VII
Fondo dell' Inquisizione, busta 288, Carteggi Diversi, 1600–1769

Oxford, Bodleian Library

The Flemish Book of Hours, Oxford, Douce MS 112, fol. 160

Reggio-Emilia, Archivio Storico Diocesano di Reggio-Emilia

Litterarum trasmissarum a supremo tribunali ab anno 1598 usque ad 1611, Tomus I

Rome, Archivio della Congregazione per la Dottrina della Fede (ACDF)

Sant' Officio, Stanza Storica, AA
Sant' Officio, Stanza Storica CC. 1c
Sant' Officio, Stanza Storica, UV 24
Sant' Officio, Decreta 1610–1611
Sant' Officio, Decreta 1612
Sant' Officio, Decreta 1613
Sant' Officio, Decreta 1650
Sant' Officio, Decreta 1653

Rome, Archivio Vaticano Camera Apostolica

Registri del Ducator di Spoleto, Entrate e Uscite 22, fol. 133b

PRIMARY SOURCES

Adamnan's De Locis Sanctis. Ed. Denis Meehan. Scriptores Latini Hiberniae 3. Dublin: Dublin Institute for Advanced Studies, 1958.

Adémar de Chabannes. *Chronique*. Ed. Jules Chavanon. Paris: A. Picard, 1897.

"Admonitio in historiam imaginis Berytensis." In *Patrologiae cursus completus, series Graeca*, ed. Jacques Paul Migne, 28:797–812. Paris, 1857.

Agapius of Manbij. *Kitab al-'unvan: Histoire universelle, écrite par Agapius (Mahboub) de Menbidj* 2.2. Edited and translated by Alexandre Vasiliev. *Patrologia Orientalis* 38 (8.3). Turnhout: Brepols, 1971.

Agobardus. *Opera omnia*. Ed. Lievan van Acker. Turnhout: Brepols, 1981.

Alfonso de Madrigal. *Confessional del Tostado*. Alcalá de Henares: Arnao Guillén de Brocar, 1517.

Alfonso X. *Las Cantigas de Santa María: Códice Rico, Ms. T-I-1 Real Biblioteca del Monasterio de San Lorenzo de El Escorial*. 2 vols. Facsimile edition. Madrid: Patrimonio Nacional; Testimonio, 2011.

———. *Songs of Holy Mary of Alfonso X, the Wise: A Translation of the "Cantigas de Santa Maria."* Translated by Kathleen Kulp-Hill. Tempe: Arizona Center for Medieval and Renaissance Studies, 2000.

Almbladh, Karin, ed. *Joseph Ha-Kohen: Sefer 'Emeq Ha-Bakha' (The Vale of Tears) with the Chronicle of the Anonymous Corrector*. Uppsala: Almqvist & Wiksell, 1981.

Anonymi auctoris Chronicon ad annum Christi 1234 pertinens I: Praemissum est Chronicon anonymum ad A.D. 819 pertinens; interpretatus est. Ed. Jean-Baptiste Chabot. Louvain: Imprimerie Orientaliste, L. Durbecq, 1952.

Aquinas, Thomas. *Summa Theologiae*. Ed. Thomas Gilby. Garden City, NY: Doubleday, 1969.

Arduini, Maria Lodovica. *Ruperto di Deutz e la controversia tra Cristiani ed Ebrei nel Secolo XII: Con testo critico dell' "Anulus seu dialogus inter Christianum et Iudaeum," a cura di Rhabanus Haacke*. Rome: Istituto Storico Italiano per il Medio Evo, 1979.

Artom, Elia S. and Humbertus [Umberto] M. D. Cassuto, eds. *Statuta Iudaeorum Candiae eorumque memorabilia*. Vol. 1. Jerusalem: Mekize Nirdamim, 1943.

Benavente, Agustín de. *Segunda parte de las Luzes de Dios, resplandor de las llagas de Cristo Señor Nuestro empleo del pensamiento cristiano en la vida del mismo Señor, y su santissima Madre*. Valladolid: Antonio de Ruenda, 1647.

Berger, Albrecht, ed. *Life and Works of Saint Gregentios, Archbishop of Taphar: Introduction, Critical Edition and Translation*. With a contribution by Gianfranco Fiaccadori. Millennium-Studien 7. Berlin: De Gruyter, 2006.

Bleda, Jaime. *Quatroçientos Milagros y muchas alabanzas de la Santa Cruz con unos tratados de las cosas mas notables desta divina señal*. Valencia: Pedro Patricio Mey, 1600.

Bullarum, diplomatum et privilegiorum sanctorum romanorum pontificum. Vol. 8. Turin, 1863.

Capsali, Eliyahu (Elijah). *Seder Eliyahu Zuta*. Ed. Aryeh Shmuelevitz, Shlomo Simonsohn, and Meir Benayahu. Vol. 2. Jerusalem: Ben-Zvi Institute, 1977.

Carpenter, Dwayne E. *Alfonso X and the Jews: An Edition of and Commentary on "Siete Partides" 7.24 "De los judíos."* Berkeley: University of California Press, 1986.

Cassiodorus-Epiphanius. *Historia ecclesiastica tripartita* 11.13, ed. Walter Jacob and Rudolf Hanslik, Vienna, 1952.

———. *Historia ecclesiastica tripartita*. Corpus Scriptorum Ecclesiasticorum Latinorum 71. Ed. Walter Jacob and Rudolf Hanslik. Vienna, 1952.

Cencius Camerarius, *Le liber censuum de l'église romaine*, ed. Paul Fabre and Louis Duchesne (Paris, 1905), vol. 1.

Chronicon Paschale, 284–628 AD. Translated with introduction and notes by Michael Whitby and Mary Whitby. Liverpool: Liverpool University Press, 1990.

Delaborde, H. François, ed. *Oeuvres de Rigord et de Guillaume le Breton, historiens de Philippe-Auguste*. Vol. 1, *Chroniques de Rigord et de Guillaume le Breton*. Paris: Librairie Renouard, 1882.

Durand, William (Guillaume). *The Rationale divinorum officiorum of William Durand of Mende: A New Translation of the Prologue and Book One*. Translated by Timothy M. Thibodeau. New York: Columbia University Press, 2007.

———. *Guillelmi Duranti Rationale divinorum officiorum*. Ed. Anselme Davril and T. M. Thibodeau. 3 vols. Corpus Christianorum Series Latina, Continuatio Mediaevalis. Turnhout: Brepols, 1995–2000.

Eliezer ben Nathan, *Sefer Ra'avan: Ha Sefer Even ha-Ezer*. Jerusalem: H. Vagshal, 1984.

Eliezer ben Joel Halevi. *SeferRav'iah*. Ed. Avigdor Aptowitzer. Jerusalem: Mekize Nirdamim, 1938.

Eliezer of Metz. *Sefer Yereim ha-Shalem: Issurim she-Ra la-Shamayim Vela-Beriot*. Jerusalem, 1973.

Espina, Alonso de. "Fortalitium fidei iudeos contra saracenos aliosque Christiane fidei inimicos," incunabulum edition of Antonius Koberger, prepared and completed in Nuremburg on February 25 1494, Friedenwald collection, Edelstein Library, National Library of Jerusalem.

Eusebius of Caesarea. *De Vita Constantini: Über das Leben Konstantins*. Introduction by Bruno Bleckmann. Translation into German and commentary by Horst Schneider. Turnhout: Brepols, 2007.

Evagrius, "Altercatio inter Theophilum Christianum et Simonem Judaem," in *Patrologia cursus completus, series latina*, ed. Jacques Paul Migne (Paris, 1845) vol. 20, cols. 1165–1180.

Gautier de Coinci. *Les Miracles de Nostre Dame*. Ed. V. Frédéric Koenig. Vol. 2. Geneva: Droz, 1961.

Giordano da Rivalto. *Prediche del beato frate Giordano da Rivalto dell'ordine de' Predicatori recitate in Firenze dal MCCCIII al MCCCVI*. Ed Domenico Moreni. 2 vols. Florence: Magheri, 1831.

Gonzalo de Berceo. *Miracles of Our Lady by Gonzalo de Berceo*. Edited and translated by Richard Mount and Annette Grant Cash. Lexington: University Press of Kentucky, 1998.

Gregory of Tours (Gregorius Turonensis). *Gregory of Tours: Life of the Fathers*. Translated with introduction by Edward James. 2nd ed. Liverpool: Liverpool University Press, 1991.

———. *Gregory of Tours: Glory of the Martyrs*. Translated with introduction by Raymond Van Dam. Liverpool: Liverpool University Press, 1988.

———. *Libri historiarum X*. Ed. Bruno Krusch and Wilhelm Levison. Monumenta Germaniae Historica, Scriptores rerum Merovingicarum 1.1. Hanover, 1951.

———. *Liber in gloria martyrum*, no. 21, ed. Bruno Krusch, Monumenta Germaniae Historica, Scriptores rerum Merovingicarum (Deutsches Institut für Erforschung des Mittelalters) vol. 1.2. Hannover, 1885, 857–72.

Gui, Bernard (Bernardus Guidonis). *Practica inquisitionis heretice pravitatis*. Ed. Célestin Douais. Paris: Picard, 1886.

Guibert of Nogent. *A Monk's Confession: The Memoirs of Guibert of Nogent*. Translated with an introduction by Paul J. Archambault. University Park: Pennsylvania State University Press, 1996.

———. *De sanctis et eorum pigneribus*. In *Guitbertus Abbas Sanctae Mariae Novigenti: Quo ordine sermo fieri debeat; De bucella iudae data et de veritate dominici corporis; De sanctis et eorum pigneribus*, ed. R. B. C. Huygens, Corpus Christianorum, Continuatio Mediaevalis 127:79–175. Turnhout: Brepols, 1993.

Haim ben Isaac. *Sefer Teshuvot m. ha-R. H. Or Zaru'a*. Jerusalem: Avitan, 2002.

Helinand of Froidmont. *Chronicon*. In *Patrologiae cursus completus, series Latina*, ed. Jacques Paul Migne, 212:771–1082. Paris, 1855.

Ibn Aderet, Solomon ben Avraham (Rashba). *Sheelot u-teshuvot (Responsa)*. 7 vols. Bnei Brak, 1957–1959.

Ibn Kaspi, Joseph. *Shulhan Kesef*. Ed. Hannah Kasher. Jerusalem: Ben-Zvi Institute, 1996.

Ibn Verga, Solomon. *Shevet Yehudah*. Ed. Azriel Shochat and Yitzhak Baer. Jerusalem: Bialik Institute, 1947.

Ishbili, Yom Tov ben Avraham (Ritva). *Sheelot u-teshuvot (Responsa)*. Ed. Yoseph Kapah. Jerusalem, 1959.

Jacobus de Voragine. *The Golden Legend: Readings on the Saints*. Translated by William Granger Ryan. 2 vols. Princeton, NJ: Princeton University Press, 1995.

James, Montague Rhodes, trans. *The Apocryphal New Testament: Being the Apocryphal Gospels, Acts, Epistles, and Apocalypses, with Other Narratives and Fragments*. Corrected edition. Oxford: Clarendon Press, 1953.

John of Damascus. *Contra imaginum calumniatores orationes tres*. Vol. 3 of *Die Schriften des Johannes von Damaskos*, ed. Bonifatius Kotter. Berlin: De Gruyter, 1975.

John Chrysostom. *Adversus Judaeos Orationes* 1.6, *Patrologiae cursus completus, series Graeca*, ed. Jacques Paul Migne (Paris, 1857), vol. 48.

Joseph Official. *Sefer Yosef HaMeqanne*. Ed Judah Rosenthal. Jerusalem: Mekize Nirdamim, 1970.

Juan Gil de Zamora. *Obra Poética: Ymago, ymitago; Quid uigoris, quid amoris; Officium almiflue Virginis*. Edited and translated by Estrella Pérez Rodríguez. Madrid: Instituto de Estudios Zamoranos. "Florián de Ocampo," 2018.

Kimhi, Joseph. *Sefer ha-Berit*. Ed. Frank Talmage. Jerusalem: Bialik Institute, 1974.

———. *The Book of the Covenant*. Translated by Frank Talmage. Toronto: PIMS, 1972.

Lake, Kirsopp. *The Apostolic Fathers: with an English Translation*. 2 vols. London: Heinemann, 1965.

Leone Modena (Leo Modena). *The History of the Rites, Customes, and Manner of Life, of the Present Jews, Throughout the World*. Translated by Edmund Chilmead. London, 1650.

Llull, Ramon. *Libre de doctrina pueril*. In *Obres de Ramón Llull*, vol. 1, *Doctrina pueril; Libre del orde de cavalleria; Libre de clerecia; Art de confessió*, ed. M. Obrador y Bennassar. 1906. Facsimile ed., Palma de Mallorca: Miquel Font, 1986.

Malcolm Letts (ed.). *The Travels of Leo of Rozmital through Germany, Flanders, England, France, Spain, Portugal and Italy 1465–1467*. Abingdon, Oxon.: Routledge, 2016.

Maimonides (Moses ben Maimon; Rambam). *Commentary on the Mishnah, Avodah zarah* 1:3. Ryzman Edition Hebrew Mishnah Avodah Zara. Rahway, NJ: Artscroll Mesorah, 2012.

———. *The Guide for the Perplexed*. Translated by M. Friedländer. New York: Dover, 1956.

Maimonides Mishneh Torah: Hilchot Avodat Kochavim V'Chukkoteihem The Law of the Worship of Stars and Their Statutes, a new translation with commentaries and notes by Rabbi Eliyahu Touger (New York: Moznaim Publishing, 1990).

Marcus, Jacob Rader. *The Jew in the Medieval World: A Source Book, 315–1791.* Cincinnati: Hebrew Union College Press, 1999.

Martí, Ramón. *Pugio fidei adversus Mauros et Iudaeos.* Paris, 1651.

Matthew Paris's English History: From the Year 1235 to 1273. Translated by J. A. Giles. 3 vols. London: Henry G. Bohn, 1852–1854.

McGiffert, Arthur Cushman. *Dialogue Between a Christian and a Jew: The Greek Text, Edited with Introduction and Notes, Together with a Discussion of Christian Polemics Against the Jews.* Marburg, 1889.

Meir of Rothenburg. *Responsa Maharam II. Pesaḳim u-Minhagim.* Ed. I. Z. Kahan. Jerusalem: Mossad HaRav Kook, 1960.

Midrash Rabbah. Ed H. Freedman and Maurice Simon. 13 vols. in 10. London: Soncino Press, 1939.

Midrash Rabbah: Genesis. Translated and edited by Harry Freedman and Maurice Simon. 2 vols. London: Soncino Press, 1983.

Midrash Rabbah: Exodus. Ed. Harry Freedman and Maurice Simon. London: Soncino Press, 1981.

Mirk, John. *Mirk's Festial: A Collection of Homilies.* Ed. Theodor Erbe. London: Kegan Paul, Trench, Trübner, 1905.

Monumenta Germaniae Historica, Scriptores rerum Merovingicarum, Deutsches Institut für Erforschung des Mittelalters, Hannover and Leipzig, 1951 vol. 6, 21, 25,

Monumenta Germaniae Historica, Scriptores rerum Merovingicarum, Deutsches Institut für Erforschung des Mittelalters, Hannover, 1885, vol. 1.2.

Munitiz, Joseph A., Julian Chrysostomides, Eirene Harvalia-Crook, and Charalambos Dendrinos, eds. *The Letter of the Three Patriarchs to Emperor Theophilos and Related Texts.* Camberley, Surrey: Porphyrogenitus, 1997.

Murner, Thomas. *Enderung und Schmach der bildung Marie von den Juden* [. . .]. Strasbourg: Hüpfuff, ca. 1515.

Patrologiae cursus completus, series Graeca (PG). Ed. Jacques Paul Migne. 161 vols. Paris, 1857–1866.

Patrologiae cursus completus, series Latina (PL). Ed. Jacques Paul Migne. 221 vols. Paris, 1844–1864.

Peter the Venerable. *The Letters of Peter the Venerable.* Ed. Giles Constable. Cambridge, MA: Harvard University Press, 1967.

Petrus de Ancharano. *Consilia sive iuris response.* Venice: Apud Nicolaum Bevilaquam, 1568.

Philo. *The Works of Philo: Complete and Unabridged.* Translated by C. D. Yonge. Peabody: Hendrickson, 1993.

Pseudo-Dionysius Areopagita: De Coelesti Hierarchia, De Ecclesiastica Hierarchia, De Mystica Theologia, Epistulae. Berlin: De Gruyter, 2012.

Rashi. *The Pentateuch and Rashi's Commentary: A Linear Translation into English.* Vol. 2, *Exodus.* Translated and edited by Abraham Ben Isaiah and Benjamin Sharfman. Brooklyn: S. S. & R., 1950.

Rigord. *Vie de Philippe-Auguste.* In *Collection des mémoires relatifs à l'histoire de France,* ed. François Guizot, vol. 11, pp. 9–179. Paris: Brière, 1825.

Sacrorum conciliorum, nova et amplissima collectio. Ed. Giovanni Domenico Mansi. Florence, Venice, 1759–1798.

Sefer Chasidim. Ed. Reuven Margaliot. Jerusalem: Mossad HaRav Kook, 1923.

Sefer Chasidim: The Book of the Pious by Rabbi Yehudah HeChasid. Edited and translated by Avraham Yaakov Finkel. Northvale, NJ: Aronson, 1997.

Segre, Renata, ed. *The Jews of Piedmont*. 3 vols. Jerusalem: Israel Academy of Sciences and Humanities, 1986–1990.

Sigebert of Gembloux. *Chronicon* novaliciense. Ed. Ludwig Bethmann. In Monumenta Germaniae Historica, Scriptores (in Folio), MGH SS 6:300–374. Hannover, 1844.

Simonsohn, Shlomo, ed. *The Apostolic See and the Jews*. 7 vols. Toronto: Pontifical Institute of Mediaeval Studies, 1988–1991.

———, ed. *The Jews in the Duchy of Milan*. 4 vols. Jerusalem: Israel Academy of Sciences and Humanities 1982–1986.

Socrates Scholasticus, *Ecclesiastical History* 7.16, trans. A. C. Zenos, in *A Select Library of Nicene and Post-Nicene Fathers of the Christian Church, 2nd ser., ed. Henry Wace and Philip Schaff, vol. 2, Socrates, Sozomenus: Church Histories,* Oxford, 1891.

Spaccini, Giovan Battista. *Cronaca di Modena*. Ed Albano Biondi, Rolando Bussi, and Carlo Giovannini. 6 vols. Modena: Franco Cosimo Panini, 1993–2008.

Stow, Kenneth R., ed. *The Church and the Jews in the XIIIth Century*. Vol. 2, 1254–1314. Philadelphia: Dropsie College for Hebrew and Cognate Learning, 1989.

Theophanes Confessor. *The Chronicle of Theophanes: Anni mundi 6095–6305 (A.D. 602–813)*. Edited and translated by Harry Turtledove. Philadelphia: University of Pennsylvania Press, 1982.

Thomas of Monmouth. *The Life and Passion of William of Norwich*. Edited and translated by Miri Rubin. London: Penguin, 2014.

Toaff, Ariel. *The Jews in Umbria*. Vol. 1, *1245–1435*. Leiden: Brill, 1993.

Usque, Samuel. *Samuel Usque's Consolation for the Tribulations of Israel (Consolaçam as tribulaçoens de Israel*. Translated by Martin A. Cohen. Philadelphia: Jewish Publication Society of America, 1965.

Vincent de Beauvais. *Speculum historiale*. Ed. Michel Tarayre. In *La Vierge et le miracle: Le "Speculum historiale" de Vincent de Beauvais*. Paris: Honoré Champion, 1999.

William of Malmesbury. *The Miracles of the Blessed Virgin Mary*. Edited and translated by R. M. Thomson and M. Winterbottom. Woodbridge: Boydell Press, 2015.

Wilson, Evelyn Faye, ed. *The "Stella Maris" of John of Garland: Edited, Together with a Study of Certain Collections of Mary Legends Made in Northern France in the Twelfth and Thirteenth Centuries*. Cambridge, MA: Mediaeval Academy of America, 1946.

Worrell, William H., ed. *The Coptic Manuscripts in the Freer Collection*. New York: Macmillan, 1923.

Wright, Frederick Adam, trans. *Jerome: Select Letters*. Loeb Classical Library 262. Cambridge, MA: Harvard University Press, 1933.

Zenos, Andrew C., ed. *A Select Library of Nicene and Post-Nicene Fathers*. Oxford: Oxford University Press, 1891.

SECONDARY SOURCES

Abulafia, Anna Sapir. *Christians and Jews in the Twelfth-Century Renaissance*. London: Routledge, 1995.

———. "The Ideology of Reform and Changing Ideas Concerning Jews in the Works of Rupert of Deutz and Hermannus Quondam Iudeus." *Jewish History* 7, no. 1 (Spring 1993): 43–63.

Abulafia, Anna Sapir, and G. R. Evans, eds. *The Works of Gilbert Crispin, Abbot of Westminster.* London: Oxford University Press, 1986.

Achinstein, Sharon. "John Foxe and the Jews." *Renaissance Quarterly* 54 (2001): 86–120.

Agosti, Giovanni. "Intorno alla "Madonna della Vittoria." In *Mantegna, 1431–1506*, exhibition catalog, ed. Giovanni Agosti and Dominque Thiébaut, 297–305, 310–312. Milan: Officina Libraria, 2008.

Agus, Irving. "Democracy in the Communities of the Early Middle Ages." *Jewish Quarterly Review*, n.s., 43, (1952–1953): 153–176.

Aist, Rodney. *From Topography to Text: The Image of Jerusalem in the Writings of Eucharius, Adomnán and Bede.* Turnhout: Brepols, 2018.

———. "Adomnán, Arculf and the Source Material of *De locis sanctis.*" In *Adomnán of Iona: Theologian, Lawmaker, Peacemaker*, ed. Jonathan M. Wooding, with Rodney Aist, Thomas Owen Clancy, and Thomas O'Loughlin, 162–180. Dublin: Four Courts Press, 2010.

Ajmar-Wollheim, Marta, and Flora Dennis. *At Home in Renaissance Italy.* London: V & A Publishing, 2010.

Akbari, Suzanne Conklin. *Idols in the East: European Representations of Islam and the Orient, 1100–1450.* Ithaca, NY: Cornell University Press, 2009.

Alexakis, Alexander. *Codex Parisinus Graecus 1115 and Its Archetype.* Washington, DC: Dumbarton Oaks Research Library and Collection, 1996.

———. "Stephen of Bostra: Fragmenta Contra Iudaeos (CPG 7790): A New Edition." *Jahrbuch der Österreichischen Byzantinistik* 43 (1993): 45–60.

———. "Some Remarks on the Colophon of the Codex *Parisinus Graecus* 115." *Revue d'Histoire des Textes* 2 (1992): 131–143.

Almog, Shmuel, ed. *Antisemitism Through the Ages.* Oxford: Oxford University Press. Translated by Nathan H. Reisner, 1988.

Alpert, Michael. "Did Spanish Crypto-Jews Desecrate Christian Images and Why? The Case of the *Cristo de la Paciencia* (1629–32), the *Romance* of 1717 and the Events of November 1714 in the *Calle del Lobo.*" In *Faith and Fanaticism: Religious Fervour in Early Modern Spain*, ed. Lesley K. Twomey, 85–94. Aldershot: Ashgate, 1997.

Al Sabbagh, Luca. "L'Inquisizione di Reggio Emilia fra centro e periferia tra XVII e XVIII secolo: Il repertorio dei carteggi." Master's thesis, University of Bologna, 2013.

Alexakis, Alexander. "Some Remarks on the Colophon of the Codex Parisinus Graecus 115." *Revue d'Histoire des Textes* 2 (1992): 131–143.

———. "Codex Parisinus Graecs 1115 and Its Archetype Washington 1996." *Dumbarton Oaks Studies* 34 (1980): 170–172.

Amador de los Ríos, José. *Historia social, política y religiosa de los judíos de España y Portugal.* 3 vols. Madrid: Ediciones Turner, 1984.

Anastos, Milton V. "The Argument for Iconoclasm as Presented by the Iconoclastic Council of 754." In *Late Classical and Medieval Studies in Honor of Albert Mathias Friend Jr.*, ed. Kurt Weitzmann, 1977–188. Princeton, NJ: Princeton University Press, 1955.

Andreatta, Michaela. "The Persuasive Path: Giulio Morosini's *Derek Emunah* as a Conversion Narrative." In *Bastards and Believers: Jewish Converts and Conversion from the Bible to the Present*, ed. Theodor Dunkelgrün and Paweł Maciejko, 156–181. Philadelphia: University of Pennsylvania Press, 2020.

Andrist, Patrick. "Les *Objections des Hébreux*: Un document du premier iconoclasme?" *Revue des Études Byzantines* 57 (1999): 99–140.

Antoniazzi Villa, Anna. *Un processo contro gli ebrei nella Milano del 1488: Crescita e decline della comunità ebraica lombarda alla fine del Medioevo*. Bologna: Cappelli, 1985.

Anstey, Henry, ed. *Munimenta Academica, or Documents Illustrative of Academical Life and Studies at Oxford*. Roll Series 50. 2 vols. London: Longmans, Green, Reader, and Dyer, 1868.

Areford, David S. *The Viewer and the Printed Image in Late Medieval Europe*. London: Routledge, 2010.

Argenziano, Raffaele. *Agli inizi dell'iconografia sacra a Siena*. Florence: Sismel-Edizioni del Galluzzo, 2000.

Aron-Beller, Katherine. "*Sopra l'imputatione del delitto di sodomia con christiano*: The Proceedings Against Lazarro de Norsa (Modena, 1670)." *Genesis* 20, no. 1 (2021): 53–91, 166–167.

———. "The Jewish Image Desecrator in the *Cantigas de Santa Maria*." *Ars Judaica* 14 (2018): 27–45.

———. "Byzantine Tales of Jewish Image Desecration: Tracing a Narrative." *Jewish Culture and History* 18, no. 2 (2017): 209–235.

———. "Fictional Tales and Their Narrative Transformations: Accusations of Image Desecration Against Jews in 12th and 13th Century Europe." *Antisemitism Studies Journal* 1 (2017): 38–81.

———. "Image Desecration in Spilamberto: Jews and Christian Images in Seventeenth-Century Italy." *English Historical Review* 132 (2017): 823–862.

———. Review of *Cultural Exchange: Jews, Christians, and Art in the Medieval Marketplace*, by Joseph Shatzmiller. *Jewish History* 28, no. 2 (2014): 221–223.

———. "Outside the Ghetto: Jews and Christians in the Duchy of Modena." *Journal of Early Modern History* 17 (2013): 1–27.

———. "The Inquisition, Professing Jews and Christian Images in Early Modern Modena." *Church History: Studies in Christianity and Culture* 81, no. 3 (September 2012): 575–600.

———. *Jews on Trial: The Papal Inquisition of Modena, 1598–1638*. Manchester: Manchester University Press, 2011.

Aron-Beller, Katherine, and Christopher Black, eds. *The Roman Inquisition: Centre Versus Peripheries*. Leiden: Brill, 2018.

Aronius, Julius. *Regesten zur Geschichte der Juden im fränkischen und deutschen Reiche bis zum jahre 1273*. Berlin, 1902.

Assis, Yom Tov. "The Jews of Barcelona in Maritime Trade with the East." In *The Jew in Medieval Iberia, 1100–1500*, ed. Jonathan Ray, 180–226. Boston: Academic Studies Press, 2011.

———. *The Golden Age of Aragonese Jewry: Community and Society in the Crown of Aragon, 1213–1327*. Oxford: Littman Library of Jewish Civilization, 1997.

———. *Jewish Economy in the Medieval Crown of Aragon, 1213–1327*. Leiden: Brill, 1997.

———. "Synagogues in Medieval Spain." *Jewish Art* 18 (1992): 6–29.

Avi-Yonah, Michael. "Mosaic Pavements in Palestine." *Quarterly of the Department of Antiquities in Palestine* 2 (1933): 136–181.

Bacci, Michele. "'Quel bello miracolo onde si fa la festa del santo Salvatore': Studio sulla metamorfosi di una leggenda." In *Santa Croce e Santo Volto: Contributi allo studio dell'origine e della fortuna del culto del Salvatore (secoli IX–XV)*, ed. Gabriella Rosetti, 1–86. Pisa: GISEM–Edizione ETS, 2002.

———. "The Berardenga Antependium and the *Passio Ymaginis* Office." *Journal of the Warburg and Courtauld Institutes* 61 (1998): 1–16.

———. *Il pennello dell'Evangelista: Storia delle imagini sacre attribuite a san Luca.* Pisa: GISEM, 1998.

Baer, Fritz. *Die Juden im christlichen Spanien.* Berlin: Akademie Verlag, 1929.

Baer, Yitzhak. *A History of the Jews in Christian Spain.* Vol. 2. Philadelphia: Jewish Publication Society of America, 1961.

Baert, Barbara. *A Heritage of Holy Wood: The Legend of the True Cross in Text and Image.* Leiden: Brill, 2004.

———. "New Observations on the Genesis of Girona (1050–1100): The Iconography of the Legend of the True Cross." *Gesta* 38, no. 2 (1999): 115–126.

———. "The Retable of the Master of Tressa (Siena, 1215): Iconography and Function." *Pantheon* 57 (1999): 14–21.

Bagby, Albert I., Jr. "The Jew in the *Cántigas* of Alfonso X, El Sabio." *Speculum* 46, no. 4 (1971): 670–688.

Balboni, Maria Pia. *Gli Ebrei del Finale Emilia nel Cinquecento e nel Seicento.* Florence: Giuntina, 2005.

Baldwin, John W. *Masters, Princes, and Merchants: The Social Views of Peter the Chanter and His Circle.* 2 vols. Princeton, NJ: Princeton University Press, 1970.

Bale, Anthony. *The Jew in the Medieval Book: English Antisemitism, 1350–1500.* Cambridge: Cambridge University Press, 2006.

———. "Fictions of Judaism in England Before 1290." In *Jews in Medieval Britain: Historical, Literary and Archaeological Perspectives*, ed. Patricia Skinner, 129–144. Woodbridge: Boydell, 2003.

Baranov, Vladamir. "The Doctrine of the Icon-Eucharist for the Byzantine Iconoclasts." *Studia Patristica* 44 (2010): 41–46.

Baras, Zvi. "Jewish-Christian Religious Disputation in Jerusalem (932)." [In Hebrew.] *Cathedra* 63 (1992): 31–51.

Barasch, Moshe. *Blindness: The History of a Mental Image in Western Thought.* New York: Routledge, 2001.

———. *Icon: Study in the History of an Idea.* New York: New York University Press, 1993.

Barber, Charles. *Figure and Likeness: On the Limits of Representation in Byzantine Iconoclasm.* Princeton, NJ: Princeton University Press, 2002.

———. "The Truth in Painting: Iconoclasm and Identity in Early-Medieval Art." *Speculum* 72 (1997): 1019–1039.

Barnard, Leslie W. "The Theology of Images." In *Iconoclasm*, ed. Anthony Bryer and Judith Herrin, 7–15. Birmingham: University of Birmingham Press, 1977.

———. "The Jews and the Byzantine Iconoclastic Controversy." *Eastern Churches Review* 5 (1973): 125–135.

Barnay, Sylvie. *El cielo en la tierra: Las apariciones de la Virgen en la Edad Media.* Madrid: Encuentro, 1999.

Batterman, Michael. "Bread of Affliction, Emblem of Power: The Passover Matzah in Haggadah Manuscripts from Christian Spain." In *Imagining the Self, Imagining the Other: Visual Representation and Jewish-Christian Dynamics in the Middle Ages and Early Modern Period*, ed. Eva Frojmovic, 53–89. Leiden: Brill, 2002.

Baumgarten, Albert I. "Herod's Eagle." In *"Go Out and Study the Land" (Judges 18:2): Archaeological, Historical and Textual Studies in Honor of Hanan Eshel*, ed. Aren M. Maeir, Jodi Magness, and Lawrence H. Schiffman, 7–21. Leiden: Brill, 2011.

Bayless, Martha. *Sin and Filth in Medieval Culture: The Devil in the Latrine.* London: Routledge, 2011.

Baynes, Norman H. "Idolatry and the Early Church." In *Byzantine Studies and Other Essays*, 116–143. London: Athlone Press, 1960.

———. "The Icons Before Iconoclasm." *Harvard Theological Review* 44 (1951): 93–106.

———. "The Finding of the Virgin's Robe." *Annuaire de l'institut de philologie et d'histoire orientales et slaves* 9 (1949): 87–95.

Beinart, Haim. *Conversos on Trial: The Inquisition in Ciudad Real.* Jerusalem: Magnes Press, 1981.

———. "A Prophesying Movement in Cordova in 1499–1502." [In Hebrew.] In *Yitzhak F. Baer Memorial Volume, 1888–1980*, ed. H. Beinart, S. Ettinger, and M. Stern, 190–200. Jerusalem: Historical Society of Israel, 1980.

———, ed. *Hispania Judaica.* Jerusalem: Magnes Press, 1978.

———, ed. *Records of the Trials of the Spanish Inquisition in Ciudad Real.* Jerusalem: Magnes Press, 1974.

Belting, Hans. *Likeness and Presence: A History of the Image Before the Era of Art.* Translated by Edmund Jephcott. Chicago: University of Chicago Press, 1994.

———. *The Image and Its Public in the Middle Ages: Form and Function of Early Paintings of the Passion.* Translated by Mark Bartusis and Raymond Meyer. New Rochelle, NY: Aristide D. Caratzas, 1990.

Berger, David. *Persecution, Polemic and Dialogue: Essays in Jewish-Christian Relations (Judaism and Jewish Life).* Boston: Academic Studies Press, 2010.

———. *The Jewish-Christian Debate in the High Middle Ages: A Critical Edition of the Nizzahon Vetus with an Introduction, Translation, and Commentary.* Philadelphia: Jewish Publication Society of America, 1979.

Bethencourt, Cardozo de. "The Jews in Portugal from 1773 to 1902." *Jewish Quarterly Review* 15, no. 2 (1903): 251–274.

Bethencourt, Francisco. *The Inquisition: A Global History, 1478–1834.* Cambridge: Cambridge University Press, 2009.

Biale, David. *Blood and Belief: The Circulation of a Symbol Between Jews and Christians.* Berkeley: University of California Press, 2007.

———. "Counter-History and Jewish Polemics Against Christianity: The *Sefer toldot yeshu* and the *Sefer zerubavel*." *Jewish Social Studies*, n.s., 6, no. 1 (Autumn 1999): 130–145.

Bidez, Joseph. *Philostorgius Kirchengeschichte.* GCS 21. Leipzig, 1913.

Bildhauer, Bettina. *Medieval Blood.* Cardiff: University of Wales Press, 2009.

Bland, Kalman. *The Artless Jew: Medieval and Modern Affirmations and Denial of the Visual.* Princeton, NJ: Princeton University Press, 2001.

Blidstein, Gerald J. "R. Yohanan, Idolatry, and Public Privilege." *Journal for the Study of Judaism in the Persian, Hellenistic, and Roman Period* 5, no. 2 (1974): 154–161.

Boes, Maria R. "Jews in the Criminal-Justice System of Early Modern Germany." *Journal of Interdisciplinary History* 30, no. 3 (Winter 1999): 407–435.

Boldrick, Stacy, Leslie Brubaker, and Richard Clay, eds. *Striking Images, Iconoclasms Past and Present.* Burlington, VT: Ashgate, 2013.

Bollo-Panadero, Maria Dolores. "Heretics and Infidels: The *Cantigas de Santa María* as Ideological Instrument of Cultural Codification." *Romance Quarterly* 55, no. 3 (2008): 163–173.

Bolzoni, Lina. *La rete delle immagini: Predicazione in volgare dalle origini a Bernardino da Siena*. Turin: Einaudi, 2002.

Bonfil, Robert. *History and Folklore in a Medieval Jewish Chronicle: The Family Chronicle of Ahima'az ben Paltiel*. Leiden: Brill, 2009.

———. "Jewish Attitudes Toward History and Historical Writing in Pre-Modern Times." *Jewish History* 11, no. 1 (1997): 7–40.

Bonfil, Robert, Oded Irshai, Guy G. Stroumsa, and Rina Talgam, eds. *Jews in Byzantium: Dialectics of Minority and Majority Cultures*. Leiden: Brill, 2012.

Bonora, Elena. "The Takeover of the Roman Inquisition." In *A Companion to Heresy Inquisitions*, ed. Donald S. Prudlo, 249–279. Leiden: Brill, 2019.

Borgehammar, Stephan. *How the Holy Cross Was Found: From Event to Medieval Legend*. Bibliotheca Theologiae Practicae, Kyrkovetenskapliga Studier 47. Stockholm: Almqvist & Wiksell International, 1991.

Bori, Pier Cesare. *The Golden Calf and the Origins of the Anti-Jewish Controversy*. Translated by David Ward. Atlanta: Scholars Press, 1990.

Bornstein, Daniel E. "Spiritual Kinship and Domestic Devotions." In *Gender and Society in Renaissance Italy*, ed. Judith C. Brown and Robert C. Davis, 173–192. New York: Longman, 1998.

———. *The Bianchi of 1399: Popular Devotion in Late Medieval Italy*. Ithaca, NY: Cornell University Press, 1993.

Borýsek, Martin. "The Jews of Venetian Candia: The Challenges of External Influences and Internal Diversity as Reflected in *Takkanot Kandiyah*." *Al-Masāq: Journal of the Medieval Mediterranean* 26, no. 3 (2014): 241–266.

Boshof, Egon. *Erzbischof Agobard von Lyon: Leben und Werk*. Cologne: Böhlau, 1969.

Boustan, Ra'anan S. "Immolating Emperors: Spectacles of Imperial Suffering and the Making of a Jewish Minority Culture in Late Antiquity." In *Violence, Scripture, and Textual Practices in Early Judaism and Christianity*, ed. Ra'anan S. Boustan, Alex P. Jassen, and Calvin J. Roetzel, 204–234. Leiden: Brill, 2010. Also published in *Biblical Interpretation* 17, nos. 1–2 (2009): 207–238.

Boyarin, Adrienne Williams. *Miracles of the Virgin in Medieval England: Law and Jewishness in Marian Tales*. Cambridge: Cambridge University Press, 2010.

Boyarin, Daniel. *Border Lines: The Partition of Judaeo-Christianity*. Philadelphia: University of Pennsylvania Press, 2004.

Boyd, Beverly. *The Middle English Miracles of the Virgin*. San Marino, CA: Huntingdon Library, 1964.

Bräcker, Antje. "The Series 'Stanza Storica' of the Sanctum Officium in the Archive of the Congregation for the Doctrine of the Faith as a Source for the History of the Jews." In *The Roman Inquisition, the Index and the Jews: Contexts, Sources and Perspectives*, ed. Stephan Wendehorst, 169–176. Leiden: Brill, 2004.

Bredekamp, Horst. *Kunst als Medium sozialer Konflikte: Bilderkämpfe von der Spätantike bis zur Hussitenrevolution*. Frankfurt: Suhrkamp Verlag, 1975.

Brennan, Brian. "The Conversion of the Jews of Clermont in AD 576." *Journal of Theological Studies*, n.s., 36, pt. 2 (October 1985): 321–337.

Brown, Peter. "Images as a Substitute for Writing." In *East and West: Modes of Communication; Proceedings of the First Plenary Conference at Merida*, ed. Evangelos Chrysos and Ian Wood, 15–34. Leiden: Brill, 1999.

———. "Society and the Supernatural: A Medieval Change." In "Wisdom, Revelation, and Doubt: Perspectives on the First Millennium B.C." Special issue, *Daedalus* 104, no. 2 (Spring 1975): 133–151.

Brown, Richard D. "Microhistory and the Post-Modern Challenge." *Journal of the Early Republic* 23, no.1 (Spring, 2003): 1–20.

Brubaker, Leslie. *Inventing Byzantine Iconoclasm*. London: Bristol Classical Press, 2012.

Brubaker, Leslie, and John Haldon. *Byzantium in the Iconoclastic Era, c. 680–850: A History*. Cambridge: Cambridge University Press, 2011.

Bruscino, Andrea. "Una presenza ebraica di lungo periodo: La famiglia da San Miniato ad Empoli (secc. XIV–XVI)." PhD diss., Università di Pisa, 2006.

Brucker, Gene A. *Firenze nel Rinascimento*. Florence: La Nuova Italia, 1980.

Burckhardt, Jacob. *The Civilization of the Renaissance in Italy*. London: Penguin Classics, 1990.

Burns, Robert I. "Christian-Islamic Confrontation in the West: The Thirteenth-Century Dream of Conversion." *American Historical Review*, 76, no. 5 (1971): 1386–1434.

Bynum, Caroline Walker. "Are Things 'Indifferent'? How Objects Change Our Understanding of Religious History." *German History* 34, no. 1 (2016): 88–112.

———. *Christian Materiality: An Essay on Religion in Late Medival Europe*. New York: Zone Books, 2011.

———. *Wonderful Blood: Theology and Practice in Late Medieval Northern Germany and Beyond*. Philadelphia: University of Pennsylvania, 2007.

———. "The Blood of Christ in the Later Middle Ages." *Church History* 71, no. 1 (2002): 685–714.

———. *Fragmentation and Redemption: Essays on Gender and the Human Body in Medieval Religion*. New York: Zone Books, 1991.

———. *Jesus as Mother: Studies in the Spirituality of the High Middle Ages*. Berkeley: University of California Press, 1982.

Caffiero, Marina. *Legami pericolosi: Ebrei e cristiani tra eresia, libri proibiti e stregoneria*. Turin: G. Einaudi, 2012.

———. *Forced Baptisms: Histories of Jews, Christians, and Converts in Papal Rome*. Berkeley: University of California Press, 2011.

Callahan, Daniel F. "Ademar of Chabannes, Millennial Fears and the Development of Western Anti-Judaism." *Journal of Ecclesiastical History* 46, no. 1 (1995): 19–35.

Cameron, Averil. "How to Read Heresiology." In *The Cultural Turn in Late Ancient Studies: Gender, Asceticism, and Historiography*, ed. Dale B. Martin and Patricia Cox Miller, 193–212. Durham, NC: Duke University Press, 2005.

———. "Blaming the Jews: The Seventh-Century Invasions of Palestine in Context." *Travaux et Mémoires* 14 (2002): 57–78.

———. "Byzantines and Jews: Some Recent Work on Early Byzantium." *Byzantine and Modern Greek Studies* 26 (1996): 249–274.

———. "The Language of Images: The Rise of Icons and Christian Representation." In *The Church and the Arts*, Studies in Church History 28, ed. Diane Wood, 1–42. Oxford: Oxford University Press, 1992.

———. "Disputations, Polemical Literature and the Formation of Opinion in the Early Byzantine Period." In *Dispute Poems and Dialogues in the Ancient and Medieval Near East: Forms and Types of Literary Debate in Semitic and Related Literatures*, ed. G. J. Reinink and H. L. J. Vanstiphout, 91–108. Louvain: Peeters, 1991.

———. "The History of the Image of Edessa: The Telling of a Story." *Harvard Ukrainian Studies* 7 (1983): 80–94.

———. "The Virgin's Robe: An Episode in the History of Early Seventh-Century Constantinople." *Byzantion* 49 (1979): 42–56.

Camille, Michael. *The Gothic Idol: Ideology and Image-Making in Medieval Art*. Cambridge Studies in New Art History and Criticism. Cambridge: Cambridge University Press, 1991.

Camporesi, Piero. *Juice of Life: The Symbolic and Magic Significance of Blood*. Translated by Robert R. Barr. New York: Continuum, 1995.

Canosa, Romano. *Storia dell'Inquisizione in Italia dalla metà del Cinquecento alla fine del Settecento*. 5 vols. Rome: Sapere 2000, 1986–1990.

Capriotti, Giuseppe. "L'infamante accusa di deicidio. Propaganda antiebraica nella pittura italiana del Quattrocento: Zanino di Pietro, Giovanni Boccati, Luca di Paolo e Carlo Crivelli." In *Antigiudaismo, Antisemitismo, Memoria: Un approccio pluridisciplinare*, ed. Giuseppe Capriotti, 51–97. Macareta: EUM, 2009.

———. "L'iconografia di S. Elena nella leggenda della "vera croce" e il problema ebraico nelle Marche del XV secolo." In *L'Abbazia di S. Elena nella valle dell'Esino: Storia, arte e architettura*, ed. Marta Paraventi, 221–262. Jesi: Tipografia Stampanova, 2008.

Caro Baroja, Julio, ed. *Los judíos en la España moderna y contemporánea*. Vol. 2 Madrid: Ediciones Arion, 1961.

Carroll, Michael P. *Veiled Threats: The Logic of Popular Catholicism in Italy*. Baltimore: Johns Hopkins University Press, 1996.

Carter, Peter. "The Historical Content of William of Malmesbury's Miracles of the Virgin Mary." In *The Writing of History in the Middle Ages: Essays Presented to Richard William Southern*, ed. R. H. C. Davis and J. M. Wallace-Hadrill, 127–165. Oxford: Clarendon Press, 1981.

Cassuto, Umberto. *Gli Ebrei a Firenze nell'età del Rinascimento*. Florence: Tipografia Galletti cocci, 1918.

———. "Un ignoto capitolo di storia ebraica." In *Judaica: Festschrift zu Hermann Cohens siebzigstem Geburtstage*, ed. Ismar Elbogen, Benzion Kellermann, and Eugen Mittwoch, 389–404. Berlin: B. Cassirer, 1912.

Cátedra, Pedro M. *Sermón, sociedad y literatura en la Edad Media: San Vicente Ferrer en Castilla (1411–1412)*. Valladolid: Junta de Castilla y León, 1994.

Chaîne, P. M. "Sermon sur la pénitence attribué a Saint Cyrille d' Alexandrie: Textes traduits et annotés." *Melanges de la Faculté orientale* 6 (1913): 493–528.

Chambers, David S., and Trevor Dean, eds. *Clean Hands and Rough Justice: An Investigating Magistrate in Renaissance Italy*. Ann Arbor: University of Michigan Press, 1981.

Chapman, David W. *Ancient Jewish and Christian Perceptions of Crucifixion*. Tübingen: Baker Academic, 2008.

Chartier, Roger, ed. *The Culture of Print: Power and the Uses of Print in Early Modern Europe*. Translated by Lydia G. Cochrane. Princeton, NJ: Princeton University Press, 1987.

Chazan, Robert, *From Anti-Judaism to Anti-Semitism: Ancient and Medieval Christian Constructions of Jewish History*. Cambridge: Cambridge University Press, 2016.

———. *Fashioning Jewish Identity in Medieval Western Christendom*. Cambridge: Cambridge University Press, 2004.

———. *The Hebrew First Crusade Narratives*. Berkeley: University of California Press, 2000.

———. *Barcelona and Beyond: The Disputation of 1263 and Its Aftermath*. Berkeley: University of California Press, 1992.

———. *European Jewry and the First Crusade.* Berkeley: University of California Press, 1987.
———. "The Hebrew First-Crusade Chronicles." *Revue des Études Juives* 133 (1974): 235–254.
———. "The Persecution of 992." *Revue des Études Juives* 129 (1970): 217–221.
Chazelle, Celia M. "Images, Scripture, the Church, and the Libri Carolini." *Proceedings of the PMR Conference* 16–17 (1993): 53–76.
Christian, William A., Jr. *Moving Crucifixes in Modern Spain.* Princeton, NJ: Princeton University Press, 1992.
———. *Local Religion in Sixteenth-Century Spain.* Princeton, NJ: Princeton University Press, 1981.
Ciappelli, Giovanni. "La devozione domestica nelle ricordanze fiorentine (fine XIII–inizio XVI secolo) in religione domestica." *Quaderni di storia religiosa* 8 (2001): 79–115.
Claman, Henry N. *Jewish Images in the Christian Church: Art as the Mirror of the Jewish-Christian Conflict, 200–1250 C.E.* Macon, GA: Mercer University Press, 2000.
Classen, Albrecht, ed. *Laughter in the Middle Ages and Early Modern Times: Epistemology of a Fundamental Human Behavior, Its Meaning and Consequences.* Berlin: De Gruyter, 2010.
Clayton, Mary. *The Cult of the Virgin Mary in Anglo-Saxon England.* Cambridge: Cambridge University Press, 1990.
Cluse, Christoph, ed. *The Jews of Europe in the Middle Ages (Tenth to Fifteenth Centuries): Proceedings of the International Symposium Held at Speyer, 20–25 October 2002.* Turnhout: Brepols, 2004.
———. "Stories of Breaking and Taking the Cross: A Possible Context for the Oxford Incident of 1268." *Revue d'Histoire Ecclésiastique* 90 (1995): 396–442.
Cohen, Jeremy. *A Historian in Exile: Solomon ibn Verga, "Shevet Yehudah," and the Jewish-Christian Encounter.* Philadelphia: University of Pennsylvania Press, 2017.
———. "From Solomon bar Samson to Solomon Ibn Verga: Tales and Ideas of Jewish Martyrdom in *Shevet Yehudah.*" In *Studies in Medieval Jewish Intellectual and Social History: Festschrift in Honor of Robert Chazan*, ed. David Engel, Lawrence H. Schiffman, and Elliot R. Wolfson, 279–297. Leiden: Brill, 2012.
———. "The Blood Libel in Solomon ibn Verga's *Shevet Yehudah.*" In *Jewish Blood: Reality and Metaphor in History, Religion, and Culture*, ed. Mitchell B. Hart, 116–135. London: Routledge, 2009.
———. *Christ Killers: The Jews and the Passion from the Bible to the Big Screen.* Oxford: Oxford University Press, 2007.
———. *Sanctifying the Name of God: Jewish Martyrs and Jewish Memories of the First Crusade.* Philadelphia: University of Pennyslvania Press, 2004.
———. *Living Letters of the Law: Ideas of the Jew in Medieval Christianity.* Berkeley: University of California Press, 1999.
———. "*Gezerot Tatnu*: Martyrdom and Martyrology in the Hebrew Chronicles of 1096." [In Hebrew.] *Zion* 59 (1994): 169–208.
———. *The Friars and the Jews: The Evolution of Medieval Anti-Judaism.* Ithaca, NY: Cornell University Press, 1982.
Colafemmina, Cesare. *Per la storia degli ebrei in Calabria: Saggi e documenti.* Messina: Rubbettino, 1996.
Connell, William J., and Giles Constable. "Sacrilege and Redemption in Renaissance Florence: The Case of Antonio Rinaldeschi." *Journal of the Warburg and Courtauld Institutes* 61(1998): 53–98.
Constable, Giles. *Three Studies in Medieval Religious and Social Thought.* Cambridge: Cambridge University Press, 1995.

Constantinou, Stavroula, and Christian Høgel, eds. *Metaphrasis: A Byzantine Concept of Rewriting and Its Hagiographical Products*. With the assistance of Andria Andreou. Leiden: Brill, 2021.

Conybeare, Frederick C. "Antiochus Strategos' Account of the Sack of Jerusalem in A.D. 614." *English Historical Review* 25 (1910): 502–517.

Corrigan, Kathleen. *Visual Polemics in the Ninth-Century Byzantine Psalters*. Cambridge: Cambridge University Press, 1992.

Corry, Maya, Marco Faini, and Alessia Meneghin, eds. *Domestic Devotions in Early Modern Italy*. Leiden: Brill, 2019.

Corry, Maya, Deborah Howard, and Mary Laven, eds. *Madonnas and Miracles: The Holy Home in Renaissance Italy*. London: Philip Wilson, in association with the Fitzwilliam Museum, 2017.

Creasman, Allyson F. "The Virgin Mary Against the Jews: Anti-Jewish Polemic in the Pilgrimage to the Schöne Maria of Regensburg, 1519–25." *Sixteenth Century Journal* 33, no. 4 (2002): 963–980.

Cuffel, Alexandra. *Gendering Disgust in Medieval Religious Polemic*. Notre Dame, IN: University of Notre Dame Press, 2007.

D'Abrera, Anna Ysabel. *The Tribunal of Zaragoza and Crypto-Judaism, 1484–1515*. Turnhout: Brepols, 2008.

D'Addario, Maria Vittoria. "La casa." In *Vita privata a Firenze nei secoli XIV e XV*, 53–73. Florence: Leo Olschki, 1966.

Dahan, Gilbert. *The Christian Polemic Against the Jews in the Middle Ages*. Translated by Jody Gladding. Notre Dame, IN: University of Notre Dame Press, 1998.

———. "Les Juifs dans les Miracles de Gautier de Coincy." *Archives Juives* 16 (1980): 41–9, 59–68.

Dall'Olio, Guido. "L'inquisizione romana e gli ebrei nella Ferrara del Seicento: Prime indagini." In *Le Inquisizioni cristiane e gli ebrei: Tavola rotonda nell'ambito della Conferenza annuale della ricerca (Roma, 20–21 dicembre 2001)*, ed. Giuseppe Galasso, 297–321. Rome: Accademia Nazionale dei Lincei, 2003.

Dan, Joseph. "*Shevet Yehuda*: Past and Future History." In *Jewish Mysticism*, vol. 4, *General Characteristics and Comparative Studies*, 25–56. Northvale, NJ: Jason Aronson, 1999.

Davidson, Israel. *Thesaurus of Medieval Hebrew Poetry*. [In Hebrew.] 4 vols. New York: Ktav, 1970.

De Bruyne, Donatien. "Le plus ancien catalogue des reliques d'Oviedo." *Analecta Bollandiana* 45 (1927): 93–95.

Delany, Sheila. "Chaucer's Prioress, the Jews, and the Muslims." *Medieval Encounters* 5, no. 2 (1999): 198–213.

Delitzsch-Vorlesungen, Franz, and Bernhard Blumenkranz. *Juden und Judenturm in der mittelalterlichen Kunst*. Stuttgart: W. Kohlhammer Verlag, 1965.

Del Plato, Joan. "On Jews and the Old Testament Precedent for Sacred Art Production: The Views of Some Twelfth-Century Abbots." *Comitatus: A Journal of Medieval and Renaissance Studies* 18 (1987): 34–44.

Del Río Barredo, María José. "Imágenes callejeras y rituales públicos en el Madrid del siglo XVII." In *La imagen religiosa en la Monarquía hispánica: Usos y espacios*, ed. María Cruz de Carlos, Pierre Civil, Felipe Pereda, and Cécile Vincent-Cassy, 197–218. Madrid: Casa de Velázquez, 2008.

Déroche, Vincent. "L'*Apologie contre les juifs* de Léontios de Néapolis." *Travaux et Mémoires* 12 (1994): 45–104.

———. "La polémique anti-judaïque au VIe et au VIIe siècle: Un mémento inédit, les *Képhalaia.*" *Travaux et Mémoires* 11 (1991): 275–311.

Di Castro, Daniela, ed. *Et ecce gaudium: The Roman Jews and the Investiture of the Popes.* Translated by Lenore Rosenberg. Exhibition catalog. Rome: Museo Ebraica di Roma, 2010.

Diemling, Maria. "Navigating Christian Space: Jewish Responses to Christian Imagery in Early Modern German Lands." In *Visualizing Jews Through the Ages*, ed. Hannah Ewence and Helen Spurling, 181–198. London: Routledge, 2015.

Divina, Giuseppe. *Storia del beato Simone de Trento.* 2 vols. Trento: Artigianelli, 1902.

Dobson, Richard Barrie. *The Jewish Communities of Medieval England: The Collected Essays of Richard Barrie Dobson.* Ed. Helen Birkett. York: University of York, Borthwick Institute, 2010.

Dodds, Jerrilynn D., María Rosa Menocal, and Abigail Krasner Balbale. *The Arts of Intimacy: Christians, Jews, and Muslims in the Making of Castilian Culture.* New Haven, CT: Yale University Press, 2008.

Drijvers, Jan Willem, and John W. Watt, eds. *Portraits of Spiritual Authority: Religious Power in Early Christianity, Byzantium and the Christian Orient.* Leiden: Brill, 1999.

Dundes, Alan, ed. *The Blood Libel Legend: A Casebook in Anti-Semitic Folklore.* Madison: University of Wisconsin Press, 1991.

Eastmond, Antony, and Liz James, eds. *Icon and Word: The Power of Images in Byzantium; Studies Presented to Robin Cormack.* Aldershot: Ashgate, 2003.

Eidelberg, Shlomo, trans. and ed. *The Jews and the Crusaders: The Hebrew Chronicles of the First and Second Crusades.* Madison: University of Wisconsin Press, 1977.

Eire, Carlos M.N. *War Against the Idols: The Reformation of Worship from Erasmus to Calvin.* New York: Cambridge University Press, 1986.

Elliott, Jessica Marin. "Jews 'Feigning Devotion': Christian Representations of Converted Jews in French Chronicles Before and After the Expulsion of 1306." In *Jews and Christians in Thirteenth-Century France*, ed. Elisheva Baumgarten and Judah D. Galinsky, 169–182. New York: Palgrave Macmillan, 2015.

Elsner, Jaś. "Iconoclasm as Discourse: From Antiquity to Byzantium." *Art Bulletin* 94, no. 3 (September 2012): 368–394.

———. *Roman Eyes: Visuality and Subjectivity in Art and Text.* Princeton, NJ: Princeton University Press, 2007.

Engel, David, Lawrence Schiffmann, and Elliot Wolfson, eds. *Studies in Medieval Jewish Intellectual and Social History: Festschrift in Honor of Robert Chazan.* Leiden: Brill, 2012.

Epstein, Marc Michael. *The Medieval Haggadah: Art, Narrative, and Religious Imagination.* New Haven, CT: Yale University Press, 2011.

Espí Forcén, Carlos. "De Oriente a Occidente: La leyenda Bizantina de la *Passio Imaginis* en el siglio XV en la corona de Aragón." *Estudios bizantinos* 2 (2014): 205–229.

———. "Jews Desecrating a Crucifix: A *Passio Imaginis* Altarpiece from Mallorca." *Iconographica: Rivista di Iconografia medievale e moderna* 8 (2009): 83–97.

———. *Recrucificando a Cristo: Los judíos de la "Passio Imaginis" en la isla de Mallorca.* Palma de Mallorca: Objeto Perdido, 2009.

Evans, Helen C., and William D. Wixom, eds. *The Glory of Byzantium: Art and Culture of the Middle Byzantine Era, A.D. 843–1261.* New York: Metropolitan Museum of Art, 1997.

Faini, Marco, and Alessia Meneghin, eds. *Domestic Devotions in the Early Modern World.* Leiden: Brill, 2002.

Faur, José. "The Legal Thinking of Tosafot: An Historical Approach." *Dine Israel* 6 (1975): xliii–lxxii.

Feci, Simona. "Guardare e vedere al di là del muro: Immagini sacre e iconoclastia ebraica a Roma in età moderna." In *Le Inquisizioni cristiane e gli ebrei: Tavola rotonda nell'ambito della Conferenza annuale della ricerca (Roma, 20–21 dicembre 2001)*, ed. Giuseppe Galasso, 407–429. Rome: Accademia Nazionale dei Lincei, 2003.

Ferreres, Juan B. *Historia del misal romano: Su origen (sacramentarios, antifonarios, epistolarios, etc.), el misal plenario, el misal de curia, su variadísimo desarrollo en la edad media, su unidad desde San Pío V, su brillante coronación con la fiesta de Cristo Rey.* Barcelona: Eugenio Subirana, 1929.

Ferretti, Massimo. "Ai margini di Dosso (tre altari in San Pietro a Modena)." *Ricerche di storia dell' arte* 17 (1982): 57–75.

Fidalgo, Elvira, ed. *Las Cantigas de Santa María.* Vigo: Edicións Xerais de Galicia, 2002.

Fine, Steven. *Art and Judaism in the Greco-Roman World: Toward a New Jewish Archaeology.* Cambridge: Cambridge University Press, 2005.

———. "Iconoclasm and the Art of Late Antique Palestinian Synagogues." In *From Dura to Sepphoris: Studies in Jewish Art and Society in Late Antiquity*, ed. Lee Levine and Ze'ev Weiss, 183–193. Portsmouth, RI: Journal of Roman Archaeology, 2000.

Finkelstein, Louis. *Jewish Self-Goverment in the Middle Ages.* New York: Philipp Feldheim, 1964.

Fishman-Duker, Rivkah. "Anti-Jewish Arguments in the Chronicon Paschale." In *Contra Iudaeos: Ancient and Medieval Polemics Between Christians and Jews*, ed. Ora Limor and Guy G. Stroumsa, 105–118. Tübingen: J. C. B. Mohr, 1996.

Fita, Fidel. "Cincuenta leyendas por Gil de Zamora combinadas con las Cantigas de Alfonso el Sabio." *Boletín de la Real Academia de la Historia* 7 (1885): 54–144.

Foote, G. W., and J. M. Wheeler, ed. and trans. *The Jewish Life of Christ, Being the Sepher Toldoth Jeshu, or Book of the Generation of Jesus.* 1885. Reprint, London: Pioneer Press, 1919.

Forlin Patrucco, Marcella. "Il 'miracolo del sangue' nella tarda antichità: Tipologia e valenze politico-teologiche." In *Sangue e antropologia biblica nella patristica: Atti della settimana, Roma, 23–28 novembre 1981*, ed. Francesco Vattioni, 2:693–712. Rome: Pia Unione Preziosissimo Sangue, 1982.

Fosi, Irene. *Convertire lo straniero.* Rome: Viella, 2011.

Franceschini, Adriano. *Artisti a Ferrara in età umanistica e rinascimentale: Testimonianze archivistiche.* Part 2, vol. 2, *Dal 1493 al 1516.* Ferrara: Gabriele Corbo, 1997.

Franceschini, Chiara. "Arti figurative e Inquisizione: La rappresentazione." In *Dizionario storico dell'Inquisizione*, vol.1, ed. Adriano Prosperi, 105–107. Pisa: Scuola Normale Superiore, 2010.

Francesconi, Federica. *Invisible Enlighteners: The Jewish Merchants of Modena, from the Renaissance to the Emancipation.* Philadelphia: University of Pennsylvania Press, 2021.

Francesconi, Federica, and Luisa Levi D'Ancona. *Vita e società ebraica di Modena e Reggio Emilia: L'età dei ghetto.* Modena: Edizioni Panini, 2007.

Frassetto, Michael, ed. *Christian Attitudes Toward the Jews in the Middle Ages: A Casebook.* London: Taylor and Francis, 2007.

Freedberg, David. *The Power of Images: Studies in the History and Theory of Response.* Chicago: University of Chicago Press, 1991.

Frendo, Joseph D. "Who Killed Anastasius II?" *Jewish Quarterly Review* 72 (1982): 202–204.

Frey, Jean-Baptiste. "La question des images chez les Juifs à la lumière des récentes découvertes." *Biblica* 15 (1934): 265–300.

Furstenberg, Yair. "Idolatry Annulment: Rabbinic Dialogue with Paganism Under the Roman Empire." [In Hebrew.] *Reshit: The Shalom Hartman Institute Academic Annual* 1 (2009): 117–144.

Galasso, Giuseppe, ed. *Le Inquisizioni cristiane e gli ebrei: Tavola rotonda nell'ambito della Conferenza annuale della ricerca (Roma, 20–21 dicembre 2001).* Rome: Accademia Nazionale dei Lincei, 2003.

Gamboni, Dario. *The Destruction of Art: Iconoclasm and Vandalism Since the French Revolution.* New Haven, CT: Yale University Press, 1997.

García Avilés, Alejandro. "Imágenes 'vivientes': Idolatría y herejía en las Cantigas de Alfonso X el Sabio." *Goya* 321 (2007) 324–342.

Gentilcore, David. "Methods and Approaches in the Social History of the Counter-Reformation in Italy." *Social History* 17, no. 1 (1992): 73–98.

Gerli, E. Michael. "Poet and Pilgrim: Discourse, Language, Imagery, and Audience in Berceo's *Milagros de Nuestra Señora.*" In *Hispanic Medieval Studies in Honor of Samuel G. Armistead*, ed. E. Michael Gerli and Harvey L. Sharrer, 139–151. Madison, WI: Hispanic Seminary of Medieval Studies, 1992.

Giakalis, Ambrosios. *Images of the Divine: The Theology of Icons at the Seventh Ecumenical Council.* Rev. ed. Leiden: Brill, 2005.

Gitlitz, David M. *Secrecy and Deceit: The Religion of Crypto-Jews.* Philadelphia: Jewish Publishing Society, 1996.

———. "Las presuntas profanaciones judías del ritual cristiano en el decreto de expulsión." In *Judíos, sefarditas, conversos: La expulsion de 1492 y sus consecuencias*, ed. Angel Alcalá Galve, 150–169. Valladolid: Ambito Ediciones, 1995.

Goedeke, Karl. *Pamphilus Gengenbach.* Hannover: Rümpler, 1856.

Goitein, Shelomo Dov. *Palestinian Jewry in Early Islamic and Crusader Times.* [In Hebrew.] Jerusalem: Magnes Press, 1980.

Goldin, Simha. *Apostasy and Jewish Identity in High Middle Ages Northern Europe: "Are You Still My Brother?"* Translated by Jonathan Chipman. Manchester: Manchester University Press, 2014.

———. "The Socialisation for *Kiddush ha-Shem* Among Medieval Jews." *Journal of Medieval History* 23, no. 2 (1997): 117–138.

Grayzel, Solomon. "Jews and the Ecumenical Councils." *Jewish Quarterly Review* 57 (1967): 287–311.

———. "References to the Jews in the Correspondence of John XXII." *Hebrew Union College Annual* 23, no. 2 (1950–1951): 37–80.

———. *The Church and the Jews in the XIIIth Century: A Study of Their Relations During the Years 1198–1254, Based on the Papal Letters and the Conciliar Decrees of the Period.* Philadelphia: Dropsie College for Hebrew and Cognate Learning, 1933.

Griffith, Sidney H. "Theodore Abū Qurrah's Arabic Tract on the Christian Practice of Venerating Images." *Journal of the American Oriental Society* 105, no. 1 (1985): 53–73.

Grossman, Avraham. "The Cultural and Social Background of Jewish Martyrdom in Germany in 1096." In *Juden und Christen zur Zeit der Kreuzzüge*, ed. Alfred Haverkamp, 73–87. Konstanzer Arbeitkreis für mittelalterliche Geschichte, Vorträge und Forschungen 47. Sigmaringen: Jan Thorbecke, 1999.

———. "Rashi's Commentary on the Psalms and the Jewish-Christian Disputation." In *Studies in Bible and Education Presented to Professor Moshe Ahrend*, ed. Dov Rappel, 59–74. Jerusalem: Touro College, 1996.

———. *The Early Sages of Ashkenaz: Their Lives, Leadership and Works.* [In Hebrew.] Jerusalem: Magnes Press, 1981.

Gudiol, José. *The Arts of Spain*. London: Thames and Hudson, 1964.

Gutmann, Joseph. "Deuteronomy: Religious Reformation or Iconoclastic Revolution?" In *The Image and the Word: Confrontations in Judaism, Christianity and Islam*, 5–25. Missoula, MT: Scholars Press, 1977.

———. "Abraham in the Fire of the Chaldeans: A Jewish Legend in Jewish, Christian, and Islamic Art." *Frühmittelalterliche Studien* 7, no. 1 (1973): 342–352.

Habermann, Abraham Meir, ed. *Sefer Gezerot Ashkenaz Ve-Tsarfat: Divre Zikhronot Mi-Bene Ha-Dorot Shebi-Tekufat Mas'e Ha-Tselav U-Mivhar Piyutehem*. Jerusalem: Mosad HaRav Kook, 1945.

Hachez, Félix. "La littérature du sacrilège de Cambron." *Annales du cercle archéologique de Mons* 27 (1897): 97–152.

Halbertal, Moshe, and Avishai Margalit. *Idolatry*. Translated by Naomi Goldblum. Cambridge, MA: Harvard University Press, 1992.

Hall, Marcia B. "Savonarola's Preaching and the Patronage of Art." In *Christianity and the Renaissance: Image and Religious Imagination in the Quattrocento*, ed. Timothy Verdon and John Henderson, 493–522. Syracuse, NY: Syracuse University Press, 1990.

Hames, Harvey J. "Urinating on the Cross: Christianity as Seen in the *SeferYoseph ha-Mekaneh* (ca. 1260) and in Light of Paris 1240." In *Ritus Infidelium: Miradas interconfesionales sobre las prácticas religiosas en la Edad Media*, ed. José Martínez Gázquez and John Victor Tolan, 209–220. Collection de la Casa de Velázquez 138. Madrid: Casa Velazquez, 2013.

Hamilton, Bernard. "The Jews and the Byzantine Iconoclastic Controversy." *Eastern Churches Review* 5, no. 2 (Autumn 1973): 125–135.

Harris, Julie. "Polemical Images in the Golden Haggadah (British Library, Add. MS 27210)." *Medieval Encounters* 8 (2002): 105–122.

Hatton, Vikki, and Angus MacKay. "Anti-Semitism in the *Cantigas de Santa Maria*." *Bulletin of Hispanic Studies* 60 (1983): 189–199.

Haverkamp, Eva, ed. *Hebräische Berichte über die Judenverfolgungen während des Ersten Kreuzzugs*. Hannover: Hahnsche Buchhandlung, 2005.

Hayes, Christine Elizabeth. *Between the Babylonian and Palestinian Talmuds: Accounting for Halakhic Difference in Selected Sugyot from Tractate Avodah Zarah*. Oxford: Oxford University Press, 1997.

Heal, Bridget, and Ole Peter Grell, eds. *The Impact of the European Reformation: Princes, Clergy and People*. Aldershot: Ashgate, 2008.

Hertz, Robert. "Saint Besse: Étude d'un culte alpestre." In *Mélanges de sociologie religieuse et folklore*. Paris: Librairie Félix Alcan, 1928.

Herzig, Tamar. *A Convert's Tale: Art, Crime, and Jewish Apostasy in Renaissance Italy*. Cambridge, MA: Harvard University Press, 2019.

Hill, Rosalind, ed. *The Deeds of the Franks and the Other Pilgrims to Jerusalem*. London: Thomas Nelson and Sons, 1962.

Hill, Thomas D. "Time, Liturgy and History in the Old English *Elene*." In *Imagining the Jew in Anglo-Saxon Literature and Culture*, ed. Samantha Zacher, 156–166. Toronto: University of Toronto Press, 2016.

Hillaby, Joe. *The Palgrave Dictionary of Medieval Anglo-Jewish History*. London: Palgrave Macmillan, 2011.

———. "The London Jewry: William I to John." *Transactions of the Jewish Historical Society of England* 33 (1992–1994): 1–44.

Ho, H. L. (Ho Hock Lai). "The Legitimacy of Medieval Proof." *Journal of Law and Religion* 19, no. 2 (2003): 259–298.

Hoeps, Reinhard. "Gottes Gegenwart im Bild? Vom Streit zwischen Bild und Sakrament." In *Christusbild: Icon + Ikone; Wege zu Theorie und Theologie des Bildes*, ed. Peter Hofmann and Andreas Matena, 101–116. Paderborn: Ferdinand Schöningh, 2010.

———. *Aus dem Schatten des goldenen Kalbes: Skulptur in theologischer Perspektive*. Ikon Bild + Theologie. Paderborn: F. Schöningh, 1999.

Holmes, Megan. *The Miraculous Image in Renaissance Florence*. New Haven, CT: Yale University Press, 2013.

———. "Miraculous Images in Renaissance Florence." *Art History* 34, no. 3 (2011): 432–465.

Homza, Lu Ann, ed. and trans. *The Spanish Inquisition, 1478–1614: An Anthology of Sources*. Indianapolis: Hackett, 2006.

Horowitz, Elliott. *Reckless Rites: Purim and the Legacy of Jewish Violence*. Princeton, NJ: Princeton University Press, 2006.

———. "'The Vengeance of the Jews Was Stronger Than Their Avarice': Modern Historians and the Persian Conquest of Jerusalem in 614." *Jewish Social Studies* 4 (1998): 1–39.

Hsia, Ronnie Po-chia. "Jews as Magicians in Reformation Germany." In *Anti-Semitism in Times of Crisis*, ed. Sander L. Gilman and Steven T. Katz, 115–139. New York: New York University Press, 1991.

Ihnat, Kati. *Mother of Mercy, Bane of the Jews: Devotion to the Virgin Mary in Anglo-Norman England*. Princeton, NJ: Princeton University Press, 2016.

———. "Getting the Punchline: Deciphering Anti-Jewish Humour in Anglo-Norman England." *Journal of Medieval History* 38, no. 4 (2012): 408–423.

Ihnat, Kati, and Katelyn Mesler. "From Christian Devotion to Jewish Sorcery: The Curious History of Wax Figurines in Medieval Europe." In *Entangled Histories: Knowledge, Authority, and Jewish Culture in the Thirteenth Century*, ed. Elisheva Baumgarten, Ruth Mazo Karras, and Katelyn Mesler, 134–158. Philadelphia: University of Pennsylvania Press, 2017.

Ioly Zorattini, Pier Cesare. "*Derekh Teshuvah*: La via del ritorno." In *L'Identità dissimulata: Giudaizzanti iberici nell'Europa cristiana dell'età moderna*, ed. Pier Cesare Ioly Zorattini, 195–248. Florence: Olschki, 2000.

———, ed. *Processi del S. Uffizio di Venezia contro ebrei e giudaizzanti (1548–60)*. Vols. 4 and 10. Florence: Olschki, 1980.

Izbicki, Thomas M. *The Eucharist in Medieval Canon Law*. Cambridge: Cambridge University Press, 2015.

Jackson, Deidre. *Marvellous to Behold: Miracles in Medieval Manuscripts*. London: British Library, 2007.

Jacobs, Martin. *Islamische Geschichte in jüdischen Chroniken: Hebräische Historiographie des 16. und 17. Jahrhunderts*. Tübingen: Mohr Siebeck, 2004.

Jennings, J. C. "The Writings of Prior Dominic of Evesham." *English Historical Review* 77 (1962): 298–304.

Johnson, Geraldine A., and Sara F. Matthews Grieco, eds. *Picturing Women in Renaissance and Baroque Italy*. Cambridge: Cambridge University Press, 2012.

Johnson Timothy J., ed. *Franciscans and Preaching: Every Miracle from the Beginning of the World Came About Through Words*. Leiden: Brill, 2002.

Jordan, William Chester. *The French Monarchy and the Jews: From Philip Augustus to the Last Capetians*. Philadelphia: University of Pennsylvania Press, 1989.

Jütte, Daniel. "'They Shall Not Keep Their Doors or Windows Open': Urban Space and the Dynamics of Conflict and Contact in Premodern Jewish-Christian Relations." *European History Quarterly* 46, no. 2 (2016): 209–36.

———. *The Age of Secrecy: Jews, Christians, and the Economy of Secrets, 1400–1800*. Translated by Jeremiah Riemer. New Haven, CT: Yale University Press, 2015.

———. *The Strait Gate: Thresholds of Power in Western History*. New Haven, CT: Yale University Press, 2015.

Kanarfogel, Ephraim. *Brothers from Afar: Rabbinic Approaches to Apostasy and Reversion in Medieval Europe*. Detroit: Wayne State University Press, 2020.

Kartsonis, Anna D. *Anastasis: The Making of an Icon*. Princeton, NJ: Princeton University Press, 1986.

Katz, Dana E. *The Jewish Ghetto and the Visual Imagination of Early Modern Venice*. Cambridge: Cambridge University Press, 2017.

———. "'Clamber Not You up to the Casements': On Ghetto Views and Viewing." *Jewish History* 24 (2010): 127–153.

———. *The Jew in the Art of the Italian Renaissance*. Philadelphia: University of Pennsylvania Press, 2008.

———. "Painting and the Politics of Persecution: Representing the Jew in Fifteenth-Century Mantua." *Art History* 23, no. 4 (2000): 475–495.

Katz, Jacob. *Exclusiveness and Tolerance: Studies in Jewish-Gentile Relations in Medieval and Modern Times*. Oxford: Oxford University Press, 1961.

Kaufmann, Thomas. *Luther's Jews: A Journey into Anti-Semitism*. Translated by Lesley Sharpe and Jeremy Noakes. Oxford: Oxford University Press, 2017.

Keely, Avril. "Arians and Jews in the 'Histories' of Gregory of Tours." *Journal of Medieval History* 23 (1997): 103–115.

Keller, John Esten. "Daily Living as Presented in the *Canticles* of Alfonso the Learned." *Speculum* 33, no. 4 (1958): 484–489.

Keller, John Esten, and Annette Grant Cash. *Daily Life Depicted in the "Cantigas de Santa Maria."* Lexington: University of Kentucky Press, 1998.

Kelley, Christopher Pierce. "Who Did the Iconoclasm in the Dura Synagogue?" *Bulletin of the American Schools of Oriental Research* 295 (1994): 57–72.

Kessler, Herbert L. *Spiritual Seeing: Picturing God's Invisibility in Medieval Art*. Philadelphia: University of Pennsylvania Press, 2000.

———. "'Pictures Fertile with Truth': How Christians Managed to Make Images of God Without Violating the Second Commandment." *Journal of the Walters Art Gallery* 49/50 (1991/1992): 53–65.

Kessler, Herbert L., and David Nirenberg, eds. *Judaism and Christian Art: Aesthetic Anxieties from Catacombs to Colonialism*. Philadelphia: University of Pennsylvania Press, 2001.

Kilde, Jeanne Halgren. *Sacred Power, Sacred Space: An Introduction to Christian Architecture and Worship*. Oxford: Oxford Univerity Press, 2008.

Kitzinger, Ernst. *The Art of Byzantium and the Medieval West: Selected Studies*. Bloomington: Indiana University Press, 1976.

———. "The Cult of Images in the Age Before Iconoclasm." *Dumbarton Oaks Papers* 8 (1954): 83–150.

Klein, Elka. *Jews, Christian Society, and Royal Power in Medieval Barcelona*. Ann Arbor: University of Michigan Press, 2006.

Kogman-Appel, Katrin. "The Tree of Death and the Tree of Life: The Hanging of Haman in Medieval Jewish Manuscript Painting." In *Between the Image and the Word: Essays in Honor of John Plummer*, ed. Colum Hourihane, 187–208. University Park: Pennsylvania State University Press, 2005.

———. "Coping with Christian Pictorial Sources: What Did Jewish Miniaturists Not Paint?" *Speculum* 75 (2000): 816–858.

Koopmans, Rachel. *Wonderful to Relate: Miracle Stories and Miracle Collecting in High Medieval England*. Philadelphia: University of Pennsylvania Press, 2010.

Kosman, Admiel. *Women's Tractate: Wisdom, Love, Faithfulness, Passion, Beauty, Sex, Holiness*. [In Hebrew.] Jerusalem: Keter, 2007.

Kretzenbacher, Leopold. *Das verletzte Kultbild: Voraussetzungen, Zeitschichten und Aussagewandel eines abendländischen Legendentypus*. Munich: Bayerischen Akademie der Wissenschaften, 1977.

Kühnel, Bianca. "Jewish Art and 'Iconoclasm': The Case of Sepphoris." In *Representation in Religion: Studies in Honor of Moshe Barasch*, ed. Jan Assmann and Alfred I. Baumgarten, 161–180. Leiden: Brill, 2000.

———. "The Synagogue Floor Mosaic in Sepphoris: Between Paganism and Christianity." In *From Dura to Sepphoris: Studies in Jewish Art and Society in Late Antiquity*, ed. Lee I. Levine and Ze'ev Weiss, 31–43. Portsmouth, RI: Journal of Roman Archaeology, 2000.

———. "Jewish and Christian Art in the Middle Ages: The Dynamics of a Relationship." In *Juden und Christen zur Zeit der Kreuzzüge*, ed. Alfred Haverkamp, 1–16. Sigmaringen: Jan Thorbecke, 1999.

Kupfer, Marcia, ed. *The Passion Story: From Visual Representation to Social Drama*. University Park: Pennsylvania State University Press, 2008.

Lackner, Jacob. "Violent Men and Malleable Women: Gender and Jewish Conversion to Christianity in Medieval Sermon Exempla." *Nashim: A Journal of Jewish Women's Studies & Gender Issues* 30 (2016): 24–47.

Landau, David, and Peter Parshall. *The Renaissance Print, 1470–1550*. New Haven, CT: Yale University Press, 1994.

Landes, Richard. *Relics, Apocalypse, and the Deceits of History: Ademar of Chabannes, 989–1034*. Cambridge, MA: Harvard University Press, 1995.

Langmuir, Gavin I. *History, Religion, and Antisemitism*. Berkeley: University of California Press, 1990.

———. *Toward a Definition of Antisemitism*. Berkeley: University of California Press, 1990.

Lasker, Daniel J. "Jewish Knowledge of Christianity in the Twelfth and Thirteenth Centuries." In *Studies in Medieval Jewish Intellectual and Social History: Festschrift in Honor of Robert Chazan*, ed. David Engel, Lawrence H. Schiffman, and Elliot R. Wolfson, 97–109. Leiden: Brill, 2012.

Lawee, Eric. "Graven Images, Astromagical Cherubs, and Mosaic Miracles: A Fifteenth-Century Curial-Rabbinic Exchange." *Speculum* 18, no. 2 (2006): 754–795.

Leder, Stefan. "The Attitude of the Population, Especially the Jews, Towards the Arab-Islamic Conquest of Bilad al-Sham and the Question of Their Role Therein." *Die Welt des Orients* 18 (1987): 64–71.

Lejeune, Théophile. "La vierge miraculeuse de Cambron." *Annales du cercle archéologique de Mons* 7 (1867): 66–95.

Lepore, Jill. "Historians Who Love Too Much: Reflections on Microhistory and Biography." *Journal of American History* 88, no. 1 (2001): 129–44.

Lévi, Israel. "L'Apocalypse de Zorobabel et le roi de Perse Siroès." *Revue des Études Juives* 68 (1914): 126–160.

———. "Le Juif de la légende." *Revue des Études Juives* 22 (1891): 233–235.

Levine, Lee I., and Ze'ev Weiss, eds. *From Dura to Sepphoris: Studies in Jewish Art and Society in Late Antiquity*. Portsmouth, RI: Journal of Roman Archaeology, 2000.

Liebeschutz, Hans. "The Crusading Movement and Its Bearing on the Christian Attitude Towards Jewry." *Journal of Jewish Studies* 10 (1959): 97–111.

Limor, Ora. "Polemical Varieties: Religious Disputations in 13th Century Spain." *Iberia Judaica* 2 (2010): 55–79.

———. "'Holy Journey': Pilgrimage and Christian Sacred Landscape." In *Christians and Christianity in the Holy Land: From the Origins to the Latin Kingdoms*, ed. Ora Limor and Guy G. Stroumsa, 321–355. Turnhout: Brepols, 2006.

———. "Mary and the Jews: Story, Controversy and Testimony." *Historein* 6 (2006): 55–71.

———. "Christian Sacred Space and the Jew." In *From Witness to Witchcraft: Jews and Judaism in Medieval Christian Thought*, Wolfenbütteler Mittelalter-Studien 11, ed. Jeremy Cohen, 55–77. Wiesbaden: Harrassowitz, 1996.

———, ed. *Die Disputationen zu Ceuta (1179) und Mallorca (1286): Zwei antijüdische Schriften aus dem mittelalterlichen Genua*. Munich: Monumenta Germaniae Historica, 1994.

Linder, Amnon. "'The Jews Too Were Not Absent . . . Carrying Moses's Law on Their Shoulders': The Ritual Encounter of Pope and Jews from the Middle Ages to Modern Times." *Jewish Quarterly Review* 99, no. 3 (2009) 323–395.

———. *The Jews in Roman Imperial Legislation*. Detroit: Wayne State University Press, 1987.

———. "Jerusalem as a Focus of Confrontation Between Judaism and Christianity." In *Vision and Conflict in the Holy Land*, ed. Richard I. Cohen, 1–22. Jerusalem: Yad Izhak Ben-Zvi; New York: St. Martin's Press, 1985.

———. "Ecclesia and Synagoga in the Medieval Myth of Constantine the Great." *Revue belge de philologie et d'histoire* 54, no. 4 (1976): 1019–1060.

———. "The Myth of Constantine the Great in the West: Sources and Hagiographic Commemoration." *Studi Medievali*, 3rd ser., 16, no. 1 (1975): 43–95.

Lipton, Sara. *Dark Mirror: The Medieval Origins of Anti-Jewish Iconography*. New York: Metropolitan Books, 2014.

———. "Images and Their Uses." In *The Cambridge History of Christianity*, vol. 4, *Christianity in Western Europe, c. 1000–c. 1500*, ed. Miri Rubin and Walter Simons, 254–283. Cambridge: Cambridge University Press, 2009.

———. "Images in the World: Reading the Crucifixion." In *Medieval Christianity in Practice*, ed. Miri Rubin, 173–188. Princeton, NJ: Princeton University Press, 2009.

———. "Where Are the Gothic Jewish Women? On the Non-Iconography of the Jewess in the *Cantigas de Santa Maria*." *Jewish History* 22 (2008): 139–177.

———. "The Sweet Lean of His Head: Writing About Looking at the Crucifix in the High Middle Ages." *Speculum* 80, no. 4 (2005): 1172–1208.

———. *Images of Intolerance: The Representation of Jews and Judaism in the "Bible moralisée."* Berkeley: University of California Press, 1999.

Little, Lester K. *Religious Poverty and the Profit Economy in Medieval Europe.* Ithaca, NY: Cornell University Press, 1983.

Loewe, Heinrich. *Die Juden in der katholischen Legende.* Berlin: Jüdischer Verlag, 1912.

Lollini, Fabrizio. "'Lo strepito degli ostinati giudei': Iconografia antiebraica a Bologna e in Emilia-Romagna." In *Banchi ebraica Bologna nel XV secolo,* ed. Maria Giuseppina Muzzarelli, 269–328. Bologna: Il Mulino, 1994.

Luzzati, Michele. "Sulle tentazioni iconoclaste ebraiche in Italia fra tardo Medioevo e prima età moderna" In *"Conosco un ottimo storico dell'arte . . .": Per Enrico Castelnuovo; Scritti di allievi e amici pisani,* ed. Maria Monica Donato and Massimo Ferretti, 227–234. Pisa: Edizioni della normale, Scuola Normale Superiore, 2010.

———."'Satis est quod tecum dormivit': Vero, verosimile e falso nelle incriminazioni di ebrei; Un caso di presunta sodomia (Lucca, 1471–1472)." In *Una manna buona per Mantova: Man Tov le-Man Tovah; Studi in onore di Vittore Colorni per il suo 92° compleanno,* ed. Mauro Perani, 261–280. Florence: Olschki, 2004.

———. "Il convertito maestro Vincenzo primo titolare di una cattedra di ebraico presso lo Studio Bolognese (1464–1490)." In *La cultura ebraica a Bologna tra medioevo e rinascimento,* ed. Mauro Perani, 167–174. Bologna: Giuntina, 2000.

———. *La sinagoga di Pisa dalle origini al restauro ottocentesco di Marco Treves.* Florence: Edifir, 1997.

———, ed. *L'Inquisizione e gli ebrei in Italia.* Rome: Laterza, 1994.

———. "Vescovi ed ebrei nell'Italia tardomedievale." In *Vescovi e diocese in Italia dal XIV alla metà del XVI secolo,* ed. Giuseppina De Sandre Gasparini, 1099–1123. Rome: Herder, 1990.

———. "Ebrei, chiesa locale, 'principe' e popolo: Due episodi di distruzione di immagini sacre alla fine del Quattrocento." In *La casa dell'ebreo,* 205–234. Pisa: Nistri-Lischi, 1985.

Maccoby, Hyam, ed. and trans. *Judaism on Trial: Jewish-Christian Disputations in the Middle Ages.* London: Littman Library of Jewish Civilization, 1993.

Macy, Gary. *The Theologies of the Eucharist in the Early Scholastic Period.* Oxford: Oxford University Press, 1984.

Magnússon, Sigurdur. "The Singularization of History: Social History and Microhistory Within the Postmodern State of Knowledge." *Journal of Social History* 36, no. 3 (Spring 2003): 701–735.

Maguire, Henry. "Garments Pleasing to God: The Significance of Domestic Textile Designs in the Early Byzantine Period." *Dumbarton Oak Papers* 44 (1990): 215–224.

Maifreda, Germano. *Italya: Storie di ebrei, storia italiana.* Bari: Gius. Laterza & Figli, 2021.

Maimon, Arye, Mordechai Breuer, and Yacov Guggenheim, eds. *Germania Judaica.* Vol. 3, *1350–1519.* Part 3. Tübingen: Mohr Siebeck, 2003.

Malkiel, David. *Reconstructing Ashkenaz: The Human Face of Franco-German Jewry, 1000–1250.* Stanford, CA: Stanford University Press, 2008.

Mann, Vivian B. "The Unknown Jewish Artists of Medieval Iberia." In *The Jew in Medieval Iberia, 1100–1555,* ed. Jonathan Ray, 138–175. Boston: Academic Press, 2011.

———, ed. *Uneasy Communion: Jews, Christians, and the Altarpieces of Medieval Spain.* New York: Museum of Biblical Art, 2010.

———. *Jewish Texts on the Visual Arts.* Cambridge: Cambridge University Press, 2000.

———, ed. *Gardens and Ghettos: The Art of Jewish Life in Italy.* Berkeley: University of California Press, 1989.

Marcus, Ivan G. "A Jewish-Christian Symbiosis: The Culture of Early Ashkenaz." In *Cultures of the Jews: A New History*, ed. David Biale, 449–516. New York: Schocken Books, 2002.

———. "From Politics to Martyrdom: Paradigms in the Hebrew Narratives of the 1096 Crusade Riots." *Prooftexts* 2, no. 1 (January 1982): 40–52.

———. *Piety and Society: The Jewish Pietists of Medieval Germany*. Leiden: Brill, 1981.

Martín, José-Luis, and Antonio Linage Conde. *Religión y sociedad medieval: El catecismo de Pedro de Cuéllar (1325)*. Valladolid: Junta, 1987.

Martínez Martínez, María José. "El Santo Cristo de Burgos y los cristos dolorosos articulados." *Boletín del Seminario de Estudios de Arte y Arqueología* 69–70 (2003–2004): 207–246.

Mayer-Thurman, Christa C. *Raiment for the Lord's Service: A Thousand Years of Western Vestments*. Chicago: Art Institute of Chicago, 1975.

McKay, John W. *Religion in Judah Under the Assyrians, 732–609 BC*. Naperville, IL: Allenson, 1973.

McMichael, Steven J. *Was Jesus of Nazareth the Messiah? Alphonso de Espina's Argument Against the Jews in the "Fortalitium Fidei" (c. 1464)*. Atlanta, GA: Scholars Press, 1994.

Meeks, Wayne A. and Robert L. Wilken, Jews and Christians in Antioch in the First Four Centuries of the Common Era. Missoula, MT: Scholars Press, 1978.

Meisen, Karl, Matthias Zender, and Franz Josef Heyen. *Nikolauskult und Nikolausbrauch im Abendlande: Eine kult geographisch-volks kundliche Untersuchung*. Düsseldorf: Schwann; Mainz: Im Selbstverlag der Gesellschaft für Mittelrheinische Kirchengeschichte, 1981.

Melammed, Reneé Levine. *Heretics or Daughters of Israel? The Crypto-Jewish Women of Castile*. New York: Oxford University Press, 1999.

Mell, Julie L. *The Myth of the Medieval Jewish Moneylender*. New York: Palgrave Macmillan, 2017.

Mellinkoff, Ruth. *Antisemitic Hate Signs in Hebrew Illuminated Manuscripts from Medieval Germany*. Jerusalem: Center for Jewish Art, 1999.

Menache, Sophia. "Matthew Paris's Attitudes Toward Anglo-Jewry." *Journal of Medieval History* 23 (1997): 139–162.

Menozzi, Danielle. *La Chiesa e le immagini: I testi fondamentali sulle arti figurativi dalle origini ai nostri giorni*. Milan: San Paolo Edizioni, 1995.

Menzione, Andrea. *Preghiera e diletto: Immagini domestiche a Pisa nel Seicento*. Pisa: Edizione Plus, 2010.

Merback, Mitchell B. *Pilgrimage and Pogrom: Violence, Memory, and Visual Culture at the Host-Miracle Shrines of Germany and Austria*. Chicago: University of Chicago Press, 2013.

———, ed. *Beyond the Yellow Badge: Anti-Judaism and Antisemitism in Medieval and Early Modern Visual Culture*. Leiden: Brill, 2010.

———. "Fount of Mercy, City of Blood: Cultic Anti-Judaism and the Pulkau Passion Altarpiece." *Art Bulletin* 87, no. 4 (2005): 589–642.

Meyerson, Mark D. *A Jewish Renaissance in Fifteenth-Century Spain*. Princeton, NJ: Princeton University Press, 2004.

———. *Jews in an Iberian Frontier Kingdom: Society, Economy, and Politics in Morvedre, 1248–1391*. Leiden: Brill, 2004.

Michelson, Emily. "How to Write a Conversionary Sermon: Rhetorical Influences and Religious Identity." In *Religious Orders and Religious Identity Formation, ca. 1420–1620: Discourses and Strategies of Observance and Pastoral Engagement*, ed. Bert Roest and Johanneke Uphoff, 235–251. Leiden: Brill, 2016.

Miles, Margaret R. *A Complex Delight: The Secularization of the Breast, 1350–1750*. Berkeley: University of California Press, 2008.

Miller, Patricia Cox. *The Corporeal Imagination: Signifying the Holy in Late Ancient Christianity*. Philadelphia: University of Pennsylvania Press, 2016.

Mills, Robert. *Suspended Animation: Pain, Pleasure and Punishment in Medieval Culture*. London: Reaktion Books, 2005.

Mimouni, Simon C. "Pour une définition nouvelle du judéo-christianisme ancien." *New Testament Studies* 38, no. 2 (1992): 161–186.

Molina Figueras, Joan. "La imagen y su contexto: Perfiles de la iconografía antijudía en la España medieval." In *Els jueus a la Girona medieval (XII ciclo de conferencias Girona a l'Abast)*, 33–85. Girona: Bell-lloc, 2008.

Mormando, Franco. *The Preacher's Demons: Bernardino of Siena and the Social Underworld of Early Renaissance Italy*. Chicago: University of Chicago Press, 1999.

Morrison, Karl F. *Conversion and Text: The Cases of Augustine of Hippo, Herman-Judah, and Constantine Tsatsos*. Charlottesville: University Press of Virginia, 1992.

Möschter, Angela. "Norme giuridiche e vita quotidiana: Costruzioni di 'interstizi' tra ebrei e cristiani nel tardo medioevo a Treviso." In *"Interstizi": Culture Ebraico-Cristiane a Venezia e nei suoi domini dal medioevo all'età moderna*, ed. Uwe Israel, Robert Jütte, and Reinhold C. Mueller, 155–190. Rome: Edizioni di Storia e letteratura, 2010.

———. *Juden im venezianischen Treviso (1389–1509)*. Hannover: Tuntematon Sidosasu, 2008.

———. "*Et Verbum caro factum est*: Begegnungen und Differenzen von Juden und Christen beim Fleischmahl." In *Campana pulsante convocati: Festschrift anlässlich der Emeritierung von Alfred Haverkamp*, ed. Frank G. Hirschmann and Gerd Mentgen, 361–362 and 386–388. Trier: Kliomedia, 2005.

Muir, Edward. "The Virgin on the Street Corner: The Place of the Sacred in Italian Cities." In *Religion and Culture in the Renaissance and Reformation*, ed. Steven Ozment, 25–40. Kirksville, MO: Sixteenth Century Journal Publishers, 1989.

Muldoon, James. *Popes, Lawyers, and Infidels: The Church and the Non-Christian World 1250–1550*. Philadelphia: University of Pennsylvania Press, 1979.

Mundill, Robin R. *The King's Jews: Money, Massacre and Exodus in Medieval England*. New York: Continuum, 2010.

Murray, Alexander C., ed. *A Companion to Gregory of Tours*. Leiden: Brill, 2016.

Muzzarelli, Maria Giuseppina. "Ebrei a convegno in epoca medieval." In *Gli ebrei a Cento e Pieve di Cento fra medioevo ed età moderna: Atti del convegno di studi storici, Cento, 22 aprile 1993*, ed. Maria Giuseppina Muzzarelli, Antonio Samaritani, and Paolo Ravenna, 13–28. Cento: Fondazione Cassa di Risparmio di Cento, 1994.

Neis, Rachel. "Religious Lives of Image-Things, *Avodah Zarah*, and Rabbis in Late Antique Palestine." *Archivfür Religions-Geschichte* 17, no. 1 (2016): 91–121.

———. "Pilgrimage Itineraries: Seeing the Past Through Rabbinic Eyes." *Jewish Studies Quarterly* 20 (2013): 224–256.

———. *The Sense of Sight in Rabbinic Culture: Jewish Ways of Seeing in Late Antiquity*. Cambridge: Cambridge University Press, 2013.

———. "Eyeing Idols: Rabbinic Viewing Practices in Late Antiquity." *Jewish Quarterly Review* 102, no. 4 (Fall 2012): 533–560.

Nelson, Benjamin, and Joshua Starr. "The Legend of Divine Surety and the Jewish Moneylender." *Annuaire de l'Institut de Philologie et d'Histoire Orientales et Slaves* 7 (1939–1944): 289–338.

Nicolaisen, Jan. "Einige Beobachtungen zur 'Privatisierung' des gedruckten Bildes im 15. Jahrhundert: Publikum und Gebrauch des Kupferstichs." In *Spiegel der Seligkeit: Privates Bild und Frömmigkeit im Spätmittelalter*, ed. Frank Matthias Kammel, 84–96. Nuremberg: Verlag des Germanischen Nationalmuseums Nürnberg, 2000.

Nirenberg, David. *Aesthetic Theology and Its Enemies: Judaism in Christian Painting, Poetry, and Politics*. Waltham, MA: Brandeis University Press, 2015.

———. *Anti-Judaism: The History of a Way of Thinking*. New York: W. W. Norton, 2013.

———. "The Historical Body of Christ." In James Clifton, David Nirenberg and Linda Elaine Neagley, *The Body of Christ in the Art of Europe and New Spain, 1150–1800*, 17–26. Munich: Prestel, 1997.

———. *Communities of Violence: Persecution of Minorities in the Middle Ages*. Princeton, NJ: Princeton University Press, 1995.

Noack, Friedrich. *Das Deutschtum in Rom seit dem Ausgang des Mittelalters*. Vol. 1. Stuttgart: Deutsche Verlags-Anstalt, 1927.

Noble, Thomas F. X. *Images, Iconoclasm, and the Carolingians*. Philadelphia: University of Pennsylvania Press, 2009.

Novak, David. *Jewish-Christian Dialogue: A Jewish Justification*. New York: Oxford University Press, 1989.

Novotný, Kamil, and Emanuel Poche. *The Charles Bridge of Prague*. Prague: V. Poláček, 1947.

O'Callaghan, Joseph F. *Alfonso X, the Justinian of His Age: Law and Justice in Thirteenth-Century Castile*. Ithaca, NY: Cornell University Press, 2019.

———. *Alfonso X and the "Cantigas de Santa Maria": A Poetic Biography*. Leiden: Brill, 1998.

Ocker, Christopher. "Ritual Murder and the Subjectivity of Christ: A Choice in Medieval Christianity." *Harvard Theological Review* 91, no. 2 (1998): 153–92.

Oelman, Timothy, ed. *Marrano Poets of the Seventeenth Century*. London: Littman Library, 1982.

O'Loughlin, Thomas. "The Exegetical Purpose of Adomnán's *De Locis Sanctis*." *Cambridge Medieval Celtic Studies* 24 (Winter 1992): 37–53.

Olster, David M. *Roman Defeat, Christian Response, and the Literary Construction of the Jew*. Philadelphia: University of Pennsylvania Press, 1994.

Ongania, Ferdinando. *Documenti per la storia dell'augusta ducale basilica di San Marco in Venezia*. Venice, 1886.

Oz, Amos. *Judas*. Translated from the Hebrew by Nicholas de Lange. London: Chatto & Windus, 1988.

Paetow, Louis J. "The Crusading Ardor of John of Garland." In *The Crusades, and Other Historical Essays, Presented to Dana C. Munro by His Former Students*, ed. Louis J. Paetow, 207–222. New York: F. S. Crofts, 1928.

Palumbo, Giuseppe. *Collezione Federico Mason Perkins: Sacro Convento di S. Francesco, Assisi*. Rome: Tip. Staderini, 1973.

Paoletti, John T., and Gary M. Radke. *Art in Renaissance Italy*. 3rd ed. Upper Saddle River, NJ: Pearson/Prentice Hall, 2005.

Paoli, Marco. *Arte e committenza privata a Lucca nel Trecento e nel Quattrocento: Produzione artistic e cultura libraria*. Lucca: Maria Pacini Fazzi, 1986.

Papaconstantinou, Arietta. "Saints and Saracens: On Some Miracle Accounts of the Early Arab Period." In *Byzantine Religious Culture Studies in Honor of Alice-Mary Talbot*, ed. Denis Sullivan, Elizabeth Fisher, and Stratis Papaioannou, 323–339. Leiden: Brill, 2012.

Patton, Pamela A. *Art of Estrangement: Redefining Jews in Reconquest Spain*. University Park: Pennsylvania State University Press, 2012.

Paudice, Aleida. *Between Several Worlds: The Life and Writings of Elia Capsali; The Historical Works of a 16th-Century Cretan Rabbi.* Munich: Peter Lang, 2010.

Pearce, Sarah, ed. *The Image and Its Prohibition in Jewish Antiquity.* Oxford: Journal of Jewish Studies, 2013.

Peers, Glenn. *Sacred Shock: Framing Visual Experience in Byzantium.* University Park: Pennsylvania State University Press, 2004.

Pereda, Felipe. "La conversion por la imagen y la imagen de la conversion: Notas sobre la cultura figurativa castellana en el umbral de la edad moderna." In *Cartografías visuales y arquitectónicas de la modernidad: Siglos XV–XVIII*, ed. Sílvia Canalda, Carme Narváez, and Joan Sureda, 228–241. Barcelona: Publicacions i Edicions de la Universitat de Barcelona, 2011.

———. *Las imágenes de la discordia: Política y poética de la imagen sagrada en la España del 400.* Madrid: Marcial Pons Historia, 2007.

———. "El debate sobre la imagen en la España del siglo XV: Judíos, cristianos y conversos." *Anuario del Departamento de Historia y Teoría del Arte* 14 (2002): 59–79.

Perles, J. "Ahron ben Gerson Aboulrabi." *Revue des Études Juives* 21 (1890): 246–269.

Pesaro, Abramo. *Memorie storiche sulla Comunità Israelitica ferrarese.* Ferrara, 1878–1880. Reprint, Bologna: Forni, 1967.

Peters, F. E. *Jerusalem: The Holy City in the Eyes of Chroniclers, Visitors, Pilgrims, and Prophets from the Days of Abraham to the Beginnings of Modern Times.* Princeton, NJ: Princeton University Press, 1985.

Pon, Lisa. *A Printed Icon in Early Modern Italy: Forlì's Madonna of the Fire.* Cambridge: Cambridge University Press, 2015.

Poncelet, Albertus. "Catalogus codicum hagiographicorum latinorum: Bibliothecae nationalis Taurinensis." *Analecta Bollandiana* 28 (1909): 417–478.

Poni, Carlo. "Tecnologie, organizzazione produttiva e divisione sessuale del lavoro: Il caso dei mulini da seta." In *Il lavoro delle donne*, ed. Angela Groppi, 269–296. Bari: Laterza, 1996.

———. "All'origine del sistema di fabbrica: Tecnologia e organizzazione produttiva dei mulini da seta nell' Italia settentrionale (sec. XVII–XVIII)." *Rivista Storica Italiana* 88, no. 3 (1976): 444–497.

———. "Archéologie de la fabrique: La diffusion des moulins à soie 'alla bolognese' dans les États vénitiens du XVIe au XVIIIe siècle." *Annales: Économies, Sociétés, Civilisations* 27, no. 6 (1972): 1475–1496.

Pringle, Denys. *The Churches of the Crusader Kingdom of Jerusalem: A Corpus.* Vol. 2. Cambridge: Cambridge University Press, 2009.

Prodi, Paolo. "Ricerca sulla teorica delle arti figurative nella riforma cattolica." *Archivio italiano per la storia della pieta* 4 (1962): 124–212.

Prosperi, Adriano. "Il condannato a morte: Santo o criminale?" In *Il delitto narrato al popolo: Immagini di giustizia e stereotipi di criminalità in età moderna*, ed. Roberto de Romanis and Rosamaria Loretelli, 219–227. Palermo: Sellerio, 1999.

———. "Incontri rituali: Il papa e gli ebrei." *Storia d'Italia* 11 (1996): 495–520.

Pulido Serrano, Juan Ignacio. *Injurias a Cristo: Religión, política y antijudaísmo en el siglo XVII (análisis de las corrientes antijudías durante la Edad Moderna).* Alcalá de Henares: Instituto Internacional de Estudios Sefardiés y Andalusíes, Universidad de Alcalá, Servicio de Publicaciones, 2002.

Pullan, Brian S. *The Jews of Europe and the Inquisition of Venice, 1550–1670.* Oxford: Basil Blackwell, 1983.

———. *Rich and Poor in Renaissance Venice: The Social Institutions of a Catholic State to 1620.* Oxford: Oxford University Press, 1971.

Rabinowitz, Zvi M., ed. *The Liturgical Poetry of Rabbi Yannai.* Jerusalem: Bialik Institute, 1985–1987.

Ravid, Benjamin. "An Introduction to the Charters of the Jewish Merchants of Venice." In *The Mediterranean and the Jews*, ed. Elliott Horowitz and Moises Orfali, 203–246. Jerusalem: Bar-Ilan University Press, 2002.

Raviv, Rivka. "The End of Idolatry in Israel During the Persian Period." [In Hebrew.] *Bekhol Derakhekha Daehu—Journal of Torah and Scholarship* 25 (2011): 83–92.

Raw, Barbara. *Anglo-Saxon Crucifixion Iconography and the Art of the Monastic Revival.* Cambridge: Cambridge University Press, 1990.

Ray, Jonathan, ed. *The Jew in Medieval Iberia, 1100–1500.* Boston: Academic Studies Press, 2011.

Régné, Jean. *History of the Jews in Aragon: Regesta and Documents, 1213–1327.* Edited by Yom Tov Assis. Hispania Judaica 1. Jerusalem: Magnes Press, 1978.

———. "Rapports entre l'inquisition et les juifs d'après le mémorial de l'inquisiteur d'Aragon (fin du XIV siècle)." *Revue des Études Juives* 53 (1906): 224–233.

Reinhardt, Klaus, and Horacio Santiago-Otero. *Biblioteca bíblica ibérica medieval.* Madrid: Editorial CSIC–CSIC Press, 1986.

Resnick, Irven "Jews and Abuse of the Cross in the Middle Ages: A Cross Desecration Libel? *Jewish Quarterly Review* 111, no. 4 (Fall 2021): 582–604.

———. *Marks of Distinction: Christian Perceptions of Jews in the High Middle Ages.* Washington, DC: Catholic University of America Press, 2012.

Revel-Neher, Elisabeth. *The Image of the Jew in Byzantine Art.* Translated by David Maizel. Oxford: Pergamon Press, 1992.

Riley-Smith, Jonathan. *The First Crusade and the Idea of Crusading.* Philadelphia: University of Pennsylvania Press, 2009.

Ringbom, Sixten. "Devotional Images and Imaginative Devotions: Notes on the Place of Art in Late Medieval Private Piety." *Gazette des Beaux-Arts*, 6th ser., 73 (1969): 159–170.

Rist, Rebecca. *Popes and Jews, 1095–1291.* Oxford: Oxford University Press, 2015.

Robinson, Cynthia. *Imagining the Passion in a Multiconfessional Castile: The Virgin, Christ, Devotions, and Images in the Fourteenth and Fifteenth Centuries.* University Park: Pennsylvania State University Press, 2013.

———. "Preaching to the Converted: Valladolid's *Cristianos nuevos* and the *Retablo de don Sancho de Rojas* (1415)." *Speculum* 83 (2008): 112–163.

Rodríguez Barral, Paulino. *La imagen del judío en la España medieval: El conflicto entre cristianismo y judaísmo en las artes visuales góticas.* Memoria artium 8. Bellaterra: Universitat Autònoma de Barcelona, Servei de Publicacions; Barcelona: Publicacions i Ediciones de la Universitat Barcelona, 2008.

———. "La dialéctica texto-imagen: A propósito de la representación del judío en las *Cantigas de Santa María* de Alfonso X." *Anuario de Estudios Medievales* 37, no. 1 (2007): 213–244.

Rodríguez G. de Ceballos, Alfonso. "Image and Counter-Reformation in Spain and Spanish America." In *Sacred Spain: Art and Belief in the Spanish World*, ed. Ronda Kasl, 15–36. Indianapolis: Indianapolis Museum of Art, 2009.

Rokéah, Zefira Entin. "The Jewish Church-Robbers and Host Desecrators of Norwich (ca. 1285)." *Revue des Études Juives* 141 (1982): 331–362.

Rosen-Zvi, Ishay. "The Polemic on the Obligation to Destroy Idolatry in Tannaitic Literature." [In Hebrew.] *Reshit: The Shalom Hartman Institute Academic Annual* 1 (2009): 91–116.

Roth, Cecil. *The Jews of Medieval Oxford*. Oxford Historical Society, vol. 9. Oxford: Oxford University Press, 1951.

Roth, Norman. *Conversos, Inquisition, and the Expulsion of the Jews from Spain*. Madison: University of Wisconsin Press, 1995.

———. "New Light on the Jews of Mozarabic Toledo." *Association of Jewish Studies Review* 11, no. 2 (1986): 189–220.

Rowe, Nina. *The Jew, the Cathedral, and the Medieval City: Synagoga and Ecclesia in the Thirteenth Century*. Cambridge: Cambridge University Press, 2015.

Rubin, Miri. *Emotion and Devotion: The Meaning of Mary in Medieval Religious Cultures*. Budapest: Central European University Press, 2009.

———. *Mother of God: A History of the Virgin Mary*. New Haven, CT: Yale University Press, 2009.

———. *Gentile Tales: The Narrative Assault on Late Medieval Jews*. Philadelphia: University of Pennsylvania Press, 2004.

———. "Imagining the Jew: The Late Medieval Eucharistic Discourse." In *In and Out of the Ghetto: Jewish-Gentile Relations in Late Medieval and Early Modern Germany*, ed. R. Po-Chia Hsia and Hartmut Lehmann, 177–208. Cambridge: Cambridge University Press, 1995.

———. *Corpus Christi: The Eucharist in Late Medieval Culture*. Cambridge: Cambridge University Press, 1992.

———. "Desecration of the Host: The Birth of an Accusation." In *Christianity and Judaism*, ed. Diana Wood, 169–189. Oxford: Blackwell, 1992.

Rublack, Ulinka. Ed. *The Oxford Handbook of the Protestant Reformations*. Oxford: Oxford University Press, 2019.

Rudolph, Conrad. *The "Things of Greater Importance": Bernard of Clairvaux's "Apologia" and the Medieval Attitude Toward Art*. Philadelphia: University of Pennsylvania Press, 1990.

Ruether, Rosemary Radford. "The *Adversus Judaeos* Tradition in the Church Fathers: The Exegesis of Christian Anti-Judaism." In *Essential Papers on Judaism and Christianity in Conflict: From Late Antiquity to the Reformation*, ed. Jeremy Cohen, 174–189. New York: New York University Press, 1991.

Russell, Norman. *Theophilus of Alexandria*. London: Routledge, 2007.

Sabar, Shalom. "'The Right Path for an Artist': The Approach of Leone da Modena to Visual Art." In *Hebraica Hereditas: Studi in onore di Cesare Colofemmina*, ed. Giancarlo Lacerenza, 1–36. Naples: Instituto Universitario orientale, Seminario di studi asiatici, 2005.

———. "Messianic Aspirations and Renaissance Urban Ideals: The Image of Jerusalem in the Venice Haggadah, 1609." *Jewish Art* 23 (1998): 294–312.

Sahas, Daniel J. *John of Damascus on Islam*. Leiden: Brill, 1972.

Salfeld, Siegmund. *Das Martyrologium des Nürnberger Memorbuches*. Berlin: Simion, 1898.

Salvadori, Roberto G., and Giorgio Sacchetti. *Presenze ebraiche nell' Aretino dal XIV al XX secolo*. Florence: L. S. Olschki, 1990.

Salzberg, Rosa M. "'Selling Stories and Many Other Things In and Through the City': Peddling Print in Renaissance Florence and Venice." *Sixteenth Century Journal* 42, no. 3 (2011): 737–759.

Scalia, Giuseppe. "La consecrazione della cattedrale pisana 26 Settembre 1118." *Bollettino Storico Pisana* 61 (1992): 1–31.

Scaramello, Pierroberto. "La campagna contro i giudaizzanti nel Regno di Napoli (1569–1582): Antecedenti e risvolti di un'azione inquisitoriale." In *Le Inquisizioni cristiane e gli ebrei: Tavola rotonda nell'ambito della Conferenza annuale di ricerca, Roma, 20–21 Dicembre 2001*, ed. Giuseppe Galasso, 357–373. Rome: Accademia Nazionale dei Lincei, 2003.

Schadler, Peter. *John of Damascus and Islam: Christian Heresiology and the Intellectual Background to Earliest Christian-Muslim Relations*. Leiden: Brill, 2018.

Schäfer, Peter. *Jesus in the Talmud*. Princeton, NJ: Princeton University Press, 2007.

———. "Jews and Gentiles in Yerushalmi Avodah Zarah." In *The Talmud Yerushalmi and Graeco-Roman Culture*, vol. 3, ed. Peter Schäfer, 335–352. Tübingen: Mohr Siebeck, 2002.

Schiaparelli, Attilio. *La casa fiorentina e i suoi arredi nei secoli XIV e XV*. Florence: G. C. Sansoni, 1908.

Schick, Robert. *The Christian Communities of Palestine from Byzantine to Islamic Rule: A Historical and Archaeological Study*. Princeton, NJ: Darwin Press, 1995.

Schmidlin, Joseph. *Geschichte der Deutschen Nationalkirche in Rom S. Maria dell' Anima*. Freiburg im Breisgau: Herder, 1906.

Schmitt, Jean-Claude. *The Conversion of Herman the Jew: Autobiography, History, and Fiction in the Twelfth Century*. Translated by Alex J. Novikoff. Philadelphia: University of Pennsylvania Press, 2010.

———. "De Nicée II à Thomas d'Aquin: L'émancipation de l'image religieuse en occident." In *Le corps des images: Essais sur la culture visuelle au Moyen Âge*, 63–127. Paris: Éditions Gallimard, 2002.

———. "La question des images dans les debats entre juifs et chrétiens au xii siècle." In *Spannungen und Widersprüche: Gedenkschrift für František Graus*, ed. Susanna Burghartz et al., 245–254. Sigmaringen: Jan Thorbecke, 1992.

Schonfield, Hugh J. *According to the Hebrews*. London: Duckworth, 1937.

Schreckenberg, Heinz. *Die christlichen Adversus-Judaeos-Texte und ihr literarisches und historisches Umfeld (13.-20. Jh.): Mit einer Ikonographie des Judentums bis zum 4. Laterankonzil*. 3rd ed., rev. Frankfurt am Main: Lang, 1997.

———. *The Jews in Christian Art: An Illustrated History*. New York: Continuum, 1996.

Schroeder, Henry Joseph. *Disciplinary Decrees of the General Councils: Text, Translation, and Commentary*. St. Louis, MO: Herder, 1937.

Schwartz, Daniel R. "Josephus and Philo on Pontius Pilate." In *The Jerusalem Cathedra: Studies in the History, Archaeology, Geography, and Ethnography of the Land of Israel*, vol. 3, ed. Lee I. Levine, 26–45. Jerusalem: Yad Izhak Ben-Zvi Institute, 1983.

Schwartz, Seth. "The Rabbi in Aphrodite's Bath: Palestinian Society and Jewish Identity in the High Roman Empire." In *Being Greek Under Rome: Cultural Identity, the Second Sophistic and the Development of Empire*, ed. Simon Goldhill, 335–361. Cambridge: Cambridge University Press, 2007.

Scott, James C. *Domination and the Arts of Resistance: Hidden Transcripts*. New Haven, CT: Yale University Press, 1990.

Scribner, Robert W. "Incombustible Luther: The Image of the Reformer in Early Modern Germany." *Past & Present* 110, no. 1 (1986): 38–68.

———. *For the Sake of Simple Folk: Popular Propaganda for the German Reformation*. Cambridge: Cambridge University Press, 1981.

Sella, Domenico. "Contributo alla storia delle fonti di energia: I filatori idraulici nella Valle Pandana durante il secolo XVII." In *Studi in onore di Amintore Fanfani*, 5:619–631. Milan: Giuffrè, 1962.

Shalev-Eyni, Sarit. *Jews Among Christians: Hebrew Book Illumination from Lake Constance*. Turnhout: Harvey Miller, 2010.

Shapiro, Marc. "Torah Study on Christmas Eve." *Journal of Jewish Thought and Philosophy* 8 (1999): 319–353.

Shatzmiller, Joseph. *Cultural Exchange: Jews, Christians, and Art in the Medieval Marketplace*. Princeton, NJ: Princeton University Press, 2013.

———. "Desecrating the Cross: A Rare Medieval Accusation." [In Hebrew.] *Mehqarim be-Toledot 'Am Yisrael ve-Erez Yisrael* 5 (1980): 159–173.

———. "Les Juifs de Provence pendant la Peste Noire." *Revue des Études Juives* 133 (1974): 457–480.

———. *Recherches sur la communauté juive de Manosque au moyen-âge (1241–1329)*. Paris: Mouton, 1973.

Shea, Jennifer. "Adgar's *Gracial* and Christian Images of Jews in Twelfth-Century Vernacular Literature." *Journal of Medieval History* 33, no. 2 (2007): 181–196.

Shoham-Steiner, Ephraim. "The Virgin Mary, Miriam, and Jewish Reactions to Marian Devotion in the High Middle Ages." *AJS Review* 37, no. 1 (2013): 75–91.

———. "Jews and Healing at Medieval Saints' Shrines: Participation, Polemics, and Shared Cultures." *Harvard Theological Review* 103, no. 1 (2010): 111–129.

Sicroff, Albert A. "Spanish Anti-Judaism: A Case of Religious Racism." In *Encuentros and Desencuentros: Spanish Jewish Cultural Interaction Throughout History*, ed. Carlos Carrete Parrondo et al., 589–613. Tel Aviv: Tel Aviv University Press, 2000.

Sigal, Pierre-André. "L'ex-voto au moyen âge dans les régions du nord-ouest de la Méditerranée (XIIe–XVe siècles)." *Provence historique* 33 (1983): 13–31.

Simonsohn, Shlomo. *Between Scylla and Charybdis: The Jews in Sicily*. Leiden: Brill, 2011.

———. "Some Well-Known Jewish Converts During the Renaissance." *Revue des Études Juives* 148, nos. 1–2 (1989): 17–52.

———. *History of the Jews in the Duchy of Mantua*. Jerusalem: Kiryath Sepher, 1977.

Sivan, Hagith. "From Byzantine to Persian Jerusalem: Jewish Perspectives and Jewish/Christian Polemics." *Greek, Roman and Byzantine Studies* 41 (2000): 277–306.

Soloveitchik, Haym. "Pawnbroking: A Study in *Ribbit* and of the Halakah in Exile." *Proceedings of American Academy for Jewish Research* 38–39 (1970–1971): 203–268.

Southern, Richard. "The English Origins of the 'Miracles of the Virgin.'" *Medieval and Renaissance Studies* 4 (1958): 176–216.

Soyer, François. *Antisemitic Conspiracy Theories in the Early Modern Iberian World: Narratives of Fear and Hatred*. Leiden: Brill, 2020.

———. "The Passion of Christ in the Church of San Cristóbal de Rapaz: An Example of Medieval Anti-Jewish Iconography in Colonial Peru?" *eHumanista/Conversos* 5 (2017): 392–416.

———. "The Massacre of the New Christians of Lisbon in 1506: A New Eyewitness Account." *Cadernos de Estudos Sefarditas* 7 (2007): 221–243.

Speck, Paul. "The Apocalypse of Zerubbabel and Christian Icons." *Jewish Studies Quarterly* 4, no. 2 (1997): 183–190.

———. *Ich bin's nicht, Kaiser Konstantin ist es gewesen: Die Legenden vom Einfluß des Teufels, des Juden und des Moslem auf den Ikonoklasmus*. Bonn: R. Habelt, 1990.

Stacey, Robert. "From Ritual Crucifixion to Host Desecration: Jews and the Body of Christ." *Jewish History* 12, no. 1 (1998): 11–28.

Starr, Joshua. "Byzantine Jewry on the Eve of the Arab Conquest (565–638)." *Journal of the Palestine Oriental Society* 15 (1935): 280–293.

———. "An Iconodulic Legend and Its Historical Basis." *Speculum* 8, no. 4 (1933): 500–503.

Starr-LeBeau, Gretchen. "Mari Sánchez and Inés González: Conflict and Cooperation Among Crypto-Jews." In *Women in the Inquisition: Spain and the New World*, ed. Mary E. Giles, 19–41. Baltimore: Johns Hopkins University Press, 1999.

Stern, Sacha. "Pagan Images in Late Antique Palestinian Synagogues." In *Ethnicity and Culture in Late Antiquity*, ed. Stephen Mitchell and Geoffrey Greatrex, 241–252. London: Duckworth and Classical Press of Wales, 2000.

Stewart, Peter. "The Destruction of Statues in Late Antiquity." In *Constructing Identities in Late Antiquity*, ed. Richard Miles, 159–189. London: Routledge, 1999.

Stock, Brian. *The Implications of Literacy: Written Language and Models of Interpretation in the Eleventh and Twelfth Centuries*. Princeton, NJ: Princeton University Press, 1983.

Taitz, Emily. *The Jews of Medieval France: The Community of Champagne*. Westport, CT: Greenwood Press, 1994.

Tanner, Norman P., ed. *Decrees of the Ecumenical Councils*. 2 vols. Washington, DC: Georgetown University Press, 2016.

Tartakoff, Paola. *Conversion, Circumcision, and Ritual Murder in Medieval Europe*. Philadelphia: University of Pennsylvania Press, 2020.

———. "Martyrdom, Conversion, and Shared Cultural Repertoires in Late Medieval Europe." *Jewish Quarterly Review* 109 (Fall 2019): 500–533.

———. *Between Christian and Jew: Conversion and Inquisition in the Crown of Aragon, 1250–1391*. Philadelphia: University of Pennsylvania Press, 2013.

Tasca, Cecilia. *Ebrei e società in Sardegna nel XV secolo: Fonti archivistiche e nuovi spunti di ricerca*. Florence: Giuntina, 2008.

Tavares, Maria José Pimenta Ferro. *Judaísmo e Inquisição: Estudos*. Lisbon: Presença, 1987.

Terpstra, Nicholas, *Lost Girls: Sex and Death in Renaissance Florence*. Baltimore: Johns Hopkins University Press, 2012.

———. "Working the Cocoon: Gendered Charitable Enclosures and the Silk Industry in Early Modern Europe." In *Worth and Repute: Valuing Gender in Late Medieval and Early Modern Europe; Essays in Honour of Barbara Todd*, ed. Kim Kippen and Lori Woods, 39–72. Toronto: Centre for Renaissance and Reformation Studies, 2011.

———. *The Art of Executing Well: Rituals of Execution in Renaissance Italy*. Early Modern Studies 1. Kirksville, MO: Truman State University Press, 2008.

Teter, Magda. *Blood Libel: On the Trail of an Antisemitic Myth*. Cambridge, MA: Harvard University Press, 2019.

———. *Sinners on Trial: Jews and Sacrilege After the Reformation*. Cambridge, MA: Harvard University Press, 2011.

Theuli, Bonaventura. *Teatro Historico di Velletri*. Bologna: Alfonso dell' Isola, 1644.

Thornton, Peter. *The Italian Renaissance Interior, 1400–1600*. New York: H. N. Abrams, 1991.

Thornton, T. C. G. "The Crucifixion of Haman and the Scandal of the Cross." *Journal of Theological Studies* 37, no. 2 (1986): 419–426.

Throop, Susanna A. *Crusading as an Act of Vengeance, 1095–1216*. Burlington, VT: Ashgate, 2011.

Thümmel, Hans Georg. *Die Frühgeschichte der ostkirchlichen Bilderlehre: Texte und Untersuchungen zur Zeit vor dem Bilderstreit*. Texte und Untersuchungen zur Geschichte der altchristlichen Literatur 139. Berlin: Akademie-Verlag, 1992.

Thunø, Erik. *Image and Relic: Mediating the Sacred in Early Medieval Rome*. Rome: "L'Erma" di Bretschneider, 2002.

Thunø, Erik, and Gerhard Wolf, eds. *The Miraculous Image in the Late Middle Ages and Renaissance*. Rome: "L'Erma" di Bretschneider, 2004.

Tiktiner, Rivkah bat Meir. *The Meneket Rivkah: A Manual of Wisdom and Piety for Jewish Women*. Ed. Frauke von Rohden. *Meneket Rivkah* translated by Samuel Spinner. Introduction and commentary translated by Maurice Tszorf. Philadelphia: Jewish Publication Society, 2009.

Toaff, Ariel. *Pasque di Sangue: Ebrei d'Europa e omicidi rituali*. Bologna: Il Mulino, 2007.

———. *Love, Work and Death: Jewish Life in Medieval Umbria*. Translated by Judith Landry. London: Littman Library of Jewish Civilization, 1996.

———. *Il vino e la carne: Una comunità ebraica nel Medioevo*. Bologna: Il Mulino, 1989.

Tolan, John V. *Faces of Muhammad: Western Perceptions of the Prophet of Islam from the Middle Ages to Today*. Princeton, NJ: Princeton University Press, 2019.

———. *Saracens: Islam in the Medieval European Imagination*. New York: Columbia University Press, 2002.

Trachtenberg, Joshua. *The Devil and the Jews: The Medieval Conception of the Jew and Its Relation to Modern Antisemitism*. Philadelphia: Jewish Publication Society of America, 1943.

Traniello, Elisabetta. *Gli ebrei e le piccolo città: Economia e società nel Polesine del Quattrocento*. Rovigo: Minelliana, 2004.

———. "Presenze ebraiche nel Polesine di Rovigo nel XV secolo." *Materia giudaica* 7, no. 1 (2002): 118–119.

Trexler, Richard. "Florentine Religious Experience: The Sacred Image." *Studies in the Renaissance* 19 (1972): 7–41.

Trivellato, Francesca. *The Familiarity of Strangers: The Sephardic Diaspora, Livorno, and Cross-Cultural Trade in the Early Modern Period*. New Haven, CT: Yale University Press, 2009.

Turner, Victor. *The Ritual Process: Structure and Anti-Structure*. Ithaca, NY: Cornell University Press, 1977.

———. *Dramas, Fields, and Metaphors: Symbolic Action in Human Society*. Ithaca, NY: Cornell University Press, 1974.

Twyman, Susan. *Papal Ceremonial at Rome in the Twelfth Century*. Woodbridge: Boydell Press 2002.

Urbach, Ephraim E. *The Tosaphists: Their History, Writings and Methods*. [In Hebrew.] 4th ed., enl. 2 vols. Jerusalem: Bialik Institute, 1980.

———. "The Rabbinical Laws of Idolatry in the Second and Third Centuries in Light of Archaeological and Historical Facts." *Eretz Israel* 5 (1958): 189–205.

———. *Ba'alei Ha-Tosafot*. Jerusalem: Bialik Institute, 1955.

Vajda, Georges. "Un chapitre de l'histoire du conflit entre la kabbale et la philosophie: La polémique anti-intellectualiste de Joseph ben Shalom Ashkenazi de Catalogne." *Archives d'histoire doctrinale et littéraire du Moyen Age* 23 (1956): 45–144.

Van Dam, Raymond. *Saints and Their Miracles in Late Antique Gaul*. Princeton, NJ: Princeton University Press, 1993.

Vandermeersch, Patrick. "Self-Flagellation in the Early Modern Era." In *The Sense of Suffering: Constructions of Physical Pain in Early Modern Culture*, ed. Jan Frans van Dijkhuizen and Karl A. E. Enenkel, 253–265. Leiden: Brill, 2008.

Van der Toorn, Karel. "The Iconic Book: Analogies Between the Babylonian Cult of Images and the Veneration of the Torah." In *The Image and the Book: Iconic Cults, Aniconism, and the Rise of Book Religion in Israel and the Ancient Near East*, ed. Karel Van der Toorn, 229–250. Leuven: Peeters, 1998.

Varner, Eric R. *Mutilation and Transformation: Damnatio Memoriae and Roman Imperial Portraiture.* Leiden: Brill, 2004.

Vasiliev, A. A. "The Iconoclastic Edict of the Caliph Yazid II, A.D. 721." *Dumbarton Oaks Papers* 9/10 (1956): 23–47.

Vassilaki, Maria. "Bleeding Icons." In *Icon and Word: The Power of Images in Byzantium*, ed. Antony Eastmond and Liz James, 121–129. Aldershot: Ashgate, 2003.

Vincent, Nicholas. *Holy Blood: King Henry III and the Westminster Blood Relic.* Cambridge: Cambridge University Press, 2001.

Waelput, Gérard. "Les Juifs à Mons au Moyen Âge." Part 2. *Le Moyen Age* 107, nos. 3–4 (2001): 503–508.

Wagner, Richard. *"The Art-Work of the Future" and Other Works.* Translated by William Ashton Ellis. Lincoln: University of Nebraska Press, 1993.

Waldman, Louis. "A Late Work by Andrea della Robbia Rediscovered: The Jews' Tabernacle at Empoli." *Apollo* 150 (September 1999): 13–20.

Walpole, A. S. *Early Latin Hymns.* Cambridge: Cambridge University Press, 1922.

Ward, Benedicta. *Miracles and the Medieval Mind: Theory, Record and Event 1000–1215.* Philadelphia: University of Pennsylvania Press, 1982.

Ward, H. L. D. *Catalogue of Romances in the Department of Manuscripts in the British Museum.* Vol. 2. 1893. Reprint, London: British Museum, 1962.

Warnke, Martin. *Bildersturm: Die Zerstörung des Kunstwerks.* Munich: Carl Hanser, 1973.

Watt, Jeffrey R. *The Scourge of Demons: Possession, Lust, and Witchcraft in a Seventeenth-Century Italian Convent.* Rochester, NY: University of Rochester Press, 2009.

Webster, Susan Verdi. *Art and Ritual in Golden-Age Spain: Sevillian Confraternities and the Processional Sculpture of Holy Week.* Princeton, NJ: Princeton University Press, 1998.

Weiss, Ze'ev. "Decorating the Sacred Realm: Biblical Depictions in Synagogues and Churches of Ancient Palestine." In *Jewish Art in Its Late Antique Context*, ed. Uzi Leibner and Catherine Hezser, 121–138. Tübingen: Mohr Siebeck, 2016.

Wendehorst, Stephan. "The Roman Inquisition, the Index and the Jews: Sources and Perspectives for Research." *Jewish History* 17 (2003): 55–76.

Wickersham, Jane K. *Rituals of Prosecution: The Roman Inquisition and the Prosecution of Philo-Protestants in Sixteenth-Century Italy.* Toronto: University of Toronto Press, 2012.

Wiedl, Birgit. "Sacred Objects in Jewish Hands: Two Case Studies." In *Jews and Christians in Medieval Europe: The Historiographical Legacy of Bernhard Blumenkranz*, Philippe Buc, Martha Keil, and John Tolan, 57–78. Turnhout: Brepols, 2016.

Wilken, Robert Louis. *The Land Called Holy: Palestine in Christian History and Thought.* New Haven, CT: Yale University Press, 1992.

Williams, A. Lukyn. *Adversus Judaeos: A Bird's-Eye View of Christian Apologiae Until the Renaissance.* Cambridge: Cambridge University Press, 1935.

Williamson, Beth. *The Madonna of Humility: Development, Dissemination and Reception, c. 1340–1400.* Woodbridge: Boydell Press, 2010.

Wirth, Jean. "Structures et fonctions de l'image chez Saint Thomas d'Aquin." In *L'image: Fonctions et usages des images dans l'Occident médiéval*, ed. Jérôme Baschet and Jean-Claude Schmitt, 39–57. Paris: Le Léopard d'Or, 1996.

Wood, Christopher S. "In Defense of Images: Two Local Rejoinders to the Zwinglian Iconoclasm." *Sixteenth Century Journal* 19, no. 1 (1988): 25–44.

Woods, David. "Arculf's Luggage: The Sources for Adomnán's *De locis sanctis*." *Ériu* 52 (2002): 25–52.

Yahalom, Joseph. *Yehuda Halevi: Poetry and Pilgrimage*. Jerusalem: Hebrew University Magnes Press, 2009.

Yassif, Eli. *The Hebrew Folktale: History, Genre, Meaning*. Translated by Jacqueline S. Teitelbaum. Bloomington: Indiana University Press, 1999.

Yavneh, Naomi. "To Bare or Not to Bare: Sofonisba Anguissola's Nursing Madonna and the Womanly Art of Breastfeeding." In *Maternal Measures: Figuring Caregiving in the Early Modern Period*, ed. Naomi J. Miller and Naomi Yavneh, 65–81. Aldershot: Ashgate, 2000.

Yerushalmi, Yosef Hayim. *Zakhor: Jewish History and Jewish Memory*. Seattle: University of Washington Press, 1982.

———. *The Lisbon Massacre of 1506 and the Royal Image in the Shebet Yehudah*. Hebrew Union College Annual Supplements 1. Cincinnati: Hebrew Union College, 1976.

———. *From Spanish Court to Italian Ghetto: Isaac Cardoso; A Study in Seventeenth-Century Marranism and Jewish Apologetics*. New York: Columbia University Press, 1971.

———. "The Inquisition and the Jews of France in the Time of Bernard Gui." *Harvard Theological Review* 63, no. 3 (1970): 317–376.

Yuval-Hacham, Noa. "'You Shall Not Make for Yourself Any Graven Image . . .': On Jewish Iconoclasm in Late Antiquity." *Ars Judaica* 6 (2010): 7–22.

Zafran, Eric M. "An Alleged Case of Image Desecration by the Jews and Its Representation in Art: The Virgin of Cambron." *Journal of Jewish Art* 2 (1974): 62–71.

———. "The Iconography of Antisemitism: A Study of the Representation of the Jews in the Visual Arts of Europe, 1400–1600." PhD diss., New York University, 1973.

Zeitler, Barbara. "The Migrating Image: Uses and Abuses of Byzantine Icons in Western Europe." In *Icon and Word: The Power of Images in Byzantium*, ed. Antony Eastmond and Liz James, 185–204. Aldershot: Ashgate, 2003.

Zeldes, Nadia. *"The Former Jews of This Kingdom": Sicilian Converts After the Expulsion, 1492–1516*. Leiden: Brill, 2003.

Zeri, Federico. *La collezione Federico Mason Perkins (Sala Alitalia, Museo-Tesoro della Basilica di S. Francesco)*. Assisi: Casa Editrice Francescana Assisi, 1988.

Zervas, Diane. *Orsanmichele a Firenze / Orsanmichele Florence*. 2 vols. Modena: Franco Cosimo Panini, 1996.

Index

Acknowledgments

My book is dedicated to the memory of Brian S. Pullan, the great social and economic historian of Venice, whose knowledge, guidance, and sage counsel have, during the past thirty-five years, accompanied me on my academic and intellectual journey. He became a beloved friend and I remain indebted to him.

I am also deeply grateful to the colleagues and friends who have helped make this book possible. Robert Eisen, Megan Holmes, and Gretchen Starr-LeBeau have kindly read earlier drafts of chapters, and Shulamit Laderman, Shalom Sabar, and Yosefa Wruble have given sound scholarly guidance. Jessica Setbon and Noam Zion have helped me with translations from Hebrew, and Christopher Black provided me with a copy of a manuscript from Rome. Katelyn Mesler shared her translation of a Hebrew text before publication, and Kati Ihnat gave me access to part of her manuscript.

For their generosity in answering queries regarding certain points I thank Rodney Aist, Luca Al Sabbagh, Michele Bacci, Giuseppe Capriotti, Carlos Espí Forcén, Laura Giles, Irene Fosi, Federica Francesconi, Tamar Herzig, Admiel Kosman, Amnon Linder, Sara Lipton, Germano Maifreda, Pam Manix, Emily Michelson, Rachel Misrati, Rachel Neis, Miri Rubin, Leah Salkin-Monzan, Rosa Salzberg, Ephraim Shoham-Steiner, and Paola Tartakoff.

I thank the dedicated staff at the different libraries where I spent time over the years, in particular, Lucia Frattarelli in the Archivio di Stato di Livorno and Alberto Palladini in the Archivio di Stato di Modena. Special thanks go also to my students at the Hebrew University, Tel Aviv University, and Schechter Institute of Jewish Studies in Jerusalem who have asked crucial questions over the years and helped me examine my opinions further.

My thanks also go to the staff at the University of Pennsylvania Press, especially to Jerome Singerman and Elisabeth Maselli who have helped me bring this project to fruition.

I owe a special debt of gratitude to my mother, Diana Aron, who has helped in more ways than I can mention, and my aunt Judith Litherland, who has read the manuscript (more than once), providing a host of useful and intelligent suggestions for improving it.

To research and write a book without sabbaticals has been a challenge, and I could not have done it without the patience, support, and devotion of Jonathan Beller, my life partner. My book is also dedicated to our dear children—Sam, Josh, and Naama—whose love continually nourishes our lives.

Printed in the USA
CPSIA information can be obtained
at www.ICGtesting.com
LVHW050311060124
768269LV00004B/279